Classic American Philosophers

CLASSIC
AMERICAN PHILOSOPHERS

Peirce • James • Royce
Santayana • Dewey
Whitehead

Selections from their Writings with Introductory Essays by

MAX H. FISCH
General Editor

ARTHUR W. BURKS PAUL HENLE GAIL KENNEDY
OTTO F. KRAUSHAAR VICTOR LOWE PHILIP B. RICE

Preface by
NATHAN HOUSER

FORDHAM UNIVERSITY PRESS
New York
1996

LC 95-47029
ISBN 0-8232-1657-8 (hardcover)
ISBN 0-8232-1658-6 (paperback)
ISSN 1073-2764
Second Edition

Published by arrangement with Prentice-Hall,
a division of Simon & Schuster, Inc.

American Philosophy Series, no. 2
Vincent M. Colapietro, Editor
Vincent G. Potter (1929–1994), Founding Editor

Library of Congress Catalgoing-in-Publication Data

Classic American philosophers : Peirce, James, Royce, Santayana,
    Dewey, Whitehead / Max H. Fisch, general editor ; preface by
Nathan Houser.
        p.   cm.—(American philosophy series ; no. 2)
    Includes index.
    ISBN 0-8232-1657-8 (hardcover).—ISBN 0-8232-1658-6 (pbk.)
    1. Philosophy, American–19th century.   2. Philosophy,
American—20th century.   3. Philosophy.   I. Fisch, Max Harold,
1900–   .   II. Series.
B935.F5   1996
191—dc20   95-47029
                                                            CIP

Printed in the United States of America

Contents

Preface to the 1996 Edition

Max H. Fisch began his preface to the fifth printing (1966) by informing his readers that the last two of the six classic American philosophers had died since the first printing in 1951, and that two of the editors were also deceased. Now, almost thirty years later, of the seven editors, only Arthur W. Burks is still alive. Max Fisch died on January 6, 1995, in California, the state of his youth. With his death, American philosophy lost one of its great champions.

Had Max Fisch lived to write this preface for the new Fordham edition, probably he would have reviewed the movements that have taken place in American philosophy during the last three decades. Although the philosophic scene has changed in many ways since the fifth printing, perhaps the change that is most significant for readers of this book is the revival of pragmatism. It is true that in some of its modern forms one is hard pressed to find the guiding hand of a classic pragmatist; still there are promising signs of a rebirth of interest in the ideas of the classic philosophers and of American philosophy more generally. One such sign is that the writings of four of our six philosophers (James, Dewey, Peirce, and Santayana) have become the subjects of critical editions (the first two now complete except for volumes of correspondence). Another sign is the growing number of Ph.D. dissertations which focus on pragmatism or American philosophy.

Over the years, *Classic American Philosophers* (CAP) has contributed to this revival by introducing hundreds of readers to six of America's great thinkers. For the new edition, I have made a number of corrections to the text and additions to the index, almost all based on Max Fisch's annotated copies of the first and fifth printings. I am grateful to Arthur W. Burks, who updated the supplementary note to his chapter on Charles S. Pierce (pp. 113–114), and to William Davenport, who supplied additional corrections. I have not attempted to update Fisch's general introduction or the references—although I have revised a few of the supplementary notes to the introduction—and the appendix of readings (pp. 447ff.) reflects the state of scholarship as it was thirty years ago. Students will want to consult current bibliographies for each of the classic philosophers and may find the most convenient sources to be the forthcoming supplemental volumes to Edwards's *Encyclopedia of Philosophy* and the new Routledge *Encyclopedia of Philosophy.*

With respect to the choice of classic philosophers and the text selections themselves, as late as 1966, in his Preface to the Fifth Printing, Fisch attested to the soundness of the decisions that were made in 1951. As possible additions to the canon, Fisch named C. I. Lewis and G. H. Mead, and he mentioned Chauncey Wright as "the great forerunner of our classic six." Many today might wish to include Emerson and Thoreau, along with Mead at least, but it is instructive to examine with care the argument of Fisch's general introduction, which limits the canon to Peirce, Royce, James, Santayana, Dewey, and Whitehead. All in all, CAP has stood the test of time and is well designed to continue for many years to come to introduce readers to one of the richest periods of American thought.

Perhaps it would be fitting to conclude this brief preface with a reminder of how things were when CAP first appeared. In a 1952 review in *The Christian Century* (January 2, pp. 17–18). Charles F. S. Virtue wrote: "When this reviewer was an undergraduate, his major instructor, the author of one of the best-known histories of philosophy, asserted, 'There is no American philosophy.' Now Prof. Max H. Fisch and six other professors collaborate to present what they confidently assert to be 'the classic period in American philosophy.'" Fisch's title no longer comes as a surprise. This is the book that opened the portal on what Whitehead called "the American renaissance."

NATHAN HOUSER

Preface

It is increasingly apparent that American philosophy has had its classical period, corresponding to the Greek classical period from Democritus through Aristotle, the medieval Christian from Abelard through Thomas Aquinas and Duns Scotus, the British from Bacon through Hume, the German from Kant through Hegel.

Our classical period began just after our Civil War and ended just before the Second World War. Its canon is already nearly fixed. It includes six philosophers. They are Charles Sanders Peirce, William James, Josiah Royce, George Santayana, John Dewey, and Alfred North Whitehead.

The primary purpose of the present volume is to introduce these philosophers to readers who do not yet know their writings at first hand. My collaborators and I have agreed on the philosophers to be included, and on the general plan of the volume. Our collaboration extends further to the reading and criticism of each collaborator's work by all the others, as well as by Professor Lamprecht, the general editor of the series in which the volume appears. But each collaborator has been free to adopt or reject the suggestions of his fellows, and each accepts full responsibility for the part that bears his name. In the case of those who have written introductions to the individual philosophers, the responsibility extends to the selections that follow.

This freedom and responsibility of each collaborator has resulted in certain disparities, both in the selections and in the introductions. Some of the introductions are more biographical, others more expository, still others more critical. Some are synoptic or comprehensive, others emphasize certain aspects of the philosopher's work and ignore the rest. Some of the groups of selections consist entirely or predominantly of complete essays or chapters, others include mosaics of shorter passages. In each case, the collaborator aimed to introduce the philosopher in question as effectively as he knew how. The reader must decide for himself which of the philosophers he wishes to know better. The Appendix will suggest how he may then proceed.

There are several histories of American philosophy as a whole, and of the period here represented in particular. Most of these are listed in the Appendix. The present volume is not intended as a substitute for such a history. The general introduction sketches some of the prominent features of the thought of the period, with reference primarily to the philosophers here represented, and with a view to suggesting certain relationships among them, or between them and their contemporaries. Its purpose, like that of the volume as a whole, is introductory. It does not aim at the comprehensiveness or balance of a definitive history, or even of a synoptic outline.

In a longer general introduction, we might have inquired how far the tendencies discerned in America were prevalent elsewhere. We might also have given some account of the influence of our philosophers upon the thought and life of their time. A quite different introduction might have been organized in terms of their contributions to the major fields of philosophy—metaphysics, theory of knowledge, semantics, logic, philosophy of science, ethics, aesthetics, general theory of value, social philosophy, philosophy of religion. Such an introduction would have avoided the chief defect of this one: its neglect of the five fields last named. Still another introduction might have focused on the major problems, and in particular on such shifts as that from the question "How do we know?" to the question "What do we mean?" The present introduction cannot possess the virtues of these or other alternatives, but we trust it may have virtues of its own.

We say to the reader, then: here you will find yourself in the company of the six major philosophers who have taught and written in these United States in the past three-quarters of a century, and here is enough of the best work of each to represent him fairly and to recommend him, if anything will, to your better acquaintance. Whatever it is you ask of philosophy, if you find no part or promise of it here, will be hard to find elsewhere.

MAX H. FISCH

Preface to the Fifth Printing (1966)

Two of our six philosophers were still living when the first printing appeared, but died in the following year: Dewey in New York on June 1 and Santayana in Rome on September 26, 1952. Two of the editors have also died: Philip Rice in 1956 and Paul Henle in 1962.

In the fifteen years that have elapsed since the first printing, there have been many changes in the philosophic scene. This is not the place for an account of them, but a few may be briefly mentioned. All are matters of degree. The movement with the widest general appeal by far has been existentialism. Phenomenology has flourished, often in association with existentialism. Logical positivism has waned if not expired. The vogue of "ordinary language" philosophy and of related forms of linguistic and logical analysis, applied particularly to the philosophy of mind and to ethics, has culminated and is now abating. The fields in which the most original work by American philosophers has been done are philosophy of science, mathematical logic, logic for computers, decision theory, "operations research," social philosophy with a focus on city planning, and, above all, aesthetics. There has been some lessening of emphasis on the history of philosophy, both in the training of philosophers and in courses for the general student. Our younger philosophers care less than their elders did about constructing systems themselves or studying the systems of the past. The usual unit for fresh construction is the journal article, and the unit selected for study from the philosophic literature of the past is the single argument bearing on a single question. Textbooks are for the most part simply topical collections of such units. Only logic is still taught systematically.

In the light of these and other changes, the surviving editors have considered whether the general conception of our book is still tenable and whether our canon should be changed, by addition or subtraction or both. Since all six of our philosophers continue to be studied by representatives of all current tendencies, our conception still seems valid, and we find no reason for subtraction. If we were making additions, C. I. Lewis would be our unanimous first choice among the pragmatists, though the claims of G. H. Mead have been strengthened by the recent appearance of *Selected Writings* of his, edited by Andrew J. Reck. Among idealists and realists a choice would be more difficult. (The chief possibilities, short of the present, are reviewed by Reck in his *Recent American Philosophy*.) In two books on Chauncey

Wright and in a volume of selections from his *Philosophical Writings,*
Edward H. Madden has shown that he was the great forerunner of our
classical six. But our conclusion has been that no philosopher among
us has risen to such eminence as to displace one of the six, or be added
to them.

For this printing, the Appendix has been entirely rewritten, but there
are only minor alterations elsewhere. The selections remain as before,
and also the general introduction and the introductions to the selections from Peirce, James and Santayana. There are slight revisions in
those to Royce and Whitehead. The last paragraph of the original
preface has been dropped. Supplementary notes have been added on
pages 39–40, 113, 127, and 335.

If more extensive revision were feasible, we could now shed fresh
light at many points throughout. I offer here a single example, touching line 10 on page 4.

In the spring of 1951, after visiting Santayana in Rome and leaving
a copy of our newly published book, I sent him a note inquiring as to
the accuracy of the statement that he had taken no notice of Peirce.
Though it was doubtless true, he replied, that he had nowhere mentioned Peirce in print, he remembered one of his Harvard lectures. "It
was about signs, and made a lasting impression upon me; that all
ideas, in so far as they convey *knowledge,* are signs has become a
favourite doctrine of mine. But I have never studied his published
works, and it is from your book that I have first gained a general view
of his achievement. If he had built his philosophy on *signs* I might
have been his disciple." (That he *did* in some sense build his philosophy on signs might perhaps have been guessed from page 29, but
the Peirce who conceived logic as semiotic or general theory of signs
is not prominent in our book.)

More recently, Justus Buchler has published extracts from an earlier
letter, of 1937, in which Santayana recalled the same lecture. A part
of it, he wrote, "seemed *ex tempore* and whimsical. But I remember
and have often used in my own thought, if not in actual writing, a
classification he made that evening of signs into indexes and symbols
and images." (Peirce's term for the last was "icons.")

Still more recently it has transpired that, in a still earlier letter,
of 1926, Santayana, being asked if he would consider editing some
of Peirce's papers, replied: "I am glad to hear that Charles Peirce left
copious materials yet unpublished, but I am not at all the person to
undertake editing any portion of them." He went on to refer to the
same lecture, and then added: "As a philosopher Peirce has come
late to be recognized, but his quality is unmistakably good, far better
logically than Wm. James's and anything speculative from his pen
would be welcomed, I think, by the learned public."

The lecture Santayana remembered so well for nearly half a century was almost certainly the third lecture in Peirce's Harvard series on "Pragmatism as a Principle and Method of Right Thinking," on April 8, 1903. Since that lecture also expounded Peirce's three categories and explained icons as firsts, indexes as seconds, and symbols as thirds, it is probable that Peirce's firsts were one of the sources of Santayana's essences, and therefore also of Whitehead's eternal objects.[1]

MAX H. FISCH

[1] A Lewis volume is forthcoming in The Library of Living Philosophers to join the Dewey, Santayana and Whitehead volumes. For Santayana's letter to Buchler, see *Journal of Philosophy* 51: 54, 1954. Reprinted in John Lachs (ed.), *Animal Faith and Spiritual Life: Previously Unpublished and Uncollected Writings by George Santayana with Critical Essays on His Thought* (New York: Appleton-Century-Crofts, 1967), pp. 68–69. For the letter of 1926, see *The Letters of George Santayana* (1955), pp. 233 f. For Peirce's lecture, see his *Collected Papers,* 5.66–91 and especially 5.73. (It is not unlikely that Peirce repeated extempore the language of shock he had used in the preceding lecture in explaining secondness; sec 5.45, and cf. 1.332–336. If he did, the "shocks" of *Scepticism and Animal Faith* may be further reverberations of this lecture; see pp. 284 ff. below, and cf. p. 93.) On essences and eternal objects, see p. 30 n. 101 below and the supplement to that note on p. 39. For another possible connection between Peirce and Santayana, see Morris R. Cohen, *American Thought* (1954), p. 273 n. 11.

Acknowledgments

Our thanks are extended to the following for permission to reprint or quote from copyright material.

Harvard University Press, for quotations from the *Collected Papers of Charles Sanders Peirce.*

Henry Holt and Company, for the selection from Dewey's *The Influence of Darwin on Philosophy.*

The Editors of the *Journal of Philosophy,* for James's "Does 'Consciousness' Exist?"

The Trustees of Lake Forest College, for selections from Royce's *The Sources of Religious Insight.*

The Library of Living Philosophers, for selections and quotations from *The Philosophy of George Santayana,* and quotations from other volumes in the series.

The Macmillan Company, for selections and quotations from Whitehead's *Science and the Modern World, Religion in the Making, Process and Reality, Adventures of Ideas,* and *Modes of Thought.*

The Open Court Publishing Company, for Peirce's "The Architecture of Theories" and "The Doctrine of Necessity Examined."

The Philosophical Library, Inc., for quotations from Whitehead's *Essays in Science and Philosophy.*

Princeton University Press, for quotations from Whitehead's *The Function of Reason.*

G. P. Putnam's Sons, for selections from Dewey's *The Quest for Certainty* and *Philosophy and Civilization* and from *The Philosopher of the Common Man.*

Paul R. Reynolds & Son, for selections from James's *The Will to Believe, Pragmatism* and *A Pluralistic Universe.*

Stephen Royce, for the selections from his father's *The Problem of Christianity.*

Charles Scribner's Sons, for selections and quotations from Santayana's *The Life of Reason, Scepticism and Animal Faith, Obiter Scripta,* and *The Realm of Matter,* and for quotations from his other writings.

General Introduction

The Classic Period in American Philosophy
by Max H. Fisch

THE HISTORY OF philosophy in western civilization has a general continuity from which no single thinker or local movement is quite cut off. There emerge, however, certain widely separated periods within which the continuity is more pervasive and intensive. Such periods are those from Democritus and Socrates through Aristotle in Greek philosophy, from Abelard through Thomas Aquinas and Duns Scotus in medieval Christian culture, from Bacon through Hume in Great Britain, from Descartes through Leibniz on the continent at about the same time, and from Kant through Hegel in Germany.

We may call such a period classic in the sense that the leading philosophic tendencies of the culture in which it arises reach within it a fulness of expression, a mutual definition, a synthesis or equilibrium, and a permanent embodiment in texts which rapidly acquire the status of a canon and which determine the directions in which further reflection moves for generations or centuries thereafter.

Such a classic period may now be discerned in American philosophy, beginning just after the Civil War and continuing to the eve of the Second World War. Its major figures are Peirce, Royce, James, Santayana, Dewey, and Whitehead. The major texts in its canon are Peirce's *Collected Papers*, James's *Principles of Psychology* and *Pragmatism*, Royce's *The World and the Individual*, Santayana's *The Life of Reason* and *Realms of Being*, Dewey's *Experience and Nature* and *Logic*, and Whitehead's *Process and Reality*.

The continuity within the period may be illustrated by reference to (A) the personal relations and mutual attractions between the major figures; (B) the general social and intellectual influences to which they were all in varying degrees subject; and (C) the philosophic tendencies within the period to which all or most of them contributed, though again in varying ways and degrees. We shall give some indications under each of these heads. Our emphasis here is on continuities, on common influences and common traits. For what is unique or emphatic in each philosopher, the reader is referred to the special introductions.

A. Personal Relations

James, Royce, and Santayana were colleagues at Harvard University in the years of its philosophic ascendancy. The crowning period of

Whitehead's career, during which his major philosophic works were produced, was spent in the same department, after James and Royce had died and Santayana had retired, but while their memory was still fresh in Emerson Hall and the Harvard Yard. Peirce was never a member of the department, though but for President Eliot's dislike he might have been. His father, a brother, and a cousin were Harvard professors of mathematics. In his earlier years he himself was an assistant in the Harvard Observatory, and he was University Lecturer on the logic of science in 1864-65, on the British logicians in 1869-70, and on general logic in 1870-71. In his later years he gave several series of lectures under the auspices of the philosophy department and of the philosophy club. Upon his death, his unpublished manuscripts came into the care of the department. After fifteen years of study, sifting and ordering, his *Collected Papers* were edited by members of the department and published (in Whitehead's time) by the Harvard Press. Peirce was the Harvard department's great might-have-been. Thus, of our canonical six, only Dewey was not associated with Harvard University. And even Dewey, as William James Lecturer in the winter and spring of 1931, was briefly a colleague of Whitehead, and delivered at Harvard the lectures from which his *Art as Experience* grew.

Of more substantial importance, perhaps, were the brief associations of four of the six—James and Peirce as teachers, and Royce and Dewey as students—with the Johns Hopkins University during its first decade, when it was not only the nation's newest university but its only real one, when it was establishing the standards of research and of graduate study later emulated at Harvard and elsewhere, and when it bade fair to have the leading department in philosophy as in so many other fields.[1]

James and Peirce were lifelong friends, beginning in 1861 when Peirce was a year ahead of James in the Lawrence Scientific School at Harvard. For many years they had a common older companion in Chauncey Wright, an admirer of J. S. Mill and of Darwin. In the early 1870's, all three were members of a fortnightly "Metaphysical Club," along with a brilliant lawyer named Nicholas St. John Green, and with James's friend Oliver Wendell Holmes, Jr. Wright and Green exerted a strong pull toward empiricism and utilitarianism on the exuberant speculations of Peirce, James, and Holmes. It was in this group, under the influence of Green and Wright, that Peirce and James developed pragmatism, and that Holmes worked out its application to law.[2]

[1] *Cf.* Max H. Fisch and Jackson I. Cope: "Peirce at the Johns Hopkins University," in the forthcoming *Studies in the Philosophy of Charles S. Peirce* (New York, Bollingen Foundation, Inc., 1950?).

[2] *Cf.* M. H. Fisch: "Justice Holmes, the Prediction Theory of Law, and Pragmatism," *Journal of Philosophy* 39:85-97, 12 Feb. 1942; "Evolution in American

James and Peirce recommended each other for professorships in the new Johns Hopkins University in the later 1870's. James was Visiting Lecturer in Psychology there in 1878, and Peirce was Lecturer in Logic from 1879 to 1884 and organized a metaphysical club which echoed in topics discussed as well as in name the club at Cambridge of which he and James had been members.

Royce heard James's lectures at Hopkins in 1878 and was thus "for a brief time his pupil." From 1882 onwards he was James's colleague at Harvard. Each was the chief stimulus to the other's philosophic development, in part by attraction, in part by repulsion and defense. After James's death, Royce ranked him with Jonathan Edwards and Emerson as a representative American philosopher, giving classic expression to a distinct stage of our culture.[3]

Royce was also acquainted with Peirce, followed his work with increasing interest, and was increasingly influenced by it. He and James alike acknowledged their indebtedness to Peirce in their published writings and referred to him frequently in their lectures and seminars. James professed to have learned more from Peirce's writings than from those of anyone else but Royce. Royce would probably have said the same of Peirce and James. Of Peirce's lectures at Cambridge in 1898, arranged by James, Royce later wrote that they would always remain quite epoch-making for him. "They started me on such new tracks." [4] Peirce thought James a greater psychologist than philosopher and even greater in the practice than in the theory of psychology.[5] He said the argument of Royce's *The World and the Individual* was weak but the opinions developed in it were near his own.[6]

Santayana was a pupil of James and Royce. Under the latter's direction he wrote his doctor's thesis on the philosophy of Lotze, with whom Royce had studied in Germany, and whom James called the "deepest philosopher" of the day and "the most exquisite of contemporary minds." [7] From 1889 to 1911 he was a colleague of James and Royce in the Harvard department. He has indicated his indebtedness

Philosophy," *Philosophical Review* 56:357-373, July 1947; and the recent book by Philip P. Wiener, *Evolution and the Founders of Pragmatism* (Cambridge, Mass., Harvard University Press, 1949).

[3] Josiah Royce: *William James and Other Essays* (New York, The Macmillan Co., 1911), pp. 8 f.

[4] R. B. Perry: *The Thought and Character of William James* (Boston, Little, Brown, and Co., 1935), II, 421; *cf.* I, 788, 792; II, 413.

[5] *Collected Papers of Charles Sanders Peirce*, edited by Charles Hartshorne and Paul Weiss (Cambridge, Mass., Harvard University Press, 6 vols., 1931-1935), 6.184 (i.e., vol. 6, paragraph 184).

[6] *Ibid.*, 5.358 n.; Perry, *op. cit.*, II, 425; *Journal of Philosophy* 13:720, 1916. See however Peirce's reviews of Royce's works in *The Nation* 70:267; 75:94-96; 79:264-265.

[7] Perry, *op. cit.*, I, 586.

to them and his divergence from them in his "General Confession"; [8] and the chapters on James and Royce in his *Character and Opinion in the United States,* though defective in sympathy, are the most brilliant of all literary portraits of American philosophers. James spoke of Santayana as "that smoothly swimming fish," "the shiningest fish in the sea." [9] Royce said he had a definite philosophy from which he never departed: the radical and complete separation of essence and existence. [10] Peirce, on the other hand, thought his philosophy eclectic, likely to have more literary than scientific value—"all that Boston has of most *précieux*." [11] Santayana took no notice of Peirce.

Dewey was a pupil of Peirce's at Hopkins and an active member of the Metaphysical Club there. At that time he was under the spell of G. S. Morris and did not learn much from Peirce; but from an idealism like Morris's and not far from Royce's, he moved gradually in the direction of James and Peirce, at first under the inspiration of James's *Psychology* and later under that of Peirce's writings. James hailed Dewey's *Studies in Logical Theory* (1903) as the foundation of a new school—"the Chicago School" [12]—and his "Beliefs and Realities" (1906) as "the weightiest pragmatist pronouncement yet made in America." [13] Peirce found in the *Studies* only a "natural history of thought," a useful preliminary to logic, but not logic itself. [14]

In his early work in the logical foundations of mathematics, Whitehead took notice of the related investigations of Peirce and Royce. Though his metaphysics was developed independently, he recognized a kinship at many points with James and at others with Dewey and Santayana; and some students of his work and of Peirce's have discerned an even closer kinship with Peirce, though he seems not to have been acquainted with Peirce's metaphysical writings. Whitehead went so far as to speak of James as a key figure in modern philosophy, marking the great shift that has taken place since the time of Descartes. He was apparently unaware that our classic period began with a conscious rejection of Descartes and all his heirs on the part of Peirce. [15]

[8] *The Philosophy of George Santayana,* edited by P. A. Schilpp (Evanston, Northwestern University, 1940), 3-30, esp. 8 ff.

[9] Dickinson Miller: "Mr. Santayana and William James," *Harvard Graduates' Magazine* 29:348-364, March 1921, at p. 356.

[10] As reported by Dewey in the *New Republic* 35:294 f., 8 Aug. 1923. Cf. *The Philosophy of George Santayana,* 497, 502, 525.

[11] *Nation* 80:461, 8 June 1905.

[12] *Collected Essays and Reviews* (New York, Longmans, Green and Co., 1920), 445 ff. (1904).

[13] Perry, *op. cit.,* II, 572.

[14] *Nation* 79:220, 15 Sept. 1904.

[15] See Part C, section 1 below. In another connection, Whitehead placed James in the company of Plato, Aristotle, and Leibniz as masters of "philosophical assemblage," and said James "had discovered intuitively the great truth with which

The continuity of the period appears in such numerous cross-fertilizations, and in particular in such a strong gravitational pull by pragmatism on all other philosophies, that none of the traditional labels is adequate to distinguish any one of our six from the others. Peirce was a pragmatist, a scholastic realist, and at the same time an idealist of the order of Schelling. In spite of logical deficiencies in its exposition, he thought Royce's idealism the soundest philosophy then before the public. Royce, nourished on German "absolute" idealism and developing his own philosophy out of it, was nevertheless in sufficient sympathy with certain features of pragmatism (which he thought he found in German idealism also) to call his own philosophy "absolute pragmatism." (Dewey, however, discerned not pragmatism but voluntarism in Royce's earliest work, with intellectualism soon setting in.[16]) Santayana's naturalism was hailed at first as a form of pragmatism; not without reason, for in their theories of knowledge the two go along together before diverging. He later called Dewey's naturalism half-hearted and short-winded, foreshortened by "the dominance of the foreground."[17] Dewey has found more to admire in and to learn from Santayana's works, and many contemporary philosophers owe them equal debts. Santayana said his "essences" could hardly be recognized more frankly than in Whitehead's descriptions of "eternal objects."[18] Even before Whitehead's major philosophic works appeared, a discerning critic pointed out the "objective relativism" which Dewey and Whitehead had in common.[19] Dewey himself has since stated the extent of his agreement with Whitehead and paid tribute to his "almost incomparable suggestiveness."[20] Though Whitehead counted himself a realist, he is often classed as an idealist, and he himself suggested that his cosmology might be considered "a transformation of some main doctrines of Absolute Idealism onto a realistic basis."[21]

Our classic period had also the continuity and the specious unity

modern logic is now wrestling"—"that every finite set of premises must indicate notions which are excluded from its direct purview." *Modes of Thought* (New York, The Macmillan Co., 1938), 2-4.

[16] *Philosophical Review* 25:253 f., 1916.

[17] "Dewey's Naturalistic Metaphysics," *Journal of Philosophy* 22:673-688, 1925; reprinted with slight changes in *The Philosophy of John Dewey*, ed. P. A. Schilpp (Evanston, Northwestern University, 1939), 245-261.

[18] *Realms of Being*, one-vol. ed. (New York, Charles Scribner's Sons, 1942), 171.

[19] Arthur E. Murphy: "Objective Relativism in Dewey and Whitehead," *Philosophical Review* 36:121-144, 1927.

[20] In: *The Philosophy of Alfred North Whitehead*, ed. P. A. Schilpp (Evanston, Northwestern University, 1941), 643-661 (quoted phrase at 659). *Cf.* "Whitehead's Philosophy," *Philosophical Review* 46:170-177, March 1937; and reviews of Whitehead's *Science and the Modern World* and *Adventures of Ideas* in *New Republic* 45:360-361 (*cf.* 46:11-13); 74:285-286. In view of attacks on Whitehead by disciples of Dewey, it is important to read what Dewey himself says.

[21] *Process and Reality* (New York, The Macmillan Co., 1929), viii.

of a period running its course within a long lifetime. Not only were all its major figures born before the period began, but three of them lived beyond it, and two are still living and writing. These two, Dewey and Santayana, reviewed nearly all the major productions of the period, and it would be instructive to consider their appraisals. Instead, we shall illustrate the point by setting down some of the more informal comments expressed in the letters of Justice Oliver Wendell Holmes, Jr., who, though an active participant in the early formulation of pragmatism, felt himself thereafter a detached but interested observer of the philosophic scene.

Holmes and James attended Peirce's Lowell Institute Lectures on "The Logic of Science: Induction and Hypothesis" in the winter of 1866–67 and discussed them together. Peirce late in life remembered Holmes as the member of the Metaphysical Club who had attained greatest distinction. After the dissolution of the Club they seem to have lost touch with each other. When Peirce applied for a grant from the newly established Carnegie Institution in 1902, it was at James's request that Holmes wrote a supporting letter in which he said:

I know Mr. Peirce's philosophy mainly at second hand from echoes in the books of James and Royce—but from these and from what I have seen of Mr. Peirce in former years I find no difficulty in believing his contributions to be of much importance. If the result of keeping him along should be the completion of his magnum opus, I should expect it to be an event of magnitude, and possibly of the first magnitude.[22]

There is no record of Holmes having read anything by Peirce until the summer of 1923, when he read the papers his friend Morris R. Cohen had just collected under the title *Chance, Love and Logic* (including the four papers reprinted in the present volume). He wrote to Cohen:

I feel Peirce's originality and depth—but he does not move me greatly— I do not sympathize with his pontifical self-satisfaction. He believes that he can, or could if you gave him time, explain the universe. He sees cosmic principles when I should not dare to see more than the limit of our capacities, and his reasoning in the direction of religion &c. seems to me to reflect what he wants to believe—in spite of his devotion to logic. That we could not assert necessity of the order of the universe I learned to believe from Chauncey Wright long ago. I suspect C. S. P. got it from the same source.[23]

---

[22] From a copy among the Peirce papers in the Houghton Library at Harvard University.

[23] "The Holmes-Cohen Correspondence," *Journal of the History of Ideas* 9:3-52, 1948, at pp. 34 f. Cf. *Holmes-Pollock Letters* (Cambridge, Mass., Harvard University Press, 1941), II, 252: "Chauncey Wright, a nearly forgotten philosopher of real merit, taught me when young that I must not say *necessary* about the universe ... So I describe myself as a *bett*abilitarian. I believe that we can bet on the behavior of the universe in its contact with us."

Though Holmes read James's *Psychology* in 1890, "every word of it," he said, "with delight and admiration," his praise thereafter was always qualified. *The Will to Believe* made demands on the universe which were "too nearly the Christian demands without the scheme of salvation." Parts of *Pragmatism*—"pedantic name"—seemed to be on the way to his own humbler formula for truth, "but I am more sceptical than you are." [24] After James's death in 1910 Holmes wrote to their mutual friend Pollock that

Wm. James's death cuts a root for me that went far into the past, but of late, indeed for many years, we had seen little of each other and had little communication except as he occasionally sent me a book. Distance, other circumstances and latterly my little sympathy with his demi spiritualism and pragmatism, were sufficient cause. His reason made him sceptical and his wishes led him to turn down the lights so as to give miracle a chance. [25]

Holmes as well as James, Royce and Santayana, had frequently attended the evening gatherings at Mrs. Henry Whitman's in Boston. John Jay Chapman writes in his memoir of her:

I remember a curious Bostonian cockfight at her studio, where Professor Royce and Judge Oliver Wendell Holmes were pitted against each other to talk about the Infinite. Royce won, of course,—somewhat after the manner of Gladstone,—by involving the subject in such adamantine cobwebs of voluminous rolling speculation that no one could regain his senses thereafter. He not only cut the ground from under everyone's feet; but he pulled down the sun and moon, and raised up the ocean, and everyone was shipwrecked and took to small planks and cups of tea. [26]

That was in 1887. A year later, Holmes spoke of Royce as "one of our most promising philosophers," but he read his *The World and the Individual* in 1902 (along with James's *Varieties of Religious Experience*) without persuasion. "Very able—but thimblerigging, I thought it, on the first rapid perusal." [27]

Santayana's *Life of Reason* and later his *Scepticism and Animal Faith* seemed much closer to Holmes's own way of thinking than either James or Royce; but "I think he improvises and obscures the foundations of his thought with too many tickling words." "Perhaps his Catholic antecedents make him like to use words that trail rainbows but disguise his meaning, especially 'spirit' and 'essence.'" Most of all Holmes ad-

[24] Perry, *op. cit.*, II, 457-462. Of the *Psychology* Holmes wrote: "Some of the chapters are schemes of all possible *belles lettres* in scientific form, yet preserving the *esprit* and richness of empirical writing."

[25] *Holmes-Pollock Letters*, I, 167. *Cf.* "Holmes-Cohen Correspondence," 43.

[26] *Memories and Milestones* (New York, Moffatt, Yard and Co., 1915), 106.

[27] *Holmes-Pollock Letters*, I, 31, 101; Perry, *op. cit.*, II, 458. Holmes to James in 1902: "Some day, here, in Heaven, or in the world outside of time and space where Royce is God, we shall talk together again with that intimacy of understanding and mutual stimulus which we have known and which I never forget."

mired *Winds of Doctrine,* and especially the opening page of the essay
on "The Intellectual Temper of the Age." So eloquently did it speak
his own mind that he wrote Santayana in high praise of it.[28]

Holmes did not discover Dewey until the latter's *Experience and
Nature* was recommended to him by a young Chinese friend. He began
it sceptically; it seemed to be so badly written. But he read it twice
in the winter of 1926-27, and wrote his impressions in five letters over
a period of a year and a half. "He seems to me," Holmes said, "to have
more of our cosmos in his head than any philosopher I have read."
Holmes reread the book in 1929 when a second edition appeared, and
recommended it to Sir Frederick Pollock. The only clearly intelligible
sentences Pollock professed to find in it were the two pages Dewey
had quoted from Holmes.[29]

Holmes read Whitehead's *Science and the Modern World* and *Process
and Reality* and "got the general drift," he hoped, but

> Whitehead talks and thinks like a mathematician and I am not in on it.
> I like one thing—that he like Dewey begins his cosmos without any conscious
> ego, and lets that come in later as *quasi* an accident. I should think W's
> mode of approach as I certainly thought Dewey's an advance on Berkeley
> and Hume. . . .[30]

Morris R. Cohen, whom Bertrand Russell was reported to consider
the outstanding American philosopher, "infinitely more important than
Dewey," dedicated his major work to his friend Holmes. On May 15,
1931, at the age of 90, Holmes wrote Pollock:

> I have just finished reading Morris Cohen's book *Reason & Nature,* a very
> thorough exposition, quickly disposing of the humbugs of which we most
> hear, and I think admirable for learning and logic. The title suggests a sort
> of challenge to John Dewey's *Experience & Nature* to which it is much
> superior as a piece of writing and in the domain of the finite. But although
> Dewey's book is incredibly ill written, it seemed to me after several rereadings
> to have a feeling of intimacy with the inside of the cosmos that I found
> unequaled. So methought God would have spoken had He been inarticulate
> but keenly desirous to tell you how it was.[31]

[28] *Holmes-Pollock Letters,* II, 132; "Holmes-Cohen Correspondence," 41; Santayana: *The Middle Span* (=*Persons and Places,* Vol. II, New York, Charles Scribner's Sons, 1945), 128 f. The opening page of *Winds of Doctrine* (New York, Charles Scribner's Sons, 1913) reads in part as follows: "The present age is a critical one and interesting to live in. The civilisation characteristic of Christendom has not disappeared, yet another civilisation has begun to take its place . . . The unconquerable mind of the East, the pagan past, the industrial socialistic future confront it with their equal authority. Our whole life and mind is saturated with the slow upward filtration of a new spirit—that of an emancipated, atheistic, international democracy. . . ."

[29] Letters to John C. H. Wu in Harry C. Shriver (ed.): *Justice Oliver Wendell Holmes: His Book Notices and Uncollected Letters and Papers* (New York, Central Book Co., 1936), 190-198; *Holmes-Pollock Letters,* II, 242.

[30] *Holmes-Pollock Letters,* II, 272.

[31] *Ibid.,* II, 287; cf. "Holmes-Cohen Correspondence," 32 f., 45.

B. The Climate of Opinion

It seemed to Holmes that of all the intellectual gaps between generations that between his father's and his own was the widest, and that it was the scientific way of looking at the world that had made the difference. He wrote to Cohen in 1919:

My father was brought up scientifically—i.e. he studied medicine in France—and I was not. Yet there was with him as with the rest of his generation a certain softness of attitude toward the interstitial miracle—the phenomenon without phenomenal antecedents—that I did not feel. The difference was in the air, although perhaps only the few of my time felt it. *The Origin of Species* I think came out while I was in college—H. Spencer had announced his intention to put the universe into our pockets—I hadn't read either of them to be sure, but as I say it was in the air. I did read Buckle—now almost forgotten—but making a noise in his day ... But I think science was at the bottom. ... [32]

The difference that science made was due not merely to the vogue of particular scientific ideas nor to particular changes wrought by science in the circumstances of life, but also to the increasing frequency with which people in all occupations turned to science for answers to problems arising in the course of business and the conduct of life. To meet the demand, there was a steady increase in the number and proportion of people engaged in scientific research and in the diffusion of scientific information, and an increasing emphasis on science in education.

The demand itself arose in large part from rapid and pervasive social changes—the industrialization and urbanization of American society; the exploitation of our natural resources; the spreading and merging of railroads and other systems of transport and communication; the surge toward bigness in industry, business, capital, labor, and education; the management problems of large-scale organization; the drift toward specialization in all occupations; and the rise of an administrative and managerial class.

Though all our major philosophers, with the exception of Santayana, have been actively interested in the social movements and questions of the day, the specific influence of these larger social changes upon their philosophies is not at once apparent, and has not been adequately studied. What does appear is rather a general recession of substance and structure and a coming forward of process and change in philosophic theory, reflecting the general fact of rapid social change and the correlated transfer from law and theology to science for leading ideas.

[32] "Holmes-Cohen Correspondence," 14 f.

Santayana has remarked that "modern philosophy is theology attenuated rather than science filled out." [33] Our classical period exhibits a shift in this respect. Theology, like law, had tended toward conservatism by its emphasis on all-embracing permanencies transcending, if not nullifying, change. Secular science, on the other hand, as the theory of change and of the sequences and correlations of changes, was not only indispensable to an age of enterprise but congenial to its mentality. And as the social and educational prestige of theology waned and that of science grew, philosophy ceased to be the handmaid of theology and became the interpreter of science.

Much more obvious in philosophy than the influence of particular social changes was that of particular sciences and particular scientific ideas. The influence of the scientific ideas of the age, however, was roughly proportional to their relevance to social change in general. By far the most influential single idea was that of evolution. To our philosophers it came to mean, among other things, (1) expelling from nature the last fixity, that of species, (2) including man and his intelligence in nature, and (3) adopting a biological view of intelligence.

In these respects as in others, the theory of evolution was reinforced by the rise of two new biological sciences, experimental physiology and experimental psychology, and by the currency of such ideas as those of ideomotor and reflex action. Experimental psychology was at first psychophysical but later behavioristic. In the earlier phase the observer was usually the subject, and the result was simply to put introspective psychology on an experimental footing. In the later phase, as in physiology, the observer was the experimenter. The former phase was transitional; only in the latter was the assimilation of psychology to biology completed.

We do well to remember that the generation of Peirce, James and Holmes was just reaching maturity when *The Origin of Species* appeared. It is worth remembering also that James was trained for medicine, that he began his career as a physiologist, and that he concentrated on psychology for fifteen years before committing himself to philosophy. Peirce, like James, was trained by the zoölogist Agassiz, and, though he counted himself as above all a logician, he was likewise an experimental psychologist; and indeed at one time he contemplated giving up the study of logic and philosophy "except experimental psychology." [34] Dewey was trained in G. Stanley Hall's first laboratory; his first book was his *Psychology;* one of his strongest early articles

[33] In *The Forum* 68:732, 1922.
[34] Letter to D. C. Gilman, 18 Dec. 1880, quoted in essay cited in n. 1 above.

was on the reflex-arc concept; [35] and the most influential of his later books was *Human Nature and Conduct, An Introduction to Social Psychology.* Royce, like Dewey and James, published a textbook of psychology. Only toward the end of our classical period did the emancipation of psychology from philosophy finally free the philosophers from special responsibility for psychology.

Also auxiliary to the idea of evolution, and permeated by it, were the sciences of man and society that arose in the late nineteenth and the early twentieth century: anthropology (physical and cultural), social psychology, comparative religion and folklore, institutional and historical economics, "the new history," and "the sociology of knowledge." Like the idea of evolution, all these influences made for an expectant if not always hopeful attitude toward social change.

Historical economics will serve as an example. As Whitehead has remarked, "The classical political economy which dominated the nineteenth century was largely based upon sociological observation of the middle classes of northern Europe and northern America in the eighteenth century." [36] The classical economists mistakenly assumed universal validity for economic laws abstracted from the practice of the particular economy in which they lived. The historical school sought to show, on the contrary, that every state of society has its own economy, the operations of which develop regularities peculiar to that economy. Their interest centered in the process by which a given economy evolves from an antecedent one and gives rise to a subsequent one. It is probable that Peirce's and Whitehead's doctrine that even the laws of nature evolve [37] owes something to the historical economists, of whom the Marxists are but the most familiar sect.

Next to evolution, the most important generalizations of the nineteenth century were the kinetic theory of gases and the laws of thermodynamics; of the early twentieth, relativity and quantum theory. These seemed even from the middle of the nineteenth century to be preparing the way for a new physical synthesis, and the biological theory of evolution was hailed almost at once as making it possible for this synthesis, unlike that of the seventeenth century, to include man and all his works. The new physics and the new biology were complementary. Each was to be interpreted in the light of the other. Furthermore, they had a common logic, which Peirce set himself to work out—the logic of statistics and probability; the logic, that is, of the social science

[35] "The Reflex Arc Concept in Psychology," *Psychological Review* 3:357-370, 1896; reprinted in *University of Chicago Contributions to Philosophy*, Vol. I, no. 1, pp. 39-52, 1896; and (under the title "The Unit of Behavior") in his *Philosophy and Civilization* (New York, G. P. Putnam's Sons, 1931), 233-248.

[36] *Adventures of Ideas* (New York, The Macmillan Co., 1933), 90 f.

[37] Part C, section 5 below.

(political economy) from which Darwin had taken the hint for his theory, as Peirce guessed before the Autobiography appeared.[38]

The crux of the theory of biological evolution was of course man, and the difficulty was not so much that of finding the links between the human organism and those of lower animals, as it was that of finding the links between animal instinct and human reason. Darwin made a beginning in those chapters of his *Descent of Man* devoted to comparison of the mental powers of man with those of lower animals, and to the development of the intellectual and moral faculties during primeval and civilized times. The naturalization of the human mind there begun was continued by our classical philosophers, and particularly by the pragmatists.

One of the pioneers of our classical period, Chauncey Wright, early established himself as a leading philosophic interpreter and defender of the Darwinian theory. With particular reference to the development of language, Darwin asked him to "take some incidental occasion to consider when a thing may properly be said to be effected by the will of man." [39] Wright visited Darwin in 1872 and a plan was laid which Wright reported to a friend as follows:

I am some time to write an essay on matters covering the ground of certain common interests and studies, and in review of his "Descent of Man," and other related works, for which the learned title is adopted of Psychozoölogy, —as a substitute for "Animal Psychology," "Instinct," and the like titles,—in order to give the requisite subordination (from our point of view) of consciousness in men and animals, to their development and general relations to nature.[40]

Wright died with the intended book unwritten, or at least unpublished, but a preliminary sketch of a part of it was written that winter and appeared in the following spring under the title "The Evolution of Self-Consciousness." In the latter part of this long essay Wright applied the principles of spontaneous variation and natural selection to Darwin's problem. In the course of the argument Wright drew a parallel between the development of language and that of law, touching by anticipation one of the themes of Holmes's great lectures on *The Common Law*, published seven years later.[41]

In November, 1872, shortly after Wright's return from his visit to Darwin, the Metaphysical Club met to hear Peirce read a paper expounding some of the views which he later said he "had been urging

[38] *Collected Papers* 5.364 n. 1; 6.293, 296-7.
[39] *Life and Letters of Charles Darwin*, II, 343.
[40] *Letters of Chauncey Wright*, 248.
[41] *North American Review* 116:303, 306, 1873; Wright: *Philosophical Discussions*, 258 f., 262. For further details see references in n. 2 above. James's *Pragmatism*, 240-242, echoes connections made between law, language and science by members of the Metaphysical Club.

all along under the name of pragmatism." [42] This paper, revised and expanded, was later published (1877-78) in the form of the two articles with which our selections from Peirce in the present volume begin. He began by saying that "each chief step in science has been a lesson in logic" and that "the Darwinian controversy is, in large part, a question of logic," as some of Wright's papers had shown it to be. "Mr. Darwin," he said, "proposed to apply the statistical method to biology . . . While unable to say what the operation of variation and natural selection in every individual case will be, [he] demonstrates that in the long run they will adapt animals to their circumstances." Peirce proceeds to outline the lesson in logic of this new step in science. The gist of the lesson turns out to be pragmatism.

The affiliation of pragmatism to the theory of evolution is thus apparent in the earliest formal exposition of the doctrine. Even more apparent, however, is the application of a psychological doctrine which remains to be mentioned.

Peirce says elsewhere that Nicholas St. John Green, the eldest of the three lawyers in the Metaphysical Club, often urged the importance of applying Bain's definition of belief as that upon which a man is prepared to act. From this definition, Peirce adds, pragmatism is scarce more than a corollary. [43] The Scotchman Alexander Bain was the author of a treatise on psychology in two volumes, *The Senses and the Intellect* (1855) and *The Emotions and the Will* (1859), which was the standard psychology in English-speaking countries for nearly half a century, rivaled only by Herbert Spencer's *Principles of Psychology* (1855). The theory of belief appeared in the second volume, under the head of Will. The essential articles in the theory are these:

(1) Belief belongs to "the active part of our being." Preparedness to act is not merely the test or criterion but the essence of belief.

(2) The opposite of belief is not disbelief but doubt or uncertainty.

(3) Belief is primary; doubt is "an after product, and not the primitive tendency." "Being under the strongest impulses to act somehow, an animal . . . seizes hold of any indication leading to an end, and abides by such instrumentality if it is found to answer. Nay more, there is the tendency to go beyond the actual experience, and not to desist until the occurrence of a positive failure or check." [44]

Bain's theory was developed quite independently of the Darwinian theory of evolution, and was published in the same year. The early pragmatists promptly put the two together. Bain's theory of spontaneous or primitive credulity was suggestive of the exuberant overproduc-

[42] *Collected Papers*, 5.13.
[43] *Ibid.* 5.12.
[44] *The Emotions and the Will* (London, John W. Parker and Son, 1859), iv, 568, 573, 580, 585.

tion of nature. The rôle of experience as confirmation or disconfirmation, not origination, was suggestive of the process of natural selection and survival of the fittest. Darwin's theory and Bain's were twinborn naturalistic variations on the old theme that man proposes and God disposes.

Bain was in the main a follower of John Stuart Mill, and it is worth a passing remark that the great classic of liberalism, Mill's *On Liberty,* was also published in 1859. The second chapter contains an argument for liberty of thought and discussion which the early pragmatists also connected with the Darwinian theory. The argument consists essentially in extending the principle of free trade from the economic to the intellectual realm.

Complete liberty of contradicting and disproving our opinion is the very condition which justifies us in assuming its truth for purposes of action; and on no other terms can a being with human faculties have any rational assurance of being right. ... The beliefs which we have most warrant for have no safeguard to rest on, but a standing invitation to the whole world to prove them unfounded.

It is but a step of rhetoric from this argument to Holmes's dictum that "the best *test* of truth is the power of the thought to get itself accepted in the competition of the market." [45] It is a somewhat farther step to Peirce's *definition* of truth as that upon which the community of investigators would agree if investigation were pushed sufficiently far.[46]

Chauncey Wright argued in 1870 that "our knowledges and rational beliefs result, *truly and literally,* from the survival of the fittest among our original and spontaneous beliefs," and suggested that the chief prejudice against this conclusion would be removed if we adopted Bain's definition of belief.[47]

About the same time another application of Bain's definition was being made by Holmes. He was developing a conception of law in terms of expectancies or predictions and the readiness to act upon them. In the *American Law Review* for July, 1872, he criticized Austin's view that command was the essence of law, that custom only became law by the tacit consent of the sovereign manifested by its adoption by the courts, and that before its adoption it was only a motive for decision. What more, Holmes asked, was the decision itself in relation to any future decision?

What more indeed is a statute; and in what other sense law, than that we believe that the motive which we think that it offers to the judges will

---

[45] Dissenting in 1919 in *Abrams* v. *United States,* 250 U. S. 616, 624 (*Dissenting Opinions,* 1929, 50); *cf. Collected Legal Papers,* 1920, 310-316.

[46] *Collected Papers* 5.407, 565. Dewey (*Logic,* 1938, 345 n.) calls this "the best definition of *truth* from the logical standpoint which is known to me."

[47] *North American Review* 111:301 n., 1870; *Philosophical Discussions,* 115 n. The essential part of this long and important note is reproduced in *Philosophical Review* 46:365 f., 1947. *Cf.* Dewey: *Experience and Nature,* 1925, 188.

prevail, and will induce them to decide a certain case in a certain way, and so shape our conduct on that anticipation? A precedent may not be followed; a statute may be emptied of its contents by construction, or may be repealed without a saving clause after we have acted on it; but we expect the reverse, and if our expectations come true, we say that we have been subject to law in the matter in hand.[48]

This was the first statement of the prediction theory of law, which Holmes elaborated in 1897 in terms like the following, and which supplied the hard core of the "legal realism" still current among us.

The object of our study . . . is prediction, the prediction of the incidence of the public force through the instrumentality of the courts. . . . The prophecies of what the courts will do in fact, and nothing more pretentious, are what I mean by the law . . . a legal duty so called is nothing but a prediction that if a man does or omits certain things he will be made to suffer in this or that way by judgment of the court; and so of a legal right. . . . The duty to keep a contract at common law means a prediction that you must pay damages if you do not keep it—and nothing else. If you commit a tort, you are liable to pay a compensatory sum. If you commit a contract, you are liable to pay a compensatory sum unless the promised event comes to pass, and that is all the difference.[49]

The experimental theory of knowledge, like the prediction theory of law, owed its prevalence among us in part to Darwinian analogies. It is but a more general form of the philosophy of science which makes much of hypothesis, prediction and experiment, and makes little of Bacon's and Mill's methods of induction. The analogies lie between the hypothesis and the spontaneous variation on the one hand, and between the experiment and natural selection on the other. What tests a legal hypothesis is future decisions, not those which suggested the hypothesis in the first place. What tests a scientific hypothesis is future experiment, not the observations from which it sprang.

This conception of science goes back to the members of the Metaphysical Club, and it appears particularly in their criticisms of the evolutionary speculations of Herbert Spencer and of his American disciple John Fiske. In an article on "The Philosophy of Herbert Spencer" in 1865, Wright said:

Ideas are developed by the sagacity of the expert, rather than by the systematic procedures of the philosopher. But when and however ideas are developed science cares nothing, for it is only by subsequent tests of sensible experience that ideas are admitted into the pandects of science. . . . Nothing justifies the development of abstract principles in science but their utility in enlarging our concrete knowledge of nature. The ideas on which mathematical Mechanics and the Calculus are founded, the morphological ideas

[48] American Law Review 6:723, 1872.
[49] Collected Legal Papers (New York, Harcourt, Brace and Howe, 1920), 167, 173, 169, 175.

of Natural History, and the theories of Chemistry are such working ideas,—finders, not merely summaries of truth.[50]

In a lecture before the Harvard Natural History Society in 1880, the main point was made by James as part of a general parallel "between the facts of social evolution on the one hand, and of zoölogical evolution as expounded by Mr. Darwin on the other." The great merit of Darwin, he said, was to discriminate clearly between the causes which originally produced variations and the causes that preserved them after they were produced.

... the new conceptions, emotions, and active tendencies which evolve are originally produced in the shape of random images, fancies, accidental out-births of spontaneous variation in the functional activity of the excessively instable human brain, which the outer environment simply confirms or refutes, adopts or rejects, preserves or destroys,—*selects*, in short, just as it selects morphological and social variations due to molecular accidents of an analogous sort. ... Even the conceiving of a law is a spontaneous variation in the strictest sense of the term. It flashes out of one brain, and no other, because the instability of that brain is such as to tip and upset itself in just that particular direction. But the important thing to notice is that the good flashes and the bad flashes, the triumphant hypotheses and the absurd conceits, are on an exact equality in respect of their origin.[51]

From this lecture it is an easy step to James's *Principles of Psychology* published a decade later, and particularly to the last chapter, on "Necessary Truths and the Effects of Experience," in which he applied the Darwinian notions of variation and selection to the a priori factors in human knowledge.

The parallel between biological evolution and the development of science was a favorite theme with Peirce also. We conclude the topic with a passage from one of his unpublished manuscripts, in which he remarks that on Darwin's original theory "the whole vast gap between the moner and man must have been bridged over by a sum of insensible variations."

That theory of Darwin's was, without any undistanced rival, the very greatest poem that man's brain ever struck out since the Great Pyramid; yet its truth always seemed to me incredible. It was too uniformitarian. Ontogeny is not so; there are certain times when it spurts: why should not Morphogeny be supposed to have done likewise? But in the parallel theory of the development of Science, while the spurts are even more marked, it is

[50] *North American Review* 100:427, 436; *Philosophical Discussions*, 47, 55 f. Joseph B. Warner, another member of the Club, echoes its similar criticisms of Fiske's *Cosmic Philosophy* in *Atlantic Monthly* 35:616-619, 1875.

[51] *The Will to Believe* (New York, Longmans, Green and Co., 1897), 216, 247, 249. Cf. James's application of the distinction between origin and value in *The Varieties of Religious Experience* (New York, Longmans, Green, and Co., 1902), ch. I.

quite unquestionable that the whole Matter of modern science has as a fact been accumulated by successive conjectures, and has had no other origin.[52]

(Readers new to philosophy may find it advantageous to postpone the remainder of the general introduction until after reading the selections from several of our six philosophers, and the special introductions to them.)

Except in the case of James, no adequate study has yet been made of the relations between our classical philosophers and their contemporaries in Great Britain and in continental Europe. From the beginning of our period, no thinker abroad was so highly esteemed by minor American philosophers as Herbert Spencer, the philosopher of evolution, until his place was taken in part by Henri Bergson, the philosopher of "creative evolution," and in much smaller part by the philosophers of "emergent evolution," such as Samuel Alexander. The British idealists, Green, Caird, Bradley, and Bosanquet; later, the realists Bertrand Russell, G. E. Moore, and C. D. Broad; and recently the German phenomenologists, existentialists and logical positivists, have had considerable followings among us.

Here as in Europe, however, it has been generally recognized that these were all epigoni. Philosophically, the nineteenth century lived in the shadow of Hegel, the pre-Darwinian philosopher of evolution, and the twentieth has scarcely emerged from it. The only subsequent philosopher of comparable scope and international stature is Benedetto Croce. Between Hegel and Croce, the philosopher whose reputation has suffered least with the passing of time is John Stuart Mill, who was still living during the most active years of the Metaphysical Club and was preëminent in its esteem. James's *Pragmatism* was dedicated to his memory.

In the prospectus of his *Principles of Philosophy* in 1893 Peirce stated that "The Principles supported by Mr. Peirce bear a close affinity with those of Hegel; perhaps are what Hegel's might have been had he been educated in a physical laboratory instead of in a theological seminary."

Though Royce was a sympathetic interpreter of German idealism generally, it was Hegel's *Phenomenology* to which he gave the most detailed consideration in his *Lectures on Modern Idealism.*

Santayana says the first impulse to write his *Life of Reason* came to him when he was studying Hegel's *Phenomenology* in Royce's seminar in 1889. In later life, he wished that his doctor's thesis had been written, not on Lotze, as it was at Royce's prompting, nor on Schopenhauer as he himself had proposed, but on Hegel.

[52] Peirce Papers, Harvard University Archives, I.B.1. box 2, p. 28 of another draft of the MS. from which *Collected Papers* 5.11-13, 464-496 were taken.

It would have meant harder work, and it would have been more inadequate; yet it would have prepared me better for professional controversies and for understanding the mind of my time. Lotze was stillborn, and I have forgotten everything that I then had to read in him and to ponder. I liked Hegel's *Phaenomenologie;* it set me planning my *Life of Reason;* and now I like even his *Logik,* not the dialectical sophistry in it, but the historical and critical lights that appear by the way. I could have written, even then, a critical thesis, say on *Logic, Sophistry, and Truth in Hegel's Philosophy.* This would have knit my own doctrine together at the beginning of my career, as I have scarcely had the chance of doing at the end.[53]

George H. Mead, who had been a pupil of Royce and had afterwards studied in Germany, was later associated with Dewey at Chicago and moved with Dewey from Hegelian idealism to pragmatism and experimentalism. He regularly gave a course in "Movements of Thought in the Nineteenth Century" in which German idealism received the most extended and surprisingly sympathetic treatment, and provided the center of reference for the consideration of later movements.

James's recognition of the kinship between his work and that of Dewey and Mead was delayed by their Hegelian inheritance. "You have all come from Hegel . . . I from empiricism," he wrote Dewey in 1903, "and though we reach much the same goal it superficially looks different from opposite sides." Yet, intermittently throughout his life, James himself studied Hegel, with polemic intent but increasing respect.[54]

In describing his own philosophical development, Dewey acknowledges that

acquaintance with Hegel has left a permanent deposit in my thinking. The form, the schematism, of his system now seems to me artificial to the last degree. But in the content of his ideas there is often an extraordinary depth; in many of his analyses, taken out of their mechanical dialectical setting, an extraordinary acuteness. Were it possible for me to be a devotee of any system, I still should believe that there is greater richness and greater variety of insight in Hegel than in any other single systematic philosopher . . .[55]

Though Whitehead never studied Hegel at first hand, he absorbed a good deal through acquaintance with two British Hegelians, McTaggart and Haldane.

[I once] read one page of Hegel. But it is true that I was influenced by Hegel. I was an intimate friend of McTaggart almost from the very first day he came to the University [Cambridge], and saw him for a few minutes

[53] *The Middle Span,* 152 f.

[54] Perry, *op. cit.,* II, 521 f.; I, 724-730. As Perry observes (II, 584), James "always had a sneaking fondness for Hegel." Ernst Mach of Vienna thanked James for giving him his "first understanding of Hegel"! *Ibid.,* II, 594.

[55] *Contemporary American Philosophy* (New York, The Macmillan Co., 1930), II, 21.

almost daily, and I had many a chat with Lord Haldane about his Hegelian point of view.[56]

Whitehead was also familiar with the philosophy of another British Hegelian, F. H. Bradley, and acknowledged that though he was in sharp disagreement with it throughout the main body of his *Process and Reality*, "the final outcome is after all not so greatly different." Whitehead's use of the term "speculative philosophy" and his general conception of it were in the Hegelian tradition. He saw an analogy less obvious to others between the Hegelian development of an idea and the concrescence of an actual entity as the development of a subjective aim in his own philosophy. "My criticism of his procedure," he said of Hegel on another occasion, "is that when in his discussion he arrives at a contradiction, he construes it as a crisis in the universe." [57]

C. Major Themes and Tendencies

From considering some of the influences that gave form and direction to the philosophy of our classical period, and from considering some of its themes in relation to these influences, we pass now to a review of the major themes themselves, in an order which may suggest some of their relations to each other.

1. THE DAMNATION OF DESCARTES

Our classical period began in 1868 with three articles by Peirce in the second volume of the *Journal of Speculative Philosophy*. "Descartes is the father of modern philosophy," he remarked; and, after examining the faculties and principles assumed by Descartes, he said that "in some or all of these respects most modern philosophers have been, in effect, Cartesians. Now without wishing to return to scholasticism, it seems to me that modern science and modern logic require us to stand upon a very different platform from this." [58] Such a platform he proceeded to erect. When he became Lecturer on Logic at the Johns Hopkins University in 1879, and founded The Metaphysical Club there, he read a paper on the same topic at its second meeting, which he abstracted as follows:

These questions ["concerning certain faculties claimed for man"] related to the hypothesis of intuitive faculties, against which it was maintained that we have a variety of facts, all of which are most readily explained on the supposition that we have no intuitive faculty of distinguishing intuitive from mediate cognition; that there is no necessity of supposing an intuitive self-

[56] *Essays in Science and Philosophy* (New York, Philosophical Library, 1947), 116.
[57] *Process and Reality*, vii, viii, 254; *Philosophical Review* 46:186, 1937.
[58] *Collected Papers* 5.264 f.

consciousness, since self-consciousness may easily be the result of inference; that we have no intuitive power of distinguishing between the subjective elements of different kinds of cognitions; that there is no reason for supposing a power of introspection, and consequently the only way of investigating a psychological question is by inference from external facts; that every thought must be interpreted in another, or that all thought is in signs; that cognition arises by a *process* of beginning, as any other change comes to pass.[59]

Peirce's "Illustrations of the Logic of Science" (1877-78)—and particularly the first two essays here reprinted—are best understood as a sustained argument to show that the scientific way of making ideas clear and of fixing beliefs is quite different from the Cartesian way.

The castigation of Descartes—his faked universal doubt, his intuitions and introspections, his clear and distinct ideas, his dualism, his exaggeration of the ego, his mechanization of nature—has been a constant theme of American philosophy ever since. Rightly or wrongly, all the evils of modern philosophy have been fathered upon him.

Most striking of all, perhaps, is the passage in Whitehead's *Science and the Modern World* in which he contrasts James's essay, "Does Consciousness Exist?" (1904), with Descartes's *Discourse on Method* (1637).

The scientific materialism and the Cartesian Ego were both challenged at the same moment, one by science and the other by philosophy, as represented by William James ... and the double challenge marks the end of a period which lasted for about two hundred and fifty years.[60]

2. THE NATURALIZING OF MIND

Assisted by the idea of evolution, by Bain's theory of belief, by experimental physiology and its substitution of the conditioned reflex for the association of ideas, our classic philosophers have put the mind back into nature. Abandoning the Platonic dichotomy of knowledge and belief, they have included knowing in believing, believing and thinking in acting, and acting in nature.

As James put it in 1880: "The theory of evolution is beginning to do very good service by its reduction of all mentality to the type of reflex action. Cognition, in this view, is but a fleeting moment, a cross-section at a certain point, of what in its totality is a motor phenomenon." [61]

According to Peirce: "There is no reason why 'thought'... should be

---

[59] *Johns Hopkins University Circulars* 1:18, Jan. 1880.
[60] *Science and the Modern World* (New York, The Macmillan Co., 1925), 205 f.
[61] *The Will to Believe*, 84.

taken in that narrow sense in which silence and darkness are favorable
to thought. It should rather be understood as covering all rational life,
so that an experiment shall be an operation of thought." [62]

Without questioning its existence, Santayana finds "no difficulty in
admitting consciousness and all its works into the web and woof of
nature"; for him, "mind is not the cause of our actions but an effect,
collateral with our actions, of bodily growth and organization." "Now,
the body is an instrument, the mind is its function, the witness and
reward of its operation. Mind is the body's entelechy, a value which
accrues to the body when it has reached a certain perfection." [63]

In Dewey's view, "The distinction between physical, psychophysical
and mental is one of levels of increasing complexity and intimacy of
interaction among natural events." [64]

3. THE MENTALIZING OF NATURE

Perhaps it is not possible to naturalize mind without in some degree
mentalizing nature. In any case, it goes without saying that in the
resolution of the Cartesian dualism adopted by idealists like Royce,
the assimilation of nature to mind was more prominent than that of
mind to nature.

It was Peirce, however, who said that "The one intelligible theory
of the universe is that of objective idealism, that matter is effete mind,
inveterate habits becoming physical laws." [65]

James was originally an idealist after the fashion of George Berkeley
and of John Stuart Mill; then a phenomenalist in Renouvier's sense,
according to which subject and object are complementary aspects of
every "phenomenon"; and only late in life a "radical empiricist." Even
then it was felt by his critics that his "pure experience," despite James's
claim that the term meant something prior to the distinction between
things and thoughts, and despite his profession of "natural realism," invariably turned out not neutral but mental. And the members of that
"pluralistic universe" which James depicted in his last complete work
were overlapping consciousnesses, great and small.

Dewey was originally an idealist of the Hegelian type, and what
Santayana called "the dominance of the foreground" in his mature
philosophy is perhaps the ghost of Hegel's *Geist*. "An empirical philosophy," Dewey says, "must replace the traditional separation of nature
and experience with the idea of continuity." [66] But what he once called

[62] *Collected Papers* 5.420.
[63] *Reason in Common Sense* (New York, Charles Scribner's Sons, 1905), 218,
206; *Winds of Doctrine*, 7.
[64] *Experience and Nature* (Chicago, Open Court Publishing Co., 1925), 261.
[65] *Collected Papers* 6.25; below, p. 95.
[66] *Intelligence in the Modern World* (New York, Modern Library, 1939), 1043.

the experiential continuum and now calls the continuum of inquiry bears a striking likeness to the continuum of mind, nature and other minds in objective idealism.[67]

Whitehead's metaphysics of feelings or "prehensions," with its rejection of the doctrine of "vacuous actuality" (existence without experience), is at once the extreme manifestation and the supreme achievement in this direction. His "actual entities" or "actual occasions," the final real things of which the world is made up, are "drops of experience, complex and interdependent." [68]

4. FROM SUBSTANCE TO PROCESS [69]

Mental substance has vanished, leaving scarcely a trace. Material substance survives only in Santayana, and its character is flux.

For Peirce, "substances" are specious derivatives of events. They are "constituted by regularities"; they are "bundles of habits." [70]

Examples of James's reduction of substance to process appear in his early "stream of consciousness" and in his later "pure experience" with its dropwise flow which Whitehead found so suggestive.

For Dewey as for Whitehead, "Every existence is an event." "Nothing but unfamiliarity stands in the way of thinking of both mind and matter as different characters of natural events." [71]

This was to invert the older view, retained by Santayana, that events are modes of substance. Hence his critique of Dewey's "pervasive quasi-Hegelian tendency to dissolve the individual into his social functions, as well as everything substantial or actual into something relative or transitional. For him events, situations, and histories hold all facts and all persons in solution." [72]

Here again, Whitehead is the extreme case. In his philosophy of organism, the ultimately real entities are events or "actual occasions," each a process of activity. "Physical endurance is the process of continuously inheriting a certain identity of character transmitted throughout a historic route of events." "The life of man is an historic route

---

[67] See for instance the statement by J. E. Creighton, the leader of this school which reigned in our universities from the 1890's into the 1920's, in *Philosophical Review* 22:522, 1917: "This historical speculative idealism, as occupying the standpoint of experience, has never separated the mind from the external order of nature. It knows no egocentric predicament, because it recognizes no ego 'alone with its states,' standing apart from the order of nature and from a society of other minds." (Reprinted in Creighton's *Studies in Speculative Philosophy*, New York, The Macmillan Co., 1925, 266.)

[68] *Process and Reality*, 28.

[69] *Cf.* W. H. Sheldon: *America's Progressive Philosophy* (New Haven, Yale University Press, 1942), esp. pp. 1-4 and ch. III.

[70] *Collected Papers* 1.411, 414.

[71] *Experience and Nature*, 71, 74.

[72] *Journal of Philosophy* 22:675, 1925; *The Philosophy of John Dewey*, 247.

of actual occasions which in a marked degree ... inherit from each other." [73]

5. THE OBSOLESCENCE OF THE ETERNAL

The eternity that belonged to Plato's ideas, to truth, and to God, survives only in Santayana's realms of essence and truth, and, somewhat doubtfully, in Whitehead's "eternal objects" and Royce's Absolute.

The notion of eternal truths independent of thought is retained only by Santayana. The shift from eternalism to temporalism, the cult of "taking time seriously," reaches its extreme limit in James's version of the pragmatic theory of truth. Truth and falsity have no *meaning* apart from propositions actually asserted or hypotheses actually entertained, and they have no *being* apart from the actual fulfilment or disappointment of expectations involved in the propositions or hypotheses so asserted or entertained.

The truth of an idea is not a stagnant property inherent in it. Truth *happens* to an idea. It *becomes* true, is *made* true by events. Its verity *is* in fact an event, a process: the process namely of its verifying itself, its veri-*fication*. Its validity is the process of its valid-*ation*.[74]

Hegel's evolutionary logic, in which the evolution was in some sense non-temporal, becomes in Dewey avowedly temporal. The logical forms or categories themselves evolve in the continuum of inquiry.

One of the insistent themes in Dewey is the shift from the eternal to the temporal as the object of knowledge also.

In the old scheme, knowledge, as science, signified precisely and exclusively turning away from change to the changeless. In the new experimental science, knowledge is obtained in exactly the opposite way, namely, through deliberate institution of a definite and specified course of change. *The* method of physical inquiry is to introduce some change in order to see what other change ensues; the correlation between these changes, when measured by a series of operations, constitutes the definite and desired object of knowledge.[75]

Nor are the correlations themselves presumed to be exact or changeless. As there are no immutable species since Darwin, so there are no eternal laws of nature since Peirce and Whitehead. It seemed to Peirce that law, more than anything else, needed explaining, and that "the only possible way of accounting for the laws of nature and for uniformity in general is to suppose them results of evolution." [76] As Whitehead later put it, "the evolution of laws of nature is concurrent with

---

[73] *Science and the Modern World*, 159; *Process and Reality*, 137.
[74] *Pragmatism* (New York, Longmans, Green, and Co., 1907), 201.
[75] *The Quest for Certainty* (New York, Minton, Balch & Co., 1929), 84.
[76] *Collected Papers* 6:12, 13; below, p. 91.

the evolution of enduring pattern." [77] Peirce, however, seems to have assumed evolution in a fixed direction, in spite of sports and spurts. Whitehead supposed a succession of cosmic epochs each evolving its own set of laws but not connected by any law of succession.

The arbitrary, as it were 'given,' elements in the laws of nature warn us that we are in a special cosmic epoch. . . . This epoch is characterized by electronic and protonic actual entities. . . . the laws of nature . . . are statistical expressions of the prevalent types of interaction. . . .[78]

As for Whitehead's eternal objects, their being is their envisagement in the primordial nature of God, and their functioning as determinants in the becoming of actual occasions; and, though their envisagement is complete, and there are therefore no novel eternal objects, the ultimate category is nevertheless that of the continuous creativity by which, in each event or actual occasion, the many become one and are increased by one. And the consequent nature of God, affected by each event, is temporal; so that, even in God, actuality is process.

6. THE REDUCTION OF YESTERDAY TO TOMORROW

One of the negative traits of Cartesian rationalism was its blindness to history. Our classic period, though reacting against Descartes chiefly on other grounds, was anti-Cartesian also in its preoccupation with history. Of our canonical six, all but James were in some sense historians. Peirce gave a course of twelve Lowell Lectures on the history of science in 1892-93; the first of the twelve volumes of his projected *Principles of Philosophy* was a *Review of the Leading Ideas of the Nineteenth Century;* the ninth was to be devoted to *Studies in Comparative Biography;* and he made an elaborate study of "The Logic of Research into Ancient History." Royce wrote a history of California from 1846 to 1856, and his *Spirit of Modern Philosophy* and *Lectures on Modern Idealism* are masterly if now somewhat outmoded historical interpretations of the German romantic movement. History and criticism, alternating and fused, bulk large in Santayana's works and are the main burden of many of them; and, if we include contemporary history, this is nearly as true of Dewey. Whitehead's *Science and the Modern World* and *Adventures of Ideas,* though containing much else, are works of genius in historical interpretation.

Yet there was never a period of which it was truer to say that its backward looks were for the sake of forward looks. Whitehead's *Science and the Modern World,* for example, concludes with a chapter on "Requisites for Social Progress," and his *Adventures of Ideas* has a

[77] *Science and the Modern World,* 156; *cf.* 159.
[78] *Process and Reality,* 139, 162.

chapter on "Foresight" which concludes with "a sketch of the Business Mind of the Future."

Perhaps the most characteristic shift in our period was in the reference of the term experience. Traditional empiricism referred ideas back to the experiences which it supposed had generated them. Our philosophers referred them forward to the experiences which they foretold and by which they were to be tested. Even in the single moment of experience their interest was in its growing point toward the future rather than in its vanishing point toward the past.

In his essay on "The Need for a Recovery of Philosophy" in the volume *Creative Intelligence,* Dewey begins with a statement of "the chief contrasts between the orthodox description of experience and that congenial to present conditions" and devotes the remainder to "a consideration of the effect of substituting the account of experience relevant to modern life for the inherited account." Perhaps the most striking contrast is the emphasis on the given and the remembered in the traditional account and on the desired and the expected in the new.

The preoccupation of experience with things which are coming (are now coming, not just to come) is obvious to anyone whose interest in experience is empirical. . . . Anticipation is therefore more primary than recollection; projection than summoning of the past; the prospective than the retrospective . . . Success and failure are the primary "categories" of life. . . . Imaginative recovery of the bygone is indispensable to successful invasion of the future, but its status is that of an instrument. . . .[79]

In Whitehead, an Englishman's sense for the continuity of history issues in a theory of the immanence or objective existence of the future in the present. "Cut away the future, and the present collapses, emptied of its proper content." [80]

The most paradoxical aspect of American futurism is, however, the pragmatic theory of meaning. Here is Peirce's phrasing of it:

The rational meaning of every proposition lies in the future. How so? The meaning of a proposition is . . . a translation of it. But of the myriads of forms into which a proposition may be translated, what is that one which is to be called its very meaning? It is, according to the pragmaticist, that form in which the proposition becomes applicable to human conduct, not in these or those special circumstances, nor when one entertains this or that special design, but that form which is most directly applicable to self-control under every situation and to every purpose. This is why he locates the meaning in future time; for future conduct is the only conduct that is subject to self-control. . . .[81]

The paradox lies in the consequence that propositions ostensibly about the past are, like all others, really about the future.

[79] *Creative Intelligence* (New York, Henry Holt and Co., 1917), 7, 8, 12, 13, 14.
[80] *Adventures of Ideas.* 246.
[81] *Collected Papers* 5.427.

As for that part of the Past that lies beyond memory, the Pragmaticist doctrine is that the meaning of its being believed to be in connection with the Past consists in the acceptance as truth of the conception that we ought to conduct ourselves according to it (like the meaning of any other belief). Thus, a belief that Christopher Columbus discovered America really refers to the future. . . .[82]

Peirce went so far in one of his unpublished notebooks as to say that all it concerns us to know is how to conduct ourselves on future occasions.

What Santayana criticized as "that strange pragmatic reduction of yesterday to tomorrow," future historians may perhaps discern in all our philosophers, including himself; for it was he who suggested that "the backward perspective of time is perhaps really an inverted expectation." [83]

7. PURPOSE IN THOUGHT

Peirce says that some of his friends (probably James among them) wished him to call his principle practicism or practicalism.

But for one who had learned philosophy out of Kant . . . *praktisch* and *pragmatisch* were as far apart as the two poles, the former belonging in a region of thought where no mind of the experimentalist type can ever make sure of solid ground under his feet, the latter expressing relation to some definite human purpose. Now quite the most striking feature of the new theory was its recognition of an inseparable connection between rational cognition and rational purpose; and that consideration it was which determined the preference for the name *pragmatism*.[84]

James himself wrote in an essay of 1879: "What now is a *conception?* It is a *teleological instrument*. It is a partial aspect of a thing which *for our purpose* we regard as its essential aspect, as the representative of the entire thing." [85] And in 1890 in his *Psychology:* "the only meaning of essence is teleological . . . classification and conception are purely teleological weapons of the mind. The essence of a thing is that one of its properties which is so *important for my interests* that in comparison with it I may neglect the rest." [86] James was concerned to show the propriety of purpose affecting moral and religious thinking by exhibiting the rôle of purpose in the most rigorous scientific thinking.

The most notable general change in the temper of philosophy in the nineteenth century was the shift from rationalism to voluntarism—from the primacy of "The Senses and the Intellect" to that of "The Emotions

[82] *Ibid.* 5.461; *cf.* 5.565 on the proposition that Caesar crossed the Rubicon.
[83] *Journal of Philosophy* 22:686, 1925; *Scepticism and Animal Faith* (New York, Charles Scribner's Sons, 1923), 36.
[84] *Collected Papers* 5.412.
[85] *Collected Essays and Reviews*, 86 f.
[86] *Principles of Psychology* (New York, Henry Holt and Co., 1890), II, 335.

and the Will," to use the titles of Bain's two volumes. The pragmatic theory of mind, in James's version more clearly than in the others, is a form of voluntarism. As he put it in an essay of 1881:

The willing department of our nature . . . dominates both the conceiving department and the feeling department; or, in plainer English, perception and thinking are only there for behavior's sake. I am sure I am not wrong in stating this result as one of the fundamental conclusions to which the entire drift of modern physiological investigation sweeps us.[87]

Dewey wrote a famous essay on "The Reflex Arc Concept" in 1896, the main point of which, as applied to perception, was neatly summarized by Mead as follows:

In the end, what we see, hear, feel, taste and smell depends upon what we are doing, and not the reverse. In our purposively organized life we inevitably come back upon previous conduct as the determining condition of what we sense at any moment, and the so-called external stimulus is the occasion for this and not its cause.[88]

In defining pragmatism for the Century Dictionary in 1909, Dewey gave the following as the net or mean sense of the term in its various uses: "The theory that the processes and the materials of knowledge are determined by practical or purposive considerations—that there is no such thing as knowledge determined by exclusively theoretical, speculative, or abstract intellectual considerations." [89]

Now it is a matter of considerable interest that this is precisely the dominant theme in Royce's philosophy from beginning to end. One of his earliest papers, which was read before Peirce's Metaphysical Club at The Johns Hopkins University, bore the title "Purpose in Thought." [90] The argument of his major work, *The World and the Individual,* turns on distinguishing the "internal meaning" of ideas—their intent or purpose—from their external meaning, and on subordinating the latter to the former. Peirce said of this work: "Royce's . . . insistence on the element of purpose in intellectual concepts is essentially the pragmatistic position." [91]

This, in fact, is one of the many respects in which pragmatism is a form of idealism. Marx in his Theses on Feuerbach acknowledged the idealistic derivation of the same aspect of his own doctrine. The chief defect of all previous materialism, he said, was its contemplative char-

[87] *The Will to Believe,* 114.

[88] *Decennial Publications of the University of Chicago,* 1st ser., vol. III, pt. II, p. 98. *Cf.* n. 35 above.

[89] *The Century Dictionary Supplement* (New York, The Century Co., 1909), II, 1050; *cf.* I, viii.

[90] *Johns Hopkins University Circulars* 1:84; Royce: *Fugitive Essays* (Cambridge, Mass., Harvard University Press, 1920), 219-260.

[91] *Journal of Philosophy* 13:720, 1916.

acter. "Hence it came about that the active side was developed by idealism in opposition to materialism."

8. EXIT THE SPECTATOR

In one of his condescending accounts of James's pragmatism, Santayana wrote in 1911 that

There is a feeling abroad now, to which biology and Darwinism lend some color, that theory is simply an instrument for practice, and intelligence merely a help toward material survival . . . Intelligence . . . is no miraculous, idle faculty, by which we mirror passively any or everything that happens to be true, reduplicating the real world to no purpose . . . It does not essentially serve to picture other parts of reality, but to connect them . . . Ideas are not mirrors, they are weapons . . .[92]

The rejection of the spectator theory of knowledge was most vigorously expressed by James as early as 1878 in his first original philosophical article, "Remarks on Spencer's Definition of Mind as Correspondence." He argued that in the working out of his theory Spencer made mind "pure product" and ignored the rôle of emotion, volition, and action.

I, for my part, cannot escape the consideration, forced upon me at every turn, that the knower is not simply a mirror floating with no foot-hold anywhere, and passively reflecting an order that he comes upon and finds simply existing. The knower is an actor, and co-efficient of the truth on one side, whilst on the other he registers the truth which he helps to create. Mental interests, hypotheses, postulates, so far as they are bases for human action—action which to a great extent transforms the world—help to *make* the truth which they declare. In other words, there belongs to mind, from its birth upward, a spontaneity, a vote. It is in the game, and not a mere looker-on.[93]

In Peirce, Royce, Dewey, and Santayana, the rejection takes various forms: the conception of ideas as plans of action; the experimental conception of knowing (not as being for the sake of other doings but) as itself involving doing; the denial of immediate knowledge; the distinguishing of knowledge from immediate experiences often confused with it, such as those of having, possessing, enjoying, suffering; and the discrediting of the notion of knowledge as disclosure of antecedent reality.

In Santayana's case the contemplative spirit traditionally associated with the spectator theory of knowledge still bears the palm, but the object of contemplation is essence, not fact, and the intuition of essences is not knowledge.

In the very course of improving our conceptual formulation of "the nature of things," Whitehead quietly rejects the spectator theory by

---

[92] *Winds of Doctrine*, 205-207.
[93] *Collected Essays and Reviews*, 67.

abolishing the detached mind and relegating consciousness to a subordinate metaphysical position;[94] by shifting the emphasis from "perception in the mode of presentational immediacy" to "perception in the mode of causal efficacy"; and by transforming the theory of propositions.

> The interest in logic, dominating overintellectualized philosophers, has obscured the main function of propositions in the nature of things...A proposition is an element in the objective lure *proposed for feeling*, and when admitted into feeling it constitutes *what is felt....* it is more important that a proposition be interesting than that it be true...[95]

9. THE THEORY OF SIGNS

In the first of his three articles of 1868 with which our classical period began, Peirce concluded that "all thought is in signs" and that "every thought must be interpreted in another."[96] One of the major tasks to which Peirce devoted his life was therefore the construction of a theory of signs.

Not the least merit of this conception of thought in Peirce's eyes was that it rounded out his theory of the categories by providing a model of "thirdness." As feeling is a single and volition a double consciousness, so "cognition is...a triple consciousness: of the sign, of the real object cognized, and of the meaning or interpretation of the sign, which the cognition connects with that object."[97] Peirce called this doctrine "cognitionism" and said that he and James had probably taken it from Chauncey Wright, who perhaps had taken it from John Stuart Mill.[98] Wright's formulations of it, at any rate, provided one of the bridges between British associationism and American pragmatism. Here is a statement of it from 1866:

> The idea of externality involves the function of sensations as signs...and their proper function as signs is to produce a state of expectation with reference to the things signified, without being themselves the objects of any expectation...In being as a sign unexpected, the idea [i.e., sensation or group of sensations] has the mark of externality in it; and by producing a state of expectation it possesses the mark of reality, and is thus the sign of an external reality....so far as an idea is a sign at all in a cognition, it is the sign of the unknown cause, not of itself, but of other actual or possible sensations, the existence of which as pleasures or pains constitutes the reality and the efficiency of the cognition; and the general expectation of these sensations is our general sense of an external reality. The idea is not a sign of an external existence numerically distinct from itself and a counterpart of

---

[94] *Process and Reality*, 88, 211.

[95] *Ibid.*, 283, 284 f., 395 f.

[96] *Collected Papers* 5.253.

[97] "Pragmatism Made Easy," unpublished MS., Peirce Papers, Harvard University Archives, I.B.1. box 1, pp. 7 f.

[98] "Quest of Quest," MS., I.B.2. box 11, §6, p. 32.

itself, but only a sign of the sources of those other mental states which as real pleasures and pains can be expected as concomitants or consequences of it.[99]

Royce's doctrine of a community of interpretation, to which a large place is given in our selections, was worked out in conscious dependence upon Peirce's theory of signs.

George H. Mead, whose philosophy is closely related to that of Dewey, developed a social psychology based in large part on a behavioristic theory of signs. Dewey's latest work, in collaboration with Arthur F. Bentley, is a fresh departure in this direction.[100]

For Santayana, knowledge is belief—"animal faith"—mediated by symbols. Though this doctrine bulks large in his philosophic system, it receives no technical development.

In all departments of Whitehead's work, the concept of symbolism plays an important part. As a mathematical logician, he emphasized the tremendous importance of sign-systems; but he seems, in his modernized Platonism, to have thought of them always as means for extending the thinker's grasp of "eternal objects"—thus maintaining a distinction which most other sign-conscious philosophers of his time either blurred or, as nominalists, rejected outright. In his discussions of human civilization, Whitehead like many of his contemporaries assigned an indispensable rôle to symbolism. And in his account of man's relation to nature, he developed the idea that sense-perception is the human animal's automatic symbolization of vaguely felt environmental realities by clear-cut sense-data. Here the symbolization is a biological instrument for attaining—not without risk of error—that higher level of experience which is our conscious awareness of the external world.[101]

A host of quite heterogeneous investigations is proceeding at present under the general head of theory of signs. Most of the investigators differ from Peirce and Whitehead by avoiding metaphysics, or at least by forswearing it.

10. LABORATORY VS. SEMINARY PHILOSOPHY

Our classical period witnessed the rise among us of the university and the transfer of intellectual leadership from the college to the university.

In 1891 Peirce defined "university" for the Century Dictionary as

[99] *North American Review* 103:264 f., 1866.

[100] Dewey & Bentley, *Knowing and the Known* (Boston, Beacon Press, 1949).

[101] It is not clear how far Whitehead was indebted to Santayana in this connection. *Cf. Symbolism, Its Meaning and Effect* (New York, The Macmillan Co., 1927), vii, 28 f., 32 f.; *Process and Reality,* 83, 125, 215 f., 231; *Adventures of Ideas,* 279 n.

An association of men for the purpose of study, which confers degrees which are acknowledged as valid throughout Christendom, is endowed, and is privileged by the state, in order that the people may receive intellectual guidance and that the theoretical problems which present themselves in the development of civilization may be resolved.

Two years later, in August 1893, John Jay Chapman spent a long evening in Peirce's company at the Century Club in New York and put his impressions into two letters, in one of which he said:

Charles Peirce wrote the definition of University in the Century Diction-ary. He called it an institution for purposes of study. They wrote to him that their notion had been that a university was an institution for instruction. He wrote back that if they had any such notion they were grievously mis-taken, that a university had not and never had had anything to do with instruction and that until we got over this idea we should not have any university in this country. He commended Johns Hopkins and Gilman...[102]

It was a favorite dictum of Peirce that "the chief obstacle to the ad-vance of science among students of science in the modern era has been that they were teachers." [103] In soberer moments, however, he took the view, not that universities had nothing to do with instruction, but that their teaching function should be subordinate to their research function and directed toward securing continuity of the latter.[104] It seemed to him that the proper balance was most nearly achieved at the Johns Hopkins University, where he had taught for five years and where Royce and Dewey had been trained.

In such an atmosphere it was natural that philosophy should also come to be conceived as a field for research, inviting original contri-butions. Thus we ceased to be merely perpetuators of a tradition, learners from the older countries of Europe, and struck out in direc-tions of our own.

It may be of interest to compare two views of our progress in this respect at the end of the nineteenth century. To Peirce in 1898 it seemed that the still backward condition of philosophy among us was due to the fact that

during this century it has chiefly been pursued by men who have not been nurtured in dissecting-rooms and other laboratories, and who consequently have not been animated by the true scientific *Eros;* but who have on the contrary come from theological seminaries, and have consequently been in-flamed with a desire to amend the lives of themselves and others, a spirit no doubt more important than the love of science, for men in average situa-tions, but radically unfitting them for the task of scientific investigation.[105]

[102] M. A. DeWolfe Howe: *John Jay Chapman and His Letters* (Boston, Hough-ton Mifflin Co., 1937), 96 f.
[103] J. M. Baldwin (ed.): *Dictionary of Philosophy and Psychology,* II, 502.
[104] *Science* n.s. 11:621, 20 April 1900.
[105] *Collected Papers* 1.620.

Royce was more optimistic, at least in addressing a foreign public. In 1897 he wrote in a German philosophic journal:

Since the middle of the seventies, the academic life of America has been deeply influenced by a tendency towards the alteration of our institutions of higher learning . . . in the direction of more thorough and liberal scholarship, of more untrammelled and minute scientific investigation, and of a favoring of the functions of research in addition to the functions of instruction. . . . our former neglect of philosophy was merely due to the predominance, in academic life, of philosophy's dogmatic rival and counterpart—theology. . . . the modern heresy-hunter is becoming more and more transformed after the fashion long since exemplified in the evolution of the pointer-dog. He no longer leaps upon the prey, but contents himself with cautiously pointing.[106]

11. SCIENCE AS COÖPERATIVE INQUIRY

In part because of the general shift from theology to science and from college and seminary to university leadership, there was a change in the conception of science. It ceased to mean primarily systematized knowledge and came to mean investigation or inquiry. Peirce could say at the turn of the century:

The glory of the nineteenth century has been its science. . . . It was my inestimable privilege to have felt as a boy the warmth of the steadily burning enthusiasm of the scientific generation of Darwin, most of the leaders of which at home I knew intimately, and some very well in almost every country of Europe. . . . The word *science* was one often in those men's mouths, and I am quite sure they did not mean by it "systematized knowledge," as former ages had defined it, nor anything set down in a book, but, on the contrary, a mode of life; not knowledge, but the devoted, well-considered life-pursuit of knowledge; devotion . . . to the truth that the man is not yet able to see but is striving to obtain. The word was thus, from the etymological point of view, already a misnomer. And so it remains with the scientists of to-day. What they meant, and still mean, by "science" ought, etymologically, to be called *philosophy*.[107]

One of the many consequences of viewing science in this way was the accentuation of its social character. The old question of the classification of the sciences, for example, was thus put in a new light, as Peirce argued in an unpublished manuscript.

I use "science" in the sense of a business, that is, of a total of real acts exerting reciprocal effects upon one another and concerned with closely analogous purposes. When I speak of any given heuretic science, I mean the body of doings in past and future time, not too remote from the present, of the members of a certain social group. These persons constitute a social group in their acquaintance with, understanding of, and sympathy for one another's doings. And the peculiarities which make it a *scientific* group are, first, that the members are devoted to ascertaining truths of a given kind on

[106] *Archiv für systematische Philosophie* 3:244-247, 1897.
[107] *The 19th Century* (New York, G. P. Putnam's Sons, 1901), 314 f.

account of their speculative interest in the matters, that they have each of them some special facilities or capacities for such research, that they employ approved methods, and that each seeks aid from the results of the others. From this point of view, the question whether a given class of investigations is to be regarded as belonging to this science or to that is not to be settled by mere logical analysis but is a question of fact; namely, it is the question whether the men who in our day will undertake in a scientific way investigations of the class in question will naturally mingle with one group or with another group.[108]

In much the same way, in the first quarter of the twentieth century, philosophy itself came to be conceived as "essentially a collective and coöperative business." [109] The philosophers followed the scientists in abandoning the Cartesian ideal of a science or a system of philosophy sprung, Minerva-like, full-grown and fully armed from the head of a solitary thinker. The typical record of philosophic inquiry was no longer the system nor even the one-author book, but, as in the sciences, the journal article, and, on occasion, the collaborative volume. Among examples of the latter, perhaps the most noteworthy are: *Studies in Logical Theory* (1903); *The New Realism* (1912); *Creative Intelligence* (1917); *Essays in Critical Realism* (1920); and, more recently, The Library of Living Philosophers, inaugurated by volumes devoted to Dewey (1939), Santayana (1940), and Whitehead (1941). More recently still, the language of the report of investigations in progress is most noticeable in the work of Dewey and Bentley, *Knowing and the Known* (1949).

Least representative in this respect is Santayana; but even he yielded to the tendency of the age so far as to contribute to *Essays in Critical Realism* and to coöperate on the volume devoted to his philosophy in The Library of Living Philosophers.

12. THE SUPREMACY OF METHOD

In an age dominated by science, it was natural that philosophy should become increasingly preoccupied with the nature and function of science; and as science came to be conceived less as a body of doctrine and more as a human enterprise, it was natural that the philosophy of science should take the form of the theory of method. It is for this reason that there seems a peculiar appropriateness in the fact that our classic period reached a kind of culmination, if not a terminus, in Dewey's *Logic: The Theory of Inquiry* (1938).

The conception of logic as "first philosophy" derives from Peirce. Though other definitions of it occur in his writings, the one he used in his teaching at The Johns Hopkins University, when Dewey was a

---

[108] Peirce Papers, Harvard University Archives, I.B.2. box 5, §7(e)2, pp. 12-15.
[109] A. O. Lovejoy: *The Revolt Against Dualism* (New York, W. W. Norton & Co., 1930), ix.

student there, was that it is the art of devising methods of research—
"the method of methods." In his public introductory lecture in September 1882 he said:

This is the age of methods; and the university which is to be the exponent
of the living condition of the human mind, must be the university of
methods.

Now I grant you that to say that this is the age of the development of
new methods of research is so far from saying that it is the age of the theory
of methods, that it is almost to say the reverse. Unfortunately practice generally precedes theory, and it is the usual fate of mankind to get things done
in some boggling way first, and find out afterward how they could have
been done much more easily and perfectly. And it must be confessed that
we students of the science of modern methods are as yet but a voice crying
in the wilderness, and saying prepare ye the way for this lord of the sciences
which is to come.[110]

Another of Dewey's teachers, the idealist George Sylvester Morris,
disparaged formal logic in favor of the "real" logic which he found in
Aristotle and Hegel. During the early years of his teaching at the University of Michigan, Dewey worked at an intermediate kind of logic
that should be neither merely formal nor a logic of the constitution of
things, but a logic of the processes by which knowledge is reached. A
book by Dewey to be called *Principles of Instrumental Logic* was announced as forthcoming in Muirhead's Library of Philosophy, but it
never appeared.[111] At that time Dewey was unconscious of any influence of Peirce's teaching on the direction of his investigation, and he
was still far from his later instrumentalism; but he was on the way.

Peirce's conception of logic is suggestive of Whitehead's dictum:
"The greatest invention of the nineteenth century was the invention of
the method of invention."[112] One of the values Peirce saw in logic
was facilitation of the extension to other sciences, with suitable modification, of methods that had proved fruitful in any one of them. One
of the dangers Whitehead saw was the tendency to make philosophic
principles out of methods of restricted applicability. "The man with a
method good for purposes of his dominant interests, is a pathological
case in respect to his wider judgment on the coördination of this
method with a more complete experience."[113] But he would perhaps
have agreed that this is a reason for, not against, a general theory of
method developed by non-partisans. It is this, presumably, to which
Dewey's *Logic* aspires to contribute. He acknowledges his great indebtedness to Peirce for the general position taken. "As far as I am

[110] *Johns Hopkins University Circulars* 2:11, Nov. 1882.
[111] *The Philosophy of John Dewey*, 18.
[112] *Science and the Modern World*, 141.
[113] *The Function of Reason* (Princeton University Press, 1929), 8.

aware, he was the first writer on logic to make inquiry and its methods the primary and ultimate source of logical subject-matter." [114]

13. SCIENCE AND SOCIETY

With the abandonment of the spectator theory of knowledge and the adoption of modern experimental science as the type of knowledge there came a changed conception of nature. As Dewey puts it: "Nature as it already exists ceases to be something which must be accepted and submitted to, endured or enjoyed, just as it is. It is now something to be modified, to be intentionally controlled." [115]

Under conditions of modern society, however, it is impossible to control nature without controlling men. Furthermore, the nineteenth and twentieth centuries have witnessed the rise of new sciences of man and society. If the purpose of natural science is control of nature, what is the purpose of the social sciences if not the extension of such control to society itself? It seemed for a time, to be sure, that their purpose was to demonstrate that social control was unnecessary, but it turned out that the real issue was who should do the controlling and what form it should take.

So far, much of it has taken the form of control of increasing numbers of men by diminishing numbers of directors of private corporate enterprise, with profit and power as primary motives. The wasteful and irresponsible exploitation of natural resources which was generally prevalent in the nineteenth century and which, in spite of checks at certain points, still prevails, has been accompanied by tragic exploitation of human resources.

The concentration of financial and labor power in private hands on the one side, and, on the other, two world wars with a great depression between, and, more recently, the cold war against a collectivized state, have driven us steadily in the direction of public enterprise and of public control of private enterprise, with collective and individual security and welfare as the professed motives.

Against this tendency one of the many objections has been that we do not know enough—that social control presupposes social science, and that the social sciences are still too immature for the purpose.

The obvious answer to this has been the extension of experimentalism from the natural to the social sciences. In Dewey's words,

it is a complete error to suppose that efforts at social control depend upon the prior existence of a social science. The reverse is the case. . . . Only the knowledge which is itself the fruit of a technology can breed further technology. . . . if we want something to which the name "social science" may

[114] *Logic: The Theory of Inquiry* (New York, Henry Holt and Co., 1938), 9 n. 1.
[115] *The Quest for Certainty,* 100; below, p. 349.

be given, there is only one way to go about it, namely, by entering upon the path of social planning and control.[116]

Though Whitehead prefers the language of adventure to that of experiment, his philosophy, like Peirce's, Royce's and Dewey's, departs radically from the assumptions of earlier modern individualism. He has remarked the congeniality between that individualism and the Cartesian dualism of "bodies and minds as independent individual substances, each existing in its own right apart from any necessary reference to each other." [117]

14. THE GREAT COMMUNITY

Our classic period began with Peirce's assertion of the doctrine of the community as against the Cartesian assumption "that the ultimate test of certainty is to be found in the individual consciousness."

In sciences in which men come to agreement, when a theory has been broached it is considered to be on probation until . . . agreement is reached. After it is reached, the question of certainty becomes an idle one, because there is no one left who doubts it. We individually cannot reasonably hope to attain the ultimate philosophy which we pursue; we can only seek it, therefore, for the *community* of philosophers. . . .
So the social principle is rooted intrinsically in logic. . . . For he who recognizes the logical necessity of complete self-identification of one's own interests with those of the community, and its potential existence in man, even if he has it not himself, will perceive that only the inferences of that man who has it are logical, and so views his own inferences as being valid only so far as they would be accepted by that man. But so far as he has this belief, he becomes identified with that man. And that ideal perfection of knowledge by which we have seen that reality is constituted must thus belong to a community in which this identification is complete.[118]

In the essay of 1877 with which our selections begin, "the problem becomes how to fix belief, not in the individual merely, but in the community," and the scientific method is presented as the only method by which in the long run this can be accomplished. In one of the later

[116] *New Republic* 67:276 f., 29 July 1931; *Intelligence in the Modern World*, 951, 952, 954.

[117] *Science and the Modern World*, 279. More than any of our canonical six, however, it is Elijah Jordan, in his *Forms of Individuality* (Indianapolis, Charles W. Laut and Co., 1927) and *Theory of Legislation* (Indianapolis, Progress Publishing Co., 1930), who has developed a social philosophy conducive to experimental politics. As he puts it in the latter work (p. 35): "Knowledge of public affairs is gained, like other knowledge, through experimentation, and involves no more and no less danger and as much and as little promise as investigation in other fields, and for the same reasons." Cf. his *The Good Life* (Chicago, University of Chicago Press, 1949), 347: "Experimentalism is only timidly recognized as yet as a valid political method, and its full ethical significance must await its fuller development in practice." The note of adventure is also prominent in Jordan, as in Whitehead.

[118] *Collected Papers* 5.265.(2), 354, 356.

essays in the same series of "Illustrations of the Logic of Science," under the title "The Doctrine of Chances," Peirce again concludes that

logicality inexorably requires that our interests shall not be limited. They must not stop at our own fate, but must embrace the whole community. This community, again, must not be limited, but must extend to all races of beings with whom we can come into immediate or mediate intellectual relation.... Logic is rooted in the social principle....

It may seem strange that I should put forward three sentiments, namely, interest in an indefinite community, recognition of the possibility of this interest being made supreme, and hope in the unlimited continuance of intellectual activity, as indispensable requirements of logic. Yet, when we consider that logic depends on a mere struggle to escape doubt, which, as it terminates in action, must begin in emotion, and that, furthermore, the only cause of our planting ourselves on reason is that other methods of escaping doubt fail on account of the social impulse, why should we wonder to find social sentiment presupposed in reasoning? As for the other two sentiments which I find necessary, they are so only as supports and accessories of that. It interests me to notice that these three sentiments seem to be pretty much the same as that famous trio of Charity, Faith, and Hope, which, in the estimation of St. Paul, are the finest and greatest of spiritual gifts.[119]

Near the end of his life, Royce felt that his deepest motives and problems had centered about the Idea of the Community, although this idea had come only gradually to his clear consciousness.[120] He acknowledged his indebtedness to Peirce for the conception of a community of interpretation. The attention he gave to insurance as an illustration may also have been suggested by Peirce's "The Doctrine of Chances." On the whole, it was the moral and religious rather than the scientific community that most concerned him, but from his earliest work he saw in the latter a model for the former.

When one considers the work of a company of scientific specialists—how each one lives for his science, and how, when the specialty is advanced and well organized, no one in official expressions of his purely scientific purposes dares either to give himself airs of importance as an individual, or to show any benevolence or favoritism or fear in considering and testing the work of anybody else; when one sees how impersonal is this idea of the scientific life, how no self of them all is supposed to have a thought about his science because it pleases him, but solely because it is true—when one considers all this, one sees faintly what the ideal relation of mankind would be, if the ideal work for all men were found. This devoted scientific spirit is itself only an ideal even today; and all sorts of personal motives still interfere to disturb its purity. But here, at all events, one sees dimly in a concrete instance what the organization of life may yet become.[121]

---

[119] Ibid., 2.654 f.

[120] The Hope of the Great Community (New York, The Macmillan Co., 1916), 129.

[121] The Religious Aspect of Philosophy (Boston: Houghton Mifflin and Co., 1885), 213 f.

Dewey follows Peirce in regarding modern philosophy since Descartes as a great apostasy, the first misstep of which was "to place the mind of the individual as such in contrast to both nature and institutions." "Wholesale revolt against tradition led to the illusion of equally wholesale isolation of mind as something wholly individual." And the remedy prescribed by German idealism and adopted in Royce's early philosophy was almost as bad as the disease.

Thinkers may start out with a naïve assumption of minds connected with separate individuals. But developments soon show the inadequacy of such "minds" to carry the burden of science and objective institutions, like the family and state. The consequence was revealed to be sceptical, disintegrative, malicious. A transcendental supra-empirical self, making human, or "finite," selves its medium of manifestation, was the logical recourse.... When the movement terminates, as in the later philosophy of Josiah Royce, with a "community of selves," the circle has returned to the empirical fact with which it might properly have started out; but the intervening insertion of a transcendent ego remains as a plague. It isolates the community of selves from natural existence and in order to get nature again in connection with mind, is compelled to reduce it to a system of volitions, feelings and thoughts.[122]

Dewey preferred, on the whole, to think in terms of "the situation," "the public," or "the social as a category continuous with and inclusive of the categories of the physical, vital and mental." Like Peirce and Royce, however, he saw in the community of investigators a pattern for society at large. In particular, "the operation of coöperative intelligence as displayed in science is a working model of the union of freedom and authority," of collective authority and individual freedom, upon which the future of society depends.

In spite of science's dependence for its development upon the free initiative, invention, and enterprise of individual inquirers, the authority of science issues from and is based upon collective activity, coöperatively organized....
No scientific inquirer can keep what he finds to himself or turn it to merely private account without losing his scientific standing. Everything discovered belongs to the community of workers. Every new idea and theory has to be submitted to this community for confirmation and test. There is an expanding community of coöperative effort and of truth.... The general adoption of the scientific attitude in human affairs would mean nothing less than a revolutionary change in morals, religion, politics and industry.... A vision of a day in which the natural sciences and the technologies that flow

---

[122] *Experience and Nature*, 224 f. (A reference to Whitehead's social philosophy would be in place here, but its relation to those of Peirce, Royce and Dewey has not yet been clarified. One of the salient features of his cosmology is its generalization of the notions of "society," "social order," and "inheritance." The interpretations of human society in the last chapters of *Science and the Modern World* and *Symbolism* and throughout *Adventures of Ideas* are thus to be understood against the background of what might be called a societal metaphysics.)

from them are used as servants of a humane life constitutes the imagination that is relevant to our own time . . .[123]

That was before the atom bomb, the large-scale militarization of science, and the absorption of important areas of it into the secret service of governments. The scientific community, as Peirce and Dewey conceived it, no longer exists. (Indeed, it never did quite obtain among scientists in the employ of private industry.) It begins to appear that it will not be restored anywhere unless and until it can be made world-wide. The ideal stands, however, as our classic period's sovereign design for the Good Society.

[123] *Intelligence in the Modern World*, 359, 459 f.

Supplementary Notes

(These notes are to be added to the previous
notes with the same numbers.)

[1] The *Studies* were edited by Philip P. Wiener and Frederic H. Young and published by the Harvard University Press in 1952.

[2] For further details, see Max H. Fisch, "Was There a Metaphysical Club in Cambridge?", in *Studies in the Philosophy of Charles Sanders Peirce, Second Series*, edited by Moore and Robin, University of Massachusetts Press, 1964, pp. 3–32; "A Chronicle of Pragmaticism, 1865–1879," *The Monist* 48: 441–466, 1964.

[6] Cf. *Collected Papers* 8:39–54, 100–131. Reviews by Peirce of other works of Royce: *Nation* 65: 524–525; 80: 71–72.

[11] For a correction of the next sentence in the text, see the preface to the fifth printing.

[15] On 2 January 1936 Whitehead wrote to Charles Hartshorne describing the United States of America as the developing center of worthwhile philosophy. He identified Charles Peirce and William James as the founders of the American renaissance and wrote that "of these men, W.J. is the analogue to Plato, and C.P. to Aristotle." This letter is quoted in Victor Law, *Alfred North Whitehead: The Man and His Work*, ed. J. B. Schneewind (Baltimore: Johns Hopkins University Press, 1990), 2: 345.

[23-31] Holmes's impressions may now be further illustrated from *The Holmes-Laski Letters* (1953) and *The Holmes-Einstein Letters* (1964).

[43-44] See Max H. Fisch, "Alexander Bain and the Genealogy of Pragmatism," *Journal of the History of Ideas* 15: 413–444, 1954. Reprinted in *Peirce, Semiotic, and Pragmatism; Essays by Max H. Fisch*, eds. Kenneth L. Ketner and Christian J. W. Kloesel (Indiana University Press, 1986).

[52] Ms. 318 in the numbering of the Papers recently adopted.

[90] This paper was read to the Metaphysical Club in Royce's absence.

[93] Compare with this a passage quoted on p. 332 from Dewey's *Psychology* (1887), when his outlook was still Hegelian. "Mind has not remained a passive spectator of the universe, but has produced and is producing certain results. These results are objective, can be studied as all objective historical facts may be, and are permanent. They are the most fixed, certain, and universal signs to us of the way in which mind works. Such objective manifestations of mind are, in the realm of intelligence, phenomena like language and science; in that of will, social and political institutions; in that of feeling, art; in that of the whole self, religion."

97 Ms. 325.

98 Ms. 655.

101 Whitehead in conversation acknowledged that Santayana's doctrine of essence had influenced him toward his own conception of eternal objects. His copy of *Scepticism and Animal Faith,* Victor Lowe informs me, "is elaborately marked up—much more than any of his books that I've seen."

108 Ms. 499.

122 The parenthesis is not in place here. Whitehead did not take the scientific community as any sort of model; nor did James or Santayana.

123 A briefer statement of "Some General Characteristics of American Philosophy" may be found in *Basis of the Contemporary Philosophy: Essays in the Philosophical Analysis,* edited by Seizi Uyeda (Tokyo: Waseda University Press, 1960). See also Dewey's "Search for the Great Community," Chap. 5 of *The Public and Its Problems* (New York: Henry Holt and Co., 1927).

I

CHARLES SANDERS PEIRCE

✣

Introduction

CHARLES SANDERS PEIRCE was born in 1839 in Cambridge, Massachusetts, the son of Benjamin Peirce, leading American mathematician and astronomer of the day. His educational opportunities were ideal: from childhood his mind was carefully trained and disciplined by his father; he associated in his youth with such men as William James and Justice Holmes; and he received a good formal training in mathematics and the physical sciences at Harvard University. Yet for all that, Peirce was, judged by ordinary standards, a failure. Though one of the most original thinkers of his time, he was only once able to obtain an academic position (at Johns Hopkins from 1879 to 1884). His highly independent nature, coupled with the circumstance of early marital difficulties and a subsequent divorce, had cut him off from an academic career. He was forced to work most of his life as a physicist for the U. S. Coast Survey (intermittently from 1861 to 1891). He did achieve some fame for his government researches: he received international recognition for his accurate determination of the gravitational constant. But as an empirical scientist Peirce has long since been forgotten, and it has become increasingly clear that his contributions to mathematical logic and philosophy constitute his real title to lasting fame. His scientific work is important today only because of the strong influence it had on his philosophy.

About 1890, Peirce retired on a small legacy to Milford, Pennsylvania, to devote all of his efforts to philosophy. There are important differences in his work before and after approximately this time, so that it is enlightening to distinguish the early and later periods of his thought. In the later period Peirce attempted to build a grand philosophic system, after the manner of Plato and Aristotle, using the ideas of the early period as a basis. But he did not succeed in this theoretical task, perhaps because he was a practical failure. Writing in an extremely technical and non-popular style, and possessed of a personality that often antagonized others, he was unable to attract followers or to find publishers for his work. Moreover, because of financial mis-

41

management he was reduced to penury, sometimes being without funds for food or fuel. As a consequence he did not produce the *magnum opus* which would have given us his entire system of philosophy. Instead, his writings were highly fragmentary, "a mere table of contents, so abstract, a very snarl of twine" as he put it. Because of the fragmentary nature of his work, the understanding and appreciation that were Peirce's due have long been delayed. Only recently has it been recognized that this "table of contents" is a rich source of ideas of lasting importance.

It is impossible in a group of selections of this size to include material representative of all of Peirce's important philosophic ideas. What we have chosen are essays which represent his thought of both periods and which illustrate both the pragmatic and the metaphysical sides of his philosophy. In "The Fixation of Belief" and "How to Make Our Ideas Clear" Peirce presents the pragmatic analysis of belief, derives the pragmatic criterion of meaning from it, and argues that scholastic realism is the metaphysical basis of pragmatism. These articles are of the early period, but since in the later period Peirce changed his mind on some important points in them, we have included a number of his later revisions and footnotes. "The Architecture of Theories" and "The Doctrine of Necessity Examined" are of the later period. In them Peirce makes his attack on determinism and presents his metaphysical theory of cosmic evolution as an alternative to it.

Peirce's pragmatic criterion of meaning is a consequence, both historically and logically, of his pragmatic theory of belief. A belief, he says, is a conscious, deliberate habit of action: "... what we think is to be interpreted in terms of what we are prepared to do ..." (5.35).[1] Let us consider just how Peirce interprets a belief as a deliberate habit of behavior in terms of an example. Suppose you believe that there is a dumbbell on the floor. Your belief is a rule of action in the following way: if you walk across the room you go around the dumbbell in order not to trip on it; if you reach to pick it up you adjust the tension of your muscles in accordance with your expectation that it is heavy; and so on. Peirce calls the consequences that you expect when you hold a belief its "practical consequences," and according to him your belief that the dumbbell exists consists of the sum total of such conscious

[1] This and similar references below are to the volumes and numbered paragraphs of the most complete edition of Peirce's works: *Collected Papers of Charles Sanders Peirce*, edited by Charles Hartshorne and Paul Weiss, six volumes, published by Harvard University Press from 1931 to 1935. This edition, however, does not contain all of Peirce's published works, nor all of his unpublished manuscripts. Most of the unpublished papers are at the Widener Library, Harvard University. Page references (p.), on the other hand, are to subsequent pages of the present volume.

habits of expecting practical consequences; and similarly with all of your beliefs.

Doubt arises in one's experience when such an actually functioning habit of action or expectation is blocked or interrupted, i.e., when the actual practical effects of an action are different from the expected practical consequences of that action. Suppose that on hoisting the dumbbell your arm flew up because you expected it to be heavy when in fact it was very light. You would, of course, be surprised: the feeling of certainty which accompanied your habit of action while it was successful (uninterrupted) would give way to a feeling of uncertainty. This feeling of dissatisfaction would motivate you to seek a new belief habit which would not be so interrupted, that is, a belief habit with different practical consequences. You would investigate and discover, say, that what you had taken to be a dumbbell was actually a carefully constructed paper model of one; and you would readjust your habits of reaction accordingly. On Peirce's view, every genuine inquiry or problem is stimulated in this way by the observation "of some surprising phenomenon, some experience which either disappoints an expectation, or breaks in upon some habit of expectation . . ." (6.469); and it is terminated when a habit of expectation is found that (so far as we know) shall not be disappointed.

Peirce's pragmatic criterion of meaning follows quite logically and directly from his analysis of belief. For if a belief is a rule of action, then two apparently different beliefs which do not differ as to the practical consequences implied have the same meaning. *"In order to ascertain the meaning of an intellectual conception one should consider what practical consequences might conceivably result by necessity from the truth of that conception; and the sum of these consequences will constitute the entire meaning of the conception"* (5.9). But the application of such a criterion of meaning hinges upon an understanding of precisely what is to be included under "practical consequences." Suppose someone argues: "My belief that God exists has practical consequences, for 'God exists' implies that nature is ordered, and this is a consequence we verify every time we find a case of order in nature, i.e., every time science succeeds in explaining a phenomenon." Assuming that this is in fact a verifiable consequence and that it is the only such consequence, we may conclude from the pragmatic criterion of meaning that 'God exists' and 'Nature is ordered' have the same meaning. But suppose our imaginary speaker goes on to argue: " 'God exists' has *for me* practical consequences that 'Nature is ordered' does not have. For one thing, 'God exists' implies that the world is moral and purposive. However it may be with others, I derive a lot of satisfaction from my belief in God that I do not derive from a belief in the orderliness of nature. Hence the former is, for me, a more *useful* belief, and is, by the pragmatic theory, different in meaning from the latter." Are these individualistic, utilitarian consequences admissible *practical* consequences in the sense in which Peirce uses 'practical'?

The consequence that the soul is immortal is not directly testable in this world, though presumably if it is true it can be verified in a future world. This kind of evidence, however, is clearly not admitted by the practising scientist, and Peirce's pragmatic criterion arose out of his reflections on his work in science; yet Peirce does, at least in his later period, seem to have allowed such consequences (cf. p. 78; 1.624, 5.541). But without question, he did not wish to include private satisfactions and emotional responses within the scope of 'practical'. For Peirce truth is public: the true is that on which the community of investigators will ultimately approach agreement. Hence there are, for Peirce, no private practical consequences. Furthermore, the emotional associations of beliefs are not part of their practical consequences: Peirce distinguishes the consequences of a belief from the consequences of holding that belief. A belief habit consists of an expectation of certain sensible effects, or of a habit of consciously reacting to objects in a certain way; and two apparently different habits that involve the same reactions and the same expectations are the same belief, according to Peirce, even though their emotional associations differ.

To many people this interpretation of 'practical' would not sound *pragmatic*. For it is usual to think of pragmatism as a philosophy that makes truth individual, relative, and useful, rather than public, absolute, and theoretical. There is an historical explanation for the confusion surrounding the term, 'pragmatism'. Both the idea of pragmatism and its name originated with Peirce: he invented the doctrine and named it 'pragmatism' in the early 1870's; and though he did not use the name in print until much later, he published the idea in 1878 in "How to Make Our Ideas Clear." [2] But Peirce's writings never attracted much attention in his own day, and the doctrine did not become well known until James, Dewey, Schiller, etc., developed their versions of it. The fact that some of these formulations are individualistic, relativistic, and utilitarian accounts for the common notion that all formulations (including Peirce's) are. This view is often accompanied by a notion even further from the historical truth, namely, that pragmatism arose out of the worship of practical success and the attitude that science and philosophy should be concerned with the practical and immediately useful rather than the theoretical. As we have seen, Peirce

[2] 5.13, 412, 414 n., 6.482. See also Peirce's own anticipation of his idea in his "Review of Fraser's *Works of George Berkeley,*" *North American Review* 113 (1871) 469. Compare 5.453.

Of course, as Peirce recognized, pragmatism had its historical antecedents in the philosophies of Socrates, Aristotle, Locke, Berkeley, Kant, etc.

was not a practical man in the sense in which 'practical' is used in the world of business and commerce. He was a laboratory scientist and a student of pure mathematics and logic, and, historically speaking, he formulated his pragmatic analysis of belief and his pragmatic theory of meaning as a result of his studies of scientific method.

It was during Peirce's later period that these other writers developed their versions of pragmatism. Peirce made it very clear at that time that he wished to dissociate himself from the individualistic, relativistic, and utilitarian interpretations of his doctrine. He pointed out that his original statement of pragmatism had been intellectualistic rather than voluntaristic and nominalistic (p. 78 n. 24). And he explained that he had deliberately chosen 'pragmatism' in preference to 'practicalism' to avoid such interpretations, but that since 'pragmatism' was no longer suitable for his doctrine he would adopt another name for it, 'pragmaticism,' "which is ugly enough to be safe from kidnappers" (5.414). He also revised his formulation of the doctrine of pragmatism during his later period, probably partly in reaction to the more popular versions. He began to emphasize the difference between theory and practice, saying that theoretical investigation, not utilitarian knowledge, is the proper concern of science and philosophy. ("True science is distinctly the study of useless things. For the useful things will get studied without the aid of scientific men" [1.76].) He rejected the implication, drawn by some pragmatists, that we are ready to apply scientific method to the solution of the social and moral problems of the world. In worldly matters we should rely on instinct, sentiment, and common sense, he argued, for philosophy is still in too rudimentary a state to be trusted in such matters. Again, in his later period Peirce began to use 'experimental' as well as 'practical' in his formulations of pragmatism. "... if one can define accurately all of the conceivable experimental phenomena which the affirmation or denial of a concept could imply, one will have therein a complete definition of the concept, and *there is absolutely nothing more in it*" (5.412). Since pragmatism arose out of Peirce's reflections on scientific method, 'experimental' is in many ways a more suitable term than 'practical'—certainly one which is less open to misunderstanding.

Peirce proposed the doctrine of pragmatism as a logical maxim for guiding our thought: it tells us how we ought to proceed in order to clarify our ideas. The most important application that he made of it was to the subject of metaphysics. Peirce was impressed by the contrast between the definite intellectual progress of empirical scientists and the lack of agreement even on fundamentals characteristic of metaphysicians. He attributed this to a difference of logical method and believed that pragmatism, if employed in metaphysics, would clarify that subject and raise it to the status of an exact science. He held that many metaphysical disputes arise only because of a confusion of thought and that these can be resolved by applying the pragmatic criterion of meaning to them. This method of resolving a dispute is fundamentally different from the ordinary procedure of marshalling evidence for or against a given position, for it amounts to showing that when the parties to the dispute disagree they really aren't saying anything! That is, the pragmatist uses his criterion of meaning to show that the two apparently opposed doctrines have the same practical consequences and so have the same meaning, and hence that in a literal sense there never really was any cognitive disagreement at all.

An interesting metaphysical dispute to which to apply this pragmatic principle is the controversy between the Cartesian dualist and the subjective idealist over the nature of physical objects.[3] According to the dualist a physical object exists independently of the knowing mind, possessing intrinsically the primary qualities of size, shape, solidity, etc., along with various causal properties (e.g., obeying the laws of gravitation). The secondary qualities of an object (e.g., looking brown, feeling smooth, tasting salty) are not properties of the object itself but only of the appearances of it (sense data) in the observer's mind. The idealist holds, on the other hand, that these mental appearances or sense data (past, present, and future) are all there is to the physical object: physical objects are really mental in character and have no existence apart from minds. To resolve this controversy by the pragmatic criterion of meaning, we consider whether the dualist and the idealist react to physical objects in different ways. They clearly do not: their habits of action in each case are the same, that is, are determined by an expectation of the same practical consequences. Since the real meaning of a belief is, for the pragmatist, the sum of its practical consequences, the differences between the two positions are only apparent, and there is no real dispute at all.

A somewhat different method of resolving metaphysical issues, based more directly on his analysis of belief than on his criterion of meaning, is sometimes employed by Peirce. From the fact that a belief is a habit of expecting certain practical consequences and not expecting their opposites it follows that doubt arises only when this habit is interrupted by the occurrence of an unexpected practical effect. Thus what Peirce calls a genuine problem can arise only when one is confronted with an actual exception to the general rule. Such an interruption is, in Peirce's terminology, a true doubt, and is to be distinguished from a feigned doubt, one not based on positive evidence. Suppose, having

---

[3] Neither this example (which originated with C. H. Langford) nor the next is Peirce's.

observed that objects released above the surface of the earth fall, and being ignorant of balloons, one asserted that all released objects fall. A sceptic who doubted this generalization without producing a case where it failed would be merely feigning doubt, and on Peirce's view he would not have posed a genuine problem. But if he pointed out that a balloon rises, he would be exhibiting genuine doubt and raising a genuine problem. Feigned doubt may be useful (it may lead to genuine doubt), but until a genuine doubt is raised there is, for Peirce, no genuine problem.

Let us apply Peirce's theory of doubt to show that Descartes never really doubted the existence of the external world or of other minds. Though Descartes pointed to exceptions to the general rule that *all* apparently perceived objects exist, he never exhibited an exception to the general rule that *some* external objects exist. By pointing to cases where particular belief habits were interrupted, e.g., a perceptual illusion, a dream, he evidenced genuine doubt of the existence of this or that object. But he failed to point to an interruption in the general belief that some external objects exist, i.e., the belief that, while some of our perceptual experiences are illusory, some are not. In fact, his habits of action or expectation showed that he had found no such interruption and that he really believed in the existence of the external world.

The use of Peirce's pragmatic analysis of belief to resolve metaphysical questions is not fundamentally different from the use of his pragmatic criterion of meaning for the same purpose. Both methods attempt to resolve the issues by maintaining that there is no genuine problem involved. Thus we can say that, according to the analysis of belief, Descartes never doubted the existence of the external world; or that, according to the criterion of meaning, there was no real cognitive difference in Descartes' beliefs concerning the external world before, during, or after his sceptical period. It is easy to see why the two methods give the same result in these cases when we consider how they are both based on the idea of a 'practical consequence.' The fundamental fact about a belief in the external world and the alternative of solipsism is that both have the same practical consequences. Hence by the pragmatic criterion of meaning they have the same meaning. And by the analysis of belief, since one belief cannot be interrupted by an unexpected practical consequence without the other being so interrupted, it is impossible really to doubt one without doubting the other.

Both of these pragmatic doctrines were attempts by Peirce to formulate into philosophic principles the procedures of the exact sciences, so that both of them amount to an application of the methods of the exact sciences to metaphysical questions. The distinction between real and feigned doubt conforms to scientific procedure; for when a theory is well established in science it is relevant only to make specific objections, based on positive evidence, to it.[4] The burden of proof is thrown on the doubter, and so, as we saw in the case of Descartes and his doubting the existence of the external world, all universal scepticisms are ruled out: Hume's doubts concerning causality, for example, play no rôle in science. The pragmatic criterion of meaning also conforms to scientific method; for it allows as meaningful only the practical consequences of a metaphysical position, that is, those consequences which can be observed and verified. Any metaphysical problem which cannot be so treated is simply eliminated.

Let us now turn to an examination of Peirce's own metaphysical doctrines, to determine whether they will stand the test of his pragmatic criterion of meaning, or whether they too must be cast aside as meaningless. Peirce, in both his early and his later periods, held to a highly metaphysical doctrine, the doctrine of scholastic realism, or what he calls "the reality of Thirdness." If it can be shown that his own pragmatism, which he formulated as a link between scientific method and metaphysics, when applied to his scholastic realism eliminates that doctrine, Peirce will clearly be forced to give up either his pragmatism or his metaphysics.

Peirce's realism includes several separate, though related, theses, all of which he held to be foundational to science and pragmatism. One is his theory of cosmic evolution, according to which the cosmos is progressing in a gradual, evolutionary manner to an ideal state, this process of growth being governed by cosmic purposes or final causes. Peirce thought this theory of cosmic evolution did have experimental (i.e., observable or verifiable) consequences (pp. 99 f.). But if it has empirical consequences they are not of the kind that can be treated by the methods of the well-established sciences. For the years since Peirce's time have seen them enter the ranks of the metaphysical debatables rather than the ranks of the theories accepted or rejected on the basis of scientific method.

Another thesis more patently fundamental to science is that there are objective, publicly knowable laws and things, concerning which we can approach agreement. Peirce was aware that our knowledge at any specific time is subject to error and never perfectly precise: in fact, he

---

[4] This approach is also characteristic of common sense. If a man has a belief it ordinarily takes positive evidence to upset it, and if he has a doubt it takes positive evidence to remove it. In this connection it is interesting to note that one of Peirce's doctrines is Critical Common-Sensism, which he says is an outgrowth of pragmatism.

was among the first to recognize the approximate nature of modern scientific knowledge. Likewise, as a pragmatist, Peirce admitted a large element of convention and arbitrary choice in the formulation of laws. Yet he maintained that there is a residue of fact which is real and not conventional and which can be ascertained by scientific method; and that though we cannot expect at any one time to have the perfectly true version of a law, there is, or will be, such a true version which we can more and more nearly approximate.[5]

Peirce's views concerning the nature of causal laws are different in his early and later periods. In his early period he held a nominalistic theory of law, as we shall see. In his later period he proposed a theory of law which constitutes a third thesis of his scholastic realism. This is the theory that a causal law is not reducible to a summary of facts, as the nominalist would have it, but involves what Peirce calls genuine "would-be's" as well. A law is "general in referring to all possible things, and not merely to those that happen to exist. No collection of facts can constitute a law; for the law goes beyond any accomplished facts and determines how facts that *may be,* but *all* of which never can have happened, shall be characterized" (1.420, *cf.* 422). "Now what *would* be, can, it is true, only be learned through observation of what happens to be; but nevertheless no collection of happenings can constitute one trillionth of one *per cent* of what might be, and would be under supposable conditions . . ." (6.327, *cf.* 1.213, 5.467).

Peirce's distinction between the "would-be" and the "happens-to-be" is a subtle one and needs elaboration. Consider the sentence 'This eraser was released and fell.' This sentence is true if it happened that the eraser was released and fell, and it is false if such was not the case: the sentence refers to what "happened to be." In contrast, consider the sentence, uttered after one has almost dropped a glass, 'If you had dropped that glass it would have broken.' While such a contrary-to-fact sentence in the subjunctive mood would be true only in the case where the glass actually was *not* dropped, it nevertheless expresses more than the fact that the glass wasn't dropped, i.e., more than what "happened to be." For it states what would have been the case had the universe been different. In Peirce's terminology, this sentence refers to a "would-be."

---

[5] Note that Peirce did not believe that this assumption is equivalent to the assumption of the uniformity of nature (that the causal laws of the universe are invariant with respect to space and time). It is generally held that the uniformity of nature is assumed by all inductive inference, since such inference proceeds from data concerning part of the universe to a law or theory believed to hold throughout the universe; e.g., in a prediction, the inference is from data gathered in the past to the future. In "The Doctrine of Necessity Examined" (pp. 102 ff.) Peirce argues that this is not the case. Furthermore, according to his theory of cosmic evolution the laws of nature evolve and hence are not invariant with respect to time.

We shall find it more convenient to substitute the terms 'actuality' and 'potentiality' for Peirce's "happens-to-be" and "would-be." Thus we may say that the sentence 'If you had dropped that glass it would have broken' refers to a potentiality, as well as to an actuality, whereas the sentence 'This eraser was released and fell' refers only to an actuality.[6] Again, the sentence 'If this piece of chalk is released it will fall' refers to an actuality: it asserts that either this piece of chalk will not actually be released or it will actually fall. In contrast, the following sentences expressed in the subjunctive mood refer to potentialities as well as actualities: 'If you were to drop this glass it would break' and 'If you do not drop this glass, then it will be true to say that if you had dropped it it would have broken.'

With our new terminology we are ready to state Peirce's theory of causal law. For Peirce, some universal or 'all' statements (e.g., 'All the books on my desk are in English') refer only to actualities, while others (e.g., 'All released objects fall') refer to potentialities as well. All statements of laws, he maintains, are of the latter type, and hence from laws we can correctly infer statements about potentialities. Thus we shouldn't infer 'If this book had been placed on my desk it would have been in English' from the non-law 'All the books on my desk are in English.' But we can correctly infer 'If this object had been released it would have fallen' and 'If that object is not released it will nevertheless be true to say that if it had been released it would have fallen' from the causal law 'All released objects fall.' That is to say, the causal law refers not only to actualities, but to potentialities as well.

Let us next consider whether this metaphysical doctrine of scholastic realism can withstand the application of Peirce's criterion of meaning. Now according to the pragmatic criterion of meaning, the realist's view of law as involving causal potentialities differs from the nominalist's view of law as a mere universal summary of facts only if there are practical consequences implied by one and not the other. So let us see, first, what differences there are between the realist's and the nominalist's conception of law, and second, whether these differences have any practical consequences.

According to the nominalist the statement 'Diamonds are hard' is a summary of the tests actually made, or to be made, on diamonds: it

---

[6] Note that we say that the first sentence refers to a potentiality *as well as to an actuality*. The actuality referred to is the implication that the glass was not in fact dropped; the potentiality is the additional element referred to by the sentence, i.e., the element which cannot be stated in the indicative mood. Our usage may differ from Peirce's in this respect, for it is not clear whether he would say that this sentence refers to a "happens-to-be" as well as to a "would-be," or to a "would-be" alone.

Note too that in ordinary usage 'potentiality' refers only to the future, while we apply it to the past as well as to the future.

says that no diamond actually rubbed (in the past, present, or future) by another material is scratched by it. In other words, the nominalist infers from this all the facts expressible by the indicative mood (such as 'If this diamond was tested it was not scratched' and 'If that diamond is tested it will not be scratched') that the realist infers from it. The predictions of actual events which the realist deduces from a law are in no wise different from the predictions which a nominalist makes; the same is true for inferences made from the present state of the universe back to some previous actual state. Thus the nominalist and the realist agree as to the actualities covered by a law.

Wherein, then, lies the difference between nominalism and realism? Clearly in the notion of causal potentialities which the realist includes in his concept of law and the nominalist does not. The realist allows you to infer 'If this diamond had been tested it would not have been scratched' from the law 'All diamonds are hard' (together with the assertion that this diamond was not tested). Similarly, he holds that the law implies of any future diamond that 'If this diamond is not tested it will nevertheless be true to say that if it had been tested it would not have been scratched.' The nominalist, on the other hand, does not allow such inferences; he maintains that a law concerns only actualities and that there are no such entities as potentialities. On his view everything that a law covers can be stated in the indicative mood, and hence a law has no subjunctive consequences.

Thus the sole difference between the nominalist's and the realist's conception of law has to do with potentialities; and there can be a genuine dispute between the two only if propositions involving potentialities alone have practical consequences. But clearly they do not. It can make no practical difference to say of a diamond that has not been and never will be tested whether it would or would not have been scratched if it had been tested. So long as we agree to the law 'All diamonds are hard' and to its practical consequence that 'If this diamond is tested it will not be scratched,' then it can make no practical difference what we hold of a diamond that is never tested. An untested diamond is beyond practical interest. Another way of putting the matter is to say that action is based on actualities, not on potentialities, and that potentialities cannot affect conduct.[7] That is, as far as action is concerned everything we need to know to guide our conduct can be stated in the indicative mood.

[7] It is of course true that we act on potentialities in the sense that feelings of regret are based upon a belief in such propositions as 'If I had done otherwise I would have succeeded' and feelings of regret affect our actions. On Peirce's view such effects are not consequences of the belief itself, however, but rather are consequences of holding the belief, i.e., they are effects of emotional associations of the belief. As we saw earlier, Peirce (unlike such pragmatists as James) does not include these effects among the practical consequences of a belief.

Since statements about potentialities alone do not have practical consequences, there is, according to the pragmatic criterion of meaning, no real difference between the nominalist's and the realist's conception of causal law, and their dispute is eliminated by pragmatism. It follows, then, that Peirce's pragmatism rules out his own realistic metaphysics, just as it ruled out other metaphysical theories. Indeed, because Peirce firmly believed that his pragmatism was based on his realistic metaphysics, he is faced with the paradox that pragmatism assumes a theory to be true (and hence meaningful) which by its own criterion of meaning is meaningless!

One naturally wonders how such a contradiction arose in Peirce's thought and why he did not at least suspect its being there. The answer is to be found partly in the evolution of his thought. In his early period Peirce advanced a nominalistic theory of law. Indeed, he even argued convincingly that pragmatism implies such a view. In "How to Make Our Ideas Clear" he maintained that there is no *practical* difference between the assertion that the untested diamond was soft and the assertion that it was hard, since by hypothesis the diamond was not put to the test. He concluded that whether we say of such a diamond that it is hard or soft is a matter of linguistic convenience and not of scientific fact. "There is absolutely no difference between a hard thing and a soft thing so long as they are not brought to the test" (p. 79; *cf.* 5.339).

When, in his later period, Peirce proposed his realistic theory of law he rejected as nominalistic his earlier view that a statement referring to potentialities alone has no practical consequences (5.453, 457) and broadened his concept of practical consequences to include references to potentialities. Accordingly, he included in the meaning of a concept those cases which don't actually affect human action but which under appropriate circumstances would affect human action. "The pragmaticist has always explicitly stated that the intellectual purport of a concept consists in the truth of certain *conditional* propositions asserting that if the concept be applicable, and the utterer of the proposition or his fellow have a certain purpose in view, he *would* act in a certain way" (5.528, italics added).[8] But never in his later period did Peirce advance any argument to show that his earlier argument was wrong, that is, to show that a statement referring to potentialities does have practical consequences in the sense in which he originally employed that term. Now to broaden the meaning of 'practical consequence' arbi-

---

[8] Similarly, he stated that a belief involves potentiality as well as actuality (4.580, 5.453, 482, 517 n., 526-528, 6.485, and the footnotes to pp. 54-87). See also 2.661-668 where Peirce revised his early definition of probability.

trarily so as to include references to potentialities is to destroy pragmatism's ability to resolve metaphysical issues. For practical consequences would no longer be *practical* in the sense that they are observable and verifiable by scientific method; differences between opposing views other than scientific differences (i.e., differences which have no practical effect on human conduct) would have to be counted as meaningful; and metaphysical disputes eliminated as meaningless by the original formulation of pragmatism would come back into being.

Peirce's realistic theory of causal law is typical of his work in many ways. Despite his insistence on the central rôle this theory was to play in his philosophy, his writings on causal potentiality are few and fragmentary. He failed to make a thorough, systematic study of this later theory of causal law and of its repercussions on his early views; and it is probably for this reason that he never realized its full implications for his pragmatic philosophy. Here is a specific instance of the general fact that Peirce never did develop the complete system of philosophy which he had outlined. Nonetheless, Peirce showed original insight of the highest order in arriving at the idea of causal potentiality. Moreover, he was decades ahead of his time in maintaining that existing logical concepts and symbols are inadequate for expressing causal laws (4.546, 580-584), for only recently have logicians recognized the difficulty of symbolizing statements about potentialities in the existing formal logics. Though Peirce did not succeed in his ambition to be one of the great system builders of philosophy, as an originator of important philosophic ideas he is hard to surpass. Pragmatism and the realistic theory of causal law are just two of many such ideas that he created. That Peirce failed to see the incompatibility of these two ideas is not nearly so significant as the fact that he originated them.

ARTHUR W. BURKS

UNIVERSITY OF MICHIGAN

A Supplementary Note on Pragmatism and Realism has been added on page 113.

1. The Fixation of Belief [1]

I

FEW PERSONS CARE to study logic, because everybody conceives himself to be proficient enough in the art of reasoning already. But I observe that this satisfaction is limited to one's own ratiocination, and does not extend to that of other men.

We come to the full possession of our power of drawing inferences the last of all our faculties, for it is not so much a natural gift as a long and difficult art. The history of its practice would make a grand subject for a book. The medieval schoolmen, following the Romans, made logic the earliest of a boy's studies after grammar, as being very easy. So it was, as they understood it. Its fundamental principle, according to them, was, that all knowledge rests on either authority or reason; but that whatever is deduced by reason depends ultimately on a premise derived from authority. Accordingly, as soon as a boy was perfect in

---

[1] *Popular Science Monthly* 12 (Nov. 1877) 1-15, with some of Peirce's later revisions and annotations (as given in 5.358-387) included in the editor's footnotes. These revisions and annotations are reprinted by permission of the publishers from *Collected Papers of Charles Sanders Peirce,* edited by Charles Hartshorne and Paul Weiss, vol. 5, Cambridge, Mass., Harvard University Press, 1934.

In this and the following three selections Peirce's original footnotes are indicated by asterisks, while the editor's are indicated by numerals.

This and the following selection are the first two of six papers of a series entitled "Illustrations of the Logic of Science" originally published in vols. 12 and 13 of the *Popular Science Monthly*. This series of papers gives Peirce's early views on logic and the philosophy of science. The complete list of these papers is as follows:

(1) "The Fixation of Belief," 5.358-387.
(2) "How to Make Our Ideas Clear," 5.388-410.
(3) "The Doctrine of Chances," 2.645-660.
(4) "The Probability of Induction," 2.669-693.
(5) "The Order of Nature," 6.395-427.
(6) "Deduction, Induction, and Hypothesis," 2.619-644.

About 1903 Peirce formed the first two papers into a single essay, never published, entitled "My Plea for Pragmatism," for which he wrote the following introduction: "The two chapters composing this Essay were first published, without any title for the whole in the *Popular Science Monthly* for November 1877 and January 1878. A French version by the author (the second having in fact been first written in French on board a steamer in September 1877) appeared in the *Revue Philosophique*, vols. 6 and 7. They received as little attention as they laid claim to; but some years later the potent pen of Professor James brought their chief thesis to the attention of the philosophic world (pressing it, indeed, further than the tether of their author would reach, who continues to acknowledge, not indeed the Existence, but yet the Reality, of the Absolute, nearly as it has been set forth, for example, by Royce in his *The World and the Individual*, a work not free from faults of logic, yet valid in the main). The doctrine of this pair of chapters had already for some years been known among friends of the writer by the name he had proposed for it, which was 'Pragmatism.'"

the syllogistic procedure, his intellectual kit of tools was held to be complete.

To Roger Bacon, that remarkable mind who in the middle of the thirteenth century was almost a scientific man, the schoolmen's conception of reasoning appeared only an obstacle to truth. He saw that experience alone teaches anything—a proposition which to us seems easy to understand, because a distinct conception of experience has been handed down to us from former generations; which to him also seemed perfectly clear, because its difficulties had not yet unfolded themselves. Of all kinds of experience, the best, he thought, was interior illumination, which teaches many things about Nature which the external senses could never discover, such as the transubstantiation of bread.

Four centuries later, the more celebrated Bacon, in the first book of his "Novum Organum," gave his clear account of experience as something which must be open to verification and reëxamination. But, superior as Lord Bacon's conception is to earlier notions, a modern reader who is not in awe of his grandiloquence is chiefly struck by the inadequacy of his view of scientific procedure. That we have only to make some crude experiments, to draw up briefs of the results in certain blank forms, to go through these by rule, checking off everything disproved and setting down the alternatives, and that thus in a few years physical science would be finished up—what an idea! "He wrote on science like a Lord Chancellor," indeed.

The early scientists, Copernicus, Tycho Brahe, Kepler, Galileo, and Gilbert, had methods more like those of their modern brethren. Kepler undertook to draw a curve through the places of Mars; * and his greatest service to science was in impressing on men's minds that this was the thing to be done if they wished to improve astronomy; that they were not to content themselves with inquiring whether one system of epicycles was better than another, but that they were to sit down to the figures and find out what the curve, in truth, was. He accomplished this by his incomparable energy and courage, blundering along in the most inconceivable way (to us), from one irrational hypothesis to another, until, after trying twenty-two of these, he fell, by the mere exhaustion of his invention, upon the orbit which a mind well furnished with the weapons of modern logic would have tried almost at the outset.[2]

---

* Not quite so, but as nearly so as can be told in a few words.

[2] In 1893 Peirce added the following footnote: "I am ashamed at being obliged to confess that this volume contains a very false and foolish remark about Kepler. When I wrote it, I had never studied the original book as I have since. It is now my deliberate opinion that it is the most marvellous piece of inductive reasoning I have been able to find." See also 1.71-74, 2.96-97, 5.362 n.l.

In the same way, every work of science great enough to be remembered for a few generations affords some exemplification of the defective state of the art of reasoning of the time when it was written; and each chief step in science has been a lesson in logic. It was so when Lavoisier and his contemporaries took up the study of chemistry. The old chemist's maxim had been, *"Lege, lege, lege, labora, ora, et relege."* Lavoisier's method was not to read and pray, not [3] to dream that some long and complicated chemical process would have a certain effect, to put it into practice with dull patience, after its inevitable failure to dream that with some modification it would have another result, and to end by publishing the last dream as a fact: his way was to carry his mind into his laboratory, and to make of his alembics and cucurbits instruments of thought, giving a new conception of reasoning, as something which was to be done with one's eyes open, by manipulating real things instead of words and fancies.

The Darwinian controversy is, in large part, a question of logic. Mr. Darwin proposed to apply the statistical method to biology.[4] The same thing had been done in a widely different branch of science, the theory of gases. Though unable to say what the movements of any particular molecule of a gas would be on a certain hypothesis regarding the constitution of this class of bodies, Clausius and Maxwell were yet able, by the application of the doctrine of probabilities, to predict that in the long run such and such a proportion of the molecules would, under given circumstances, acquire such and such velocities; that there would take place, every second, such and such a number of collisions, etc.; and from these propositions were able to deduce certain properties of gases, especially in regard to their heat-relations. In like manner, Darwin, while unable to say what the operation of variation and natural selection in any individual case will be, demonstrates that in the long run they will [5] adapt animals to their circumstances. Whether or not existing animal forms are due to such action, or what position the theory ought to take, forms the subject of a discussion in which questions of fact and questions of logic are curiously interlaced.

---

[3] In 5.363 "not" has been replaced by "but," though without any explanation as to why the change was made. It is clear that "not" is correct, however, for the process of dreaming outside of the laboratory, working in the laboratory without direction, and publishing the last dream is surely characteristic of the alchemists rather than Lavoisier.

[4] In 1903 Peirce added the following footnote: "What he did, a most instructive illustration of the logic of science, will be described in another chapter [where?]; and we now know what was authoritatively denied when I first suggested it, that he took a hint from Malthus' book on Population."

[5] Later changed to read "will, or would."

II

The object of reasoning is to find out, from the consideration of what we already know, something else which we do not know. Consequently, reasoning is good if it be such as to give a true conclusion from true premises, and not otherwise. Thus, the question of its validity is purely one of fact and not of thinking. A being the premises and B the conclusion, the question is, whether these facts are really so related that if A is B is.[6] If so, the inference is valid; if not, not. It is not in the least the question whether, when the premises are accepted by the mind, we feel an impulse to accept the conclusion also. It is true that we do generally reason correctly by nature. But that is an accident; the true conclusion would remain true if we had no impulse to accept it; and the false one would remain false, though we could not resist the tendency to believe in it.

We are, doubtless, in the main logical animals, but we are not perfectly so. Most of us, for example, are naturally more sanguine and hopeful than logic would justify. We seem to be so constituted that in the absence of any facts to go upon we are happy and self-satisfied; so that the effect of experience is continually to contract our hopes and aspirations. Yet a lifetime of the application of this corrective does not usually eradicate our sanguine disposition. Where hope is unchecked by any experience, it is likely that our optimism is extravagant. Logicality in regard to practical matters [7] is the most useful quality an animal can possess, and might, therefore, result from the action of natural selection; but outside of these it is probably of more advantage to the animal to have his mind filled with pleasing and encouraging visions, independently of their truth; and thus, upon unpractical subjects, natural selection might occasion a fallacious tendency of thought.[8]

That which determines us, from given premises, to draw one inference rather than another, is some habit of mind, whether it be constitutional or acquired. The habit is good or otherwise, according as it produces true conclusions from true premises or not; and an inference is regarded as valid or not, without reference to the truth or falsity of its conclusion specially, but according as the habit which determines it is such as to produce true conclusions in general or not. The particular habit of mind which governs this or that inference may

[6] "if A is B is" later changed to "if A were B would generally be."

[7] About 1910 Peirce added: "(if this be understood, not in the old sense, but as consisting in a wise union of security with fruitfulness of reasoning)."

[8] In 1903 Peirce added the following footnote: "Let us not, however, be cocksure that natural selection is the only factor of evolution; and until this momentous proposition has been much better proved than as yet it has been, let it not blind us to the force [of] very sound reasoning."

be formulated in a proposition whose truth depends on the validity of the inferences which the habit determines; and such a formula is called a *guiding principle* of inference. Suppose, for example, that we observe that a rotating disk of copper quickly comes to rest when placed between the poles of a magnet, and we infer that this will happen with every disk of copper. The guiding principle is, that what is true of one piece of copper is true of another. Such a guiding principle with regard to copper would be much safer than with regard to many other substances—brass, for example.

A book might be written to signalize all the most important of these guiding principles of reasoning. It would probably be, we must confess, of no service to a person whose thought is directed wholly to practical subjects, and whose activity moves along thoroughly-beaten paths. The problems which present themselves to such a mind are matters of routine which he has learned once for all to handle in learning his business. But let a man venture into an unfamiliar field, or where his results are not continually checked by experience, and all history shows that the most masculine intellect will ofttimes lose his orientation and waste his efforts in directions which bring him no nearer to his goal, or even carry him entirely astray. He is like a ship in the open sea, with no one on board who understands the rules of navigation. And in such a case some general study of the guiding principles of reasoning would be sure to be found useful.

The subject could hardly be treated, however, without being first limited; since almost any fact may serve as a guiding principle. But it so happens that there exists a division among facts, such that in one class are all those which are absolutely essential as guiding principles, while in the others are all which have any other interest as objects of research. This division is between those which are necessarily taken for granted in asking whether a certain conclusion follows from certain premises, and those which are not implied in that question. A moment's thought will show that a variety of facts are already assumed when the logical question is first asked. It is implied, for instance, that there are such states of mind as doubt and belief—that a passage from one to the other is possible, the object of thought remaining the same, and that this transition is subject to some rules which all minds are alike bound by. As these are facts which we must already know before we can have any clear conception of reasoning at all, it cannot be supposed to be any longer of much interest to inquire into their truth or falsity. On the other hand, it is easy to believe that those rules of reasoning which are deduced from the very idea of the process are the ones which are the most essential; and, indeed, that so long as it conforms to these it will, at least, not lead to false conclusions from true premises. In point of fact, the importance of what may be deduced from the assumptions involved in the logical question turns out to be greater than might be supposed, and this for reasons which it is difficult to exhibit at the outset. The only one which I shall here mention is, that conceptions which are really products of logical reflection, without being readily seen to be so, mingle with our ordinary thoughts, and are frequently the causes of great confusion. This is the case, for example, with the conception of quality. A quality as such is never an object of observation. We can see that a thing is blue or green, but the quality of being blue and the quality of being green are not things which we see; they are products of logical reflection. The truth is, that common-sense, or thought as it first emerges above the level of the narrowly practical, is deeply imbued with that bad logical quality to which the epithet *metaphysical* is commonly applied; and nothing can clear it up but a severe course of logic.

III

We generally know when we wish to ask a question and when we wish to pronounce a judgment, for there is a dissimilarity between the sensation of doubting and that of believing.

But this is not all which distinguishes doubt from belief. There is a practical difference. Our beliefs guide our desires and shape our actions. The Assassins, or followers of the Old Man of the Mountain, used to rush into death at his least command, because they believed that obedience to him would insure everlasting felicity. Had they doubted this, they would not have acted as they did. So it is with every belief, according to its degree. The feeling of believing is a more or less sure indication of there being established in our nature some habit which will determine our actions. Doubt never has such an effect.

Nor must we overlook a third point of difference. Doubt is an uneasy and dissatisfied state from which we struggle to free ourselves and pass into the state of belief; [9] while the latter is a calm and satisfactory state which we do not wish to avoid, or to change to a belief in anything else.[*] On the contrary, we cling tenaciously, not merely to believing, but to believing just what we do believe.

Thus, both doubt and belief have positive effects upon us, though

[9] In 1893 Peirce added the following footnote: "In this, it is like any other stimulus. It is true that just as men may, for the sake of the pleasures of the table, like to be hungry and take means to make themselves so, although hunger always involves a desire to fill the stomach, so for the sake of the pleasures of inquiry, men may like to seek out doubts. Yet, for all that, doubt essentially involves a struggle to escape it."

[*] I am not speaking of secondary effects occasionally produced by the interference of other impulses.

very different ones. Belief does not make us act at once, but puts us into such a condition that we shall behave in a certain way, when the occasion arises. Doubt has not the least effect of this sort, but stimulates us to action [10] until it is destroyed. This reminds us of the irritation of a nerve and the reflex action produced thereby; while for the analogue of belief, in the nervous system, we must look to what are called nervous associations—for example, to that habit of the nerves in consequence of which the smell of a peach will make the mouth water.[11]

IV

The irritation of doubt causes a struggle to attain a state of belief. I shall term this struggle *inquiry,* though it must be admitted that this is sometimes not a very apt designation.

The irritation of doubt is the only immediate motive for the struggle to attain belief. It is certainly best for us that our beliefs should be such as may truly guide our actions so as to satisfy our desires; and this reflection will make us reject any belief which does not seem to have been so formed as to insure this result. But it will only do so by creating a doubt in the place of that belief. With the doubt, therefore, the struggle begins, and with the cessation of doubt it ends. Hence, the sole object of inquiry is the settlement of opinion. We may fancy that this is not enough for us, and that we seek, not merely an opinion, but a true opinion. But put this fancy to the test, and it proves groundless; for as soon as a firm belief is reached we are entirely satisfied, whether the belief be true or false. And it is clear that nothing out of the sphere of our knowledge can be our object, for nothing which does not affect the mind can be the motive for a mental effort. The most that can be maintained is, that we seek for a belief that we shall *think*

[10] "action" later replaced by "inquiry."

[11] In 1893 Peirce added the following footnote (editor's italics): "Doubt, however, is not usually hesitancy about what is to be done then and there. It is anticipated hesitancy about what I shall do hereafter, or a feigned hesitancy about a fictitious state of things. It is the power of making believe we hesitate, together with the pregnant fact that the decision upon the merely make-believe dilemma goes toward forming a bona fide habit that will be operative in a real emergency. It is these two things in conjunction that constitute us intellectual beings.

"Every answer to a question that has any meaning is a decision as to how we *would* act under imagined circumstances, or how the world *would be* expected to react upon our senses. Thus, suppose I am told that if two straight lines in one plane are cut by a third making the sum of the internal angles on one side less than two right angles, then those lines if sufficiently produced will meet on the side on which the said sum is less than two right angles. This means to me that if I had two lines drawn on a plane and wished to find where they would meet, I could draw a third line cutting them and ascertaining on which side the sum of the two internal angles was less than two right angles, and should lengthen the lines on that side. In like manner, all doubt is a state of hesitancy about an *imagined* state of things."

to be true. But we think each one of our beliefs to be true, and, indeed, it is mere tautology to say so.[12]

That the settlement of opinion is the sole end of inquiry is a very important proposition. It sweeps away, at once, various vague and erroneous conceptions of proof. A few of these may be noticed here.

1. Some philosophers have imagined that to start an inquiry it was only necessary to utter a question or set it down upon paper, and have even recommended us to begin our studies with questioning everything! But the mere putting of a proposition into the interrogative form does not stimulate the mind to any struggle after belief. There must be a real and living doubt, and without this all discussion is idle.[13]

2. It is a very common idea that a demonstration must rest on some ultimate and absolutely indubitable propositions. These, according to one school, are first principles of a general nature; according to another, are first sensations. But, in point of fact, an inquiry, to have that completely satisfactory result called demonstration, has only to start with propositions perfectly free from all actual doubt. If the premises are not in fact doubted at all, they cannot be more satisfactory than they are.[14]

3. Some people seem to love to argue a point after all the world is fully convinced of it. But no further advance can be made. When doubt ceases, mental action on the subject comes to an end; and, if it did go on, it would be without a purpose.

[12] In 1903 Peirce added the following footnote (editor's italics): "For truth is neither more nor less than that character of a proposition which consists in this, that belief in the proposition *would*, with sufficient experience and reflection, lead us to such conduct as *would* tend to satisfy the desires we should then have. To say that truth means more than this is to say that it has no meaning at all."

[13] In 1893 Peirce added the following footnote: "So long as we cannot put our fingers on our erroneous opinions, they remain our opinions, still. It will be wholesome enough for us to make a general review of the causes of our beliefs; and the result will be that most of them have been taken upon trust and have been held since we were too young to discriminate the credible from the incredible. Such reflections may awaken real doubts about some of our positions. But in cases where no real doubt exists in our minds inquiry will be an idle farce, a mere whitewashing commission which were better let alone. This fault in philosophy was very widespread in those ages in which Disputations were the principal exercises in the universities; that is, from their rise in the thirteenth century down to the middle of the eighteenth, and even to this day in some Catholic institutions. But since those disputations went out of vogue, this philosophic disease is less virulent."

[14] In 1893 Peirce added the following footnote: "We have to acknowledge that doubts about them may spring up later; but we can find no propositions which are not subject to this contingency. We ought to construct our theories so as to provide for such discoveries; first, by making them rest on as great a variety of different considerations as possible, and second, by leaving room for the modifications which cannot be foreseen but which are pretty sure to prove needful. Some

V

If the settlement of opinion is the sole object of inquiry, and if belief is of the nature of a habit, why should we not attain the desired end, by taking any answer to a question which we may fancy, and constantly reiterating it to ourselves, dwelling on all which may conduce to that belief, and learning to turn with contempt and hatred from anything which might disturb it? This simple and direct method is really pursued by many men. I remember once being entreated not to read a certain newspaper lest it might change my opinion upon free-trade. "Lest I might be entrapped by its fallacies and misstatements," was the form of expression. "You are not," my friend said, "a special student of political economy. You might, therefore, easily be deceived by fallacious arguments upon the subject. You might, then, if you read this paper, be led to believe in protection. But you admit that free-trade is the true doctrine; and you do not wish to believe what is not true." I have often known this system to be deliberately adopted. Still oftener, the instinctive dislike of an undecided state of mind, exaggerated into a vague dread of doubt, makes men cling spasmodically to the views they already take. The man feels that, if he only holds to his belief without wavering, it will be entirely satisfactory. Nor can it be denied that a steady and immovable faith yields great peace of mind. It may, indeed, give rise to inconveniences, as if a man should resolutely continue to believe that fire would not burn him, or that he would be eternally damned if he received his *ingesta* otherwise than through a stomach-pump. But then the man who adopts this method will not allow that its inconveniences are greater than its advantages. He will say, "I hold steadfastly to the truth, and the truth is always wholesome." And in many cases it may very well be that the pleasure he derives from his calm faith overbalances any inconveniences resulting from its deceptive character. Thus, if it be true that death is annihilation, then the man who believes that he will certainly go straight to heaven when he dies, provided he have fulfilled certain simple observances in this life, has a cheap pleasure which will not be followed by the least disappointment.[15] A similar consideration seems to have weight with many persons in religious topics, for we frequently hear it said, "Oh, I could not believe so-and-so, because I should be wretched if I did." When an ostrich buries its head in the sand as danger ap-

systems are much more open to this criticism than others. All those which repose heavily upon an 'inconceivability of the opposite' have proved particularly fragile and short-lived. Those, however, which rest upon positive evidences and which avoid insisting upon the absolute precision of their dogmas are hard to destroy."

[15] In 1903 Peirce added the following footnote: "Although it certainly may be that it will cause a line of conduct leading to pains that deeper reflection would have avoided."

proaches, it very likely takes the happiest course. It hides the danger, and then calmly says there is no danger; and, if it feels perfectly sure there is none, why should it raise its head to see? A man may go through life, systematically keeping out of view all that might cause a change in his opinions, and if he only succeeds—basing his method, as he does, on two fundamental psychological laws—I do not see what can be said against his doing so. It would be an egotistical impertinence to object that his procedure is irrational, for that only amounts to saying that his method of settling belief is not ours. He does not propose to himself to be rational, and, indeed, will often talk with scorn of man's weak and illusive reason. So let him think as he pleases.

But this method of fixing belief, which may be called the method of tenacity, will be unable to hold its ground in practice. The social impulse is against it. The man who adopts it will find that other men think differently from him, and it will be apt to occur to him, in some saner moment, that their opinions are quite as good as his own, and this will shake his confidence in his belief. This conception, that another man's thought or sentiment may be equivalent to one's own, is a distinctly new step, and a highly important one. It arises from an impulse too strong in man to be suppressed, without danger of destroying the human species. Unless we make ourselves hermits, we shall necessarily influence each other's opinions; so that the problem becomes how to fix belief, not in the individual merely, but in the community.

Let the will of the state act, then, instead of that of the individual. Let an institution be created which shall have for its object to keep correct doctrines before the attention of the people, to reiterate them perpetually, and to teach them to the young; having at the same time power to prevent contrary doctrines from being taught, advocated, or expressed. Let all possible causes of a change of mind be removed from men's apprehensions. Let them be kept ignorant, lest they should learn of some reason to think otherwise than they do. Let their passions be enlisted, so that they may regard private and unusual opinions with hatred and horror. Then, let all men who reject the established belief be terrified into silence. Let the people turn out and tar-and-feather such men, or let inquisitions be made into the manner of thinking of suspected persons, and, when they are found guilty of forbidden beliefs, let them be subjected to some signal punishment. When complete agreement could not otherwise be reached, a general massacre of all who have not thought in a certain way has proved a very effective means of settling opinion in a country. If the power to do this be wanting, let a list of opinions be drawn up, to which no man of the least independence of thought can assent, and let the faithful be required to accept all these propositions, in order to segregate them as radically as possible from the influence of the rest of the world.

This method has, from the earliest times, been one of the chief means of upholding correct theological and political doctrines, and of preserving their universal or catholic character. In Rome, especially, it has been practised from the days of Numa Pompilius to those of Pius Nonus. This is the most perfect example in history; but wherever there is a priesthood—and no religion has been without one—this method has been more or less made use of. Wherever there is an aristocracy, or a guild, or any association of a class of men whose interests depend or are supposed to depend on certain propositions, there will be inevitably found some traces of this natural product of social feeling. Cruelties always accompany this system; and when it is consistently carried out, they become atrocities of the most horrible kind in the eyes of any rational man. Nor should this occasion surprise, for the officer of a society does not feel justified in surrendering the interests of that society for the sake of mercy, as he might his own private interests. It is natural, therefore, that sympathy and fellowship should thus produce a most ruthless power.

In judging this method of fixing belief, which may be called the method of authority, we must, in the first place, allow its immeasurable mental and moral superiority to the method of tenacity. Its success is proportionately greater; and, in fact, it has over and over again worked the most majestic results. The mere structures of stone which it has caused to be put together—in Siam, for example, in Egypt, and in Europe—have many of them a sublimity hardly more than rivaled by the greatest works of Nature. And, except the geological epochs, there are no periods of time so vast as those which are measured by some of these organized faiths. If we scrutinize the matter closely, we shall find that there has not been one of their creeds which has remained always the same; yet the change is so slow as to be imperceptible during one person's life, so that individual belief remains sensibly fixed. For the mass of mankind, then, there is perhaps no better method than this. If it is their highest impulse to be intellectual slaves, then slaves they ought to remain.

But no institution can undertake to regulate opinions upon every subject. Only the most important ones can be attended to, and on the rest men's minds must be left to the action of natural causes. This imperfection will be no source of weakness so long as men are in such a state of culture that one opinion does not influence another—that is, so long as they cannot put two and two together. But in the most priestridden states some individuals will be found who are raised above that condition. These men possess a wider sort of social feeling; they see that men in other countries and in other ages have held to very different doctrines from those which they themselves have been brought up to believe; and they cannot help seeing that it is the mere accident of their having been taught as they have, and of their having been surrounded with the manners and associations they have, that has caused them to believe as they do and not far differently. And their candor cannot resist the reflection that there is no reason to rate their own views at a higher value than those of other nations and other centuries; and this gives rise to doubts in their minds.

They will further perceive that such doubts as these must exist in their minds with reference to every belief which seems to be determined by the caprice either of themselves or of those who originated the popular opinions. The willful adherence to a belief, and the arbitrary forcing of it upon others, must, therefore, both be given up, and a new method of settling opinions must be adopted, which shall not only produce an impulse to believe, but shall also decide what proposition it is which is to be believed. Let the action of natural preferences be unimpeded, then, and under their influence let men, conversing together and regarding matters in different lights, gradually develop beliefs in harmony with natural causes. This method resembles that by which conceptions of art have been brought to maturity. The most perfect example of it is to be found in the history of metaphysical philosophy. Systems of this sort have not usually rested upon any observed facts, at least not in any great degree. They have been chiefly adopted because their fundamental propositions seemed "agreeable to reason." This is an apt expression; it does not mean that which agrees with experience, but that which we find ourselves inclined to believe. Plato, for example, finds it agreeable to reason that the distances of the celestial spheres from one another should be proportional to the different lengths of strings which produce harmonious chords. Many philosophers have been led to their main conclusions by considerations like this; but this is the lowest and least developed form which the method takes, for it is clear that another man might find Kepler's theory, that the celestial spheres are proportional to the inscribed and circumscribed spheres of the different regular solids, more agreeable to *his* reason. But the shock of opinions will soon lead men to rest on preferences of a far more universal nature. Take, for example, the doctrine that man only acts selfishly—that is, from the consideration that acting in one way will afford him more pleasure than acting in another. This rests on no fact in the world, but it has had a wide acceptance as being the only reasonable theory.

This method is far more intellectual and respectable from the point of view of reason than either of the others which we have noticed. But its failure has been the most manifest. It makes of inquiry something similar to the development of taste; but taste, unfortunately, is always more or less a matter of fashion, and accordingly metaphysicians have never come to any fixed agreement, but the pendulum has swung backward and forward between a more material and a more spiritual philosophy, from the earliest times to the latest. And so from this, which has been called the *a priori* method, we are driven, in Lord Bacon's phrase, to a true induction. We have examined into this *a priori* method as something which promised to deliver our opinions from their accidental and capricious element. But development, while it is a process which eliminates the effect of some casual circumstances, only magnifies that of others. This method, therefore, does not differ in a very essential way from that of authority. The government may not have lifted its finger to influence my convictions; I may have been left outwardly quite free to choose, we will say, between monogamy and polygamy, and, appealing to my conscience only, I may have concluded that the latter practice is in itself licentious. But when I come to see that the chief obstacle to the spread of Christianity among a people of as high culture as the Hindoos has been a conviction of the immorality of our way of treating women, I cannot help seeing that, though governments do not interfere, sentiments in their development will be very greatly determined by accidental causes. Now, there are some people, among whom I must suppose that my reader is to be found, who, when they see that any belief of theirs is determined by any circumstance extraneous to the facts, will from that moment not merely admit in words that that belief is doubtful, but will experience a real doubt of it, so that it ceases to be a belief.

To satisfy our doubts, therefore, it is necessary that a method should be found by which our beliefs may be caused by nothing human, but by some external permanency—by something upon which our thinking has no effect.[16] Some mystics imagine that they have such a method in a private inspiration from on high. But that is only a form of the method of tenacity, in which the conception of truth as something public is not yet developed. Our external permanency would not be external, in our sense, if it was restricted in its influence to one individual. It must be something which affects, or might affect, every man. And, though these affections are necessarily as various as are individual conditions, yet the method must be such that the ultimate conclusion of every man shall be the same.[17] Such is the method of science. Its fundamental hypothesis, restated in more familiar language, is this: There are real things, whose characters are entirely independent of our opinions about them; those realities affect our senses according to regular laws, and, though our sensations are as different as our relations to the objects, yet, by taking advantage of the laws of per-

---

[16] In 1903 Peirce added the following footnote: "But which, on the other hand, unceasingly tends to influence thought; or in other words, by something Real."

[17] In 1903 Peirce added the following footnote (editor's italics): "Or *would be* the same if inquiry were sufficiently persisted in."

ception, we can ascertain by reasoning how things really are, and any man, if he have sufficient experience and reason enough about it, will be led to the one true conclusion. The new conception here involved is that of reality. It may be asked how I know that there are any realities. If this hypothesis is the sole support of my method of inquiry, my method of inquiry must not be used to support my hypothesis. The reply is this: 1. If investigation cannot be regarded as proving that there are real things, it at least does not lead to a contrary conclusion; but the method and the conception on which it is based remain ever in harmony. No doubts of the method, therefore, necessarily arise from its practice, as is the case with all the others. 2. The feeling which gives rise to any method of fixing belief is a dissatisfaction at two repugnant propositions. But here already is a vague concession that there is some *one* thing to which a proposition should conform. Nobody, therefore, can really doubt that there are realities, or, if he did, doubt would not be a source of dissatisfaction. The hypothesis, therefore, is one which every mind admits. So that the social impulse does not cause me to doubt it. 3. Everybody uses the scientific method about a great many things, and only ceases to use it when he does not know how to apply it. 4. Experience of the method has not led me to doubt it, but, on the contrary, scientific investigation has had the most wonderful triumphs in the way of settling opinion. These afford the explanation of my not doubting the method or the hypothesis which it supposes; and not having any doubt, nor believing that anybody else whom I could influence has, it would be the merest babble for me to say more about it. If there be anybody with a living doubt upon the subject, let him consider it.[18]

To describe the method of scientific investigation is the object of this series of papers. At present I have only room to notice some points of contrast between it and other methods of fixing belief.

This is the only one of the four methods which presents any distinc-

---

[18] In 1893 Peirce added the following footnote: "Changes of opinion are brought about by events beyond human control. All mankind were so firmly of opinion that heavy bodies must fall faster than light ones, that any other view was scouted as absurd, eccentric, and probably insincere. Yet as soon as some of the absurd and eccentric men could succeed in inducing some of the adherents of common sense to look at their experiments—no easy task—it became apparent that nature would not follow human opinion, however unanimous. So there was nothing for it but human opinion must move to nature's position. That was a lesson in humility. A few men, the small band of laboratory men, began to see that they had to abandon the pride of an opinion assumed absolutely final in any respect, and to use all their endeavors to yield as unresistingly as possible to the overwhelming tide of experience, which must master them at last, and to listen to what nature seems to be telling us. The trial of this method of experience in natural science for these three centuries—though bitterly detested by the majority of men—encourages us to hope that we are approaching nearer and nearer to an opinion which is not destined to be broken down—though we cannot expect ever quite to reach that ideal goal."

tion of a right and a wrong way. If I adopt the method of tenacity and shut myself out from all influences, whatever I think necessary to doing this is necessary according to that method. So with the method of authority: the state may try to put down heresy by means which, from a scientific point of view, seem very ill-calculated to accomplish its purposes; but the only test *on that method* is what the state thinks, so that it cannot pursue the method wrongly. So with the *a priori* method. The very essence of it is to think as one is inclined to think. All metaphysicians will be sure to do that, however they may be inclined to judge each other to be perversely wrong. The Hegelian system recognizes every natural tendency of thought as logical, although it be certain to be abolished by counter-tendencies. Hegel thinks there is a regular system in the succession of these tendencies, in consequence of which, after drifting one way and the other for a long time, opinion will at last go right. And it is true that metaphysicians get the right ideas at last; Hegel's system of Nature represents tolerably the science of that day; and one may be sure that whatever scientific investigation has put out of doubt will presently receive *a priori* demonstration on the part of the metaphysicians. But with the scientific method the case is different. I may start with known and observed facts to proceed to the unknown; and yet the rules which I follow in doing so may not be such as investigation would approve. The test of whether I am truly following the method is not an immediate appeal to my feelings and purposes, but, on the contrary, itself involves the application of the method. Hence it is that bad reasoning as well as good reasoning is possible; and this fact is the foundation of the practical side of logic.

It is not to be supposed that the first three methods of settling opinion present no advantage whatever over the scientific method. On the contrary, each has some peculiar convenience of its own. The *a priori* method is distinguished for its comfortable conclusions. It is the nature of the process to adopt whatever belief we are inclined to, and there are certain flatteries to the vanity of man which we all believe by nature, until we are awakened from our pleasing dream by some rough facts. The method of authority will always govern the mass of mankind; and those who wield the various forms of organized force in the state will never be convinced that dangerous reasoning ought not to be suppressed in some way. If liberty of speech is to be untrammeled from the grosser forms of constraint, then uniformity of opinion will be secured by a moral terrorism to which the respectability of society will give its thorough approval. Following the method of authority is the path of peace. Certain non-conformities are permitted; certain others (considered unsafe) are forbidden. These are different in different countries and in different ages; but, wherever you are, let it be known that you seriously hold a tabooed belief, and you may be perfectly sure of being treated with a cruelty less brutal but more refined than hunting you like a wolf. Thus, the greatest intellectual benefactors of mankind have never dared, and dare not now, to utter the whole of their thought; and thus a shade of *prima facie* doubt is cast upon every proposition which is considered essential to the security of society. Singularly enough, the persecution does not all come from without; but a man torments himself and is oftentimes most distressed at finding himself believing propositions which he has been brought up to regard with aversion. The peaceful and sympathetic man will, therefore, find it hard to resist the temptation to submit his opinions to authority. But most of all I admire the method of tenacity for its strength, simplicity, and directness. Men who pursue it are distinguished for their decision of character, which becomes very easy with such a mental rule. They do not waste time in trying to make up their minds what they want, but, fastening like lightning upon whatever alternative comes first, they hold to it to the end, whatever happens, without an instant's irresolution. This is one of the splendid qualities which generally accompany brilliant, unlasting success. It is impossible not to envy the man who can dismiss reason, although we know how it must turn out at last.

Such are the advantages which the other methods of settling opinion have over scientific investigation. A man should consider well of them; and then he should consider that, after all, he wishes his opinions to coincide with the fact, and that there is no reason why the results of these three methods should do so. To bring about this effect is the prerogative of the method of science. Upon such considerations he has to make his choice—a choice which is far more than the adoption of any intellectual opinion, which is one of the ruling decisions of his life, to which, when once made, he is bound to adhere. The force of habit will sometimes cause a man to hold on to old beliefs, after he is in a condition to see that they have no sound basis. But reflection upon the state of the case will overcome these habits, and he ought to allow reflection its full weight. People sometimes shrink from doing this, having an idea that beliefs are wholesome which they cannot help feeling rest on nothing. But let such persons suppose an analogous though different case from their own. Let them ask themselves what they would say to a reformed Mussulman who should hesitate to give up his old notions in regard to the relations of the sexes; or to a reformed Catholic who should still shrink from reading the Bible. Would they not say that these persons ought to consider the matter fully, and clearly understand the new doctrine, and then ought to embrace it, in its entirety? But, above all, let it be considered that what is more wholesome than any particular belief is integrity of belief, and that to avoid looking into the support of any belief from a fear that it may turn out rotten is quite as immoral as it is disadvantageous. The person who confesses that there is such a thing as truth, which is distinguished from falsehood simply by this, that if acted on it will carry [19] us to the point we aim at and not astray, and then, though convinced of this, dares not know the truth and seeks to avoid it, is in a sorry state of mind indeed.

Yes, the other methods do have their merits: a clear logical conscience does cost something—just as any virtue, just as all that we cherish, costs us dear. But we should not desire it to be otherwise. The genius of a man's logical method should be loved and reverenced as his bride, whom he has chosen from all the world. He need not contemn the others; on the contrary, he may honor them deeply, and in doing so he only honors her the more. But she is the one that he has chosen, and he knows that he was right in making that choice. And having made it, he will work and fight for her, and will not complain that there are blows to take, hoping that there may be as many and as hard to give, and will strive to be the worthy knight and champion of her from the blaze of whose splendors he draws his inspiration and his courage.

2. How to Make Our Ideas Clear [20]

I

WHOEVER HAS LOOKED into a modern treatise on logic of the common sort, will doubtless remember the two distinctions between *clear* and *obscure* conceptions, and between *distinct* and *confused* conceptions. They have lain in the books now for nigh two centuries, unimproved and unmodified, and are generally reckoned by logicians as among the gems of their doctrine.

A clear idea is defined as one which is so apprehended that it will be recognized wherever it is met with, and so that no other will be mistaken for it. If it fails of this clearness, it is said to be obscure.

This is rather a neat bit of philosophical terminology; yet, since it is clearness that they were defining, I wish the logicians had made their definition a little more plain. Never to fail to recognize an idea, and under no circumstances to mistake another for it, let it come in how recondite a form it may, would indeed imply such prodigious force and clearness of intellect as is seldom met with in this world. On the

---

[19] "will carry" later replaced by "should, on full consideration, carry."

[20] *Popular Science Monthly* 12 (Jan. 1878) 286-302, with some of the revisions and footnotes of the later period (as given in 5.388-410) included in the editor's footnotes by permission of the Harvard University Press.

other hand, merely to have such an acquaintance with the idea as to have become familiar with it, and to have lost all hesitancy in recognizing it in ordinary cases, hardly seems to deserve the name of clearness of apprehension, since after all it only amounts to a subjective feeling of mastery which may be entirely mistaken. I take it, however, that when the logicians speak of "clearness," they mean nothing more than such a familiarity with an idea, since they regard the quality as but a small merit, which needs to be supplemented by another, which they call *distinctness*.

A distinct idea is defined as one which contains nothing which is not clear. This is technical language; by the *contents* of an idea logicians understand whatever is contained in its definition. So that an idea is *distinctly* apprehended, according to them, when we can give a precise definition of it, in abstract terms. Here the professional logicians leave the subject; and I would not have troubled the reader with what they have to say, if it were not such a striking example of how they have been slumbering through ages of intellectual activity, listlessly disregarding the enginery of modern thought, and never dreaming of applying its lessons to the improvement of logic. It is easy to show that the doctrine that familiar use and abstract distinctness make the perfection of apprehension has its only true place in philosophies which have long been extinct; and it is now time to formulate the method of attaining to a more perfect clearness of thought, such as we see and admire in the thinkers of our own time.

When Descartes set about the reconstruction of philosophy, his first step was to (theoretically) permit skepticism and to discard the practice of the schoolmen of looking to authority as the ultimate source of truth. That done, he sought a more natural fountain of true principles, and professed to find it in the human mind; thus passing, in the directest way, from the method of authority to that of apriority, as described in my first paper. Self-consciousness was to furnish us with our fundamental truths, and to decide what was agreeable to reason. But since, evidently, not all ideas are true, he was led to note, as the first condition of infallibility, that they must be clear. The distinction between an idea *seeming* clear and really being so, never occurred to him. Trusting to introspection, as he did, even for a knowledge of external things, why should he question its testimony in respect to the contents of our own minds? But then, I suppose, seeing men, who seemed to be quite clear and positive, holding opposite opinions upon fundamental principles, he was further led to say that clearness of ideas is not sufficient, but that they need also to be distinct, i.e., to have nothing unclear about them. What he probably meant by this (for he did not explain himself with precision) was, that they must sustain the test of dialectical examination; that they must not only seem clear at the outset, but that discussion must never be able to bring to light points of obscurity connected with them.

Such was the distinction of Descartes, and one sees that it was precisely on the level of his philosophy. It was somewhat developed by Leibnitz. This great and singular genius was as remarkable for what he failed to see as for what he saw. That a piece of mechanism could not do work perpetually without being fed with power in some form, was a thing perfectly apparent to him; yet he did not understand that the machinery of the mind can only transform knowledge, but never originate it, unless it be fed with facts of observation. He thus missed the most essential point of the Cartesian philosophy, which is, that to accept propositions which seem perfectly evident to us is a thing which, whether it be logical or illogical, we cannot help doing. Instead of regarding the matter in this way, he sought to reduce the first principles of science to formulas which cannot be denied without self-contradiction,[21] and was apparently unaware of the great difference between his position and that of Descartes. So he reverted to the old formalities of logic, and, above all, abstract definitions played a great part in his philosophy. It was quite natural, therefore, that on observing that the method of Descartes labored under the difficulty that we may seem to ourselves to have clear apprehensions of ideas which in truth are very hazy, no better remedy occurred to him than to require an abstract definition of every important term. Accordingly, in adopting the distinction of *clear* and *distinct* notions, he described the latter quality as the clear apprehension of everything contained in the definition; and the books have ever since copied his words. There is no danger that his chimerical scheme will ever again be overvalued. Nothing new can ever be learned by analyzing definitions. Nevertheless, our existing beliefs can be set in order by this process, and order is an essential element of intellectual economy, as of every other. It may be acknowledged, therefore, that the books are right in making familiarity with a notion the first step toward clearness of apprehension, and the defining of it the second. But in omitting all mention of any higher perspicuity of thought, they simply mirror a philosophy which was exploded a hundred years ago. That much-admired "ornament of logic"—the doctrine of clearness and distinctness—may be pretty enough, but it is high time to relegate to our cabinet of curiosities the antique *bijou,* and to wear about us something better adapted to modern uses.

The very first lesson that we have a right to demand that logic shall teach us is, how to make our ideas clear; and a most important one it is, depreciated only by minds who stand in need of it. To know what

---

[21] "formulas which cannot be denied without self-contradiction" later replaced by "two classes, those which cannot be denied without self-contradiction, and those which result from the principle of sufficient reason (of which more anon)."

we think, to be masters of our own meaning, will make a solid foundation for great and weighty thought. It is most easily learned by those
whose ideas are meagre and restricted; and far happier they than such
as wallow helplessly in a rich mud of conceptions. A nation, it is true,
may, in the course of generations, overcome the disadvantage of an
excessive wealth of language and its natural concomitant, a vast, un-
fathomable deep of ideas. We may see it in history, slowly perfecting
its literary forms, sloughing at length its metaphysics, and, by virtue
of the untirable patience which is often a compensation, attaining great
excellence in every branch of mental acquirement. The page of history
is not yet unrolled which is to tell us whether such a people will or
will not in the long run prevail over one whose ideas (like the words
of their language) are few, but which possesses a wonderful mastery
over those which it has. For an individual, however, there can be no
question that a few clear ideas are worth more than many confused
ones. A young man would hardly be persuaded to sacrifice the greater
part of his thoughts to save the rest; and the muddled head is the least
apt to see the necessity of such a sacrifice. Him we can usually only
commiserate, as a person with a congenital defect. Time will help him,
but intellectual maturity with regard to clearness comes rather late,
an unfortunate arrangement of Nature, inasmuch as clearness is of less
use to a man settled in life, whose errors have in great measure had
their effect, than it would be to one whose path lies before him. It is
terrible to see how a single unclear idea, a single formula without
meaning, lurking in a young man's head, will sometimes act like an
obstruction of inert matter in an artery, hindering the nutrition of the
brain, and condemning its victim to pine away in the fullness of his
intellectual vigor and in the midst of intellectual plenty. Many a man
has cherished for years as his hobby some vague shadow of an idea,
too meaningless to be positively false; he has, nevertheless, passionately
loved it, has made it his companion by day and by night, and has given
to it his strength and his life, leaving all other occupations for its sake,
and in short has lived with it and for it, until it has become, as it were,
flesh of his flesh and bone of his bone; and then he has waked up some
bright morning to find it gone, clean vanished away like the beautiful
Melusina of the fable, and the essence of his life gone with it. I have
myself known such a man; and who can tell how many histories of
circle-squarers, metaphysicians, astrologers, and what not, may not be
told in the old German story?

II

The principles set forth in the first of these papers lead, at once, to
a method of reaching a clearness of thought of a far higher grade than
the "distinctness" of the logicians. We have there found that the action

of thought is excited by the irritation of doubt, and ceases when belief is attained; so that the production of belief is the sole function of thought. All these words, however, are too strong for my purpose. It is as if I had described the phenomena as they appear under a mental microscope. Doubt and Belief, as the words are commonly employed, relate to religious or other grave discussions. But here I use them to designate the starting of any question, no matter how small or how great, and the resolution of it. If, for instance, in a horse-car, I pull out my purse and find a five-cent nickel and five coppers, I decide, while my hand is going to the purse, in which way I will pay my fare. To call such a question Doubt, and my decision Belief, is certainly to use words very disproportionate to the occasion. To speak of such a doubt as causing an irritation which needs to be appeased, suggests a temper which is uncomfortable to the verge of insanity. Yet, looking at the matter minutely, it must be admitted that, if there is the least hesitation as to whether I shall pay the five coppers or the nickel (as there will be sure to be, unless I act from some previously contracted habit in the matter), though irritation is too strong a word, yet I am excited to such small mental activity as may be necessary to deciding how I shall act. Most frequently doubts arise from some indecision, however momentary, in our action. Sometimes it is not so. I have, for example, to wait in a railway-station, and to pass the time I read the advertisements on the walls, I compare the advantages of different trains and different routes which I never expect to take, merely fancying myself to be in a state of hesitancy, because I am bored with having nothing to trouble me. Feigned hesitancy, whether feigned for mere amusement or with a lofty purpose, plays a great part in the production of scientific inquiry. However the doubt may originate, it stimulates the mind to an activity which may be slight or energetic, calm or turbulent. Images pass rapidly through consciousness, one incessantly melting into another, until at last, when all is over—it may be in a fraction of a second, in an hour, or after long years—we find ourselves decided as to how we should act under such circumstances as those which occasioned our hesitation. In other words, we have attained belief.

In this process we observe two sorts of elements of consciousness, the distinction between which may best be made clear by means of an illustration. In a piece of music there are the separate notes, and there is the air. A single tone may be prolonged for an hour or a day, and it exists as perfectly in each second of that time as in the whole taken together; so that, as long as it is sounding, it might be present to a sense from which everything in the past was as completely absent as the future itself. But it is different with the air, the performance of which occupies a certain time, during the portions of which only portions of it are played. It consists in an orderliness in the succession of sounds which strike the ear at different times; and to perceive it there must be some continuity of consciousness which makes the events of a lapse of time present to us. We certainly only perceive the air by hearing the separate notes; yet we cannot be said to directly hear it, for we hear only what is present at the instant, and an orderliness of succession cannot exist in an instant. These two sorts of objects, what we are *immediately* conscious of and what we are *mediately* conscious of, are found in all consciousness. Some elements (the sensations) are completely present at every instant so long as they last, while others (like thought) are actions having beginning, middle, and end, and consist in a congruence in the succession of sensations which flow through the mind. They cannot be immediately present to us, but must cover some portion of the past or future. Thought is a thread of melody running through the succession of our sensations.

We may add that just as a piece of music may be written in parts, each part having its own air, so various systems of relationship of succession subsist together between the same sensations. These different systems are distinguished by having different motives, ideas, or functions. Thought is only one such system, for its sole motive, idea, and function, is to produce belief, and whatever does not concern that purpose belongs to some other system of relations. The action of thinking may incidentally have other results; it may serve to amuse us, for example, and among *dillettanti* it is not rare to find those who have so perverted thought to the purposes of pleasure that it seems to vex them to think that the questions upon which they delight to exercise it may ever get finally settled; and a positive discovery which takes a favorite subject out of the arena of literary debate is met with ill-concealed dislike. This disposition is the very debauchery of thought. But the soul and meaning of thought, abstracted from the other elements which accompany it, though it may be voluntarily thwarted, can never be made to direct itself toward anything but the production of belief. Thought in action has for its only possible motive the attainment of thought at rest; and whatever does not refer to belief is no part of the thought itself.

And what, then, is belief? It is the demi-cadence which closes a musical phrase in the symphony of our intellectual life. We have seen that it has just three properties: First, it is something that we are aware of; second, it appeases the irritation of doubt; and, third it involves the establishment in our nature of a rule of action, or, say, for short, a *habit*. As it appeases the irritation of doubt, which is the motive for thinking, thought relaxes, and comes to rest for a moment when belief is reached. But, since belief is a rule for action, the application of which involves further doubt and further thought, at the same time that it is a stopping-place, it is also a new starting-place for thought. That is why I have permitted myself to call it thought at rest, although thought is essentially an action. The *final* upshot of thinking is the exercise of volition, and of this thought no longer forms a part; but belief is only a stadium of mental action, an effect upon our nature due to thought, which will influence future thinking.

The essence of belief is the establishment of a habit, and different beliefs are distinguished by the different modes of action to which they give rise. If beliefs do not differ in this respect, if they appease the same doubt by producing the same rule of action, then no mere differences in the manner of consciousness of them can make them different beliefs, any more than playing a tune in different keys is playing different tunes. Imaginary distinctions are often drawn between beliefs which differ only in their mode of expression;—the wrangling which ensues is real enough, however. To believe that any objects are arranged [22] as in Fig. 1, and to believe that they are

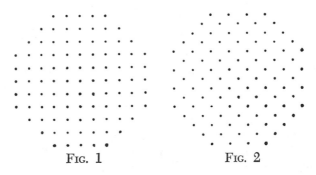

FIG. 1　　　　　　FIG. 2

arranged [as] in Fig. 2, are one and the same belief; yet it is conceivable that a man should assert one proposition and deny the other. Such false distinctions do as much harm as the confusion of beliefs really different, and are among the pitfalls of which we ought constantly to beware, especially when we are upon metaphysical ground. One singular deception of this sort, which often occurs, is to mistake the sensation produced by our own unclearness of thought for a character of the object we are thinking. Instead of perceiving that the obscurity is purely subjective, we fancy that we contemplate a quality of the object which is essentially mysterious; and if our conception be afterward presented to us in a clear form we do not recognize it as the same, owing to the absence of the feeling of unintelligibility. So long as this deception lasts, it obviously puts an impassable barrier in the way of perspicuous thinking; so that it equally interests the opponents of rational thought to perpetuate it, and its adherents to guard against it.

[22] "among themselves" added later.

Another such deception is to mistake a mere difference in the grammatical construction of two words for a distinction between the ideas they express. In this pedantic age, when the general mob of writers attend so much more to words than to things, this error is common enough. When I just said that thought is an *action,* and that it consists in a *relation,* although a person performs an action but not a relation, which can only be the result of an action, yet there was no inconsistency in what I said, but only a grammatical vagueness.

From all these sophisms we shall be perfectly safe so long as we reflect that the whole function of thought is to produce habits of action; and that whatever there is connected with a thought, but irrelevant to its purpose, is an accretion to it, but no part of it. If there be a unity among our sensations which has no reference to how we shall act on a given occasion, as when we listen to a piece of music, why we do not call that thinking. To develop its meaning, we have, therefore, simply to determine what habits it produces, for what a thing means is simply what habits it involves. Now, the identity of a habit depends on how it might lead us to act, not merely under such circumstances as are likely to arise, but under such as might possibly occur, no matter how improbable they may be. What the habit is depends on *when* and *how* it causes us to act. As for the *when,* every stimulus to action is derived from perception; as for the *how,* every purpose of action is to produce some sensible result. Thus, we come down to what is tangible and [23] practical, as the root of every real distinction of thought, no matter how subtile it may be; and there is no distinction of meaning so fine as to consist in anything but a possible difference of practice.

To see what this principle leads to, consider in the light of it such a doctrine as that of transubstantiation. The Protestant churches generally hold that the elements of the sacrament are flesh and blood only in a tropical sense; they nourish our souls as meat and the juice of it would our bodies. But the Catholics maintain that they are literally just that; although they possess all the sensible qualities of wafer-cakes and diluted wine. But we can have no conception of wine except what may enter into a belief, either—

1. That this, that, or the other, is wine; or,
2. That wine possesses certain properties.

Such beliefs are nothing but self-notifications that we should, upon occasion, act in regard to such things as we believe to be wine according to the qualities which we believe wine to possess. The occasion of such action would be some sensible perception, the motive of it to produce some sensible result. Thus our action has exclusive reference

[23] "conceivably" added later.

to what affects the senses, our habit has the same bearing as our action, our belief the same as our habit, our conception the same as our belief; and we can consequently mean nothing by wine but what has certain effects, direct or indirect, upon our senses; and to talk of something as having all the sensible characters of wine, yet being in reality blood, is senseless jargon. Now, it is not my object to pursue the theological question; and having used it as a logical example I drop it, without caring to anticipate the theologian's reply. I only desire to point out how impossible it is that we should have an idea in our minds which relates to anything but conceived sensible effects of things. Our idea of anything *is* our idea of its sensible effects; and if we fancy that we have any other we deceive ourselves, and mistake a mere sensation accompanying the thought for a part of the thought itself. It is absurd to say that thought has any meaning unrelated to its only function. It is foolish for Catholics and Protestants to fancy themselves in dis-agreement about the elements of the sacrament, if they agree in regard to all their sensible effects, here or hereafter.

It appears, then, that the rule for attaining the third grade of clear-ness of apprehension is as follows: Consider what effects, which might conceivably have practical bearings, we conceive the object of our conception to have. Then, our conception of these effects is the whole of our conception of the object.[24]

---

[24] In "Consequences of Pragmaticism," 1906, Peirce wrote: "Note that in these three lines one finds, 'conceivably,' 'conceive,' 'conception,' 'conception,' 'concep-tion.' Now I find there are many people who detect the authorship of my unsigned screeds; and I doubt not that one of the marks of my style by which they do so is my inordinate reluctance to repeat a word. This employment five times over of derivates of *concipere* must then have had a purpose. In point of fact it had two. One was to show that I was speaking of meaning in no other sense than that of *intellectual purport*. The other was to avoid all danger of being understood as attempting to explain a concept by percepts, images, schemata, or by anything but concepts. I did not, therefore, mean to say that acts, which are more strictly singu-lar than anything, could constitute the purport, or adequate proper interpretation, of any symbol. I compared action to the finale of the symphony of thought, belief being a demicadence. Nobody conceives that the few bars at the end of a musical movement are the *purpose* of the movement. They may be called its upshot. But the figure obviously would not bear detailed application. I only mention it to show that the suspicion I myself expressed (Baldwin's *Dictionary* Article, *Pragmatism*) after a too hasty rereading of the forgotten magazine paper, that it expressed a stoic, that is, a nominalistic, materialistic, and utterly philistine state of thought, was quite mistaken.

"No doubt, Pragmaticism makes thought ultimately *apply* to action exclusively—to *conceived* action. But between admitting that and either saying that it makes thought, in the sense of the purport of symbols, to consist in acts, or saying that the true ultimate purpose of thinking is action, there is much the same difference as there is between saying that the artist-painter's living art is applied to dabbing paint upon canvas, and saying that that art-life consists in dabbing paint, or that its ultimate aim is dabbing paint. Pragmaticism makes thinking to consist in the living inferential metaboly of symbols whose purport lies in conditional general resolutions to act...." (5.402 n. 3).

III

Let us illustrate this rule by some examples; and, to begin with the simplest one possible, let us ask what we mean by calling a thing *hard*. Evidently that it will not be scratched by many other substances. The whole conception of this quality, as of every other, lies in its conceived effects. There is absolutely no difference between a hard thing and a soft thing so long as they are not brought to the test. Suppose, then, that a diamond could be crystallized in the midst of a cushion of soft cotton, and should remain there until it was finally burned up. Would it be false to say that that diamond was soft? This seems a foolish question, and would be so, in fact, except in the realm of logic. There such questions are often of the greatest utility as serving to bring logical principles into sharper relief than real discussions ever could. In studying logic we must not put them aside with hasty answers, but must consider them with attentive care, in order to make out the principles involved. We may, in the present case, modify our question, and ask what prevents us from saying that all hard bodies remain perfectly soft until they are touched, when their hardness increases with the pressure until they are scratched. Reflection will show that the reply is this: there would be no *falsity* in such modes of speech. They would involve a modification of our present usage of speech with regard to the words hard and soft, but not of their meanings. For they represent no fact to be different from what it is; only they involve arrangements of facts which would be exceedingly maladroit. This leads us to remark that the question of what would occur under circumstances which do not actually arise is not a question of fact, but only of the most perspicuous arrangement of them. For example, the question of free-will and fate in its simplest form, stripped of verbiage, is something like this: I have done something of which I am ashamed; could I, by an effort of the will, have resisted the temptation, and done otherwise? The philosophical reply is, that this is not a question of fact, but only of the arrangement of facts. Arranging them so as to exhibit what is particularly pertinent to my question—namely, that I ought to blame myself for having done wrong—it is perfectly true to say that, if I had willed to do otherwise than I did, I should have done otherwise. On the other hand, arranging the facts so as to exhibit another important consideration, it is equally true that, when a temptation has once been allowed to work, it will, if it has a certain force, produce its effect, let me struggle how I may. There is no objection to a contradiction in what would result from a false supposition. The *reductio ad absurdum* consists in showing that contradictory results would follow from a hypothesis which is consequently judged to be false. Many questions are involved in the free-will discussion, and I am far from desiring to say that both sides are equally right. On the contrary, I am of opinion that one side denies important facts, and that the other does not. But what I do say is, that the above single question was the origin of the whole doubt; that, had it not been for this question, the controversy would never have arisen; and that this question is perfectly solved in the manner which I have indicated.

Let us next seek a clear idea of Weight. This is another very easy case. To say that a body is heavy means simply that, in the absence of opposing force, it will fall. This (neglecting certain specifications of how it will fall, etc., which exist in the mind of the physicist who uses the word) is evidently the whole conception of weight. It is a fair question whether some particular facts may not *account* for gravity; but what we mean by the force itself is completely involved in its effects.

This leads us to undertake an account of the idea of Force in general. This is the great conception which, developed in the early part of the seventeenth century from the rude idea of a cause, and constantly improved upon since, has shown us how to explain all the changes of motion which bodies experience, and how to think about all physical phenomena; which has given birth to modern science, and changed the face of the globe; and which, aside from its more special uses, has played a principal part in directing the course of modern thought, and in furthering modern social development. It is, therefore, worth some pains to comprehend it. According to our rule, we must begin by asking what is the immediate use of thinking about force; and the answer is, that we thus account for changes of motion. If bodies were left to themselves, without the intervention of forces, every motion would continue unchanged both in velocity and in direction. Furthermore, change of motion never takes place abruptly; if its direction is changed, it is always through a curve without angles; if its velocity alters, it is by degrees. The gradual changes which are constantly taking place are conceived by geometers to be compounded together according to the rules of the parallelogram of forces. If the reader does not already know what this is, he will find it, I hope, to his advantage to endeavor to follow the following explanation; but if mathematics are insupportable to him, pray let him skip three paragraphs rather than that we should part company here.

A *path* is a line whose beginning and end are distinguished. Two paths are considered to be equivalent, which, beginning at the same point, lead to the same point. Thus the two paths, A B C D E and A F G H E (Fig. 3), are equivalent. Paths which do *not* begin at the same point are considered to be equivalent, provided that, on moving either of them without turning it, but keeping it always parallel to its original position, when its beginning coincides with that of the other path, the ends also coincide. Paths are considered as geometrically added together, when one begins where the other ends; thus the path *A E* is conceived to be a sum of *A B*, *B C*, *C D*, and *D E*. In the parallelogram of Fig. 4 the diagonal *A C* is the sum of *A B* and *B C*; or, since *A D* is geometrically equivalent to *B C*, *A C* is the geometrical sum of *A B* and *A D*.

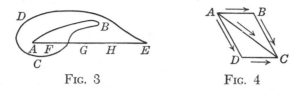

FIG. 3   FIG. 4

All this is purely conventional. It simply amounts to this: that we choose to call paths having the relations I have described equal or added. But, though it is a convention, it is a convention with a good reason. The rule for geometrical addition may be applied not only to paths, but to any other things which can be represented by paths. Now, as a path is determined by the varying direction and distance of the point which moves over it from the starting-point, it follows that anything which from its beginning to its end is determined by a varying direction and a varying magnitude is capable of being represented by a line. Accordingly, *velocities* may be represented by lines, for they have only directions and rates. The same thing is true of *accelerations*, or changes of velocities. This is evident enough in the case of velocities; and it becomes evident for accelerations if we consider that precisely what velocities are to positions—namely, states of change of them—that accelerations are to velocities.

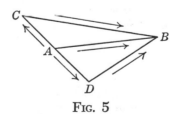

FIG. 5

The so-called "parallelogram of forces" is simply a rule for compounding accelerations. The rule is, to represent the accelerations by paths, and then to geometrically add the paths. The geometers, however, not only use the "parallelogram of forces" to compound different accelerations, but also to resolve one acceleration into a sum of several. Let *A B* (Fig. 5) be the path which represents a certain acceleration—say, such a change in the motion of a body that at the end of one second the body will, under the influence of that change, be in a position different from what it would have had if its motion had continued unchanged, such that a path equivalent to *A B* would lead from the latter position to the former. This acceleration may be considered as the sum of the accelerations represented by *A C* and *C B*. It may also be considered as the sum of the very different accelerations represented by *A D* and *D B*, where *A D* is almost the opposite of *A C*. And it is clear that there is an immense variety of ways in which *A B* might be resolved into the sum of two accelerations.

After this tedious explanation, which I hope, in view of the extraordinary interest of the conception of force, may not have exhausted the reader's patience, we are prepared at last to state the grand fact which this conception embodies. This fact is that if the actual changes of motion which the different particles of bodies experience are each resolved in its appropriate way, each component acceleration is precisely such as is prescribed by a certain law of Nature, according to which bodies in the relative positions which the bodies in question actually have at the moment,* always receive certain accelerations, which, being compounded by geometrical addition, give the acceleration which the body actually experiences.

This is the only fact which the idea of force represents, and whoever will take the trouble clearly to apprehend what this fact is, perfectly comprehends what force is. Whether we ought to say that a force *is* an acceleration, or that it *causes* an acceleration, is a mere question of propriety of language, which has no more to do with our real meaning than the difference between the French idiom *"Il fait froid"* and its English equivalent *"It is cold."* Yet it is surprising to see how this simple affair has muddled men's minds. In how many profound treatises is not force spoken of as a "mysterious entity," which seems to be only a way of confessing that the author despairs of ever getting a clear notion of what the word means! In a recent admired work on "Analytic Mechanics" it is stated that we understand precisely the effect of force, but what force itself is we do not understand! This is simply a self-contradiction. The idea which the word force excites in our minds has no other function than to affect our actions, and these actions can have no reference to force otherwise than through its effects. Consequently, if we know what the effects of force are, we are acquainted with every fact which is implied in saying that a force exists, and there is nothing more to know. The truth is, there is some vague notion afloat that a question may mean something which the mind cannot conceive; and when some hair-splitting philosophers have been confronted with the absurdity of such a view, they have invented an empty distinction between positive and negative conceptions, in the attempt to give

---

* Possibly the velocities also have to be taken into account.

their non-idea a form not obviously nonsensical. The nullity of it is sufficiently plain from the considerations given a few pages back; and, apart from those considerations, the quibbling character of the distinction must have struck every mind accustomed to real thinking.

IV

Let us now approach the subject of logic, and consider a conception which particularly concerns it, that of *reality*. Taking clearness in the sense of familiarity, no idea could be clearer than this. Every child uses it with perfect confidence, never dreaming that he does not understand it. As for clearness in its second grade, however, it would probably puzzle most men, even among those of a reflective turn of mind, to give an abstract definition of the real. Yet such a definition may perhaps be reached by considering the points of difference between reality and its opposite, fiction. A figment is a product of somebody's imagination; it has such characters as his thought impresses upon it. That whose characters are independent of how you or I think is an external reality. There are, however, phenomena within our own minds, dependent upon our thought, which are at the same time real in the sense that we really think them. But though their characters depend on how we think, they do not depend on what we think those characters to be. Thus, a dream has a real existence as a mental phenomenon, if somebody has really dreamt it; that he dreamt so and so, does not depend on what anybody thinks was dreamt, but is completely independent of all opinion on the subject. On the other hand, considering, not the fact of dreaming, but the thing dreamt, it retains its peculiarities by virtue of no other fact than that it was dreamt to possess them. Thus we may define the real as that whose characters are independent of what anybody may think them to be.

But, however satisfactory such a definition may be found, it would be a great mistake to suppose that it makes the idea of reality perfectly clear. Here, then, let us apply our rules. According to them, reality, like every other quality, consists in the peculiar sensible effects which things partaking of it produce. The only effect which real things have is to cause belief, for all the sensations which they excite emerge into consciousness in the form of beliefs. The question therefore is, how is true belief (or belief in the real) distinguished from false belief (or belief in fiction). Now, as we have seen in the former paper, the ideas of truth and falsehood, in their full development, appertain exclusively to the scientific method [25] of settling opinion. A person who arbitrarily chooses the propositions which he will adopt can use the word truth only to emphasize the expression of his determination to hold on to his

[25] "scientific method" later changed to "experiential method."

choice. Of course, the method of tenacity never prevailed exclusively; reason is too natural to men for that. But in the literature of the dark ages we find some fine examples of it. When Scotus Erigena is commenting upon a poetical passage in which hellebore is spoken of as having caused the death of Socrates, he does not hesitate to inform the inquiring reader that Helleborus and Socrates were two eminent Greek philosophers, and that the latter having been overcome in argument by the former took the matter to heart and died of it! What sort of an idea of truth could a man have who could adopt and teach, without the qualification of a perhaps, an opinion taken so entirely at random? The real spirit of Socrates, who I hope would have been delighted to have been "overcome in argument," because he would have learned something by it, is in curious contrast with the naïve idea of the glossist, for whom discussion would seem to have been simply a struggle. When philosophy began to awake from its long slumber, and before theology completely dominated it, the practice seems to have been for each professor to seize upon any philosophical position he found unoccupied and which seemed a strong one, to intrench himself in it, and to sally forth from time to time to give battle to the others. Thus, even the scanty records we possess of those disputes enable us to make out a dozen or more opinions held by different teachers at one time concerning the question of nominalism and realism. Read the opening part of the "Historia Calamitatum" of Abelard, who was certainly as philosophical as any of his contemporaries, and see the spirit of combat which it breathes. For him, the truth is simply his particular stronghold. When the method of authority prevailed, the truth meant little more than the Catholic faith. All the efforts of the scholastic doctors are directed toward harmonizing their faith in Aristotle and their faith in the Church, and one may search their ponderous folios through without finding an argument which goes any further. It is noticeable that where different faiths flourish side by side, renegades are looked upon with contempt even by the party whose belief they adopt; so completely has the idea of loyalty replaced that of truth-seeking. Since the time of Descartes, the defect in the conception of truth has been less apparent. Still, it will sometimes strike a scientific man that the philosophers have been less intent on finding out what the facts are, than on inquiring what belief is most in harmony with their system. It is hard to convince a follower of the *a priori* method by adducing facts; but show him that an opinion he is defending is inconsistent with what he has laid down elsewhere, and he will be very apt to retract it. These minds do not seem to believe that disputation is ever to cease; they seem to think that the opinion which is natural for one man is not so for another, and that belief will, consequently, never be settled. In contenting themselves with fixing their own opinions by a method which would lead another man to a different result, they betray their feeble hold of the conception of what truth is.

On the other hand, all the followers of science are fully persuaded that the processes of investigation, if only pushed far enough, will give one certain solution to every question to which they can be applied. One man may investigate the velocity of light by studying the transits of Venus and the aberration of the stars; another by the oppositions of Mars and the eclipses of Jupiter's satellites; a third by the method of Fizeau; a fourth by that of Foucault; a fifth by the motions of the curves of Lissajous; a sixth, a seventh, an eighth, and a ninth, may follow the different methods of comparing the measures of statical and dynamical electricity. They may at first obtain different results, but, as each perfects his method and his processes, the results will move steadily together toward a destined centre. So with all scientific research. Different minds may set out with the most antagonistic views, but the progress of investigation carries them by a force outside of themselves to one and the same conclusion. This activity of thought by which we are carried, not where we wish, but to a foreordained goal, is like the operation of destiny. No modification of the point of view taken, no selection of other facts for study, no natural bent of mind even, can enable a man to escape the predestinate opinion. This great law is embodied in the conception of truth and reality. The opinion which is fated * to be ultimately agreed to by all who investigate, is what we mean by the truth, and the object represented in this opinion is the real. That is the way I would explain reality.

But it may be said that this view is directly opposed to the abstract definition which we have given of reality, inasmuch as it makes the characters of the real to depend on what is ultimately thought about them. But the answer to this is that, on the one hand, reality is independent, not necessarily of thought in general, but only of what you or I or any finite number of men may think about it; and that, on the other hand, though the object of the final opinion depends on what that opinion is, yet what that opinion is does not depend on what you or I or any man thinks. Our perversity and that of others may indefinitely postpone the settlement of opinion; it might even conceivably cause an arbitrary proposition to be universally accepted as long as the human race should last. Yet even that would not change the nature of the belief, which alone could be the result of investigation carried sufficiently far; and if, after the extinction of our race, another should arise with faculties and disposition for investigation, that true opinion

---

* Fate means merely that which is sure to come true, and can nohow be avoided. It is a superstition to suppose that a certain sort of events are ever fated, and it is another to suppose that the word fate can never be freed from its superstitious taint. We are all fated to die.

must be the one which they would ultimately come to. "Truth crushed to earth shall rise again," and the opinion which would finally result from investigation does not depend on how anybody may actually think. But the reality of that which is real does depend on the real fact that investigation is destined to lead, at last, if continued long enough, to a belief in it.

But I may be asked what I have to say to all the minute facts of history, forgotten never to be recovered, to the lost books of the ancients, to the buried secrets.

> Full many a gem of purest ray serene
> The dark, unfathomed caves of ocean bear;
> Full many a flower is born to blush unseen,
> And waste its sweetness on the desert air.

Do these things not really exist because they are hopelessly beyond the reach of our knowledge? And then, after the universe is dead (according to the prediction of some scientists), and all life has ceased forever, will not the shock of atoms continue though there will be no mind to know it? To this I reply that, though in no possible state of knowledge can any number be great enough to express the relation between the amount of what rests unknown and the amount of the known, yet it is unphilosophical to suppose that, with regard to any given question (which has any clear meaning), investigation would not bring forth a solution of it, if it were carried far enough. Who would have said, a few years ago, that we could ever know of what substances stars are made whose light may have been longer in reaching us than the human race has existed? Who can be sure of what we shall not know in a few hundred years? Who can guess what would be the result of continuing the pursuit of science for ten thousand years, with the activity of the last hundred? And if it were to go on for a million, or a billion, or any number of years you please, how is it possible to say that there is any question which might not ultimately be solved?

But it may be objected, "Why make so much of these remote considerations, especially when it is your principle that only practical distinctions have a meaning?" Well, I must confess that it makes very little difference whether we say that a stone on the bottom of the ocean, in complete darkness, is brilliant or not—that is to say, that it *probably* makes no difference, remembering always that that stone *may* be fished up tomorrow. But that there are gems at the bottom of the sea, flowers in the untraveled desert, etc., are propositions which, like that about a diamond being hard when it is not pressed, concern much more the arrangement of our language than they do the meaning of our ideas.

It seems to me, however, that we have, by the application of our rule, reached so clear an apprehension of what we mean by reality, and of the fact which the idea rests on, that we should not, perhaps, be making a pretension so presumptuous as it would be singular, if we were to offer a metaphysical theory of existence for universal acceptance among those who employ the scientific method of fixing belief. However, as metaphysics is a subject much more curious than useful, the knowledge of which, like that of a sunken reef, serves chiefly to enable us to keep clear of it, I will not trouble the reader with any more Ontology at this moment. I have already been led much further into that path than I should have desired; and I have given the reader such a dose of mathematics, psychology, and all that is most abstruse, that I fear he may already have left me, and that what I am now writing is for the compositor and proof-reader exclusively. I trusted to the importance of the subject. There is no royal road to logic, and really valuable ideas can only be had at the price of close attention. But I know that in the matter of ideas the public prefer the cheap and nasty; and in my next paper [26] I am going to return to the easily intelligible, and not wander from it again. The reader who has been at the pains of wading through this month's paper, shall be rewarded in the next one by seeing how beautifully what has been developed in this tedious way can be applied to the ascertainment of the rules of scientific reasoning.

We have, hitherto, not crossed the threshold of scientific logic. It is certainly important to know how to make our ideas clear, but they may be ever so clear without being true. How to make them so, we have next to study. How to give birth to those vital and procreative ideas which multiply into a thousand forms and diffuse themselves everywhere, advancing civilization and making the dignity of man, is an art not yet reduced to rules, but of the secret of which the history of science affords some hints.

3. The Architecture of Theories [27]

Of the fifty or hundred systems of philosophy that have been advanced at different times of the world's history, perhaps the larger

[26] See footnote 1.

[27] *The Monist* 1 (Jan. 1891) 161-176; reprinted in 6.7-34. This and the following selection are the first two of a series of five articles (originally published in vols. 1, 2, and 3 of *The Monist*) in which Peirce develops his metaphysics of cosmic evolution. The complete list of these papers is as follows:

    (1) "The Architecture of Theories," 6.7-34.
    (2) "The Doctrine of Necessity Examined," 6.35-65.
    (3) "The Law of Mind," 6.102-163.
    (4) "Man's Glassy Essence," 6.238-271.

number have been, not so much results of historical evolution, as happy thoughts which have accidently occurred to their authors. An idea which has been found interesting and fruitful has been adopted, developed, and forced to yield explanations of all sorts of phenomena. The English have been particularly given to this way of philosophising; witness, Hobbes, Hartley, Berkeley, James Mill. Nor has it been by any means useless labor; it shows us what the true nature and value of the ideas developed are, and in that way affords serviceable materials for philosophy. Just as if a man, being seized with the conviction that paper was a good material to make things of, were to go to work to build a *papier mâché* house, with roof of roofing-paper, foundations of pasteboard, windows of paraffined paper, chimneys, bath tubs, locks, etc., all of different forms of paper, his experiment would probably afford valuable lessons to builders, while it would certainly make a detestable house, so those one-idea'd philosophies are exceedingly interesting and instructive, and yet are quite unsound.

The remaining systems of philosophy have been of the nature of reforms, sometimes amounting to radical revolutions, suggested by certain difficulties which have been found to beset systems previously in vogue; and such ought certainly to be in large part the motive of any new theory. This is like partially rebuilding a house. The faults that have been committed are, first, that the dilapidations have generally not been sufficiently thoroughgoing, and second, that not sufficient pains has been taken to bring the additions into deep harmony with the really sound parts of the old structure.

When a man is about to build a house, what a power of thinking he has to do, before he can safely break ground! With what pains he has to excogitate the precise wants that are to be supplied! What a study to ascertain the most available and suitable materials, to determine the mode of construction to which those materials are best adapted, and to answer a hundred such questions! Now without riding the metaphor too far, I think we may safely say that the studies preliminary to the construction of a great theory should be at least as deliberate and thorough as those that are preliminary to the building of a dwelling-house.

That systems ought to be constructed architectonically has been

---

(5) "Evolutionary Love," 6.287-317.

According to Peirce there are three factors involved in the process of cosmic evolution: Chance, Logic, and Love. Consequently, his metaphysics of cosmic evolution involves three doctrines: Tychism, the doctrine that there is objective *chance;* Synechism, the *logical* principle of continuity governing development; and Agapism, the philosophy of evolutionary *love.* The whole theory is outlined in article (1); tychism is developed in (2) in connection with Peirce's criticism of determinism; synechism is discussed chiefly in (3) and (4) and agapism chiefly in (5).

preached since Kant, but I do not think the full import of the maxim has by any means been apprehended. What I would recommend is that every person who wishes to form an opinion concerning fundamental problems, should first of all make a complete survey of human knowledge, should take note of all the valuable ideas in each branch of science, should observe in just what respect each has been successful and where it has failed, in order that in the light of the thorough acquaintance so attained of the available materials for a philosophical theory and of the nature and strength of each, he may proceed to the study of what the problem of philosophy consists in, and of the proper way of solving it. I must not be understood as endeavoring to state fully all that these preparatory studies should embrace; on the contrary, I purposely slur over many points, in order to give emphasis to one special recommendation, namely, to make a systematic study of the conceptions out of which a philosophical theory may be built, in order to ascertain what place each conception may fitly occupy in such a theory, and to what uses it is adapted.

The adequate treatment of this single point would fill a volume, but I shall endeavor to illustrate my meaning by glancing at several sciences and indicating conceptions in them serviceable for philosophy. As to the results to which long studies thus commenced have led me, I shall just give a hint at their nature.

We may begin with dynamics—field in our day of perhaps the grandest conquest human science has ever made—I mean the law of the conservation of energy. But let us revert to the first step taken by modern scientific thought—and a great stride it was—the inauguration of dynamics by Galileo. A modern physicist on examining Galileo's works is surprised to find how little experiment had to do with the establishment of the foundations of mechanics. His principal appeal is to common sense and *il lume naturale*. He always assumes that the true theory will be found to be a simple and natural one. And we can see why it should indeed be so in dynamics. For instance, a body left to its own inertia moves in a straight line, and a straight line appears to us the simplest of curves. In *itself*, no curve is simpler than another. A system of straight lines has intersections precisely corresponding to those of a system of like parabolas similarly placed, or to those of any one of an infinity of systems of curves. But the straight line appears to us simple, because, as Euclid says, it lies evenly between its extremities; that is, because viewed endwise it appears as a point. That is, again, because light moves in straight lines. Now, light moves in straight lines because of the part which the straight line plays in the laws of dynamics. Thus it is that our minds having been formed under the influence of phenomena governed by the laws of mechanics, certain conceptions entering into those laws become implanted in our minds, so that we readily guess at what the laws are. Without such a natural prompting, having to search blindfold for a law which would suit the phenomena, our chance of finding it would be as one to infinity. The further physical studies depart from phenomena which have directly influenced the growth of the mind, the less we can expect to find the laws which govern them "simple," that is, composed of a few conceptions natural to our minds.

The researches of Galileo, followed up by Huygens and others, led to those modern conceptions of *Force* and *Law*, which have revolutionized the intellectual world. The great attention given to mechanics in the seventeenth century soon so emphasized these conceptions as to give rise to the Mechanical Philosophy, or doctrine that all the phenomena of the physical universe are to be explained upon mechanical principles. Newton's great discovery imparted a new impetus to this tendency. The old notion that heat consists in an agitation of corpuscles was now applied to the explanation of the chief properties of gases. The first suggestion in this direction was that the pressure of gases is explained by the battering of the particles against the walls of the containing vessel, which explained Boyle's law of the compressibility of air. Later, the expansion of gases, Avogadro's chemical law, the diffusion and viscosity of gases, and the action of Crookes's radiometer were shown to be consequences of the same kinetical theory; but other phenomena, such as the ratio of the specific heat at constant volume to that at constant pressure, require additional hypotheses, which we have little reason to suppose are simple, so that we find ourselves quite afloat. In like manner with regard to light, that it consists of vibrations was almost proved by the phenomena of diffraction, while those of polarization showed the excursions of the particles to be perpendicular to the line of propagation; but the phenomena of dispersion, etc., require additional hypotheses which may be very complicated. Thus, the further progress of molecular speculation appears quite uncertain. If hypotheses are to be tried haphazard, or simply because they will suit certain phenomena, it will occupy the mathematical physicists of the world say half a century on the average to bring each theory to the test, and since the number of possible theories may go up into the trillions, only one of which can be true, we have little prospect of making further solid additions to the subject in our time. When we come to atoms, the presumption in favor of a simple law seems very slender. There is room for serious doubt whether the fundamental laws of mechanics hold good for single atoms, and it seems quite likely that they are capable of motion in more than three dimensions.

To find out much more about molecules and atoms, we must search out a natural history of laws of nature, which may fulfil that function which the presumption in favor of simple laws fulfilled in the early days of dynamics, by showing us what kind of laws we have to expect and by answering such questions as this: Can we with reasonable prospect of not wasting time, try the supposition that atoms attract one another inversely as the seventh power of their distances, or can we not? To suppose universal laws of nature capable of being apprehended by the mind and yet having no reason for their special forms, but standing inexplicable and irrational, is hardly a justifiable position. Uniformities are precisely the sort of facts that need to be accounted for. That a pitched coin should sometimes turn up heads and sometimes tails calls for no particular explanation; but if it shows heads every time, we wish to know how this result has been brought about. Law is *par excellence* the thing that wants a reason.

Now the only possible way of accounting for the laws of nature and for uniformity in general is to suppose them results of evolution. This supposes them not to be absolute, not to be obeyed precisely. It makes an element of indeterminacy, spontaneity, or absolute chance in nature. Just as, when we attempt to verify any physical law, we find our observations cannot be precisely satisfied by it, and rightly attribute the discrepancy to errors of observation, so we must suppose far more minute discrepancies to exist owing to the imperfect cogency of the law itself, to a certain swerving of the facts from any definite formula.

Mr. Herbert Spencer wishes to explain evolution upon mechanical principles. This is illogical, for four reasons. First, because the principle of evolution requires no extraneous cause; since the tendency to growth can be supposed itself to have grown from an infinitesimal germ accidentally started. Second, because law ought more than anything else to be supposed a result of evolution. Third, because exact law obviously never can produce heterogeneity out of homogeneity; and arbitrary heterogeneity is the feature of the universe the most manifest and characteristic. Fourth, because the law of the conservation of energy is equivalent to the proposition that all operations governed by mechanical laws are reversible; so that an immediate corollary from it is that growth is not explicable by those laws, even if they be not violated in the process of growth. In short, Spencer is not a philosophical evolutionist, but only a half-evolutionist,—or, if you will, only a semi-Spencerian. Now philosophy requires thoroughgoing evolutionism or none.

The theory of Darwin was that evolution had been brought about by the action of two factors: first, heredity, as a principle making offspring nearly resemble their parents, while yet giving room for "sporting," or accidental variations—for very slight variations often, for wider ones rarely; and, second, the destruction of breeds or races that are unable to keep the birth rate up to the death rate. This Darwinian principle is plainly capable of great generalization. Wherever there are large numbers of objects, having a tendency to retain certain characters unaltered, this tendency, however, not being absolute but giving room for chance variations, then, if the amount of variation is absolutely limited in certain directions by the destruction of everything which reaches those limits, there will be a gradual tendency to change in directions of departure from them. Thus, if a million players sit down to bet at an even game, since one after another will get ruined, the average wealth of those who remain will perpetually increase. Here is indubitably a genuine formula of possible evolution, whether its operation accounts for much or little in the development of animal and vegetable species.

The Lamarckian theory also supposes that the development of species has taken place by a long series of insensible changes, but it supposes that those changes have taken place during the lives of the individuals, in consequence of effort and exercise, and that reproduction plays no part in the process except in preserving these modifications. Thus, the Lamarckian theory only explains the development of characters for which individuals strive, while the Darwinian theory only explains the production of characters really beneficial to the race, though these may be fatal to individuals.* But more broadly and philosophically conceived, Darwinian evolution is evolution by the operation of chance, and the destruction of bad results, while Lamarckian evolution is evolution by the effect of habit and effort.

A third theory of evolution is that of Mr. Clarence King. The testimony of monuments and of rocks is that species are unmodified or scarcely modified, under ordinary circumstances, but are rapidly altered after cataclysms or rapid geological changes. Under novel circumstances, we often see animals and plants sporting excessively in reproduction, and sometimes even undergoing transformations during individual life, phenomena no doubt due partly to the enfeeblement of vitality from the breaking up of habitual modes of life, partly to changed food, partly to direct specific influence of the element in which the organism is immersed. If evolution has been brought about in this way, not only have its single steps not been insensible, as both Darwinians and Lamarckians suppose, but they are furthermore neither haphazard on the one hand, nor yet determined by an inward striving on the other, but on the contrary are effects of the changed environment, and have a positive general tendency to adapt the organism to that environment, since variation will particularly affect organs at once enfeebled and stimulated. This mode of evolution, by external forces and the breaking up of habits, seems to be called for by some of the broadest and most important facts of biology and paleontology; while

* The neo-Darwinian, Weismann, has shown that mortality would almost necessarily result from the action of the Darwinian principle.

it certainly has been the chief factor in the historical evolution of institutions as in that of ideas; and cannot possibly be refused a very prominent place in the process of evolution of the universe in general.

Passing to psychology, we find the elementary phenomena of mind fall into three categories. First, we have Feelings, comprising all that is immediately present, such as pain, blue, cheerfulness, the feeling that arises when we contemplate a consistent theory, etc. A feeling is a state of mind having its own living quality, independent of any other state of mind. Or, a feeling is an element of consciousness which might conceivably override every other state until it monopolized the mind, although such a rudimentary state cannot actually be realized, and would not properly be consciousness. Still, it is conceivable, or supposable, that the quality of blue should usurp the whole mind, to the exclusion of the ideas of shape, extension, contrast, commencement and cessation, and all other ideas, whatsoever. A feeling is necessarily perfectly simple, *in itself,* for if it had parts these would also be in the mind, whenever the whole was present, and thus the whole could not monopolize the mind.*

Besides Feelings, we have Sensations of reaction; as when a person blindfold suddenly runs against a post, when we make a muscular effort, or when any feeling gives way to a new feeling. Suppose I had nothing in my mind but a feeling of blue, which were suddenly to give place to a feeling of red; then, at the instant of transition there would be a shock, a sense of reaction, my blue life being transmuted into red life. If I were further endowed with a memory, that sense would continue for some time, and there would also be a peculiar feeling or sentiment connected with it. This last feeling might endure (conceivably I mean) after the memory of the occurrence and the feelings of blue and red had passed away. But the *sensation* of reaction cannot exist except in the actual presence of the two feelings blue and red to which it relates. Wherever we have two feelings and pay attention to a relation between them of whatever kind, there is the sensation of which I am speaking. But the sense of action and reaction has two types; it may either be a perception of relation between two ideas, or it may be a sense of action and reaction between feeling and something out of feeling. And this sense of external reaction again has two forms; for it is either a sense of something happening to us, by no act of ours, we being passive in the matter, or it is a sense of resistance, that is, of our expending feeling upon something without. The sense of reaction is thus a sense of connection or comparison between feelings, either,

---

* A feeling may certainly be compound, but only in virtue of a perception which is not that feeling nor any feeling at all.

A, between one feeling and another, or *B,* between feeling and its absence or lower degree; and under *B* we have, First, the sense of the access of feeling, and Second, the sense of remission of feeling.

Very different both from feelings and from reaction-sensations or disturbances of feeling are general conceptions. When we think, we are conscious that a connection between feelings is determined by a general rule, we are aware of being governed by a habit. Intellectual power is nothing but facility in taking habits and in following them in cases essentially analogous to, but in non-essentials widely remote from, the normal cases of connections of feelings under which those habits were formed.

The one primary and fundamental law of mental action consists in a tendency to generalization. Feeling tends to spread; connections between feelings awaken feelings; neighboring feelings become assimilated; ideas are apt to reproduce themselves. These are so many formulations of the one law of the growth of mind. When a disturbance of feeling takes place, we have a consciousness of gain, the gain of experience; and a new disturbance will be apt to assimilate itself to the one that preceded it. Feelings, by being excited, become more easily excited, especially in the ways in which they have previously been excited. The consciousness of such a habit constitutes a general conception.

The cloudiness of psychological notions may be corrected by connecting them with physiological conceptions. Feeling may be supposed to exist, wherever a nerve-cell is in an excited condition. The disturbance of feeling, or sense of reaction, accompanies the transmission of disturbance between nerve-cells or from a nerve-cell to a muscle-cell or the external stimulation of a nerve-cell. General conceptions arise upon the formation of habits in the nerve-matter, which are molecular changes consequent upon its activity and probably connected with its nutrition.

The law of habit exhibits a striking contrast to all physical laws in the character of its commands. A physical law is absolute. What it requires is an exact relation. Thus, a physical force introduces into a motion a component motion to be combined with the rest by the parallelogram of forces; but the component motion must actually take place exactly as required by the law of force. On the other hand, no exact conformity is required by the mental law. Nay, exact conformity would be in downright conflict with the law; since it would instantly crystallize thought and prevent all further formation of habit. The law of mind only makes a given feeling *more likely* to arise. It thus resembles the "non-conservative" forces of physics, such as viscosity and the like, which are due to statistical uniformities in the chance encounters of trillions of molecules.

The old dualistic notion of mind and matter, so prominent in Carte-sianism, as two radically different kinds of substance, will hardly find defenders today. Rejecting this, we are driven to some form of hylop-athy, otherwise called monism. Then the question arises whether physical laws on the one hand, and the psychical law on the other are to be taken—

(A) as independent, a doctrine often called *monism*, but which I would name *neutralism*; or,

(B) the psychical law as derived and special, the physical law alone as primordial, which is *materialism*; or,

(C) the physical law as derived and special, the psychical law alone as primordial, which is *idealism*.

The materialistic doctrine seems to me quite as repugnant to scien-tific logic as to common sense; since it requires us to suppose that a certain kind of mechanism will feel, which would be a hypothesis absolutely irreducible to reason—an ultimate, inexplicable regularity; while the only possible justification of any theory is that it should make things clear and reasonable.

Neutralism is sufficiently condemned by the logical maxim known as Ockham's razor, i.e., that not more independent elements are to be supposed than necessary. By placing the inward and outward aspects of substance on a par, it seems to render both primordial.

The one intelligible theory of the universe is that of objective ideal-ism, that matter is effete mind, inveterate habits becoming physical laws. But before this can be accepted it must show itself capable of explaining the tridimensionality of space, the laws of motion, and the general characteristics of the universe, with mathematical clearness and precision; for no less should be demanded of every Philosophy.

Modern mathematics is replete with ideas which may be applied to philosophy. I can only notice one or two. The manner in which mathe-maticians generalize is very instructive. Thus, painters are accustomed to think of a picture as consisting geometrically of the intersections of its plane by rays of light from the natural objects to the eye. But geome-ters use a generalized perspective. For instance, in the figure let O be the eye, let A B C D E be the edgewise view of any plane, and let a f e D c be the edgewise view of another plane. The geometers draw rays through O cutting both these planes, and treat the points of inter-section of each ray with one plane as representing the point of inter-section of the same ray with the other plane. Thus, e represents E, in the painter's way. D represents itself. C is represented by c, which is further from the eye; and A is represented by a which is on the other side of the eye. Such generalization is not bound down to sensuous images. Further, according to this mode of representation every point on one plane represents a point on the other, and every point on the

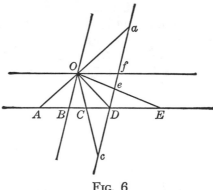

Fig. 6

latter is represented by a point on the former. But how about the point *f* which is in a direction from *O* parallel to the represented plane, and how about the point *B* which is in a direction parallel to the representing plane? Some will say that these are exceptions; but modern mathematics does not allow exceptions which can be annulled by generalization. As a point moves from *C* to *D* and thence to *E* and off toward infinity, the corresponding point on the other plane moves from *c* to *D* and thence to *e* and toward *f*. But this second point can pass through *f* to *a;* and when it is there the first point has arrived at *A.* We therefore say that the first point has passed *through infinity,* and that every line joins into itself somewhat like an oval. Geometers talk of the parts of lines at an infinite distance as points. This is a kind of generalization very efficient in mathematics.

Modern views of measurement have a philosophical aspect. There is an indefinite number of systems of measuring along a line; thus, a perspective representation of a scale on one line may be taken to measure another, although of course such measurements will not agree with what we call the distances of points on the latter line. To establish a system of measurement on a line we must assign a distinct number to each point of it, and for this purpose we shall plainly have to suppose the numbers carried out into an infinite number of places of decimals. These numbers must be ranged along the line in unbroken sequence. Further, in order that such a scale of numbers should be of any use, it must be capable of being shifted into new positions, each number continuing to be attached to a single distinct point. Now it is found that if this is true for "imaginary" as well as for real points (an expression which I cannot stop to elucidate), any such shifting will necessarily leave two numbers attached to the same points as before. So that when the scale is moved over the line by any continuous series of shiftings of one kind, there are two points which no numbers on the scale can ever reach, except the numbers fixed there. This pair of points, thus unattainable in measurement, is called the Absolute. These two points may be distinct and real, or they may coincide, or they may be both imaginary. As an example of a linear quantity with a double absolute we may take probability, which ranges from an unattainable absolute certainty *against* a proposition to an equally unattainable absolute certainty *for* it. A line, according to ordinary notions, we have seen is a linear quantity where the two points at infinity coincide. A velocity is another example. A train going with infinite velocity from Chicago to New York would be at all the points on the line at the very same instant, and if the time of transit were reduced to less than nothing it would be moving in the other direction. An angle is a familiar example of a mode of magnitude with no real immeasurable values. One of the questions philosophy has to consider is whether the development of the universe is like the increase of an angle, so that it proceeds forever without tending toward anything unattained, which I take to be the Epicurean view, or whether the universe sprang from a chaos in the infinitely distant past to tend toward something different in the infinitely distant future, or whether the universe sprang from nothing in the past to go on indefinitely toward a point in the infinitely distant future, which, were it attained, would be the mere nothing from which it set out.

The doctrine of the absolute applied to space comes to this, that either—

First, space is, as Euclid teaches, both *unlimited* and *immeasurable,* so that the infinitely distant parts of any plane seen in perspective appear as a straight line, in which case the sum of the three angles of a triangle amounts to 180°; or,

Second, space is *immeasurable* but *limited,* so that the infinitely distant parts of any plane seen in perspective appear as a circle, beyond which all is blackness, and in this case the sum of the three angles of a triangle is less than 180° by an amount proportional to the area of the triangle; or,

Third, space is *unlimited* but *finite* (like the surface of a sphere), so that it has no infinitely distant parts; but a finite journey along any straight line would bring one back to his original position, and looking off with an unobstructed view one would see the back of his own head enormously magnified, in which case the sum of the three angles of a triangle exceeds 180° by an amount proportional to the area.

Which of these three hypotheses is true we know not. The largest triangles we can measure are such as have the earth's orbit for base, and the distance of a fixed star for altitude. The angular magnitude resulting from subtracting the sum of the two angles at the base of such a triangle from 180° is called the star's *parallax.* The parallaxes of only about forty stars have been measured as yet. Two of them come out

negative, that of Arided (α Cygni), a star of magnitude 1½, which is
— 0."082, according to C. H. F. Peters, and that of a star of magnitude
7¾, known as Piazzi III 422, which is — 0."045 according to R. S. Ball.
But these negative parallaxes are undoubtedly to be attributed to errors
of observation; for the probable error of such a determination is about
± 0."075, and it would be strange indeed if we were to be able to see,
as it were, more than half way round space, without being able to see
stars with larger negative parallaxes. Indeed, the very fact that of all
the parallaxes measured only two come out negative would be a strong
argument that the smallest parallaxes really amount to + 0."1, were
it not for the reflexion that the publication of other negative parallaxes
may have been suppressed. I think we may feel confident that the
parallax of the furthest star lies somewhere between — 0."05 and
+ 0."15, and within another century our grandchildren will surely
know whether the three angles of a triangle are greater or less than
180°,—that they are *exactly* that amount is what nobody ever can be
justified in concluding. It is true that according to the axioms of geometry the sum of the three angles of a triangle is precisely 180°; but these
axioms are now exploded, and geometers confess that they, as geometers, know not the slightest reason for supposing them to be precisely
true. They are expressions of our inborn conception of space, and as
such are entitled to credit, so far as their truth could have influenced
the formation of the mind. But that affords not the slightest reason for
supposing them exact.

Now metaphysics has always been the ape of mathematics. Geometry
suggested the idea of a demonstrative system of absolutely certain
philosophical principles; and the ideas of the metaphysicians have at
all times been in large part drawn from mathematics. The metaphysical
axioms are imitations of the geometrical axioms; and now that the latter
have been thrown overboard, without doubt the former will be sent
after them. It is evident, for instance, that we can have no reason to
think that every phenomenon in all its minutest details is precisely
determined by law. That there is an arbitrary element in the universe
we see—namely, its variety. This variety must be attributed to spontaneity in some form.

Had I more space, I now ought to show how important for philosophy is the mathematical conception of continuity. Most of what is
true in Hegel is a darkling glimmer of a conception which the mathematicians had long before made pretty clear, and which recent researches have still further illustrated.

Among the many principles of Logic which find their application in
Philosophy, I can here only mention one. Three conceptions are perpetually turning up at every point in every theory of logic, and in the
most rounded systems they occur in connection with one another. They

are conceptions so very broad and consequently indefinite that they are hard to seize and may be easily overlooked. I call them the conceptions of First, Second, Third. First is the conception of being or existing independent of anything else. Second is the conception of being relative to, the conception of reaction with, something else. Third is the conception of mediation, whereby a first and second are brought into relation. To illustrate these ideas, I will show how they enter into those we have been considering. The origin of things, considered not as leading to anything, but in itself, contains the idea of First, the end of things that of Second, the process mediating between them that of Third. A philosophy which emphasizes the idea of the One, is generally a dualistic philosophy in which the conception of Second receives exaggerated attention; for this One (though of course involving the idea of First) is always the other of a manifold which is not one. The idea of the Many, because variety is arbitrariness and arbitrariness is repudiation of any Secondness, has for its principal component the conception of First. In psychology Feeling is First, Sense of reaction Second, General conception Third, or mediation. In biology, the idea of arbitrary sporting is First, heredity is Second, the process whereby the accidental characters become fixed is Third. Chance is First, Law is Second, the tendency to take habits is Third. Mind is First, Matter is Second, Evolution is Third.

Such are the materials out of which chiefly a philosophical theory ought to be built, in order to represent the state of knowledge to which the nineteenth century has brought us. Without going into other important questions of philosophical architectonic, we can readily foresee what sort of a metaphysics would appropriately be constructed from those conceptions. Like some of the most ancient and some of the most recent speculations it would be a Cosmogonic Philosophy. It would suppose that in the beginning,—infinitely remote,—there was a chaos of unpersonalised feeling, which being without connection or regularity would properly be without existence. This feeling, sporting here and there in pure arbitrariness, would have started the germ of a generalizing tendency. Its other sportings would be evanescent, but this would have a growing virtue. Thus, the tendency to habit would be started; and from this with the other principles of evolution all the regularities of the universe would be evolved. At any time, however, an element of pure chance survives and will remain until the world becomes an absolutely perfect, rational, and symmetrical system, in which mind is at last crystallized in the infinitely distant future.

That idea has been worked out by me with elaboration. It accounts for the main features of the universe as we know it—the characters of time, space, matter, force, gravitation, electricity, etc. It predicts many more things which new observations can alone bring to the test. May some future student go over this ground again, and have the leisure to give his results to the world.

4. The Doctrine of Necessity Examined [28]

In *The Monist* for January, 1891, I endeavored to show what elementary ideas ought to enter into our view of the universe. I may mention that on those considerations I had already grounded a cosmical theory, and from it had deduced a considerable number of consequences capable of being compared with experience. This comparison is now in progress, but under existing circumstances must occupy many years.

I propose here to examine the common belief that every single fact in the universe is precisely determined by law. It must not be supposed that this is a doctrine accepted everywhere and at all times by all rational men. Its first advocate appears to have been Democritus the atomist, who was led to it, as we are informed, by reflecting upon the "impenetrability, translation, and impact of matter." That is to say, having restricted his attention to a field where no influence other than mechanical constraint could possibly come before his notice, he straightway jumped to the conclusion that throughout the universe that was the sole principle of action—a style of reasoning so usual in our day with men not unreflecting as to be more than excusable in the infancy of thought. But Epicurus, in revising the atomic doctrine and repairing its defences, found himself obliged to suppose that atoms swerve from their courses by spontaneous chance; and thereby he conferred upon the theory life and entelechy. For we now see clearly that the peculiar function of the molecular hypothesis in physics is to open an entry for the calculus of probabilities. Already, the prince of philosophers had repeatedly and emphatically condemned the dictum of Democritus (especially in the "Physics," Book II, chapters iv, v, vi), holding that events come to pass in three ways, namely, (1) by external compulsion, or the action of efficient causes, (2) by virtue of an inward nature, or the influence of final causes, and (3) irregularly without definite cause, but just by absolute chance; and this doctrine is of the inmost essence of Aristotelianism. It affords, at any rate, a valuable enumeration of the possible ways in which anything can be supposed to have come about. The freedom of the will, too, was admitted both by Aristotle and by Epicurus. But the Stoa, which in every department seized upon the most tangible, hard, and lifeless element, and blindly denied the existence of every other, which, for example, impugned the

[28] *The Monist* 2 (April 1892) 321-337; reprinted in 6.35-65.

validity of the inductive method and wished to fill its place with the *reductio ad absurdum,* very naturally became the one school of ancient philosophy to stand by a strict necessitarianism, thus returning to the single principle of Democritus that Epicurus had been unable to swallow. Necessitarianism and materialism with the Stoics went hand in hand, as by affinity they should. At the revival of learning, Stoicism met with considerable favor, partly because it departed just enough from Aristotle to give it the spice of novelty, and partly because its superficialities well adapted it for acceptance by students of literature and art who wanted their philosophy drawn mild. Afterwards, the great discoveries in mechanics inspired the hope that mechanical principles might suffice to explain the universe; and though without logical justification, this hope has since been continually stimulated by subsequent advances in physics. Nevertheless, the doctrine was in too evident conflict with the freedom of the will and with miracles to be generally acceptable, at first. But meantime there arose that most widely spread of philosophical blunders, the notion that associationalism belongs intrinsically to the materialistic family of doctrines; and thus was evolved the theory of motives; and libertarianism became weakened. At present, historical criticism has almost exploded the miracles, great and small; so that the doctrine of necessity has never been in so great vogue as now.

The proposition in question is that the state of things existing at any time, together with certain immutable laws, completely determine the state of things at every other time (for a limitation to *future* time is indefensible). Thus, given the state of the universe in the original nebula, and given the laws of mechanics, a sufficiently powerful mind could deduce from these data the precise form of every curlicue of every letter I am now writing.

Whoever holds that every act of the will as well as every idea of the mind is under the rigid governance of a necessity coördinated with that of the physical world, will logically be carried to the proposition that minds are part of the physical world in such a sense that the laws of mechanics determine everything that happens according to immutable attractions and repulsions. In that case, that instantaneous state of things from which every other state of things is calculable consists in the positions and velocities of all the particles at any instant. This, the usual and most logical form of necessitarianism, is called the mechanical philosophy.

When I have asked thinking men what reason they had to believe that every fact in the universe is precisely determined by law, the first answer has usually been that the proposition is a "presupposition" or postulate of scientific reasoning. Well, if that is the best that can be said for it, the belief is doomed. Suppose it be "postulated": that does not make it true, nor so much as afford the slightest rational motive for yielding it any credence. It is as if a man should come to borrow money, and when asked for his security, should reply he "postulated" the loan. To "postulate" a proposition is no more than to hope it is true. There are, indeed, practical emergencies in which we act upon assumptions of certain propositions as true, because if they are not so, it can make no difference how we act. But all such propositions I take to be hypotheses of individual facts. For it is manifest that no universal principle can in its universality be compromised [29] in a special case or can be requisite for the validity of any ordinary inference. To say, for instance, that the demonstration by Archimedes of the property of the lever would fall to the ground if men were endowed with free-will, is extravagant; yet this is implied by those who make a proposition incompatible with the freedom of the will the postulate of all inference. Considering, too, that the conclusions of science make no pretense to being more than probable, and considering that a probable inference can at most only suppose something to be most frequently, or otherwise approximately, true, but never that anything is precisely true without exception throughout the universe, we see how far this proposition in truth is from being so postulated.

But the whole notion of a postulate being involved in reasoning appertains to a by-gone and false conception of logic. Non-deductive, or ampliative inference is of three kinds: induction, hypothesis, and analogy. If there be any other modes, they must be extremely unusual and highly complicated, and may be assumed with little doubt to be of the same nature as those enumerated. For induction, hypothesis, and analogy, as far as their ampliative character goes, that is, so far as they conclude something not implied in the premises, depend upon one principle and involve the same procedure. All are essentially inferences from sampling. Suppose a ship arrives in Liverpool laden with wheat in bulk. Suppose that by some machinery the whole cargo be stirred up with great thoroughness. Suppose that twenty-seven thimblefuls be taken equally from the forward, midships, and aft parts, from the starboard, center, and larboard parts, and from the top, half depth, and lower parts of her hold, and that these being mixed and the grains counted, four fifths of the latter are found to be of quality A. Then we infer, experientially and provisionally, that approximately four fifths of all the grain in the cargo is of the same quality. I say we infer this *experientially* and *provisionally*. By saying that we infer it *experientially*, I mean that our conclusion makes no pretension to knowledge of wheat-in-itself, our *alētheia*, as the derivation of that word implies, has nothing to do with *latent* wheat. We are dealing only with the

---

[29] Should this be "comprised"? See 6.39.

matter of possible experience—experience in the full acceptation of the term as something not merely affecting the senses but also as the subject of thought. If there be any wheat hidden on the ship, so that it can neither turn up in the sample nor be heard of subsequently from purchasers—or if it be half-hidden, so that it may, indeed, turn up, but is less likely to do so than the rest—or if it can affect our senses and our pockets, but from some strange cause or causelessness cannot be reasoned about—all such wheat is to be excluded (or have only its proportional weight) in calculating that true proportion of quality A, to which our inference seeks to approximate. By saying that we draw the inference *provisionally*, I mean that we do not hold that we have reached any assigned degree of approximation as yet, but only hold that if our experience be indefinitely extended, and if every fact of whatever nature, as fast as it presents itself, be duly applied, according to the inductive method, in correcting the inferred ratio, then our approximation will become indefinitely close in the long run; that is to say, close to the experience *to come* (not merely close by the exhaustion of a finite collection) so that if experience in general is to fluctuate irregularly to and fro, in a manner to deprive the ratio sought of all definite value, we shall be able to find out approximately within what limits it fluctuates, and if, after having one definite value, it changes and assumes another, we shall be able to find that out, and in short, whatever may be the variations of this ratio in experience, experience indefinitely extended will enable us to detect them, so as to predict rightly, at last, what its ultimate value may be, if it have any ultimate value, or what the ultimate law of succession of values may be, if there be any such ultimate law, or that it ultimately fluctuates irregularly within certain limits, if it do so ultimately fluctuate. Now our inference, claiming to be no more than thus experiential and provisional, manifestly involves no postulate whatever.

For what is a postulate? It is the formulation of a material fact which we are not entitled to assume as a premise, but the truth of which is requisite to the validity of an inference. Any fact, then, which might be supposed postulated, must either be such that it would ultimately present itself in experience, or not. If it will present itself, we need not postulate it now in our provisional inference, since we shall ultimately be entitled to use it as a premise. But if it never would present itself in experience, our conclusion is valid but for the possibility of this fact being otherwise than assumed, that is, it is valid as far as possible experience goes, and that is all that we claim. Thus, every postulate is cut off, either by the provisionality or by the experientiality of our inference. For instance, it has been said that induction postulates that, if an indefinite succession of samples be drawn, examined, and thrown back each before the next is drawn, then in the long run every grain will be drawn as often as any other, that is to say postulates that the ratio of the numbers of times in which any two are drawn will indefinitely approximate to unity. But no such postulate is made; for if, on the one hand, we are to have no other experience of the wheat than from such drawings, it is the ratio that presents itself in those drawings and not the ratio which belongs to the wheat in its latent existence that we are endeavoring to determine; while if, on the other hand, there is some other mode by which the wheat is to come under our knowledge, equivalent to another kind of sampling, so that after all our care in stirring up the wheat, some experiential grains will present themselves in the first sampling operation more often than others in the long run, this very singular fact will be sure to get discovered by the inductive method, which must avail itself of every sort of experience; and our inference, which was only provisional, corrects 'tself at last. Again, it has been said, that induction postulates that under like circumstances like events will happen, and that this postulate is at bottom the same as the principle of universal causation. But this is a blunder, or *bévue,* due to thinking exclusively of inductions where the concluded ratio is either 1 or 0. If any such proposition were postulated, it would be that under like circumstances (the circumstances of drawing the different samples) different events occur in the same proportions in all the different sets—a proposition which is false and even absurd. But in truth no such thing is postulated, the experiential character of the inference reducing the condition of validity to this, that if a certain result does not occur, the opposite result will be manifested, a condition assured by the provisionality of the inference. But it may be asked whether it is not conceivable that every instance of a certain class destined to be ever employed as a datum of induction should have one character, while every instance destined not to be so employed should have the opposite character. The answer is that in that case, the instances excluded from being subjects of reasoning would not be experienced in the full sense of the word, but would be among these *latent* individuals of which our conclusion does not pretend to speak.

To this account of the rationale of induction I know of but one objection worth mention: it is that I thus fail to deduce the full degree of force which this mode of inference in fact possesses; that according to my view, no matter how thorough and elaborate the stirring and mixing process had been, the examination of a single handful of grain would not give me any assurance, sufficient to risk money upon, that the next handful would not greatly modify the concluded value of the ratio under inquiry, while, in fact, the assurance would be very high that this ratio was not greatly in error. If the true ratio of grains of quality A were 0.80 and the handful contained a thousand grains, nine such handfuls out of every ten would contain from 780 to 820 grains of quality A. The answer to this is that the calculation given is correct when we know that the units of this handful and the quality inquired into have the normal independence of one another, if for instance the stirring has been complete and the character sampled for has been settled upon in advance of the examination of the sample. But in so far as these conditions are not known to be complied with, the above figures cease to be applicable. Random sampling and predesignation of the character sampled for should always be striven after in inductive reasoning, but when they cannot be attained, so long as it is conducted honestly, the inference retains some value. When we cannot ascertain how the sampling has been done or the sample-character selected, induction still has the essential validity which my present account of it shows it to have.

I do not think a man who combines a willingness to be convinced with a power of appreciating an argument upon a difficult subject can resist the reasons which have been given to show that the principle of universal necessity cannot be defended as being a postulate of reasoning. But then the question immediately arises whether it is not proved to be true, or at least rendered highly probable, by observation of nature.

Still, this question ought not long to arrest a person accustomed to reflect upon the force of scientific reasoning. For the essence of the necessitarian position is that certain continuous quantities have certain exact values. Now, how can observation determine the value of such a quantity with a probable error absolutely *nil?* To one who is behind the scenes, and knows that the most refined comparisons of masses, lengths, and angles, far surpassing in precision all other measurements, yet fall behind the accuracy of bank-accounts, and that the ordinary determinations of physical constants, such as appear from month to month in the journals, are about on a par with an upholsterer's measurements of carpets and curtains, the idea of mathematical exactitude being demonstrated in the laboratory will appear simply ridiculous. There is a recognized method of estimating the probable magnitudes of errors in physics—the method of least squares. It is universally admitted that this method makes the errors smaller than they really are; yet even according to that theory an error indefinitely small is indefinitely improbable; so that any statement to the effect that a certain continuous quantity has a certain exact value, if well-founded at all, must be founded on something other than observation.

Still, I am obliged to admit that this rule is subject to a certain qualification. Namely, it only applies to continuous * quantity. Now, certain

* *Continuous* is not exactly the right word, but I let it go to avoid a long and irrelevant discussion.

kinds of continuous quantity are discontinuous at one or at two limits, and for such limits the rule must be modified. Thus, the length of a line cannot be less than zero. Suppose, then, the question arises how long a line a certain person had drawn from a marked point on a piece of paper. If no line at all can be seen, the observed length is zero; and the only conclusion this observation warrants is that the length of the line is less than the smallest length visible with the optical power employed. But indirect observations—for example, that the person supposed to have drawn the line was never within fifty feet of the paper —may make it probable that no line at all was made, so that the concluded length will be strictly zero. In like manner, experience no doubt would warrant the conclusion that there is absolutely *no* indigo in a given ear of wheat, and absolutely *no* attar in a given lichen. But such inferences can only be rendered valid by positive experiential evidence, direct or remote, and cannot rest upon a mere inability to detect the quantity in question. We have reason to think there is no indigo in the wheat, because we have remarked that wherever indigo is produced it is produced in considerable quantities, to mention only one argument. We have reason to think there is no attar in the lichen, because essential oils seem to be in general peculiar to single species. If the question had been whether there was iron in the wheat or the lichen, though chemical analysis should fail to detect its presence, we should think some of it probably was there, since iron is almost everywhere. Without any such information, one way or the other, we could only abstain from any opinion as to the presence of the substance in question. It cannot, I conceive, be maintained that we are in any *better* position than this in regard to the presence of the element of chance or spontaneous departures from law in nature.

Those observations which are generally adduced in favor of mechanical causation simply prove that there is an element of regularity in nature, and have no bearing whatever upon the question of whether such regularity is exact and universal, or not. Nay, in regard to this *exactitude*, all observation is directly *opposed* to it; and the most that can be said is that a good deal of this observation can be explained away. Try to verify any law of nature, and you will find that the more precise your observations, the more certain they will be to show irregular departures from the law. We are accustomed to ascribe these, and I do not say wrongly, to errors of observation; yet we cannot usually account for such errors in any antecedently probable way. Trace their causes back far enough, and you will be forced to admit they are always due to arbitrary determination, or chance.

But it may be asked whether if there were an element of real chance in the universe it must not occasionally be productive of signal effects such as could not pass unobserved. In answer to this question, without stopping to point out that there is an abundance of great events which one might be tempted to suppose were of that nature, it will be simplest to remark that physicists hold that the particles of gases are moving about irregularly, substantially as if by real chance, and that by the principles of probabilities there must occasionally happen to be concentrations of heat in the gases contrary to the second law of thermodynamics, and these concentrations, occurring in explosive mixtures, must sometimes have tremendous effects. Here, then, is in substance the very situation supposed; yet no phenomena ever have resulted which we are forced to attribute to such chance concentration of heat, or which anybody, wise or foolish, has ever dreamed of accounting for in that manner.

In view of all these considerations, I do not believe that anybody, not in a state of casehardened ignorance respecting the logic of science, can maintain that the precise and universal conformity of facts to law is clearly proved, or even rendered particularly probable, by any observations hitherto made. In this way, the determined advocate of exact regularity will soon find himself driven to *a priori* reasons to support his thesis. These received such a socdolager from Stuart Mill in his examination of Hamilton, that holding to them now seems to me to denote a high degree of imperviousness to reason; so that I shall pass them by with little notice.

To say that we cannot help believing a given proposition is no argument, but it is a conclusive fact if it be true; and with the substitution of "I" for "we," it is true in the mouths of several classes of minds, the blindly passionate, the unreflecting and ignorant, and the person who has overwhelming evidence before his eyes. But that which has been inconceivable today has often turned out indisputable on the morrow. Inability to conceive is only a stage through which every man must pass in regard to a number of beliefs—unless endowed with extraordinary obstinacy and obtuseness. His understanding is enslaved to some blind compulsion which a vigorous mind is pretty sure soon to cast off.

Some seek to back up the *a priori* position with empirical arguments. They say that the exact regularity of the world is a natural belief, and that natural beliefs have generally been confirmed by experience. There is some reason in this. Natural beliefs, however, if they generally have a foundation of truth, also require correction and purification from natural illusions. The principles of mechanics are undoubtedly natural beliefs; but, for all that, the early formulations of them were exceedingly erroneous. The general approximation to truth in natural beliefs is, in fact, a case of the general adaptation of genetic products to recognizable utilities or ends. Now, the adaptations of nature, beautiful and often marvellous as they verily are, are never found to be quite perfect;

so that the argument is quite *against* the absolute exactitude of any natural belief, including that of the principle of causation.

Another argument, or convenient commonplace, is that absolute chance is *inconceivable*. This word has eight current significations. The Century Dictionary enumerates six. Those who talk like this will hardly be persuaded to say in what sense they mean that chance is inconceivable. Should they do so, it would easily be shown either that they have no sufficient reason for the statement or that the inconceivability is of a kind which does not prove that chance is non-existent.

Another *a priori* argument is that chance is unintelligible; that is to say, while it may perhaps be conceivable, it does not disclose to the eye of reason the how or why of things; and since a hypothesis can only be justified so far as it renders some phenomenon intelligible, we never can have any right to suppose absolute chance to enter into the production of anything in nature. This argument may be considered in connection with two others. Namely, instead of going so far as to say that the supposition of chance can *never* properly be used to explain any observed fact, it may be alleged merely that no facts are known which such a supposition could in any way help in explaining. Or again, the allegation being still further weakened, it may be said that since departures from law are not unmistakably observed, chance is not a *vera causa*,[30] and ought not unnecessarily to be introduced into a hypothesis.

These are no mean arguments, and require us to examine the matter a little more closely. Come, my superior opponent, let me learn from your wisdom. It seems to me that every throw of sixes with a pair of dice is a manifest instance of chance.

"While you would hold a throw of deuce-ace to be brought about by necessity?" [The opponent's supposed remarks are placed in quotation marks.]

Clearly one throw is as much chance as another.

"Do you think throws of dice are of a different nature from other events?"

I see that I must say that *all* the diversity and specificalness of events is attributable to chance.

"Would you, then, deny that there is any regularity in the world?"

That is clearly undeniable. I must acknowledge there is an approximate regularity, and that every event is influenced by it. But the diversification, specificalness, and irregularity of things I suppose is chance. A throw of sixes appears to me a case in which this element is particularly obtrusive.

[30] Peirce gives a definition of this term in 6.242: "By a *vera causa*, in the logic of science, is meant a state of things known to exist in some cases and supposed to exist in other cases, because it would account for observed phenomena."

"If you reflect more deeply, you will come to see that *chance* is only a name for a cause that is unknown to us."

Do you mean that we have no idea whatever what kind of causes could bring about a throw of sixes?

"On the contrary, each die moves under the influence of precise mechanical laws."

But it appears to me that it is not these *laws* which made the die turn up sixes; for these laws act just the same when other throws come up. The chance lies in the diversity of throws; and this diversity cannot be due to laws which are immutable.

"The diversity is due to the diverse circumstances under which the laws act. The dice lie differently in the box, and the motion given to the box is different. These are the unknown causes which produce the throws, and to which we give the name of chance; not the mechanical law which regulates the operation of these causes. You see you are already beginning to think more clearly about this subject."

Does the operation of mechanical law not increase the diversity?

"Properly not. You must know that the instantaneous state of a system of particles is defined by six times as many numbers as there are particles, three for the coördinates of each particle's position, and three more for the components of its velocity. This number of numbers, which expresses the amount of diversity in the system, remains the same at all times. There may be, to be sure, some kind of relation between the coördinates and component velocities of the different particles, by means of which the state of the system might be expressed by a smaller number of numbers. But, if this is the case, a precisely corresponding relationship must exist between the coördinates and component velocities at any other time, though it may doubtless be a relation less obvious to us. Thus, the intrinsic complexity of the system is the same at all times."

Very well, my obliging opponent, we have now reached an issue. You think all the arbitrary specifications of the universe were introduced in one dose, in the beginning, if there was a beginning, and that the variety and complication of nature has always been just as much as it is now. But I, for my part, think that the diversification, the specification, has been continually taking place. Should you condescend to ask me why I so think, I should give my reason as follows:

1) Question any science which deals with the course of time. Consider the life of an individual animal or plant, or of a mind. Glance at the history of states, of institutions, of language, of ideas. Examine the successions of forms shown by paleontology, the history of the globe as set forth in geology, or what the astronomer is able to make out concerning the changes of stellar systems. Everywhere the main fact is growth and increasing complexity. Death and corruption are mere

accidents or secondary phenomena. Among some of the lower organisms, it is a moot point with biologists whether there be anything which ought to be called death. Races, at any rate, do not die out except under unfavorable circumstances. From these broad and ubiquitous facts we may fairly infer, by the most unexceptionable logic, that there is probably in nature some agency by which the complexity and diversity of things can be increased; and that consequently the rule of mechanical necessity meets in some way with interference.

2) By thus admitting pure spontaneity or life as a character of the universe, acting always and everywhere though restrained within narrow bounds by law, producing infinitesimal departures from law continually, and great ones with infinite infrequency, I account for all the variety and diversity of the universe, in the only sense in which the really *sui generis* and new can be said to be accounted for. The ordinary view has to admit the inexhaustible multitudinous variety of the world, has to admit that its mechanical law cannot account for this in the least, that variety can spring only from spontaneity, and yet denies without any evidence or reason the existence of this spontaneity, or else shoves it back to the beginning of time and supposes it dead ever since. The superior logic of my view appears to me not easily controverted.

3) When I ask the necessitarian how he would explain the diversity and irregularity of the universe, he replies to me out of the treasury of his wisdom that irregularity is something which from the nature of things we must not seek to explain. Abashed at this, I seek to cover my confusion by asking how he would explain the uniformity and regularity of the universe, whereupon he tells me that the laws of nature are immutable and ultimate facts, and no account is to be given of them. But my hypothesis of spontaneity does explain irregularity, in a certain sense; that is, it explains the general fact of irregularity, though not, of course, what each lawless event is to be. At the same time, by thus loosening the bond of necessity, it gives room for the influence of another kind of causation, such as seems to be operative in the mind in the formation of associations, and enables us to understand how the uniformity of nature could have been brought about. That single events should be hard and unintelligible, logic will permit without difficulty: we do not expect to make the shock of a personally experienced earthquake appear natural and reasonable by any amount of cogitation. But logic does expect things *general* to be understandable. To say that there is a universal law, and that it is a hard, ultimate, unintelligible fact, the why and wherefore of which can never be inquired into, at this a sound logic will revolt; and will pass over at once to a method of philosophising which does not thus barricade the road of discovery.

4) Necessitarianism cannot logically stop short of making the whole action of the mind a part of the physical universe. Our notion that we

decide what we are going to do, if as the necessitarian says, it has been calculable since the earliest times, is reduced to illusion. Indeed, consciousness in general thus becomes a mere illusory aspect of a material system. What we call red, green, and violet are in reality only different rates of vibration. The sole reality is the distribution of qualities of matter in space and time. Brain-matter is protoplasm in a certain degree and kind of complication—a certain arrangement of mechanical particles. Its feeling is but an inward aspect, a phantom. For, from the positions and velocities of the particles at any one instant, and the knowledge of the immutable forces, the positions at all other times are calculable; so that the universe of space, time, and matter is a rounded system uninterfered with from elsewhere. But from the state of feeling at any instant, there is no reason to suppose the states of feeling at all other instants are thus exactly calculable; so that feeling is, as I said, a mere fragmentary and illusive aspect of the universe. This is the way, then, that necessitarianism has to make up its accounts. It enters consciousness under the head of sundries, as a forgotten trifle; its scheme of the universe would be more satisfactory if this little fact could be dropped out of sight. On the other hand, by supposing the rigid exactitude of causation to yield, I care not how little—be it but by a strictly infinitesimal amount—we gain room to insert mind into our scheme, and to put it into the place where it is needed, into the position which, as the sole self-intelligible thing, it is entitled to occupy, that of the fountain of existence; and in so doing we resolve the problem of the connection of soul and body.

5) But I must leave undeveloped the chief of my reasons, and can only adumbrate it. The hypothesis of chance-spontaneity is one whose inevitable consequences are capable of being traced out with mathematical precision into considerable detail. Much of this I have done and find the consequences to agree with observed facts to an extent which seems to me remarkable. But the matter and methods of reasoning are novel, and I have no right to promise that other mathematicians shall find my deductions as satisfactory as I myself do, so that the strongest reason for my belief must for the present remain a private reason of my own, and cannot influence others. I mention it to explain my own position; and partly to indicate to future mathematical speculators a veritable goldmine, should time and circumstances and the abridger of all joys prevent my opening it to the world.

If now I, in my turn, inquire of the necessitarian why he prefers to suppose that all specification goes back to the beginning of things, he will answer me with one of those last three arguments which I left unanswered.

First, he may say that chance is a thing absolutely unintelligible, and therefore that we never can be entitled to make such a supposition.

But does not this objection smack of naïve impudence? It is not mine, it is his own conception of the universe which leads abruptly up to hard, ultimate, inexplicable, immutable law, on the one hand, and to inexplicable specification and diversification of circumstances on the other. My view, on the contrary, hypothetises nothing at all, unless it be hypothesis to say that all specification came about in some sense, and is not to be accepted as unaccountable. To undertake to account for anything by saying baldly that it is due to chance would, indeed, be futile. But this I do not do. I make use of chance chiefly to make room for a principle of generalization, or tendency to form habits, which I hold has produced all regularities. The mechanical philosopher leaves the whole specification of the world utterly unaccounted for, which is pretty nearly as bad as to baldly attribute it to chance. I attribute it altogether to chance, it is true, but to chance in the form of a spontaneity which is to some degree regular. It seems to me clear at any rate that one of these two positions must be taken, or else specification must be supposed due to a spontaneity which develops itself in a certain and not in a chance way, by an objective logic like that of Hegel. This last way I leave as an open possibility, for the present; for it is as much opposed to the necessitarian scheme of existence as my own theory is.

Secondly the necessitarian may say there are, at any rate, no observed phenomena which the hypothesis of chance could aid in explaining. In reply, I point first to the phenomenon of growth and developing complexity, which appears to be universal, and which though it may possibly be an affair of mechanism perhaps, certainly presents all the appearance of increasing diversification. Then, there is variety itself, beyond comparison the most obtrusive character of the universe: no mechanism can account for this. Then, there is the very fact the necessitarian most insists upon, the regularity of the universe which for him serves only to block the road of inquiry. Then, there are the regular relationships between the laws of nature—similarities and comparative characters, which appeal to our intelligence as its cousins, and call upon us for a reason. Finally, there is consciousness, feeling, a patent fact enough, but a very inconvenient one to the mechanical philosopher.

Thirdly, the necessitarian may say that chance is not a *vera causa*, that we cannot know positively there is any such element in the universe. But the doctrine of the *vera causa* has nothing to do with elementary conceptions. Pushed to that extreme, it at once cuts off belief in the existence of a material universe; and without that necessitarianism could hardly maintain its ground. Besides, variety is a fact which must be admitted; and the theory of chance merely consists in supposing this diversification does not antedate all time. Moreover, the avoidance of hypotheses involving causes nowhere positively known to act

—is only a recommendation of logic, not a positive command. It cannot be formulated in any precise terms without at once betraying its untenable character—I mean as rigid rule, for as a recommendation it is wholesome enough.

I believe I have thus subjected to fair examination all the important reasons for adhering to the theory of universal necessity, and have shown their nullity. I earnestly beg that whoever may detect any flaw in my reasoning will point it out to me, either privately or publicly; for if I am wrong, it much concerns me to be set right speedily. If my argument remains unrefuted, it will be time, I think, to doubt the absolute truth of the principle of universal law: and when once such a doubt has obtained a living root in any man's mind, my cause with him, I am persuaded, is gained.[31]

[31] Paul Carus, editor of *The Monist,* took up this challenge. See his articles: "Mr. Charles S. Peirce's Onslaught on the Doctrine of Necessity," *The Monist* 2 (1892) 560-582; "The Idea of Necessity, Its Basis and Its Scope," *The Monist* 3 (1892) 68-96. See also *The Monist* 1 (1891) 241-244 and 2 (1892) 442. Peirce's reply to Carus is given in "Reply to the Necessitarians," *The Monist* 3 (1893) 526-570; reprinted in 6.588-618. Carus concludes this debate in "The Founder of Tychism, His Methods, Philosophy, and Criticism," *The Monist* 3 (1893) 571-622.

A Note on Peirce's Pragmatism and Metaphysical Evolutionism

I wrote my introduction to these Peirce articles 45 years ago, when logical positivism was a prominent philosophical school. Peirce was correctly seen as having anticipated the positivist's verifiability theory of meaning in the first two essays printed here. But the positivists declared metaphysics to be meaingless, whereas Peirce was highly metaphysical, as is evident in the last two essays printed here. Indeed, his pragmatism was an application of his earlier metaphysical doctrine that humanity is an infinite community of sign users, and truth is what will "be ultimately agreed to by all who investigate" (p. 85, above).

Peirce announced his cosmic evolutionism in "The Architecture of Theories":

. . . in the beginning,—infinitely remote,—there was a chaos of unpersonalised feeling. . . . This feeling, sporting here and there in pure arbitrariness, would have started the germ of a generalizing tendency . . . and from this . . . all the regularities of the universe would be evolved. At any time, however, an element of pure chance survives and will remain until the world becomes an absolutely perfect, rational, and symmetrical system, in which mind is at last crystallized in the infinitely distant future [p. 99, above].

Thus Peirce's pragmatism was only one step in his philosophical development of a grand theory of evolution, in which human sign using and scientific inquiry are stages of an evolutionary process that will continue into the infinite future under the guidance of "would be's" (cf. pp. 50–51, above) and final causes toward an absolutely perfect and rational form.

For a systematic account of Peirce's cosmic evolutionism, see my "Peirce's Evolutional Pragmatic Idealism," to be published in the journal *Synthèse* in 1996 or soon thereafter. I have devoted much of my research to understanding Peirce's writings, and those writings have greatly influenced by own philosophy. I expound my views on pragmatism, causality, and probability along with his in *Cause, Chance, Reason* (Chicago: The University of Chicago Press, 1977). My own philosophy of logical mechanism is fundamentally different from Peirce's idealism, but nevertheless owes much to him. Merrilee H. Salmon edited a work on my philosophy: *The Philosophy of Logical Mechanism: Essays in Honor of Arthur W. Burks* (Boston: Kluwer Academic, 1990); my responses are in Part II.

ARTHUR W. BURKS

II

WILLIAM JAMES

≥ଔଵ

Introduction

MORE THAN ANYONE ELSE, William James stands in the eyes of the world as the representative American philosopher. His life (1842-1910) marks the period in which American academic thought ceased to follow European philosophy and displayed a marked originality. James himself contributed greatly to this development. His philosophy was distinctively American in its formulation and phraseology. Although some European developments approximated it, the idea of pragmatism also was hailed as native American. His frequent travels in Europe, his command of languages, and his great personal charm, all contributed to the spread of his ideas. These factors, together with the intrinsic importance of what he had to say, have resulted in the translation of his works into all major languages. James is probably the one American philosopher who has been read the world over.

James achieved an international reputation in psychology before turning his full attention to philosophy. Many of his philosophical views are foreshadowed or even developed in his psychological work, and all of them are influenced by the intellectual climate produced by the spread of the theory of evolution. A complete account of James's philosophy would take full cognizance of these and other influences. Since, however, they have been discussed in the general introduction, and since space is limited, it is necessary here to confine attention to his strictly philosophical work.

Central in James's entire philosophy is the theory of meaning, the analysis of the conditions under which statements are significant. In the broadest outlines of his theory, James agreed with Peirce and freely acknowledged his indebtedness (see p. 129). With Peirce, he held that the way to understand an idea is to envisage its possible consequences in experience. Thus, to say "My pipe has gone out" is implicitly to predict, among other things, that if I draw on it, I will experience no taste; if I stick my finger into the bowl, I will not be burned; and so with innumerable other consequences. These are all ways in which my experience will be different if the pipe has gone out.

So far, there is nothing new or startling in the theory. From any point of view, an investigation of the consequences of an idea may contribute to its understanding. What was both new and startling in Peirce's theory, however, and again James agreed, was that the entire meaning of any statement could be given by these consequences in experience. Given that, if I draw on the pipe, I will taste nothing, that I may stick my finger in the bowl without burning it, and the vast number of other similar experiential consequences which might be drawn, then one has the entire meaning of saying that my pipe has gone out. The analysis in the case of my pipe is simple, but James would hold that any conception could be reduced in this way to a set of differences in experience—actual or possible experience. This is the pragmatic theory of meaning.

Such a theory has the effect of reducing disputes to concrete terms and getting away from purely verbal arguments. Consider the pair of statements, "This table is exactly one yard long" and "This table is not quite a yard long, but it is so close that no measuring instrument can detect the difference." At first sight, the statements would appear to be incompatible and to contradict each other. Applying the pragmatic criterion of meaning, however, what each statement comes to is that the table measures a yard regardless of the instrument employed. Thus the experiential consequences are the same in the two cases and the meanings are seen to be identical. Instead of a conflict, we have alternative verbal formulations of the same idea.

It may happen again that a statement which appears meaningful actually lacks meaning. Suppose I were to tell you that there is an imp sitting in the corner of the room, an imp about three feet tall with a long pointed tail. Suppose I were to add that our imp is perfectly transparent, that he keeps out of the reach of people, that he dodges when things are thrown at him, that he is altogether silent, and is so thoroughly washed as to have no detectable odor. In what way would you be the wiser for this information? From James's point of view, the answer is clear. In no way would experience be different if there were such an imp or if there were not. Hence there is no choice between the alternatives and no meaning to the entire description.

Still, the description seems intelligible. The reason is that at one time it was perfectly meaningful to say that there was an imp about. It meant that one was likely, quite inexplicably, to have his ears tweaked; that if one turned suddenly, he might catch a glimpse of a shadowy figure disappearing; and that if one sniffed carefully, he might detect the faintest aroma of brimstone. In our description, however, all these meanings have been cancelled out and what remains comes simply to nothing.

So far, in consideration of what ideas are meaningful, we have considered only the direct consequences of the statement itself. Under some conditions, James is willing to go further than this and broaden his theory of meaning. An illustration may make the position clear. Take such an issue as the existence of God. James is convinced that the traditional attempts to demonstrate His existence are a complete failure. On the other hand there is no disproof of the existence of God. There seems to be no possible appeal to experience, no way in which our experience would be different, in the foreseeable future at least, if God exists or does not. By the criteria we have been sketching, therefore, the issue is meaningless. Still, a belief in God makes a difference in people's lives; they feel different and may even act differently. Hence there is a difference in people's experience caused by a belief in God, and this difference, James believes, is enough to give the issue meaning.

Thus, James construes broadly the difference which a statement must make in possible experience to be meaningful. It may be that there are consequences of the statement subject to scientific test; or it may be that there are no such consequences, but that belief in the statement makes a difference. In any case, however, the general principle holds; wherever there is meaning there is a difference in some possible experience.

James's first and most striking application of this doctrine is to the problem of truth. The tradition in Western philosophy has accorded truth an awe and reverence approaching that given to deity itself. Science has professed a devotion to truth and to truth alone. James raises the question why. As the ancient sceptics pointed out, true and false statements may look quite similar and there may be as much evidence for one as for the other. If truth is stranger than fiction, fiction is often more interesting. Why then this devotion to truth? James's answer is to give a pragmatic analysis of the meaning of the term "true." If a statement is true, what difference does this make in any experience, actual or possible? So far as James can see, the difference comes to this: If one acts on a true statement, he will not be disappointed in his expectations; if he acts on a false one, he is likely to be disappointed.

Thus, truth is a good guide to conduct, falsity is not. Here, then, is the difference between truth and falsity in experience and, since experience determines meanings, this is the meaning of the term "truth."

James's view can be put in other terms. In science, an hypothesis is accepted or rejected because of its ability or inability to explain certain data and give rise to successful predictions. So long as a theory enables one to anticipate the outcome of experiments it is accepted and held to be a "good" theory. James's view is equivalent to holding that all our beliefs are to be treated as if they were scientific theories; to be accepted as good or true to the extent, and only to the extent, that they enable us to anticipate the course of events. Thus, even so simple a statement as "My pipe has gone out" is to be regarded not as a picture of the nature of things, but rather as an explanation of my present sensations as I suck and as a suggestion that it is safe to put my finger in the bowl. To the extent that future experience bears this out, it is a good theory and, by James's analysis, a true statement.

James formulates his view in other terms as well. The true is what is better to believe. The true is what agrees with reality, meaning by "reality" subsequent experience. The true is what "works." All of these statements are loose, probably intentionally so, and are liable to misinterpretation. James's critics took full advantage of this possibility of misrepresentation. Suppose, for example, I am invited to dinner by an utter bore and invent a previous engagement even though I have no plans for the evening in question. The man is satisfied, arranges dinner without me, and I am spared a tedious evening. In a sense, this works and, in a sense, if I dislike the man sufficiently, this is a good guide for conduct. Thus pragmatists were accused of saying what they pleased and calling it the truth.

But this is not the sense of working or being a good guide to conduct that James intended, and he was careful to make the point entirely explicit. Before one can say that a theory works, one must recall what work it is supposed to do. We have seen that the function of beliefs is to anticipate experience and, in the case of a deliberate lie such as we have been considering, there is no accurate clue to what is coming. Someone might, for example, try to locate me on the assumption that I had a previous engagement and call all my friends' houses. The last place one would look would be my home where, in all probability, I should be. Thus though the excuse would work in one sense, this is not the sense that James requires for a statement to qualify as true.

In order to work and be a good guide to conduct, then, a belief must not be arbitrary but must take account of the realities with which it deals. There are other limitations as well. A belief which came in conflict with most of our other beliefs would lead only to confusion. We would anticipate one sort of future on the basis of our previous beliefs and another on the basis of the new one. Hence James requires that, to be counted as true, a belief be consistent with previous opinions, at least so far as is possible. It is true of course, especially in the case of new scientific theories, that consistency with all that was previously believed is usually impossible and something must be sacrificed. Even here, however, the sacrifice of old beliefs must be kept at a minimum and the entire system of truths brought into consistency, with the least abandonment of the old.

In spite of these strict requirements on what may be considered true, there are cases in which one has the right and even is forced simply to decide what he will believe. These are cases in which there are neither immediate evidences from experience nor conclusive implications of other truths. Consider, as James does in one essay, the question, is life worth living? Conclusive evidence in the form of a demonstration one way or the other is lacking. One may decide that it is not worth living and the pessimism induced thereby will probably result in a life that indeed is not worth living. Or one may decide that the evidence is inconclusive and be left by one's doubts in a state hardly more worth enduring. Or, finally, one may adopt a faith that life is worth living and through that determination make it so. In this case belief freely adopted creates its own truth. The attitude, once taken and adhered to, creates its own verification in subsequent experience. This possibility of arriving at a truth by other than intellectual means, was a cardinal point of James's philosophy and the theory of it is developed in "The Will to Believe." It is important to notice, however, that James allows this method of settling problems only as a last resort, only when there is no possibility of obtaining evidence by any ordinary method. Even then, there are further restrictions.

It is a corollary of James's theory of truth that truth is a matter of degree. A belief may work, or be a good guide to conduct, not absolutely, but to a limited extent. James is ready to say that the belief is true to that extent but no further. It follows, also, and this aspect of his theory outraged his contemporaries most, that truth may change. At the very least, truth grows as new theories are developed and confirmed.

We have seen that in one formulation James considered the truth as what was better to believe, thus making truth one species of good and raising the question as to what constitutes good and what general ethical principles can be established. James answers the question in an essay, "The Moral Philosopher and the Moral Life," most of which is reprinted in the accompanying selections. This essay has been the basis of a number of developments in ethics and in attempts to work out a general theory embracing ethics and esthetics.

James begins the essay with the same sort of treatment which characterized his discussion as to whether or not life is worth living, by a bold assertion, made in the hope that it will be self-justifying, that there is an ethical truth. He definitely rejects a complete relativism or, as he calls it, an "ethical skepticism." The problem then becomes not "Is there an ethical norm?" but rather "What is it?"

But although James insists that an ethical standard is possible, he is not willing to set up his own beliefs or preferences as absolute standards. To do this would be to renounce the attempt to attain objectivity and simply add one more to the many systems of ethics. Rather the philosopher must compare the various standards of values which have been advocated in the attempt to discover something universal in all of them. James argues that one common element in all moral situations is the presence of some conscious being or agent and he appeals to the reader to agree that, if there were no conscious beings, there could be no good or bad. To be good is to be good in the eyes of some one, and a universe devoid of life would be simply amoral. Continuing this line of reasoning, it is an easy step to conclude that what is common to all things which are good is that they satisfy some sort of demand or appeal to some one. This being the case, James is ready to say that to be good is to satisfy demand. This gives a standard which is at once universal, giving a basis for an ethical theory, and at the same time avoids the peculiar preferences of any one philosopher.

The equation of good with satisfaction of demand requires some explanation. If an act satisfies the demands of one person and not of others, how is it to be evaluated? James claims that no demand, as such, is preferable to any other and that, in case of conflict, the action which satisfies the most demands should prevail. Similarly in cases where an individual is torn by a conflict of his own demands, the better line of conduct is what satisfies the most, or more persistent, or strongest demands. To be good, then, is to satisfy demand; the ideal would be to satisfy all demands, but, since this is impossible in practice, that is better which satisfies more demands.

This is a general account of the procedure of solving ethical problems, but it does not give the answer to any specific problem. James is content to leave the matter in this state, maintaining that, for the solution of specific problems, specific factual knowledge is necessary. To decide what line of action will produce the most satisfaction, requires a knowledge of the consequences of that action, as well as of the way in which people will react to it. Thus the question goes out of the domain in which the philosopher has peculiar competence and into that where practice and experience hold sway.

James's ethical position was formulated long before he wrote his lectures on pragmatism. As a result the language is somewhat different, but the underlying thought is the same. When James enquires into the characteristics of moral situations and concludes that there could be no good in a world where there are no sentient beings, what he is doing is to raise, in pragmatic terms, the question of the meaning of the term "good." The difference which is made by something being good, in experiential terms, is simply that a demand is satisfied; or, to be more accurate, that more demands are satisfied than frustrated. Since this is the concrete difference made by something being good, this is the meaning of the term. What James has done, then, in his ethical analysis is to apply the pragmatic theory, both in his act of faith in declaring that there is an answer to the problems and in his development of just how the answer is to be obtained.

Turning to other aspects of his philosophy, we find James calling his theory of mind and matter *radical empiricism*. The theory was never worked out fully and is represented only by a series of articles which were published in book form posthumously. The excerpts from "Does 'Consciousness' Exist?" represent this phase of James's work. In his thought, unquestionably, radical empiricism is an outgrowth of the pragmatic method, but the view can be arrived at in other ways and it has influenced the American neo-realists and even such arch-enemies of pragmatism as Bertrand Russell.

In essence, the doctrine of radical empiricism consists in two points, the first of which differentiates it from the older British empiricism. Locke, Berkeley, and Hume had tried to analyze knowledge in terms of simple sensations and then to reconstitute it out of these components. In this discussion the relations between simple sensations were largely imposed on them and, in later times, this became the central point of attack upon the empiricists by their idealist critics. James admitted the point of the criticism but reaffirmed the empirical position by contending that relations are given in the same sense as the terms they relate. The relation of one thing being on another, for example, is given in the same way as the sensations of the things one of which is on the other. Thus James holds that relations are not a mental addition to the given elements of experience, but rather a part and parcel of the given, presented in the same manner as other aspects. The result is an empiricism more adequate than that developed by James's predecessors.

The other basic point of radical empiricism is that the same element of experience may function in different contexts. In particular, it may function both as an element of consciousness and as a part of physical reality. When I look at my pipe, for example, my percept, what I see, may at once be part of my consciousness and part of the physical pipe. There is no need to speak of a mental image duplicating the physical reality; what is given may be at once mental and physical, mental if considered as part of my pattern of thought, physical if considered along with the other aspects which constitute the pipe. The pipe itself may be regarded simply as the sum-total of its actual and possible appearances. This view of matter is closely related to Berkeley's and differs only in allowing possible appearances an existence outside of mind. Mind and matter, then, instead of being different kinds of stuff, become different organizations of the same material. The difference between them is one of entering into different relationships, not of being different substances.

If we take the two main theses of radical empiricism together, it is clear that the way is paved for a monistic view of the world which does not require mind as something over and beyond experience necessary to supply the relationships which link the various parts of experience. The relations are there as aspects of the experience. Neither is mind reduced in the manner of the materialists to something inert and completely non-mental. Rather the entire world is thought of as constituted of entities mental, in that they enter into the constitution of minds, and physical, in that a different organization of them gives physical objects. "Pure experience" is the name James gives to this neutral stuff.

A reader of the essay "Does 'Consciousness' Exist?", which sets forth the essentials of this view, cannot fail to see in it an application of James's theory of meaning. The main purpose of the essay is to deny the existence of consciousness in the sense of a Cartesian mind, or independently existing substance. The argument throughout insists on raising the question of the difference which consciousness makes and, in proper pragmatic fashion, taking this to be the meaning of consciousness.

James's views of radical empiricism are further developed in *A Pluralistic Universe* to sketch an entire cosmology. Just as James holds in the *Essays in Radical Empiricism* that the same percept may be an aspect of both physical and mental entities, so here he maintains that the same percept may be an element of more than one consciousness. It is possible that any of my thoughts may be a part, not merely of my consciousness, but also of some higher and more inclusive consciousness. The thought might appear differently in the two consciousnesses, but still might be a constituent of both. Fechner had suggested this idea of a compounding of consciousness and James was enthusiastic in adopting it. Thus there would appear to be the possibility of a world-soul embracing in one inclusive consciousness the thoughts of all human beings. These thoughts might be differently organized, to be sure, but the same content might appear in a human mind and in this more inclusive consciousness. Here is the idea of a god who is not completely distinct from the world, as in much of traditional theology, nor is he the mere sum total of existence, as in some pantheisms, but rather there is a suggestion of how a god might have something in common with the world and still retain his own unique consciousness.

This compounding of consciousness need not, moreover, be confined to a single stage. There is no reason why there should not be a plurality of such more inclusive consciousnesses, some completely distinct, some included in others. James calls up the picture of an ever-expanding series of world-consciousnesses. He is unwilling, however, to say that there is one all-embracing consciousness which is the consciousness of the universe and which might be called an Absolute in Royce's sense.

The reason for this refusal lies in James's taking seriously the traditional problem of evil. If there is a single mind of the universe whose thoughts are the totality of existence, then he is responsible for everything that goes on in the universe. And much that goes on is evil. Even though the good in the world may outweigh the evil, the evil is there and it is not to be explained away as a hidden form of good. Either God is responsible for it or he is powerless to prevent it. James prefers the latter alternative and so holds that a single consciousness, however vast its reaches, never includes everything. God, like us, is concerned with the issue between good and evil, striving, without assurance of success, to bring about a better state of affairs. It is impossible to rest complacently in the belief that everything in the world will turn out for the best. The issue may hang in balance and, for this reason, human efforts acquire an importance that they might not have on another view.

This position involves the assumption, of course, that human beings are free to make the choice between what is better and what is worse. The insistence that the human will is free is one of the oldest strains of thought in James's philosophy. Man can choose, can decide, in spite of all hereditary and environmental influences, which course he will pursue. Since the whole outcome of the universe is undecided, human decisions take on a cosmic importance. James counts on this situation to induce a "strenuous mood" in men, an attitude not merely of favoring what they consider better, but of striving whole-heartedly to attain it.

The picture of the universe sketched here is fanciful in the extreme. A cautious reader will demand at once what proof James has for all these assertions. In the conventional sense, James has none and thinks none is necessary. There is nothing in the picture here given which contradicts any known facts. It might be true. It is an attractive view. It were well if it were true. There is no reason, therefore, why it should not be held to be true. And so, James proclaims, it is true. In short, James's cosmology rests on the will to believe.

There remains only to consider James's philosophy of religion. It is characteristic of James that he places no credence in, and even disregards, the traditional proofs of the existence of God. Rather he seeks evidence for the value of religion from the phenomena of religious life itself. Prayer, religious conversion, and mystical experiences had always interested him and they are thoroughly investigated in *The Varieties of Religious Experience*. After a detailed consideration of their psychological aspects, James attempts to assess their philosophic significance. Prayer and mystical experiences, he finds, cause changes in personality. A religious person may find himself weak, tired and uncertain and, after prayer, stronger, refreshed and assured. For such persons, prayer is thus a source of energy, and James seeks to trace the origin of this energy. James's own work in psychology as well as that of his contemporaries had assured him of the existence of an unconscious mind, a mind broader than our consciousness at any moment, but similar to it in character. Matters which we are not attending to as well as desires which do not come to the level of consciousness were included in its scope, although the theory was not worked out with anything like the elaboration that Freud was to give it later. With such a notion of an unconscious mind, James can say with assurance that the energy acquired in religious experience comes from the unconscious mind. So far this is a purely naturalistic explanation which would class religious experience among the phenomena of abnormal psychology.

James is convinced that religious experience is an abnormal phenomenon. But is it merely that? Granted that the energy in question comes to consciousness from the unconscious mind, did it originate there? Or perhaps does it come from some greater mind separate from our own which operates through our unconscious mind? James does not know of any evidence which would enable us to decide between these alternatives. He considers it therefore a case for free choice of belief. Without trying to compel the reader, he himself chooses the view that prayer and other forms of religious experience do involve actual communication with a power greater than our own minds. Here again we have the doctrine of the will to believe.[1]

This in outline, then, represents James's point of view in philosophy. If by a system of philosophy is meant fitting everything in the universe into its proper logically demarcated compartment, James has no system of philosophy. In this sense he hated system and his own picture of the world leaves it full of loose ends and uncompleted processes. This he considered the only true description of the world as we find it.

If, on the other hand, one means by a system of philosophy the answering of a wide variety of problems in terms of a few basic principles, then James is systematic. We have seen that his theory of truth,

---

[1] In this and other uses of the will to believe, the question naturally arises whether there is one belief which is better for everyone to hold and so is true for everyone, or whether different beliefs may be better for different people and so there would be a plurality of divergent truths. James himself is not clear on the matter. In every case, he argues that one belief is more satisfactory for everyone than the others. If, however, some perverse person found the opposite view more satisfactory, there would seem to be no reason why it should not constitute the truth for him. Thus, if some one had been brought up to lead a strenuous, God-fearing life which he loathed, the discovery that the existence of God was a proper place for the exercise of the will to believe might lead him to embrace atheism. James might not like the result but, if it satisfied the man's most persistent demands, he would have to admit that it was true for the man.

In cases where the will to believe is not involved, this situation does not arise and, as is clear from the foregoing discussion, one belief must be at least "truer" than the others.

his views on ethics, his radical empiricism, his cosmology and his philosophy of religion, are all based on his theory of meaning. They form a coherent and integrated description of the universe. This is the more remarkable because these works were written over a span of more than thirty-five years and the order of composition is not at all the order into which I have thrown them for the sake of systematic exposition. His work, taken as a whole, is much more unified than the writings of many philosophers who made greater pretences of systematic philosophy.

If this description of James's philosophy is at all correct, any attempt to assess and evaluate it must be concerned primarily with the theory of meaning which is the core of the whole point of view. In this connection, it will be useful to employ a distinction which James draws in the first chapter of *Pragmatism* between those philosophers whom he calls "tough-minded" and those who are "tender-minded." James describes the tough-minded as being empiricists, pluralists, and irreligious; the tender-minded have the opposite characteristics. James suggests pragmatism as a view to appeal to both types of philosopher. In this contention I think James is right; but he achieves his result only by employing two theories of meaning, the one to appeal to the tough-minded and the other to the tender-minded philosophers. The two theories cover different ground, and so are complementary rather than contradictory; but I believe they are distinct and represent different points of view.

To take first what may be called the tough-minded theory, we have seen that the basic tenet of pragmatism is that the meaning of any statement consists in its consequences for possible experience. Where there are no such consequences, there is no meaning. A rigid adherence to this theory would yield a view more closely related to Dewey's instrumentalism and in many respects similar to contemporary positivism. It would rule out many metaphysical issues, including such questions as the existence of God.

But James finds this theory of meaning too narrow. A belief in God makes a difference in the life of the believer and so must be accounted meaningful. But notice that in this case it is not the statement itself which has consequences for experience, but rather the believing of the statement. One deduces consequences, not from the statement, but from the fact that someone believes it. Thus it is not the existence of God which makes a difference in what one will experience, but rather it is the belief which colors one's attitude toward life and so makes a difference. Thus the will to believe may be differentiated from the other aspects of James's pragmatism in that it considers not properly the consequences of a statement, but the consequences of believing the statement.

There is a further point, however, in this connection. Suppose that a belief in God, as James suggests, affects a person's emotional outlook and mode of conduct, and consider the meaning of the statement "God exists" from the point of view of the person holding the belief. If it is to be believed, the statement must itself have meaning. This meaning cannot be the consequences of holding the belief, since, for the believer, these consequences are the result of holding the belief, not the meaning of the statement itself. Thus if a person is to feel relief because he is sure God exists, the relief is not the meaning of saying that God exists, but rather the result of the belief. Neither can the statement have meaning in the tough-minded sense previously discussed, since admittedly there is no experimental test for the existence of God. Thus there must be another, unexplained sense of meaning in which James is ready to allow that the statement "God exists" is meaningful. This might be called the tender-minded view of meaning, a view which would allow meaning to any statement whatsoever, provided only that believing it makes a difference in the attitude or conduct of the believer.

To summarize James's theory of meaning: A statement is meaningful if either (a) it has experiential consequences, or (b) it has no such consequences, but belief in it has experiential consequences. In case (a) the experiential consequences constitute the meaning. This is the tough-minded view. In case (b) there is no explanation of what constitutes the meaning and we are left with the bare criterion of meaningfulness. This is the tender-minded view.[2]

James uses the two standards of meaning in a complementary fashion, being willing to make use of any statement which is meaningful by either criterion. Even though Professor A. O. Lovejoy pointed out the difference in standards in unmistakable terms, James was not impressed and continued to use the two without distinction.

It is easy to trace the two views of meaning through the remainder of James's philosophy. The doctrine of the will to believe is clearly dependent on the tender-minded view. So are his cosmology and his philosophy of religion which depend on the will to believe. The radical empiricism, on the other hand, is an outgrowth of the tough-minded view, insisting as it does on taking reality as just what it shows itself to be. The ethics shows a combination of the two views employing the will to believe and the tender-minded theory in the insistence that there is an ethical truth and the tough-minded view in the determina-

---

[2] It is tempting to say that in case (b) the consequences of the belief constitute the meaning. It would be possible to read parts of Chapter III of *Pragmatism* in support of this interpretation. But section V of "The Moral Philosopher and the Moral Life" (omitted from our selections), as well as the discussions of philosophy of religion, rule it out, for reasons indicated above.

tion of what that truth is. This dualism of theory of meaning, then, runs through James's entire philosophy, some of his doctrines having the one source, some the other. This is not to claim that there is any gap or inconsistency in the entire philosophy. It is merely that different parts of it rest on different theories of meaning. The parts, however, in James's thought fit together as neatly as the white and yolk of an egg.

Perhaps it is merely the temper of the age which followed him, or perhaps a difference in the intrinsic worth of the two aspects of his philosophy, but at any rate, that side of James's philosophy which I have called tough-minded has been much more influential than the other. In general, James's cosmology has been neglected, his philosophy of religion has lost much of its influence, and the theory of the will-to-believe has few, if any, followers. The pragmatic theory of meaning is, however, very much alive and, indeed, holds almost exclusive sway in contemporary discussions of semantics. Similarly, the radical empiricism, as well as aspects of the ethics and theory of truth, while not always discussed in James's terminology, are in the forefront of present-day discussion. This side of James's philosophy has as much vitality today as on the day it was written.

PAUL HENLE

UNIVERSITY OF MICHIGAN

Supplementary Note

For the exchange between Lovejoy and James referred to in the second sentence of the third paragraph on page 126, see *The Thought and Character of William James*, by R. B. Perry (1935), II, 480-481. "Consequences of true ideas *per se*, and consequences of ideas *qua believed by us*, are logically different consequences," James conceded, "and the whole 'will to believe' business has got to be re-edited with explicit uses made of the distinction."

1. What Pragmatism Means [1]

SOME YEARS AGO, being with a camping party in the mountains, I returned from a solitary ramble to find every one engaged in a ferocious metaphysical dispute. The *corpus* of the dispute was a squirrel—a live squirrel supposed to be clinging to one side of a tree-trunk; while over against the tree's opposite side a human being was imagined to stand. This human witness tries to get sight of the squirrel by moving rapidly round the tree, but no matter how fast he goes, the squirrel moves as fast in the opposite direction, and always keeps the tree between himself and the man, so that never a glimpse of him is caught. The resultant metaphysical problem now is this: *Does the man go round the squirrel or not?* He goes round the tree, sure enough, and the squirrel is on the tree; but does he go round the squirrel? In the unlimited leisure of the wilderness, discussion had been worn threadbare. Every one had taken sides, and was obstinate; and the numbers on both sides were even. Each side, when I appeared therefore appealed to me to make it a majority. Mindful of the scholastic adage that whenever you meet a contradiction you must make a distinction, I immediately sought and found one, as follows: "Which party is right," I said, "depends on what you *practically mean* by 'going round' the squirrel. If you mean passing from the north of him to the east, then to the south, then to the west, and then to the north of him again, obviously the man does go round him, for he occupies these successive positions. But if on the contrary you mean being first in front of him, then on the right of him, then behind him, then on his left, and finally in front again, it is quite as obvious that the man fails to go round him, for by the compensating movements the squirrel makes, he keeps his belly turned towards the man all the time, and his back turned away. Make the distinction, and there is no occasion for any farther dispute. You are both right and both wrong according as you conceive the verb 'to go round' in one practical fashion or the other."

Although one or two of the hotter disputants called my speech a shuffling evasion, saying they wanted no quibbling or scholastic hair-splitting, but meant just plain honest English 'round,' the majority seemed to think that the distinction had assuaged the dispute.

I tell this trivial anecdote because it is a peculiarly simple example of what I wish now to speak of as *the pragmatic method*. The pragmatic

[1] Pages 43-65 from chapter II of *Pragmatism* (copyright 1907 by William James and 1934 by Henry James), reprinted by permission of Paul R. Reynolds. In this and the following selections, the present editor's notes are indicated by numerals, and James's original notes by asterisks. In subsequent selections, some of James's notes are omitted.

method is primarily a method of settling metaphysical disputes that otherwise might be interminable. Is the world one or many?—fated or free?—material or spiritual?—here are notions either of which may or may not hold good of the world; and disputes over such notions are unending. The pragmatic method in such cases is to try to interpret each notion by tracing its respective practical consequences. What difference would it practically make to any one if this notion rather than that notion were true? If no practical difference whatever can be traced, then the alternatives mean practically the same thing, and all dispute is idle. Whenever a dispute is serious, we ought to be able to show some practical difference that must follow from one side or the other's being right.

A glance at the history of the idea will show you still better what pragmatism means. The term is derived from the same Greek word *pragma*, meaning action, from which our words 'practice' and 'practical' come. It was first introduced into philosophy by Mr. Charles Peirce in 1878. In an article entitled 'How to Make Our Ideas Clear,' in the *Popular Science Monthly* for January of that year, Mr. Peirce, after pointing out that our beliefs are really rules for action, said that, to develop a thought's meaning, we need only determine what conduct it is fitted to produce: that conduct is for us its sole significance. And the tangible fact at the root of all our thought-distinctions, however subtle, is that there is no one of them so fine as to consist in anything but a possible difference of practice. To attain perfect clearness in our thoughts of an object, then, we need only consider what conceivable effects of a practical kind the object may involve—what sensations we are to expect from it, and what reactions we must prepare. Our conception of these effects, whether immediate or remote, is then for us the whole of our conception of the object, so far as that conception has positive significance at all.

This is the principle of Peirce, the principle of pragmatism. It lay entirely unnoticed by any one for twenty years, until I, in an address before Professor Howison's philosophical union at the University of California, brought it forward again and made a special application of it to religion. By that date (1898) the times seemed ripe for its reception. The word 'pragmatism' spread, and at present it fairly spots the pages of the philosophic journals. On all hands we find the 'pragmatic movement' spoken of, sometimes with respect, sometimes with contumely, seldom with clear understanding. It is evident that the term applies itself conveniently to a number of tendencies that hitherto have lacked a collective name, and that it has 'come to stay.'

To take in the importance of Peirce's principle, one must get accustomed to applying it to concrete cases. I found a few years ago that Ostwald, the illustrious Leipzig chemist, had been making perfectly distinct use of the principle of pragmatism in his lectures on the philosophy of science, though he had not called it by that name.

"All realities influence our practice," he wrote me, "and that influence is their meaning for us. I am accustomed to put questions to my classes in this way: In what respects would the world be different if this alternative or that were true? If I can find nothing that would become different, then the alternative has no sense."

That is, the rival views mean practically the same thing, and meaning, other than practical, there is for us none. Ostwald in a published lecture gives this example of what he means. Chemists have long wrangled over the inner constitution of certain bodies called 'tautomerous.' Their properties seemed equally consistent with the notion that an instable hydrogen atom oscillates inside of them, or that they are instable mixtures of two bodies. Controversy raged, but never was decided. "It would never have begun," says Ostwald, "if the combatants had asked themselves what particular experimental fact could have been made different by one or the other view being correct. For it would then have appeared that no difference of fact could possibly ensue; and the quarrel was as unreal as if, theorizing in primitive times about the raising of dough by yeast, one party should have invoked a 'brownie,' while another insisted on an 'elf' as the true cause of the phenomenon." *

It is astonishing to see how many philosophical disputes collapse into insignificance the moment you subject them to this simple test of tracing a concrete consequence. There can *be* no difference anywhere that doesn't *make* a difference elsewhere—no difference in abstract truth that doesn't express itself in a difference in concrete fact and in conduct consequent upon that fact, imposed on somebody, somehow, somewhere, and somewhen. The whole function of philosophy ought to be to find out what definite difference it will make to you and me, at definite instants of our life, if this world-formula or that world-formula be the true one.

There is absolutely nothing new in the pragmatic method. Socrates was an adept at it. Aristotle used it methodically. Locke, Berkeley, and Hume made momentous contributions to truth by its means. Shadworth Hodgson keeps insisting that realities are only what they are 'known as.' But these forerunners of pragmatism used it in fragments: they were preluders only. Not until in our time has it generalized itself,

---

* 'Theorie und Praxis,' *Zeitsch. des Oesterreichischen Ingenieur u. Architecten-Vereines,* 1905, Nr. 4 u. 6. I find a still more radical pragmatism than Ostwald's in an address by Professor W. S. Franklin: "I think that the sickliest notion of physics, even if a student gets it, is that it is 'the science of masses, molecules, and the ether.' And I think that the healthiest notion, even if a student does not wholly get it, is that physics is the science of the ways of taking hold of bodies and pushing them!" (*Science,* January 2, 1903.)

become conscious of a universal mission, pretended to a conquering destiny. I believe in that destiny, and I hope I may end by inspiring you with my belief.

Pragmatism represents a perfectly familiar attitude in philosophy, the empiricist attitude, but it represents it, as it seems to me, both in a more radical and in a less objectionable form than it has ever yet assumed. A pragmatist turns his back resolutely and once for all upon a lot of inveterate habits dear to professional philosophers. He turns away from abstraction and insufficiency, from verbal solutions, from bad *a priori* reasons, from fixed principles, closed systems, and pretended absolutes and origins. He turns towards concreteness and adequacy, towards facts, towards action and towards power. That means the empiricist temper regnant and the rationalist temper sincerely given up. It means the open air and possibilities of nature, as against dogma, artificiality, and the pretense of finality in truth.

At the same time it does not stand for any special results. It is a method only. But the general triumph of that method would mean an enormous change in what I called in my last lecture the 'temperament' of philosophy. Teachers of the ultra-rationalistic type would be frozen out, much as the courtier type is frozen out in republics, as the ultramontane type of priest is frozen out in protestant lands. Science and metaphysics would come much nearer together, would in fact work absolutely hand in hand.

Metaphysics has usually followed a very primitive kind of quest. You know how men have always hankered after unlawful magic, and you know what a great part in magic *words* have always played. If you have his name, or the formula of incantation that binds him, you can control the spirit, genie, afrite, or whatever the power may be. Solomon knew the names of all the spirits, and having their names, he held them subject to his will. So the universe has always appeared to the natural mind as a kind of enigma, of which the key must be sought in the shape of some illuminating or power-bringing word or name. That word names the universe's *principle*, and to possess it is after a fashion to possess the universe itself. 'God,' 'Matter,' 'Reason,' 'the Absolute,' 'Energy,' are so many solving names. You can rest when you have them. You are at the end of your metaphysical quest.

But if you follow the pragmatic method, you cannot look on any such word as closing your quest. You must bring out of each word its practical cash-value, set it at work within the stream of your experience. It appears less as a solution, then, than as a program for more work, and more particularly as an indication of the ways in which existing realities may be *changed*.

Theories thus become instruments, not answers to enigmas, in which we can rest. We don't lie back upon them, we move forward, and, on occasion, make nature over again by their aid. Pragmatism unstiffens all our theories, limbers them up and sets each one at work. Being nothing essentially new, it harmonizes with many ancient philosophic tendencies. It agrees with nominalism for instance, in always appealing to particulars; with utilitarianism in emphasizing practical aspects; with positivism in its disdain for verbal solutions, useless questions and metaphysical abstractions.

All these, you see, are *anti-intellectualist* tendencies. Against rationalism as a pretension and a method pragmatism is fully armed and militant. But, at the outset, at least, it stands for no particular results. It has no dogmas, and no doctrines save its method. As the young Italian pragmatist Papini has well said, it lies in the midst of our theories, like a corridor in a hotel. Innumerable chambers open out of it. In one you may find a man writing an atheistic volume; in the next some one on his knees praying for faith and strength; in a third a chemist investigating a body's properties. In a fourth a system of idealistic metaphysics is being excogitated; in a fifth the impossibility of metaphysics is being shown. But they all own the corridor, and all must pass through it if they want a practicable way of getting into or out of their respective rooms.

No particular results then, so far, but only an attitude of orientation, is what the pragmatic method means. *The attitude of looking away from first things, principles, 'categories,' supposed necessities; and of looking towards last things, fruits, consequences, facts.*

So much for the pragmatic method! You may say that I have been praising it rather than explaining it to you, but I shall presently explain it abundantly enough by showing how it works on some familiar problems. Meanwhile the word pragmatism has come to be used in a still wider sense, as meaning also a certain *theory of truth*. I mean to give a whole lecture to the statement of that theory, after first paving the way, so I can be very brief now. But brevity is hard to follow, so I ask for your redoubled attention for a quarter of an hour. If much remains obscure, I hope to make it clearer in the later lectures.

One of the most successfully cultivated branches of philosophy in our time is what is called inductive logic, the study of the conditions under which our sciences have evolved. Writers on this subject have begun to show a singular unanimity as to what the laws of nature and elements of fact mean, when formulated by mathematicians, physicists and chemists. When the first mathematical, logical, and natural uniformities, the first *laws,* were discovered, men were so carried away by the clearness, beauty and simplification that resulted, that they believed themselves to have deciphered authentically the eternal thoughts of the Almighty. His mind also thundered and reverberated in syllogisms. He also thought in conic sections, squares and roots and ratios, and geometrized like Euclid. He made Kepler's laws for the planets to follow; he made velocity increase proportionally to the time in falling bodies; he made the law of the sines for light to obey when refracted; he established the classes, orders, families and genera of plants and animals, and fixed the distances between them. He thought the archetypes of all things, and devised their variations; and when we rediscover any one of these his wondrous institutions, we seize his mind in its very literal intention.

But as the sciences have developed farther, the notion has gained ground that most, perhaps all, of our laws are only approximations. The laws themselves, moreover, have grown so numerous that there is no counting them; and so many rival formulations are proposed in all the branches of science that investigators have become accustomed to the notion that no theory is absolutely a transcript of reality, but that any one of them may from some point of view be useful. Their great use is to summarize old facts and to lead to new ones. They are only a man-made language, a conceptual shorthand, as some one calls them, in which we write our reports of nature; and languages, as is well known, tolerate much choice of expression and many dialects.

Thus human arbitrariness has driven divine necessity from scientific logic. If I mention the names of Sigwart, Mach, Ostwald, Pearson, Milhaud, Poincaré, Duhem, Ruyssen, those of you who are students will easily identify the tendency I speak of, and will think of additional names.

Riding now on the front of this wave of scientific logic Messrs. Schiller and Dewey appear with their pragmatistic account of what truth everywhere signifies. Everywhere, these teachers say, 'truth' in our ideas and beliefs means the same thing that it means in science. It means, they say, nothing but this, *that ideas (which themselves are but parts of our experience) become true just in so far as they help us to get into satisfactory relation with other parts of our experience,* to summarize them and get about among them by conceptual shortcuts instead of following the interminable succession of particular phenomena. Any idea upon which we can ride, so to speak; any idea that will carry us prosperously from any one part of our experience to any other part, linking things satisfactorily, working securely, simplifying, saving labor; is true for just so much, true in so far forth, true *instrumentally.* This is the 'instrumental' view of truth taught so successfully at Chicago, the view that truth in our ideas means their power to 'work,' promulgated so brilliantly at Oxford.

Messrs. Dewey, Schiller and their allies, in reaching this general conception of all truth, have only followed the example of geologists, biologists and philologists. In the establishment of these other sciences, the successful stroke was always to take some simple process actually

observable in operation—as denudation by weather, say, or variation
from parental type, or change of dialect by incorporation of new words
and pronunciations—and then to generalize it, making it apply to all
times, and produce great results by summating its effects through the
ages.

The observable process which Schiller and Dewey particularly
singled out for generalization is the familiar one by which any individual settles into *new opinions*. The process here is always the same.
The individual has a stock of old opinions already, but he meets a
new experience that puts them to a strain. Somebody contradicts them;
or in a reflective moment he discovers that they contradict each other;
or he hears of facts with which they are incompatible; or desires arise
in him which they cease to satisfy. The result is an inward trouble
to which his mind till then had been a stranger, and from which he
seeks to escape by modifying his previous mass of opinions. He saves
as much of it as he can, for in this matter of belief we are all extreme
conservatives. So he tries to change first this opinion, and then that
(for they resist change very variously), until at last some new idea
comes up which he can graft upon the ancient stock with a minimum
of disturbance of the latter, some idea that mediates between the stock
and the new experience and runs them into one another most felicitously and expediently.

This new idea is then adopted as the true one. It preserves the older
stock of truths with a minimum of modification, stretching them just
enough to make them admit the novelty, but conceiving that in ways
as familiar as the case leaves possible. An *outrée* explanation, violating
all our preconceptions, would never pass for a true account of a novelty. We should scratch round industriously till we found something less
excentric. The most violent revolutions in an individual's beliefs leave
most of his old order standing. Time and space, cause and effect, nature
and history, and one's own biography remain untouched. New truth is
always a go-between, a smoother-over of transitions. It marries old
opinion to new fact so as ever to show a minimum of jolt, a maximum
of continuity. We hold a theory true just in proportion to its success in
solving this 'problem of maxima and minima.' But success in solving
this problem is eminently a matter of approximation. We say this theory
solves it on the whole more satisfactorily than that theory; but that
means more satisfactorily to ourselves, and individuals will emphasize
their points of satisfaction differently. To a certain degree, therefore,
everything here is plastic.

The point I now urge you to observe particularly is the part played
by the older truths. Failure to take account of it is the source of much
of the unjust criticism levelled against pragmatism. Their influence is
absolutely controlling. Loyalty to them is the first principle—in most

cases it is the only principle; for by far the most usual way of handling phenomena so novel that they would make for a serious re-arrangement of our preconception is to ignore them altogether, or to abuse those who bear witness for them.

You doubtless wish examples of this process of truth's growth, and the only trouble is their superabundance. The simplest case of new truth is of course the mere numerical addition of new kinds of facts, or of new single facts of old kinds, to our experience—an addition that involves no alteration in the old beliefs. Day follows day, and its contents are simply added. The new contents themselves are not true, they simply *come* and *are*. Truth is *what we say about them,* and when we say that they have come, truth is satisfied by the plain additive formula.

But often the day's contents oblige a re-arrangement. If I should now utter piercing shrieks and act like a maniac on this platform, it would make many of you revise your ideas as to the probable worth of my philosophy. 'Radium' came the other day as part of the day's content, and seemed for a moment to contradict our ideas of the whole order of nature, that order having come to be identified with what is called the conservation of energy. The mere sight of radium paying heat away indefinitely out of its own pocket seemed to violate that conservation. What to think? If the radiations from it were nothing but an escape of unsuspected 'potential' energy, pre-existent inside of the atoms, the principle of conservation would be saved. The discovery of 'helium' as the radiation's outcome, opened a way to this belief. So Ramsay's view is generally held to be true, because, although it extends our old ideas of energy, it causes a minimum of alteration in their nature.

I need not multiply instances. A new opinion counts as 'true' just in proportion as it gratifies the individual's desire to assimilate the novel in his experience to his beliefs in stock. It must both lean on old truths and grasp new fact; and its success (as I said a moment ago) in doing this, is a matter for the individual's appreciation. When old truth grows, then, by new truth's addition, it is for subjective reasons. We are in the process and obey the reasons. That new idea is truest which performs most felicitously its function of satisfying our double urgency. It makes itself true, gets itself classed as true, by the way it works; grafting itself then upon the ancient body of truth, which thus grows much as a tree grows by the activity of a new layer of cambium.

Now Dewey and Schiller proceed to generalize this observation and to apply it to the most ancient parts of truth. They also once were plastic. They also were called true for human reasons. They also mediated between still earlier truths and what in those days were novel observations. Purely objective truth, truth in whose establishment the function of giving human satisfaction in marrying previous parts of experience with newer parts played no rôle whatever, is nowhere to be found. The reason why we call things true is the reason why they *are* true, for 'to be true' *means* only to perform this marriage-function.

The trail of the human serpent is thus over everything. Truth independent; truth that we *find* merely; truth no longer malleable to human need; truth incorrigible, in a word; such truth exists indeed superabundantly—or is supposed to exist by rationalistically minded thinkers; but then it means only the dead heart of the living tree, and its being there means only that truth also has its paleontology, and its 'prescription,' and may grow stiff with years of veteran service and petrified in men's regard by sheer antiquity. But how plastic even the oldest truths nevertheless really are has been vividly shown in our day by the transformation of logical and mathematical ideas, a transformation which seems even to be invading physics. The ancient formulas are reinterpreted as special expressions of much wider principles, principles that our ancestors never got a glimpse of in their present shape and formulation. . . .

2. The Will to Believe [2]

I

LET US GIVE the name of *hypothesis* to anything that may be proposed to our belief; and just as the electricians speak of live and dead wires, let us speak of any hypothesis as either *live* or *dead*. A live hypothesis is one which appeals as a real possibility to him to whom it is proposed. If I ask you to believe in the Mahdi, the notion makes no electric connection with your nature—it refuses to scintillate with any credibility at all. As an hypothesis it is completely dead. To an Arab, however (even if he be not one of the Mahdi's followers), the hypothesis is among the mind's possibilities: it is alive. This shows that deadness and liveness in an hypothesis are not intrinsic properties, but relations to the individual thinker. They are measured by his willingness to act. The maximum of liveness in an hypothesis means willingness to act irrevocably. Practically, that means belief; but there is some believing tendency wherever there is willingness to act at all.

Next, let us call the decision between two hypotheses an *option*. Options may be of several kinds. They may be—1, *living* or *dead*; 2, *forced* or *avoidable*; 3, *momentous* or *trivial*, and for our pur-

[2] Pages 2-14, 22-30 of *The Will to Believe and Other Essays in Popular Philosophy* (copyright 1896 by William James), reprinted by permission of Paul R. Reynolds. (From an address read to the philosophical clubs of Yale and Brown Universities in April and May, 1896, and published in *The New World* for June of the same year. The complete address may be found in *Essays on Faith and Morals* by William James, New York, Longmans, Green and Co., 1943.)

poses we may call an option a *genuine* option when it is of the forced, living, and momentous kind.

1. A living option is one in which both hypotheses are live ones. If I say to you: "Be a theosophist or be a Mohammedan," it is probably a dead option, because for you neither hypothesis is likely to be alive. But if I say: "Be an agnostic or be a Christian," it is otherwise: trained as you are, each hypothesis makes some appeal, however small, to your belief.

2. Next, if I say to you: "Choose between going out with your umbrella or without it," I do not offer you a genuine option, for it is not forced. You can easily avoid it by not going out at all. Similarly, if I say, "Either love me or hate me," "Either call my theory true or call it false," your option is avoidable. You may remain indifferent to me, neither loving nor hating, and you may decline to offer any judgment as to my theory. But if I say, "Either accept this truth or go without it," I put on you a forced option, for there is no standing place outside of the alternative. Every dilemma based on a complete logical disjunction, with no possibility of not choosing, is an option of this forced kind.

3. Finally, if I were Dr. Nansen and proposed to you to join my North Pole expedition, your option would be momentous; for this would probably be your only similar opportunity, and your choice now would either exclude you from the North Pole sort of immortality altogether or put at least the chance of it into your hands. He who refuses to embrace a unique opportunity loses the prize as surely as if he tried and failed. *Per contra*, the option is trivial when the opportunity is not unique, when the stake is insignificant, or when the decision is reversible if it later prove unwise. Such trivial options abound in the scientific life. A chemist finds an hypothesis live enough to spend a year in its verification: he believes in it to that extent. But if his experiments prove inconclusive either way, he is quit for his loss of time, no vital harm being done.

It will facilitate our discussion if we keep all these distinctions well in mind.

II

The next matter to consider is the actual psychology of human opinion. When we look at certain facts, it seems as if our passional and volitional nature lay at the root of all our convictions. When we look at others, it seems as if they could do nothing when the intellect had once said its say. Let us take the latter facts up first.

Does it not seem preposterous on the very face of it to talk of our opinions being modifiable at will? Can our will either help or hinder our intellect in its perceptions of truth? Can we, by just willing it, believe that Abraham Lincoln's existence is a myth, and that the portraits of him in *McClure's Magazine* are all of some one else? Can we, by any effort of our will, or by any strength of wish that it were true, believe ourselves well and about when we are roaring with rheumatism in bed, or feel certain that the sum of the two one-dollar bills in our pocket must be a hundred dollars? We can *say* any of these things, but we are absolutely impotent to believe them; and of just such things is the whole fabric of the truths that we do believe in made up—matters of fact, immediate or remote, as Hume said, and relations between ideas, which are either there or not there for us if we see them so, and which if not there cannot be put there by any action of our own.

In Pascal's *Thoughts* there is a celebrated passage known in literature as Pascal's wager. In it he tries to force us into Christianity by reasoning as if our concern with truth resembled our concern with the stakes in a game of chance. Translated freely his words are these: You must either believe or not believe that God is—which will you do? Your human reason cannot say. A game is going on between you and the nature of things which at the day of judgment will bring out either heads or tails. Weigh what your gains and your losses would be if you should stake all you have on heads, or God's existence: if you win in such case, you gain eternal beatitude; if you lose, you lose nothing at all. If there were an infinity of chances, and only one for God in this wager, still you ought to stake your all on God; for though you surely risk a finite loss by this procedure, any finite loss is reasonable, even a certain one is reasonable, if there is but the possibility of infinite gain. Go, then, and take holy water, and have masses said; belief will come and stupefy your scruples—*Cela vous fera croire et vous abêtira.* Why should you not? At bottom, what have you to lose?

You probably feel that when religious faith expresses itself thus, in the language of the gaming-table, it is put to its last trumps. Surely Pascal's own personal belief in masses and holy water had far other springs; and this celebrated page of his is but an argument for others, a last desperate snatch at a weapon against the hardness of the unbelieving heart. We feel that a faith in masses and holy water adopted wilfully after such a mechanical calculation would lack the inner soul of faith's reality; and if we were ourselves in the place of the Deity, we should probably take particular pleasure in cutting off believers of this pattern from their infinite reward. It is evident that unless there be some pre-existing tendency to believe in masses and holy water, the option offered to the will by Pascal is not a living option. Certainly no Turk ever took to masses and holy water on its account; and even to us Protestants these means of salvation seem such foregone impossibilities that Pascal's logic, invoked for them specifically, leaves us unmoved. As well might the Mahdi write to us, saying, "I am the Expected

One whom God has created in his effulgence. You shall be infinitely happy if you confess me; otherwise you shall be cut off from the light of the sun. Weigh, then, your infinite gain if I am genuine against your finite sacrifice if I am not!" His logic would be that of Pascal; but he would vainly use it on us, for the hypothesis he offers us is dead. No tendency to act on it exists in us to any degree.

The talk of believing by our volition seems, then, from one point of view, simply silly. From another point of view it is worse than silly, it is vile. When one turns to the magnificent edifice of the physical sciences, and sees how it was reared; what thousands of disinterested moral lives of men lie buried in its mere foundations; what patience and postponement, what choking down of preference, what submission to the icy laws of outer fact are wrought into its very stones and mortar; how absolutely impersonal it stands in its vast augustness—then how besotted and contemptible seems every little sentimentalist who comes blowing his voluntary smoke-wreaths, and pretending to decide things from out of his private dream! Can we wonder if those bred in the rugged and manly school of science should feel like spewing such subjectivism out of their mouths? The whole system of loyalties which grow up in the schools of science go dead against its toleration; so that it is only natural that those who have caught the scientific fever should pass over to the opposite extreme, and write sometimes as if the incorruptibly truthful intellect ought positively to prefer bitterness and unacceptableness to the heart in its cup.

> It fortifies my soul to know
> That, though I perish, Truth is so—

sings Clough, while Huxley exclaims: "My only consolation lies in the reflection that, however bad our posterity may become, so far as they hold by the plain rule of not pretending to believe what they have no reason to believe, because it may be to their advantage so to pretend [the word 'pretend' is surely here redundant], they will not have reached the lowest depth of immorality." And that delicious *enfant terrible* Clifford writes: "Belief is desecrated when given to unproved and unquestioned statements for the solace and private pleasure of the believer. ... Whoso would deserve well of his fellows in this matter will guard the purity of his belief with a very fanaticism of jealous care, lest at any time it should rest on an unworthy object, and catch a stain which can never be wiped away. ... If [a] belief has been accepted on insufficient evidence [even though the belief be true, as Clifford on the same page explains] the pleasure is a stolen one. ... It is sinful because it is stolen in defiance of our duty to mankind. That duty is to guard ourselves from such beliefs as from a pestilence which may shortly master our own body and then spread to the rest of the town.

... It is wrong always, everywhere, and for every one, to believe anything upon insufficient evidence."

III

All this strikes one as healthy, even when expressed, as by Clifford, with somewhat too much of robustious pathos in the voice. Free-will and simple wishing do seem, in the matter of our credences, to be only fifth wheels to the coach. Yet if any one should thereupon assume that intellectual insight is what remains after wish and will and sentimental preference have taken wing, or that pure reason is what then settles our opinions, he would fly quite as directly in the teeth of the facts.

It is only our already dead hypotheses that our willing nature is unable to bring to life again. But what has made them dead for us is for the most part a previous action of our willing nature of an antagonistic kind. When I say 'willing nature,' I do not mean only such deliberate volitions as may have set up habits of belief that we cannot now escape from—I mean all such factors of belief as fear and hope, prejudice and passion, imitation and partisanship, the circumpressure of our caste and set. As a matter of fact we find ourselves believing, we hardly know how or why. Mr. Balfour gives the name of 'authority' to all those influences, born of the intellectual climate, that make hypotheses possible or impossible for us, alive or dead. Here in this room, we all of us believe in molecules and the conservation of energy, in democracy and necessary progress, in Protestant Christianity and the duty of fighting for 'the doctrine of the immortal Monroe,' all for no reasons worthy of the name. We see into these matters with no more inner clearness, and probably with much less, than any disbeliever in them might possess. His unconventionality would probably have some grounds to show for its conclusions; but for us, not insight, but the *prestige* of the opinions, is what makes the spark shoot from them and light up our sleeping magazines of faith. Our reason is quite satisfied, in nine hundred and ninety-nine cases out of every thousand of us, if it can find a few arguments that will do to recite in case our credulity is criticized by some one else. Our faith is faith in some one else's faith, and in the greatest matters this is most the case. Our belief in truth itself, for instance, that there is a truth, and that our minds and it are made for each other—what is it but a passionate affirmation of desire, in which our social system backs us up? We want to have a truth; we want to believe that our experiments and studies and discussions must put us in a continually better and better position towards it; and on this line we agree to fight out our thinking lives. But if a pyrrhonistic sceptic asks us *how we know* all this, can our logic find a reply? No! certainly it cannot. It is just one volition against another

—we willing to go in for life upon a trust or assumption which he, for his part, docs not care to make.

As a rule we disbelieve all facts and theories for which we have no use. Clifford's cosmic emotions find no use for Christian feelings. Huxley belabors the bishops because there is no use for sacerdotalism in his scheme of life. Newman, on the contrary, goes over to Romanism, and finds all sorts of reasons good for staying there, because a priestly system is for him an organic need and delight. Why do so few 'scientists' even look at the evidence for telepathy, so called? Because they think, as a leading biologist, now dead, once said to me, that even if such a thing were true, scientists ought to band together to keep it suppressed and concealed. It would undo the uniformity of Nature and all sorts of other things without which scientists cannot carry on their pursuits. But if this very man had been shown something which as a scientist he might *do* with telepathy, he might not only have examined the evidence, but even have found it good enough. This very law which the logicians would impose upon us—if I may give the name of logicians to those who would rule out our willing nature here—is based on nothing but their own natural wish to exclude all elements for which they, in their professional quality of logicians, can find no use.

Evidently, then, our non-intellectual nature does influence our convictions. There are passional tendencies and volitions which run before and others which come after belief, and it is only the latter that are too late for the fair; and they are not too late when the previous passional work has been already in their own direction. Pascal's argument, instead of being powerless, then sccms a regular clincher, and is the last stroke needed to make our faith in masses and holy water complete. The state of things is evidently far from simple; and pure insight and logic, whatever they might do ideally, are not the only things that really do produce our creeds.

IV

Our next duty, having recognized this mixed-up state of affairs, is to ask whether it be simply reprehensible and pathological, or whether, on the contrary, we must treat it as a normal element in making up our minds. The thesis I defend is, briefly stated, this: *Our passional nature not only lawfully may, but must, decide an option between propositions, whenever it is a genuine option that cannot by its nature be decided on intellectual grounds; for to say, under such circumstances, "Do not decide, but leave the question open," is itself a passional decision—just like deciding yes or no—and is attended with the same risk of losing the truth.* The thesis thus abstractly expressed will, I trust, soon become quite clear. But I must first indulge in a bit more of preliminary work.

V

It will be observed that for the purposes of this discussion we are on 'dogmatic' ground—ground, I mean, which leaves systematic philosophical scepticism altogether out of account. The postulate that there is truth, and that it is the destiny of our minds to attain it, we are deliberately resolving to make, though the sceptic will not make it. We part company with him, therefore, absolutely, at this point. But the faith that truth exists, and that our minds can find it, may be held in two ways. We may talk of the *empiricist* way and of the *absolutist* way of believing in truth. The absolutists in this matter say that we not only can attain to knowing truth, but we can *know when* we have attained to knowing it; while the empiricists think that although we may attain it, we cannot infallibly know when. To *know* is one thing, and to know for certain *that* we know is another. One may hold to the first being possible without the second; hence the empiricists and the absolutists, although neither of them is a sceptic in the usual philosophic sense of the term, show very different degrees of dogmatism in their lives.

If we look at the history of opinions, we see that the empiricist tendency has largely prevailed in science, while in philosophy the absolutist tendency has had everything its own way. The characteristic sort of happiness, indeed, which philosophies yield has mainly consisted in the conviction felt by each successive school or system that by it bottom-certitude has been attained. "Other philosophies are collections of opinions, mostly false; *my* philosophy gives standing-ground forever"— who does not recognize in this the key-note of every system worthy of the name? A system, to be a system at all, must come as a *closed* system, reversible in this or that detail, perchance, but in its essential features never!

Scholastic orthodoxy, to which one must always go when one wishes to find perfectly clear statement, has beautifully elaborated this absolutist conviction in a doctrine which it calls that of 'objective evidence.' If, for example, I am unable to doubt that I now exist before you, that two is less than three, or that if all men are mortal then I am mortal too, it is because these things illumine my intellect irresistibly. The final ground of this objective evidence possessed by certain propositions is the *adæquatio intellectûs nostri cum rê*. The certitude it brings involves an *aptitudinem ad extorquendum certum assensum* on the part of the truth envisaged, and on the side of the subject a *quietem in cognitione*, when once the object is mentally received, that leaves no possibility of doubt behind; and in the whole transaction nothing operates but the *entitas ipsa* of the object and the *entitas ipsa* of the mind. We slouchy modern thinkers dislike to talk in Latin—indeed, we dislike to talk in set terms at all; but at bottom our own state of mind is very much like this whenever we uncritically abandon ourselves: You believe in objective evidence, and I do. Of some things we feel that we are certain: we know, and we know that we know. There is something that gives a click inside of us, a bell that strikes twelve, when the hands of our mental clock have swept the dial and meet over the meridian hour. The greatest empiricists among us are only empiricists on reflection: when left to their instincts, they dogmatize like infallible popes. When the Cliffords tell us how sinful it is to be Christians on such 'insufficient evidence,' insufficiency is really the last thing they have in mind. For them the evidence is absolutely sufficient, only it makes the other way. They believe so completely in an anti-Christian order of the universe that there is no living option: Christianity is a dead hypothesis from the start. . . .

IX

Moral questions immediately present themselves as questions whose solution cannot wait for sensible proof. A moral question is a question not of what sensibly exists, but of what is good, or would be good if it did exist. Science can tell us what exists; but to compare the *worths*, both of what exists and of what does not exist, we must consult not science, but what Pascal calls our heart. Science herself consults her heart when she lays it down that the infinite ascertainment of fact and correction of false belief are the supreme goods for man. Challenge the statement, and science can only repeat it oracularly, or else prove it by showing that such ascertainment and correction bring man all sorts of other goods which man's heart in turn declares. The question of having moral beliefs at all or not having them is decided by our will. Are our moral preferences true or false, or are they only odd biological phenomena, making things good or bad for *us*, but in themselves indifferent? How can your pure intellect decide? If your heart does not *want* a world of moral reality, your head will assuredly never make you believe in one. Mephistophelian scepticism, indeed, will satisfy the head's play-instincts much better than any rigorous idealism can. Some men (even at the student age) are so naturally cool-hearted that the moralistic hypothesis never has for them any pungent life, and in their supercilious presence the hot young moralist always feels strangely ill at ease. The appearance of knowingness is on their side, of *naïveté* and gullibility on his. Yet, in the inarticulate heart of him, he clings to it that he is not a dupe, and that there is a realm in which (as Emerson says) all their wit and intellectual superiority is no better than the cunning of a fox. Moral scepticism can no more be refuted or proved by logic than intellectual scepticism can. When we stick to it that there *is* truth (be it of either kind), we do so with our whole nature, and resolve to stand or fall by the results. The sceptic with his whole nature adopts the doubting attitude; but which of us is the wiser, Omniscience only knows.

Turn now from these wide questions of good to a certain class of questions of fact, questions concerning personal relations, states of mind between one man and another. *Do you like me or not?*—for example. Whether you do or not depends, in countless instances, on whether I meet you half-way, am willing to assume that you must like me, and show you trust and expectation. The previous faith on my part in your liking's existence is in such cases what makes your liking come. But if I stand aloof, and refuse to budge an inch until I have objective evidence, until you shall have done something apt, as the absolutists say, *ad extorquendum assensum meum,* ten to one your liking never comes. How many women's hearts are vanquished by the mere sanguine insistence of some man that they *must* love him! he will not consent to the hypothesis that they cannot. The desire for a certain kind of truth here brings about that special truth's existence; and so it is in innumerable cases of other sorts. Who gains promotions, boons, appointments, but the man in whose life they are seen to play the part of live hypotheses, who discounts them, sacrifices other things for their sake before they have come, and takes risks for them in advance? His faith acts on the powers above him as a claim, and creates its own verification.

A social organism of any sort whatever, large or small, is what it is because each member proceeds to his own duty with a trust that the other members will simultaneously do theirs. Wherever a desired result is achieved by the coöperation of many independent persons, its existence as a fact is a pure consequence of the precursive faith in one another of those immediately concerned. A government, an army, a commercial system, a ship, a college, an athletic team, all exist on this condition, without which not only is nothing achieved, but nothing is even attempted. A whole train of passengers (individually brave enough) will be looted by a few highwaymen, simply because the latter can count on one another, while each passenger fears that if he makes a movement of resistance, he will be shot before any one else backs him up. If we believed that the whole car-full would rise at once with us, we should each severally rise, and train-robbing would never even be attempted. There are, then, cases where a fact cannot come at all unless a preliminary faith exists in its coming. *And where faith in a fact can help create the fact,* that would be an insane logic which should say that faith running ahead of scientific evidence is the 'lowest kind of immorality' into which a thinking being can fall. Yet such is the logic by which our scientific absolutists pretend to regulate our lives!

X

In truths dependent on our personal action, then, faith based on desire is certainly a lawful and possibly an indispensable thing.

But now, it will be said, these are all childish human cases, and have nothing to do with great cosmical matters, like the question of religious faith. Let us then pass on to that! Religions differ so much in their accidents that in discussing the religious question we must make it very generic and broad. What then do we now mean by the religious hypothesis? Science says things are; morality says some things are better than other things; and religion says essentially two things.

First, she says that the best things are the more eternal things, the overlapping things, the things in the universe that throw the last stone, so to speak. and say the final word. "Perfection is eternal"—this phrase of Charles Secrétan seems a good way of putting this first affirmation of religion, an affirmation which obviously cannot yet be verified scientifically at all.

The second affirmation of religion is that we are better off even now if we believe her first affirmation to be true.

Now, let us consider what the logical elements of this situation are *in case the religious hypothesis in both its branches be really true.* (Of course, we must admit that possibility at the outset. If we are to discuss the question at all, it must involve a living option. If for any of you religion be a hypothesis that cannot by any living possibility be true, then you need go no farther. I speak to the 'saving remnant' alone.) So proceeding, we see, first, that religion offers itself as a *momentous* option. We are supposed to gain, even now, by our belief, and to lose by our non-belief, a certain vital good. Secondly, religion is a *forced* option, so far as that good goes. We cannot escape the issue by remaining sceptical and waiting for more light, because, although we do avoid error in that way *if religion be untrue,* we lose the good, *if it be true,* just as certainly as if we positively chose to disbelieve. It is as if a man should hesitate indefinitely to ask a certain woman to marry him because he was not perfectly sure that she would prove an angel after he brought her home. Would he not cut himself off from that particular angel-possibility as decisively as if he went and married some one else? Scepticism, then, is not avoidance of option; it is option of a certain particular kind of risk. *Better risk loss of truth than chance of error—* that is your faith-vetoer's exact position. He is actively playing his stake as much as the believer is; he is backing the field against the religious hypothesis, just as the believer is backing the religious hypothesis against the field. To preach scepticism to us as a duty until 'sufficient evidence' for religion be found, is tantamount therefore to telling us, when in presence of the religious hypothesis, that to yield to our fear of its being error is wiser and better than to yield to our hope that it may be true. It is not intellect against all passions, then; it is only intellect with one passion laying down its law. And by what, forsooth, is the supreme wisdom of this passion warranted? Dupery for dupery, what proof is there that dupery through hope is so much worse than dupery through fear? I, for one, can see no proof; and I simply refuse obedience to the scientist's command to imitate his kind of option, in a case where my own stake is important enough to give me the right to choose my own form of risk. If religion be true and the evidence for it be still insufficient, I do not wish, by putting your extinguisher upon my nature (which feels to me as if it had after all some business in this matter), to forfeit my sole chance in life of getting upon the winning side—that chance depending, of course, on my willingness to run the risk of acting as if my passional need of taking the world religiously might be prophetic and right.

All this is on the supposition that it really may be prophetic and right, and that, even to us who are discussing the matter, religion is a live hypothesis which may be true. Now, to most of us religion comes in a still further way that makes a veto on our active faith even more illogical. The more perfect and more eternal aspect of the universe is represented in our religions as having personal form. The universe is no longer a mere *It* to us, but a *Thou*, if we are religious; and any relation that may be possible from person to person might be possible here. For instance, although in one sense we are passive portions of the universe, in another we show a curious autonomy, as if we were small active centres on our own account. We feel, too, as if the appeal of religion to us were made to our own active good-will, as if evidence might be forever withheld from us unless we met the hypothesis half-way. To take a trivial illustration: just as a man who in a company of gentlemen made no advances, asked a warrant for every concession, and believed no one's word without proof, would cut himself off by such churlishness from all the social rewards that a more trusting spirit would earn—so here, one who should shut himself up in snarling logicality and try to make the gods extort his recognition willy-nilly, or not get it at all, might cut himself off forever from his only opportunity of making the gods' acquaintance. This feeling, forced on us we know not whence, that by obstinately believing that there are gods (although not to do so would be so easy both for our logic and our life) we are doing the universe the deepest service we can, seems part of the living essence of the religious hypothesis. If the hypothesis *were* true in all its parts, including this one, then pure intellectualism, with its veto on our making willing advances, would be an absurdity; and some participation of our sympathetic nature would be logically required. I, therefore, for one, cannot see my way to accepting the agnostic rules for truth-seeking, or wilfully agree to keep my willing nature out of the game. I cannot do so for this plain reason, that *a rule of thinking which would absolutely prevent me from acknowledging certain kinds of truth if those kinds of truth were really there, would be an irrational rule.* That for me is the long and short of the formal logic of the situation, no matter what the kinds of truth might materially be.

I confess I do not see how this logic can be escaped. But sad experience makes me fear that some of you may still shrink from radically saying with me, *in abstracto,* that we have the right to believe at our own risk any hypothesis that is live enough to tempt our will. I suspect, however, that if this is so, it is because you have got away from the abstract logical point of view altogether, and are thinking (perhaps without realizing it) of some particular religious hypothesis which for you is dead. The freedom to 'believe what we will' you apply to the case of some patent superstition; and the faith you think of is the faith defined by the schoolboy when he said, "Faith is when you believe something that you know ain't true." I can only repeat that this is misapprehension. *In concreto,* the freedom to believe can only cover living options which the intellect of the individual cannot by itself resolve; and living options never seem absurdities to him who has them to consider. When I look at the religious question as it really puts itself to concrete men, and when I think of all the possibilities which both practically and theoretically it involves, then this command that we shall put a stopper on our heart, instincts, and courage, and *wait*— acting of course meanwhile more or less as if religion were *not* true *—till doomsday, or till such time as our intellect and senses working together may have raked in evidence enough—this command, I say, seems to me the queerest idol ever manufactured in the philosophic cave. Were we scholastic absolutists, there might be more excuse. If we had an infallible intellect with its objective certitudes, we might feel ourselves disloyal to such a perfect organ of knowledge in not trusting to it exclusively, in not waiting for its releasing word. But if we are empiricists, if we believe that no bell in us tolls to let us know for certain when truth is in our grasp, then it seems a piece of idle

* Since belief is measured by action, he who forbids us to believe religion to be true, necessarily also forbids us to act as we should if we did believe it to be true. The whole defense of religious faith hinges upon action. If the action required or inspired by the religious hypothesis is in no way different from that dictated by the naturalistic hypothesis, then religious faith is a pure superfluity, better pruned away, and controversy about its legitimacy is a piece of idle trifling, unworthy of serious minds. I myself believe, of course, that the religious hypothesis gives to the world an expression which specifically determines our reactions, and makes them in a large part unlike what they might be on a purely naturalistic scheme of belief.

fantasticality to preach so solemnly our duty of waiting for the bell. Indeed we *may* wait if we will—I hope you do not think that I am denying that—but if we do so, we do so at our peril as much as if we believed. In either case we *act,* taking our life in our hands. No one of us ought to issue vetoes to the other, nor should we bandy words of abuse. We ought, on the contrary, delicately and profoundly to respect one another's mental freedom: then only shall we bring about the intellectual republic; then only shall we have that spirit of inner tolerance without which all our outer tolerance is soulless, and which is empiricism's glory; then only shall we live and let live, in speculative as well as in practical things. . . .

3. Does 'Consciousness' Exist? [3]

. . . To DENY PLUMPLY that 'consciousness' exists seems so absurd on the face of it—for undeniably 'thoughts' do exist—that I fear some readers will follow me no farther. Let me then immediately explain that I mean only to deny that the word stands for an entity, but to insist most emphatically that it does stand for a function. There is, I mean, no aboriginal stuff or quality of being, contrasted with that of which material objects are made, out of which our thoughts of them are made; but there is a function in experience which thoughts perform, and for the performance of which this quality of being is invoked. That function is *knowing.* 'Consciousness' is supposed necessary to explain the fact that things not only are, but get reported, are known. Whoever blots out the notion of consciousness from his list of first principles must still provide in some way for that function's being carried on.

I

My thesis is that if we start with the supposition that there is only one primal stuff or material in the world, a stuff of which everything is composed, and if we call that stuff 'pure experience,' then knowing can easily be explained as a particular sort of relation towards one another into which portions of pure experience may enter. The relation itself is a part of pure experience; one of its 'terms' becomes the subject or bearer of the knowledge, the knower,* the other becomes the object known. This will need much explanation before it can be understood.

[3] Reprinted, by permission of the Editors, from the *Journal of Philosophy* 1:477-491, Sept. 1, 1904, omitting the first two paragraphs and the last, and some of the notes. The complete text may be found in *Essays in Radical Empiricism* (New York, Longmans, Green and Co., 1912).
* In my *Psychology* [I, 338 ff.] I have tried to show that we need no knower other than the 'passing thought.'

The best way to get it understood is to contrast it with the alternative view; and for that we may take the recentest alternative, that in which the evaporation of the definite soul-substance has proceeded as far as it can go without being yet complete. If neo-Kantism has expelled earlier forms of dualism, we shall have expelled all forms if we are able to expel neo-Kantism in its turn.

For the thinkers I call neo-Kantian, the word consciousness today does no more than signalize the fact that experience is indefeasibly dualistic in structure. It means that not subject, not object, but object-plus-subject is the minimum that can actually be. The subject-object distinction meanwhile is entirely different from that between mind and matter, from that between body and soul. Souls were detachable, had separate destinies; things could happen to them. To consciousness as such nothing can happen, for, timeless itself, it is only a witness of happenings in time, in which it plays no part. It is, in a word, but the logical correlative of 'content' in an Experience of which the peculiarity is that *fact comes to light* in it, that *awareness of content* takes place. Consciousness as such is entirely impersonal—'self' and its activities belong to the content. To say that I am self-conscious, or conscious of putting forth volition, means only that certain contents, for which 'self' and 'effort of will' are the names, are not without witness as they occur.

Thus, for these belated drinkers at the Kantian spring, we should have to admit consciousness as an 'epistemological' necessity, even if we had no direct evidence of its being there.

But in addition to this, we are supposed by almost every one to have an immediate consciousness of consciousness itself. When the world of outer fact ceases to be materially present, and we merely recall it in memory, or fancy it, the consciousness is believed to stand out and to be felt as a kind of impalpable inner flowing, which, once known in this sort of experience, may equally be detected in presentations of the outer world. "The moment we try to fix our attention upon consciousness and to see *what*, distinctly, it is," says a recent writer, "it seems to vanish. It seems as if we had before us a mere emptiness. When we try to introspect the sensation of blue, all we can see is the blue; the other element is as if it were diaphanous. Yet it *can* be distinguished, if we look attentively enough, and know that there is something to look for." * "Consciousness" (*Bewusstheit*), says another philosopher, "is inexplicable and hardly describable, yet all conscious experiences have this in common that what we call their content has this peculiar reference to a centre for which 'self' is the name, in virtue of which reference alone the content is subjectively given, or appears. . . . While in this way consciousness, or reference to a self, is the only thing which distinguishes a conscious content from any sort of being that might be

* G. E. Moore: *Mind*, vol. xii, n.s. [1903], p. 450.

there with no one conscious of it, yet this only ground of the distinction defies all closer explanations. The existence of consciousness, although it is the fundamental fact of psychology, can indeed be laid down as certain, can be brought out by analysis, but can neither be defined nor deduced from anything but itself." *

'Can be brought out by analysis,' this author says. This supposes that the consciousness is one element, moment, factor—call it what you like—of an experience of essentially dualistic inner constitution, from which, if you abstract the content, the consciousness will remain revealed to its own eye. Experience, at this rate, would be much like a paint of which the world pictures were made. Paint has a dual constitution, involving, as it does, a menstruum (oil, size or what not) and a mass of content in the form of pigment suspended therein. We can get the pure menstruum by letting the pigment settle, and the pure pigment by pouring off the size or oil. We operate here by physical subtraction; and the usual view is, that by mental subtraction we can separate the two factors of experience in an analogous way—not isolating them entirely, but distinguishing them enough to know that they are two.

II

Now my contention is exactly the reverse of this. *Experience, I believe, has no such inner duplicity; and the separation of it into consciousness and content comes, not by way of subtraction, but by way of addition*—the addition, to a given concrete piece of it, of other sets of experiences, in connection with which severally its use or function may be of two different kinds. The paint will also serve here as an illustration. In a pot in a paint-shop, along with other paints, it serves in its entirety as so much saleable matter. Spread on a canvas, with other paints around it, it represents, on the contrary, a feature in a picture and performs a spiritual function. Just so, I maintain, does a given undivided portion of experience, taken in one context of associates, play the part of a knower, of a state of mind, of 'consciousness'; while in a different context the same undivided bit of experience plays the part of a thing known, of an objective 'content.' In a word, in one group it figures as a thought, in another group as a thing. And, since it can figure in both groups simultaneously we have every right to speak of it as subjective and objective both at once. The dualism connoted by such double-barrelled terms as 'experience,' 'phenomenon,' 'datum,' 'Vorfindung'—terms which, in philosophy at any rate, tend more and more to replace the single-barrelled terms of 'thought' and 'thing'—that dualism, I say, is still preserved in this account, but reinterpreted, so that, instead of being mysterious and elusive, it becomes

* Paul Natorp: *Einleitung in die Psychologie,* 1888, pp. 14, 112.

verifiable and concrete. It is an affair of relations, it falls outside, not inside, the single experience considered, and can always be particularized and defined.

The entering wedge for this more concrete way of understanding the dualism was fashioned by Locke when he made the word 'idea' stand indifferently for thing and thought, and by Berkeley when he said that what common sense means by realities is exactly what the philosopher means by ideas. Neither Locke nor Berkeley thought his truth out into perfect clearness, but it seems to me that the conception I am defending does little more than consistently carry out the 'pragmatic' method which they were the first to use.

If the reader will take his own experiences, he will see what I mean. Let him begin with a perceptual experience, the 'presentation,' so called, of a physical object, his actual field of vision, the room he sits in, with the book he is reading as its centre; and let him for the present treat this complex object in the common-sense way as being 'really' what it seems to be, namely, a collection of physical things cut out from an environing world of other physical things with which these physical things have actual or potential relations. Now at the same time it is just *those self-same things* which his mind, as we say, perceives; and the whole philosophy of perception from Democritus's time downwards has been just one long wrangle over the paradox that what is evidently one reality should be in two places at once, both in outer space and in a person's mind. 'Representative' theories of perception avoid the logical paradox, but on the other hand they violate the reader's sense of life, which knows no intervening mental image but seems to see the room and the book immediately just as they physically exist.

The puzzle of how the one identical room can be in two places is at bottom just the puzzle of how one identical point can be on two lines. It can, if it be situated at their intersection; and similarly, if the 'pure experience' of the room were a place of intersection of two processes, which connected it with different groups of associates respectively, it could be counted twice over, as belonging to either group, and spoken of loosely as existing in two places, although it would remain all the time a numerically single thing.

Well, the experience is a member of diverse processes that can be followed away from it along entirely different lines. The one self-identical thing has so many relations to the rest of experience that you can take it in disparate systems of association, and treat it as belonging with opposite contexts. In one of these contexts it is your 'field of consciousness'; in another it is 'the room in which you sit,' and it enters both contexts in its wholeness, giving no pretext for being said to attach itself to consciousness by one of its parts or aspects, and to outer reality by another. What are the two processes, now, into which the room-experience simultaneously enters in this way?

One of them is the reader's personal biography, the other is the history of the house of which the room is part. The presentation, the experience, the *that* in short (for until we have decided *what* it is it must be a mere *that*) is the last term of a train of sensations, emotions, decisions, movements, classifications, expectations, etc., ending in the present, and the first term of a series of similar 'inner' operations extending into the future, on the reader's part. On the other hand, the very same *that* is the *terminus ad quem* of a lot of previous physical operations, carpentering, papering, furnishing, warming, etc., and the *terminus a quo* of a lot of future ones, in which it will be concerned when undergoing the destiny of a physical room. The physical and the mental operations form curiously incompatible groups. As a room, the experience has occupied that spot and had that environment for thirty years. As your field of consciousness it may never have existed until now. As a room, attention will go on to discover endless new details in it. As your mental state merely, few new ones will emerge under attention's eye. As a room, it will take an earthquake, or a gang of men, and in any case a certain amount of time, to destroy it. As your subjective state, the closing of your eyes, or any instantaneous play of your fancy will suffice. In the real world, fire will consume it. In your mind, you can let fire play over it without effect. As an outer object, you must pay so much a month to inhabit it. As an inner content, you may occupy it for any length of time rent-free. If, in short, you follow it in the mental direction, taking it along with events of personal biography solely, all sorts of things are true of it which are false, and false of it which are true if you treat it as a real thing experienced, follow it in the physical direction, and relate it to associates in the outer world.

III

So far, all seems plain sailing, but my thesis will probably grow less plausible to the reader when I pass from percepts to concepts, or from the case of things presented to that of things remote. I believe, nevertheless, that here also the same law holds good. If we take conceptual manifolds, or memories, or fancies, they also are in their first intention mere bits of pure experience, and, as such, are single *thats* which act in one context as objects, and in another context figure as mental states. By taking them in their first intention, I mean ignoring their relation to possible perceptual experiences with which they may be connected, which they may lead to and terminate in, and which then they may be supposed to 'represent.' Taking them in this way first, we confine the problem to a world merely 'thought-of' and not directly felt or seen. This world, just like the world of percepts, comes to us at first as a chaos of experiences, but lines of order soon get traced. We find that any bit of it which we may cut out as an example is connected with distinct groups of associates, just as our perceptual experiences are, that these associates link themselves with it by different relations,* and that one forms the inner history of a person, while the other acts as an impersonal 'objective' world, either spatial and temporal, or else merely logical or mathematical, or otherwise 'ideal.'

The first obstacle on the part of the reader to seeing that these non-perceptual experiences have objectivity as well as subjectivity will probably be due to the intrusion into his mind of *percepts*, that third group of associates with which the non-perceptual experiences have relations, and which, as a whole, they 'represent,' standing to them as thoughts to things. This important function of the non-perceptual experiences complicates the question and confuses it; for, so used are we to treat percepts as the sole genuine realities that, unless we keep them out of the discussion, we tend altogether to overlook the objectivity that lies in non-perceptual experiences by themselves. We treat them, 'knowing' percepts as they do, as through and through subjective, and say that they are wholly constituted of the stuff called consciousness, using this term now for a kind of entity, after the fashion which I am seeking to refute.

Abstracting, then, from percepts altogether, what I maintain is, that any single non-perceptual experience tends to get counted twice over, just as a perceptual experience does, figuring in one context as an object or field of objects, in another as a state of mind: and all this without the least internal self-diremption on its own part into consciousness and content. It is all consciousness in one taking; and, in the other, all content.

I find this objectivity of non-perceptual experiences, this complete parallelism in point of reality between the presently felt and the remotely thought, so well set forth in a page of Münsterberg's *Grundzüge*, that I will quote it as it stands.

"I may only think of my objects," says Professor Münsterberg; "yet, in my living thought they stand before me exactly as perceived objects would do, no matter how different the two ways of apprehending them may be in their genesis. The book here lying on the table before me, and the book in the next room of which I think and which I mean to get, are both in the same sense given realities for me, realities which

---

* Here as elsewhere the relations are of course *experienced* relations, members of the same originally chaotic manifold of non-perceptual experience of which the related terms themselves are parts. [For the "logical realism" which James approaches here, see his *Meaning of Truth*, pp. 49, 195 n.; *A Pluralistic Universe*, 339-340; *Some Problems of Philosophy*, 50-57, 67-70, 106.]

I acknowledge and of which I take account. If you agree that the perceptual object is not an idea within me, but that percept and thing, as indistinguishably one, are really experienced *there, outside,* you ought not to believe that the merely thought-of object is hid away inside of the thinking subject. The object of which I think, and of whose existence I take cognizance without letting it now work upon my senses, occupies its definite place in the outer world as much as does the object which I directly see."

"What is true of the here and the there, is also true of the now and the then. I know of the thing which is present and perceived, but I know also of the thing which yesterday was but is no more, and which I only remember. Both can determine my present conduct, both are parts of the reality of which I keep account. It is true that of much of the past I am uncertain, just as I am uncertain of much of what is present if it be but dimly perceived. But the interval of time does not in principle alter my relation to the object, does not transform it from an object known into a mental state.... The things in the room here which I survey, and those in my distant home of which I think, the things of this minute and those of my long-vanished boyhood, influence and decide me alike, with a reality which my experience of them directly feels. They both make up my real world, they make it directly, they do not have first to be introduced to me and mediated by ideas which now and here arise within me.... This not-me character of my recollections and expectations does not imply that the external objects of which I am aware in those experiences should necessarily be there also for others. The objects of dreamers and hallucinated persons are wholly without general validity. But even were they centaurs and golden mountains, they still would be 'off there,' in fairy land, and not 'inside' of ourselves." [4]

This certainly is the immediate, primary, naïf, or practical way of taking our thought-of world. Were there no perceptual world to serve as its 'reductive,' in Taine's sense, by being 'stronger' and more genuinely 'outer' (so that the whole merely thought-of world seems weak and inner in comparison), our world of thought would be the only world, and would enjoy complete reality in our belief. This actually happens in our dreams, and in our day-dreams so long as percepts do not interrupt them.

And yet, just as the seen room (to go back to our late example) is *also* a field of consciousness, so the conceived or recollected room is *also* a state of mind; and the doubling-up of the experience has in both cases similar grounds.

The room thought-of, namely, has many thought-of couplings with many thought-of things. Some of these couplings are inconstant, others

[4] Hugo Münsterberg: *Grundzüge der Psychologie,* I, 48.

are stable. In the reader's personal history the room occupies a single date—he saw it only once perhaps, a year ago. Of the house's history, on the other hand, it forms a permanent ingredient. Some couplings have the curious stubbornness, to borrow Royce's term, of fact; others show the fluidity of fancy—we let them come and go as we please. Grouped with the rest of its house, with the name of its town, of its owner, builder, value, decorative plan, the room maintains a definite foothold, to which, if we try to loosen it, it tends to return, and to reassert itself with force. With these associates, in a word, it coheres, while to other houses, other towns, other owners, etc., it shows no tendency to cohere at all. The two collections, first of its cohesive, and, second, of its loose associates, inevitably come to be contrasted. We call the first collection the system of external realities, in the midst of which the room, as 'real,' exists; the other we call the stream of our internal thinking, in which, as a 'mental image,' it for a moment floats. *
The room thus again gets counted twice over. It plays two different rôles, being *Gedanke* and *Gedachtes*, the thought-of-an-object, and the object-thought-of, both in one; and all this without paradox or mystery, just as the same material thing may be both low and high, or small and great, or bad and good, because of its relations to opposite parts of an environing world.

As 'subjective' we say that the experience represents; as 'objective' it is represented. What represents and what is represented is here numerically the same; but we must remember that no dualism of being represented and representing resides in the experience *per se*. In its pure state, or when isolated, there is no self-splitting of it into consciousness and what the consciousness is 'of.' Its subjectivity and objectivity are functional attributes solely, realized only when the experience is 'taken,' *i.e.*, talked-of, twice, considered along with its two differing contexts respectively, by a new retrospective experience, of which that whole past complication now forms the fresh content.

The instant field of the present is at all times what I call the 'pure' experience. It is only virtually or potentially either object or subject as yet. For the time being, it is plain, unqualified actuality, or existence, a simple *that*. In this *naïf* immediacy it is of course *valid*; it is *there*; we *act* upon it; and the doubling of it in retrospection into a state of mind and a reality intended thereby, is just one of the acts. The 'state of mind,' first treated explicitly as such in retrospection, will stand corrected or confirmed, and the retrospective experience in its turn

---

* For simplicity's sake I confine my exposition to 'external' reality. But there is also the system of ideal reality in which the room plays its part. Relations of comparison, of classification, serial order, value, also are stubborn, assign a definite place to the room, unlike the incoherence of its places in the mere rhapsody of our successive thoughts.

will get a similar treatment; but the immediate experience in its passing is always 'truth,' practical truth, *something to act on*, at its own
movement. If the world were then and there to go out like a candle,
it would remain truth absolute and objective, for it would be 'the last
word,' would have no critic, and no one would ever oppose the thought
in it to the reality intended.

I think I may now claim to have made my thesis clear. Consciousness connotes a kind of external relation, and does not denote a special
stuff or way of being. *The peculiarity of our experiences, that they not
only are, but are known, which their 'conscious' quality is invoked to
explain, is better explained by their relations—these relations themselves being experiences—to one another.*

IV

Were I now to go on to treat of the knowing of perceptual by conceptual experiences, it would again prove to be an affair of external
relations. One experience would be the knower, the other the reality
known; and I could perfectly well define, without the notion of 'consciousness,' what the knowing actually and practically amounts to—
leading-towards, namely, and terminating-in percepts, through a series
of transitional experiences which the world supplies. But I will not
treat of this, space being insufficient.[5] I will rather consider a few
objections that are sure to be urged against the entire theory as it
stands.

V

First of all, this will be asked: "If experience has not 'conscious'
existence, if it be not partly made of 'consciousness,' of what then is
it made? Matter we know, and thought we know, and conscious content we know, but neutral and simple 'pure experience,' is something
we know not at all. Say *what* it consists of—for it must consist of something—or be willing to give it up."

To this challenge the reply is easy. Although for fluency's sake I
myself spoke early in this article of a stuff of pure experience, I have
now to say that there is no *general* stuff of which experience at large
is made. There are as many stuffs as there are 'natures' in the things
experienced. If you ask what any one bit of pure experience is made
of, the answer is always the same: "It is made of *that*, just what appears,
of space, of intensity, of flatness, brownness, heaviness, or what not.". . .
Experience is only a collective name for all these sensible natures, and
save for time and space (and, if you like, for 'being') there appears no
universal element of which all things are made.

[5] See *The Meaning of Truth*, 1-42, 43-50; *Essays in Radical Empiricism*, 52-61.

VI

The next objection is more formidable, in fact it sounds quite crushing when one hears it first.

"If it be the self-same piece of pure experience, taken twice over, that serves now as thought and now as thing"—so the objection runs—"how comes it that its attributes should differ so fundamentally in the two takings. As thing, the experience is extended; as thought, it occupies no space or place. As thing, it is red, hard, heavy; but who ever heard of a red, hard or heavy thought? Yet even now you said that an experience is made of just what appears, and what appears is just such adjectives. How can the one experience in its thing-function be made of them, consist of them, carry them as its own attributes, while in its thought-function it disowns them and attributes them elsewhere. There is a self-contradiction here from which the radical dualism of thought and thing is the only truth that can save us. Only if the thought is one kind of being can the adjectives exist in it 'intentionally' (to use the scholastic term); only if the thing is another kind, can they exist in it constitutively and energetically. No simple subject can take the same adjective and at one time be qualified by it, and at another time be merely 'of' it, as of something only meant or known."

The solution insisted on by this objector, like many other common-sense solutions, grows the less satisfactory the more one turns it in one's mind. To begin with, *are* thought and thing as heterogeneous as is commonly said?

No one denies that they have some categories in common. Their relations to time are identical. Both, moreover, may have parts (for psychologists in general treat thoughts as having them); and both may be complex or simple. Both are of kinds, can be compared, added and subtracted and arranged in serial orders. All sorts of adjectives qualify our thoughts which appear incompatible with consciousness, being as such a bare diaphaneity. For instance, they are natural and easy, or laborious. They are beautiful, happy, intense, interesting, wise, idiotic, focal, marginal, insipid, confused, vague, precise, rational, casual, general, particular, and many things besides. Moreover, the chapters on 'Perception' in the psychology-books are full of facts that make for the essential homogeneity of thought with thing. How, if 'subject' and 'object' were separated 'by the whole diameter of being,' and had no attributes in common, could it be so hard to tell, in a presented and recognized material object, what part comes in through the sense-organs and what part comes 'out of one's own head'? Sensations and apperceptive ideas fuse here so intimately that you can no more tell where one begins and the other ends, than you can tell, in those cunning circular panoramas that have lately been exhibited, where the real foreground and the painted canvas join together.

Descartes for the first time defined thought as the absolutely unextended, and later philosophers have accepted the description as correct. But what possible meaning has it to say that, when we think of a foot-rule or a square yard, extension is not attributable to our thought? Of every extended object the *adequate* mental picture must have all the extension of the object itself. The difference between objective and subjective extension is one of relation to a context solely. In the mind the various extents maintain no necessarily stubborn order relatively to each other, while in the physical world they bound each other stably, and, added together, make the great enveloping Unit which we believe in and call real Space. As 'outer,' they carry themselves adversely, so to speak, to one another, exclude one another and maintain their distances; while, as 'inner,' their order is loose, and they form a *durcheinander* in which unity is lost.* But to argue from this that inner experience is absolutely inextensive seems to me little short of absurd. The two worlds differ, not by the presence or absence of extension, but by the relations of the extensions which in both worlds exist.

Does not this case of extension now put us on the track of truth in the case of other qualities? It does; and I am surprised that the facts should not have been noticed long ago. Why, for example, do we call a fire hot, and water wet, and yet refuse to say that our mental state, when it is 'of' these objects, is either wet or hot? 'Intentionally,' at any rate, and when the mental state is a vivid image, hotness and wetness are in it just as much as they are in the physical experience. The reason is this, that, as the general chaos of all our experiences gets sifted, we find that there are some fires that will always burn sticks and always warm our bodies, and that there are some waters that will always put out fires; while there are other fires and waters that will not act at all. The general group of experiences that *act*, that do not only possess their natures intrinsically, but wear them adjectively and energetically, turning them against one another, comes inevitably to be contrasted with the group whose members, having identically the same natures, fail to manifest them in the 'energetic' way. I make for myself now an experience of blazing fire; I place it near my body; but it does not warm me in the least. I lay a stick upon it, and the stick either burns or remains green, as I please. I call up water, and pour it on the fire, and absolutely no difference ensues. I account for all such facts by calling this whole train of experiences unreal, a mental train. Mental fire is what won't burn real sticks; mental water is what won't necessarily

---

* I speak here of the complete inner life in which the mind plays freely with its materials. Of course the mind's free play is restricted when it seeks to copy real things in real space.

(though of course it may) put out even a mental fire. Mental knives may be sharp, but they won't cut real wood. Mental triangles are pointed, but their points won't wound. With 'real' objects, on the contrary, consequences always accrue; and thus the real experiences get sifted from the mental ones, the things from our thoughts of them, fanciful or true, and precipitated together as the stable part of the whole experience-chaos, under the name of the physical world. Of this our perceptual experiences are the nucleus, they being the originally *strong* experiences. We add a lot of conceptual experiences to them, making these strong also in imagination, and building out the remoter parts of the physical world by their means; and around this core of reality the world of laxly connected fancies and mere rhapsodical objects floats like a bank of clouds. In the clouds, all sorts of rules are violated which in the core are kept. Extensions there can be indefinitely located; motion there obeys no Newton's laws.

VII

There is a peculiar class of experiences to which, whether we take them as subjective or as objective, we *assign* their several natures as attributes, because in both contexts they affect their associates actively, though in neither quite as 'strongly' or as sharply as things affect one another by their physical energies. I refer here to *appreciations,* which form an ambiguous sphere of being, belonging with emotion on the one hand, and having objective 'value' on the other, yet seeming not quite inner nor quite outer, as if a diremption had begun but had not made itself complete.

Experiences of painful objects, for example, are usually also painful experiences; perceptions of loveliness, of ugliness, tend to pass muster as lovely or as ugly perceptions; intuitions of the morally lofty are lofty intuitions. Sometimes the adjective wanders as if uncertain where to fix itself. Shall we speak of seductive visions or of visions of seductive things? Of wicked desires or of desires for wickedness? Of healthy thoughts or of thoughts of healthy objects? Of good impulses, or of impulses towards the good? Of feelings of anger, or of angry feelings? Both in the mind and in the thing, these natures modify their context, exclude certain associates and determine others, have their mates and incompatibles. Yet not as stubbornly as in the case of physical qualities, for beauty and ugliness, love and hatred, pleasant and painful can, in certain complex experiences, coexist.

If one were to make an evolutionary construction of how a lot of originally chaotic pure experiences became gradually differentiated into an orderly inner and outer world, the whole theory would turn upon one's success in explaining how or why the quality of an experience, once active, could become less so, and, from being an energetic attribute in some cases, elsewhere lapse into the status of an inert or merely internal 'nature.' This would be the 'evolution' of the psychical from the bosom of the physical, in which the esthetic, moral and otherwise emotional experiences would represent a halfway stage.

VIII

But a last cry of *non possumus* will probably go up from many readers. "All very pretty as a piece of ingenuity," they will say, "but our consciousness itself intuitively contradicts you. We, for our part, *know* that we are conscious. We *feel* our thought, flowing as a life within us, in absolute contrast with the objects which it so unremittingly escorts. We can not be faithless to this immediate intuition. The dualism is a fundamental *datum:* Let no man join what God has put asunder."

My reply to this is my last word, and I greatly grieve that to many it will sound materialistic. I can not help that, however, for I, too, have my intuitions and I must obey them. Let the case be what it may in others, I am as confident as I am of anything that, in myself, the stream of thinking (which I recognize emphatically as a phenomenon) is only a careless name for what, when scrutinized, reveals itself to consist chiefly of the stream of my breathing. The 'I think' which Kant said must be able to accompany all my objects, is the 'I breathe' which actually does accompany them. There are other internal facts besides breathing (intracephalic muscular adjustments, etc., of which I have said a word in my larger *Psychology* [6]), and these increase the assets of 'consciousness,' so far as the latter is subject to immediate perception; but breath, which was ever the original of 'spirit,' breath moving outwards, between the glottis and the nostrils, is, I am persuaded, the essence out of which philosophers have constructed the entity known to them as consciousness. *That entity is fictitious, while thoughts in the concrete are fully real. But thoughts in the concrete are made of the same stuff as things are....*

4. The Continuity of Experience [7]

... THE CONCRETE PULSES of experience appear pent in by no such definite limits as our conceptual substitutes for them are confined by. They run into one another continuously and seem to interpenetrate. What in them is relation and what is matter related is hard to discern. You feel no one of them as inwardly simple, and no two as wholly with-

[6] I, 299-305.
[7] From *A Pluralistic Universe* (copyright 1909 by William James and 1936 by Henry James), pp. 282-290, 309-312; by permission of Paul R. Reynolds & Son.

out confluence where they touch. There is no datum so small as not to show this mystery, if mystery it be. The tiniest feeling that we can possibly have comes with an earlier and a later part and with a sense of their continuous procession.... If we do not feel both past and present in one field of feeling, we feel them not at all. We have the same many-in-one in the matter that fills the passing time. The rush of our thought forward through its fringes is the everlasting peculiarity of its life. We realize this life as something always off its balance, something in transition, something that shoots out of a darkness through a dawn into a brightness that we feel to be the dawn fulfilled. In the very midst of the continuity our experience comes as an alteration. 'Yes,' we say at the full brightness, '*this* is what I just meant.' 'No,' we feel at the dawning, 'this is not yet the full meaning, there is more to come.' In every crescendo of sensation, in every effort to recall, in every progress towards the satisfaction of desire, this succession of an emptiness and fulness that have reference to each other and are one flesh is the essence of the phenomenon. In every hindrance of desire the sense of an ideal presence which is absent in fact, of an absent, in a word, which the only function of the present is to *mean,* is even more notoriously there. And in the movement of pure thought we have the same phenomenon. When I say *Socrates is mortal,* the moment *Socrates* is incomplete; it falls forward through the *is* which is pure movement, into the *mortal* which is indeed bare mortal on the tongue, but for the mind is *that mortal,* the *mortal Socrates,* at last satisfactorily disposed of and told off.

Here, then, inside of the minimal pulses of experience, is realized that very inner complexity which the transcendentalists say only the absolute can genuinely possess. The gist of the matter is always the same—something ever goes indissolubly with something else. You cannot separate the same from its other, except by abandoning the real altogether and taking to the conceptual system. What is immediately given in the single and particular instance is always something pooled and mutual, something with no dark spot, no point of ignorance. No one elementary bit of reality is eclipsed from the next bit's point of view, if only we take reality sensibly and in small enough pulses—and by us it has to be taken pulse-wise, for our span of consciousness is too short to grasp the larger collectivity of things except nominally and abstractly. No more of reality collected together at once is extant anywhere, perhaps, than in my experience of reading this page, or in yours of listening; yet within those bits of experience as they come to pass we get a fulness of content that no conceptual description can equal. Sensational experiences *are* their 'own others,' then, both internally and externally. Inwardly they are one with their parts, and outwardly they pass continuously into their next neighbors, so that events separated by years of time in a man's life hang together unbrokenly by the intermediary events. Their *names,* to be sure, cut them into separate conceptual entities, but no cuts existed in the continuum in which they originally came.

If, with all this in our mind, we turn to our own particular predicament, we see that our old objection to the self-compounding of states of consciousness, our accusation that it was impossible for purely logical reasons, is unfounded in principle. Every smallest state of consciousness, concretely taken, overflows its own definition. Only concepts are self-identical; only 'reason' deals with closed equations; nature is but a name for excess; every point in her opens out and runs into the more; and the only question, with reference to any point we may be considering, is how far into the rest of nature we may have to go in order to get entirely beyond its overflow. In the pulse of inner life immediately present now in each of us is a little past, a little future, a little awareness of our own body, of each other's persons, of these sublimities we are trying to talk about, of the earth's geography and the direction of history, of truth and error, of good and bad, and of who knows how much more? Feeling, however dimly and subconsciously, all these things, your pulse of inner life is continuous with them, belongs to them and they to it. You can't identify it with either one of them rather than with the others, for if you let it develop into no matter which of those directions, what it develops into will look back on it and say, 'That was the original germ of me.'

In *principle,* then, the real units of our immediately-felt life are unlike the units that intellectualist logic holds to and makes its calculations with. They are not separate from their own others, and you have to take them at widely separated dates to find any two of them that seem unblent. Then indeed they do appear separate even as their concepts are separate; a chasm yawns between them; but the chasm itself is but an intellectualist fiction, got by abstracting from the continuous sheet of experiences with which the intermediary time was filled. It is like the log carried first by William and Henry, then by William, Henry, and John, then by Henry and John, then by John and Peter, and so on. All real units of experience *overlap.* Let a row of equidistant dots on a sheet of paper symbolize the concepts by which we intellectualize the world. Let a ruler long enough to cover at least three dots stand for our sensible experience. Then the conceived changes of the sensible experience can be symbolized by sliding the ruler along the line of dots. One concept after another will apply to it, one after another drop away, but it will always cover at least two of them, and no dots less than three will ever adequately cover *it.* You falsify it if you treat it conceptually, or by the law of dots.

What is true here of successive states must also be true of simultaneous characters. They also overlap each other with their being. My present field of consciousness is a centre surrounded by a fringe that shades insensibly into a subconscious more. I use three separate terms here to describe this fact; but I might as well use three hundred, for the fact is all shades and no boundaries. Which part of it properly is in my consciousness, which out? If I name what is out, it already has come in. The centre works in one way while the margins work in another, and presently overpower the centre and are central themselves. What we conceptually identify ourselves with and say we are thinking of at any time is the centre; but our *full* self is the whole field, with all those indefinitely radiating subconscious possibilities of increase that we can only feel without conceiving, and can hardly begin to analyze. The collective and the distributive ways of being coexist here, for each part functions distinctly, makes connection with its own peculiar region in the still wider rest of experience and tends to draw us into that line, and yet the whole is somehow felt as one pulse of our life—not conceived so, but felt so.

In principle, then, as I said, intellectualism's edge is broken; it can only approximate to reality, and its logic is inapplicable to our inner life, which spurns its vetoes and mocks at its impossibilities. Every bit of us at every moment is part and parcel of a wider self, it quivers along various radii like the wind-rose on a compass, and the actual in it is continuously one with possibles not yet in our present sight.* And just as we are co-conscious with our own momentary margin, may not we ourselves form the margin of some more really central self in things which is co-conscious with the whole of us? May not you and I be confluent in a higher consciousness, and confluently active there, tho we now know it not? . . . .

In spite of rationalism's disdain for the particular, the personal, and the unwholesome, the drift of all the evidence we have seems to me to sweep us very strongly towards the belief in some form of super-human life with which we may, unknown to ourselves, be co-conscious. We may be in the universe as dogs and cats are in our libraries, seeing the books and hearing the conversation, but having no inkling of the meaning of it all. The intellectualist objections to this fall away when the authority of intellectualist logic is undermined by criticism, and then the positive empirical evidence remains. The analogies with ordinary psychology and with the facts of pathology, with those of psychical research, so called, and with those of religious experience, establish, when taken together, a decidedly *formidable* probability in favor of a

---

* The conscious self of the moment, the central self, is probably determined to this privileged position by its functional connection with the body's imminent or present acts. It is the present *acting* self. Tho the more that surrounds it may be 'subconscious' to us, yet if in its 'collective capacity' it also exerts an active function, it may be conscious in a wider way, conscious, as it were, over our heads.

general view of the world almost identical with Fechner's. The out-lines of the superhuman consciousness thus made probable must re-main, however, very vague, and the number of functionally distinct 'selves' it comports and carries has to be left entirely problematic. It may be polytheistically or it may be monotheistically conceived of. Fechner, with his distinct earth-soul functioning as our guardian angel, seems to me clearly polytheistic; but the word 'polytheism' usually gives offence, so perhaps it is better not to use it. Only one thing is certain, and that is the result of our criticism of the absolute: the only way to escape from the paradoxes and perplexities that a consist-ently thought-out monistic universe suffers from as from a species of auto-intoxication—the mystery of the 'fall' namely, of reality lapsing into appearance, truth into error, perfection into imperfection; of evil, in short; the mystery of universal determinism, of the block-universe eternal and without a history, etc.;—the only way of escape, I say, from all this is to be frankly pluralistic and assume that the superhuman consciousness, however vast it may be, has itself an external environ-ment, and consequently is finite. Present day monism carefully repudi-ates complicity with spinozistic monism. In that, it explains, the many get dissolved in the one and lost, whereas in the improved idealistic form they get preserved in all their manyness as the one's eternal ob-ject. The absolute itself is thus represented by absolutists as having a pluralistic object. But if even the absolute has to have a pluralistic vision, why should we ourselves hesitate to be pluralistic on our own sole account? Why should we envelop our many with the 'one' that brings so much poison in its train?

The line of least resistance, then, as it seems to me, both in theology and in philosophy, is to accept, along with the superhuman conscious-ness, the notion that it is not all-embracing, the notion, in other words, that there is a God, but that he is finite, either in power or in knowl-edge, or in both at once. These, I need hardly tell you, are the terms in which common men have usually carried on their active commerce with God; and the monistic perfections that make the notion of him so paradoxical practically and morally are the colder addition of remote professorial minds operating *in distans* upon conceptual substitutes for him alone.

Why cannot 'experience' and 'reason' meet on this common ground? Why cannot they compromise? May not the godlessness usually but needlessly associated with the philosophy of immediate experience give way to a theism now seen to follow directly from that experience more widely taken? and may not rationalism, satisfied with seeing her *a priori* proofs of God so effectively replaced by empirical evidence, abate something of her absolutist claims? Let God but have the least infinitesimal *other* of any kind beside him, and empiricism and rationalism might strike hands in a lasting treaty of peace. Both might then leave abstract thinness behind them, and seek together, as scientific men seek, by using all the analogies and data within reach, to build up the most probable approximate idea of what the divine consciousness concretely may be like. . . .

5. The Moral Philosopher and the Moral Life [8]

THE MAIN PURPOSE of this paper is to show that there is no such thing possible as an ethical philosophy dogmatically made up in advance. We all help to determine the content of ethical philosophy so far as we contribute to the race's moral life. In other words, there can be no final truth in ethics any more than in physics, until the last man has had his experience and said his say. In the one case as in the other, however, the hypotheses which we now make while waiting, and the acts to which they prompt us, are among the indispensable conditions which determine what that 'say' shall be.

First of all, what is the position of him who seeks an ethical philosophy? To begin with, he must be distinguished from all those who are satisfied to be ethical sceptics. He *will* not be a sceptic; therefore so far from ethical scepticism being one possible fruit of ethical philosophizing, it can only be regarded as that residual alternative to all philosophy which from the outset menaces every would-be philosopher who may give up the quest discouraged, and renounce his original aim. That aim is to find an account of the moral relations that obtain among things, which will weave them into the unity of a stable system, and make of the world what one may call a genuine universe from the ethical point of view. So far as the world resists reduction to the form of unity, so far as ethical propositions seem unstable, so far does the philosopher fail of his ideal. The subject-matter of his study is the ideals he finds existing in the world; the purpose which guides him is this ideal of his own, of getting them into a certain form. This ideal is thus a factor in ethical philosophy whose legitimate presence must never be overlooked; it is a positive contribution which the philosopher himself necessarily makes to the problem. But it is his only positive contribution. At the outset of his inquiry he ought to have no other ideals. Were he interested peculiarly in the triumph of any one kind

[8] Pages 184-210 of *The Will to Believe and Other Essays in Popular Philosophy* (copyright 1896 by William James), reprinted by permission of Paul R. Reynolds. (From an address to the Yale Philosophical Club, published in the *International Journal of Ethics*, April, 1891. The complete text may also be found in *Essays on Faith and Morals* by William James, New York, Longmans, Green and Co., 1943.)

of good, he would *pro tanto* cease to be a judicial investigator, and become an advocate for some limited element of the case.

There are three questions in ethics which must be kept apart. Let them be called respectively the *psychological* question, the *metaphysical* question, and the *casuistic* question. The psychological question asks after the historical *origin* of our moral ideas and judgments; the metaphysical question asks what the very *meaning* of the words 'good,' 'ill,' and 'obligation' are; the casuistic question asks what is the *measure* of the various goods and ills which men recognize, so that the philosopher may settle the true order of human obligations.

I

The psychological question is for most disputants the only question. When your ordinary doctor of divinity has proved to his own satisfaction that an altogether unique faculty called 'conscience' must be postulated to tell us what is right and what is wrong; or when your popular-science enthusiast has proclaimed that 'apriorism' is an exploded superstition, and that our moral judgments have gradually resulted from the teaching of the environment, each of these persons thinks that ethics is settled and nothing more is to be said. The familiar pair of names, Intuitionist and Evolutionist, so commonly used now to connote all possible differences in ethical opinion, really refer to the psychological question alone. The discussion of this question hinges so much upon particular details that it is impossible to enter upon it at all within the limits of this paper. I will therefore only express dogmatically my own belief, which is this—that the Benthams, the Mills, and the Bains have done a lasting service in taking so many of our human ideals and showing how they must have arisen from the association with acts of simple bodily pleasures and reliefs from pain. Association with many remote pleasures will unquestionably make a thing significant of goodness in our minds; and the more vaguely the goodness is conceived of, the more mysterious will its source appear to be. But it is surely impossible to explain all our sentiments and preferences in this simple way. The more minutely psychology studies human nature, the more clearly it finds there traces of secondary affections, relating the impressions of the environment with one another and with our impulses in quite different ways from those mere associations of coexistence and succession which are practically all that pure empiricism can admit. Take the love of drunkenness; take bashfulness, the terror of high places, the tendency to sea-sickness, to faint at the sight of blood, the susceptibility to musical sounds; take the emotion of the comical, the passion for poetry, for mathematics, or for metaphysics—no one of these things can be wholly explained by either association or utility. They *go with* other things that can be so explained, no doubt; and some of them are prophetic of future utilities, since there is nothing in us for which some use may not be found. But their origin is in incidental complications to our cerebral structure, a structure whose original features arose with no reference to the perception of such discords and harmonies as these.

Well, a vast number of our moral perceptions also are certainly of this secondary and brain-born kind. They deal with directly felt fitnesses between things, and often fly in the teeth of all the prepossessions of habit and presumptions of utility. The moment you get beyond the coarser and more commonplace moral maxims, the Decalogues and Poor Richard's Almanacs, you fall into schemes and positions which to the eye of common-sense are fantastic and overstrained. The sense for abstract justice which some persons have is as eccentric a variation, from the natural-history point of view, as is the passion for music or for the higher philosophical consistencies which consumes the soul of others. The feeling of the inward dignity of certain spiritual attitudes, as peace, serenity, simplicity, veracity; and of the essential vulgarity of others, as querulousness, anxiety, egoistic fussiness, etc.—are quite inexplicable except by an innate preference of the more ideal attitude for its own pure sake. The nobler thing *tastes* better, and that is all that we can say. 'Experience' of consequences may truly teach us what things are *wicked,* but what have consequences to do with what is *mean* and *vulgar?* If a man has shot his wife's paramour, by reason of what subtile repugnancy in things is it that we are so disgusted when we hear that the wife and the husband have made it up and are living comfortably together again? Or if the hypothesis were offered us of a world in which Messrs. Fourier's and Bellamy's and Morris's utopias should all be outdone, and millions kept permanently happy on the one simple condition that a certain lost soul on the far-off edge of things should lead a life of lonely torture, what except a specifical and independent sort of emotion can it be which would make us immediately feel, even though an impulse arose within us to clutch at the happiness so offered, how hideous a thing would be its enjoyment when deliberately accepted as the fruit of such a bargain? To what, once more, but subtile brain-born feelings of discord can be due all these recent protests against the entire race-tradition of retributive justice? —I refer to Tolstoi with his ideas of non-resistance, to Mr. Bellamy with his substitution of oblivion for repentance (in his novel of Dr. Heidenhain's Process), to M. Guyau with his radical condemnation of the punitive ideal. All these subtleties of the moral sensibility go as much beyond what can be ciphered out from the 'laws of association' as the delicacies of sentiment possible between a pair of young lovers go beyond such precepts of the 'etiquette to be observed during engagement' as are printed in the manuals of social form.

No! Purely inward forces are certainly at work here. All the higher, more penetrating ideals are revolutionary. They present themselves far less in the guise of effects of past experience than in that of probable causes of future experience, factors to which the environment and the lessons it has so far taught us must learn to bend.

This is all I can say of the psychological question now. In the last chapter of a recent work * I have sought to prove in a general way the existence, in our thought, of relations which do not merely repeat the couplings of experience. Our ideals have certainly many sources. They are not all explicable as signifying corporeal pleasures to be gained, and pains to be escaped. And for having so constantly perceived this psychological fact, we must applaud the intuitionist school. Whether or not such applause must be extended to that school's other characteristics will appear as we take up the following questions.

The next one in order is the metaphysical question, of what we mean by the words 'obligation,' 'good,' and 'ill.'

II

First of all, it appears that such words can have no application or relevancy in a world in which no sentient life exists. Imagine an absolutely material world, containing only physical and chemical facts, and existing from eternity without a God, without even an interested spectator: would there be any sense in saying of that world that one of its states is better than another? Or if there were two such worlds possible, would there be any rhyme or reason in calling one good and the other bad—good or bad positively, I mean, and apart from the fact that one might relate itself better than the other to the philosopher's private interests? But we must leave these private interests out of the account, for the philosopher is a mental fact, and we are asking whether goods and evils and obligations exist in physical facts *per se*. Surely there is no *status* for good and evil to exist in, in a purely insentient world. How can one physical fact, considered simply as a physical fact, be 'better' than another? Betterness is not a physical relation. In its mere material capacity, a thing can no more be good or bad than it can be pleasant or painful. Good for what? Good for the production of another physical fact, do you say? But what in a purely physical universe demands the production of that other fact? Physical facts simply *are* or are *not;* and neither when present or absent, can they be supposed to make demands. If they do, they can only do so by having desires; and then they have ceased to be purely physical facts, and have become facts of conscious sensibility. Goodness, badness, and obligation must

* *The Principles of Psychology* (New York, H. Holt & Co., 1890).

be *realized* somewhere in order really to exist; and the first step in ethical philosophy is to see that no merely inorganic 'nature of things' can realize them. Neither moral relations nor the moral law can swing *in vacuo*. Their only habitat can be a mind which feels them; and no world composed of merely physical facts can possibly be a world to which ethical propositions apply.

The moment one sentient being, however, is made a part of the universe, there is a chance for goods and evils really to exist. Moral relations now have their *status*, in that being's consciousness. So far as he feels anything to be good, he *makes* it good. It *is* good, for him; and being good for him, is absolutely good, for he is the sole creator of values in that universe, and outside of his opinion things have no moral character at all.

In such a universe as that it would of course be absurd to raise the question of whether the solitary thinker's judgments of good and ill are true or not. Truth supposes a standard outside of the thinker to which he must conform; but here the thinker is a sort of divinity, subject to no higher judge. Let us call the supposed universe which he inhabits a *moral solitude*. In such a moral solitude it is clear that there can be no outward obligation, and that the only trouble the god-like thinker is liable to have will be over the consistency of his own several ideals with one another. Some of these will no doubt be more pungent and appealing than the rest, their goodness will have a profounder, more penetrating taste; they will return to haunt him with more obstinate regrets if violated. So the thinker will have to order his life with them as its chief determinants, or else remain inwardly discordant and unhappy. Into whatever equilibrium he may settle, though, and however he may straighten out his system, it will be a right system; for beyond the facts of his own subjectivity there is nothing moral in the world.

If now we introduce a second thinker with his likes and dislikes into the universe, the ethical situation becomes much more complex, and several possibilities are immediately seen to obtain.

One of these is that the thinkers may ignore each other's attitude about good and evil altogether, and each continue to indulge his own preferences, indifferent to what the other may feel or do. In such a case we have a world with twice as much of the ethical quality in it as our moral solitude, only it is without ethical unity. The same object is good or bad there, according as you measure it by the view which this one or that one of the thinkers takes. Nor can you find any possible ground in such a world for saying that one thinker's opinion is more correct than the other's, or that either has the truer moral sense. Such a world, in short, is not a moral universe but a moral dualism. Not only is there no single point of view within it from which the values of things can be unequivocally judged, but there is not even a demand for such a point of view, since the two thinkers are supposed to be indifferent to each other's thoughts and acts. Multiply the thinkers into a pluralism, and we find realized for us in the ethical sphere something like that world which the antique sceptics conceived of—in which individual minds are the measures of all things, and in which no 'objective' truth, but only a multitude of 'subjective' opinions, can be found.

But this is the kind of world with which the philosopher, so long as he holds to the hope of a philosophy, will not put up. Among the various ideals represented, there must be, he thinks, some which have the more truth or authority; and to these the others *ought* to yield, so that system and subordination may reign. Here in the word 'ought' the notion of *obligation* comes emphatically into view, and the next thing in order must be to make its meaning clear.

Since the outcome of the discussion so far has been to show us that nothing can be good or right except so far as some consciousness feels it to be good, or thinks it to be right, we perceive on the very threshold that the real superiority and authority which are postulated by the philosopher to reside in some of the opinions, and the really inferior character which he supposes must belong to others, cannot be explained by any abstract moral 'nature of things' existing antecedently to the concrete thinkers themselves with their ideals. Like the positive attributes good and bad, the comparative ones better and worse must be *realized* in order to be real. If one ideal judgment be objectively better than another, that betterness must be made flesh by being lodged concretely in some one's actual perception. It cannot float in the atmosphere, for it is not a sort of meteorological phenomenon, like the aurora borealis or the zodiacal light. Its *esse* is *percipi*, like the *esse* of the ideals themselves between which it obtains. The philosopher, therefore, who seeks to know which ideal ought to have supreme weight and which one ought to be subordinated, must trace the *ought* itself to the *de facto* constitution of some existing consciousness, behind which, as one of the data of the universe, he as a purely ethical philosopher is unable to go. This consciousness must make the one ideal right by feeling it to be right, the other wrong by feeling it to be wrong. But now what particular consciousness in the universe *can* enjoy this prerogative of obliging others to conform to a rule which it lays down?

If one of the thinkers were obviously divine, while all the rest were human, there would probably be no practical dispute about the matter. The divine thought would be the model, to which the others should conform. But still the theoretic question would remain, What is the ground of the obligation, even here?

In our first essays at answering this question, there is an inevitable tendency to slip into an assumption which ordinary men follow when they are disputing with one another about questions of good and bad. They imagine an abstract moral order in which the objective truth resides; and each tries to prove that this pre-existing order is more accurately reflected in his own ideas than in those of his adversary. It is because one disputant is backed by this overarching abstract order that we think the other should submit. Even so, when it is a question no longer of two finite thinkers, but of God and ourselves—we follow our usual habit, and imagine a sort of *de jure* relation, which antedates and overarches the mere facts, and would make it right that we should conform our thoughts to God's thoughts, even though he made no claim to that effect, and though we preferred *de facto* to go on thinking for ourselves.

But the moment we take a steady look at the question, *we see not only that without a claim actually made by some concrete person there can be no obligation, but that there is some obligation wherever there is a claim.* Claim and obligation are, in fact, coextensive terms; they cover each other exactly. Our ordinary attitude of regarding ourselves as subject to an overarching system of moral relations, true 'in themselves,' is therefore either an out-and-out superstition, or else it must be treated as a merely provisional abstraction from that real Thinker in whose actual demand upon us to think as he does our obligation must be ultimately based. In a theistic ethical philosophy that thinker in question is, of course, the Deity to whom the existence of the universe is due.

I know well how hard it is for those who are accustomed to what I have called the superstitious view, to realize that every *de facto* claim creates in so far forth an obligation. We inveterately think that something which we call the 'validity' of the claim is what gives to it its obligatory character, and that this validity is something outside of the claim's mere existence as a matter of fact. It rains down upon the claim, we think, from some sublime dimension of being, which the moral law inhabits, much as upon the steel of the compass-needle the influence of the Pole rains down from out of the starry heavens. But again, how can such an inorganic abstract character of imperativeness, additional to the imperativeness which is in the concrete claim itself, *exist?* Take any demand, however slight, which any creature, however weak, may make. Ought it not, for its own sole sake, to be satisfied? If not, prove why not. The only possible kind of proof you could adduce would be the exhibition of another creature who should make a demand that ran the other way. The only possible reason there can be why any phenomenon ought to exist is that such a phenomenon actually is desired. Any desire is imperative to the extent of its amount; it *makes* itself valid by the fact that it exists at all. Some desires, truly enough, are small desires; they are put forward by insignificant persons, and we customarily make light of the obligations which they bring. But the fact that such personal demands as these impose small obligations does not keep the largest obligations from being personal demands.

If we must talk impersonally, to be sure we can say that 'the universe' requires, exacts, or makes obligatory such or such an action, whenever it expresses itself through the desires of such or such a creature. But it is better not to talk about the universe in this personified way, unless we believe in a universal or divine consciousness which actually exists. If there be such a consciousness, then its demands carry the most of obligation simply because they are the greatest in amount. But it is even then not *abstractly* right that we should respect them. It is only *concretely* right—or right after the fact, and by virtue of the fact, that they are actually made. Suppose we do not respect them, as seems largely to be the case in this queer world. That ought not to be, we say; that is wrong. But in what way is this fact of wrongness made more acceptable or intelligible when we imagine it to consist rather in the laceration of an *à priori* ideal order than in the disappointment of a living personal God? Do we, perhaps, think that we cover God and protect him and make his impotence over us less ultimate, when we back him up with this *à priori* blanket from which he may draw some warmth of further appeal? But the only force of appeal to *us*, which either a living God or an abstract ideal order can wield, is found in the 'everlasting ruby vaults' of our own human hearts, as they happen to beat responsive and not irresponsive to the claim. So far as they do feel it when made by a living consciousness, it is life answering to life. A claim thus livingly acknowledged is acknowledged with a solidity and fulness which no thought of an 'ideal' backing can render more complete; while if, on the other hand, the heart's response is withheld, the stubborn phenomenon is there of an impotence in the claims which the universe embodies, which no talk about an eternal nature of things can glaze over or dispel. An ineffective *à priori* order is as impotent a thing as an ineffective God; and in the eye of philosophy it is as hard a thing to explain.

We may now consider that what we distinguished as the metaphysical question in ethical philosophy is sufficiently answered, and that we have learned what the words 'good,' 'bad,' and 'obligation' severally mean. They mean no absolute natures, independent of personal support. They are objects of feeling and desire, which have no foothold or anchorage in Being, apart from the existence of actually living minds.

Wherever such minds exist, with judgments of good and ill, and demands upon one another, there is an ethical world in its essential features. Were all other things, gods and men and starry heavens, blotted out from this universe, and were there left but one rock with two loving souls upon it, that rock would have as thoroughly moral a constitution as any possible world which the eternities and immensities could harbor. It would be a tragic constitution, because the rock's inhabitants would die. But while they lived, there would be real good things and real bad things in the universe; there would be obligations, claims, and expectations; obediences, refusals, and disappointments; compunctions, and longings for harmony to come again, and inward peace of conscience when it was restored; there would, in short, be a moral life, whose active energy would have no limit but the intensity of interest in each other with which the hero and heroine might be endowed.

We, on this terrestrial globe, so far as the visible facts go, are just like the inhabitants of such a rock. Whether a God exist, or whether no God exist, in yon blue heaven above us bent, we form at any rate an ethical republic here below. And the first reflection which this leads to is that ethics have as genuine and real a foothold in a universe where the highest consciousness is human, as in a universe where there is a God as well. 'The religion of humanity' affords a basis for ethics as well as theism does. Whether the purely human system can gratify the philosopher's demand as well as the other is a different question, which we ourselves must answer ere we close.

III

The last fundamental question in Ethics was, it will be remembered, the *casuistic* question. Here we are, in a world where the existence of a divine thinker has been and perhaps always will be doubted by some of the lookers-on, and where, in spite of the presence of a large number of ideals in which human beings agree, there are a mass of others about which no general consensus obtains. It is hardly necessary to present a literary picture of this, for the facts are too well known. The wars of the flesh and the spirit in each man, the concupiscences of different individuals pursuing the same unshareable material or social prizes, the ideals which contrast so according to races, circumstances, temperaments, philosophical beliefs, etc.—all form a maze of apparently inextricable confusion with no obvious Ariadne's thread to lead one out. Yet the philosopher, just because he is a philosopher, adds his own peculiar ideal to the confusion (with which if he were willing to be a sceptic he would be passably content), and insists that over all these individual opinions there is a *system of truth* which he can discover if he only takes sufficient pains.

We stand ourselves at present in the place of that philosopher, and must not fail to realize all the features that the situation comports. In the first place we will not be sceptics; we hold to it that there is a truth to be ascertained. But in the second place we have just gained the insight that that truth cannot be a self-proclaiming set of laws, or an abstract 'moral reason,' but can only exist in act, or in the shape of an opinion held by some thinker really to be found. There is, however, no visible thinker invested with authority. Shall we then simply proclaim our own ideals as the lawgiving ones? No; for if we are true philosophers we must throw our own spontaneous ideals, even the dearest, impartially in with that total mass of ideals which are fairly to be judged. But how then can we as philosophers ever find a test; how avoid complete moral scepticism on the one hand, and on the other escape bringing a wayward personal standard of our own along with us, on which we simply pin our faith?

The dilemma is a hard one, nor does it grow a bit more easy as we revolve it in our minds. The entire undertaking of the philosopher obliges him to seek an impartial test. That test, however, must be incarnated in the demand of some actually existent person; and how can he pick out the person save by an act in which his own sympathies and prepossessions are implied?

One method indeed presents itself, and has as a matter of history been taken by the more serious ethical schools. If the heap of things demanded proved on inspection less chaotic than at first they seemed, if they furnished their own relative test and measure, then the casuistic problem would be solved. If it were found that all goods *quâ* goods contained a common essence, then the amount of this essence involved in any one good would show its rank in the scale of goodness, and order could be quickly made; for this essence would be *the* good upon which all thinkers were agreed, the relatively objective and universal good that the philosopher seeks. Even his own private ideals would be measured by their share of it, and find their rightful place among the rest.

Various essences of good have thus been found and proposed as bases of the ethical system. Thus, to be a mean between two extremes; to be recognized by a special intuitive faculty; to make the agent happy for the moment; to make others as well as him happy in the long run; to add to his perfection or dignity; to harm no one; to follow from reason or flow from universal law; to be in accordance with the will of God; to promote the survival of the human species on this planet—are so many tests, each of which has been maintained by somebody to constitute the essence of all good things or actions so far as they are good.

No one of the measures that have been actually proposed has, however, given general satisfaction. Some are obviously not universally present in all cases—*e.g.*, the character of harming no one, or that of following a universal law; for the best course is often cruel; and many acts are reckoned good on the sole condition that they be exceptions, and serve not as examples of a universal law. Other characters, such as following the will of God, are unascertainable and vague. Others again, like survival, are quite indeterminate in their consequences, and leave us in the lurch where we most need their help: a philosopher of the Sioux Nation, for example, will be certain to use the survival-criterion in a very different way from ourselves. The best, on the whole, of these marks and measures of goodness seems to be the capacity to bring happiness. But in order not to break down fatally, this test must be taken to cover innumerable acts and impulses that never *aim* at happiness; so that, after all, in seeking for a universal principle we inevitably are carried onward to the *most* universal principle—that *the essence of good is simply to satisfy demand.* The demand may be for anything under the sun. There is really no more ground for supposing that all our demands can be accounted for by one universal underlying kind of motive than there is ground for supposing that all physical phenomena are cases of a single law. The elementary forces in ethics are probably as plural as those of physics are. The various ideals have no common character apart from the fact that they are ideals. No single abstract principle can be so used as to yield to the philosopher anything like a scientifically accurate and genuinely useful casuistic scale.

A look at another peculiarity of the ethical universe, as we find it, will still further show us the philosopher's perplexities. As a purely theoretic problem, namely, the casuistic question would hardly ever come up at all. If the ethical philosopher were only asking after the best *imaginable* system of goods he would indeed have an easy task; for all demands as such are *primâ facie* respectable, and the best simply imaginary world would be one in which *every* demand was gratified as soon as made. Such a world would, however, have to have a physical constitution entirely different from that of the one which we inhabit. It would need not only a space, but a time, 'of *n*-dimensions,' to include all the acts and experiences incompatible with one another here below, which would then go on in conjunction—such as spending our money, yet growing rich; taking our holiday, yet getting ahead with our work; shooting and fishing, yet doing no hurt to the beasts; gaining no end of experience, yet keeping our youthful freshness of heart; and the like. There can be no question that such a system of things, however brought about, would be the absolutely ideal system; and that if a philosopher could create universes *à priori*, and provide all the mechanical conditions, that is the sort of universe which he should unhesitatingly create.

But this world of ours is made on an entirely different pattern, and the casuistic question here is most tragically practical. The actually possible in this world is vastly narrower than all that is demanded; and there is always a *pinch* between the ideal and the actual which can only be got through by leaving part of the ideal behind. There is hardly a good which we can imagine except as competing for the possession of the same bit of space and time with some other imagined good. Every end of desire that presents itself appears exclusive of some other end of desire. Shall a man drink and smoke, *or* keep his nerves in condition?—he cannot do both. Shall he follow his fancy for Amelia, *or* for Henrietta?—both cannot be the choice of his heart. Shall he have the dear old Republican party, *or* a spirit of unsophistication in public affairs?—he cannot have both, etc. So that the ethical philosopher's demand for the right scale of subordination in ideals is the fruit of an altogether practical need. Some part of the ideal must be butchered, and he needs to know which part. It is a tragic situation, and no mere speculative conundrum, with which he has to deal.

Now *we* are blinded to the real difficulty of the philosopher's task by the fact that we are born into a society whose ideals are largely ordered already. If we follow the ideal which is conventionally highest, the others which we butcher either die and do not return to haunt us; or if they come back and accuse us of murder, every one applauds us for turning to them a deaf ear. In other words, our environment encourages us not to be philosophers but partisans. The philosopher, however, cannot, so long as he clings to his own ideal of objectivity, rule out any ideal from being heard. He is confident, and rightly confident, that the simple taking counsel of his own intuitive preferences would be certain to end in a mutilation of the fulness of the truth. The poet Heine is said to have written 'Bunsen' in the place of 'Gott' in his copy of that author's work entitled "God in History," so as to make it read 'Bunsen in der Geschichte.' Now, with no disrespect to the good and learned Baron, is it not safe to say that any single philosopher, however wide his sympathies, must be just such a Bunsen in der Geschichte of the moral world, so soon as he attempts to put his own ideas of order into that howling mob of desires, each struggling to get breathing-room for the ideal to which it clings? The very best of men must not only be insensible, but be ludicrously and peculiarly insensible, to many goods. As a militant, fighting free-handed that the goods to which he *is* sensible may not be submerged and lost from out of life, the philosopher, like every other human being, is in a natural position. But think of Zeno and of Epicurus, think of Calvin and of Paley, think of Kant and Schopenhauer, of Herbert Spencer and John Henry Newman, no longer as one-sided champions of special ideals, but as schoolmasters deciding what all must think—and what more grotesque topic could a satirist wish for on which to exercise his pen? The fabled attempt of Mrs. Partington to arrest the rising tide of the North Atlantic with her broom was a reasonable spectacle compared with their effort to substitute the content of their clean-shaven systems for that exuberant mass of goods with which all human nature is in travail, and groaning to bring to the light of day. Think, furthermore, of such individual moralists, no longer as mere schoolmasters, but as pontiffs armed with the temporal power, and having authority in every concrete case of conflict to order which good shall be butchered and which shall be suffered to survive—and the notion really turns one pale. All one's slumbering revolutionary instincts waken at the thought of any single moralist wielding such powers of life and death. Better chaos forever than an order based on any closet-philosopher's rule, even though he were the most enlightened possible member of his tribe. No! if the philosopher is to keep his judicial position, he must never become one of the parties to the fray.

What can he do, then, it will now be asked, except to fall back on scepticism and give up the notion of being a philosopher at all?

But do we not already see a perfectly definite path of escape which is open to him just because he is a philosopher, and not the champion of one particular ideal? Since everything which is demanded is by that fact a good, must not the guiding principle for ethical philosophy (since all demands conjointly cannot be satisfied in this poor world) be simply to satisfy at all times *as many demands as we can?* That act must be the best act, accordingly, which makes for the *best whole,* in the sense of awakening the least sum of dissatisfactions. In the casuistic scale, therefore, those ideals must be written highest which *prevail at the least cost,* or by whose realization the least possible number of other ideals are destroyed. Since victory and defeat there must be, the victory to be philosophically prayed for is that of the more inclusive side—of the side which even in the hour of triumph will to some degree do justice to the ideals in which the vanquished party's interests lay. The course of history is nothing but the story of men's struggles from generation to generation to find the more and more inclusive order. *Invent some manner* of realizing your own ideals which will also satisfy the alien demands—that and that only is the path of peace! Following this path, society has shaken itself into one sort of relative equilibrium after another by a series of social discoveries quite analogous to those of science. Polyandry and polygamy and slavery, private warfare and liberty to kill, judicial torture and arbitrary royal power have slowly succumbed to actually aroused complaints; and though some one's ideals are unquestionably the worse off for each improvement, yet a vastly greater total number of them find shelter in our civilized society than in the older savage ways. So far then, and up to date, the casuistic scale is made for the philosopher already far better than he can ever make it for himself. An experiment of the most searching kind has proved that the laws and usages of the land are what yield the maximum of satisfaction to the thinkers taken all together. The presumption in cases of conflict must always be in favor of the conventionally recognized good. The philosopher must be a conservative, and in the construction of his casuistic scale must put the things most in accordance with the customs of the community on top.

And yet if he be a true philosopher he must see that there is nothing final in any actually given equilibrium of human ideals, but that, as our present laws and customs have fought and conquered other past ones, so they will in their turn be overthrown by any newly discovered order which will hush up the complaints that they still give rise to, without producing others louder still. "Rules are made for man, not man for rules"—that one sentence is enough to immortalize Green's Prolegomena to Ethics. And although a man always risks much when he breaks away from established rules and strives to realize a larger ideal whole than they permit, yet the philosopher must allow that it is at all times open to any one to make the experiment, provided he fear not to stake his life and character upon the throw. The pinch is always here. Pent in under every system of moral rules are innumerable persons whom it weighs upon, and goods which it represses; and these are always rumbling and grumbling in the background, and ready for any issue by which they may get free. See the abuses which the institution of private property covers, so that even today it is shamelessly asserted among us that one of the prime functions of the national government is to help the adroiter citizens to grow rich. See the unnamed and unnamable sorrows which the tyranny, on the whole so beneficent, of the marriage-institution brings to so many, both of the married and the unwed. See the wholesale loss of opportunity under our *régime* of so-called equality and industrialism, with the drummer and the counter-jumper in the saddle, for so many faculties and graces which could flourish in the feudal world. See our kindliness for the humble and the outcast, how it wars with that stern weeding-out which until now has been the condition of every perfection in the breed. See everywhere the struggle and the squeeze; and everlastingly the problem how to make them less. The anarchists, nihilists, and free-lovers; the free-silverites, socialists, and single-tax men; the free-traders and civil-service reformers; the prohibitionists and anti-vivisectionists; the radical darwinians with their idea of the suppression of the weak—these and all the conservative sentiments of society arrayed against them, are simply deciding through actual experiment by what sort of conduct the maximum amount of good can be gained and kept in this world. These experiments are to be judged, not *à priori*, but by actually finding, after the fact of their making, how much more outcry or how much appeasement comes about. What closet-solutions can possibly anticipate the result of trials made on such a scale? Or what can any superficial theorist's judgment be worth, in a world where every one of hundreds of ideals has its special champion already provided in the shape of some genius expressly born to feel it, and to fight to death in its behalf? The pure philosopher can only follow the windings of the spectacle, confident that the line of least resistance will always be towards the richer and the more inclusive arrangement, and that by one tack after another some approach to the kingdom of heaven is incessantly made.

IV

All this amounts to saying that, so far as the casuistic question goes, ethical science is just like physical science, and instead of being deducible all at once from abstract principles, must simply bide its time, and be ready to revise its conclusions from day to day. The presumption of course, in both sciences, always is that the vulgarly accepted opinions are true, and the right casuistic order that which public opinion believes in; and surely it would be folly quite as great, in most of us, to strike out independently and to aim at originality in ethics as in physics. Every now and then, however, some one is born with the right to be original, and his revolutionary thought or action may bear prosperous fruit. He may replace old 'laws of nature' by better ones; he may, by breaking old moral rules in a certain place, bring in a total condition of things more ideal than would have followed had the rules been kept.

On the whole, then, we must conclude that no philosophy of ethics is possible in the old-fashioned absolute sense of the term. Everywhere the ethical philosopher must wait on facts. The thinkers who create the ideals come he knows not whence, their sensibilities are evolved he knows not how; and the question as to which of two conflicting ideals will give the best universe then and there, can be answered by him only through the aid of the experience of other men. I said some time ago, in treating of the 'first' question, that the intuitional moralists deserve credit for keeping most clearly to the psychological facts. They do much to spoil this merit on the whole, however, by mixing with it that dogmatic temper which, by absolute distinctions and unconditional 'thou shalt nots,' changes a growing, elastic, and continuous life into a superstitious system of relics and dead bones. In point of fact, there are no absolute evils, and there are no non-moral goods; and the *highest* ethical life—however few may be called to bear its burdens—

consists at all times in the breaking of rules which have grown too narrow for the actual case. There is but one unconditional commandment, which is that we should seek incessantly, with fear and trembling, so to vote and to act as to bring about the very largest total universe of good which we can see. Abstract rules indeed can help; but they help the less in proportion as our intuitions are more piercing, and our vocation is the stronger for the moral life. For every real dilemma is in literal strictness a unique situation; and the exact combination of ideals realized and ideals disappointed which each decision creates is always a universe without a precedent, and for which no adequate previous rule exists. The philosopher, then, *quâ* philosopher, is no better able to determine the best universe in the concrete emergency than other men. He sees, indeed, somewhat better than most men what the question always is—not a question of this good or that good simply taken, but of the two total universes with which these goods respectively belong. He knows that he must vote always for the richer universe, for the good which seems most organizable, most fit to enter into complex combinations, most apt to be a member of a more inclusive whole. But which particular universe this is he cannot know for certain in advance; he only knows that if he makes a bad mistake the cries of the wounded will soon inform him of the fact. In all this the philosopher is just like the rest of us non-philosophers, so far as we are just and sympathetic instinctively, and so far as we are open to the voice of complaint. His function is in fact indistinguishable from that of the best kind of statesman at the present day. His books upon ethics, therefore, so far as they truly touch the moral life, must more and more ally themselves with a literature which is confessedly tentative and suggestive rather than dogmatic—I mean with novels and dramas of the deeper sort, with sermons, with books on statecraft and philanthropy and social and economical reform. Treated in this way ethical treatises may be voluminous and luminous as well; but they never can be *final*, except in their abstractest and vaguest features; and they must more and more abandon the old-fashioned, clear-cut, and would-be 'scientific' form....

III

JOSIAH ROYCE

≫≪

Introduction

IDEALISM IS THE oldest and most persistent philosophy in America. Stemming from the Platonism of Jonathan Edwards and nourished by the moral idealism of the American enlightenment, it inspired the transcendental movement and reached philosophic maturity in the academic awakening of the nineteenth century. It has never been long without able champions or popular following. That so old a philosophy should enjoy such a long and vigorous life in a new country is no anomaly. Santayana once observed, "America is a young country with an old mentality . . ." [1] The peoples who sought a new life on this continent brought with them settled religious and moral ideals, the deposit of centuries of experience and reflection. Many came here in search of something more than physical adventure, economic security, or commercial success. To that idealism which, in Emerson's words, "is a hypothesis to account for nature by other principles than those of carpentry and chemistry," they were no strangers. Moreover, philosophical idealism with its passionate search for wholeness and spiritual security mirrored the struggle of disparate peoples to create, on this continent, order out of wilderness, thereby to become one nation. In the light of these facts the persistence of idealistic modes of thought in the United States is no puzzle.

American idealism was a long time extricating itself from the toils of religious orthodoxy and systematic theology so as to be free to develop in a truly philosophic way. The idealism of Jonathan Edwards was essentially a Platonic graft on the stern parent-stem of Calvinism. By the time Emerson and the Concord School were in the ascendant, the grip of religious orthodoxy had relaxed; but the method of transcendentalism was intuitive and literary rather than philosophical. It was not until the advent of Josiah Royce that idealism of a philosophic sort, free from sectarian loyalties, appeared in the United States.

His philosophy took the form of absolute or objective idealism, although in its mature form he chose to call it absolute voluntarism. It is a thing of searching moods and multiple facets, reflecting the heroic

[1] *Winds of Doctrine* (1913), p. 187.

proportions of its author's mind. Royce was constantly recasting his argument, giving it new turns, illustrating and exemplifying his ideas in novel ways. But from first to last his thought is controlled by a single theme of which each successive embodiment is but another variation. It was his conviction that we are all members of one body, one community, the divine, infinite, eternal whole, the source of whatever meaning and purpose may be embodied in finite experience. He did not come by this conviction wholly through an impartial examination of evidence; rather, it seems to have been somehow in him from the beginning. This was Royce, his faith, his being. The measure of Royce, the philosopher, is the resourcefulness, persistence and intellectual eminence which he displayed in verifying this insight and in seeking to give it precise, logical articulation.

The Making of a Frontier Idealist

Josiah Royce had an uncommon background. He was born in the uncouth High Sierras mining camp of Grass Valley, California, in 1855, to parents who but six years before had completed the long, hazardous forty-niner trek in search of gold. Since there were no schools in Grass Valley, young Josiah's first instruction was imparted by his mother, a pious Christian lady of steadfast, intrepid character,[2] whose influence was decisive in shaping his sense of values. In 1866 the family moved to San Francisco, and Josiah completed his schooling there and in Oakland. He was, by his own admission, an awkward lad, red-haired, freckled, countrified—a poor mixer who all his life found it difficult to be effective socially, the while he felt a deep yearning for love and companionship.[3] At home the solicitude of his mother and two older sisters was a barrier to the development of a normal boyhood. But the boys at grammar school gave him, he observed, his first and grievous introduction to "the majesty of the community." He never forgot it.

In 1871 he entered the infant University of California. The intellectual fare there did not yet include courses in philosophy, but he read Herbert Spencer and John Stuart Mill on his own, studied science under Joseph LeConte, a philosophical geologist, and English under the poet Edward Rowland Sill. Four years later he took his bachelor's degree with a thesis on *The Theology of Aeschylus's Prometheus*, and had so impressed a group of affluent San Franciscans that they furnished him with the means for a year's study in Germany.

There he attended the lectures of Lotze, read Schopenhauer and Kant, and lived vicariously in the Gothic world of romantic poetry.

[2] Josiah persuaded his mother to write her memoirs of the journey westward. See *A Frontier Lady,* ed. R. H. Gabriel (1932).

[3] See "Words of Professor Royce," in *Papers in Honor of Josiah Royce,* ed. J. E. Creighton (1916), pp. 279-86.

While these influences helped to fix the general form of Royce's philosophy, they also provoked a compensatory interest in logic and mathematics. He determined to conquer these fields also in order to forge new weapons for the arsenal of idealism.

Upon his return to the United States a fellowship awaited him at Johns Hopkins. Here he came under the tutelage of George S. Morris, who, like many American philosophers of that day, had deserted Scottish realism and sought in German idealism a more adequate basis for religion and morality. At Hopkins Royce confessed his philosophical aspirations to a visiting lecturer named William James, who assured the young philosopher that "a young man might rightfully devote his life to philosophy if he chose." [4] By 1878 Royce had completed a thesis, "Of the Interdependence of Human Knowledge," and tucked a Ph.D. under his arm. But, alas, there were no openings in philosophy. So he returned to the University of California to teach—logic and rhetoric. He made the most of the limited opportunity. He composed a *Primer of Logical Analysis for Composition Students*, lectured on philosophy and psychology, published articles on Schiller, Shelley, and other literary and philosophical subjects,[5] and in his spare time, we learn from his correspondence with James, he admits "reviewing parts of the calculus, and dabbling in modern geometry and quaternions." [6]

Four years of zealous devotion to his duties and study [7] were rewarded, in 1882, by an appointment to Harvard, where Royce was an immediate success and became in time a legend. He was a major star in that Harvard constellation which, at the turn of the century, included James, Santayana, Münsterberg, and Palmer.

The First Proof of the Absolute

When at age twenty-seven Royce assumed his new teaching duties the central theme which he was to elaborate and defend for the rest of his career was already fixed in his massive head. Reality is the divine, timeless many-in-one, the source of all being and perfection. This nebulous idea had been nourished by Royce's training in Christianity and his study of post-Kantian romantic idealism, especially Fichte, Schelling, and Goethe. From Hegel he learned system-building, but accepted little else without important reservations. The reading of Schopenhauer

---

[4] R. B. Perry, *The Thought and Character of William James* (1935), I, p. 779.
[5] See "A Bibliography of the Writings of Josiah Royce," in *Papers*, cited above in footnote 3.
[6] R. B. Perry, *op. cit.*, I, p. 785.
[7] The spirit in which he pursued his work may be gleaned from an entry in his "Diary," dated Feb. 12, 1879: "I am a Californian, and day after day, by the order of the World Spirit (whose commands we all do ever obey, whether we will it or no), I am accustomed to be found at my tasks ... Here as I do my work I often find time for contemplation." *Fugitive Essays* (1925), ed. J. Lowenberg, p. 6.

made him sensitive to the existence of evil. And he had sharpened his wits in the study of logic and mathematics.

Such was Royce's mental cargo when in 1885 he plumbed the solemn deeps of existence in his first major work, *The Religious Aspect of Philosophy*. The style and content are reminiscent of Fichte's flamboyant homily, *The Vocation of Man*. Royce's title is prophetic of his life-long preoccupation with religious themes. He had little respect for blind faith and took a dim view of sectarian theology. But he never doubted that the ultimate objects of faith could or should be securely established by logical demonstration. And this was, to his way of thinking, the crucial piece of unfinished business in philosophy. This book marks his first assault on the problem; but it plots a course of thought which he pursued ever after.

The problem assumed the following form: "Is there then, anywhere in the universe, any real thing of Infinite Worth?" (p. 8). Scouting the historical "warfare of ideals" in a skeptical vein, Royce reviews Greek and Christian ideals, morals resting on self-love, sympathy and altruism, only to conclude that no one of these is final, since each has its source in "physical fact," that is, some liking or disliking that is not obligatory. As a consequence, the will becomes helpless, morbid and frustrated. But the mood of pessimism harbors a dim apprehension of an inclusive, higher ideal in which the conflicting ends are harmonized. Royce states this ideal in the form of the following practical maxim: "In so far as in thee lies, act as if thou wert at once thy neighbor and thyself. Treat these two lives as one life" (p. 149). Man in his aloneness is a meaningless fragment; if his life is to have meaning and content, it must be interpreted in the light of his relations to others, to the community of purposes and ends. The ideal life is attained in part, Royce suggests, in scientific research and in the spiritual community of Christian believers. The dependence of Royce's highest ethical principle on Kant's "good will" and "realm of ends" is obvious.

Royce applied this pattern of thinking, in the second part of the book, to the problem of reality, the central problem of metaphysics. Again he launches his skeptical shafts, showing that the traditional theories of reality are fraught with doubt and error. The way out lies through an analysis of error. How is error possible? In answering this question Royce built the argument that he considered the clincher in the case for idealism. Just as he slew the dragon of pessimism by showing that it implies the reality of a higher moral principle in which ethical conflicts are resolved, so now, borrowing a chapter from his Ph. D. thesis, he argues that the recognition of error implies the acknowledgment of the existence of absolute truth. Error consists in the lack of agreement or correspondence between a judgment and its intended object. 'Peter is in error about Paul' means that Peter's idea of Paul does not agree with the real or true idea of Paul. But, says Royce, warming to his argument, the error of Peter's idea could never be ascertained unless there is in fact a more inclusive thought which includes both Peter's erroneous idea *and* the true idea of Paul; for the error of Peter's idea is detectable only by comparison with the whole truth about Paul.

The unregenerate skeptic may protest: 'Royce, you have merely made a case for the *possibility* of such an all-inclusive thought, but you have not demonstrated its actuality.' Royce has his answer at hand. Since error is actual, the conditions under which error is possible must be actual also. And since there can be no error except in the presence of an inclusive error-correcting truth, the actuality of error establishes the necessary existence of absolute truth. The skeptic, still unconvinced, declares: 'Your all-inclusive thought seems unreal to me; you are in error.' Royce retorts: 'How can you assert this unless you grant that there is an absolute truth in the light of which my thought is erroneous?' And he rushes confidently to his grand climax: 'My error, this finite fragment of thought, is an element in an all-seeing consciousness wherein my fragment of thought is fulfilled. There is no stopping-place short of the Absolute.' "All reality must be present to the Unity of Infinite Thought" (p. 433). In this insight both philosophy and religion may rest.

Armed with this conclusion Royce returns to the problem of morals. If the infinite thought, the "Divine Life," is in possession of the whole truth, it must have an absolute knowledge of good and evil. In a mode typical of romantic idealists, Royce identifies the completed whole of thought with the infinite perfection of the real. "The world then, as a whole, is and must be absolutely good, since the infinite thought must know what is desirable, and knowing it, must have present in itself the true objects of desire" (p. 444). The summit of practical endeavor is "the progressive realization by men of the eternal life of an Infinite Spirit" (p. 441). This is the core of Royce's religious and moral ideal.

The Religious Aspect of Philosophy also records Royce's first bout with his black angel—the existence of evil—with which he was destined to wrestle ceaselessly. He was in a perpetual dilemma. In the logic of his monistic metaphysics all finite evil is rectified in the perfection of the completed Absolute. But he was not one to dismiss the reality of evil in cavalier fashion. He knew what it was to suffer; measured by his own severe ethics he was a heroic character. Finite evil is there, undeniably. But how can this be in a perfect universe? Royce's solution of this problem parallels his reflections on error. Just as error is a fragment, a detail, torn from the whole truth, so also evil is an episode which in the total scheme of things is conquered by good, on the cosmic plane. Moreover, the existence of evil is morally necessary, for it is in the struggle against evil that the good is realized. But the labor of cleaning out the stables is not merely Herculean but endless. Evil can never be eradicated wholly from the finite world. The crown of virtue is for those who battle heroically and keep a keen edge on their consciences. For, virtue does not consist of ends attained or goods enjoyed, but in fighting the good fight. Royce's was a strenuous, essentially tragic conception of life, buttressed by romanticism and Calvinism.

Alarums and Excursions

The freshness and originality of Royce's treatment of old themes, to which a brief digest of his thought cannot hope to do justice, made his first book a notable success and established his reputation. Here was a son of the West expounding an old-world philosophy; a frontiersman defending the genteel tradition. His classroom teaching added to his reputation for oracular wisdom. There he stressed exact and thorough scholarship in the history of philosophy, but discouraged slavish adherence to past ideas. His students saw before them a face of unexampled homeliness crowned by a massive brow—"an indecent exposure of forehead," James called it—the whole resting on a body rather too spare and compact. A comparison with Socrates was inevitable. What his students heard was even more arresting. For Royce was a man of prodigious memory and vast erudition which sat not too lightly on him. The hard work of thinking appeared to refresh him, though at times the very weight of his learning seemed an impediment to the free flow of his own thought. He was an inveterate teacher, ever eager to enlighten and edify, be the audience one student or a full lecture hall, whether off or on the campus, by talk or printed word—it did not matter. He was one of the great inexhaustible talkers of his time.[8] In his style he achieved a sort of ponderous eloquence; it was rich and full; he was, James observed, "the Rubens of philosophy."[9] The tone was serious and homiletic, occasionally enlivened by dignified humor. He had a weakness for sententious quotations, for italics and upper-case type. But his intellectual eminence and nobility of mind were such as to command the respect even of the sophisticated. That he was no mere closet philosopher became evident when he published a history of California and a novel of frontier life—interests he never ceased cultivating. And among his friends admiration for his integrity grew when it became known that the impecunious professor had been asked to give the Lowell lectures for a fat fee, but refused when he learned

[8] John Jay Chapman recorded a wonderfully vivid impression of Royce, "the John L. Sullivan of Philosophy," "ready for all comers." See "Portrait of Josiah Royce," *Outlook* 122 (1919), p. 372.

[9] R. B. Perry, *op. cit.*, I, p. 810.

that he must first sign a simple statement of religious belief. Obviously, here was a man of whom much could be expected.

The next phase of Royce's development was conditioned by his intimate friendship with his neighbor and philosophical sparring-partner, William James. They were as different in most respects as night and day.[10] Royce had come early into possession of his central philosophical theme, while James, an agile and flexible mind, groped his way slowly to a position where he was satisfied to stand. As a result, Royce, James's junior by thirteen years and his protégé, exerted a strong influence upon the suggestible James during the eighties and early nineties. But thereafter Royce was obliged to go on the defensive against the powerful anti-monistic arguments James employed in his frontal assault upon absolutisms of all sorts. Royce never really shifted, however, from the general position expounded in his first book; but James's critique did at length cause him to make some important concessions.

James greeted Royce's first book with lavish praise; [11] but this, like the artful flattery of Socrates, was a prelude to the argument proper. During the many gate-post discussions James and Royce indulged in before their Irving Street homes in Cambridge, the pluralistic and empirical traits of James's thought directed a running fire at Royce's monism and rationalism. Royce was sensitive to these criticisms because, unlike some of his idealistic predecessors, he attached great weight to the deliverances of experience and the reality of persons. James's attack proved to be such a continual harassment that Royce was at pains to show that his Absolute is empirically grounded, and that the world of finitude is not simply a stooge for the Absolute. The arguments of certain pluralistic idealists, notably those of George H. Howison, put Royce on the defensive in much the same respects.

The results are evident in his second major work, *The Conception of God*. The positive, triumphant tone of the *Religious Aspect* is superseded now by caution, circumspection, and a greater concern for experience and finite particulars. There is space here for only a brief comment about the *Conception of God*. In it Royce resorts to a fresh analysis of experience in order to undergird his argument purporting to prove the reality of the Absolute from the existence of error.

Sensory experience, he observes, is passing and fragmentary. But there is always more in it than we perceive at the first look. We interpret the stray facts of the immediately given by fitting such facts into organized systems of knowledge, such as the sciences. Experience thus

[10] For an instructive comparison of Royce and James by one who knew them both see R. B. Perry's *In the Spirit of William James* (1938), ch. I.

[11] He described it as "one of the very freshest, profoundest, solidest, most human bits of philosophical work I've seen for a long time." See R. B. Perry, *Thought and Character of William James* (1935), I, p. 797.

organized "fulfils" the fragmentary perceptions by revealing their coherence with the community of facts and ideas. Thus, absolute truth
and reality would be absolutely organized experience fulfilling all possible finite facts and systems of facts. But is there such a reality? Royce
here invokes the argument of his first book. To assert that the realm of
splintered experience is finite involves a contradiction. For that proposition contains an assertion about the absolute whole of experience.
To say, 'all is finite,' is to assert a proposition which itself transcends
the finite. Yet we constantly do assert such propositions in science and
philosophy. Since we cannot interpret experience without transcending it, our thought points toward the absolute whole of experience,
thought fulfilled completely, absolute knowledge of good and evil,
self-hood fully attained, in short, God.

But what now of human life? James had already arraigned Royce's
Absolute as another instance of a "block universe" wherein all differences vanish; and Howison saw in it an "oriental pantheism" wherein
persons are absorbed in the great homogeneous limbo. These attacks
provoked Royce to a full rejoinder in the final essay of the *Conception
of God*. "I shall try to show," he writes, "... that the Absolute, as I
have ventured to define the conception, has room for ethical individuality without detriment to its true unity..." (p. 137). The principle
of individuation fixed on by Royce is the factor of purpose, of will, in
human experience. Every idea embodies an intention; it selects and
focuses attention upon only certain determinate objects or relations,
namely, those relevant to the purpose; and thus an idea represents
many items brought into convergence by the controlling purpose. To
be an individual, then, means to embody a purpose. Knowledge or
intellect, in the purely cognitive sense, cannot individuate; for they
traffic in universals. The concrete 'thatness' of a specific thing consists
in its being the embodiment of a specific, dynamic purpose. Royce
stressed this doctrine to a point where, in his later books, he obliterated
the distinction between the cognitive and voluntaristic aspects of ideas.

The Absolute, then, is an individual writ large. God is not simply
the all-knower; above all he is cosmic purpose, the end upon which
all purposes of finite individuals converge. It is the divine will, God's
loving purpose, that individuates a world of objects out of his cosmic
thoughts. And since finite individuals are projections of the infinite
person, they can find their fulfilment only in so far as they exemplify
self-transcending purposes and loyalty to more and more inclusive
ends. Personal freedom is attained only through conscious participation
in the life of the Absolute. "A world of individuals more separate than
this ... would be a world of anarchy ... a moral hell" (p. 275).

Royce was not satisfied for long with this statement of his case,
although he never doubted the validity of the pattern of thought he

was seeking to expound. He was convinced that empiricism and pluralism trade in truncated half-truths; and so he was constantly calling to mind neglected considerations in the upper reaches of experience. He would be satisfied with nothing less than that whole truth which would complete the half-truths of empiricism. But the passionate earnestness of his search betrayed him into dialectical equivocation, from which he strove to redeem his philosophy each time by a fresh attempt.

The Mature System of Absolute Voluntarism

An invitation to deliver the Gifford Lectures of 1899 and 1900 in Scotland provided Royce with the next opportunity to restate and clarify his position. Most of his major works were first delivered as lectures, many before semi-popular audiences. Like Emerson, he was in his element as a lecturer.[12] Both cultivated a didactic style especially adapted to vocal delivery, and burdened, consequently, with repetition and diffuseness in the printed text. The resemblance goes deeper. They are alike also in the vision of the sublime many-in-one; although in Royce this vision was subjected to the discipline of logic, whereas Emerson spoke often in the tongue of mysticism. If Emerson was the poet and prophet of transcendentalism, Royce may fairly be called the belated philosopher of the movement.[13]

The Gifford Lectures, appearing in two thick volumes entitled *The World and the Individual*, represent Royce's supreme effort to give systematic and definitive utterance to his philosophy. It is the only major work in which he treats of philosophical problems in their own right without permitting religious themes to preëmpt the center of the stage. In the fashion typical of idealists he approaches the central problem, What is reality? by way of an analysis of "ideas." The emphasis is again on the volitional aspect; ideas are not purely cognitive entities, they belong also to the motor side of life; they are at bottom expressions of conscious purpose or intention. In short, an idea is primarily a "nascent deed" or a "plan of action." But ideas also represent "outer facts," imitate them or correspond to them. And this Royce calls their "external meaning," whereas the embodied purpose is the "inner meaning." The melody I hum corresponds to a theme from Beethoven, but it also expresses my purpose at the moment.

With internal and external meanings thus contrasted, how can they be harmonized, how can our purposes and the world of outer fact become compatible?

In probing for an answer to this question, Royce undertakes a

[12] To Dickinson Miller is credited the *bon mot*, "Royce finds lecturing the easiest mode of breathing."

[13] For Royce's appreciation of Emerson (and Jonathan Edwards) see his *William James and Other Essays* (1911), Essay I.

methodical critique of the three reigning theories of reality—realism, mysticism, and critical rationalism. Realism assumes the existence of a common-sense world of independent things-in-themselves, but ends with a void; for it cannot on its premises account for the evident inter-dependence of outer fact and knowing mind. Mysticism would solve the latter problem by premising the immediate identity of knower and known, but at the cost of obliterating the reality of the finite and "quenching" the activity of discursive thought. Critical rationalism of the Kantian sort fares no better; for it reduces 'being' to a set of cognitive categories; that is, 'to be' means to be true or valid. But, Royce protests, we can never by reasoning alone comprehend the simple thatness of any thing. To be real does not mean 'to conform to some test of thought.' 'Being' is given. Thought must find and correspond to reality, but it cannot generate or constitute being. Thought without reality, without something other and beyond, remains a mere empty possibility.

The problem of the simultaneous duality and union of thought and reality obliges Royce to press on to a "fourth, unnamed conception of being." The crux of this conception is the purposive, teleological character of ideas, their internal meaning. He called this theory sometimes "absolute pragmatism." The test of true correspondence of idea and outer facts is the degree to which the latter fulfil or embody the purpose which is the core of the idea. A thing is real only if, and to the extent that, it fulfils the internal meaning of ideas. Now outer facts serve to modify purposes, while implemented purposes also modify outer facts. But taken in the perspective of the cosmos, 'purpose' is determinative of 'reality.' For what passes before us as outer fact, only partly relevant to our purposes, is an expression of the completely determinate and absolutely fulfilled purpose of the Absolute. To the extent, then, that our purposes become ever broader and more inclusive, ever more self-transcending, to that extent our ideas are more adequately fulfilled, we come into possession of more and more truth and reality and we become more truly individuated. Ideas are true if they work; but the only ideas that will 'work' are those that harmonize with the purposes of the Absolute, with reality. This is absolute pragmatism.

In this trinity of interlocking notions—individuality, truth, and being—Royce, mindful of the criticisms of empiricists and personalists, gives special stress to individuality. "The essence of the Real is to be Individual, or to permit no other of its own kind" (I, p. 348). But since finite persons know in part only and there is always more in intention than can be realized in any moment, such persons are individual only in tendency and aspiration. While no finite view is wholly illusory, the only perfect individual is the whole, God, the perfect fulness of life and thought, the complex harmony of infinitely various individuals.

Royce recognized that his whole argument stands or falls with the notion of the Absolute; he must prove by irrefragable logic that the Absolute exists. To this end he tapped a new vein of argument to which Charles S. Peirce had called his attention. His debt to this seminal thinker was to become very great.[14] In the present connection the study of Peirce's essays in mathematical logic helped Royce overcome the acute arguments of F. H. Bradley, British idealist. That keen analyst argued, in his *Appearance and Reality*, that the Absolute is an ideal notion simply and concluded that the *existence* of an infinite multitude is a self-contradictory notion. If this argument were allowed to prevail it would knock the props out from under Royce's system. He propounds his answer in a long, technical "Supplementary Essay," appended to his *World and the Individual*. He aims to establish a sound analogy between the mathematician's definition of a determinate infinite and the actual many-in-one. A mathematical series is said to be infinite when it is similar (or stands in a one-to-one correspondence) to a constituent part of itself. In such a system the relations between members resemble the structure of the series as a whole. Think of a bottle which has a picture of itself on the label. This in turn pictures itself, and so on, *ad infinitum*. Each representation has a next member, although the original bottle, the archetype embracing them all, is not itself the image of any other. Such a relationship of whole and members is perfectly definable, even though there be infinite members. The series of whole numbers offers a more precise illustration. It is endless, but still determinate, because the manner in which numbers are generated is represented also by many included series, such as the series of even numbers, of odd numbers, of squares, etc.

But the number series is ideal whereas the Absolute is alleged to be actual. Thus far the argument has only established the logical possibility of a determinate infinite. To prove not only its actuality but its necessity, Royce has recourse to another argument. Self-representation, he contends, is a genetic principle of thought which is empirically verifiable. The thought of a thought, the consciousness of consciousness of self, loyalty to the ideal of loyalty—these are illustrations of actual ordered series of self-representation fundamental to all knowledge. Without such progressions there is no truth, no reality; for Royce has already shown that truth and reality are comprehensible only as particular ideas are fitted into ordered systems or connected series. Either,

---

[14] Royce relates of presenting one of his books to Peirce and receiving from that candid genius the following acknowledgment: "But, when I read you, I do wish that you would study logic. You need it so much." *Problem of Christianity* (1913), II, p. 117.

then, the Absolute is real, or there is no knowledge, no truth, no reality, and no finite things.

The actual Absolute, thus, is a determinate, infinite whole, the series of self-representative series, the self represented in endlessly various persons. Being both subject and object, it images itself eternally, generating representations of itself endlessly in the finite. The Absolute is the melody, we are the notes. God knows and appreciates the composition as a whole, and also attends to each note or phrase in contrapuntal harmonies of the universe. But we can hear only stray notes or perhaps now and again a strain of the divine music.

Having 'saved' the Absolute once more, Royce turns to the interpretation of the finite world and the moral order. He calls to mind his earlier distinction between the worlds of *description* and *appreciation*.[15] The former is the world of brute fact, of nature; the latter is the inner world of values and purposes, preëminently a social world. Metaphysically considered, brute facts as well as values are individuations within the divine life. In the world of description, facts become intelligible, are fulfilled, only as they are interpreted by ordered systems of ideas. But the ordering of facts is itself a fact, one which relates nature to life and the world of appreciation. For, Royce holds, our knowledge of nature, our science, reflect the social values and coöperating interests of men living in a world of intercommunication. Each element in the world of description is in the status of an as yet unfulfilled purpose awaiting its ultimate realization in that wider social consciousness of the Absolute.

Royce suggests that beyond the organized but limited book-keeping of science, nature may embody meanings and purposes of her own, just as each finite person does. Sticks and stones, though not themselves conscious of purposes, may well be parts of a larger conscious process with a time-span in which aeons are as moments. For time is a function of the tension between purpose and fulfillment. The oceans and stars may have a rhythm of original purpose and ultimate realization harmonizing with a total, divine cosmic plan not discernible to human beings who live in *allegro tempi*. The purposes of nature may be likened to the sustained bass notes, while human purposes, each with a relatively brief time-span, are as the vivacious voice parts, blending with the more massive elements of the divine composition.

In this scheme of things each human self has its unique individuating life-span requiring other complementary personalities as well as external nature for its fulfillment. A self in isolation is incapable of realizing a life-plan, and is, therefore, not truly a self. It is not free. Freedom is just that reciprocity with other selves and with nature, in virtue of

---

[15] Cf. *The Spirit of Modern Philosophy* (1892), Lect. XII.

which each self approaches its fulfillment. The infinity of intercommunicating, mutually interpreting selves constitutes one body, one community: the Absolute self. God can be one only by being many. While the finite parts are dependent upon the whole, the whole is the sum and conscious unity of all the parts.

Royce persisted in calling this position theism; but his critics argued that his position is actually nearer pantheism than theism.

Royce's design to 'save' the finite individual from absorption in the One is evident also in his moral philosophy. What meaning can there be in moral obligation in view of the eternal perfection of the whole? Royce made repeated assaults on this problem. If the triumph of righteousness is written in the stars, does this not reduce morality either to a form of cosmic pressure, or to an inexplicable, pathetic delusion of mankind? Royce could not tolerate moral fatalism, nor could he follow Spinoza in conceiving nature to be beyond good and evil. He chose instead the slippery alternative, aiming to show that even though the Absolute has perfect knowledge of good and evil and all happenings are ultimately for the best, still men are not simply the pawns of the Absolute. Royce says in effect: You are free to follow or to ignore the moral law; if you choose evil, the world-order will neutralize your deed because other finite agents, striving to overcome the evil you have done, will somewhere succeed. For the perfection of the whole requires that every evil deed must be atoned for not only by the evil-doer but by all others as well. The imperfection of the moral will in ourselves and others is thus the primary cause of suffering in the finite. And yet the imperfection of the will is the very condition of virtue, which is just the perpetual struggle against evil. The agonized conscience can find comfort in the fact that the sorrows of finitude are God's sorrows as well, for he knows all and experiences all.

Royce's reflections on evil provide a good measure of the validity and value of his thought, for his philosophy stands first and last upon the quality of his moral and religious insight. It is instructive, in this connection, to compare him with William James. Royce's thinking was controlled, at bottom, by a tragic sense of life, while James was uncompromisingly optimistic in an almost Nietzschean fashion. Each in his own way gloried in the struggle against evil. What James could not tolerate in Royce's philosophy was the admission of the *necessary* existence of evil, tantamount to a theological concession of original sin. James once remarked that the monists wanted "not the absence of vice, but vice there, and virtue holding her by the throat..." [16] Or, as Santayana, one of Royce's most unsympathetic critics, observed, Royce's world is good only because it is good to strangle. "What calm

[16] *The Will to Believe* (1897), p. 169.

could there be in the double assurance that it was really right that things should be wrong, but that it was really wrong not to strive to right them?" [17] Royce and James agreed that evil is something to be hated and overcome. But James could find in this pluralistic strung-along universe no guarantee for the success of this project. Such a view coupled with James's reliance upon man's subjective sense of right seemed to Royce a frivolous and dangerous moral anarchy. He was familiar with the stock objections to his own theory. He could reply only by reiterating his whole metaphysics, emphasizing that by the Absolute he did not mean a sterile, frozen perfection, but a community of organic purposes converging upon a common universal end; like a family or community intent upon improving the lot of each by working for the well-being of the whole.

Royce's Absolute, like his ethics and religion, is first of all a *social* conception. This is evident especially in the final stage of his development.

Towards the Great Community

The last and in some respects most revolutionary phase of Royce's development finds him once again immersed in the study of logic. Between the publication of the *World and the Individual* in 1901 and his death in 1916, he published two monographs [18] and no less than six articles dealing primarily with problems of general and mathematical logic. These studies were decisive in establishing the character of the final revision of his system.

From the first Royce defended logical realism and rejected all philosophies which, like mentalism, relativism and psychologism, reduce objective knowledge to the status of private experience. This was the root of his persisting quarrel with James's version of pragmatism. Royce held that concepts, laws, numbers, and other entities belonging to the ideal world of mind, are no less real than the concrete 'thats' of sense perception. The reality of concepts is not spatio-temporal like that of things, but consists of fitting logically into the context of valid relations between ideas and systems of ideas. Thus, the mathematician is as much a student of given facts as the engineer or farmer. In this respect Royce's idealism stood nearer to Plato's than to Hegel's; and he was justified in protesting the label of "Hegelian" which his critics continued to apply to his works.

Logical realism is the clue to Royce's conception of the science of logic. He defined logic as "the general science of order, the theory of

---

[17] *Character and Opinion in the United States* (1920), p. 126.
[18] "The Relation of the Principles of Logic to the Foundations of Geometry," *Trans. Am. Math. Soc.*, VI (1905), no. 3; and "Principien der Logik," *Encycl. der philos. Wissenschaften* (1912), I; trans. B. E. Meyer in *Encycl. of Philos. Sciences* (1913), I, pp. 67-135.

the forms of any orderly realm of objects, real or ideal." [19] 'Order' is not some arbitrary arrangement the mind imposes upon the ready-made facts of nature; it is an essential constituent of reality. Reality is expressed always in verified, ordered series of ideas; anything less than that is a senseless fragment. This is just as true of reality as of thought. Nothing can be understood in absolute isolation. The clue to reality is the connectedness of things. Hence the importance of logic.

This seemingly intellectualistic account of reality was compromised by Royce's tenacious voluntarism. Following Schopenhauer, Royce affirmed the centrality of the will and purpose in the cosmic process. The primary and essential nature of individuals, infinite or finite, is revealed by their purposes, their will. We are real and individual because we act purposively and not because we think. But Royce, unlike Schopenhauer, was loath to see reality split into "world as idea" and "world as will." He emphasized that without cognition and knowledge there could be no fulfilment of purposes. Hence, an accurate description of intellectual functions and how these coöperate with the will was a project of special importance to Royce.

To these tasks he devoted the second volume of his last major work, *The Problem of Christianity,* published in 1913. It is essentially an interpretation of meaning in social, teleological terms leading to the construction of the Absolute as the grand community of intercommunicating, mutually interpreting spirits. In this connection Royce has recourse to a theory of knowledge developed by C. S. Peirce. Peirce criticized the traditional epistemologies for having neglected certain special and growing meanings which he called "signs." These are neither percepts nor concepts, strictly considered, but symbols invested with meanings by the accumulating experience of the community. Almost anything may come to function as a sign—a smile, 'Post no Bills,' a barometric reading, a bank check, social unrest. The process whereby things, relations, or qualities become endowed with meanings and function as signs Peirce called "interpretation." It is a social process involving three terms: the sign, the interpreter, and the interpretee. The interpreter interprets the sign to the interpretee. The latter may be the interpreter himself or another person. Interpretation is an endless process; for a given interpretation may function as sign in subsequent interpretations, and so on without limit. The world of interpretation is thus inexhaustible and steadily enriched by changing social relations, by memories of the past and hopes and plans for the future. Interpretation, Royce concluded, is the foundation of community, of our spiritual solidarity with our fellows; it is the true sense of the Christian ideal of the kingdom of heaven. "The world is the Community. The world contains its own interpreter. Its processes are infinite in their

[19] *Encyclopaedia of the Philosophical Sciences,* p. 69.

temporal varieties. But their interpreter, the spirit of this universal community—never absorbing varieties or permitting them to blend—compares and, through a real life, interprets them all" (II, p. 324).[20]

With the Absolute thus redefined as the world-community of mutually interpreting persons, Royce's ethics underwent a corresponding transformation. Interpretation suggested a mode of expressing the moral ideal in concrete, practical terms. The general form of Royce's ethics was determined, from the first, by his monistic metaphysics. The duty of finite man is to rise above the local, transitory and selfish and seek the good of the whole. In *The Philosophy of Loyalty* he interprets this general duty to promote unity in a new way. The ideal community, existing for the moral consciousness in aspiration rather than in fact, is the true object of love and loyalty. Dedication to self-transcending causes, even though these may be limited at first, is training for community. But once the essence of community is grasped the true moral maxim is perceived to be "loyalty to loyalty." Royce did not take this to mean, as naïve critics often asserted, blind devotion to an abstract principle, or allegiance to any self-transcending cause, however pointless or futile or ill-advised it may be. Loyalty to loyalty is a formula expressing the supreme love and respect of the whole community, not only some limited part of it. For the community is the surrogate of God in the finite and the source of being for the individual.

The Great Community is Royce's exalted dream of that ultimate unity of purpose attained when loyalty and love triumph over conflict and war; when competition and discord melt before the beneficent warmth of coöperation and harmony. Royce sees the beginnings of such a community in the society of scientists coöperating in the search for truth, and in the Christian community of believers modeled on the Pauline church. Whatever creates and promotes sharable values strengthens and sustains the community. Royce did not regard the political state or the nation as being communities in the true sense, for they foster a spirit of partisanship, exclusiveness and animosity towards other states and nations.

While he was occupied with these thoughts the First World War broke out. His friends wondered: Would Royce regard the war as being in the serene, cosmic scheme of things merely an episode which would, in due course, be rectified, while, in the meantime, it enlarged the opportunities for virtue? He himself delivered the answer in a

[20] Some of Royce's contemporaries wondered whether, in this new tack of his thought, he had abandoned the old doctrine of the Absolute. See, *e.g.*, G. H. Howison's essay in *Papers in Honor of Josiah Royce* (1916), p. 13. We have it from Royce himself that this was not the case. He commented: "These reflections [on interpretation] constitute for me, not something inconsistent with my former position, but ... a new attainment,—I believe a new growth." See "Letter to M. W. Calkins," *ibid.*, p. 66.

dramatic public denunciation of the aggressors.[21] Here was evil rampant, and he rose up and called it by name. The ideal of the great community provided Royce with a definite criterion of good and evil that helped him to overcome the indecisiveness of his earlier meditations on evil.

As an earnest of his profound interest in deepening the sense of community Royce proposed, in his last years, a quixotic scheme of insurance against war.[22] The idea of insurance appealed to him; it is a way of uniting men into groups of greater stability; it involves a triadic relation of social interdependency between insured, insurer and beneficiary; and it helps people bear each other's burdens. The extension of insurance, he believed, would help to establish a tangible community of interpretation.

Royce's inability to elicit for this scheme any active support served to deepen his pathetic awareness that he was "unpractical" and "a poor helper of concrete social enterprises." [23] Far-fetched and confused as this plan appears to the present-day reader, it was to Royce's way of thinking just one more application of his teaching that "we are saved through community." His was the impractical nature of one who sought his whole life long to understand and abet the workings of the spirit. His failures were those of a mind unaccustomed to dealing with anything less than Promethean problems. But in the spirit of good will, in the sincere endeavor to be of service, in the desire to see the good and truth prevail, Royce was without a peer.

Royce's Philosophy: An Evaluation

The philosophical literature between 1890 and 1920 is replete with attack and defense of Royce's position as a whole and of its characteristic features.[24] So much water has gone over the dams of thought since then that it would serve no good purpose to review those controversies. It is more profitable to appraise the general significance of Royce's thought in the light of recent developments in philosophy.

In this perspective, Royce is the last of a long line of monistic idealists aiming to solve the perennial problems of philosophy and life in a frame of reference perfected in the religious and moral environment of the eighteenth century. The equivocations of Royce's system make it evident, however, that this mode of thought was ill adapted to found a compelling philosophy for the twentieth century. Ever since the early decades of the nineteenth century there has been an accelerated aug-

[21] See chapters 1-3 and 5 in *The Hope of the Great Community* (1916).
[22] *War and Insurance* (1914).
[23] See "Words of Professor Royce," in *Papers in Honor of Josiah Royce* (1916), p. 282.
[24] See the Appendix, section 4, for selected examples of this literature.

mentation of concrete data, making it more and more hazardous for
the metaphysician who would detect *the* cosmic design in the welter
of facts. Eventually the old ontological schemes, unable to accommo-
date this accumulating wealth of new facts, burst at every seam. Royce
strove conscientiously to assimilate the new, to appreciate the significance of science, to defend individuality and concreteness. But the
combination of exuberant romanticism and systematic rationalism to
which he was committed was no longer equal to the task, not even
after the logical tinkering and refurbishing which Royce undertook in
the interest of bolstering the old way of thinking.

Royce thus represents a stage half way between the old and the
new in contemporary western thought. His fundamental insights—the
reality and self-transcendence of the concrete person, the fact that the
whole is implicit in its parts, the notion of interpretation and of community—are as vivid and significant now as when he defended them.
But his conception of that whole was one that left a chasm between
the Absolute and the world of concrete particulars. That no isolated
fact or individual is self-sufficient, that meanings emerge only in a
context of interpretation—all this is richly verified in experience and
is affirmed, furthermore, in many living systems of thought today. But
does this suffice to prove that there exists in fact a completed absolute
whole of the sort described by Royce? Does the existence of interdependent parts imply just this actualized unity? The evidence does
not permit of so definite a conclusion. Royce's confidence was a leap
of faith, an aspiration that he sought to justify in the court of 'dry
logic.'

In view of this fact it is not surprising that there are few disciples
of Royce in the strict sense. The dominant philosophies of this century
—Whitehead's philosophy of organism, Dewey's contextualism, Bergson's spiritual philosophy of nature, Santayana's synthesis of naturalism
and Platonism, phenomenology—begin, not by positing the completed
unity of finite fact, but by seeking in experience for specific modes of
empirical interdependence which, speculatively projected, may serve
to make a case for one world in the making. Viewed in the light of this
tendency, Royce's argument for the Absolute, based on the implications
of thought instead of on experience of the actual workings of the
whole in the parts, does not appear logically coercive to the twentieth
century mind. Royce seemed to sense this in the last phase of his
development. In *The Problem of Christianity* he addressed himself to
the task of *constructing* the Absolute by way of the actual community
of interpretation. But the bonds tying him to his original argument for
the completed, perfect Absolute, the archetype of all lesser workings,

were still too strong to permit of a radical transformation in his conception of the One.

Royce was in his time a respected and eloquent spokesman for many sensitive and troubled souls who were searching for spiritual peace in a world wracked by the convulsive disturbances attending the growth of modern, scientific technology. Like so many of his compatriots he was too deeply imbued with scientific rationalism to embrace a faith which could not be squared with reason. But he was, at the same time, too deeply religious to accept the verdict of scientific thought as the final or whole truth. He was dedicated to the healing mission of making life whole again. Although he did not succeed in this endeavor, he wrote a significant chapter in the struggle of modern western man to conquer the tragic sense of alienation from a world of his own making. His philosophy survived his times because Royce possessed both the courage and the intellectual power to treat of the perennial, universal themes of the great tradition in philosophy.

OTTO F. KRAUSHAAR

GOUCHER COLLEGE

1. The Nature of Community [1]

MOTIVES WHICH ARE as familiar as they are hard to analyze have convinced us all, before we begin to philosophize, that our human world contains a variety of individually distinct minds or selves, and that some, for us decisively authoritative, principle of individuation, keeps these selves apart, and forbids us to regard their various lives merely as incidents, or as undivided phases of a common life. This conviction—the stubborn pluralism of our present and highly cultivated social consciousness—tends indeed, under criticism, to be subject to various doubts and modifications—the more so as, in case we are once challenged to explain who we are, none of us find it easy to define the precise boundaries of the individual self, or to tell wherein it differs from the rest of the world, and, in particular, from the selves of other men.

But to all such doubts our social common sense replies by insisting upon three groups of facts. These facts combine to show that the individual human selves are sundered from one another by gaps which, as it would seem, are in some sense impassable.

First, in this connection, our common sense insists upon the empirical sundering of the feelings—that is, of the immediate experiences of various human individuals. One man does not feel, and, speaking in terms of direct experience, cannot feel, the physical pains of another man. Sympathy may try its best to bridge the gulf thus established by nature. Love may counsel me to view the pangs of my fellow *as if they were* my own. But, as a fact, my sensory nerves do not end in my fellow's skin, but in mine. And the physical sundering of the organisms corresponds to a persistent sundering of our streams of immediate feeling. Even the most immediate and impressive forms of sympathy with the physical pangs of another human being only serve the more to illustrate how our various conscious lives are thus kept apart by gulfs which we cannot cross. When a pitiful man shrinks, or feels faint, or is otherwise overcome with emotion, at what is called "the sight" of another's suffering—how unlike are the sufferings of the shrinking or terrified or overwhelmed spectator, and the pangs of the one with whom he is said to sympathize. As a fact, the sympathizer does not feel the sufferer's pain. What he feels is his own emotional reverberation at the sight of its symptoms. That is, in general, something very different, both in quality and in intensity, from what the injured man feels.

We appear, then, to be individuated by the diversity and the sepa-

[1] From *The Problem of Christianity* (New York, The Macmillan Co., 1913), vol. II, Lectures IX and X, with omissions. The topical headings and the footnotes have been supplied by the editor.

rateness of our streams of immediate feeling. My toothache cannot directly become an item in my neighbor's mind. Facts of this sort form the first group of evidences upon which common sense depends for its pluralistic view of the world of human selves.

The facts of the second group are closely allied to the former, but lie upon another level of individual life—namely, upon the level of our more organized ideas.

"One man," so says our social common sense, "can only indirectly discover the intentions, the thoughts, the ideas of another man." Direct telepathy, if it ever occurs at all, is a rare and, in most of our practical relations, a wholly negligible fact. By nature, every man's plans, intents, opinions, and range of personal experience are secrets, except in so far as his physical organism indirectly reveals them. His fellows can learn these secrets only through his expressive movements. Control your expression, keep silence, avoid the unguarded look and the telltale gesture; and then nobody can discover what is in your mind. No man can directly read the hearts of his fellows. This seems, for our common sense, to be one of the deepest-seated laws of our social experience. It is often expressed as if it were not merely an empirical law, but a logical necessity. How could I possibly possess or share or become conscious of the thoughts and purposes of another mind, unless I were myself identical with that mind? So says our ordinary common sense. The very supposition that I could be conscious of a thought or of an intent which was all the while actually present to the consciousness of another individual man, is often regarded as a supposition not only contrary to fact, but also contrary to reason. Such a supposition, it is often said, would involve a direct self-contradiction.

Otherwise expressed, the facts of this second group, and the principles which they exemplify, are summed up by asserting, as our social common sense actually asserts: We are individuated by the law that our trains of conscious thought and purpose are mutually inaccessible through any mode of direct intuition. Each of us lives within the charmed circle of his own conscious will and meaning—each of us is more or less clearly the object of his own inspection, but is hopelessly beyond the direct observation of his fellows.

Of separate streams of feeling—of mutually inaccessible and essentially secret trains of ideas—we men are thus constituted. By such forms and by such structure of mental life, by such divisions which no human power can bring into one unity of insight, individual human minds are forced to exist together upon terms which make them, in so far, appear to resemble Leibnizian monads. Their only windows appear to be those which their physical organisms supply.[2]

[2] In the ingenious system of G. W. Leibniz (1646-1716) the ultimate constituents of reality are monads, which are said to be "windowless" because they are incapable of communicating with or influencing one another directly.

The third group of facts here in question is the group upon which our cultivated social common sense most insists whenever ethical problems are in question; and therefore it is precisely this third group of facts which has most interest in its bearings upon the idea of the community.

"We are all members one of another." So says the doctrine of the community. "On the contrary," so our social common sense insists: "We are beings, each of whom has a soul of his own, a destiny of his own, rights of his own, worth of his own, ideals of his own, and an individual life in which this soul, this destiny, these rights, these ideals, get their expression. No other man can do my deed for me. When I choose, my choice coalesces with the voluntary decision of no other individual." Such, I say, is the characteristic assertion to which this third group of facts leads our ordinary social pluralism.

In brief: We thus seem to be individuated by our deeds. The will whereby I choose my own deed, is not my neighbor's will. My act is my own. Another man can perform an act which repeats the type of my act, or which helps or hinders my act. But if the question arises concerning any one act: Who hath done this?—such a question admits of only one true answer. Deeds and their doers stand in one-one correspondence. Such is the opinion of our cultivated modern ethical common sense...

Nevertheless, all these varieties of individual experience, these chasms which at any one present moment seem to sunder mind and mind, and these ethical considerations which have taught us to think of one man as morally independent of another, do not tell us the whole truth about the actual constitution of the social realm. There are facts that seem to show that these many are also one. These, then, are facts which force upon us the problem of the community...

We may be aided in making a more decisive advance towards understanding what a community is by emphasizing at this point a motive which we have not before mentioned, and which no doubt plays a great part in the psychology of the social consciousness.

Any notable case wherein we find a social organization which we can call, in the psychological sense, either a highly developed community or the creation or product of such a community, is a case where some process of the nature of a history—that is, of coherent social evolution—has gone on, and has gone on for a long time, and is more or less remembered by the community in question. If, ignoring history, you merely take a cross-section of the social order at any one moment; and if you thus deal with social groups that have little or no history, and confine your attention to social processes which occur during a short period of time—for example, during an hour, or a day, or a year —what then is likely to come to your notice takes either the predominantly pluralistic form of the various relatively independent doings of detached individuals, or else the social form of the confused activities of a crowd. A crowd, whether it be a dangerous mob, or an amiably joyous gathering at a picnic, is not a community. It has a mind, but no institutions, no organization, no coherent unity, no history, no traditions. It may be a unit, but is then of the type which suggests James's mere blending of various consciousnesses [3]—a sort of mystical loss of personality on the part of its members. On the other hand, a group of independent buyers at market, or of the passers-by in a city street, is not a community. And it also does not suggest to the onlooker any blending of many selves in one. Each purchaser seeks his own affairs. There may be gossip, but gossip is not a function which establishes the life of a community. For gossip has a short memory. But a true community is essentially a product of a time-process. A community has a past and will have a future. Its more or less conscious history, real or ideal, is a part of its very essence. A community requires for its existence a history and is greatly aided in its consciousness by a memory . . .

The psychological unity of many selves in one community is bound up, then, with the consciousness of some lengthy social process which has occurred, or is at least supposed to have occurred. And the wealthier the memory of a community is, and the vaster the historical processes which it regards as belonging to its life, the richer—other things being equal—is its consciousness that it *is* a community, that its members are somehow made one in and through and with its own life . . .

The rule that time is needed for the formation of a conscious community is a rule which finds its extremely familiar analogy within the life of every individual human self. Each one of us knows that he just now, at this instant, cannot find more than a mere fragment of himself present. The self comes down to us from its own past. It needs and is a history. Each of us can see that his own idea of himself as this person is inseparably bound up with his view of his own former life, of the plans that he formed, of the fortunes that fashioned him, and of the accomplishments which in turn he has fashioned for himself. A self is, by its very essence, a being with a past. One must look lengthwise backwards in the stream of time in order to see the self, or its shadow, now moving with the stream, now eddying in the currents from bank to bank of its channel, and now strenuously straining onwards in the pursuit of its own chosen good.

At this present moment I am indeed here, as this creature of the moment—sundered from the other selves. But nevertheless, if consid-

---

[3] Royce probably has in mind William James's essay on "The Compounding of Consciousness." See *A Pluralistic Universe,* essay V; also pp. 160-165 above.

ered simply in this passing moment of my life, I am hardly a self at all. I am just a flash of consciousness—the mere gesticulation of a self— not a coherent personality. Yet memory links me with my own past— and not, in the same way, with the past of anyone else. This joining of the present to the past reveals a more or less steady tendency—a sense about the whole process of my remembered life. And this tendency and sense of my individual life agree, on the whole, with the sense and the tendencies that belong to the entire flow of the time-stream, so far as it has sense at all. My individual life, my own more or less well-sundered stream of tendency, not only is shut off at each present moment by various barriers from the lives of other selves—but also constitutes an intelligible sequence in itself, so that, as I look back, I can say: "What I yesterday intended to pursue, that I am today still pursuing." "My present carries farther the plan of my past." Thus, then, I am one more or less coherent plan expressed in a life. "The child is father to the man." My days are "bound each to each by mutual piety."

Since I am this self, not only by reason of what now sunders me from the inner lives of other selves, but by reason of what links me, in significant fashion, to the remembered experiences, deeds, plans, and interests of my former conscious life, I need a somewhat extended and remembered past to furnish the opportunity for my self to find, when it looks back, a long process that possesses sense and coherence. In brief, my idea of myself is an interpretation of my past—linked also with an interpretation of my hopes and intentions as to my future.

Precisely as I thus define myself with reference to my own past, so my fellows also interpret the sense, the value, the qualifications, and the possessions of my present self by virtue of what are sometimes called my antecedents. In the eyes of his fellow-men, the child is less of a self than is the mature man; and he is so not merely because the child just now possesses a less wealthy and efficient conscious life than a mature man possesses, but because the antecedents of his present self are fewer than are the antecedents of the present self of the mature man. The child has little past. He has accomplished little. The mature man bears the credit and the burden of his long life of deeds. He not only possesses, but in great part is, for his fellow-men, a record.

These facts about our individual self-consciousness are indeed well known. But they remind us that our idea of the individual self is no mere present datum, or collection of data, but is based upon an interpretation of the sense, of the tendency, of the coherence, and of the value of a life to which belongs the memory of its own past. And therefore these same facts will help us to see how the idea of the community is also an idea which is impressed upon us whenever we make a sufficiently successful and fruitful effort to interpret the sense, the coherent interest, and the value of the relations in which a great number of different selves stand to the past...

Just as each one of many present selves, despite the psychological or ethical barriers which now keep all of these selves sundered, may accept the same past fact or event as a part of himself, and say, "That belonged to my life," even so, each one of many present selves, despite these same barriers and sunderings, may accept the same future event, which all of them hope or expect, as part of his own personal future. Thus, during a war, all of the patriots of one of the contending nations may regard the termination of the war, and the desired victory of their country, so that each one says: "I shall rejoice in the expected surrender of that stronghold of the enemy. That surrender will be my triumph."

Now when many contemporary and distinct individual selves so interpret, each his own personal life, that each says of an individual past or of a determinate future event or deed: "That belongs to my life;" "That occurred, or will occur, to me," then these many selves may be defined as hereby constituting, in a perfectly definite and objective, but also in a highly significant, sense, a community. They may be said to constitute a community *with reference* to that particular past or future event, or group of events, which each of them accepts or interprets as belonging to his own personal past or to his own individual future. A community constituted by the fact that each of its members accepts as part of his own individual life and self the same *past* events that each of his fellow-members accepts, may be called a *community of memory*. Such is any group of persons who individually either remember or commemorate the same dead—each one finding, because of personal affection or of reverence for the dead, that those whom he commemorates form for him a part of his own past existence.

A community constituted by the fact that each of its members accepts, as part of his own individual life and self, the same expected *future* events that each of his fellows accepts, may be called a *community of expectation*, or upon occasion, a *community of hope*.

A community, whether of memory or of hope, exists relatively to the past or future facts to which its several members stand in the common relation just defined. The concept of the community depends upon the interpretation which each individual member gives to his own self—to his own past—and to his own future. Every one of us does, for various reasons, extend his interpretation of his own individual self so that from his own point of view, his life includes many far-away temporal happenings. The complex motives of such interpretations need not now be further examined. Enough—these motives may vary from self to self with all the wealth of life. Yet when these interests of each self lead it to accept any part or item of the same past or the same future which another self accepts as its own—then pluralism of the selves is perfectly consistent with their forming a community, either of memory or of hope. How rich this community is in meaning, in value, in membership, in significant organization, will depend upon the selves that enter into the community, and upon the ideals in terms of which they define themselves, their past, and their future.

With this definition in mind, we see why long histories are needed in order to define the life of great communities. We also see that, if great new undertakings enter into the lives of many men, a new community of hope, unified by the common relations of its individual members to the same future events, may be, upon occasion, very rapidly constituted, even in the midst of great revolutions.

The concept of the community, as thus analyzed, stands in the closest relation to the whole nature of the time-process, and also involves recognizing to the full both the existence and the significance of individual selves. In what sense the individual selves constitute the community we can in general see, while we are prepared to find that, for the individual selves, it may well prove to be the case that a real community of memory or of hope is necessary in order to secure their significance. Our own definition of a community can be illustrated by countless types of political, religious, and other significant communities which you will readily be able to select for yourselves. Without ignoring our ordinary social pluralism, this definition shows how and why many selves may be viewed as actually brought together in an historical community. Without presupposing any one metaphysical interpretation of experience, or of time, our definition shows where, in our experience and in our interpretation of the time-process, we are to look for a solution of the problem of the community. Without going beyond the facts of human life, of human memory, and of human interpretation of the self and of its past, our definition clears the way for a study of the constitution of the real world of the spirit. . .

Our definition presupposes that there exist many individual selves. Suppose these selves to vary in their present experiences and purposes as widely as you will. Imagine them to be sundered from one another by such chasms of mutual mystery and independence as, in our natural social life, often seem hopelessly to divide and secrete the inner world of each of us from the direct knowledge and estimate of his fellows. But let these selves be able to look beyond their present chaos of fleeting ideas and of warring desires, far away into the past whence they came, and into the future whither their hopes lead them. As they thus look, let each one of them ideally enlarge his own individual life, extending himself into the past and future, so as to say of some far-off event, belonging, perhaps, to other generations of men, "I view that event as a part of my own life." "That former happening or achievement so predetermined the sense and the destiny which are now mine, that I am moved to regard it as belonging to my own past." Or again: "For that coming event I wait and hope as an event of my own future."

And further, let the various ideal extensions, forwards and backwards, include at least one common event, so that each of these selves regards that event as a part of his own life.

Then, *with reference to the ideal common past and future in question, I say that these selves constitute a community.* This is henceforth to be our definition of a community. The present variety of the selves who are the members of the spiritual body so defined, is not hereby either annulled or slighted. The motives which determine each of them thus ideally to extend his own life, may vary from self to self in the most manifold fashion.

Our definition will enable us, despite all these varieties of the mem‹ bers, to understand in what sense any such community as we have defined exists, and is one.

Into this form, which, when thus summarily described, seems so abstract and empty, life can and does pour the rich contents and ideals which make the communities of our human world so full of dramatic variety and significance.

The *first* condition upon which the existence of a community, in our sense of the word, depends, is the power of an individual self to extend his life, in ideal fashion, so as to regard it as including past and future events which lie far away in time, and which he does not now personally remember. That this power exists, and that man has a self which is thus ideally extensible in time without any definable limit, we all know.

This power itself rests upon the principle that, however a man may come by his idea of himself, the self is no mere datum, but is in its essence a life which is interpreted, and which interprets itself, and which, apart from some sort of ideal interpretation, is a mere flight of ideas, or a meaningless flow of feelings, or a vision that sees nothing, or else a barren abstract conception. How deep the process of interpretation goes in determining the real nature of the self, we shall only later be able to estimate.

There is no doubt that what we usually call our personal memory does indeed give us assurances regarding our own past, so far as memory extends and is trustworthy. But our trust in our memories is itself an interpretation of their data. All of us regard as belonging, even to our recent past life, much that we cannot just now remember. And the future self shrinks and expands with our hopes and our energies. No one can merely, from without, set for us the limits of the life of the self, and say to us: "Thus far and no farther."

In my ideal extensions of the life of the self, I am indeed subject to some sort of control—to what control we need not here attempt to formulate. I must be able to give myself some sort of reason, personal, or social, or moral, or religious, or metaphysical, for taking on or throwing off the burden, the joy, the grief, the guilt, the hope, the glory of past and of future deeds and experiences; but I must also myself personally share in this task of determining how much of the past and the future shall ideally enter into my life, and shall contribute to the value of that life.

And if I choose to say, "There is a sense in which *all* the tragedy and the attainment of an endless past and future of deeds and of fortunes enter into my own life," I say only what saints and sages of the most various creeds and experiences have found their several reasons for saying. The fact and the importance of such ideal extensions of the self must therefore be recognized. Here is the first basis for every clear idea of what constitutes a community...

The *second* condition upon which the existence of a community depends is the fact that there are in the social world a number of distinct selves capable of social communication, and, in general, engaged in communication.

The distinctness of the selves we have illustrated at length in our previous discussion. We need not here dwell upon the matter further, except to say, expressly, that a community does not become one, in the sense of my definition, by virtue of any reduction or melting of these various selves into a single merely present self, or into a mass of passing experience. That mystical phenomena may indeed form part of the life of a community, just as they may also form part of the life of an individual human being, I fully recognize...

The *third* of the conditions for the existence of the community which my definition emphasizes consists in the fact that the ideally extended past and future selves of the members include at least some events which are, for all these selves, identical. This third condition is the one which furnishes both the most exact, the most widely variable, and the most important of the motives which warrant us in calling a community a real unit. The Pauline metaphor of the body and the members finds, in this third condition, its most significant basis—a basis capable of exact description...

Men do not form a community, in our present restricted sense of that word, merely in so far as the men coöperate. They form a community, in our present limited sense, when they not only coöperate, but accompany this coöperation with that ideal extension of the lives of individuals whereby each coöperating member says: "This activity which we perform together, this work of ours, its past, its future, its sequence, its order, its sense,—all these enter into my life, and are the life of my own self writ large."...

But we have now been led to a narrower application of the term "community." It is an application to which we have restricted the term simply because of our special purpose in this inquiry. Using this restricted definition of the term "community," we see that groups which coöperate may be very far from constituting communities in our narrower sense. We also see how, in general, a group whose coöperative activities are very highly complex will require a correspondingly long period of time to acquire that sort of tradition and of common expectation which is needed to constitute a community in our sense—that is, a community conscious of its own life.

Owing to the psychological conditions upon which social coöperation depends, such coöperation can very far outstrip, in the complexity of its processes, the power of any individual man's wit to understand its intricacies. In modern times, when social coöperation both uses and is so largely dominated by the industrial arts, the physical conditions of coöperative social life have combined with the psychological conditions to make any thorough understanding of the coöperative processes upon which we all depend simply hopeless for the individual, except within some narrow range. Experts become well acquainted with aspects of these forms of coöperation which their own callings involve. Less expert workers understand a less range of the coöperative processes in which they take part. Most individuals, in most of their work, have to coöperate as the cogs coöperate in the wheels of a mechanism. They work together; but few or none of them know how they coöperate, or what they must do.

But the true community, in our present restricted sense of the word, depends for its genuine common life upon such coöperative activities that the individuals who participate in these common activities understand enough to be able, first, to direct their own deeds of coöperation; secondly, to observe the deeds of their individual fellow workers, and thirdly to know that, without just this combination, this order, this interaction of the coworking selves, just this deed could not be accomplished by the community. So, for instance, a chorus or an orchestra carries on its coöperative activities. In these cases coöperation is a conscious art. If hereupon these coöperative deeds, thus understood by the individual coworker, are viewed by him as linked, through an extended history with past and future deeds of the community, and if he then identifies his own life with this common life, and if his fellow members agree in this identification, then indeed the community both has a common life, and is aware of the fact. For then the individual coworker not only says: "This past and future fortune of the community belongs to my life"; but also declares: "This past and future deed of coöperation belongs to my life." "This, which none of us could have done alone—this, which all of us together could not have accomplished unless we were ordered and linked in precisely this way—this we together accomplished, or shall yet accomplish; and this deed of all of us belongs to my life."

A community thus constituted is essentially a community of those who are artists in some form of coöperation, and whose art constitutes, for each artist, his own ideally extended life. But the life of an artist depends upon his love for his art.

The community is made possible by the fact that each member includes in his own ideally extended life the deeds of coöperation which the members accomplish. When these deeds are hopelessly complex, how shall the individual member be able to regard them as genuinely belonging to his own ideally extended life? He can no longer understand them in any detail. He takes part in them, willingly or unwillingly. He does so because he is social, and because he must. He works in his factory, or has his share, whether greedily or honestly, in the world's commercial activities. And his coöperations may be skillful; and this fact also he may know. But his skill is largely due to external training, not to inner expansion of the ideals of the self. And the more complex the social order grows, the more all this coöperation must tend to appear to the individual as a mere process of nature, and not as his own work—as a mechanism and not as an ideal extension of himself— unless indeed love supplies what individual wit can no longer accomplish.

If a social order, however complex it may be, actually wins and keeps the love of its members; so that—however little they are able to understand the details of their present coöperative activities- they still—with all their whole hearts and their minds and their souls, and their strength —desire, each for himself, that such coöperations should go on; and if each member, looking back to the past, rejoices in the ancestors and the heroes who have made the present life of this social group possible; and if he sees in these deeds of former generations the source and support of his present love; and if each member also looks forward with equal love to the future—then indeed love furnishes that basis for the consciousness of the community which intelligence, without love, in a highly complex social realm, can no longer furnish. Such love—such loyalty—depends not upon losing sight of the variety of the callings of individuals, but upon seeing in the successful coöperation of all the members precisely that event which the individual member most eagerly loves as his own fulfillment.

When love of the community, nourished by common memories, and common hope, both exists and expresses itself in devoted individual lives, it can constantly tend, despite the complexity of the present social order, to keep the consciousness of the community alive. And when this takes place, the identification of the loyal individual self with the life of the community will tend, both in ideal and in feeling, to identify each self not only with the distant past and future of the community, but with the present activities of the whole social body.

Thus, for instance, when the complexities of business life, and the dreariness of the factory, have, to our minds, deprived our present social coöperations of all or of most of their common significance, the great communal or national festivity, bringing to memory the great events of past and future, not only makes us, for the moment, feel and think as a community with reference to those great past and future events, but in its turn, as a present event, reacts upon next day's ordinary labors. The festivity says to us: "We are one because of our common past and future, because of the national heroes and victories and hopes, and because we love all these common memories and hopes." Our next day's mood, consequent upon the festivity, bids us say: "Since we are thus possessed of this beloved common past and future, let this consciousness lead each of us even today to extend his ideal self so as to include the daily work of all his fellows, and to view his fellow members' life as his own."

Thus memory and hope tend to react upon the present self, which finds the brotherhood of present labor more significant, and the ideal identification of the present self with the self of the neighbor easier, because the ideal extension of the self into past and future has preceded.

And so, first, each of us learns to say: "This beloved past and future life, by virtue of the ideal extension, is my own life." Then, finding that our fellows have and love this past and future in common with us, we learn further to say: "In this respect we are all one loving and beloved community." Then we take a further step and say: "Since we are all members of this community, therefore, despite our differences, and our mutual sunderings of inner life, each of us can, and will, ideally extend his present self so as to include the present life and deeds of his fellow."...

Love, when it exists and triumphs over the complexities which obscure and confuse the common life, thus completes the consciousness of the community, in the forms which that consciousness can assume under human conditions. Such love, however, must be one that has the common deeds of the community as its primary object. No one understands either the nature of the loyal life, or the place of love in the constitution of the life of a real community, who conceives such love as merely a longing for the mystical blending of the selves or for their mutual interpenetration, and for that only. Love says to the individual: "So extend yourself, in ideal, that you aim, with all your heart and your soul and your mind and your strength, at *that* life of perfectly definite deeds which never can come to pass unless all the members, despite their variety and their natural narrowness, are in perfect coöperation. Let this life be your art and also the art of all your fellow members. Let your community be as a chorus, and not as a company who forget themselves in a common trance.". . .

2. Interpretation [4]

IN DEFINING what constitutes a community I have repeatedly mentioned processes of Interpretation. The word "interpretation" is well known; and students of the humanities have special reasons for using it frequently. When one calls an opinion about the self an interpretation, one is not employing language that is familiar only to philosophers. When a stranger in a foreign land desires the services of an interpreter, when a philologist offers his rendering of a text, when a judge construes a statute, some kind of interpretation is in question. And the process of interpretation, whatever it is, is intended to meet human needs which are as well known as they are vital. Such needs determine, as we shall see, whatever is humane and articulate in the whole conduct and texture of our lives.

Yet if we ask, What is an interpretation?—the answer is not easy. Nor is it made much easier by stating the question in the form: What does one desire who seeks for an interpretation? What does one gain, or create, or acknowledge who accepts an interpretation?

Our investigation has reached the point where it is necessary to face these questions, as well as some others closely related to them. For, as a fact, to inquire what the process of interpretation is, takes us at once to the very heart of philosophy, throws a light both on the oldest and on the latest issues of metaphysical thought. . .

. . . A community, as we have seen, depends for its very constitution upon the way in which each of its members interprets himself and his life. For the rest, nobody's self is either a mere datum or an abstract conception. A self is a life whose unity and connectedness depend upon some sort of interpretation of plans, of memories, of hopes, and of deeds. If, then, there are communities, there are many selves who, despite their variety, so interpret their lives that all these lives, taken together, get the type of unity which our last lecture characterized. Were there, then, no interpretations in the world, there would be neither selves nor communities. Thus our effort to study matters of fact led us back to problems of interpretation. These latter problems obviously dominate every serious inquiry into our problem of Christianity.

What, however, is any philosophy but an interpretation either of

[4] From *The Problem of Christianity*, vol. II, Lectures XI and XII, with omissions. Some references to Royce's intellectual debt to Peirce are contained in the omissions.

life, or of the universe, or of both? Does there exist, then, any student of universally interesting issues who is not concerned with an answer to the question, What is an interpretation?

Possibly these illustrations of our topic, few as they are, seem already so various in their characters as to suggest that the term "interpretation" may be too vague in its applications to admit of precise definition. A rendering of a text written in a foreign tongue; a judge's construction of a statute; a man's interpretation of himself and of his own life; our own philosophical interpretation of this or of that religious idea; and the practical interpretation of our destiny, or of God, which a great historical religion itself seems to have taught to the faithful; or, finally, a metaphysical interpretation of the universe—what—so you may ask— have all these things in common? What value can there be in attempting to fix by a definition such fluent and uncontrollable interests as inspire what various people may call by the common name interpretation?

I reply that, beneath all this variety in the special motives which lead men to interpret objects, there exists a very definable unity of purpose. Look more closely, and you shall see that to interpret, or to attempt an interpretation, is to assume an attitude of mind which differs, in a notable way, from the other attitudes present in the intelligent activities of men; while this attitude remains essentially the same amidst very great varieties, both in the individual interpreters and in the interpretations which they seek, or undertake, or accept. Interpretation, viewed as a mental process, or as a type of knowledge, differs from other mental processes and types of knowledge in the objects to which it is properly applied, in the relations in which it stands to these objects, and in the ends which it serves.

In order to show you that this is the case, I must summarize in my own way some still neglected opinions which were first set forth, in outline, more than forty years ago by our American logician, Mr. Charles Peirce. . .[5]

The contrast between the cognitive processes called, respectively, perception and conception, dominates a great part of the history of philosophy. This contrast is usually so defined as to involve a dual classification of our cognitive processes. When one asks which of the two processes, perception or conception, gives us the more significant guidance, or is the original from which the other is derived, or is the ideal process whereof the other is the degenerate fellow, such a dual classification is in possession of the field. . .

[5] Royce here refers to four articles Peirce published in 1867-1869, which may now be found in Peirce's *Collected Papers* 1.545-559; 5.213-357. He adds a reference to Peirce's article on "Signs" in Baldwin's *Dictionary of Philosophy and Psychology*, which may also be found in *Collected Papers* 2.303-304.

Despite this prevalence of the dual classification of our cognitive processes, most of us will readily acknowledge that, in our real life, we human beings are never possessed either of pure perception or of pure conception. In ideal, we can define an intuitive type of knowledge, which should merely see, and which should never think. In an equally ideal fashion, we can imagine the possibility of a pure thought, which should be wholly absorbed in conceptions, which should have as its sole real object a realm of universals, and which should ignore all sensible data. But we mortals live the intelligent part of our lives through some sort of more or less imperfect union or synthesis of conception and perception.

When, a number of years ago, I began a general metaphysical inquiry by defining an idea as a "plan of action," and thereupon developed a theory of knowledge and of reality, upon bases which this definition helped me to formulate, I was making my own use of thoughts which, in their outlines, are at the present day common property. The outcome of my own individual use of this definition was a sort of absolute pragmatism, which has never been pleasing either to rationalists or to empiricists, either to pragmatists or to the ruling type of absolutists. But in so far as I simply insisted upon the active meaning of ideas, my statement has something in common with many forms of current opinion which agree with one another in hardly any other respect. Only the more uncompromising of the mystics still seek for knowledge in a silent land of absolute intuition, where the intellect finally lays down its conceptual tools, and rests from its pragmatic labors, while its works do not follow it, but are simply forgotten, and are as if they never had been. Those of us who are not such uncompromising mystics, view accessible human knowledge neither as pure perception nor as pure conception, but always as depending upon the marriage of the two processes. . .

We shall here be aided by a very familiar instance, suggested by the very illustration which Bergson uses in pointing out the contrast between perception and conception, and in emphasizing the secondary and purely instrumental character of the process of conception. Gold coin, as Bergson reminds us, corresponds, in its value for the ordinary business of buying and selling, to perceptions as they appear in our experience. Bank-notes correspond, in an analogous fashion, to conceptions. The notes are promises to pay cash. The conceptions are useful guides to possible perceptions. The link between the note and its cash-value is the link which the activity of making and keeping the promises of a solvent bank provides. The link between the conception and its corresponding perception is the link which some active synthesis, such as voluntary seeking, or creative action, or habitual conduct, or intention, supplies. The illustration is clear. In a special way perceptions do indeed correspond to cash-value, and conceptions to credit-values. But in the world of commercial transactions there are other values than simple cash-values and credit-values. Perhaps, therefore, in the realm of cognitive processes there may be analogous varieties.

Recall the familiar case wherein a traveller crosses the boundary of a foreign country. To the boundary he comes provided, let us say, with the gold and with bank-notes of his own country, but without any letter of credit. This side of the boundary his bank-notes are good because of their credit-value. His gold is good because, being the coinage of the realm, it possesses cash-value and is legal tender. But beyond the boundary, in the land to which he goes, the coin which he carries is no longer legal tender, and possibly will not pass at all in ordinary transactions. His bank-notes may be, for the moment, valueless, not because the promise stamped upon their face is irredeemable, but because the gold coin itself into which they could be converted upon presentation at the bank in question, would not be legal tender beyond the boundary.

Consequently, at the boundary, a new process may be convenient, if not, for the traveller's purpose, indispensable. It is the process of exchanging coin of the realm which he leaves for that of the foreign land which he enters. The process may be easy or difficult, may be governed by strict rules or else may be capricious, according to the conditions which prevail at the boundary. But it is a third process, which consists neither in the presentation of cash-values nor in the offering or accepting of credit-values. It is a process of interpreting the cash-values which are recognized by the laws and customs of one realm in terms of the cash-values which are legal tender in another country. It is also a process of proceeding to act upon the basis of this interpretation. We are not concerned with the principles which make this interpretation possible, or which guide the conduct either of the traveller or of the money-changer at the boundary. What interests us here is simply the fact that a new type of transaction is now in question. It is a process of money-changing—a special form of exchange of values, but a form not simply analogous to the type of the activities whereby conceptions are provided with their corresponding perceptions. And this form is not reducible to that of the simple contrast between credit-values and cash-values.

Each of us, in every new effort to communicate with our fellow-men, stands, like the traveller crossing the boundary of a new country, in the presence of a largely strange world of perceptions and of conceptions. Our neighbor's perceptions, in their immediate presence, we never quite certainly share. Our neighbor's conceptions, for various reasons which I need not here enumerate, are so largely communicable that they can often be regarded, with a high degree of probability, as identical, in certain aspects of their meaning, with our own. But the active syntheses, the practical processes of seeking and of construction, the volitions, the promises, whereby we pass from our own concepts to our own percepts, are often in a high degree individual. In that case it may be very difficult to compare them to the corresponding processes of our neighbors; and then a mutual understanding, in respect of our activities and their values, is frequently as hard to obtain as is a direct view of one another's sensory perceptions. "I never loved you," so says Hamlet to Ophelia. "My lord, you made me believe so." Here is a classic instance of a problem of mutual interpretation. Who of us can solve this problem for Hamlet and Ophelia?

Therefore, in our efforts to view the world as other men view it, our undertaking is very generally analogous to the traveller's financial transactions when he crosses the boundary. We try to solve the problem of learning how to exchange the values of our own lives into the terms which can hope to pass current in the new or foreign spiritual realms whereto, when we take counsel together, we are constantly attempting to pass. Both the credit-values and the cash-values are not always easily exchanged.

I have no hope of showing, in the present discussion, how and how far we can make sure that, in a given case of human social intercourse, we actually succeed in fairly exchanging the coinage of our perceptions and the bank-notes of our conceptions into the values which pass current in the realm beyond the boundary. What measure of truth our individual interpretations possess, and by what tests we verify that truth, I have not now to estimate. But I am strongly interested in the fact, that, just as the process of obtaining cash for our bank-notes is not the same as the process of exchanging our coins for foreign coins when we pass the border, precisely so the process of verifying our concepts through obtaining the corresponding percepts is not the same as the process of interpreting our neighbors' minds.

A philosophy which, like that of Bergson, defines the whole problem of knowledge in terms of the classic opposition between conception and perception, and which then declares that, if our powers of perception were unlimited, the goal of knowledge would be reached, simply misses the principal problem, both of our daily human existence and of all our higher spiritual life, as well as of the universe. And in bidding us seek the solution of our problems in terms of perception, such a doctrine simply forbids us to pass any of the great boundaries of the spiritual world, or to explore the many realms wherein the wealth of the spirit is poured out. For neither perception nor conception, nor any combination of the two, nor yet their synthesis in our practical activities, constitutes the whole of any interpretation. Interpretation, however, is what we seek in all our social and spiritual relations; and without some process of interpretation, we obtain no fulness of life.

It would be wrong to suppose, however, that interpretation is needed and is used only in our literal social relations with other individual human beings. For it is important to notice that one of the principal problems in the life of each of us is the problem of interpreting himself. The bare mention of Hamlet's words reminds us of this fact. Ophelia does not understand Hamlet. But does he understand himself?

In our inner life it not infrequently happens that we have—like the traveller, or like Hamlet in the ghost-scene, or like Macbeth when there comes the knocking on the gate—to pass a boundary, to cross into some new realm, not merely of experience, but of desire, of hope, or of resolve. It is then our fortune not merely that our former ideas, as the pragmatists say, no longer "work," and that our bank-notes can no longer be cashed in terms of the familiar inner perceptions which we have been accustomed to seek. Our situation is rather this: that *both* our ideas *and* our experiences, both our plans and our powers to realize plans, both our ideas with their "leadings" and our intuitions, are in process of dramatic transformation. At such times we need to know, like Pharaoh, both our dream and the interpretation thereof...

At such times we are impressed with the fact that there is no royal road to self-knowledge. Charles Peirce, in the earliest of the essays to which I am calling your attention, maintained (quite rightly, I think) that there is no direct intuition or perception of the self. Reflection, as Peirce there pointed out, involves what is, in its essence, an interior conversation, in which one discovers one's own mind through a process of inference analogous to the very modes of inference which guide us in a social effort to interpret our neighbors' minds. Such social inference is surely no merely conceptual process. But it cannot be reduced to the sort of perception which Bergson invited you, in his Oxford lectures, to share. Although you are indeed placed in the "interior" of yourself, you can never so far retire into your own inmost recesses of intuition as merely to find the true self presented to an inner sense...

Interpretation always involves a relation of three terms. In the technical phrase, interpretation *is* a triadic relation. That is, you cannot express any complete process of interpreting by merely naming two terms—persons, or other objects—and by then telling what dyadic relation exists between one of these two and the other.

Let me illustrate: Suppose that an Egyptologist translates an inscription. So far two beings are indeed in question: the translator and his text. But a genuine translation cannot be merely a translation in the abstract. There must be some language into which the inscription is translated. Let this translation be, in a given instance, an English translation. Then the translator interprets something; but he interprets it only to one who can read English. And if a reader knows no English, the translation is for such a reader no interpretation at all. That is, a triad of beings—the Egyptian text, the Egyptologist who translates, and the possible English reader—are equally necessary in order that such an English interpretation of an Egyptian writing should exist. Whenever anybody translates a text, the situation remains, however you vary texts or languages or translators, essentially the same. There must exist some one, or some class of beings, to whose use this translation is adapted; while the translator is somebody who expresses himself by mediating between two expressions of meanings, or between two languages, or between two speakers or two writers. The mediator or translator, or interpreter, must, in cases of this sort, himself know both languages, and thus be intelligible to both the persons whom his translation serves. The triadic relation in question is, in its essence, non-symmetrical—that is, unevenly arranged with respect to all three terms. Thus somebody (let us say A)—the translator or interpreter—interprets somebody (let us say B) to somebody (let us say C). If you transpose the order of the terms—A, B, C—an account of the happening which constitutes an interpretation must be altered, or otherwise may become either false or meaningless.

Thus an interpretation is a relation which not only involves three terms, but brings them into a determinate order. One of the three terms is the interpreter; a second term is the object—the person or the meaning or the text—which is interpreted; the third is the person to whom the interpretation is addressed.

This may, at first, seem to be a mere formality. But nothing in the world is more momentous than the difference between a pair and a triad of terms may become, if the terms and the relations involved are themselves sufficiently full of meaning.

You may observe that, when a man perceives a thing, the relation is dyadic. A perceives B. A pair of members is needed, and suffices, to make the relation possible. But when A interprets B to C, a triad of members (whereof, as in case of other relations, two or all three members may be wholly, or in part, identical) must exist in order to make the interpretation possible. Let illustrations show us how important this formal condition of interpretation may become.

When a process of conscious reflection goes on, a man may be said to interpret himself to himself. In this case, although but one personality, in the usual sense of the term, is in question, the relation is still really a triadic relation. And, in general, in such a case, the man who is said to be reflecting remembers some former promise or resolve of his own, or perhaps reads an old letter that he once wrote, or an entry in a diary. He then, at some present time, interprets this expression of his past self.

But, usually, he interprets this bit of his past self to his future self. "This," he says, "is what I meant when I made that promise." "This is what I wrote or recorded or promised." "Therefore," he continues, addressing his future self, "I am now committed to doing thus," "planning thus," and so on.

The interpretation in question still constitutes, therefore, a triadic relation. And there are three men present in and taking part in the interior conversation: the man of the past whose promises, notes, records, old letters, are interpreted; the present self who interprets them; and the future self to whom the interpretation is addressed. Through the present self the past is so interpreted that its counsel is conveyed to the future self.

The illustration just chosen has been taken from the supposed experience of an individual man. But the relations involved are capable of a far-reaching metaphysical generalization...

The relations exemplified by the man who, at a given present moment, interprets his own past to his own future, are precisely analogous to the relations which exist when any past state of the world is, at any present moment, so linked, through a definite historical process, with the coming state of the world, that an intelligent observer who happened to be in possession of the facts could, were he present, interpret to a possible future observer the meaning of the past. Such interpretation might or might not involve definite predictions of future events. History or biography, physical or mental processes, might be in question; fate or free will, determinism or chance, might rule the region of the world which was under consideration. The most general distinctions of past, present, and future appear in a new light when considered with reference to the process of interpretation.

In fact, what our own inner reflection exemplifies is outwardly embodied in the whole world's history. For what we all mean by past time is a realm of events whose historical sense, whose records, whose lessons, we may now interpret, in so far as our memory and the documents furnish us the evidences for such interpretation. We may also observe that what we mean by future time is a realm of events which we view as more or less under the control of the present will of voluntary agents, so that it is worth while to give to ourselves, or to our fellows, counsel regarding this future. And so, wherever the world's processes are recorded, wherever the records are preserved, and wherever they influence in any way the future course of events, we may say that (at least in these parts of the world) the present potentially interprets the past to the future, and continues so to do *ad infinitum*.

Such, for instance, is the case when one studies the crust of a planet.

The erosions and the deposits of a present geological period lay down the traces which, if read by a geologist, would interpret the past history of the planet's crust to the observers of future geological periods.

Thus the Colorado Cañon, in its present condition, is a geological section produced by a recent stream. Its walls record, in their stratification, a vast series of long-past changes. The geologist of the present may read these traces, and may interpret them for future geologists of our own age. But the present state of the Colorado Cañon, which will erc long pass away as the walls crumble, and as the continents rise or sink, will leave traces that may be used at some future time to interpret these now present conditions of the earth's crust to some still more advanced future, which will come to exist after yet other geological periods have passed away.

In sum, if we view the world as everywhere and always recording its own history, by processes of aging and weathering, or of evolution, or of stellar and nebular clusterings and streamings, we can simply define the time order, and its three regions—past, present, future—as an order of possible interpretation. That is, we can define the present as, potentially, the interpretation of the past to the future. The triadic structure of our interpretations is strictly analogous, both to the psychological and to the metaphysical structure of the world of time. And each of these structures can be stated in terms of the other.

This analogy between the relational structure of the whole time-process and the relations which are characteristic of any system of acts of interpretation seems to me to be worthy of careful consideration...

Psychologically speaking, the mental process which thus involves three members differs from perception and conception in three respects. First, interpretation is a conversation, and not a lonely enterprise. There is some one, in the realm of psychological happenings, who addresses some one. The one who addresses interprets some object to the one addressed. In the second place, the interpreted object is itself something which has the nature of a mental expression. Peirce uses the term "sign" to name this mental object which is interpreted. Thirdly, since the interpretation is a mental act, and is an act which is expressed, the interpretation itself is, in its turn, a Sign. This new sign calls for further interpretation. For the interpretation is addressed to somebody. And so—at least in ideal—the social process involved is endless. Thus wealthy, then, in its psychological consequences, is the formal character of a situation wherein any interpretation takes place.

Perception has its natural terminus in some object perceived; and therewith the process, as would seem, might end, were there nothing else in the world to perceive. Conception is contented, so to speak, with defining the universal type, or ideal form which chances to become an object of somebody's thought. In order to define a new universal, one needs a new act of thought whose occurrence seems, in so far, an arbitrary additional cognitive function. Thus both perception and conception are, so to speak, self-limiting processes. The wealth of their facts comes to them from without, arbitrarily.

But interpretation both requires as its basis the sign or mental expression which is to be interpreted, and calls for a further interpretation of its own act, just because it addresses itself to some third being. Thus interpretation is not only an essentially social process, but also a process which, when once initiated, can be terminated only by an external and arbitrary interruption, such as death or social separation. By itself, the process of interpretation calls, in ideal, for an infinite sequence of interpretations. For every interpretation, being addressed to somebody, demands interpretation from the one to whom it is addressed.

Thus the formal difference between interpretation on the one hand, and perception and conception on the other hand, is a difference involving endlessly wealthy possible psychological consequences.

Perception is indeed supported by the wealth of our sensory processes; and is therefore rightly said to possess an endless fecundity.

But interpretation lives in a world which is endlessly richer than the realm of perception. For its discoveries are constantly renewed by the inexhaustible resources of our social relations, while its ideals essentially demand, at every point, an infinite series of mutual interpretations in order to express what even the very least conversational effort, the least attempt to find our way in the life that we would interpret, involves.

Conception is often denounced, in our day, as "sterile." But perception, taken by itself, is intolerably lonesome. And every philosophy whose sole principle is perception invites us to dwell in a desolate wilderness where neither God nor man exists. For where either God or man is in question, interpretation is demanded. And interpretation —even the simplest, even the most halting and trivial interpretation of our daily life—seeks what eye hath not seen, and ear hath not heard, and what it hath not entered into the heart of man to conceive—namely, the successful interpretation of somebody to somebody.

Interpretation seeks an object which is essentially spiritual. The abyss of abstract conception says of this object: It is not in me. The heaven of glittering immediacies which perception furnishes answers the quest by saying: It is not in me. Interpretation says: It is nigh thee —even in thine heart; but shows us, through manifesting the very nature of the object to be sought, what general conditions must be met if any one is to interpret a genuine Sign to an understanding mind.

And withal, interpretation seeks a city out of sight, the homeland where, perchance, we learn to understand one another...

Recent pragmatism, both in the form emphasized by James and (so far as I know) in all its other now prominent forms, depends upon conceiving two types of cognitive processes, perception and conception, as mutually opposed, and as in such wise opposed that conception merely defines the bank-notes, while only perception can supply the needed cash. In consequence of this dualistic view of the cognitive process, and in view of other considerations recently emphasized, the essential doctrine of pragmatism has come to include the two well-known theses: That truth is mutable; and that the sole criterion of the present state of the truth is to be found in the contents of particular perceptions...

Whoever insists upon the mutability of truth, speaks in terms of the dual classification of cognitive processes. But let one learn to know that our very conception of our temporal experience, as of all happenings, is neither a conception nor a perception, but an interpretation. Let one note that every present judgment bearing upon future experience is indeed, as the pragmatists tell us, a practical activity. But let one also see that, for this very reason, every judgment, whose meaning is concrete and practical, so interprets past experience as to counsel a future deed. Let one consider that when my present judgment, addressing my future self, counsels: "Do this," this counsel, if followed, leads to an individual deed, which henceforth irrevocably stands on the score of my life, and can never be removed therefrom.

Hence, just as what is done cannot be undone, just so what is truly or falsely counselled by any concrete and practical judgment remains permanently true or false. For the deed which a judgment counsels remains forever done, when once it has been done...

The interpreter, the mind to which he addresses his interpretation, the mind which he undertakes to interpret—all these appear, in our explicitly human and social world, as three distinct selves—sundered by chasms which, under human conditions, we never cross, and contrasting in their inner lives in whatever way the motives of men at any moment chance to contrast.

The Will to Interpret undertakes to make of these three selves a Community. In every case of ideally serious and loyal effort truly to interpret this is the simplest, but, in its deepest motives, the most purely spiritual of possible communities. Let us view that simple and ideal community as the interpreter himself views it, precisely in so far as he is sincere and truth-loving in his purpose as interpreter.

I, the interpreter, regard you, my neighbor, as a realm of ideas, of "leadings," of meanings, of pursuits, of purposes. This realm is not wholly strange and incomprehensible to me. For at any moment, in my life as interpreter, I am dependent upon the results of countless previous efforts to interpret. The whole past history of civilization has resulted in that form and degree of interpretation of you and of my other fellow-men which I already possess, at any instant when I begin afresh the task of interpreting your life or your ideas. You are to me, then, a realm of ideas which lie outside of the centre which my will to interpret can momentarily illumine with the clearest grade of vision. But I am discontent with my narrowness and with your estrangement. I seek unity with you. And since the same will to interpret you is also expressive of my analogous interests in all my other neighbors, what I here and now specifically aim to do is this: I mean to interpret you to somebody else, to some other neighbor, who is neither yourself nor myself. Three of us, then, I seek to bring into the desired unity of interpretation.

Now if I could succeed in interpreting you to another man as fully as, in my clearest moments, I interpret one of my ideas to another, my process of interpretation would simply reduce to a conscious comparison of ideas. I should then attain, as I succeeded in my interpretation, a luminous vision of your ideas, of my own, and of the ideas of the one to whom I interpret you. This vision would look down, as it were, from above. In the light of it, we, the selves now sundered by the chasms of the social world, should indeed not interpenetrate. For our functions as the mind interpreted, and the interpreter, would remain as distinct as now they are. There would be no melting together, no blending, no mystic blur, and no lapse into mere intuition. But for me the vision of the successful interpretation would simply be the attainment of my own goal as interpreter. This attainment would as little confound our persons as it would divide our substance. We should remain, for me, many, even when viewed in this unity.

Yet this vision, if I could win it, would constitute an event wherein your will to be interpreted would also be fulfilled. For if you are indeed ready to accept my service as interpreter, you even now possess this will to be interpreted. And if there exists the one to whom I can interpret you, that other also wills that you should be interpreted to him, and that I should be the interpreter.

If, then, I am worthy to be an interpreter at all, we three—you, my neighbor, whose mind I would fain interpret—you, my kindly listener, to whom I am to address my interpretation—we three constitute a Community. Let us give to this sort of community a technical name. Let us call it a Community of Interpretation.

The form of such a community is determinate.

One goal lies before us all, one event towards which we all direct our efforts when we take part in this interpretation. This ideal event is a goal, unattainable under human social conditions, but definable, as an ideal, in terms of the perfectly familiar experience which every successful comparison of ideas involves. It is a goal towards which we all may work together: you, when you give me the signs that I am to interpret; our neighbor, when he listens to my interpretation; I, when I devote myself to the task.

This goal:—Our individual experience of our successful comparisons of our own ideas shows us wherein it consists, and that it is no goal which an abstract conception can define in terms of credit-values, and that it is also no goal which a possible perception can render to me in the cash of any set of sensory data. Yet it is a goal which each of us can accept as his own. I can at present aim to approach that goal through plans, through hypotheses regarding you which can be inductively tested. I can view that goal as a common future event. We can agree upon that goal. And herewith I interpret not only you as the being whom I am to interpret, but also myself as in ideal the interpreter who aims to approach the vision of the unity of precisely this community. And you, and my other neighbor to whom I address my interpretation, can also interpret yourselves accordingly.

The conditions of the definition of our community will thus be perfectly satisfied. We shall be many selves with a common ideal future event at which we aim. Without essentially altering the nature of our community, our respective offices can be, at our pleasure, interchanged. You, or my other neighbor, can at any moment assume the function of interpreter; while I can pass to a new position in the new community. And yet, we three shall constitute as clearly as before a Community of Interpretation. The new community will be in a perfectly definite relation to the former one; and may grow out of it by a process as definite as is every form of conscious interpretation.

Thus there can arise, in our community, no problem regarding the one and the many, the quest and the goal, the individual who approaches the goal by one path or by another—no question to which the definition of the community of interpretation will not at once furnish a perfectly precise answer.

Such an answer will be based upon the perfectly fundamental triadic relation which is essential to every process of interpretation, whether such process takes place within the inner life of an individual human being, or goes on in the world of ordinary social intercourse...

In a community thus defined, the interpreter obviously assumes, in a highly significant sense, the chief place. For the community is one of interpretation. Its goal is the ideal unity of insight which the interpreter would possess were these who are now his neighbors transformed into ideas of his own which he compared; that is, were they ideas between which his own interpretation successfully mediated. The interpreter appears, then, as the one of the three who is most of all the spirit of the community, dominating the ideal relations of all three members.

But the one who is, in ideal, this chief, is so because he is first of all servant. His office it is to conform to the mind which he interprets, and to the comprehension of the mind to which he addresses his interpretation. And his own ideas can "work" only if his self-surrender, and his conformity to ideas which are not his own, is actually a successful conformity; and only if his approach to a goal which, as member of a human community of interpretation, he can never reach, is a real approach.

Such are the relationships which constitute a Community of Interpretation. I beg you to observe, as we close, the ethical and religious significance which the structure of such a community makes possible. In case our interpretations actually approach success, a community of interpretation possesses such ethical and religious significance, with increasing definiteness and beauty as the evolution of such a community passes from simpler to higher stages.

Upon interpretation, as we have already seen, every ideal good that we mortals win together, under our human social conditions, depends. Whatever else men need, they need their communities of interpretation.

It is indeed true that such communities can exist, at any time, in the most various grades of development, of self-consciousness, and of ideality. The communities of interpretation which exist in the market-places of the present social world, or that lie at the basis of the diplomatic intercourse of modern nations, are communities whose ideal goal is seldom present to the minds of their members; and it is not love which often seems to be their consciously ruling motive.

Yet, on the whole, it is not perception, and it is not conception; while it certainly is interpretation which is the great humanizing factor in our cognitive processes and which makes the purest forms of love for communities possible. Loyalty to a community of interpretation enters into all the other forms of true loyalty. No one who loves mankind can find a worthier and more significant way to express his love than by increasing and expressing among men the Will to Interpret. This will inspires every student of the humanities; and is present wherever charity enters into life. When Christianity teaches us to hope for the community of all mankind, we can readily see that the Beloved Community, whatever else it is, will be, when it comes, a Community of Interpretation. When we consider the ideal form and the goal of such a community, we see that in no other form, and with no other ideal, can we better express the constitution of the ideal Church, be that conceived as the Church on earth, or as the Church triumphant in some ideal realm of superhuman and all-seeing insight, where I shall know even as I am known.

And, if, in ideal, we aim to conceive the divine nature, how better can we conceive it than in the form of the Community of Interpretation, and above all in the form of the Interpreter, who interprets all to all, and each individual to the world, and the world of spirits to each individual.

In such an interpreter, and in his community, the problem of the One and the Many would find its ideally complete expression and solution. The abstract conceptions and the mystical intuitions would be at once transcended, and illumined, and yet retained and kept clear and distinct, in and through the life of one who, as interpreter, was at once servant to all and chief among all, expressing his will through all, yet, in his interpretations, regarding and loving the will of the least of these his brethren. In him the Community, the Individual, and the Absolute would be completely expressed, reconciled, and distinguished.

This, to be sure, is, at this point of our discussion, still merely the expression of an ideal, and not the assertion of a metaphysical proposition. But in the Will to Interpret, the divine and the human seem to be in closest touch with each other.

The mere form of interpretation may be indeed momentarily misused for whatever purpose of passing human folly you will. But if the ideal of interpretation is first grasped; and if then the Community of Interpretation is conceived as inclusive of all individuals; and as unified by the common hope of the far-off event of complete mutual understanding; and, finally, if love for this community is awakened—then indeed this love is able to grasp, in ideal, the meaning of the Church Universal, of the Communion of Saints, and of God the Interpreter.

Merely to define such ideals is not to solve the problems of metaphysics. But it is to remove many obstacles from the path that leads towards insight...

3. Reality [6]

... Now WHAT IS the warrant for believing in the reality of such a community?

For a general answer to this question let us hereupon consult the philosophers. The philosophers differ sadly amongst themselves. They do not at present form a literal human community of mutual enlightenment and of growth in knowledge, to any such extent as do the workers in the field of any one of the natural sciences. The philosophers are thus far individuals rather than consciously members one of another. The charity of mutual interpretation is ill developed amongst them. They frequently speak with tongues and do not edify. And they are

[6] From *The Problem of Christianity*, Lectures XIII and XIV, with omissions.

especially disposed to contend regarding their spiritual gifts. We cannot expect them, then, at present to agree regarding any one philosophical opinion. Nevertheless, if we consider them in a historical way, there is one feature about their work to which, at this point, I need to call especial attention.

I have already more than once asserted that the principal task of the philosopher is one, not of perception, not of conception, but of interpretation. This remark refers in the first place to the office which the philosophers have filled in the history of culture.

Common opinion classes philosophy among the humanities. It ought so to be classed. Philosophers have actually devoted themselves, in the main, neither to perceiving the world, nor to spinning webs of conceptual theory, but to interpreting the meaning of the civilizations which they have represented, and to attempting the interpretation of whatever minds in the universe, human or divine, they believed to be real. That the philosophers are neither the only interpreters, nor the chiefs among those who interpret, we now well know. The artists, the leaders of men, and all the students of the humanities, make interpretation their business; and the triadic cognitive function, as the last lecture showed, has its applications in all the realms of knowledge. But in any case the philosopher's ideals are those of an interpreter. He addresses one mind and interprets another. The unity which he seeks is that which is characteristic of a community of interpretation.

The historical proofs of this thesis are manifold. A correct summary of their meaning appears in the common opinion which classes philosophy amongst the humanities. This classification is a perfectly just one. The humanities are busied with interpretations. Individual illustrations of the historical office of philosophy could be furnished by considering with especial care precisely those historical instances which the philosophers furnish who, like Plato or like Bergson, have most of all devoted their efforts to emphasizing as much as possible one of the other cognitive processes, instead of interpretation. For the more exclusively such a philosopher lays stress upon perception alone, or conception alone, the better does he illustrate our historical thesis.

Plato lays stress upon conception as furnishing our principal access to reality. Bergson has eloquently maintained the thesis that pure perception brings us in contact with the real. Yet each of these philosophers actually offers us an interpretation of the universe. That is, each of them begins by taking account of certain mental processes which play a part in human life. Each asks us to win some sort of touch with a higher type of consciousness than belongs to our natural human existence. Each declares that, through such a transformation of our ordinary consciousness, either through a flight from the vain show of sense into the realm of pure thought, or else through an abandonment of the merely practical labors of that user of tools, the intellect, we shall find the pathway to reality. Each in his own way interprets our natural mode of dealing with reality to some nobler form of insight which he believes to be corrective of our natural errors, or else, in turn, interprets the supposed counsels of a more divine type of knowledge to the blindness or to the barrenness or to the merely practical narrowness of our ordinary existence.

Each of these philosophers mediates, in his own way, between the spiritual existence of those who sit in the darkness of the cave of sense, or who, on the other hand, wander in the wilderness of evolutionary processes and of intellectual theories;—he mediates, I say, between these victims of error on the one hand, and that better, that richer, spiritual life and the truer insight, on the other hand, of those who, in this philosopher's opinion, find the homeland—be that land the Platonic realm of the eternal forms of being, or the dwelling-place which Bergson loves—where the artists see their beautiful visions of endless change.

In brief, there is no philosophy of pure conception, and there is no philosophy of pure perception. Plato was a leader of the souls of those men to whom he showed the way out of the cave, and in whom he inspired the love of the eternal. Bergson winningly devotes himself to saying, as any artist says, "Come and intuitively see what I have intuitively seen."

Such speech, however, is the speech neither of the one who trusts to mere conception, nor of one who finds the real merely in perception. It is the speech of an interpreter, who, addressing himself to one form of personality or of life, interprets what he takes to be the meaning of some other form of life.

This thesis, that the philosopher is an interpreter, simply directs our attention to the way in which he is required to define his problems. And the universality of these problems makes this purely elementary task of their proper definition at once momentous and difficult. We shall not lose by any consideration which rightly fixes our attention upon an essential aspect of the process of knowledge which the philosopher seeks to control. For the philosopher is attempting to deal with the world as a whole, with reality in general.

Why is it that the philosopher has to be an interpreter even when, like Bergson or like Plato, he tries to subordinate interpretation either to conception alone or to perception alone? Why is it that when, in his loftiest speculative flights, he attempts to seize upon some intuition of reason, or upon some form of direct perception, which shall reveal to him the inmost essence of reality, he nevertheless acts as interpreter?

The answer to this question is simple.

If, as a fact, we could, at least in ideal, and as a sort of speculative experiment, weld all our various ideas, our practical ideas as well as our theoretical ideas, together into some single idea, whose "leading" we could follow wherever it led, from concept to percept, or from percept to concept; and if we could reduce our problem of reality simply to the question, Is this one idea expressive of the nature of reality?— then indeed some such philosophy as that of Bergson, or as that of Plato, might be formulated in terms either of pure perception or of pure conception. Then the philosopher who thus welded his ideas into one idea, and who then assured himself of the success of that one idea, would no longer be an interpreter.

Thus, let us imagine that we could, with Spinoza, weld together into the one idea of Substance, the totality of ideas, that is of pragmatic leadings, which all men, at all times, are endeavoring to follow through their experience, or to express through their will. Suppose that this one idea could be shown to be successful. Then our philosophy could assume the well-known form which Spinoza gave to his own:—

By substance, Spinoza means that which is "in itself" and which needs no other to sustain or in any ideal fashion to contain it. Hereupon the philosopher finds it easy to assert that whatever is in any sense real must indeed be either "in itself" or "in another." No other idea need be used in estimating realities except the idea thus defined. The only question as to any object is: Is this a substance or not? A very brief and simple process of conceptual development, then, brings us to Spinoza's result that whatever is "in another" is not in the highest sense real at all. Therefore there remains in our world only that which is real "in itself." The one idea can be realized only in a world which is, once for all, the Substance. The tracks of all finite creatures that are observed near the edge of the cave of this Substance lead (as was long ago said of Spinoza's substance) only inwards. The world is defined in terms of the single idea, all other human ideas or possible ideas being but special cases of the one idea. The real world is purely conceptual, and is also monistic.

Suppose, on the other hand, that we indeed recognize with Bergson, and with the pragmatists, an endless and empirical wealth of ideas which, in practical life, lead or do not lead from concepts to percepts, as experience may determine. Suppose, however, that, with Bergson, we first notice that all these ideal leadings of the intellect constitute, at best, but an endlessly varied using of tools. Suppose that hereupon, with Bergson and with the mystics, we come to regard all this life of the varied ideas, this mechanical using of mere tools, this mere pragmatism, as an essentially poorer sort of life from which nature has long since delivered the nobler of the insects, from which the artists can and do escape, and from which it is the loftiest ideal of philosophy to liberate those who are indeed to know reality.

Then indeed, though not at all in Spinoza's way, all the ideal leadings which the philosopher has henceforth to regard as essentially illuminating, will simply blend into a single idea. This idea will be the one idea of winning a pure intuition. We shall define reality in terms of this pure intuition. And hereupon a purely perceptual view of reality will result.

If, then, all the ideas of men, if all ideas of reality, could collapse or could blend or could otherwise be ideally welded into a single idea, then this idea could be used to define reality, just as pragmatism has come to define all the endless variety of forms of "truth" in terms of the single idea which gets the name "success" or "working" or "expediency" or "cash-value," according to the taste of the individual pragmatist.

As a fact, however, the genuine problem, whether of reality, or of truth, cannot be faced by means of any such blending of all ideal leadings into a single ideal leading.

We all of us believe that there is any real world at all, simply because we find ourselves in a situation in which, because of the fragmentary and dissatisfying conflicts, antitheses, and problems of our present ideas, an interpretation of this situation is needed, but is not now known to us. *By the "real world" we mean simply the "true interpretation" of this our problematic situation.* No other reason can be given than this for believing that there is any real world at all. From this one consideration, vast consequences follow. Let us next sketch some of these consequences.

Whoever stands in presence of the problem of reality has, at the very least, to compare two essential ideas. These ideas are, respectively, the idea of present experience and the idea of the goal of experience. The contrast in question has countless and infinitely various forms. In its ethical form the contrast appears as that between our actual life and our ideal life. It also appears as the Pauline contrast between the flesh and the spirit; or as the Stoic contrast between the life of the wise and the life of fools. It is also known to common sense as the contrast between our youthful hopes and our mature sense of our limitations. The contrast between our future life, which we propose to control, and our irrevocable past life which we can never recall, presents the same general antithesis. In the future, as we hopefully view it, the goal is naturally supposed to lie. But the past, dead as it is often said to be, determines our present need, and sets for us our ideal task.

In the world of theory the same contrast appears as that between our ignorance and our possible enlightenment, between our endlessly numerous problems and their solutions, between our innumerable uncertainties and those attainments of certainty at which our sciences and our arts aim. For our religious consciousness the contrasts between nature and grace, between good and evil, between our present state and our salvation, between God and the world, merely illustrate the antithesis.

One can also state this antithesis as that between our Will (which, as Schopenhauer and the Buddhists said, is endlessly longing) and the Fulfilment of our will. Plato, on the one hand, and the mystics on the other, attempt to conceive or to perceive some such fulfilment, according as Plato, or as some mystic, emphasizes one or the other of the two cognitive processes to which the philosophers have usually confined their attention.

This antithesis between two fundamental ideas presents to each of us the problem of the universe, and dominates that problem. For by the "real world" we mean the true interpretation of the problematic situation which this antithesis presents to us in so far as we compare what is our ideal with what is so far given to us. Whatever the real world is, its nature has to be expressed in terms of this antithesis of ideas.

Two such ideas, then, stand in contrast when we face our problem of reality. They stand as do plaintiff and defendant in court, or as do the ideas of the suffering patient and his hopes of recovery, or as do the wrongs which the litigant feels and the rights or the doom which the law allows him. The empirical shapes which the antithesis takes are simply endless in their wealth. They furnish to us the special topics which science and common sense study. But the general problem which the antithesis presents is the world-problem. *The question about what the real world is, is simply the question as to what this contrast is and means.* Neither of the two ideas can solve its own problem or be judge in its own case. Each needs a counsel, a mediator, an interpreter, to represent its cause to the other idea.

In the well-known metaphysical expression, this contrast may be called that between appearance and reality. The antithesis itself is in one sense the appearance, the phenomenon, the world-problem. The question about the real world is that furnished to us by our experience of this appearance. When we ask what the real world is, we simply ask what this appearance, this antithesis, this problem of the two contrasting ideas both is and means. So to ask, is to ask for the solution of the problem which the antithesis presents. That is, we ask: "What is the interpretation of this problem, of this antithesis?" The real world is that solution. Every special definition of reality takes the form of offering such a solution. Whether a philosopher calls himself realist or idealist, monist or pluralist, theist or materialist, empiricist or rationalist, his philosophy, wherever he states it, takes the form of saying: "The true, the genuine interpretation of the antithesis is such and such."

If you say that perhaps there is no solution of the problem, that hypothesis, if true, could be verified only by an experience that in itself would constitute a full insight into the meaning of the real contrast, and so would in fact furnish a solution. In any case, the real world is precisely that whose nature is expressed by whatever mediating idea is such that, when viewed in unity with the two antithetical ideas, it fully compares them, and makes clear the meaning of the contrast. *But an interpretation is real only if the appropriate community is real, and is true only if that community reaches its goal.*

In brief, then, the real world is the Community of Interpretation which is constituted by the two antithetic ideas, and their mediator or interpreter, whatever or whoever that interpreter may be. If the interpretation is a reality, and if it truly interprets the whole of reality, then the community reaches its goal, and the real world includes its own interpreter. *Unless both the interpreter and the community are real, there is no real world.*

After the foregoing discussion of the nature and the processes of interpretation, we are now secure from any accusation that, from this point of view, the real world is anything merely static, or is a mere idea within the mind of a finite self, or is an Absolute that is divorced from its appearances, or is any merely conceptual reality, or is "out of time," or is a "block universe," or is an object of a merely mystical intuition.

Interpretation, as we have seen in our general discussion of the cognitive process in question, demands that at least an infinite series of distinct individual acts of interpretation shall take place, unless the interpretation which is in question is arbitrarily interrupted. If, then, the real world contains the Community of Interpretation just characterized, this community of interpretation expresses its life in an infinite series of individual interpretations, each of which occupies its own place in a perfectly real order of time.

If, however, this community of interpretation reaches its goal, this whole time-process is in some fashion spanned by one insight which surveys the unity of its meaning. Such a viewing of the whole time-process by a single synopsis will certainly not be anything "timeless." It will not occur, on the other hand, at any one moment of time. But its nature is the one empirically known to us at any one moment when we clearly contrast two of our own ideas and find their mediator.

Nothing is more concretely known to us than are the nature, the value, and the goal of a community of interpretation. The most ideal as well as the most scientifically exact interests of mankind are bound up with the existence, with the purposes, with the fortunes, and with the unity of such communities.

The metaphysical doctrine just set forth in outline can be summed up thus: The problem of reality is furnished to us by a certain universal antithesis of two Ideas, or, if one prefers the word, by the antithesis of two Selves. The first thesis of this doctrine is that Reality—the solution of this problem—is the interpretation of this antithesis, the process of mediating between these two selves and of interpreting each of them to the other. Such a process of interpretation involves, of necessity, an infinite sequence of acts of interpretation. It also admits of an endless variety within all the selves which are thus mutually interpreted. These selves, in all their variety, constitute the life of a single Community of Interpretation, whose central member is that spirit of the community whose essential function we now know. In the concrete, then, the universe is a community of interpretation whose life comprises and unifies all the social varieties and all the social communities which, for any reason, we know to be real in the empirical world which our social and our historical sciences study. The history of the universe, the whole order of time, is the history and the order and the expression of this Universal Community...

We have no ground whatever for believing that there is any real world except the ground furnished by our experience, and by the fact that, in addition to our perceptions and our conceptions, we have problems upon our hands which need interpretation. Our fundamental postulate is: *The world is the interpretation of the problems which it presents.* If you deny this principle, you do so only by presenting, as Bergson does, some other interpretation as the true one. But thus you simply reaffirm the principle that the world has an interpreter.[7]

Using this principle, in your ordinary social life, you postulate your fellow-man as the interpreter of the ideas which he awakens in your mind, and which are not your own ideas. The same principle, applied to our social experience of the physical world, determines our ordinary interpretations of nature and guides our natural science. For, as we

[7] This paragraph contains in brief the nucleus of Royce's reiterated argument for the existence of the Absolute. In Lecture XI of *The Religious Aspect of Philosophy* (1885) he argued that the recognition of error and ignorance implies the existence of the absolute unity of conscious thought (i.e., absolute truth), in the light of which the error embodied in our fragmentary ideas becomes apparent. In *The Conception of God* (1897) he employed essentially the same argument, only this time focusing attention on the fact that the very denial of the existence of absolute experience involves an assertion about the absolute whole of experience. Finally, in Lecture VIII of Vol. I of *The World and the Individual* (1899), he defined the Absolute, with great technical elaboration, as the determinate infinite which fulfils all finite ideas.

The philosophy of interpretation and community is but the last of Royce's several attempts to make the sense of the infinite presence vivid and compelling for the finite individual. Royce considered this not as a repudiation of his earlier arguments, but as the simplest way of exhibiting (a) the empirical evidence on which he claimed the argument for the Absolute rests, and (b) the practical obligations and duties imposed upon men by the subsumption of the individual under the Absolute.

have seen, the physical world is an object known to the community, and through interpretation. The same principle, applied to our memories and to our expectations, gives us our view of the world of time, with all its infinite wealth of successive acts of interpretation.

In all these special instances, the application of this principle defines for us some form or grade of community, and teaches us wherein lies the true nature, the form, the real unity, and the essential life of this community.

Our Doctrine of Signs extends to the whole world the same fundamental principle. The World is the Community. The world contains its own interpreter. Its processes are infinite in their temporal varieties. But their interpreter, the spirit of this universal community—never absorbing varieties or permitting them to blend—compares and, through a real life, interprets them all.

The attitude of will which this principle expresses, is neither that of the affirmation nor that of the denial of what Schopenhauer meant by the will to live. It is the attitude which first expresses itself by saying "Alone I am lost, and am worse than nothing. I need a counsellor, I need my community. Interpret me. Let me join in this interpretation. Let there be the community. This alone is life. This alone is salvation. This alone is real." This is at once an attitude of the will and an assertion whose denial refutes itself. For if there is no interpreter, there is no interpretation. And if there is no interpretation, there is no world whatever.

In its daily form as the principle of our social common sense, this attitude of the will inspires whatever is reasonable about our worldly business and our scientific inquiry. For all such business and inquiry are in and for and of the community, or else are vanity.

In its highest form, this attitude of the will was the one which Paul knew as Charity, and as the life in and through the spirit of the Community. . .

4. Science and the Progress of Christianity [8]

THE ESSENTIAL MESSAGE of Christianity has been the word that the sense of life, the very being of the time process itself, consists in the progressive realization of the Universal Community in and through the longings, the vicissitudes, the tragedies, and the triumphs of this process of the temporal world. Now this message has been historically expressed through the symbols, through the traditions, and through the concrete life of whatever human communities have most fully em-

---

[8] From *The Problem of Christianity*, Lecture XVI, with omissions.

bodied the essential spirit of Christianity. We know not in what non-human forms the spiritual life may now or hereafter find its temporal embodiment. Our metaphysical doctrine, dealing, as it does, with universal issues, is quite unable to extend our vision to any heavenly realm of angelic powers. We have undertaken merely to defend a thesis regarding the form in which the life of the community, whether human or non-human, finds its conscious expression.

On earth, as we have seen, the universal community is nowhere visibly realized. But in the whole world, the divine life is expressed in the form of a community. Herewith, in teaching us this general but intensely practical truth, the "kindly light" seems also to show us not, in its temporal details, "the distant scene," but the "step" which we most need to see "amid the encircling gloom." And our little task it has been to learn whether, for our special purpose, that step is not, in just our present sense, "enough.". . .

I have already said that we cannot, like the founders of new religious faiths, point to any sign or wonder as the evidence that we have rightly interpreted the divine process of which the world is the expression. Yet, as I leave our argument, in its incomplete statement, to produce, if possible, some effect upon your future thoughts about these matters, I wish to call your attention—not to a further technical proof of our philosophy of interpretation, but to a closing exemplification of its main doctrine. This example may serve to bring our philosophy, which many of you will have found too recondite and too speculative, into closer touch with certain thoughtful interests which not only our own age, but many future ages of human inquiry, are certain to cherish.

I wish, namely, to indicate that our main thesis concerning the World of Interpretation is not only in harmony with the spirit which guides the researches of the empirical natural sciences, but is, in a very striking way, suggested to us afresh when we ponder the meaning which the very existence and the successes of the empirical sciences seem to imply. In other words, I wish to show you that our theory of the World of Interpretation, and our doctrine that the whole process of the temporal order is the progressive expression of a single spiritual meaning, is—not indeed proved—but lighted up, when we reconsider for a moment the question: "What manner of natural world is this in which the actual successes of our inductive sciences are possible?". . .

Every one knows that the natural sciences depend, for their existence, upon inductive inquiries. And all of us are aware, in a general way, of what is meant by induction. When one collects facts of experience and then infers, with greater or less probability, that some proposition relating to facts not yet observed, or relating to the laws of nature, is a true proposition, the thinking process which one uses is called inductive reasoning. The conditions which make a process of reasoning inductive are thus twofold. First, inductive reasoning is based upon an experience of particular facts. That is, inductions depend upon observations or experiments. Secondly, what one concludes or infers, from the observations or experiments in question, follows from these facts not necessarily, but with some more or less precisely estimable degree of probability. The terms "inductive inference" and "probable inference" are almost precisely equivalent terms. If you draw from given premises or presuppositions a conclusion such that, *in case* the premise is true, the conclusion *must* be true, the process of reasoning which is in question is called "necessary inference" or "deductive inference" (these two terms being, for our present purposes, equivalent). But if, upon assuming certain premises to be true, you find that they merely make a given conclusion *probable*, the inference which guides you to the conclusion is an inductive inference.

Examples of such inference may easily be mentioned. Thus a life insurance company, in assuming new risks, and in computing premiums, is guided by mortality tables. Such tables summarize, in a statistical fashion, facts which previous experience has furnished regarding the ages at which men have died. The insurance actuaries compute, upon the basis of the tables, the mortalities of men who are yet to be insured. The results of the tables and of the computations are probable inferences to the effect that of a certain number of men, who are now in normal condition and who are of a given age, a certain proportion will die within a year, or within ten years, or within some other chosen interval of time. Such probable inferences are used, by the insurance company, in determining the rate at which it is safe to insure a given applicant who appears to be, upon examination, a "good risk" for his age. Nobody can know when any one individual man will die; and the insurance company draws as few inferences as possible regarding the case of any one individual man...

What the insurance companies do when they reason about taking new risks is an example of a method widely used in the natural sciences. A collection of facts of observation, a statistical study of these facts, and a probable inference based upon such statistics—these, in many cases, make up a great part of the work of an inductive science.

But the statistical methods used by the insurance companies are not the only methods known to natural science. Another sort of probable inference is also known, and is, in many cases, of much more importance for natural science than is the more directly statistical method which the insurance companies use. This other method is known to you all. It is the method of forming hypotheses and of testing these hypotheses by comparing their results with experience...

... This second method of induction consists in first inventing some hypothesis A, which is adapted to the purpose of the investigator. Then the user of this method discovers, usually by some process of deductive reasoning, that, if the hypothesis A is true, some determinate fact of experience E will be found under certain conditions. The investigator hereupon looks for this predicted fact E. If he fails to find it, his hypothesis is refuted, and he must look for another. But if he finds E where his hypothesis had bidden him to look for E, then the hypothesis A begins to be rendered probable. And the more frequently A is verified, and the more unexpected and antecedently improbable are these verifications, the more probable does the hypothesis A become.

The most important and exact results of the inductive sciences are reached by methods in which the verification of hypothesis plays a very large part. Galileo used hypotheses, computed what the results would be in case the hypotheses were true, and then by further experience verified the hypotheses. So did Newton; so in a very different age, and in a very different field, did Darwin. Upon the process of inventing hypotheses, of computing their consequences, and of then appealing to experience to confirm or refute the hypotheses, the greatest single advances in physical science rest.

And the principle used in this branch of induction may be stated thus:—

When without any antecedent knowledge that the consequences of a given hypothesis are true, we find, upon a fair examination of the facts, that these consequences are unexpectedly verified, then the hypothesis in question becomes, not certainly true, but more and more probable. . .

Now a very good hypothesis depends, in general, for its high value, first upon its novelty; secondly, upon the fact that, when duly tested, it is verified. If it is not novel, the verification of its consequences will make comparatively little difference to the science in question. If it cannot be verified, and especially if experience refutes it, it does not directly contribute to the progress of science. But the more novel an hypothesis is, the more in advance of verification must it appear improbable; and the greater are the risks which its inventor seems to run when he first proposes it.

Now in what way shall a good inventor of hypotheses be guided to his invention? Shall he confine himself only to the hypotheses which, when first he proposes them, seem antecedently probable? If he does this, he condemns himself to relative infertility. For the antecedently probable hypothesis is precisely the hypothesis which lacks any very notable novelty. Even if such an hypothesis bears the test of experience, it therefore adds little to knowledge. Worthless for the purposes of any more exact natural science until it has been duly verified, the hypothesis which is to win, in the advancement of science, a really great place, must often be, at the moment of its first invention, an apparently unlikely hypothesis—a poetical creation, warranted as yet by none of the facts thus far known, and subject to all the risks which attend great human enterprises in any field. In such a position was Darwin's hypothesis regarding the origin of species through natural selection, when first he began to seek for its verification.

This, however, is not all. A highly significant scientific hypothesis must not only be a sort of poetic creation. There is another consideration to be borne in mind. The number of possible new hypotheses, in any large field of scientific inquiry, is, like the number of possible new poems, often very great. The labor of testing each one of a number of such hypotheses, sufficiently to know whether the hypothesis tested is or is not probably true, is frequently long. And the poetic skill with which the hypotheses are invented, as well as their intrinsic beauty, give, in advance of the test, no assurance that they will succeed in agreeing with experience. The makers of great scientific hypotheses— the Galileos, the Darwins—are, so to speak, poets whose inventions must be submitted to a very stern critic, namely, to the sort of experience which their sciences use. And no one can know in advance what this critic's verdict will be. Therefore, if it were left to mere chance to determine what hypotheses should be invented and tested, scientific progress would be very slow. For each new hypothesis would involve new risks, would require lengthy new tests, and would often fail.

As a fact, however, the progress of natural science, since Galileo began his work, and since the new inductive methods were first applied, has been (so Charles Peirce asserts) prodigiously faster than it could have been had mere chance guided the inventive processes of the greater scientific thinkers. In view of these facts, Charles Peirce reasons that the actual progress of science, from the sixteenth century until now, could not have been what it is, had not the human mind been, as he says, in some deep way attuned to the nature of things. The mind of man must be peculiarly fitted to invent new hypotheses such that, when tested by experience, they bear the test, and turn out to be probably true. The question hereupon arises, "To what is this aptness of the human mind for the invention of important and successful scientific hypotheses due?"

This question is not easy to answer. Were new hypotheses in science framed simply by processes analogous to those which the insurance companies employ when they take new risks, the matter would be different. For the insurance companies adapt the existing tables of mortality to their new undertakings, or else obtain modified tables gradually, by a mere process of collection and arrangement. And all the statistical sciences make use of this method; and there is, of course, no doubt that this method of gradual advance, through patient collection of facts, is one of the two great sources of scientific progress.

But the other method, the method of inventing new hypotheses which go beyond all results thus far obtained—the method which first proposes and then tests these hypotheses—involves at every stage a venture into an unknown sea. Unless some deep-lying motive guides the inventor, he will go uselessly astray, and will waste his efforts upon inventions which prove to be failures.

In many branches of science such fortunes have in fact long barred the way. Consider, for instance, the fortunes of modern pathological research, up to the present moment, in dealing with the problem fur-nished by the existence of cancer. The most patient devotion to details, the most skilful invention of hypotheses, has so far led only to defeat regarding some of the most central problems of the pathology of cancer. These problems may be solved at any moment in the near future. But up to this time it seems—according to what the leading pathologists tell us—as if the human mind had not been attuned to the invention of fitting hypotheses regarding the most fundamental problems of the "cancer-research."

How different, on the other hand, were the fortunes of mechanics from Galileo's time to that of Newton. What wonderful scientific inventiveness guided the early stages of electrical science. How rapidly some portions of pathological research have advanced. And, according to Charles Peirce, in all these most successful instances it is the happy instinct for inventing the hypotheses which has shortened a task that, if left to chance and to patience, would have proved hopelessly slow. If science had advanced mainly by the successive testing of all the possible hypotheses in any given field, the cancer-research, in its period of tedious trials and errors, and not the physical science of Galileo, with its dramatic swiftness of progress, nor yet the revolutionary changes due to the influence of Darwin, would exemplify the ruling type of scientific research. But as a fact, the great scientific advances have been due to a wonderful skill in the art of Galileo, and of the other leading inventors of new scientific ideas.

The present existence, then, and the rapid progress of the inductive sciences, have been rendered possible by an instinctive aptitude of the human mind to shorten the labors of testing hypothesis through some sort of native skill in the invention of hypotheses such as are capable of bearing the test of experience. . .

If, then, you seek for a sign that the universe contains its own inter-preter, let the very existence of the sciences, let the existence of the happy inventive power which has made their progress possible, furnish you such a sign. A being whom nature seems to have intended, in the first place, simply to be more crafty than the other animals, more skil-ful in war and in hunting, and in the arts of living in tribal unities, turns out to be so attuned to the whole of nature that, when he once gets the idea of scientific research, his discoveries soon relate to physical matters as remote from his practical needs as is the chemical constitution of the nebulae, or as is the origin and destiny of this earth, or as is the state of the natural universe countless ages ago in the past. In brief, man is not what he seems, a creature of a day, but is known to be an interpreter of nature. He is full of aptitudes to sound the depths of time and of space, and to invent hypotheses which will take ages to verify, but which will, in a vast number of cases, be verified. Full of wonders is nature. But the most wonderful of all is man the interpreter—a part and a member (if our philosophy is right) of the world's infinite Community of Interpretation.

The very existence of natural science, then, is an illustration of our thesis that the universe is endlessly engaged in the spiritual task of interpreting its own life.

The older forms of teleology, often used by the theologians of the past, frequently missed the place where the empirical illustrations of the workings of intelligence, in the universe, and where the signs of the life of the divine spirit are most to be sought. The teleology of the future will look for illustrations of the divine, and of design, neither in miracles nor in the workings of any continuously striving "will" or "vital impulse" which from moment to moment moulds things so as to meet present needs, or to guide present evolution.

Man, as we have seen, has an aptitude to invent hypotheses that, when once duly tested, throw light on things as remote in space as are the nebulae, as distant in time as is the origin of our whole stellar system. This aptitude lies deep in human nature. Its existence is indeed no miraculous event of today. Man's power to interpret his world has somehow evolved with man. The whole natural world of the past has been needed to produce man the interpreter. On the other hand, this power of man cannot have been the result of any "vital impulse" "canalizing" matter or otherwise blindly striving continuously and tentatively for light. For this scientific aptitude of man links him even now with the whole time-order. He is so attuned by nature that, imperfect as he now is, he is adapted to be or to become, in his own halting way, but not in totally blind fashion, an interpreter of the meaning of the whole of time. Now such a teleological process as this which man's scientific successes express, illustrates the teleology of a spiritual process which does not merely, from moment to moment, adapt itself to a preëxistent world. Nor does this process appear as merely one whereby an unconscious impulse squirms its way through the "canals" which it makes in matter. No, this teleology appears to illustrate a spiritual process which, in its wholeness, interprets at once the endless whole of time...

In the past, the teaching of Christian doctrine has generally depended upon some form of Christology. In recent times the traditional problems of Christology have become, in the light of our whole view of the world, of mankind, and of history, increasingly difficult and perplexing. Whoever asserts that, at one moment of human history, and only at that one moment, a unique being, at once an individual man, and at the same time also God, appeared, and performed the work which saved mankind—whoever, I say, asserts this traditional thesis, involves himself in historical, in metaphysical, in technically theological, and in elementally religious problems, which all advances in our modern sciences and in our humanities, in our spiritual life and in our breadth of outlook upon the universe, have only made, for the followers of tradition, constantly harder to face and to solve. . .

What is practically necessary is therefore this: Let your Christology be the practical acknowledgment of the Spirit of the Universal and Beloved Community. This is the sufficient and practical faith. Love this faith, use this faith, teach this faith, preach this faith, in whatever words, through whatever symbols, by means of whatever forms of creeds, in accordance with whatever practices best you find to enable you with a sincere intent and a whole heart to symbolize and to realize the presence of the Spirit in the Community. All else about your religion is the accident of your special race or nation or form of worship or training or accidental personal opinion, or devout private mystical experience—illuminating but capricious. The core, the center of the faith, is not the person of the individual founder, and is not any other individual man. Nor is this core to be found in the sayings of the founder, nor yet in the traditions of Christology. The core of the faith is the Spirit, the Beloved Community, the work of grace, the atoning deed, and the saving power of the loyal life. There is nothing else under heaven whereby men have been saved or can be saved. To say this is to found no new faith, but to send you to the heart of all true faith.

This is no vague humanitarianism, is no worship of the mere natural being called humanity, and is no private mystic experience. This is a creed at once human, divine, and practical, and religious, and universal. Assimilate and apply this creed, and you have grasped the principle of Christian institutional life in the past, and the principle which will develop countless new religious institutions in the future, *and which will survive them*. . .

. . . Henceforth view the religious ideal as one which, in the future, is to be won, if at all, by methods distinctively analogous to the methods which now prevail in the sciences of nature. It is not my thought that natural science can ever displace religion or do its work. But what I mean is that since the office of religion is to aim towards the creation on earth of the Beloved Community, the future task of religion is the task of inventing and applying the arts which shall win men over to unity, and which shall overcome their original hatefulness by the gracious love, not of mere individuals, but of communities. Now such arts are still to be discovered. Judge every social device, every proposed reform, every national and every local enterprise by the one test: *Does this help towards the coming of the universal community?* If you have a church, judge your own church by this standard; and if your church does not yet fully meet this standard, aid towards reforming your church accordingly. If, like myself, you hold the true church to be invisible, require all whom you can influence to help to render it visible. To do that, however, does not mean that you shall either conform to the church as it is, or found new sects. If the spirit of scientific investigation, or of learned research, shows signs—as it already does—of becoming one of the best of all forms of unifying mankind in free loyalty, then regard science not merely as in possible harmony with religion, but as itself already one of the principal organs of religion. Aid toward the coming of the universal community by helping to make the work of religion not only as catholic as is already the true spirit of loyalty, but as inventive of new social arts, as progressive as is now natural science. So shall you help in making, not merely happy individuals (for no power can render detached individuals permanently happy, or save them from death or from woe). You shall aid towards the unity of spirit of those who shall be at once free and loyal.

We can look forward, then, to no final form, either of Christianity or of any other special religion. But we can look forward to a time when the work and the insight of religion can become as progressive as is now the work of science.

5. The Religion of Loyalty [9]

THERE IS AN obvious contrast between the points of view from which morality and religion consider the problem of life. Whatever may be your views as to what your duty is, it is plain that the moral interest centres about this idea of duty. That is, the moral interest seeks to define right deeds and to insist that they shall be done. It estimates the rightness of deeds with reference to some ideal of life. But however it conceives this ideal, it makes its main appeal to the active individual. It says: "Do this." The religious interest, on the other hand, centres about the sense of need, or, if it is successful in finding this

[9] From *The Sources of Religious Insight* (New York, Charles Scribner's Sons, 1912), Lecture V, with omissions. By permission of the trustees of Lake Forest College.

need satisfied, it centres about the knowledge of that which has delivered the needy from their danger. It appeals for help, or waits
patiently for the Lord, or rejoices in the presence of salvation. It therefore may assume any one of many different attitudes toward the problem of duty. It may seek salvation through deeds, or again it may not,
in the minds of some men, appeal to the active nature in any vigorous
way whatever. Some religious moods are passive, contemplative, receptive, adoring rather than strenuous. It is therefore quite consistent with
the existence of a religious interest to feel suspicious of the dutiful
restlessness of many ardent souls.

"They also serve who only stand and wait."

Such is sometimes the comforting, sometimes the warning word that
seems to many to express the religious interest.

This general contrast between the two interests assumes many special
forms when we consider how moralists—that is, teachers who especially
emphasise the call of duty—may stand related to the two postulates
upon which, as we have seen, the higher religions base their appeal.
Religion, in our sense of the word, depends upon asserting: (1) That
there is some one highest end of existence, some goal of life, some
chief good; and (2) That, by nature, man is in great danger of completely failing to attain this good, so that he needs to be saved from
this danger.

Now the first of these two postulates religion has frequently, although not always, shared with the moralists, that is, with those who
devote themselves to teaching us how to act rightly. Aristotle, for
instance, based his ethical doctrine (one of the most influential books
in the history of morals) upon the postulate that there is a highest
good. Many others who have discussed or have preached morality, have
asserted that all obligations are subject to one ultimate obligation,
which is the requirement to act with reference to the highest good. Yet
this agreement as to the highest good turns out to be not quite universal when one compares the opinions of the teachers of religion, on the
one hand, and of the moralists on the other. Popular and traditional
morality often takes the form of a little hoard of maxims about right
acts—maxims whose relations to one another, and to any one highest
goal of life, remain obscure. Each maxim is supposed to define a duty.
Of course it also tells us how to win some special good or how to avoid
some particular evil. But what this special duty has to do with winning
any one highest good is not thus made explicit. And since many who
make traditional morality prominent in their minds and lives are unaware of the deeper spirit that indeed, as I hold, underlies every serious
endeavour, these persons simply remain unconscious that their morality
has any religious motive or that they are dealing with the problem of

salvation. Even some professional teachers of duty are mere legalists who do not succeed in reducing the law which they teach to any rational unity. And for such people the postulate which religion makes the head of the corner is rather a stumbling-stone. They doubt or question whether there is any highest good whatever or any pearl of great price. Yet they illustrate the essential feature of morality by insisting that certain deeds must be done.

But, however it may be with the first of the religious postulates, it is the second (the postulate that we are naturally in very great danger of missing the true goal of life) which leaves open the greater room for differences of interest as between the religious teachers and the teachers of duty. Suppose that we are in agreement in holding that there is a highest good. Nevertheless, the question: How far is man naturally in danger of missing this supreme goal? is a question which, since we are all fallible mortals, leaves room for many varieties of opinion. . . . To me the religious need seems an insistent and clear need. But many moralists are partisans of duty as a substitute for religion. And they are often much more optimistic regarding human nature than I am. In their opinion the goal can be reached, or at least steadily approached, by simple dutifulness in conduct, without any aid from other motives that should tend to our salvation.

There is, then, a pearl of great price. But—so such teachers hold— why sell all that you have to buy that pearl, when by nature you are able to win it through a reasonable effort? Dutifulness is the name for the spirit that leads to such an effort. And dutifulness, say these teachers, is as natural as any other normal function. "No general catastrophe threatens our destiny," they insist. "Why not do right? That is in your own personal power and is sufficient for your deepest need. You need cry out for no aid from above. You can be saved if you choose. There is no dark problem of salvation."

To such optimists the intensely religious often respond with that strange horror and repugnance which only very close agreement can make possible. Near spiritual kin can war together with a bitterness that mutual strangers cannot share. In this case, as you see, the goal is the same for both parties to the controversy. Both want to reach some highest good. The cheerful optimists simply feel sure of being able to reach, through action, what the earnestly devout are passionately seeking by the aid of faith. Yet each side may regard the other with a deep sense of sacred aversion. "Fanatic!" cries the partisan of duty to his religious brother. "Mere moralists," retorts the other, and feels that no ill name could carry more well-founded opprobrium. The issue involved is indeed both delicate and momentous. . . .

Let us here approach this problem from the side of our moral consciousness. For at this point we are already familiar with the religious need. Does there exist amongst men a type of morality that, in and for itself, is already essentially religious, so that it knows nothing of this conflict between duty and religion? I reply, there is such a type of morality. There is a sort of consciousness which equally demands of those whom it inspires, spiritual attainment and strenuousness, serenity and activity, resignation and vigour, life in the spirit and ceaseless enterprise in service. Is this form of consciousness something belonging only to highly and intellectually cultivated souls? Is it the fruit of abstract thinking alone? Is it the peculiar possession of the philosophers? Or, on the other hand, does it arise solely through dumb and inarticulate intuitions? Is it consistent only with a highly sensitive and mystical temperament? Does it belong only to the childhood of the spirit? Is it exclusively connected with the belief in some one creed? To all these questions I reply: No.

This sort of consciousness is possessed in a very high degree by some of the humblest and least erudite of mankind. Those in whose lives it is a notable feature may be personally known only to a few near friends. But the spirit in which they live is the most precious of humanity's possessions. And such people may be found belonging to all the ages in which we can discover any genuinely humane activities, and to all those peoples that have been able to do great work, and to all the faiths that contain any recognisable element of higher religious significance.

I can best show you what I mean by next very briefly reviewing the motives upon which the idea of duty itself rests, and by then showing to what, upon the noblest level of human effort, these motives lead.

Our moral interests have a development which, in all its higher phases, runs at least parallel to the development of our religious interests, even in cases where the two sorts of interests seem to clash. The moral problems arise through certain interactions that take place between our individual and our social experience. The reason reviews these interactions and takes interest in unifying our plan of life. The will is always, from the very nature of the case, concerned in the questions that here arise. For whatever else morality is, it is certain that your morality has to do with your conduct, and that moral goodness cannot be yours unless your will itself is good. Wealth might come to you as a mere gift of fortune. Pleasure might be brought to you from without, so far as you have the mere capacity for pleasure. The same might appear to be true even in case of salvation, if, indeed, salvation is wholly due to saving grace. But moral goodness, if you can get it at all, requires your active coöperation. You can earn it only in case you do something to possess it. . . .

Therefore the moral question always takes the form of asking: What am I to do? The first contribution to the answer is furnished, upon all levels of our self-consciousness, by our individual experience. And one apparently simple teaching that we get from this source may be stated in a maxim which wayward people often insist upon, but which only the very highest type of morality can rationally interpret: "I am to do what I choose, in case only I know what I choose and am able to do it." From this point of view, my only limitations, at first sight, seem to be those set for me by my physical weakness. There are many things that, if I had the power, I should or might choose to do. But since I frequently cannot accomplish my will, I must learn to limit myself to what I can carry out. So far, I say, our individual experience, if taken as our sole moral guide, seems at first to point out the way.

But this first teaching of our individual experience is by no means so simple as it seems. For the question arises: What is it, on the whole, that I choose to do? And, as we saw very early in these discussions, each of us is by nature so full of caprices and of various aims, that, left to ourselves, we live not only narrowly but inconsistently. Hence we spend much of our lives in finding out, after the fact, that what we chose to do at one moment of our lives has hopelessly thwarted what we intended to do at some other moment. Self-will, left to itself, means self-defeat. That is the lesson of life. And the question: What is it that, on the whole, I would choose to do if I had the power? is a question that individual experience, taken by itself, never answers in any steadily consistent way. Therefore, as we all sooner or later come to see, one of our most persistent limitations is *not* our physical weakness to accomplish what we choose, but our incapacity, when left to ourselves, to find out what it is that we propose and really choose to do. Therefore, just because individual experience, taken by itself, never gives steady guidance, we have to look elsewhere for a rule.

The question: What am I to do? is never in practice answered without consulting, more or less persistently, our social experience. Being what we are, naturally gregarious, imitative, and, when trained, conventional creatures, who, indeed, often fight with our kind, but who also love our kind, who not only cannot bear to be too much alone, but are simply helpless when wholly isolated from our fellows (unless we have already learned in their company the very arts that we may be able to use while we are alone), we can give no answer to the question: What is to be my choice? without pretty constantly consulting our social interests. And these interests are indeed plentiful and absorbing. But they too are naturally conflicting. And so, taken as they come, they give us no rule of life.

To be sure, the social will in general says to us: "Live with your fellows, for you cannot do without them. Learn from them how to live; for you have to live more or less in their way. Imitate them, coöperate with them, at least enough to win such ideas as will help you to know what you want and such skill as will make you best able to accomplish whatever, in view of your social training, you are led to choose. Do not oppose them too much, for they are many, and, if stirred up against you, can easily destroy you. Conform, then, to their will enough to get power to have your own way." And so far our ordinary social will gives us more or less consistent counsel. But beyond such really rather barren advice (the counsel of an inane worldly prudence), our social experience, as it daily comes to us, has no single ideal to furnish, no actually universal rules to lay down. For, as I go about in social relations, sometimes I love my fellows and sometimes I feel antipathy for them. Sometimes I am full of pity for their woes and long to help them. Sometimes they are my rivals; and I then naturally try to crush them. There is thus no one social tendency that, as it comes to us in the course of our ordinary social experience, gives us sufficient guidance to tell us how to escape self-defeat. For my love and pity war with my social greed and with my rivalries. I am so far left to my chaos. . . .

. . . How real and how confused this chaos is, the daily record of certain aspects of the ordinary social life of men which you see in each morning's newspaper may serve to illustrate. These princes and peoples, these rebels and executioners, these strikers and employers, these lovers and murderers, these traders and bankrupts, these who seem for the moment to triumph and these who just now appear to be ground under the opponent's or the oppressor's heel, what arts of living were they and are they all following? Well, each in his way appears to have been choosing to have his own will; yet each, being a social creature, had learned from his fellows all his vain little arts of life. Each loved some of his fellows and was the rival of others. Each had his standards of living, standards due to some more or less accidental and unstable union of all the motives thus barely suggested. The news of the day tells you how some of these won their aims, for the moment, while others were thwarted. What I ask you to note, and what the reason of every man in his more enlightened moments shows him, is that each of these who at any moment was thwarted, precisely in so far as he had any will of his own at all, was defeated not only by his fellows, but by himself. For this special will of his was some caprice not large enough to meet his own ends. The career, for instance, of that man who failed in love or in business or in politics is wrecked. His reputation is lost. Well, it was his will, as a social being, to aim at just such a career and to value just that sort of reputation. Had he chosen to be a hermit, or a saint, or a Stoic, what would just such a career and such a reputation have been to him? How could he have lost unless he had sought? And his failure, to what was it due? No doubt to some choice of his own quite as much as to his rival's skill. He wanted freedom to carry on his own speculations. He got that freedom and lost his fortune. He wanted to be free to choose whom and how to love. He had his way and defeated his own aim. He chose to follow his ambitions. They have led him where he is.

Such are perfectly reasonable reflections upon the course of ordinary social conflicts. They suggest to our more considerate moments the very sort of reflection which, at the outset of the present discussion, led us to define the religious ideal of salvation. Only now this type of reflection appears as aiming to lead us to some practical rule for guiding our active life. For our attention is now fixed, not on a condition to be called salvation, but on a rule for doing something in accordance with our own true will. This rule is, negatively stated, the following: Do *not* seek, either in your individual self as you are or in your social experience as it comes, for the whole truth either about what your own will is or about how you can get your aims. For if you confine yourself to such sources of moral insight, you will go on thwarting yourself quite as genuinely, even if by good luck, not quite as scandalously, as the bankrupt speculators and the strikers and the outcast oppressors, and the politicians and the murderers, and the deposed monarchs and the defeated revolutionists, of whom you read in the newspapers, have thwarted both their individual and their social will. In brief: Put not your trust in caprices, either individual or social. On the positive side, the rule here in question is: In order to find out what is your true choice, and how you can live without thwarting yourself, make your *principle* of life such that whatever fortune besets you, you can inwardly say: "I have not really failed, for I have acted as I intended, and also as I still intend to act, and have had my will whatever the consequences that fortune has brought to me, or however my momentary mood happens to change, or however this or that social caprice leads men to love or to despise me." Such is the moral insight that the first use of your reason, in thus reviewing life, suggests. Or, as the moral common-sense of the wise has often stated the rule here in question: So act that, upon any calm review of the sense of your individual and of your social life, you shall never have ground to regret the principle of your action, never have ground to say: "By choosing thus I thwarted my own will."

As you hear these statements, I hope that, reduced to their very lowest terms: "*So act as never to have reason to regret the principle of your action,*" they express a sort of counsel for life which is not strange to common-sense, even if it has received an abstract expression in the famous ethical philosophy of Kant. Only, as you will rightly insist, this counsel is indeed a seemingly hopeless counsel of perfection when it is addressed to the natural man, who merely has taken his instincts as he found them developing, and his social world as he has felt it fascinating or disturbing him, and who has then stumbled on, more or less prudently and obstinately trying to find out what it really is that he wants to do in life. Such a man will cry out: "But how shall I discover a principle of life such that, if I hold thereto, I shall never, upon any reasonable survey of life, regret following that principle?"

Here at length let life itself answer the question. As I was preparing these very words, and thinking what new instances to choose, in order to illustrate afresh the very principle that I have in mind, the newspaper of the day, side by side with its usual chronicle of unreason and of disaster, reported the approaching end of a public servant. This public servant was Ida Lewis, who for fifty years was the official keeper of the Lime Rock lighthouse in Narragansett Bay. She had been known for more than fifty years for her early and later repeated heroism as a life-saver. And now she was at last on her death-bed. She has since died. I know nothing of her career but what public reports have told. So far as her duty required her at her post, she kept her light burning through all the nights and the storms of those many years. She saved, in all, upon various occasions, eighteen lives of those who were in danger from wreck. Her occupation thus had its perils. It had, what must have been much harder to endure, its steady call upon daily fidelity. It was, on the whole, an obscure and humble occupation; although by chance, as well as by reason of her skill and devotion, this particular lighthouse keeper was privileged to become in a sense famous. But certainly it could have been no part of her original plan to pursue a famous career. When we seek public prominence we do not select the calling of the lighthouse keeper. I do not know how she came to find this calling. She may not even have chosen it. But she certainly chose how to live her life when she had found it. What it means for the world to have such lives lived, a very little thought will show us. What spirit is needed to live such lives as they should be lived, we seldom consider, until such a public servant, dying with the fruits of her years to some extent known to the public, reminds us of our debt and of her devotion. . . .

And now, I ask you, What is the spirit which rules such lives? It is a spirit which is familiar in song and story; for men always love to tell about it when they meet with impressive examples of its workings. What I regret is that, when men repeat such songs and stories, familiarity breeds, not indeed contempt (for our whole nature rejoices to think of such deeds), but a certain tendency to false emphasis. We notice the dramatic and heroic incidents of such lives, and are charmed with the picturesque or with the thrilling features of the tale. And so we seem to ourselves to be dealing mainly with anecdotes and with accidents. We fail sufficiently to consider that back of the exceptional show of heroism there has to be the personal character, itself the result of years of devotion and of training—the character that has made itself ready for these dramatic but, after all, not supremely significant opportunities. Only when we in mind run over series of such cases do we see that we are dealing with a spirit suited not only to great occasions, but to every moment of reasonable life, and not only to any one or two callings, but to all sorts and conditions of men.

The spirit in question is the one which is often well illustrated in the lives of warriors who willingly face death for their flag—if only they face death not merely as brutes may also face it (because their fighting blood is aroused), but as reasonable men face death who clearly see what conditions make it "man's perdition to be safe." There are two tests by which we may know whether the warriors really have the spirit of which I am speaking... The first test that the warrior and the lighthouse tender are moved by the same spirit is furnished by the fact that those warriors who are rightly filled with this spirit are as well able to live by it in peace as in war; are, for instance, able even to surrender to the foe, when fortune and duty require them to do so—to surrender, I say, with the same calm dignity and unbroken courage that Lee showed in his interview with Grant at Appomattox, and that inspired him in the years of defeat and of new toils through which he had still to live after the war. That is, the warrior, if rightly inspired, is as ready for life as for death, is as ready for peace as for war; and despises defeat as much as danger—fearing only sloth and dishonour and abandonment of the service. The other test is whether the warrior is ready to recognize and to honour, with clear cordiality, this same spirit when it is manifested in another calling, or in another service, and, in particular, is manifested by his enemy. For then the warrior knows that warfare itself is only the accident of fortune, and that the true spirit of his own act is one which could be manifested without regard to the special occasion that has required him to face death just here or to fight on this side...

...Let me say that, to my mind, the calm and laborious devotion to a science which has made possible the life-work of a Newton, or of a Maxwell, or of a Darwin is still another example, and a very great example, of this same spirit—an example full of the same strenuousness, the same fascinated love of an idealized object, and, best of all, full of the willingness to face unknown fortunes, however hard, and to abandon, when that is necessary, momentary joys, however dear, in a pursuit of one of the principal goods which humanity needs—namely, an understanding of the wonderful world in which we mortals are required to work out our destiny. It is not a superficial resemblance that the lighthouse tender and the scientific man both seek to keep and to spread light for the guidance of men....

We have illustrated the spirit. We now ask: What is the principle which dominates such lives? Is it or is it not a principle such, that one at any time wholly devoted to it could thereafter, upon a reasonable review of life, wisely regret having chosen to live thus? If it is not such a principle, if on the contrary it is a principle such that any reasonable view of life approves it, let us know what it is, let us detach it from the accidental conditions which at once adorn and disguise it for our imagination, let us read it so as to see how it applies to every sort of reasonable life—and then we shall be in possession of the solution of our moral problem. Then we shall know what it is that, if we are indeed rational, we really choose to do so soon as we learn how to live. . . .

The people whom I have in mind, and of whom such instances teach us something, are, in the first place, individuals of considerable wealth and strength of personal character. They certainly are resolute. They have a will of their own. They make choices. And so the contribution of their individual experience to their moral purpose is large. It would be wrong to say, as some do, that they are characterized by mere "altruism," by utter "self-forgetfulness," by "living solely for others." If you were on a wreck in a storm, and the lighthouse keeper were coming out to save you, you would take little comfort in the belief, if you had such a belief, that, since he was a man who had always "lived for others," he had never allowed himself the selfish delight of being fond of handling a boat with skill or of swimming for the mere love of the water. No, on the contrary, you would rejoice to believe, if you could, that he had always delighted in boating and in swimming, and was justly vain of his prowess on the water. The more of a self he had delightedly or with a just pride trained on the water, the more of a self he might have to save you with. When we are in desperate need, we never wish beings who, as some say, "have no thought of self" to help us in our plight. We want robust helpers who have been trained through their personal fondness for the skill and the prowess that they can now show in helping us. So individual self-development belongs of necessity to the people whose faithfulness we are to prize in an emergency. And if people resolve to become effectively faithful in some practical service, their principle of action includes individual self-development.

In the second place, people of the type whom I here have in mind have strong social motives. Their faithfulness is a recognition of the significance, in their eyes, of some socially important call. And this, of course, is too obvious a fact to need further mention.

But in the third place, these people are guided by a motive which distinguishes their type of social consciousness from the chance and fickle interests in this or that form of personal and social success which I exemplified a short time since. A peculiar grace has been indeed granted to them—a free gift, but one which they can only accept by being ready to earn it—a precious treasure that they cannot possess without loving and serving the life that has thus endowed them—a talent which they cannot hide, but must employ to earn new usury— a talent which seems to them not to belong to themselves, but to their master, who will require it of them, increased. This grace, this gift, is what may be called their Cause. Sometimes it appears to them in winning guise, seen in the depths of the eyes of a beloved one, or symbolized by a flag, or expressed through a song. Sometimes they think of it more austerely, and name it "science," or "the service," or "the truth." Sometimes they conceive it expressly as a religious object, and call it, not unwisely, "God's will." But however they conceive it, or whatever name they give to it, it has certain features by which you may easily know it.

The Cause, for people of this spirit, is never one individual person alone, even if, as in the lover's case, the devoted person centres it about the self of one beloved. For even the lovers know that they transfigure the beloved being, and speak of their love in terms that could not be true, unless that which they really serve were much more than any one individual. The Cause for any such devoted servant of a cause as we have been describing *is some conceived, and yet also real, spiritual unity which links many individual lives in one, and which is therefore essentially superhuman, in exactly the sense in which we found the realities of the world of the reason to be superhuman.* Yet the cause is not, on that account, any mere abstraction. It is a live something: "My home," "my family," "my country," "my service," "mankind," "the church," "my art," "my Science," "the cause of humanity," or, once more, "God's will"—such are names for the cause. One thinks of all these objects as living expressions of what perfectly concrete and needy people want and require. But one also thinks of the cause as unifying many individuals in its service, and as graciously furnishing to them what they need, namely, the opportunity to be one in spirit. The cause, then, is something based upon human needs, and inclusive of human efforts, and alive with all the warmth of human consciousness and of human love and desire and effort. One also thinks of the cause as *superhuman in the scope, the wealth, the unity, and the reasonableness of its purposes and of its accomplishments.*

Such is the cause. That the individual loves it is, in any one case, due to the chances of his temperament and of his development. That it can be conceived and served is a matter of social experience. That it is more worthy to be served than are any passing whims, individual or social, is the insight which the individual gets whenever he surveys his life in its wider unities. That to serve it requires creative effort; that it cannot be served except by positive deeds is the result of all one's knowledge of it. That in such service one finds self-expression even in and through self-surrender and is more of a self even because one gives one's self, is the daily experience of all who have found such a cause. That such service enables one to face fortune with a new courage, because, whatever happens to the servant of the cause, he is seeking not his own fortune, but that of the cause, and has therefore discounted his own personal defeats, is the result of the whole spirit here in question.

For such a practical attitude toward such a cause I know no better name than the good old word Loyalty. And hereupon we are ready for a statement of the principle which dominates loyal lives. All the foregoing cases were cases of loyalty. In each some one had found a cause, a live spiritual unity, above his own individual level. This cause is no mere heap or collection of other human beings; it is a life of many brethren in unity. The simplest statement of the principle of the loyal person was the maxim: *"Be loyal to your cause."* Somewhat more fully stated this principle would read: *"Devote your whole self to your cause."* Such a principle does not mean "Lose yourself," or "Abolish yourself," or even simply "Sacrifice yourself." It means: "Be as rich and full and strong a self as you can, and then with all your heart and your soul and your mind and your strength, devote yourself to this your cause, to this spiritual unity in which individuals may be, and (when they are loyal) actually are, united in a life whose meaning is above the separate meanings of any or of all natural human beings."

Yet even thus the principle which actually inspires every thoroughly loyal action has not been fully stated. For, as we have seen, the warriors, despite the fact that their duty requires them to compass if they can the defeat of their foes, best show their loyal spirit if they prize the loyalty of their foes and honour loyalty wherever they find it. We call such a spirit that honours loyalty in the foe a spirit of chivalry. You and I may remember that Lee was the foe of that Union in whose triumph we now rejoice. Yet we may and should look upon him as, in his own personal intent, a model of the spirit of true loyalty; for he gave all that he had and was to what he found to be his cause. Such an insight into the meaning of the loyalty of the foe, chivalry requires. Therefore, the true spirit of loyalty, including, as is reasonable, this spirit of chivalry, also requires us to state the principle of loyalty in a still deeper and more universal form. The true principle of loyalty is, in fact, a union of two principles. The first is: *Be loyal.* The second is: *So be loyal, that is, so seek, so accept, so serve your cause that thereby the loyalty of all your brethren throughout all the world, through your example, through your influence, through your own love of loyalty wherever you find it, as well as through the sort of loyalty which you exemplify in your deeds, shall be aided, furthered, increased so far as in you lies.*

Can this principle be acted out? Can it direct life? Is it a barren abstraction? Let the life and the deed of the lonely lighthouse keeper give the reply. Who, amongst us, whatever his own cause, is not instructed and aided in his loyalty by the faithful deed of such a devoted soul? Such people are then, in truth, not loyal *merely* to their own private cause. *They are loyal to the cause of all loyal people.* For, to any enlightened survey of life, all the loyal, even when chance and human blindness force them at any moment to war with one another, are, in fact, spiritual brethren. They have a common cause—the cause of furthering universal loyalty through their own choice and their own service. The spirit of chivalry simply brings this fact to mind. The loyal are inspired by the loyal, are sustained by them. Every one of them finds in the loyal his kindred, his fellow-servants. Whoever is concretely loyal, that is, whoever wholly gives himself to some cause that binds many human souls in one superhuman unity, is just in so far serving the cause not only of all mankind, but of all the rational spiritual world. I repeat then: The true principle of all the loyal is: *So be loyal to your own cause as thereby to serve the advancement of the cause of universal loyalty.*

Now of the principle thus formulated I assert that it is a principle fit to be made the basis of a universal moral code. There is no duty, there is no virtue whose warrant and whose value you cannot deduce from this one principle. Charity, justice, fidelity, decisiveness, strenuousness, truthfulness, efficiency, wise self-assertion, watchful self-restraint, patience, defiance of fortune, resignation in defeat, your daily social duties, your individual self-development, your personal rights and dignity, your obedience to the calls of duty, your justified self-sacrifices, your rational pride in the unique moral office to which you have individually been called—all these, I assert, can be rightly defined, defended, estimated, and put into practice through an accurate understanding and development of the principle of loyalty just laid down.

Since I am, indeed, speaking of sources of insight, and am not portraying at any length their results, you will not expect of me a deduction of such a moral code here. But this assertion of mine is no mere boast. I have repeatedly endeavoured, elsewhere, to portray loyalty and to apply its principles to life. For the moment it suffices to ask you to consider the lives of the loyal, in such examples as I have suggested to you, and to try for yourselves to see what they teach. To help you in such a consideration, I may here simply remind you that when one is not only loyal but enlightened, one cannot finally approve or accept any cause or any mode of living that, while seeming in itself to be a cause or a mode of living such as embodies the spirit of loyalty, still depends upon or involves contempt for the loyalty of other men, or a disposition to prey upon their loyalty and to deprive them of any cause

to which they can be loyal. No loyalty that lives by destroying the
loyalty of your neighbour is just to its own true intent. And that is why
charity and justice are fruits of the loyal spirit. And that is why, if
your cause and your loyal action are rightly accepted and carried out,
the common interests of all rational beings are served by your loyalty
precisely in so far as your powers permit. Whatever your special cause
(and your special personal cause—your love, your home, or your calling—you must have), *your true cause is the spiritual unity of all the
world of reasonable beings.* This cause you further, so far as in you
lies, by your every deed.

And that also is why the principle of loyalty, once rightly defined
and served by you—served with the whole energy and power of your
personal self—is a principle that, upon any enlightened survey of your
life you can never regret having served. This, then, is what we were
seeking—an absolute moral principle, a guide for all action.

But even this is not the whole meaning of what the spirit of loyalty
has to teach you.... For your cause can only be revealed to you
through some presence that first teaches you to love this unity of the
spiritual life. This presence will come to you in a beloved form, as
something human, dear, vitally fascinating. It may be a person—a face
—or a living community of human beings that first reveals it to you.
You can, indeed, choose it as your cause. Your will is needed. Loyalty
is no mere sentiment. It is the willing and practical and thorough-going
devotion of a self to a cause. But you can never choose your cause until
you have first found it. And you must find it in human shape. And you
must love it before you can choose its service.

, *Therefore, however far you go in loyalty, you will never regard your
loyalty as a mere morality. It will also be in essence a religion.* It will
always be to you a finding of an object that comes to you from without and above, as divine grace has always been said to come. Hence
loyalty is a source not only of moral but of religious insight. The spirit
of true loyalty is of its very essence a complete synthesis of the moral
and of the religious interests. The cause is a religious object. It finds
you in your need. It points out to you the way of salvation. Its presence
in your world is to you a free gift from the realm of the spirit—a gift
that you have not of yourself, but through the willingness of the world
to manifest to you the way of salvation. This free gift first compels
your love. Then you freely give yourself in return.

Therefore, the spirit of loyalty completely reconciles those bitter
and tragic wrangles between the mere moralists and the partisans of
divine grace. It supplies in its unity also the way to define, in harmonious fashion, the ideal of what your individual experience seeks in its
need, of what your social world, groaning and travailing in pain together, longs for as our common salvation, of what the reason conceives

as the divine unity of the world's meaning, of what the rational will requires you to serve as God's will. Through loyalty, then, not only the absolute moral insight, but the absolute religious insight, as you grow in grace and persist in service, may be and will be gradually and truthfully revealed to you.

For loyalty, though justifying no "moral holidays," [10] shows you the will of the spiritual world, the divine will, and so gives you rest in toil, peace in the midst of care. And loyalty also, though leaving you in no mystic trance, displays to you the law that holds the whole rational world together; though showing you the divine grace, calls upon you for the strenuous giving of your whole self to action; though requiring of you no philosophical training, tells you what the highest reason can but justify; and, though concerned with no mere signs and wonders, shows you the gracious and eternal miracle of a spiritual realm where, whatever fortunes and miracles and divine beings there may be, you, in so far as you are loyal, are and are to be always at home.

And all this is true because the spirit of loyalty at once expresses your own personal need and reason, and defines for you the only purpose that could be justified from the point of view of one who surveyed all voluntary and rational life. This is the purpose to further the unity of whatever spiritual life you can influence, and to do this by your every rational deed, precisely in so far as your powers permit. This is a law for all rational beings. No angels could do more than this. . . .

---

[10] William James used this phrase in criticizing the moral implications of the belief in an all-disposing, benevolent Providence. Given a world so regulated, James argued, the moral strivings of finite individuals really make no difference; so if God's in his heaven, we may as well take a moral holiday. Royce endeavored to escape this implication by showing that since finite persons are constituent parts of the Absolute, their striving for moral perfection does make a difference to whole and part alike.

IV

GEORGE SANTAYANA

꙳

Introduction

T HE INCLUSION OF George Santayana in a volume on American philosophy has its ironies: he is not an American by birth, lineage,
citizenship, nor to any considerable extent by sympathies. It is, if nothing more, a cherished fancy of his to claim that his philosophy would
have been the same whatever the century or the land in which he
might have lived. Yet only the most strident chauvinist would deny
him a place in this anthology. Santayana resided in the United States
during most of the years when his philosophy was being formed; he
was a pupil of two of the other men represented in this volume, James
and Royce; and American thought and American life not only supplied
an irritant which provoked some of his most characteristic doctrines
but may have shaped him in a positive way more than he himself has
acknowledged. A few years ago he wrote: "my intellectual relations
and labours still unite me closely to America; and it is as an American
writer that I must be counted if I am counted at all." [1]

As the Oedipus legend suggests, a man's country is where his influence works. By this criterion, we have a particular right to claim
Santayana. Although his doctrines so far have been effective in narrower circles than those of our pragmatists, it is in this country that
he has been most widely read. Possessing the ripest humanistic culture
of our philosophers, he has appealed to the literary-minded, and to
others especially concerned with the values of personal living. His
writings appeared at the most self-critical period in this country's intellectual history, and they have played a quiet but substantial part
in bringing into a somewhat provincial culture an element that is
more cosmopolitan and more broadly human. Peirce, William James,
Dewey and Royce have expressed aspects of our national genius—
traditionally pragmatic and idealistic by turns—which without them
would not have come to full development, and Santayana in his comparative aloofness has been insensitive to many of these. But he belongs
with Henry James and T. S. Eliot among those figures who have helped

---

[1] "Apologia Pro Mente Sua," in *The Philosophy of George Santayana*, edited by
P. A. Schilpp (Evanston, The Library of Living Philosophers, Inc., 1940), p. 603.

us to extend our capacities for experience by assimilating neglected elements from the European past and present.

Santayana was born in Madrid of Spanish parents on December 16, 1863. His mother's first marriage had been to George Sturgis, a Bostonian merchant prince resident in Manila, after whose death she brought their three children to Boston to be educated. On a later visit to Spain, she married Agustín Ruiz de Santayana, an old friend from her days in the Philippines, and to them was born the future philosopher. Mrs. Santayana's commitments to her first husband led her to return to Boston to continue the education of her Sturgis children. After remaining for several years with his father in Spain, George Santayana first came to the United States in his ninth year, and stayed to graduate from Boston Latin School and Harvard College. With intervals of foreign travel, and of study in Germany and at King's College, Cambridge, he lived in the United States until the eve of the First World War, when upon receipt of a legacy from his mother's estate he gave up the professorship of philosophy he had held at Harvard to spend the period of the war in England and later to make his headquarters in Rome. Santayana has written voluminously of his personal associations and his travels in his memoirs, of which only the first two volumes, *Persons and Places* and *The Middle Span,* have appeared at this writing, and in such autobiographical sketches as "A General Confession" [2] and several of the chapters in *Character and Opinion in the United States.* But Santayana's personal life and his writing have been so much of one piece that the student of his biography will not ignore his poems, his novel, *The Last Puritan,* nor for that matter his systematic philosophy. The most extensive account of his life by another hand than his own is to be found in G. W. Howgate's *George Santayana.*

Santayana's literary career has extended over more than sixty years of constant writing, and has included many genres.[3] Yet it displays a remarkable consistency, so that one may begin almost anywhere after his first efforts: it is no great exaggeration to say that his whole philosophy is contained, in large or in small, in everything that he has written. His leading ideas have been stated fully but informally in such books as *Soliloquies in England, Character and Opinion in the United States, Dialogues in Limbo, Interpretations of Poetry and Religion,* and *Three Philosophical Poets.* Twice in his lifetime he has summed them up systematically in a five-volume work, first in *The Life of Reason* (1905-06), then in *Realms of Being* (1927-1940) and its introduction, *Scepticism and Animal Faith* (1923). Santayana's ethics and

---

[2] In *The Philosophy of George Santayana,* edited by P. A. Schilpp.

[3] The most complete bibliography is included in the volume edited by Schilpp, cited above.

his philosophy of culture are given their fullest treatment in *The Life of Reason,* while the later series emphasizes his theories of knowledge and reality.

The title of *The Life of Reason* is intentionally ambiguous: in this work Santayana is writing both a biographical or historical sketch of rationality and an analysis of the rational life. The historical part of the enterprise traces some of the principal steps by which reason is attained in the development of the individual and in the course of human society. The culmination of this process is the good or rational life, which Santayana, like the great Hellenic thinkers whom he follows, conceives to be inseparable from the perfecting of human powers and institutions. Although Santayana has often been called an "aesthete"—and not merely because his *The Sense of Beauty* has been the most influential writing on aesthetics to appear in America—he has written on several occasions that he considered himself primarily a moralist. He insists that even aesthetic judgments, though they are not moralistic in any narrow sense and invoke special criteria of their own, deal with the good for man, or a part of it; and that art as a whole must be judged, as must science, religion and all other human activities, by its contribution to the rational life. But Santayana's ethics cannot be understood apart from his theory of knowledge and his cosmology, for Santayana believes that man cannot know his good without comprehending the reality which generated and environs him; that the rational life is impossible without a rational view of the cosmos.

There is no single method of approach which the philosopher must adopt in his effort to know himself and the world. Wherever we start, we find ourselves in the middle of things, and "there is no first principle of criticism." All knowledge involves a structure of assumptions; no one of these assumptions has any absolute priority to the rest. In *The Life of Reason,* Santayana follows a genetic procedure, seeking to discover how our rational techniques and standards could have arisen from more rudimentary human functions under the tutelage of experience. *Scepticism and Animal Faith* proceeds after the fashion of modern criticisms of knowledge from Descartes to Kant. Starting from the complex whole of what is accepted as "knowledge" or "experience," it tries to dissect this into its components, tracing each to its sources and asking for its credentials. How much in what is called "objective" knowledge is imposed upon us from without and how much is contributed by the structure of the human mind and the human organism?

This method can be successful only if we subject all beliefs to the most honest and rigorous doubt: "Scepticism is the chastity of the intellect, and it is shameful to surrender it too soon or to the first comer: there is nobility in preserving it coolly and proudly through a long youth, until at last, in the ripeness of instinct and discretion, it can be

safely exchanged for fidelity and happiness." [4] Santayana finds that
Descartes and Hume, those of his predecessors who have the greatest
reputation for pushing the method of doubt as far as it can go, were
faint-hearted in their scepticism. Descartes quickly tired of this method
when, after playing with it, he hastily adopted "I think, therefore I
am" as a proposition which is indubitable. Santayana asks:

What is "thinking," what is "I," what is "therefore," and what is "existence"? If there were no existence there would certainly be no persons and
no thinking, and it may be doubted . . . that anything exists at all. That any
being exists that may be called "I," so that I am not a mere essence, is a
thousand times more doubtful, and is often denied by the keenest wits. The
persuasion that in saying "I am" I have reached an indubitable fact, can
only excite a smile in the genuine sceptic. No *fact* is self-evident; and what
sort of fact is this "I," and in what sense do I "exist"? Existence does not
belong to a mere datum, nor am I a datum to myself; I am a somewhat
remote and extremely obscure object of belief.[5]

Hume, likewise, thought that he could legitimately call in question
everything except the existence of perceptions. Yet even this supposedly
ultimate belief, as Hume described it, rests upon a mass of unproved
assumptions:

Hume seems to have assumed that every perception perceived itself. He
assumed further that these perceptions lay in time and formed certain sequences. Why a given perception belonged to one sequence rather than
another, and why all simultaneous perceptions were not in the same mind,
he never considered; the questions were unanswerable, so long as he ignored
or denied the existence of bodies. He asserted also that these perceptions
were repeated, and that the repetitions were always fainter than the originals
—two groundless assertions, unless the transitive force of memory is admitted,
and impressions are distinguished from ideas externally, by calling an intuition an impression when caused by a present object, visible to a third person,
and calling it an idea when not so caused. Furthermore, he invoked an
alleged habit of perceptions always to follow one another in the same order
—something flatly contrary to fact; but the notion was made plausible by
confusion with habits of the physical world, where similar events recur when
the conditions are similar.[6]

Santayana's more radical scepticism tries to show, against Descartes
and the rationalists, that no proposition carries its truth with it as
self-evident; and, against Hume and the empiricists, that no perception carries with it assurance of its object's existence nor even of its
own existence. Truth and existence are complicated notions; neither
can be "given" in any single experience, but both rest on an elaborate
structure of reference and belief which transcends what is immediately
present. It is hard to limit oneself to what is directly "given," for this

---

[4] *Scepticism and Animal Faith* (New York, 1923), pp. 69-70.
[5] *Ibid.*, p. 290.
[6] *Ibid.*, p. 294.

is all mixed up with memory, expectation and dogma. Santayana applies the name of "intuition" to the attitude which passively contemplates the given; this attitude is contrasted with "intent," which is directed upon, or signifies, something not present. Intent usually predominates over intuition; experience is always on the wing; the animal organism is concerned with what is present as a signal of something absent, and its signals are highly fallible. If we could become wholly absorbed in intuition of what is given, we should have to suspend intent, and this would mean, in a manner of speaking, to "stop living." The complete sceptic, if one were possible, would simply stare mutely at any datum or "essence" which happened to pass before him, renouncing all interpretation of it and all belief about it. Santayana calls this ultimate step in doubt a "solipsism of the present moment."

Such scepticism is incapable of logical refutation, and also—since it is not an intellectually articulated attitude—of logical defense. All belief, even belief in scepticism, goes beyond its evidence and takes a leap into the unknown. The pressure of living, nevertheless, will not let us remain in the suspended animation in which complete intellectual scrupulousness would leave us. Intent is central in the structure of the organism. Long before any animal becomes capable of logical reasoning, it has exercised such functions as memory and expectation —assuming as they do belief in the past and the future—and its reactions presuppose the existence of "substance," or an independent order of things to which it must conform. Santayana applies the name of "animal faith" to such quasi-instinctive beliefs, whose objects are not immediately given. When their assumptions are made explicit, these beliefs lead us to an articulated faith in such objects as discourse (the systematic structure of meanings which makes reasoning possible), experience, the self, other selves, and an enduring order of nature. Belief in such objects does not rest upon inference, either deductive or inductive, since they are postulates which make inference itself possible. Their ultimate justification is pragmatic, since they constitute the minimum of assumption necessary in order to perform the basic vital functions. As the existentialists would say, we know existence in these various modes by being "involved" in it; and many of Santayana's readers will find the existentialists' handling of this topic thin beside Santayana's re-creation of the pressure, strain and zest of existence.

A fuller account of the individual's existential situation leads Santayana to an analysis of the four "Realms of Being" which constitute the most general categories of reality: Matter, Essence, Spirit and Truth. Matter or substance is the fundamental reality in space-time; it is a collective name for the executive order of nature, which is made up of such things as electrons, stars, mountains, trees, and intricate animal organisms. Matter has certain general properties, such as continuous existence and the exclusive power to do work; but Santayana leaves its detailed description to the special sciences. Essences include the forms and qualities of everything that is possible as well as everything that is actual: mythical monsters and n-dimensional geometrical figures as well as the redness and triangularity that are embodied in existence and are perceived. Essences are not powers that exert energy and beget existences, but unlike Platonic Ideas, which in some respects they resemble, they are "merely logical *loci* without authority or selectiveness of any kind."[7]

Santayana's conception of "spirit" or consciousness is a variety of the position that is known technically as epiphenomenalism. When animal bodies reach a certain level of complexity and organization, consciousness arises in them as a free gift of nature; Santayana calls it "a sort of ritual solemnising by prayer, jubilation or mourning, the chief episodes in the body's fortunes."[8] Spirit, mind or soul, like everything else that exists, is generated by matter or substance, and is an expression of it. The properties of matter are not defined by the formulae of physics alone; matter is what matter does or becomes, and "Nature" is suitable as a term for the whole of its manifestations in all their range and variety. Santayana gives a fervent statement of his naturalistic faith in his poems:

> The soul is not on earth an alien thing
> That hath her life's rich sources otherwhere;
> She is a parcel of the sacred air.
> She takes her being from the breath of Spring,
> The glance of Phoebus is her fount of light,
> And her long sleep a draught of primal night.[9]

Although spirit has no existence independent of matter, and, strictly speaking, constitutes one of its properties, it is such an important property that the philosopher not only calls spirit a new "dimension" of matter but dignifies it as a distinct, though not a separable, realm of being. Matter produces in the realm of spirit a record or reflection of some of its activities, but spirit cannot react in turn upon matter and direct its behavior. All the complicated adjustments that we make to the world are actually performed by the immensely complex bodily organization, including the nervous system. In his later writings Santayana, following a major Greek tradition, uses "the psyche" as the name for these executive functions of the organism. Only essences are directly given to spirit by perception or thought; we arrive at truth about substance—and all truth is symbolic rather than literal—by marshalling

---

[7] Santayana in a letter to Max H. Fisch, the general editor of this volume.

[8] *The Life of Reason*, vol. 1: *Reason in Common Sense* (New York, 1905), p. 213.

[9] *Poems* (New York, 1923), p. 22.

essences in the order which the shocks of experience impose upon us. Truth, defined as "the standard comprehensive description of any fact in all its relations," is thus a hybrid realm constituted by the interrelationships of matter, essence and spirit.

Reason, as Santayana conceives it, operates in a world that is in many ways irrational. We cannot explain how the world came to exist, nor why it should be as it is. To such questions Santayana answers, well in advance of the existentialists: "This world is contingency and absurdity incarnate, the oddest of possibilities masquerading momentarily as a fact." [10] We cannot, beyond a certain point, account for reason itself: our most careful and critical thinking about the world rests upon a basis of "animal faith," which assures us of an independent order of nature and of continuity in our experience. Within the environing mysteries, however, reason can discern certain regular and reliable habits in the natural world, and chastened by this knowledge it can impose its own orderly constructions of ideas upon those domains of nature which are amenable to human control.

The principal thesis of *The Life of Reason* is "that nature carries its ideal with it and that the progressive organization of irrational impulses makes a rational life." [11] Our impulses are not irrational in the sense that they are wholly disorderly, or that biological and psychological accounts of their origin and nature are irrelevant. Their irrationality consists in the fact that they impose themselves upon the individual initially without his foreseeing or willing them; and however much our goals and satisfactions may be transformed by being harmonized with each other and with the world, they are still relative to the nature of man, which, like the nature of the universe itself, could not be discovered *a priori* by purely logical reasoning, but must be accepted as a brute fact.

Like some of Santayana's critics among professional philosophers, the student may be puzzled to see how reason can have any effectiveness on Santayana's view of the nature of consciousness. Now in denying that consciousness as such does any work, Santayana does not mean to say that *thinking* or *reasoning* is useless. Reasoning, like other mental activities, has both a conscious and an unconscious or material aspect. "Ideas" have efficacy, but an idea is amphibious: it exists both in the realm of matter—as, say, a complicated operation of the brain— and in the realm of spirit as a content of consciousness. Even in our most elaborate logical thinking, according to Santayana, the psyche or the "automatic inward machinery" does the work, and consciousness merely notes its products.

It is, nevertheless, this by-product that is the justification of the life

[10] *Soliloquies in England and Later Soliloquies* (New York, 1922), p. 142.
[11] *Reason in Common Sense*, p. 291.

process. The conditions of value are two: consciousness and emotion. No matter how successfully the psyche preserved the organism and adapted it to the world, its labor would be lost if it did not give rise to awareness tinged with feeling as its "witness and reward."

The successive volumes of *The Life of Reason* illustrate, from the major branches of human activity, the principle that "the Life of Reason is the happy marriage of two elements—impulse and ideation— which if wholly divorced would reduce man to a brute or a maniac." [12] According to *Reason in Common Sense*, the first step in the conscious acquisition of rationality consists in becoming aware of our impulses and their ends. In our early commerce with the world, our knowledge of objects, of other minds, and of the self, and our elementary valuations, are built up by the interplay of impulse and ideation. *Reason in Society* begins with a discussion of love as a form of experience that is animal or material in its origin and spiritual in its possible fruits. The form that family life takes in various animal species and in various human cultures is relative to the biological needs of the species and to the circumstances of the environment. Yet the efforts of human beings to improve the organization of the family show how any such institution develops through the tensions springing from the necessity of allowing both for the biological functions that gave rise to it and for the ideal interests that grow out of it, so that in its perfect development the family would promote all of the following: natural affection, material nurture, and moral freedom. Society in general has as its rational goal the performance of a number of functions, and these manifest themselves at three different levels. Natural society is concerned with satisfying the basic human needs, and this function remains predominant in political and economic forms throughout the development of society. In so far as progress in civilization is possible, however, natural society makes some room for free society, in which individuals are not wholly occupied with gratifying their biological necessities but can pursue those activities and associations that are temperamentally congenial to them. Free society in turn generates ideal society, where one's companions are not persons but the symbols of religion, art, and science.

Although these ideal activities may be pursued largely for their own sakes, and may to a considerable extent supply their own justification, they also have their natural or material roots from which they cannot divorce themselves entirely. *Reason in Religion* conceives worship as initially a blend of ideal and practical elements, combining a luxuriant and unrestrained imaginative expression with a concern for the basic values of survival and security. Progress in religion consists in eliminat-

---

[12] *Ibid.*, p. 6.

ing the magical and superstitious elements through an increasingly accurate knowledge of the cosmos and of man, while retaining the vivid imaginative grasp of the human predicament concentrated in religious symbol and ritual. A rational religion would preserve the fundamental religious attitudes and practices, such as prayer, mythopoesis, piety, spirituality, and charity; but in order to do so, it must detach them from the misconceived and illusory objects around which they have spontaneously clustered, and link them to the real features of the world, disclosed by science and philosophical criticism, toward a discrimination of which they were inchoately groping. "The only truth of religion comes from its interpretation of life, from its symbolic rendering of that moral experience which it springs out of and which it seeks to elucidate." [13]

If Santayana thus makes of religion a kind of serious ethical and cosmological poetry, he does not thereby intend to disparage it. Poetry and the other arts play an essential rôle in the life of reason. No one, not even Mr. Dewey, has repudiated more emphatically than Santayana in *Reason in Art* the notion that art is exclusively an affair of museums. The distinction between fine art and industrial art is one of degree. All good art is "fine" in the sense that it springs from spontaneous expression, and that it is enjoyable for its own sake; yet it is practical in the sense that it answers to human needs. Poetry, for example, grows out of play with words, out of "memorable nonsense, or sound with a certain hypnotic power," and it retains something of this in its highest developments. Yet poetry can incorporate the intelligence, and can derive its intensity and poignancy from illuminating, however incidentally, the human concerns about which it plays; so that art and religion in their highest reaches coincide.

Science is continuous with common sense, and even possesses some features in common with art and religion. Like all these enterprises, it gives us no literal transcript of reality, but operates by means of symbols that are ineradicably tinged by the human perspective: "Science might . . . be called a myth conscious of its essential ideality, reduced to its fighting weight and valued only for its significance." [14] The scientific attitude, Santayana says in *Reason in Science,* may take either of two extreme directions: toward "physics" or toward "dialectic." In Santayana's very special sense of the term, "physics" would simply describe particular existences and the directly observable relations, such as their spatial connections and temporal sequences, which hold among them. Dialectic, on the other hand, exemplified by "pure" mathematics, is concerned with essences rather than with existences; it constructs systems of symbols and meanings without regard to their

[13] *The Life of Reason,* vol. 3: *Reason in Religion* (New York, 1905), p. 11.
[14] *The Life of Reason,* vol. 5: *Reason in Science* (New York, 1905), p. 17.

266 GEORGE SANTAYANA

embodiment in existence. All the empirical sciences arise from a combination of these two opposed tendencies, from observation of fact in constant interplay with elaborate constructions of theory. The science that is ordinarily called by the name of physics, for example, makes extensive use of the dialectical webs of mathematics, yet shuttles back and forth between these and the perception of relations actually existing in nature which control the selection and acceptance of certain formulae as true.

The reader may be surprised to find Santayana's ethical theory in the volume entitled *Reason in Science*. Although morality—the practice of the good life—is for him in many respects an art, nevertheless he follows the Socratic tradition in holding that ethics—the theory of the good life—is a science. Like the other sciences, it finds its materials by observing its subject-matter, which includes human desires, feelings, aspirations, and ideals. At the stage of pre-rational morality, the conscious moral ideas of a society do little more than reflect the process of trial-and-error by which that society has adjusted itself to its circumstances: these ideas are a miscellaneous jumble of hard experience, prejudice, fantasy, and local custom. With Socrates, moral experience was subjected to dialectic, and the great Athenian midwife thereby brought rational ethics to birth. A harmony of impulses is sought through a harmony in moral ideas. We become conscious not merely of our particular purposes but, in a systematic way, of the principles which are capable of organizing and directing them, and which discover features of the good for man that transcend their embodiment in local conditions. As in all the manifestations of reason, however, these ethical principles must be tested by reference to nature—the inscrutable, the ultimately contingent given order of things—and in this case, to the nature of man as manifested through his clarified satisfactions and preferences. When, from intellectual incapacity or great social tribulation, the effort at a rational ethics fails, men will once again seek a limited code which renounces the many-sided development of human powers, and they will find salvation in the cultivation of a few residual activities, often directed toward a supernatural goal. Such is post-rational morality, the recourse of a disillusioned and despairing civilization.

The Life of Reason does not contain Santayana's final word on the relation between the rational and post-rational attitudes. His later writings manifest a shift in emphasis even if not a change of doctrine. Since 1920 Santayana has given less attention to the instrumental function of reason in organizing man's manifold interests than to the contemplative or speculative exercise of reason as an end in itself. It is possible that his earlier concern with the practical uses of reason was in some measure forced upon him by the moral earnestness of American life and by his responsibilities as a teacher, and that his sojourn in Rome gave free rein to a temperament naturally inclined toward detachment—a detachment which he has preserved throughout the greatest war in history. In reply to critics who accuse him of absorption in post-rational communion with essences, Santayana asks them "to admit post-rational sentiment into the life of reason as an element, and to coördinate it with all the other profound and perennial elements in human nature." [15] Consequently, although the contemplative reason has come to the fore, both in his life and in his theory, as a separate impulse in its own right, Santayana still gives the primacy to rational ethics by insisting that the interest in contemplation is only one interest among others, and must find its place in that harmony at which the rational life always aims but in which it can never rest. If Santayana's detachment, after all this is said, seems notwithstanding excessive to some of his readers in a world horrified by new vistas of evil and new apocalypses of destruction, we can take this element in his philosophy as pointing us toward one possibility of life that may become actual when violence has been, for a period, subdued. There is small danger that American philosophy, as a whole or in these extracts, will lead us into excessive detachment; the danger is rather, even now, that our concern with the immediately practical will cause us to miss that tincture of speculative disinterestedness and its product, gentle irony, which can make action itself wiser and more rewarding.

PHILIP BLAIR RICE

KENYON COLLEGE

[15] "Apologia Pro Mente Sua," in Schilpp, *op. cit.*, p. 565.

1. Scepticism and Animal Faith

Preface [1]

HERE IS ONE more system of philosophy. If the reader is tempted to smile, I can assure him that I smile with him, and that my system—to which this volume is a critical introduction—differs widely in spirit and pretensions from what usually goes by that name. In the first place, *my system is not mine, nor new.* I am merely attempting to express for the reader the principles to which he appeals when he smiles. There are convictions in the depths of his soul, beneath all his overt parrot beliefs, on which I would build our friendship. I have a great respect for orthodoxy; not for those orthodoxies which prevail in particular schools or nations, and which vary from age to age, but for a certain shrewd orthodoxy which the sentiment and practice of laymen maintain everywhere. I think that common sense, in a rough dogged way, is technically sounder than the special schools of philosophy, each of which squints and overlooks half the facts and half the difficulties in its eagerness to find in some detail the key to the whole. I am animated by distrust of all high guesses, and by sympathy with the old prejudices and workaday opinions of mankind: they are ill expressed, but they are well grounded. What novelty my version of things may possess is meant simply to obviate occasions for sophistry by giving to everyday beliefs a more accurate and circumspect form. I do not pretend to place myself at the heart of the universe nor at its origin, nor to draw its periphery. I would lay siege to the truth only as animal exploration and fancy may do so, first from one quarter and then from another, expecting the reality to be not simpler than my experience of it, but far more extensive and complex. I stand in philosophy exactly where I stand in daily life; I should not be honest otherwise. I accept the same miscellaneous witnesses, bow to the same obvious facts, make conjectures no less instinctively, and admit the same encircling ignorance.

My system, accordingly, is *no system of the universe.* The Realms of Being of which I speak are not parts of a cosmos, nor one great cosmos together: they are only kinds or categories of things which I find conspicuously different and worth distinguishing, at least in my own thoughts. I do not know how many things in the universe at large may fall under each of these classes, nor what other Realms of Being may not exist, to which I have no approach or which I have not happened to distinguish in my personal observation of the world. Logic, like

[1] *Scepticism and Animal Faith* (New York, 1923), pp. v-x. By permission of the publishers, Charles Scribner's Sons.

language, is partly a free construction and partly a means of symbolizing and harnessing in expression the existing diversities of things; and
whilst some languages, given a man's constitution and habits, may seem
more beautiful and convenient to him than others, it is a foolish heat
in a patriot to insist that only his native language is intelligible or
right. No language or logic is right in the sense of being identical with
the facts it is used to express, but each may be right by being faithful
to these facts, as a translation may be faithful. My endeavour is to
think straight in such terms as are offered to me, to clear my mind of
cant and free it from the cramp of artificial traditions; but I do not ask
any one to think in my terms if he prefers others. Let him clean better,
if he can, the windows of his soul, that the variety and beauty of the
prospect may spread more brightly before him.

Moreover, my system, save in the mocking literary sense of the word,
is *not metaphysical*. It contains much criticism of metaphysics, and
some refinements in speculation, like the doctrine of essence, which are
not familiar to the public; and I do not disclaim being metaphysical
because I at all dislike dialectic or disdain immaterial things: indeed,
it is of immaterial things, essence, truth, and spirit that I speak chiefly.
But logic and mathematics and literary psychology (when frankly
literary) are not metaphysical, although their subject-matter is immaterial, and their application to existing things is often questionable.
Metaphysics, in the proper sense of the word, is dialectical physics, or
an attempt to determine matters of fact by means of logical or moral
or rhetorical constructions. It arises by a confusion of those Realms of
Being which it is my special care to distinguish. It is neither physical
speculation nor pure logic nor honest literature, but (as in the treatise
of Aristotle first called by that name) a hybrid of the three, materializ-
ing ideal entities, turning harmonies into forces, and dissolving natural
things into terms of discourse. Speculations about the natural world,
such as those of the Ionian philosophers, are not metaphysics, but
simply cosmology or natural philosophy. Now in natural philosophy
I am a decided materialist—apparently the only one living; and I am
well aware that idealists are fond of calling materialism, too, metaphysics, in rather an angry tone, so as to cast discredit upon it by
assimilating it to their own systems. But my materialism, for all that,
is not metaphysical. I do not profess to know what matter is in itself,
and feel no confidence in the divination of those *esprits forts* who,
leading a life of vice, thought the universe must be composed of nothing but dice and billiard-balls. I wait for the men of science to tell
me what matter is, in so far as they can discover it, and am not at
all surprised or troubled at the abstractness and vagueness of their
ultimate conceptions: how should our notions of things so remote from
the scale and scope of our senses be anything but schematic? But what-

ever matter may be, I call it matter boldly, as I call my acquaintances Smith and Jones without knowing their secrets: whatever it may be, it must present the aspects and undergo the motions of the gross objects that fill the world: and if belief in the existence of hidden parts and movements in nature be metaphysics, then the kitchen-maid is a metaphysician whenever she peels a potato.

My system, finally, though, of course, formed under the fire of contemporary discussions, is *no phase of any current movement*. I cannot take at all seriously the present flutter of the image-lovers against intelligence. I love images as much as they do, but images must be discounted in our waking life, when we come to business. I also appreciate the other reforms and rebellions that have made up the history of philosophy. I prize their sharp criticism of one another and their several discoveries; the trouble is that each in turn has denied or forgotten a much more important truth than it has asserted. The first philosophers, the original observers of life and nature, were the best; and I think only the Indians and the Greek naturalists, together with Spinoza, have been right on the chief issue, the relation of man and of his spirit to the universe. It is not unwillingness to be a disciple that prompts me to look beyond the modern scramble of philosophies: I should gladly learn of them all, if they had learned more of one another. Even as it is, I endeavour to retain the positive insight of each, reducing it to the scale of nature and keeping it in its place; thus I am a Platonist in logic and morals, and a transcendentalist in romantic soliloquy, when I choose to indulge in it. Nor is it necessary, in being teachable by any master, to become eclectic. All these vistas give glimpses of the same wood, and a fair and true map of it must be drawn to a single scale, by one method of projection, and in one style of calligraphy. All known truth can be rendered in any language, although the accent and poetry of each may be incommunicable, and as I am content to write in English, although it was not my mother-tongue, and although in speculative matters I have not much sympathy with the English mind, so I am content to follow the European tradition in philosophy, little as I respect its rhetorical metaphysics, its humanism, and its worldliness.

There is one point, indeed, in which I am truly sorry not to be able to profit by the guidance of my contemporaries. There is now a great ferment in natural and mathematical philosophy and the times seem ripe for a new system of nature, at once ingenuous and comprehensive, such as has not appeared since the earlier days of Greece. We may soon be all believing in an honest cosmology, comparable with that of Heraclitus, Pythagoras, or Democritus. I wish such scientific systems joy, and if I were competent to follow or to forecast their procedure, I should gladly avail myself of their results, which are bound to be no less picturesque than instructive. But what exists today is so tentative, obscure, and confused by bad philosophy, that there is no knowing what parts may be sound and what parts merely personal and scatter-brained. If I were a mathematician I should no doubt regale myself, if not the reader, with an electric or logistic system of the universe expressed in algebraic symbols. For good or ill, I am an ignorant man, almost a poet, and I can only spread a feast of what everybody knows. Fortunately exact science and the books of the learned are not necessary to establish my essential doctrine, nor can any of them claim a higher warrant than it has in itself: for it rests on public experience. It needs, to prove it, only the stars, the seasons, the swarm of animals, the spectacle of birth and death, of cities and wars. My philosophy is justified, and has been justified in all ages and countries, by the facts before every man's eyes; and no great wit is requisite to discover it, only (what is rarer than wit) candour and courage. Learning does not liberate men from superstition when their souls are cowed or perplexed; and, without learning, clear eyes and honest reflection can discern the hang of the world, and distinguish the edge of truth from the might of imagination. In the past or in the future, my language and my borrowed knowledge would have been different, but under whatever sky I had been born, since it is the same sky, I should have had the same philosophy.

[Ultimate Scepticism] [2]

A philosopher is compelled to follow the maxim of epic poets and to plunge *in medias res*. The origin of things, if things have an origin, cannot be revealed to me, if revealed at all, until I have traveled very far from it, and many revolutions of the sun must precede my first dawn. The light as it appears hides the candle. Perhaps there is no source of things at all, no simpler form from which they are evolved, but only an endless succession of different complexities. In that case nothing would be lost by joining the procession wherever one happens to come upon it, and following it as long as one's legs hold out. Every one might still observe a typical bit of it; he would not have understood anything better if he had seen more things; he would only have had more to explain. The very notion of understanding or explaining anything would then be absurd; yet this notion is drawn from a current presumption or experience to the effect that in some directions at least things do grow out of simpler things: bread can be baked, and dough and fire and an oven are conjoined in baking it. Such an episode is enough to establish the notion of origins and explanations, without at all implying that the dough and the hot oven are themselves primary

[2] *Ibid.*, pp. 1-2, 7-10, 21-22, 24, 25-26, 35, 39-41, 44-45. By permission of Charles Scribner's Sons. Headings in brackets are supplied by the editor.

facts. A philosopher may accordingly perfectly well undertake to find *episodes of evolution* in the world: parents with children, storms with shipwrecks, passions with tragedies. If he begins in the middle he will still begin at the beginning of something, and perhaps as much at the beginning of things as he could possibly begin.

On the other hand, this whole supposition may be wrong. Things may have had some simpler origin, or may contain simpler elements. In that case it will be incumbent on the philosopher to prove this fact; that is, to find in the complex present objects evidence of their composition out of simples. But in this proof also he would be beginning in the middle; and he would reach origins or elements only at the end of his analysis.

The case is similar with respect to first principles of discourse. They can never be discovered, if discovered at all, until they have been long taken for granted, and employed in the very investigation which reveals them. The more cogent a logic is, the fewer and simpler its first principles will turn out to have been; but in discovering them, and deducing the rest from them, they must first be employed unawares, if they are the principles lending cogency to actual discourse; so that the mind must trust current presumptions no less in discovering that they are logical—that is, justified by more general unquestioned presumptions—than in discovering that they are arbitrary and merely instinctive. . . .

To me the opinions of mankind, taken without any contrary prejudice (since I have no rival opinions to propose) but simply contrasted with the course of nature, seem surprising fictions; and the marvel is how they can be maintained. What strange religions, what ferocious moralities, what slavish fashions, what sham interests! I can explain it all only by saying to myself that intelligence is naturally forthright; it forges ahead; it piles fiction on fiction; and the fact that the dogmatic structure, for the time being, stands and grows, passes for a proof of its rightness. Right indeed it is in one sense, as vegetation is right; it is vital; it has plasticity and warmth, and a certain indirect correspondence with its soil and climate. Many obviously fabulous dogmas, like those of religion, might for ever dominate the most active minds, except for one circumstance. In the jungle one tree strangles another, and luxuriance itself is murderous. So is luxuriance in the human mind. What kills spontaneous fictions, what recalls the impassioned fancy from its improvisation, is the angry voice of some contrary fancy. Nature, silently making fools of us all our lives, never would bring us to our senses; but the maddest assertions of the mind may do so, when they challenge one another. Criticism arises out of the conflict of dogmas.

May I escape this predicament and criticize without a dogmatic criterion? Hardly; for though the criticism may be expressed hypothetically, as for instance in saying that if any child knew his own father he would be a wise child, yet the point on which doubt is thrown is a point of fact, and that there are fathers and children is assumed dogmatically. If not, however obscure the essential relation between fathers and children might be ideally, no one could be wise or foolish in assigning it in any particular instance, since no such terms would exist in nature at all. Scepticism is a suspicion of error about facts, and to suspect error about facts is to share the enterprise of knowledge, in which facts are presupposed and error is possible. The sceptic thinks himself shrewd, and often is so; his intellect, like the intellect he criticizes, may have some inkling of the true hang and connection of things; he may have pierced to a truth of nature behind current illusions. Since his criticism may thus be true and his doubt well grounded, they are certainly assertions; and if he is sincerely a sceptic, they are assertions which he is ready to maintain stoutly. Scepticism is accordingly a form of belief. Dogma cannot be abandoned; it can only be revised in view of some more elementary dogma which it has not yet occurred to the sceptic to doubt; and he may be right in every point of his criticism, except in fancying that his criticism is radical and that he is altogether a sceptic.

This vital compulsion to posit and to believe something, even in the act of doubting, would nevertheless be ignominious, if the beliefs which life and intelligence forced upon me were always false. I should then be obliged to honour the sceptic for his heroic though hopeless effort to eschew belief, and I should despise the dogmatist for his willing subservience to illusion. The sequel will show, I trust, that this is not the case; that intelligence is by nature veridical, and that its ambition to reach the truth is sane and capable of satisfaction, even if each of its efforts actually fails. To convince me of this fact, however, I must first justify my faith in many subsidiary beliefs concerning animal economy and the human mind and the world they flourish in.

That scepticism should intervene in philosophy at all is an accident of human history, due to much unhappy experience of perplexity and error. If all had gone well, assertions would be made spontaneously in dogmatic innocence, and the very notion of a *right* to make them would seem as gratuitous as in fact it is; because all the realms of being lie open to a spirit plastic enough to conceive them, and those that have ears to hear, may hear. Nevertheless, in the confused state of human speculation this embarrassment obtrudes itself automatically, and a philosopher today would be ridiculous and negligible who had not strained his dogmas through the utmost rigours of scepticism, and who did not approach every opinion, whatever his own ultimate faith, with the courtesy and smile of the sceptic.

The brute necessity of believing something so long as life lasts does not justify any belief in particular; nor does it assure me that not to live would not, for this very reason, be far safer and saner. To be dead and have no opinions would certainly not be to discover the truth; but if all opinions are necessarily false, it would at least be not to sin against intellectual honour. Let me then push scepticism as far as I logically can, and endeavour to clear my mind of illusion, even at the price of intellectual suicide. . . .

Do I know, can I know, anything? Would not knowledge be an impossible inclusion of what lies outside? May I not rather renounce all beliefs? If only I could, what peace would descend into my perturbed conscience! The spectacle of other men's folly continually reawakens in me the suspicion that I too am surely fooled; and the character of the beliefs which force themselves upon me—the fantasticality of space and time, the grotesque medley of nature, the cruel mockery called religion, the sorry history and absurd passions of mankind—all invite me to disown them and to say to what I call the world, "Come now; how do you expect me to believe in *you?*" At the same time this very incredulity and wonder in me are baseless and without credentials. What right have I to any presumptions as to what would be natural and proper? Is not the most extravagant fact as plausible as any other? Is not the most obvious axiom a wanton dogma? Yet turn whichever way I will, and refine as I may, the pressure of existence, of tyrannical absolute present being, seems to confront me. Something is evidently going on, at least in myself. I feel an instant complex strain of existence, forcing me to say that I think and that I am. Certainly the words I use in such reflection bring many images with them which may possess no truth. Thus when I say "I," the term suggests a man, one of many living in a world contrasted with his thinking, yet partly surveyed by it. These suggestions of the word "I" might well be false. This thinking might not belong to a member of the human family, and no such race as this mankind that I am thinking of might ever have existed. The natural world in which I fancy that race living, among other races of animals, might also be imaginary. Yet, in that case, what is imagination? Banish myself and my world as much as I will, the present act of banishing them subsists and is manifest; and it was this act, now unrolling itself consciously through various phases, not any particular person in any environment, that I meant when I said, "I find that I think and am."

In like manner the terms thinking and finding, which I use for want of anything better, imply contrasts and antecedents which I may disregard. It is not a particular process called thinking, nor a particular conjunction called finding, that I need assert to exist, but merely this passing unrest, whatever you choose to call it: these pulsations and phantoms which to deny is to produce and to strive to banish is to redouble. . . .

The fact of experience, then, is single and, from its own point of view, absolutely unconditioned and groundless, impossible to explain and impossible to exorcise. Yet just as it comes unbidden, so it may fade and lapse of its own accord. It constantly seems to do so; and my hold on existence is not so firm that non-existence does not seem always at hand and, as it were, always something deeper, vaster, and more natural than existence. Yet this apprehension of an imminent non-existence —an apprehension which is itself an existing fact—cannot be trusted to penetrate to a real nothingness yawning about me unless I assert something not at all involved in the present being, and something most remarkable, namely, that I know and can survey the *movement* of my existence, and that it can actually have lapsed from one state into another, as I conceive it to have lapsed.

Thus the sense of a complex strain of existence, the conviction that I am and that I am thinking, involve a sense of at least possible change. I should not speak of complexity nor of strain, if various opposed developments into the not-given were not, to my feeling, striving to take place. Doors are about to open, cords to snap, blows to fall, pulsations to repeat themselves. The flux and perspectives of being seem to be open within me to my own intuition. . . .

Doubtless, as a matter of fact, this intuition of change is itself lapsing, and yielding its place in physical time to vacancy or to the intuition of changelessness; and this lapse of the intuition in physical time is an actual change. Evidently, however, it is not a given change, since neither vacancy nor the intuition of changelessness can reveal it. It is revealed, if revealed at all, by a further intuition of specious change *taken as a report*. Actual change, if it is to be known at all, must be known by belief and not by intuition. Doubt is accordingly always possible regarding the existence of actual change. Having renounced my faith in nature, I must not weakly retain faith in experience. This intuition of change might be false; it might be the only fact in the universe, and perfectly changeless. I should then be that intuition, but it would not bring me any true knowledge of anything actual. On the contrary, it would be an illusion, presenting a false object, since it would present nothing but change, when the only actual reality, namely its own, was unchanging. On the other hand, if this intuition of change was no illusion, but a change was actually occurring and the universe had passed into its present state out of a previous state which was different (if, for instance, this very intuition of change had grown more articulate or more complex), I should then be right in hazarding a very bold assertion, namely, that it is known to me that what now is was not always, that there are things not given, that there is genesis in nature, and that time is real. . . .

The last step in scepticism is now before me. It will lead me to deny existence to any datum, whatever it may be; and as the datum, by hypothesis, is the whole of what solicits my attention at any moment, I shall deny the existence of everything, and abolish that category of thought altogether. If I could not do this, I should be a tyro in scepticism. Belief in the existence of anything, including myself, is something radically incapable of proof, and resting, like all belief, on some irrational persuasion or prompting of life. Certainly, as a matter of fact, when I deny existence I exist; but doubtless many of the other facts I have been denying, because I found no evidence for them, were true also. To bring me evidence of their existence is no duty imposed on facts, nor a habit of theirs: I must employ private detectives. The point is, in this task of criticism, to discard every belief that is a belief merely; and the belief in existence, in the nature of the case, can be a belief only. The datum is an idea, a description; I may contemplate it without belief; but when I assert that such a thing exists I am hypostatising this datum, placing it in presumptive relations which are not internal to it, and worshipping it as an idol or thing. Neither its existence nor mine nor that of my belief can be given in any datum. These things are incidents involved in that order of nature which I have thrown over; they are no part of what remains before me. . . .

Existence, then, not being included in any immediate datum, is a fact always open to doubt. I call it a fact notwithstanding, because in talking about the sceptic I am positing his existence. If he has any intuition, however little the theme of that intuition may have to do with any actual world, certainly I who think of his intuition, or he himself thinking of it afterwards, see that this intuition of his must have been an event, and his existence at that time a fact; but like all facts and events, this one can be known only by an affirmation which posits it, which may be suspended or reversed, and which is subject to error. Hence all this business of intuition may perfectly well be doubted by the sceptic: the existence of his own doubt (however confidently I may assert it for him) is not given to him then: all that is given is some ambiguity or contradiction in images; and if afterwards he is sure that he has doubted, the sole cogent evidence which that fact can claim lies in the psychological impossibility that, so long as he believes he has doubted, he should not believe it. But he may be wrong in harbouring this belief, and he may rescind it. For all an ultimate scepticism can see, therefore, there may be no facts at all, and perhaps nothing has ever existed.

Scepticism may thus be carried to the point of denying change and memory, and the reality of all facts. Such a sceptical dogma would

certainly be false, because this dogma itself would have to be entertained, and that event would be a fact and an existence: and the sceptic
in framing that dogma discourses, vacillates, and lives in the act of
contrasting one assertion with another—all of which is to exist with a
vengeance. Yet this false dogma that nothing exists is tenable intuitively and, while it prevails, is irrefutable. There are certain motives
(to be discussed later) which render ultimate scepticism precious to
a spiritual mind, as a sanctuary from grosser illusions. For the wayward
sceptic, who regards it as no truer than any other view, it also has some
utility: it accustoms him to discard the dogma which an introspective
critic might be tempted to think self-evident, namely, that he himself
lives and thinks. That he does so is true; but to establish that truth he
must appeal to animal faith. If he is too proud for that, and simply
stares at the datum, the last thing he will see is himself. . . .

The theory that the universe is nothing but a flux of appearances is
plausible to the sceptic; he thinks he is not believing much in believing
it. Yet the residuum of dogma is very remarkable in this view; and the
question at once will assail him how many appearances he shall assert
to exist, of what sort, and in what order, if in any, he shall assert them
to arise; and the various hypotheses that may be suggested concerning
the character and distribution of appearances will become fresh data
in his thought; and he will find it impossible to decide whether any
such appearances, beyond the one now passing before him, are ever
actual, or whether any of the suggested systems of appearances actually
exists. Thus existence will loom again before him, as something problematical, at a distance from that immediacy into which he thought he
had fled.

Existence thus seems to re-establish itself in the very world of appearances, so soon as these are regarded as facts and events occurring
side by side or one after the other. In each datum taken separately
there would be no occasion to speak of existence. It would be an obvious appearance; whatever appeared there would be simply and
wholly apparent, and the fact that it appeared (which would be the
only fact involved) would not appear in it at all. This fact, the existence of the intuition, would not be asserted until the appearance ceased
to be actual, and was viewed from the outside, as something that presumably had occurred, or would occur, or was occurring elsewhere.
In such an external view there might be truth or error; not so in each
appearance taken in itself, because in itself and as a whole each is a
pure appearance and bears witness to nothing further. Nevertheless,
when some term within this given appearance comes to be regarded
as a sign of some other appearance not now given, the question is pertinent whether that other appearance exists or not. Thus existence and
non-existence seem to be relevant to appearances in so far as they are

problematical and posited from outside, not in so far as they are certain and given.

Hence an important conclusion which at first seems paradoxical but which reflection will support; namely, that the notion that the datum exists is unmeaning, and if insisted upon is false. That which exists is the fact that the datum is given at that particular moment and crisis in the universe; the intuition, not the datum, is the fact which occurs; and this fact, if known at all, must be asserted at some other moment by an adventurous belief which may be true or false. That which is certain and given, on the contrary, is something of which existence cannot be predicated, and which, until it is used as a description of something else, cannot be either false or true. . . .

The Discovery of Essence [3]

The loss of faith, as I have already observed, has no tendency to banish ideas; on the contrary, since doubt arises on reflection, it tends to keep the imagination on the stretch, and lends to the whole spectacle of things a certain immediacy, suavity, and humour. All that is sordid or tragic falls away, and everything acquires a lyric purity, as if the die had not yet been cast and the ominous choice of creation had not been made. Often the richest philosophies are the most sceptical; the mind is not then tethered in its home paddock, but ranges at will over the wilderness of being. . . . In the critic, as in the painter, suspension of belief and the practical understanding is favourable to vision; the arrested eye renders every image limpid and unequivocal. . . . Living beings dwell in their expectations rather than in their senses. If they are ever to *see* what they see, they must first in a manner stop living; they must suspend the will, as Schopenhauer put it; they must photograph the idea that is flying past, veiled in its very swiftness. This swiftness is not its own fault, but that of my haste and inattention; my hold is loose on it, as in a dream; or else perhaps those veils and that swiftness are the truth of the picture; and it is they that the true artist should be concerned to catch and to eternalize, restoring to all that the practical intellect calls vague its own specious definition. Nothing is vague in itself, or other than just what it is. Symbols are vague only in respect to their signification, when this remains ambiguous. . . .

It was the fear of illusion that originally disquieted the honest mind, congenitally dogmatic, and drove it in the direction of scepticism; and it may find three ways, not equally satisfying to its honesty, in which the fear of illusion may be dispelled. One is death, in which illusion vanishes and is forgotten; but although anxiety about error, and even positive error, are thus destroyed, no solution is offered to the previous

[3] *Ibid.*, pp. 67, 68, 72-73, 73-74, 77-78. By permission of Charles Scribner's Sons

doubt: no explanation of what could have called forth that illusion or what could have dissipated it. Another way out is by correcting the error, and substituting a new belief for it: but while in animal life this is the satisfying solution, and the old habit of dogmatism may be resumed in consequence without practical inconvenience, speculatively the case is not at all advanced; because no criterion of truth is afforded except custom, comfort, and the accidental absence of doubt; and what is absent by chance may return at any time unbidden. The third way, at which I have now arrived, is to entertain the illusion without succumbing to it, accepting it openly as an illusion, and forbidding it to claim any sort of being but that which it obviously has; and then, whether it profits me or not, it will not deceive me.... The error came from a wild belief about it; and the possibility of error came from a wild propensity to belief. Relieve now the pressure of that animal haste and that hungry presumption; the error is washed out of the illusion; it is no illusion now, but an idea. Just as food would cease to be food, and poison poison, if you removed the stomach and the blood that they might nourish or infect; and just as beautiful things would cease to be beautiful if you removed the wonder and the welcome of living souls, so if you eliminate your anxiety, deceit itself becomes entertainment, and every illusion but so much added acquaintance with the realm of form. For the unintelligible accident of existence will cease to appear to lurk in this manifest being, weighting and crowding it, and threatening it with being swallowed up by nondescript neighbours. It will appear dwelling in its own world, and shining by its own light, however brief may be my glimpse of it: for no date will be written on it, no frame of full or of empty time will shut it in; nothing in it will be addressed to me, nor suggestive of any spectator. It will seem an event in no world, an incident in no experience. The quality of it will have ceased to exist: it will be merely the quality which it inherently, logically, and inalienably is. It will be an ESSENCE.

Retrenchment has its rewards. When by a difficult suspension of judgment I have deprived a given image of all adventitious significance, when it is taken neither for the manifestation of a substance nor for an idea in a mind nor for an event in a world, but simply if a colour for that colour and if music for that music, and if a face for that face, then an immense cognitive certitude comes to compensate me for so much cognitive abstention. My scepticism at last has touched bottom, and my doubt has found honourable rest in the absolutely indubitable. Whatever essence I find and note, that essence and no other is established before me. I cannot be mistaken about it, since I now have no object of intent other than the object of intuition. If for some private reason I am dissatisfied, and wish to change my entertainment, nothing prevents; but the change leaves the thing I first saw possessed of all its quality, for the sake of which I perhaps disliked or disowned it. That, while one essence is before me, some one else may be talking of another, which he calls by the same name, is nothing to the purpose; and if I myself change and correct myself, choosing a new essence in place of the old, my life indeed may have shifted its visions and its interests, but the characters they had when I harboured them are theirs without change. Indeed, only because each essence is the essence defined by instant apprehension can I truly be said to have changed my mind; for I can have discarded any one of them only by substituting something different. This new essence could not be different from the former one, if each was not unchangeably itself. . . .

. . . The realm of essence is not peopled by choice forms or magic powers. It is simply the unwritten catalogue, prosaic and infinite, of all the characters possessed by such things as happen to exist, together with the characters which all different things would possess if they existed. It is the sum of mentionable objects, of terms about which, or in which, something might be said. Thus although essences have the texture and ontological status of Platonic ideas, they can lay claim to none of the cosmological, metaphysical, or moral prerogatives attributed to those ideas. They are infinite in number and neutral in value. Greek minds had rhetorical habits; what told in debate seemed to them final; and Socrates thought it important to define in disputation the common natures designated by various words. Plato, who was initially a poet, had a warmer intuition of his ideas; but it was still grammar and moral prejudice that led him to select and to deify them. The quality or function that makes all shepherds shepherds or all goods good is an essence; but so are all the remaining qualities which make each shepherd and each good distinguishable from every other. Far from gathering up the fluidity of existence into a few norms for human language and thought to be focussed upon, the realm of essence infinitely multiplies that multiplicity, and adds every undiscriminated shade and mode of being to those which man has discriminated or which nature contains. Essence is not something invented or instituted for a purpose; it is something passive, anything that might be found, every quality of being; it therefore has not the function of reducing plurality to unity for the convenience of our poor wits or economy of language. It is far more garrulous than nature, herself not laconic. . . .

The Watershed of Criticism [4]

I have now reached the culminating point of my survey of evidence, and the entanglements I have left behind me and the habitable regions I am looking for lie spread out before me like opposite valleys. On the

[4] *Ibid.*, pp. 99-100, 101-102, 105, 106-107. By permission of Charles Scribner's Sons.

one hand I see now a sweeping reason for scepticism, over and above all particular contradictions or fancifulness of dogma. Nothing is ever present to me except some essence; so that nothing that I possess in intuition, or actually see, is ever *there;* it can never exist bodily, nor lie in that place or exert that power which belongs to the objects encountered in action. Therefore, if I regard my intuitions as knowledge of facts, all my experience is illusion, and life is a dream. At the same time I am now able to give a clearer meaning to this old adage; for life would not be a dream, and all experience would not be illusion, if I abstained from believing in them. The evidence of data is only obviousness; they give no evidence of anything else; they are not witnesses. If I am content to recognize them for pure essences, they cannot deceive me; they will be like works of literary fiction, more or less coherent, but without any claim to exist on their own account. If I hypostatise an essence into a fact, instinctively placing it in relations which are not given within it, I am putting my trust in animal faith, not in any evidence or implication of my actual experience. I turn to an assumed world about me, because I have organs for turning, just as I expect a future to reel itself out without interruption because I am wound up to go on myself. To such ulterior things no manifest essence can bear any testimony. They must justify themselves. If the ulterior fact is some intuition elsewhere, its existence, if it happens to exist, will justify that belief; but the fulfilment of my prophecy, in taking my present dream for testimony to that ulterior experience, will be found only in the realm of truth—a realm which is itself an object of belief, never by any possibility of intuition, human or divine. So too when the supposed fact is thought of as a substance, its existence, if it is found in the realm of nature, will justify that supposition; but the realm of nature is of course only another object of belief, more remote if possible from intuition than even the realm of truth. Intuition of essence, to which positive experience and certitude are confined, is therefore always illusion, if we allow our hypostatising impulse to take it for evidence of anything else....

The doctrine of essence thus renders my scepticism invincible and complete, while reconciling me with it emotionally.

If now I turn my face in the other direction and consider the prospect open to animal faith, I see that all this insecurity and inadequacy of alleged knowledge are almost irrelevant to the natural effort of the mind to describe natural things. The discouragement we may feel in science does not come from failure; it comes from a false conception of what would be success. Our worst difficulties arise from the assumption that knowledge of existences ought to be literal, whereas knowledge of existences has no need, no propensity, and no fitness to be literal. It is symbolic initially, when a sound, a smell, an indescribable feeling are signals to the animal of his dangers or chances; and it fulfils its function perfectly—I mean its moral function of enlightening us about our natural good—if it remains symbolic to the end. Can anything be more evident than that religion, language, patriotism, love, science itself speak in symbols? Given essences unify for intuition, in entirely adventitious human terms, the diffuse processes of nature; the aesthetic image—the sound, the colour, the expanse of space, the scent, taste, and sweet or cruel pressure of bodies—wears an aspect altogether unlike the mechanisms it stands for. Sensation and thought (between which there is no essential difference) work in a conventional medium, as do literature and music. The experience of essence is direct; the expression of natural facts through that medium is indirect. But this indirection is no obstacle to expression, rather its condition; and this vehicular manifestation of things may be knowledge of them, which intuition of essence is not. The theatre, for all its artifices, depicts life in a sense more truly than history, because the medium has a kindred movement to that of real life, though an artificial setting and form; and much in the same way the human medium of knowledge can perform its pertinent synthesis and make its pertinent report all the better when it frankly abandons the plane of its object and expresses in symbols what we need to know of it. . . .

Complete scepticism is accordingly not inconsistent with animal faith; the admission that nothing given exists is not incompatible with belief in things not given. I may yield to the suasion of instinct, and practise the arts with a humble confidence, without in the least disavowing the most rigorous criticism of knowledge or hypostatising any of the data of sense or fancy. . . .

I propose now to consider what objects animal faith requires me to posit, and in what order; without for a moment forgetting that my assurance of their existence is only instinctive, and my description of their nature only symbolic. I may know them by intent, based on bodily reaction; I know them initially as whatever confronts me, whatever it may turn out to be, just as I know the future initially as whatever is coming, without knowing what will come. That something confronts me here, now, and from a specific quarter, is in itself a momentous discovery. The aspect this thing wears, as it first attracts my attention, though it may deceive me in some particulars, can hardly fail to be, in some respects, a telling indication of its nature in its relation to me. Signs identify their objects for discourse, and show us where to look for their undiscovered qualities. Further signs, catching other aspects of the same object, may help me to lay siege to it from all sides; but signs will never lead me into the citadel, and if its inner chambers are ever opened to me, it must be through sympathetic imagination. I might, by some happy unison between my imagination and its generative principles, intuit the essence which is actually the essence of that thing. In that case (which may often occur when the object is a sympathetic mind) knowledge of existence, without ceasing to be instinctive faith, will be as complete and adequate as knowledge can possibly be. The given essence will be the essence of the object meant; but knowledge will remain a claim, since the intuition is not satisfied to observe the given essence passively as a disembodied essence, but instinctively affirms it to be the essence of an existence confronting me, and beyond the range of my possible apprehension. Therefore the most perfect knowledge of fact is perfect only pictorially, not evidentially, and remains subject to the end to the insecurity inseparable from animal faith, and from life itself.

Animal faith being a sort of expectation and open-mouthedness, is earlier than intuition; intuitions come to help it out and lend it something to posit. It is more than ready to swallow any suggestion of sense or fancy; and perhaps primitive credulity, as in a dream, makes no bones of any contradiction or incongruity in successive convictions, but yields its whole soul to every image. . . .

[Intuition and the Self] [5]

At the vanishing-point of scepticism, which is also the acme of life, intuition is absorbed in its object. For this reason, philosophers capable of intense contemplation—Aristotle, for instance, at those points where his thought becomes, as it were, internal to spirit—have generally asserted that in the end essence and the contemplation of essence are identical. Certainly the intuition of essence is oblivious of itself, and cognisant of essence only, to which it adds nothing whatever internally, either in character or in intensity; because the intensity of a thunderclap is the chief part of its essence, and so the peculiar intolerableness of each sort of pain, or transitiveness of each sort of pleasure. . . .

. . . In reality, essence and the intuition of essence can never be identical. If all animal predicaments were resolved, there would be no organ and no occasion for intuition; and intuition ceasing, no essences would appear. Certainly they would not be abolished by that accident in their own sphere, and each would be what it would have seemed if intuition of it had arisen; but they would all be merely logical or aesthetic themes unrehearsed, as remote as possible from life or from the intense splendour of divinity. Essence without intuition would be not merely nonexistent (as it always is), but what is worse, it would be the object of no contemplation, the goal of no effort, the secret or implicit ideal of no life. It would be valueless. All that joy and sense of liberation which pure objectivity brings to the mind would be en-

[5] *Ibid.*, pp. 126, 128-129, 129-130, 133, 145, 146-147, 148-149. By permission of Charles Scribner's Sons.

tirely absent; and essence would lose all its dignity if life lost its precarious existence....

Value accrues to any part of the realm of essence by virtue of the interest which somebody takes in it, as being the part relevant to his own life. If the organ of this life comes to perfect operation, it will reach intuition of that relevant part of essence. This intuition will be vital in the highest degree. It will be absorbed in its object. It will be unmindful of any possibility of lapse in that object, or defection on its own part; it will not be aware of itself, of time, or of circumstances. But this intuition will continue to exist, and to exist in time, and the pulsations of its existence will hardly go on without some oscillation, and probably a quick evanescence. So the intuition will be an utterly different thing from the essence intuited: it will be something existent and probably momentary; it will grow and fade; it will be perhaps delightful; that is, no essences will appear to it which are not suffused with a general tint of interest and beauty....

The first existence, then, of which a sceptic who finds himself in the presence of random essences may gather reasonable proof, is the existence of the intuition to which those essences are manifest. This is of course not the object which the animal mind first posits and believes in. The existence of things is assumed by animals in action and expectation before intuition supplies any description of what the thing is that confronts them in a certain quarter. But animals are not sceptics, and a long experience must intervene before the problem arises which I am here considering, namely, whether anything need be posited and believed in at all. And I reply that it is not inevitable, if I am willing and able to look passively on the essences that may happen to be given: but that if I consider what they are, and how they appear, I see that this appearance is an accident to them; that the principle of it is a contribution from my side, which I call intuition. The difference between essence and intuition, though men may have discovered it late, then seems to me profound and certain. They belong to two different realms of being....

Experience, when the shocks that punctuate it are reacted upon instinctively, imposes belief in something far more recondite than mental discourse, namely, a person or self; and not merely such a transcendental ego as is requisite intrinsically for any intuition, nor such a flux of sentience as discourse itself constitutes, but a substantial being preceding *all* the vicissitudes of experience, and serving as an instrument to produce them, or a soil out of which they grow....

... What shock proves, if it proves anything, is that I have a nature to which all events and all developments are not equally welcome. How could any apparition surprise or alarm me, or how could interruption of any sort overtake me, unless I was somehow running on in a certain direction, with a specific rhythm? Had I not such a positive nature, the existence of material things and their most violent impact upon one another, shattering the world to atoms, would leave me a placid observer of their movement; whereas a definite nature in me, even if disturbed only by cross-currents or by absolute accidents within my own being, would justify my sense of surprise and horror. A self, then, not a material world, is the first object which I should posit if I wish the experience of shock to enlarge my dogmas in the strict order of evidence.

But what sort of a self? In one sense, the existence of intuition is tantamount to that of a self, though of a merely formal and transparent one, pure spirit. A self somewhat more concrete is involved in discourse, when intuition has been deployed into a successive survey of constant ideal objects, since here the self not only sees, but adds an adventitious order to the themes it rehearses; traversing them in various directions, with varying completeness, and suspending or picking up the consideration of them at will; so that the self involved in discourse is a thinking mind. Now that I am consenting to build further dogmas on the sentiment of shock, and to treat it, not as an essence groundlessly revealed to me, but as signifying something pertinent to the alarm or surprise with which it fills me, I must thicken and substantialize the self I believe in, recognizing in it a nature that accepts or rejects events, a nature having a movement of its own, far deeper, more continuous and more biassed than a discoursing mind: the self posited by the sense of shock is a living psyche. . . .

. . . The natural psyche, being a habit of matter, is to be described and investigated from without, scientifically, by a behaviourist psychology; but the critical approach to it from within, as a postulate of animal faith, is extremely difficult and fraught with danger. Literary psychology, to which I am here confined, is at home only in the sentiments and ideas of the adult mind, as language has expressed them: the deeper it tries to go, the vaguer its notions; and it soon loses itself in the dark altogether. I cannot hope to discover, therefore, what precisely this psyche is, this self of mine, the existence of which is so indubitable to my active and passionate nature. The evidence for it in shock hardly goes beyond the instinctive assertion that I existed before, that I am a principle of steady life, welcoming or rejecting events, that I am a nucleus of active interests and passions. It will be easy to graft upon these passions and interests the mental discourse which I had previously asserted to be going on, and which made up, in this critical reconstruction of belief, my first notion of myself. And yet here is one of the dangers of my investigation, because mental discourse is not, and cannot be, a self nor a psyche. It is all surface; it neither precedes, nor survives, nor guides, nor posits its data; it merely notes and remembers them. Discourse is a most superficial function of the self; and if by the self I was tempted to understand a series of ideas, I should be merely reverting sceptically to that stage of philosophic denudation in which I found myself, before I had consented to accept the evidence of shock in favour of my own existence. I, if I exist, am not an idea, nor am I the fact that several ideas may exist, one of which remembers the other. If I exist, I am a living creature to whom ideas are incidents, like aeroplanes in the sky; they pass over, more or less followed by the eye, more or less listened to, recognized, or remembered; but the self slumbers and breathes below, a mysterious natural organism, full of dark yet definite potentialities; so that different events will awake it to quite disproportionate activities. The self is a fountain of joy, folly, and sorrow, a waxing and waning, stupid and dreaming creature, in the midst of a vast natural world, of which it catches but a few transient and odd perspectives.

Knowledge is Faith Mediated by Symbols [6]

... Since intuition of essence is not knowledge, knowledge can never lie in an overt comparison of one datum with another datum given at the same time; even in pure dialectic, the comparison is with a datum *believed* to have been given formerly. ...

Knowledge accordingly is belief: belief in a world of events, and especially of those parts of it which are near the self, tempting or threatening it. This belief is native to animals, and precedes all deliberate use of intuitions as signs or descriptions of things; as I turn my head to see who is there, before I see who it is. Furthermore, knowledge is true belief. It is such an enlightening of the self by intuitions arising there, that what the self imagines and asserts of the collateral thing, with which it wrestles in action, is actually true of that thing. Truth in such presumptions or conceptions does not imply adequacy, nor a pictorial identity between the essence in intuition and the constitution of the object. Discourse is a language, not a mirror. The images in sense are parts of discourse, not parts of nature: they are the babble of our innocent organs under the stimulus of things; but these spontaneous images, like the sounds of the voice, may acquire the function of names; they may become signs, if discourse is intelligent and can recapitulate its phases, for the things sought or encountered in the world. The truth which discourse can achieve is truth in its own terms, appropriate description: it is no incorporation or reproduction of the object in the mind. The mind notices and intends; it cannot incorporate or reproduce anything not an intention or an intuition. Its objects are no part of itself even when they are essences, much less when they are things. It thinks

---

[6] *Ibid.*, pp. 167, 179-181. By permission of Charles Scribner's Sons.

the essences, with that sort of immediate and self-forgetful attention which I have been calling intuition; and if it is animated, as it usually is, by some ulterior interest or pursuit, it takes the essences before it for messages, signs, or emanations sent forth to it from those objects of animal faith; and they become its evidences and its description for those objects. Therefore any degree of inadequacy and originality is tolerable in discourse, or even requisite, when the constitution of the objects which the animal encounters is out of scale with his organs, or quite heterogeneous from his possible images. A sensation or a theory, no matter how arbitrary its terms (and all language is perfectly arbitrary), will be true of the object, if it expresses some true relation in which that object stands to the self, so that these terms are not misleading as signs, however poetical they may be as sounds or as pictures.

Finally, knowledge is true belief grounded in experience, I mean, controlled by outer facts. It is not true by accident; it is not shot into the air on the chance that there may be something it may hit. It arises by a movement of the self sympathetic or responsive to surrounding beings, so that these beings become its intended objects, and at the same time an appropriate correspondence tends to be established between these objects and the beliefs generated under their influence.

In regard to the original articles of the animal creed—that there is a world, that there is a future, that things sought can be found, and things seen can be eaten—no guarantee can possibly be offered. I am sure these dogmas are often false; and perhaps the event will some day falsify them all, and they will lapse altogether. But while life lasts, in one form or another this faith must endure. It is the initial expression of animal vitality in the sphere of mind, the first announcement that anything is going on. It is involved in any pang of hunger, of fear, or of love. It launches the adventure of knowledge. The object of this tentative knowledge is things in general, whatsoever may be at work (as I am) to disturb me or awake my attention. The effort of knowledge is to discover what sort of world this disturbing world happens to be. Progress in knowledge lies open in various directions, now in the scope of its survey, now in its accuracy, now in its depth of local penetration. The ideal of knowledge is to become natural science: if it trespasses beyond that, it relapses into intuition, and ceases to be knowledge.

Belief in Substance [7]

All knowledge, being faith in an object posited and partially described, is belief in substance, in the etymological sense of this word; it is belief in a thing or event subsisting in its own plane, and waiting

[7] *Ibid.,* pp. 182-183, 189, 190-191. By permission of Charles Scribner's Sons.

for the light of knowledge to explore it eventually, and perhaps name or define it. In this way my whole past lies waiting for memory to review it, if I have this faculty; and the whole future of the world in the same manner is spread out for prophecy, scientific or visionary, to predict falsely or truly. Yet the future and the past are not ordinarily called substances; probably because the same material substance is assumed to run through both. Nevertheless, from the point of view of knowledge, every event, even if wholly psychological or phenomenal, is a substance. It is a self-existing fact, open to description from the point of view of other events, if in the bosom of these other events there is such plasticity and intent as are requisite for perception, prophecy, or memory.

When modern philosophers deny material substance, they make substances out of the sensations or ideas which they regard as ultimate facts. It is impossible to eliminate belief in substance so long as belief in existence is retained. A mistrust in existence, and therefore in substance, is not unphilosophical; but modern philosophers have not given full expression to this sceptical scruple. They have seldom been disinterested critics, but often advocates of some metaphysic that allured them, and whose rivals they wished to destroy. They deny substance in favour of phenomena, which are hypostatised essences, because phenomena are individually wholly open to intuition; but they forget that no phenomenon can intuit another, and that if it contains knowledge of that other, it must be animated by intent, and besides existing itself substantially must recognize its object as another substance, indifferent in its own being to the cognisance which other substances may take of it. In other words, although each phenomenon in passing is an object of intuition, all absent phenomena, and all their relations, are objects of faith; and this faith must be mediated by some feature in the present phenomenon which faith assumes to be a sign of the existence of other phenomena elsewhere, and of their order. So that in so far as the instinctive claims and transcendent scope of knowledge are concerned, phenomenalism fully retains the belief in substance. In order to get rid of this belief, which is certainly obnoxious to the sceptic, a disinterested critic would need to discard all claims to knowledge, and to deny his own existence and that of all absent phenomena. . . .

. . . The first thing experience reports is the existence of something, merely as existence, the weight, strain, danger, and lapse of being. . . . Animal watchfulness, lying in wait for the signals of the special senses, lends them their significance, sets them in their places, and retains them, as descriptions of things, and as symbols in its own ulterior discourse.

This animal watchfulness carries the category of substance with it, asserts existence most vehemently, and in apprehension seizes and throws on the dark screen of substance every essence it may descry. To grope, to blink, to dodge a blow, or to return it, is to have very radical and specific experiences, but probably without one assignable image of the outer senses. Yet a nameless essence, the sense of a moving existence, is there most intensely present; and a man would be a shameless, because an insincere, sceptic, who should maintain that this experience exists *in vacuo*, and does not express, as it feels it does, the operation of a missile flying, and the reaction of a body threatened or hit: motions in substance anterior to the experience, and rich in properties and powers which no experience will ever fathom.

Belief in substance, taken transcendentally, as a critic of knowledge must take it, is the most irrational, animal, and primitive of beliefs: it is the voice of hunger. But when, as I must, I have yielded to this presumption, and proceeded to explore the world, I shall find in its constitution the most beautiful justification for my initial faith, and the proof of its secret rationality. This corroboration will not have any logical force, since it will be only pragmatic, based on begging the question, and perhaps only a bribe offered by fortune to confirm my illusions. The force of the corroboration will be merely moral, showing me how appropriate and harmonious with the nature of things such a blind belief was on my part. How else should the truth have been revealed to me at all? Truth and blindness, in such a case, are correlatives, since I am a sensitive creature surrounded by a universe utterly out of scale with myself: I must, therefore, address it questioningly but trustfully, and it must reply to me in my own terms, in symbols and parables, that only gradually enlarge my childish perceptions. It is as if Substance said to Knowledge: My child, there is a great world for thee to conquer, but it is a vast, an ancient, and a recalcitrant world. It yields wonderful treasures to courage, when courage is guided by art and respects the limits set to it by nature. I should not have been so cruel as to give thee birth, if there had been nothing for thee to master; but having first prepared the field, I set in thy heart the love of adventure.

The Realm of Matter [8]

In the chase, for those who follow it, the intensity of experience is not like the intensity (limitless if you will) of contemplating pure Being—immutable, equable, and complete. The hunter and the hunted believe in something ambushed and imminent: present images are little to them but signs for coming events. Things are getting thick, agents are coming together, or disappearing; they are killing and dying. The

[8] *The Realm of Matter* (New York, 1930), pp. 9-11, 41-43. By permission of the publishers, Charles Scribner's Sons.

assurance of this sort of being is assurance of existence, and the belief in this sort of agent is belief in substance. If this belief and assurance are not illusions (which the acting animal cannot admit them to be), several properties must belong to substances and to the world they compose. These properties I may distinguish in reflection and call by philosophical names, somewhat as follows.

1. Since substance is posited, and not given in intuition, as essences may be given, *substance is external to the thought which posits it.*

2. Since it is posited in action, or in readiness for action, the substance posited is external not merely to the positing thought (as a different thought would be) but is external to the physical agent which is the organ of that action, as well as of that thought. In other words, *Substance has parts and constitutes a physical space.* Conversely, the substantial agent in action and thought is external to the surrounding portions of substance with which it can interact. *All the parts of substance are external to one another.*

3. Since substance is engaged in action, and action involves change, *substance is in flux and constitutes a physical time.* Changes are perpetually occurring in the relations of its parts, if not also in their intrinsic characters.

4. Since the agents in action and reaction are distinct in position and variable in character, and since they induce changes in one another, *substance is unequally distributed.* It diversifies the field of action, or physical time and space.

5. Since there is no occasion for positing any substance save as an agent in the field of action, all recognisable substance must lie in the same field in which the organism of the observer occupies a relative centre. Therefore, wherever it works and solicits recognition, *substance composes a relative cosmos....*

I may now add to the indispensable properties of substance others which substance seems to possess, and which, since they too are assumed in practice, may be assumed in natural philosophy.

6. *Substance,* in diversifying the field of nature, *sometimes takes the form of animals in whom there are feelings, images, and thoughts. These mental facts are immaterial.* They offer no butt for action and exercise no physical influence on one another.

7. The same *mental facts are manifestations of substance;* in their occurrence they are parts of a total natural event which, on its substantial side, belongs to the plane of action. They are therefore significant and relevant to action as signs, being created and controlled by the flux of substance beneath.

8. Beneath the intermittence of phenomena, *the phases or modes through which substance flows are continuous.*

9. As far as action and calculation can extend, *the quantity of substance remains equivalent throughout.*

10. *Each phase or mode of substance, although not contained in its antecedents, is pre-determined by them in its place and quality, and proportionate to them in extent and intensity.* An event will be repeated if ever the constellation of events which bred it should recur. This regularity in the genesis of modes or phases of substance is constantly verified in action on a small scale. To expect it in substance is the soul of science and art; but to expect it in phenomena is superstition.

When, then, in perception, action, memory, or hope experience is treated as significant, a substance is posited which must be external to thought, with its parts external to one another and each a focus of existence; a substance which passes through various phases, is unequally distributed in the field of action, and forms a relative cosmos surrounding each agent. Action on these assumptions makes it further appear that this substance is the source of phenomena unsubstantial in themselves but significant of the phases of substance which produce them; that these phases are continuous and measurable; and that each transformation, though spontaneous in itself, is repeated whenever the same conditions recur. Now a substance possessing these functions and these characteristics has a familiar name: it is called matter. Matter is the medium of calculable art. But I have found from the beginning that the impulse to act and the confidence that the opposite partner in action has specific and measurable resources, are the primary expressions of animal faith; also that animal faith is the only principle by which belief in existence of any kind can be justified or suggested to the spirit. It follows that the only object posited by animal faith is matter; and that all those images which in human experience may be names or signs for objects of belief are, in their ultimate signification, so many names or signs for matter. Their perpetual variety indicates the phases through which the flux of matter is passing in the self, or those which the self is positing in the field of action to which it is responsive. Apart from this material signification, those feelings and perceptions are simply intuitions of essences, essences to which no existence in nature can be assigned. The field of action is accordingly the realm of matter; and I will henceforth call it by that name.

The Implied Being of Truth [9]

From the beginning of discourse there is a subtle reality posited which is not a thing: I mean the truth. If intuition of essence exists anywhere without discourse, the being of truth need not be posited

[9] *Scepticism and Animal Faith*, pp. 262-263, 268-269. By permission of the publishers, Charles Scribner's Sons.

there, because intuition of itself is intransitive, and having no object other than the datum, can be neither true nor false. Every essence picked up by intuition is equally real in its own sphere; and every degree of articulation reached in intuition defines one of a series of essences, each contained in or containing its neighbour, and each equally central in that infinite progression. The central one, for apprehension, is the one that happens to appear at that moment. Therefore in pure intuition there is no fear of picking up the wrong thing, as if the object were a designated existence in the natural world; and therefore the being of truth is not broached in pure intuition.

Truth is not broached even in pure dialectic, which is only the apprehension of a system of essences so complex and finely articulated, perhaps, as to tax human attention, or outrun it if unaided by some artifice of notation, but essentially only an essence like any other. Truth, therefore, is as irrelevant to dialectic as to merely aesthetic intuition. Logic and mathematics are not true inherently, however cogent or extensive. They are ideal constructions based on ideal axioms; and the question of truth or falsity does not arise in respect to them unless the dialectic is asserted to apply to the natural world, or perhaps when a dispute comes up as to the precise essence signified by some word, such as, for instance, infinity. . . .

The word truth ought, I think, to be reserved for what everybody spontaneously means by it: the standard comprehensive description of any fact in all its relations. Truth is not an opinion, even an ideally true one; because besides the limitation in scope which human opinions, at least, can never escape, even the most complete and accurate opinion would give precedence to some terms, and have a direction of survey; and this direction might be changed or reversed without lapsing into error; so that the truth is the field which various true opinions traverse in various directions, and no opinion itself. An even more impressive difference between truth and any true discourse is that discourse is an event; it has a date not that of its subject-matter, even if the subject-matter be existential and roughly contemporary; and in human beings it is conversant almost entirely with the past only, whereas truth is dateless and absolutely identical whether the opinions which seek to reproduce it arise before or after the event which the truth describes.

The eternity of truth is inherent in it: all truths—not a few grand ones—are equally eternal. I am sorry that the word eternal should necessarily have an unction which prejudices dry minds against it, and leads fools to use it without understanding. This unction is not rhetorical, because the nature of truth is really sublime, and its name ought to mark its sublimity. Truth is one of the realities covered in the eclectic religion of our fathers by the idea of God. Awe very properly hangs about it, since it is the immovable standard and silent witness of all our memories and assertions; and the past and the future, which in our anxious life are so differently interesting and so differently dark, are one seamless garment for the truth, shining like the sun. It is not necessary to offer any evidence for this eternity of truth, because truth is not an existence that asks to be believed in, and that may be denied. It is an essence involved in positing any fact, in remembering, expecting, or asserting anything; and while no truth need be acknowledged if no existence is believed in, and none would obtain if there was no existence in fact, yet on the hypothesis that anything exists, truth has appeared, since this existence must have one character rather than another, so that only one description of it in terms of essence will be complete; and this complete description, covering all its relations, will be the truth about it. No one who understands what is meant by this eternal being of truth can possibly deny it; so that no argument is required to support it, but only enough intensity of attention to express what we already believe. . . .

Discernment of Spirit [10]

The common quality of all appearances is not spirit but mere Being; that simple and always obvious element to which I referred just now as given in all essences without distinction, and which some philosophers and saints have found so unutterably precious. . . .

By spirit I understand the light of discrimination that marks in that pure Being differences of essence, of time, of place, of value; a living light ready to fall upon things, as they are spread out in their weight and motion and variety, ready to be lighted up. Spirit is a fountain of clearness, decidedly wind-blown and spasmodic, and possessing at each moment the natural and historical actuality of an event, not the imputed or specious actuality of a datum. Spirit, in a word, is no phenomenon, not sharing the aesthetic sort of reality proper to essences when given, nor that other sort proper to dynamic and material things; its peculiar sort of reality is to be intelligence in act. Spirit, or the intuitions in which it is realised, accordingly forms a new realm of being, silently implicated in the apparition of essences and in the felt pressure of nature, but requiring the existence of nature to create it, and to call up those essences before it. By spirit essences are transposed into appearances and things into objects of belief; and (as if to compensate them for that derogation from their native status) they are raised to a strange actuality in thought—a moral actuality which in their logical being or their material flux they had never aspired to have: like those rustics and servants at an inn whom a travelling poet may take note

[10] *Ibid.*, pp. 273, 273-275, 276-279. By permission of Charles Scribner's Sons.

of and afterwards, to their astonishment, may put upon the stage with applause.

It is implied in these words, when taken as they are meant, that spirit is not a reality that can be observed; it does not figure among the *dramatis personae* of the play it witnesses. As the author, nature, and the actors, things, do not emerge from the prompter's box, or remove their make-up so as to exhibit themselves to me in their unvarnished persons, but are satisfied that I should know them only as artists (and I for my part am perfectly willing to stop there in my acquaintance with them); so the spirit in me which their art serves is content not to be put on the stage; that would be far from being a greater honour, or expressing a truer reality, than that which belongs to it as spectator, virtually addressed and consulted and required in everything that the theatre contrives. Spirit can never be observed as an essence is observed, nor encountered as a thing is encountered. It must be enacted; and the essence of it (for of course it has an essence) can be described only circumstantially, and suggested pregnantly. It is actualised in actualising something else, an image or a feeling or an intent or a belief; and it can be discovered only by implication in all discourse, when discourse itself has been posited. The witnesses to the existence of spirit are therefore the same as those to the existence of discourse; but when once discourse is admitted, the existence of spirit in it becomes self-evident; because discourse is a perusal of essence, or its recurring presence to spirit.

Now in discourse there is more than passive intuition; there is intent. This element also implies spirit, and in spirit as man possesses it intent or intelligence is almost always the dominant element. For this reason I shall find it impossible, when I come to consider the realm of spirit, to identify spirit with simple awareness, or with consciousness in the abstract sense of this abused word. Pure awareness or consciousness suffices to exemplify spirit; and there may be cold spirits somewhere that have merely that function; but it is not the only function that only spirits could perform; and the human spirit, having intent, expectation, belief, and eagerness, runs much thicker than that. Spirit is a category, not an individual being: and just as the realm of essence contains an infinite number of essences, each different from the rest, and each nothing but an essence, so the realm of spirit may contain any number of forms of spirit, each nothing but a spiritual fact. Spirit is a fruition, and there are naturally as many qualities of fruition as there are fruits to ripen. Spirit is accordingly qualified by the types of life it actualises, and is individuated by the occasions on which it actualises them. Each occasion generates an intuition numerically distinct, and brings to light an essence qualitatively different....

The occasions on which spirit arises in man are the vicissitudes of his animal life: that is why spirit in him runs so thick. In intent, in belief, in emotion a given essence takes on a value which to pure spirit it could not have. The essence then symbolises an object to which the animal is tentatively addressed, or an event through which he has just laboured, or which he is preparing to meet. This attitude of the animal may be confined to inner readjustments in the psyche, not open to gross external observation; yet it may all the more directly be raised to consciousness in the form of attention, expectation, deliberation, memory, or desire. These sentiments form a moving but habitual background for any particular essence considered; they frame it in, not only pictorially in a sensuous perspective, but morally, by its ulterior suggestions, and by the way in which, in surveying the whole field of intuition, that particular feature in it is approached or attacked or rejected. In such settings given essences acquire their felt meanings; and if they should be uprooted from that soil and exhibited in isolation, they would no longer mean the same thing to the spirit. Like a note in a melody, or a word in a sentence, they appeared in a field of essence greater than they; they were never more than a term or a feature within it. For this reason I imagine that I see things and not essences; the essences I see incidentally are embedded in the voluminous ever-present essences of the past, the world, myself, the future; master-presences which express attitudes of mine appropriate not to an essence—which is given—but to a thing—which though not given enlists all my conviction and concern.

Thus intelligence in man, being the spiritual transcript of an animal life, is transitional and impassioned. It approaches its objects by a massive attack, groping for them and tentatively spying them before it discovers them unmistakably. It is energetic and creative, in the sense of slowly focussing its object within the field of intuition in the midst of felt currents with a felt direction, themselves the running expression of animal endeavours. All this intuition of turbulence and vitality, which a cold immortal spirit could never know, fills the spirit of man, and renders any contemplation of essences in their own realm only an interlude for him or a sublimation or an incapacity. It also renders him more conscious than a purer spirit would be of his own spirit. For just as I was able to find evidence of intuition in discourse, which in the motionless vision of essence would have eluded me, so in intent, expectation, belief, and emotion, the being of my thoughts rises up and almost hides the vision of my object. Although I myself am a substance in flux, on the same level as the material thing that confronts me, the essences that reveal my own being are dramatic and moral, whereas those that express the thing are sensuous; and these dramatic and moral essences, although their presence involves spirit exactly in the same way, and no more deeply, than the presence of the sensuous essences

does, yet seem to suggest its presence more directly and more voluminously.

Hence the popular identification of spirit with the heart, the breath,
the blood, or the brain; and the notion that my substantial self and the
spirit within me are identical. In fact, they are the opposite poles of
my being, and I am neither the one nor the other exclusively. If I am
spiritually proud and choose to identify myself with the spirit, I shall
be compelled to regard my earthly person and my human thoughts as
the most alien and the sorriest of accidents; and my surprise and morti-
fication will never cease at the way in which my body and its world
monopolise my attention. If on the contrary I modestly plead guilty to
being the biped that I seem, I shall be obliged to take the spirit within
me for a divine stranger, in whose heaven it is not given me to live,
but who miraculously walks in my garden in the cool of the evening.
Yet in reality, incarnation is no anomaly, and the spirit is no intruder.
It is as much at home in any animal as in any heaven. In me, it takes
my point of view; it is the voice of my humanity; and what other man-
sions it may have need not trouble me. Each will provide a suitable
shrine for its resident deity and its native oracle. It is a prejudice to
suppose that spirit is contaminated by the flesh; it is generated there;
and the more varied its instruments and sources are, the more copiously
it will be manifested, and the more unmistakably. . . .

[Conclusion] [11]

Living when human faith is again in a state of dissolution, I have
imitated the Greek sceptics in calling doubtful everything that, in spite
of common sense, any one can possibly doubt. But since life and even
discussion forces me to break away from a complete scepticism, I have
determined not to do so surreptitiously nor at random, ignominiously
taking cover now behind one prejudice and now behind another. Instead, I have frankly taken nature by the hand, accepting as a rule in
my farthest speculations the animal faith I live by from day to day.
There are many opinions which, though questionable, are inevitable to
a thought attentive to appearance, and honestly expressive of action.
These natural opinions are not miscellaneous, such as those which the
Sophists embraced in disputation. They are superposed in a biological
order, the stratification of the life of reason. In rising out of passive
intuition, I pass, by a vital constitutional necessity, to belief in discourse, in experience, in substance, in truth, and in spirit. All these
objects may conceivably be illusory. Belief in them, however, is not
grounded on a prior probability, but all judgements of probability are
grounded on them. They express a rational instinct or instinctive reason,

[11] *Ibid.*, pp. 308-309. By permission of Charles Scribner's Sons.

the waxing faith of an animal living in a world which he can observe and sometimes remodel.

This natural faith opens to me various Realms of Being, having very different kinds of reality in themselves and a different status in respect to my knowledge of them. . . .

2. [Reason in Ethics]

Prerational Morality [12]

WHEN A polyglot person is speaking, foreign words sometimes occur to him, which he at once translates into the language he happens to be using. Somewhat in the same way, when dialectic develops an idea, suggestions for this development may come from the empirical field; yet these suggestions soon shed their externality and their place is taken by some genuine development of the original notion. In constructing, for instance, the essence of a circle, I may have started from a hoop. I may have observed that as the hoop meanders down the path the roundness of it disappears to the eye, being gradually flattened into a straight line, such as the hoop presents when it is rolling directly away from me. I may now frame the idea of a mathematical circle, in which all diameters are precisely equal, in express contrast to the series of ellipses, with very unequal diameters, which the floundering hoop has illustrated in its career. When once, however, the definition of the circle is attained, no watching of hoops is any longer requisite. The ellipse can be generated ideally out of the definition, and would have been generated, like asymptotes and hyperbolas, even if never illustrated in nature at all. Lemmas from a foreign tongue have only served to disclose a great fecundity in the native one, and the legitimate word that the context required has supplanted the casual stranger that may first have ushered it into the mind.

When the idea which dialectic is to elaborate is a moral idea, a purpose touching something in the concrete world, lemmas from experience often play a very large part in the process. Their multitude, with the small shifts in aspiration and esteem which they may suggest to the mind, often obscures the dialectical process altogether. In this case the foreign term is never translated into the native medium; we never make out what ideal connection our conclusion has with our premises, nor in what way the conduct we finally decide upon is to fulfil the purpose with which we began. Reflection merely beats about the bush, and when a sufficient number of prejudices and impulses have been driven from cover, we go home satisfied with our day's ranging, and

[12] *The Life of Reason*, vol. 5: *Reason in Science* (New York, 1905), ch. VIII, in part. By permission of the publishers, Charles Scribner's Sons.

feeling that we have left no duty unconsidered; and our last bird is our final resolution.

When morality is in this way non-dialectical, casual, impulsive, polyglot, it is what we may call prerational morality. There is indeed reason in it, since every deliberate precept expresses some reflection by which impulses have been compared and modified. But such chance reflection amounts to moral perception, not to moral science. Reason has not begun to educate her children. This morality is like knowing chairs from tables and things near from distant things, which is hardly what we mean by natural science. On this stage, in the moral world, are the judgments of Mrs. Grundy, the aims of political parties and their maxims, the principles of war, the appreciation of art, the commandments of religious authorities, special revelations of duty to individuals, and all systems of intuitive ethics.

Prerational morality is vigorous because it is sincere. Actual interests, rooted habits, appreciations the opposite of which is inconceivable and contrary to the current use of language, are embodied in special precepts; or they flare up of themselves in impassioned judgments. It is hardly too much to say, indeed, that prerational morality is morality proper. Rational ethics, in comparison, seems a kind of politics or wisdom, while postrational systems are essentially religions. If we thus identify morality with prerational standards, we may agree also that morality is no science in itself, though it may become, with other matters, a subject for the science of anthropology; and Hume, who had never come to close quarters with any rational or postrational ideal, could say with perfect truth that morality was not founded on reason. Instinct is of course not founded on reason, but *vice versa;* and the maxims enforced by tradition or conscience are unmistakably founded on instinct. They might, it is true, become materials for reason, if they were intelligently accepted, compared and controlled; but such a possibility reverses the partisan and spasmodic methods which Hume and most other professed moralists associate with ethics. Hume's own treatises on morals, it need hardly be said, are pure psychology. It would have seemed to him conceited, perhaps, to inquire what ought really to be done. He limited himself to asking what men tended to think about their doings.

The chief expression of rational ethics which a man in Hume's world would have come upon lay in the Platonic and Aristotelian writings; but these were not then particularly studied nor vitally understood. The chief illustration of postrational morality that could have fallen under his eyes, the Catholic religion, he would never have thought of as a philosophy of life, but merely as a combination of superstition and policy, well adapted to the lying and lascivious habits of Mediterranean peoples. Under such circumstances ethics could not be thought of as a science; and whatever gradual definition of the ideal, whatever prescription of what ought to be and to be done, found a place in the thoughts of such philosophers formed a part of their politics or religion and not of their reasoned knowledge.

There is, however, a dialectic of the will; and that is the science which, for want of a better name, we must call ethics or moral philosophy. The interweaving of this logic of practice with various natural sciences that have man or society for their theme, leads to much confusion in terminology and in point of view. Is the good, we may ask, what anybody calls good at any moment, or what anybody calls good on reflection, or what all men agree to call good, or what God calls good, no matter what all mankind may think about it? Or is true good something that perhaps nobody calls good nor knows of, something with no other characteristic or relation except that it is simply good?

Various questions are involved in such perplexing alternatives; some are physical questions and others dialectical. Why any one values anything at all, or anything in particular, is a question of physics; it asks for the causes of interest, judgment, and desire. To esteem a thing good is to express certain affinities between that thing and the speaker; and if this is done with self-knowledge and with knowledge of the thing, so that the felt affinity is a real one, the judgment is invulnerable and cannot be asked to rescind itself. Thus if a man said hemlock was good to drink, we might say he was mistaken; but if he explained that he meant good to drink in committing suicide, there would be nothing pertinent left to say: for to adduce that to commit suicide is not good would be impertinent. To establish that, we should have to go back and ask him if he valued anything—life, parents, country, knowledge, reputation; and if he said no, and was sincere, our mouths would be effectually stopped—that is, unless we took to declamation. But we might very well turn to the bystanders and explain what sort of blood and training this man possessed, and what happened among the cells and fibres of his brain to make him reason after that fashion. The causes of morality, good or bad, are physical, seeing that they are causes.

The science of ethics, however, has nothing to do with causes, not in that it need deny or ignore them but in that it is their fruit and begins where they end. Incense rises from burning coals, but it is itself no conflagration, and will produce none. What ethics asks is not why a thing is called good, but whether it is good or not, whether it is right or not so to esteem it. Goodness, in this ideal sense, is not a matter of opinion, but of nature. For intent is at work, life is in active operation, and the question is whether the thing or the situation responds to that intent. So if I ask, Is four really twice two? the answer is not that most people say so, but that, in saying so, I am not misunderstanding myself. To judge whether things are *really* good, intent must be made to speak;

and if this intent may itself be judged later, that happens by virtue of other intents comparing the first with their own direction.

Hence good, when once the moral or dialectical attitude has been assumed, means not what is called good but what is so; that is, what *ought* to be called good. For intent, beneath which there is no moral judgment, sets up its own standard, and ideal science begins on that basis, and cannot go back of it to ask why the obvious good is good at all. Naturally, there is a reason, but not a moral one; for it lies in the physical habit and necessity of things. The reason is simply the propulsive essence of animals and of the universal flux, which renders forms possible but unstable, and either helpful or hurtful to one another. That nature should have this constitution, or intent this direction, is not a good in itself. It is esteemed good or bad as the intent that speaks finds in that situation a support or an obstacle to its ideal. As a matter of fact, nature and the very existence of life cannot be thought wholly evil, since no intent is wholly at war with these its conditions; nor can nature and life be sincerely regarded as wholly good, since no moral intent stops at the facts; nor does the universal flux, which infinitely overflows any actual synthesis, altogether support any intent it may generate.

Philosophers would do a great discourtesy to estimation if they sought to justify it. It is all other acts that need justification by this one. The good greets us initially in every experience and in every object. Remove from anything its share of excellence and you have made it utterly insignificant, irrelevant to human discourse, and unworthy of even theoretic consideration. Value is the principle of perspective in science, no less than of rightness in life. The hierarchy of goods, the architecture of values, is the subject that concerns man most. Wisdom is the first philosophy, both in time and in authority; and to collect facts or to chop logic would be idle and would add no dignity to the mind, unless that mind possessed a clear humanity and could discern what facts and logic are good for and what not. The facts would remain facts and the truths truths; for of course values, accruing on account of animal souls and their affections, cannot possibly create the universe those animals inhabit. But both facts and truths would remain trivial, fit to awaken no pang, no interest, and no rapture. The first philosophers were accordingly sages. They were statesmen and poets who knew the world and cast a speculative glance at the heavens, the better to understand the conditions and limits of human happiness. Before their day, too, wisdom had spoken in proverbs. *It is better,* every adage began: *Better this than that.* Images or symbols, mythical or homely events, of course furnished subjects and provocations for these judgments; but the residuum of all observation was a settled estimation of things, a direction chosen in thought and life because it was better.

Such was philosophy in the beginning and such is philosophy still.

To one brought up in a sophisticated society, or in particular under an ethical religion, morality seems at first an external command, a chilling and arbitrary set of requirements and prohibitions which the young heart, if it trusted itself, would not reckon at a penny's worth. Yet while this rebellion is brewing in the secret conclave of the passions, the passions themselves are prescribing a code. They are inventing gallantry and kindness and honour; they are discovering friendship and paternity. With maturity comes the recognition that the authorised precepts of morality were essentially not arbitrary; that they expressed the genuine aims and interests of a practised will; that their alleged alien and supernatural basis (which if real would have deprived them of all moral authority) was but a mythical cover for their forgotten natural springs. Virtue is then seen to be admirable essentially, and not merely by conventional imputation. If traditional morality has much in it that is out of proportion, much that is unintelligent and inert, nevertheless it represents on the whole the verdict of reason. It speaks for a typical human will chastened by a typical human experience.

Gnomic wisdom, however, is notoriously polychrome, and proverbs depend for their truth entirely on the occasion they are applied to. Almost every wise saying has an opposite one, no less wise, to balance it; so that a man rich in such lore, like Sancho Panza, can always find a venerable maxim to fortify the view he happens to be taking. In respect to foresight, for instance, we are told, Make hay while the sun shines, A stitch in time saves nine, Honesty is the best policy, Murder will out, Woe unto you, ye hypocrites, Watch and pray, Seek salvation with fear and trembling, and *Respice finem.* But on the same authorities exactly we have opposite maxims, inspired by a feeling that mortal prudence is fallible, that life is shorter than policy, and that only the present is real; for we hear, A bird in the hand is worth two in the bush, *Carpe diem, Ars longa, vita brevis,* Be not righteous overmuch, Enough for the day is the evil thereof, Behold the lilies of the field, Judge not, that ye be not judged, Mind your own business, and It takes all sorts of men to make a world. So when some particularly shocking thing happens one man says, *Cherchez la femme,* and another says, Great is Allah.

That these maxims should be so various and partial is quite intelligible when we consider how they spring up. Every man, in moral reflection, is animated by his own intent; he has something in view which he prizes, he knows not why, and which wears to him the essential and unquestionable character of a good. With this standard before his eyes, he observes easily—for love and hope are extraordinarily keen-sighted —what in action or in circumstances forwards his purpose and what thwarts it; and at once the maxim comes, very likely in the language of the particular instance before him. Now the interests that speak in a man are different at different times; and the outer facts or measures which in one case promote that interest may, where other less obvious conditions have changed, altogether defeat it. Hence all sorts of precepts looking to all sorts of results.

Prescriptions of this nature differ enormously in value; for they differ enormously in scope. By chance, or through the insensible operation of experience leading up to some outburst of genius, intuitive maxims may be so central, so expressive of ultimate aims, so representative, I mean, of all aims in fusion, that they merely anticipate what moral science would have come to if it had existed. This happens much as in physics ultimate truths may be divined by poets long before they are discovered by investigators; the *vivida vis animi* taking the place of much recorded experience, because much unrecorded experience has secretly fed it. Such, for instance, is the central maxim of Christianity, Love thy neighbour as thyself. On the other hand, what is usual in intuitive codes is a mixture of some elementary precepts, necessary to any society, with others representing local traditions or ancient rites: so Thou shalt not kill, and Thou shalt keep holy the Sabbath day, figure side by side in the Decalogue. . . .

The objects of human desire, then, until reason has compared and experience has tested them, are a miscellaneous assortment of goods, unstable in themselves and incompatible with one another. It is a happy chance if a tolerable mixture of them recommends itself to a prophet or finds an adventitious acceptance among a group of men. Intuitive morality is adequate while it simply enforces those obvious and universal laws which are indispensable to any society, and which impose themselves everywhere on men under pain of quick extinction—a penalty which many an individual and many a nation continually prefers to pay. But when intuitive morality ventures upon speculative ground and tries to guide progress, its magic fails. Ideals are tentative and have to be critically viewed. A moralist who rests in his intuitions may be a good preacher, but hardly deserves the name of philosopher. He cannot find any authority for his maxims which opposite maxims may not equally invoke. To settle the relative merits of rival authorities and of hostile consciences it is necessary to appeal to the only real authority, to experience, reason, and human nature in the living man. No other test is conceivable and no other would be valid; for no good man would ever consent to regard an authority as divine or binding which essentially contradicted his own conscience. Yet a conscience which is irreflective and incorrigible is too hastily satisfied with itself, and not conscientious enough: it needs cultivation by dialectic. It neglects to extend to all human interests that principle of synthesis and justice by which conscience itself has arisen. And so soon as the conscience summons its own dicta for revision in the light of experience and of universal sympathy, it is no longer called conscience, but reason. So, too, when the spirit summons its traditional faiths, to subject them to a similar examination, that exercise is not called religion, but philosophy. It is true, in a sense, that philosophy is the purest religion and reason the ultimate conscience; but so to name them would be misleading. The things commonly called by those names have seldom consented to live at peace with sincere reflection. It has been felt vaguely that reason could not have produced them, and that they might suffer sad changes by submitting to it; as if reason could be the *ground* of anything, or as if everything might not find its consummation in becoming rational.

Rational Ethics [13]

A truly rational morality, or social regimen, has never existed in the world and is hardly to be looked for. What guides men and nations in their practice is always some partial interest or some partial disillusion. A rational morality would imply perfect self-knowledge, so that no congenial good should be needlessly missed—least of all practical reason or justice itself; so that no good congenial to other creatures would be needlessly taken from them. The total value which everything had from the agent's point of view would need to be determined and felt efficaciously; and, among other things, the total value which this point of view, with the conduct it justified, would have for every foreign interest which it affected. Such knowledge, such definition of purpose, and such perfection of sympathy are clearly beyond man's reach. All that can be hoped for is that the advance of science and commerce, by fostering peace and a rational development of character, may bring some part of mankind nearer to that goal; but the goal lies, as every ultimate ideal should, at the limit of what is possible, and must serve rather to measure achievements than to prophesy them.

In lieu of a rational morality, however, we have rational ethics; and this mere idea of a rational morality is something valuable. While we wait for the sentiments, customs and laws which should embody perfect humanity and perfect justice, we may observe the germinal principle of these ideal things; we may sketch the ground-plan of a true commonwealth. This sketch constitutes rational ethics, as founded by Socrates, glorified by Plato, and sobered and solidified by Aristotle. It sets forth the method of judgment and estimation which a rational morality would apply universally and express in practice. The method, being very simple, can be discovered and largely illustrated in advance, while the complete self-knowledge and sympathy are still wanting which might avail to embody that method in the concrete and to discover

[13] *Ibid.*, ch. IX, in part. By permission of Charles Scribner's Sons.

unequivocally where absolute duty and ultimate happiness may lie.

This method, the Socratic method, consists in accepting any estimation which any man may sincerely make, and in applying dialectic to it, so as to let the man see what he really esteems. What he really esteems is what ought to guide his conduct; for to suggest that a rational being ought to do what he feels to be wrong, or ought to pursue what he genuinely thinks is worthless, would be to impugn that man's rationality and to discredit one's own. With what face could any man or god say to another: Your duty is to do what you cannot know you ought to do; your function is to suffer what you cannot recognise to be worth suffering? Such an attitude amounts to imposture and excludes society; it is the attitude of a detestable tyrant, and any one who mistakes it for moral authority has not yet felt the first heart-throb of philosophy.

More even than natural philosophy, moral philosophy is something Greek: it is the appanage of freemen. The Socratic method is the soul of liberal conversation; it is compacted in equal measure of sincerity and courtesy. Each man is autonomous and all are respected; and nothing is brought forward except to be submitted to reason and accepted or rejected by the self-questioning heart. Indeed, when Socrates appeared in Athens mutual respect had passed into democracy and liberty into license; but the stalwart virtue of Socrates saved him from being a sophist, much as his method, when not honestly and sincerely used, might seem to countenance that moral anarchy which the sophists had expressed in their irresponsible doctrines. Their sophistry did not consist in the private *seat* which they assigned to judgment; for what judgment is there that is not somebody's judgment at some moment? The sophism consisted in ignoring the living moment's *intent,* and in suggesting that no judgment could refer to anything ulterior, and therefore that no judgment could be wrong: in other words that each man at each moment was the theme and standard, as well as the seat, of his judgment.

Socrates escaped this folly by force of honesty, which is what saves from folly in dialectic. He built his whole science precisely on that intent which the sophists ignored; he insisted that people should declare sincerely what they meant and what they wanted; and on that living rock he founded the persuasive and ideal sciences of logic and ethics, the necessity of which lies all in free insight and in actual will. This will and insight they render deliberate, profound, unshakable, and consistent. Socrates, by his genial midwifery, helped men to discover the truth and excellence to which they were naturally addressed. This circumstance rendered his doctrine at once moral and scientific; scientific because dialectical, moral because expressive of personal and living aspirations. His ethics was not like what has since passed under that name—a spurious physics, accompanied by commandments and threats. It was a pliant and liberal expression of ideals, inwardly grounded and spontaneously pursued. It was an exercise in self-knowledge.

Socrates' liberality was that of a free man ready to maintain his will and conscience, if need be, against the whole world. The sophists, on the contrary, were sycophants in their scepticism, and having inwardly abandoned the ideals of their race and nation—which Socrates defended with his homely irony—they dealt out their miscellaneous knowledge, or their talent in exposition, at the beck and for the convenience of others. Their theory was that each man having a right to pursue his own aims, skilful thinkers might, for money, furnish any fellow-mortal with instruments fitted to his purpose. Socrates, on the contrary, conceived that each man, to achieve his aims, must first learn to distinguish them clearly; he demanded that rationality, in the form of an examination and clarification of purposes, should precede any selection of external instruments. For how should a man recognise anything useful unless he first had established the end to be subserved and thereby recognised the good? True science, then, was that which enabled a man to disentangle and attain his natural good; and such a science is also the art of life and the whole of virtue. . . .

Rational ethics is an embodiment of volition, not a description of it. It is the expression of living interest, preference, and categorical choice. It leaves to psychology and history a free field for the description of moral phenomena. It has no interest in slipping far-fetched and incredible myths beneath the facts of nature, so as to lend a non-natural origin to human aspirations. It even recognises, as an emanation of its own force, that uncompromising truthfulness with which science assigns all forms of moral life to their place in the mechanical system of nature. But the rational moralist is not on that account reduced to a mere spectator, a physicist acknowledging no interest except the interest in facts and in the laws of change. His own spirit, small by the material forces which it may stand for and express, is great by its prerogative of surveying and judging the universe; surveying it, of course, from a mortal point of view, and judging it only by its kindliness or cruelty to some actual interest, yet, even so, determining unequivocally a part of its constitution and excellence. The rational moralist represents a force energising in the world, discovering its affinities there and clinging to them to the exclusion of their hateful opposites. He represents, over against the chance facts, an ideal embodying the particular demands, possibilities, and satisfactions of a specific being. . . .

Now will, no less than that reason which avails to render will consistent and far-reaching, animates natural bodies and expresses their functions. It has a radical bias, a foregone determinate direction, else it could not be a will nor a principle of preference. The knowledge of what other people desire does not abolish a man's own aims. Sympathy and justice are simply an expansion of the soul's interests, arising when we consider other men's lives so intently that something in us imitates and re-enacts their experience, so that we move partly in unison with their movement, recognise the reality and initial legitimacy of their interests, and consequently regard their aims in our action, in so far as our own status and purposes have become identical with theirs. We are not less ourselves, nor less autonomous, for this assimilation, since we assimilate only what is in itself intelligible and congruous with our mind and obey only that authority which can impose itself on our reason. . . .

Rational ethics, then, resembles prerational precepts and half-systems in being founded on impulse. It formulates a natural morality. It is a settled method of achieving ends to which man is drawn by virtue of his physical and rational constitution. By this circumstance rational ethics is removed from the bad company of all artificial, verbal, and unjust systems of morality, which in absolving themselves from relevance to man's endowment and experience merely show how completely irrelevant they are to life. Once, no doubt, each of these arbitrary systems expressed (like the observance of the Sabbath) some practical interest or some not unnatural rite; but so narrow a basis of course has to be disowned when the precepts so originating have been swollen into universal tyrannical laws. A rational ethics reduces them at once to their slender representative role; and it surrounds and buttresses them on every side with all other natural ideals.

Rational ethics thus differs from the prerational in being complete. There is one impulse which intuitive moralists ignore: the impulse to reflect. Human instincts are ignorant, multitudinous, and contradictory. To satisfy them as they come is often impossible, and often disastrous, in that such satisfaction prevents the satisfaction of other instincts inherently no less fecund and legitimate. When we apply reason to life we immediately demand that life be consistent, complete, and satisfactory when reflected upon and viewed as a whole. This view, as it presents each moment in its relations, extends to all moments affected by the action or maxim under discussion; it has no more ground for stopping at the limits of what is called a single life than at the limits of a single adventure. To stop at selfishness is not particularly rational. The same principle that creates the ideal of a self creates the ideal of a family or an institution.

The conflict between selfishness and altruism is like that between any two ideal passions that in some particular may chance to be opposed; but such a conflict has no obstinate existence for reason. For reason the person itself has no obstinate existence. The *character* which a man achieves at the best moment of his life is indeed something ideal and significant; it justifies and consecrates all his coherent actions and preferences. But *the man's life*, the circle drawn by biographers around the career of a particular body, from the womb to the charnel-house, and around the mental flux that accompanies that career, is no significant unity. All the substances and efficient processes that figure within it come from elsewhere and continue beyond; while all the rational objects and interests to which it refers have a transpersonal status. Self-love itself is concerned with public opinion; and if a man concentrates his view on private pleasures, these may qualify the fleeting moments of his life with an intrinsic value, but they leave the life itself shapeless and infinite, as if sparks should play over a piece of burnt paper....

If pleasure, because it is commonly a result of satisfied instinct, may by a figure of speech be called the aim of impulse, happiness, by a like figure, may be called the aim of reason. The direct aim of reason is harmony; yet harmony, when made to rule in life, gives reason a noble satisfaction which we call happiness. Happiness is impossible and even inconceivable to a mind without scope and without pause, a mind driven by craving, pleasure, and fear. The moralists who speak disparagingly of happiness are less sublime than they think. In truth their philosophy is too lightly ballasted, too much fed on prejudice and quibbles, for happiness to fall within its range. Happiness implies resource and security; it can be achieved only by discipline. Your intuitive moralist rejects discipline, at least discipline of the conscience; and he is punished by having no lien on wisdom. He trusts to the clash of blind forces in collision, being one of them himself. He demands that virtue should be partisan and unjust; and he dreams of crushing the adversary in some physical cataclysm.

Such groping enthusiasm is often innocent and romantic; it captivates us with its youthful spell. But it has no structure with which to resist the shocks of fortune, which it goes out so jauntily to meet. It turns only too often into vulgarity and worldliness. A snow-flake is soon a smudge, and there is a deeper purity in the diamond. Happiness is hidden from a free and casual will; it belongs rather to one chastened by a long education and unfolded in an atmosphere of sacred and perfected institutions. It is discipline that renders men rational and capable of happiness, by suppressing without hatred what needs to be suppressed to attain a beautiful naturalness. Discipline discredits the random pleasures of illusion, hope, and triumph, and substitutes those which are self-reproductive, perennial, and serene, because they express an equilibrium maintained with reality. So long as the result of endeavour is partly unforeseen and unintentional, so long as the will is partly blind, the Life of Reason is still swaddled in ignominy and the animal barks in the midst of human discourse. Wisdom and happiness consist in having recast natural energies in the furnace of experience. Nor is this experience merely a repressive force. It enshrines the successful expressions of spirit as well as the shocks and vetoes of circumstance; it enables a man to know himself in knowing the world and to discover his ideal by the very ring, true or false, of fortune's coin.

With this brief account we may leave the subject of rational ethics. Its development is impossible save in the concrete, when a legislator, starting from extant interests, considers what practices serve to render those interests vital and genuine, and what external alliances might lend them support and a more glorious expression. The difficulty in carrying rational policy very far comes partly from the refractory materials at hand, and partly from the narrow range within which moral science is usually confined. The materials are individual wills naturally far from unanimous, lost for the most part in frivolous pleasures, rivalries, and superstitions, and little inclined to listen to a law-giver that, like a new Lycurgus, should speak to them of unanimity, simplicity, discipline, and perfection. Devotion and singlemindedness, perhaps possible in the cloister, are hard to establish in the world; yet a rational morality requires that all lay activities, all sweet temptations, should have their voice in the conclave. Morality becomes rational precisely by refusing either to accept human nature, as it sprouts, altogether without harmony, or to mutilate it in the haste to make it harmonious. . . .

Post-Rational Morality [14]

When Socrates and his two great disciples composed a system of rational ethics they were hardly proposing practical legislation for mankind. One by his irony, another by his frank idealism, and the third by his preponderating interest in history and analysis, showed clearly enough how little they dared to hope. They were merely writing an eloquent epitaph on their country. They were publishing the principles of what had been its life, gathering piously its broken ideals, and interpreting its momentary achievement. The spirit of liberty and coöperation was already dead. The private citizen, debauched by the largesses and petty quarrels of his city, had become indolent and mean-spirited. He had begun to question the utility of religion, of patriotism, and of justice. Having allowed the organ for the ideal to atrophy in his soul, he could dream of finding some sullen sort of happiness in unreason. He felt that the austere glories of his country, as a Spartan regimen might have preserved them, would not benefit that baser part of him which alone remained. Political virtue seemed a useless tax on his material profit and freedom. The tedium and distrust proper to a dis-

---

[14] *Ibid.*, ch. X, in part. By permission of Charles Scribner's Sons.

integrated society began to drive him to artificial excitements and superstitions. Democracy had learned to regard as enemies the few in whom public interest was still represented, the few whose nobler temper and traditions still coincided with the general good. These last patriots were gradually banished or exterminated, and with them died the spirit that rational ethics had expressed. Philosophers were no longer suffered to have illusions about the state. Human activity on the public stage had shaken off all allegiance to art or reason.

The biographer of reason might well be tempted to ignore the subsequent attitudes into which moral life fell in the West, since they all embodied a more or less complete despair, and, having abandoned the effort to express the will honestly and dialectically, they could support no moral science. The point was merely to console or deceive the soul with some substitute for happiness. Life is older and more persistent than reason, and the failure of a first experiment in rationality does not deprive mankind of that mental and moral vegetation which they possessed for ages in a wild state before the advent of civilisation. They merely revert to their uncivil condition and espouse whatever imaginative ideal comes to hand, by which some semblance of meaning and beauty may be given to existence without the labour of building this meaning and beauty systematically out of its positive elements....

... Pessimism, and all the moralities founded on despair, are not pre-rational but post-rational. They are the work of men who more or less explicitly have conceived the Life of Reason, tried it at least imaginatively, and found it wanting. These systems are a refuge from an intolerable situation: they are experiments in redemption. As a matter of fact, animal instincts and natural standards of excellence are never eluded in them, for no moral experience has other terms; but the part of the natural ideal which remains active appears in opposition to all the rest and, by an intelligible illusion, seems to be no part of that natural ideal because, compared with the commoner passions on which it reacts, it represents some simpler or more attenuated hope—the appeal to some very humble or very much chastened satisfaction, or to an utter change in the conditions of life.

Post-rational morality thus constitutes, in intention if not in fact, a criticism of all experience. It thinks it is not, like pre-rational morality, an arbitrary selection from among co-ordinate precepts. It is an effort to subordinate all precepts to one, that points to some single eventual good. For it occurs to the founders of these systems that by estranging oneself from the world, or resting in the moment's pleasure, or mortifying the passions, or enduring all sufferings in patience, or studying a perfect conformity with the course of affairs, one may gain admission to some sort of residual mystical paradise; and this thought, once conceived, is published as a revelation and accepted as a panacea. It becomes in consequence (for such is the force of nature) the foundation of elaborate institutions and elaborate philosophies, into which the contents of the worldly life are gradually reintroduced.

When human life is in an acute crisis, the sick dreams that visit the soul are the only evidence of her continued existence. Through them she still envisages a good; and when the delirium passes and the normal world gradually re-establishes itself in her regard, she attributes her regeneration to the ministry of those phantoms, a regeneration due, in truth, to the restored nutrition and circulation within her. In this way post-rational systems, though founded originally on despair, in a later age that has forgotten its disillusions may come to pose as the only possible basis of morality. The philosophers addicted to each sect, and brought up under its influence, may exhaust criticism and sophistry to show that all faith and effort would be vain unless their particular nostrum was accepted; and so a curious party philosophy arises in which, after discrediting nature and reason in general, the sectary puts forward some mythical echo of reason and nature as the one saving and necessary truth. The positive substance of such a doctrine is accordingly pre-rational and perhaps crudely superstitious; but it is introduced and nominally supported by a formidable indictment of physical and moral science, so that the wretched idol ultimately offered to our worship acquires a spurious halo and an imputed majesty by being raised on a pedestal of infinite despair.

Socrates was still living when a school of post-rational morality arose among the Sophists, which after passing quickly through various phases, settled down into Epicureanism and has remained the source of a certain consolation to mankind, which if somewhat cheap, is none the less genuine. The pursuit of pleasure may seem simple selfishness, with a tendency to debauchery; and in this case the pre-rational and instinctive character of the maxim retained would be very obvious. Pleasure, to be sure, is not the direct object of an unspoiled will; but after some experience and discrimination, a man may actually guide himself by a foretaste of the pleasures he has found in certain objects and situations. The criticism required to distinguish what pays from what does not pay may not often be carried very far; but it may sometimes be carried to the length of suppressing every natural instinct and natural hope, and of turning the philosopher, as it turned Hegesias the Cyrenaic, into a eulogist of death. . . .

Even Aristippus, the first and most delightful of hedonists, who really enjoyed the pleasures he advocated and was not afraid of the incidental pains—even Aristippus betrayed the post-rational character of his philosophy by abandoning politics, mocking science, making his peace with all abuses that fostered his comfort, and venting his wit on all ambitions that exceeded his hopes. A great temperament can carry off a rough philosophy. Rebellion and license may distinguish honourable souls in an age of polite corruption, and a grain of sincerity is better, in moral philosophy, than a whole harvest of conventionalities. The violence and shamelessness of Aristippus were corrected by Epicurus; and a balance was found between utter despair and utter irresponsibility. Epicureanism retrenched much: it cut off politics, religion, enterprise, and passion. These things it convicted of vanity, without stopping to distinguish in them what might be inordinate from what might be rational. At the same time it retained friendship, freedom of soul, and intellectual light. It cultivated unworldliness without superstition and happiness without illusion. It was tender toward simple and honest things, scornful and bitter only against pretence and usurpation. It thus marked a first halting-place in the retreat of reason, a stage where the soul had thrown off only the higher and more entangling part of her burden and was willing to live, in somewhat reduced circumstances, on the remainder. Such a philosophy expresses well the genuine sentiment of persons, at once mild and emancipated, who find themselves floating on the ebb-tide of some civilisation, and enjoying its fruits, without any longer representing the forces that brought that civilisation about.

The same emancipation, without its mildness, appeared in the Cynics, whose secret it was to throw off all allegiance and all dependence on circumstance, and to live entirely on inner strength of mind, on pride and inflexible humour. The renunciation was far more sweeping than that of Epicurus, and indeed wellnigh complete; yet the Stoics, in underpinning the Cynical self-sufficiency with a system of physics, introduced into the life of the sect a contemplative element which very much enlarged and ennobled its sympathies. Nature became a sacred system, the laws of nature being eulogistically called rational laws, and the necessity of things, because it might be foretold in auguries, being called providence. There was some intellectual confusion in all this; but contemplation, even if somewhat idolatrous, has a purifying effect, and the sad and solemn review of the cosmos to which the Stoic daily invited his soul, to make it ready to face its destiny, doubtless liberated it from many an unworthy passion. The impressive spectacle of things was used to remind the soul of her special and appropriate function, which was to be rational. This rationality consisted partly in insight, to perceive the necessary order of things, and partly in conformity, to perceive that this order, whatever it might be, could serve the soul to exercise itself upon, and to face with equanimity.

Despair, in this system, flooded a much larger area of human life; everything, in fact, was surrendered except the will to endure whatever might come. The concentration was much more marked, since only a formal power of perception and defiance was retained and made the sphere of moral life; this rational power, at least in theory, was the one peak that remained visible above the deluge. But in practice much more was retained. Some distinction was drawn, however unwarrantably, between external calamities and human turpitude, so that absolute conformity and acceptance might not be demanded by the latter; although the chief occasion which a Stoic could find to practise fortitude and recognise the omnipresence of law was in noting the universal corruption of the state and divining its ruin. The obligation to conform to nature (which, strictly speaking, could not be disregarded in any case) was interpreted to signify that every one should perform the offices conventionally attached to his station. In this way a perfunctory citizenship and humanity were restored to the philosopher. But the restored life was merely histrionic: the Stoic was a recluse parading the market-place and a monk disguised in armour. His interest and faith were centred altogether on his private spiritual condition. He cultivated the society of those persons who, he thought, might teach him some virtue. He attended to the affairs of state so as to exercise his patience. He might even lead an army to battle, if he wished to test his endurance and make sure that philosophy had rendered him indifferent to the issue. . . .

Neo-Platonic morality, through a thousand learned and vulgar channels, permeated Christianity and entirely transformed it. Original Christianity was, though in another sense, a religion of redemption. The Jews, without dreaming of original sin or of any inherent curse in being finite, had found themselves often in the sorest material straits. They hoped, like all primitive peoples, that relief might come by propitiating the deity. They knew that the sins of the fathers were visited upon the children even to the third and fourth generation. They had accepted this idea of joint responsibility and vicarious atonement, turning in their unphilosophical way this law of nature into a principle of justice. Meantime the failure of all their cherished ambitions had plunged them into a penitential mood. Though in fact pious and virtuous to a fault, they still looked for repentance—their own or the world's —to save them. This redemption was to be accomplished in the Hebrew spirit, through long suffering and devotion to the Law, with the Hebrew solidarity, by vicarious attribution of merits and demerits within the household of the faith.

Such a way of conceiving redemption was far more dramatic, poignant, and individual than the Neo-Platonic; hence it was far more popular and better fitted to be a nucleus for religious devotion. However much, therefore, Christianity may have insisted on renouncing the world, the flesh, and the devil, it always kept in the background this perfectly Jewish and pre-rational craving for a delectable promised land. The journey might be long and through a desert, but milk and

honey were to flow in the oasis beyond. Had renunciation been fundamental or revulsion from nature complete, there would have been no
much-trumpeted last judgment and no material kingdom of heaven.
The renunciation was only temporary and partial; the revulsion was
only against incidental evils. Despair touched nothing but the present
order of the world, though at first it took the extreme form of calling
for its immediate destruction. This was the sort of despair and renunciation that lay at the bottom of Christian repentance; while hope in
a new order of this world, or of one very like it, lay at the bottom of
Christian joy. A temporary sacrifice, it was thought, and a partial mutilation would bring the spirit miraculously into a fresh paradise. The
pleasures nature had grudged or punished, grace was to offer as a
reward for faith and patience. The earthly life which was vain as an
experience was to be profitable as a trial. Normal experience, appropriate exercise for the spirit, would thereafter begin.

Christianity is thus a system of postponed rationalism, a rationalism
intercepted by a supernatural version of the conditions of happiness.
Its moral principle is reason—the only moral principle there is; its
motive power is the impulse and natural hope to be and to be happy.
Christianity merely renews and reinstates these universal principles
after a first disappointment and a first assault of despair, by opening
up new vistas of accomplishment, new qualities and measures of success. The Christian field of action being a world of grace enveloping
the world of nature, many transitory reversals of acknowledged values
may take place in its code. Poverty, chastity, humility, obedience, self-
sacrifice, ignorance, sickness, and dirt may all acquire a religious worth
which reason, in its direct application, might scarcely have found in
them; yet these reversed appreciations are merely incidental to a secret
rationality, and are justified on the ground that human nature, as now
found, is corrupt and needs to be purged and transformed before it can
safely manifest its congenital instincts and become again an authoritative criterion of values. In the kingdom of God men would no longer
need to do penance, for life there would be truly natural and there the
soul would be at last in her native sphere. . . .

Post-rational systems accordingly mark no real advance and offer no
genuine solution to spiritual enigmas. The saving force each of them
invokes is merely some remnant of that natural energy which animates
the human animal. Faith in the supernatural is a desperate wager made
by man at the lowest ebb of his fortunes; it is as far as possible from
being the source of that normal vitality which subsequently, if his
fortunes mend, he may gradually recover. . . . What keeps supernatural
morality, in its better forms, within the limits of sanity is the fact that
it reinstates in practice, under novel associations and for motives ostensibly different, the very natural virtues and hopes which, when seen to

be merely natural, it had thrown over with contempt. The new dispensation itself, if treated in the same spirit, would be no less contemptible; and what makes it genuinely esteemed is the restored authority of those human ideals which it expresses in a fable....

The value of post-rational morality, then, depends on a double conformity on its part with the Life of Reason. In the first place some natural impulse must be retained, some partial ideal must still be trusted and pursued by the prophet of redemption. In the second place the intuition thus gained and exclusively put forward must be made the starting-point for a restored natural morality. Otherwise the faith appealed to would be worthless in its operation, as well as fanciful in its basis, and it could never become a mould for thought or action in a civilised society.

[Postcript on the Rational Life] [15]

It may be useful to remind the reader that by rational ethics I do not understand a set of reasonable precepts contrasted with another set that are unreasonable; I understand rather reasonableness itself, something intellectual, prudential, or even aesthetic, rather than some new or "higher" moral impulse to be substituted for the old impulses of human nature. It is *prudent* to be rational up to a certain point, because if we neglect too many or too deeply rooted impulses in ourselves or in the world, our master-passion itself will come to grief; but too much rationality might be fatal to that passion at once, before it ventured to take its chance and win the prizes that were possible. So too, the impulse to be rational and to establish harmony in oneself and in the world may be itself a "higher" impulse than others, in that it presupposes them; yet the romantic impulse to be rash, or the sudden call to be converted, might be thought "higher" than rationality by many people. Reason alone can be rational, but it does not follow that reason alone is good. The criterion of worth remains always the voice of nature, truly consulted, in the person that speaks....

Now you cannot have a harmony of nothings, and rational ethics would be impossible if pre-rational morality were annulled. And as the impulse to establish harmony, and the love of order, are themselves natural and pre-rational passions, so an ulterior shift to post-rational morality introduces a new natural and pre-rational passion, the demand for harmony not merely within the human psyche or within the human world, but between this world and the psyche on the one hand and the universe, the truth, or God on the other. We have passed from morality

[15] "Apologia pro mente sua," in *The Philosophy of George Santayana*, edited by P. A. Schilpp (Evanston and Chicago, 1940), pp. 562-563, 563-565, 571, 572-573. By permission of The Library of Living Philosophers.

to religion; but not so as to destroy morality, because religion itself only adds a fresh passion (reason raised to a higher power and taking a broader view) to the passions that reason undertakes to harmonise. And religion, unless it takes the bit in its teeth and becomes fanatical, will admit the need of harmonising its inspirations with the counsels of good sense: often it goes so far as to regard itself as the only safe guardian of conventional morals. That is not my view; but I see the perfect continuity of post-rational with rational and with pre-rational morality. We begin with the instinct of animals, sometimes ferocious, sometimes placid, sometimes industrious, always self-justified and self-repeating; we proceed to a certain teachableness by experience, to a certain tradition and progress in the arts; we proceed further to general reflection, to tragic discoveries, to transformed interests. For instance, poets begin to be elegiac and to insist that everything is transitory; all is vanity; even our virtues and our prayers, before God, are impertinent. All this, that might occur to Solomon, would not have occurred to Joshua. Joshua would have been sure that God was on the side of pre-rational morality, and against the foreigner. And Solomon would have agreed that, on whatever side the Lord might be, the fear of the Lord was the beginning of wisdom.

There is one suggestion that I should remove, if I could, from the account given of these matters in *Reason in Science,* the suggestion, due to my historical manner, that these phases of morality are successive, and as it were, abolish one another. The post-rational phase, I there observe, comes of despair and belongs to ages of decadence. I was thinking of the Stoics and Epicureans in contrast to the previous spirit of Greek politics; yet the fourth century B.C. was hardly an age of decadence in general, and for Rome it was a school-age. I was perhaps thinking also of Leopardi, whose pessimism certainly expressed despair; yet the nineteenth century did not pass for an age of decadence, and Leopardi's shepherd so post-rationally questioning the moon about the uses of life, represents an adolescent sentiment, a sentiment very strong and persistent in myself when I was a schoolboy. To draw the sum total of our account, and ask what do we gain, what do we lose, is possible at any moment of reflection, whatever the wealth or paucity of our experience. But it is the impulse to reflect, not the impulse to acquire or to venture, that is here at work; and reason, instead of looking for means to achieving given ends, has become an autonomous interest capable of criticising those ends. To itself therefore it seems reason liberated rather than reason abandoned; but I think that in fact reason here has lost its judicial peace-making function (which was constantly in mind in my *Life of Reason*) and has become a separate pre-rational impulse, like any other original factor in morals. Judicial political reason therefore may well turn upon reason emancipated and ask it to take its place among the constituent interests that a life of reason should harmonise. . . .

Another version of the relations between rational and post-rational morality may be found in the Mahabharata, in the well-known scene where two armies face each other with drawn swords, awaiting the signal for battle. But the prince commanding one of the armies has pacifist scruples, which he confesses to his spiritual mentor—a god in disguise—in the most eloquent words I have ever read on that theme. His heart will not suffer him to give the word. And then the sage, while the armies stand spell-bound at arms, pours forth wisdom for eighteen cantos; yet the conclusion is simple enough. The tender prince must live the life appointed for him; he must fight this battle, *but with detachment.*

This version has the advantage of not separating natural virtue and spiritual insight into two different lives or two strands of action or interest: the two may be lived together and in the same moment. Just as rational ethics would have no materials if pre-rational preferences were abolished, so post-rational detachment would have no occasion and no reality if men and nations had no natural passions and ambitions. You cannot be detached without being previously attached; you cannot renounce or sacrifice anything significantly unless you love it. And if you withdraw from any action it must not be from timidity or laziness; that would be giving up one vain impulse for another still vainer and more physical. Your detachment will not be spiritual unless it is universal; it will then bring you liberation at once from the world and from yourself. This will neither destroy your natural gifts and duties nor add to them; but it will enable you to exercise them without illusion and in far-seeing harmony with their real function and end. Detachment leaves you content to be where you are, and what you are. Why should you hanker to be elsewhere or someone else? Yet in your physical particularity detachment makes you ideally impartial; and in enlightening your mind it is likely to render your action also more successful and generous. . . .

This reconciliation of spirit with nature does not rest, in my view, merely on moral grounds. It is inherent in my theory of the origin and place of spirit in nature. It follows from my materialism. So long as life is only tactile and digestive, it seems to remain unconscious; but when physical sensibility stretches to things at a distance and action can be focussed upon them, impressions become signals and reports, and a sense develops for the whole field of action, in which distinct movements and qualities begin to be discerned. Spirit from the beginning has the whole world and all events for its virtual object. The particular psyche that has bred this spirit has done so in the act of adapting action to distant things; this field of action then appears to the spirit, with that psyche and the body it animates strangely central and power-ful in the midst of that field. Thus the child has a different allegiance from that of the parent. The parent is Will, local, specific, blind, and indomitable; the child is Intelligence, plastic, extroverted, impartial, and universal. Up to a certain point it is useful for a busy-body to mind external things, yet it becomes disconcerting to learn too much and to begin to care for seeing for its own sake or even (worst of treasons) for the sake of the things seen. And still this disinterested speculation sends a breath of free air, a wonderful tragic light, into the dark convolutions of the psyche, always a little insecure and blustering in her egoism. She can begin to understand her housekeeping, to love it with a modesty and truth unknown before. She can become truly human, because something superhuman within her has made her peace with what is non-human outside.

3. Ultimate Religion [16]

BEFORE THIS CHOSEN audience, in this consecrated place, I may ven-ture to pass over all subsidiary matters and come at once to the last question of all: What inmost allegiance, what ultimate religion, would be proper to a wholly free and disillusioned spirit? The occasion invites us to consider this question, and to consider it with entire frankness. Great as you and I may feel our debt to be to Spinoza for his philos-ophy of nature, there is, I think, something for which we owe him an even greater debt; I mean, the magnificent example he offers us of philosophic liberty, the courage, firmness, and sincerity with which he reconciled his heart to the truth. Any clever man may sometimes see the truth in flashes; any scientific man may put some aspect of the truth into technical words; yet all this hardly deserves the name of philos-ophy so long as the heart remains unabashed, and we continue to live like animals lost in the stream of our impressions, not only in the public routine and necessary cares of life, but even in our silent thoughts and affections. Many a man before Spinoza and since has found the secret of peace: but the singularity of Spinoza, at least in the modern world, was that he facilitated this moral victory by no dubious postulates. He did not ask God to meet him half way: he did not whitewash the facts, as the facts appear to clear reason, or as they appeared to the science of his day. He solved the problem of the spiritual life after stating it in the hardest, sharpest, most cruel terms. Let us nerve ourselves today

[16] A paper read in the *Domus Spinozana* at the Hague during the commemora-tion of the tercentenary of the birth of Spinoza in 1932. Reprinted from *Obiter Scripta,* by George Santayana; copyright 1936 by Charles Scribner's Sons; used by permission of the publishers.

to imitate his example, not by simply accepting his solution, which for some of us would be easy, but by exercising his courage in the face of a somewhat different world, in which it may be even more difficult for us than it was for him to find a sure foothold and a sublime companionship.

There is a brave and humorous saying of Luther's, which applies to Spinoza better, perhaps, than to Luther himself. When asked where, if driven out of the Church, he would stand, he replied: "Under the sky." The sky of Luther was terribly clouded: there was a vast deal of myth tumbling and thundering about in it: and even in the clear sky of Spinoza there was perhaps something specious, as there is in the blue vault itself. The sun, he tells us, seemed to be about two hundred feet away: and if his science at once corrected this optical illusion, it never undermined his conviction that all reality was within easy reach of his thought. Nature was dominated, he assumed, by unquestionable scientific and dialectical principles; so that while the forces of nature might often put our bodily existence in jeopardy, they always formed a decidedly friendly and faithful object for the mind. There was no essential mystery. The human soul from her humble station might salute the eternal and the infinite with complete composure and with a certain vicarious pride. Every man had a true and adequate idea of God: and this saying, technically justified as it may be by Spinoza's definitions of terms, cannot help surprising us: it reveals such a virgin sense of familiarity with the absolute. There could not but be joy in the sweep of an intelligence that seemed so completely victorious, and no misgivings could trouble a view of the world that explained everything.

Today, however, we can hardly feel such assurance: we should be taking shelter in a human edifice which the next earthquake might shake down. Nor is it a question really of times or temperaments: anyone anywhere, if he does not wish to construct a plausible system, but to challenge his own assumptions and come to spiritual self-knowledge, must begin by abstention from all easy faith, lest he should be madly filling the universe with images of his own reason and his own hopes. I will therefore ask you today, provisionally, for an hour, and without prejudice to your ulterior reasonable convictions, to imagine the truth to be as unfavourable as possible to your desires and as contrary as possible to your natural presumptions; so that the spirit in each of us may be drawn away from its accidental home and subjected to an utter denudation and supreme trial. Yes, although the dead cannot change their minds, I would respectfully beg the shade of Spinoza himself to suspend for a moment that strict rationalism, that jealous, hard-reasoning, confident piety which he shared with the Calvinists and Jansenists of his day, and to imagine—I do not say to admit—that nature may be but imperfectly formed in the bosom of chaos, and that reason in us may be imperfectly adapted to the understanding of nature. Then, having hazarded no favourite postulates and invoked no cosmic forces pledged to support our aspirations, we may all quietly observe what we find; and whatever harmonies may then appear to subsist between our spirits and the nature of things will be free gifts to us and, so far as they go, unchallengeable possessions. We shall at last be standing unpledged and naked, under the open sky.

In what I am about to say, therefore, I do not mean to prejudge any cosmological questions, such as that of free will or necessity, theism or pantheism. I am concerned only with the sincere confessions of a mind that has surrendered every doubtful claim and every questionable assurance. Of such assurances or claims there is one which is radical and comprehensive: I mean, the claim to existence and to directing the course of events. We say conventionally that the future is uncertain: but if we withdrew honestly into ourselves and examined our actual moral resources, we should feel that what is insecure is not merely the course of particular events but the vital presumption that there is a future coming at all, and a future pleasantly continuing our habitual experience. We rely in this, as we must, on the analogies of experience, or rather on the clockwork of instinct and presumption in our bodies; but existence is a miracle, and, morally considered, a free gift from moment to moment. That it will always be analogous to itself is the very question we are begging. Evidently all interconnections and sequences of events, and in particular any consequences which we may expect to flow from our actions, are really entirely beyond our spiritual control. When our will commands and seems, we know not how, to be obeyed by our bodies and by the world, we are like Joshua seeing the sun stand still at his bidding; when we command and nothing happens, we are like King Canute surprised that the rising tide should not obey him: and when we say we have executed a great work and re-directed the course of history, we are like Chanticleer attributing the sunrise to his crowing.

What is the result? That at once, by a mere act of self-examination and frankness, the spirit has come upon one of the most important and radical of religious perceptions. It has perceived that though it is living, it is powerless to live; that though it may die, it is powerless to die; and that altogether, at every instant and in every particular, it is in the hands of some alien and inscrutable power.

Of this felt power I profess to know nothing further. To me, as yet, it is merely the counterpart of my impotence. I should not venture, for instance, to call this power almighty, since I have no means of knowing how much it can do; but I should not hesitate, if I may coin a word, to call it *omnificent*: it is to me, by definition, the doer of everything that is done. I am not asserting the physical validity of this sense of agency or cause: I am merely feeling the force, the friendliness, the hostility, the unfathomableness of the world. I am expressing an impression; and it may be long before my sense of omnipresent power can be erected, with many qualifications, into a theological theory of the omnipotence of God. But the moral presence of power comes upon a man in the night, in the desert, when he finds himself, as the Arabs say, alone with Allah. It re-appears in every acute predicament, in extremities, in the birth of a child, or in the face of death. And as for the unity of this power, that is not involved in its sundry manifestations, but rather in my own solitude; in the unity of this suffering spirit overtaken by all those accidents. My destiny is single, tragically single, no matter how multifarious may be the causes of my destiny. As I stand amazed, I am not called upon to say whether, if I could penetrate into the inner workings of things, I should discover omnificent power to be simple or compound, continuous or spasmodic, intentional or blind. I stand before it simply receptive, somewhat as, in Rome, I might stand before the great fountain of Trevi. There I see jets and cascades flowing in separate streams and in divers directions. I am not sure that a single Pontifex Maximus designed it all, and led those musical waters into just those channels. Some streams may have dried up or been diverted since the creation; some rills may have been added today by fresh rains from heaven; behind one of those artificial rocks some little demon, of his own free will, may even now be playing havoc with the conduits; and who knows how many details, in my image, may not have been misplaced or multiplied by optical tricks of my own? Yet here, for the spirit, is one total marvellous impression, one thunderous force, confronting me with this theatrical but admirable spectacle.

Yet this is not all. Power comes down upon me clothed in a thousand phenomena; and these manifestations of power open to me a new spiritual resource. In submitting to power, I learn its ways; from being passive my spirit becomes active; it begins to enjoy one of its essential prerogatives. For like a child the spirit is attracted to all facts by the mere assault of their irrational presence and variety. It watches all that happens or is done with a certain happy excitement, even at the most fearful calamities. Although the essence of spirit may be merely to think, yet some intensity and progression are essential to this thinking; thinking is a way of living, and the most vital way. Therefore all the operations of universal power, when they afford themes for perception, afford also occasions for intellectual delight. Here will and intellect, as Spinoza tells us, coincide: for omnificent power flows in part through our persons; the spirit itself is a spark of that fire, or rather the light of that flame: it cannot have an opposite principle of motion. With health a certain euphoria, a certain alacrity and sense of mastery are induced in the spirit; and a natural effect of perspective, the pathos of nearness, turns our little spark for us into a central sun. The world moves round us, and we move gladly with the world. What if the march of things be destined to overwhelm us? It cannot destroy the joy we had in its greatness and in its victory. There may even be some relief in passing from the troubled thought of ourselves to the thought of something more rich in life, yet in its own sphere and progression, untroubled: and it may be easier for me to understand the motion of the heavens and to rejoice in it than to understand or rejoice in my own motions. My own eclipse, my own vices, my own sorrows, may become a subject to me for exact calculation and a pleasing wonder. The philosophical eye may compose a cosmic harmony out of these necessary conflicts, and an infinite life out of these desirable deaths.

Does it not begin to appear that the solitude of a naked spirit may be rather well peopled? In proportion as we renounce our animal claims and commitments, do we not breathe a fresher and more salubrious air? May not the renunciation of everything disinfect everything and return everything to us in its impartial reality, at the same time disinfecting our wills also, and rendering us capable of charity? This charity will extend, of course, to the lives and desires of others, which we recognize to be no less inevitable than our own; and it will extend also to their ideas, and by a curious and blessed consequence, to the relativity and misery of our own minds. Yet this intellectual charity, since it is inspired by respect for the infinite, will by no means accept all views passively and romantically, as if they were equal and not subject to correction; but doing better justice to the holy aspiration which animates them in common, it will rise from them all, and with them all, to the conception of eternal truth.

Here we touch the crown of Spinoza's philosophy, that intellectual love of God in which the spirit was to be ultimately reconciled with universal power and universal truth. This love brings to consciousness a harmony intrinsic to existence: not an alleged harmony such as may be posited in religions or philosophies resting on faith, but a harmony which, as far as it goes, is actual and patent. In the realm of matter, this harmony is measured by the degree of adjustment, conformity, and co-operation which the part may have attained in the whole; in a word, it is measured by *health*. In the realm of truth, the same natural harmony extends as far as do capacity and pleasure in understanding the truth: so that besides health we may possess *knowledge*. And this is no passive union, no dead peace; the spirit rejoices in it; for the spirit, being, according to Spinoza, an essential concomitant of all existence, shares the movement, the *actuosa essentia* of the universe; so that we necessarily *love* health and knowledge, and *love* the things in which health and knowledge are found. In so far as omnificent power endows us with health, we necessarily love that power whose total movement makes for our own perfection; and in so far as we are able to understand the truth, we necessarily love the themes of an intense and unclouded vision, in which our imaginative faculty reaches its perfect function.

Of this religion of health and understanding Spinoza is a sublime prophet. By overcoming all human weaknesses, even when they seemed kindly or noble, and by honouring power and truth, even if they should slay him, he entered the sanctuary of an unruffled superhuman wisdom, and declared himself supremely happy, not because the world as he conceived it was flattering to his heart, but because the gravity of his heart disdained all flatteries, and with a sacrificial prophetic boldness uncovered and relished his destiny, however tragic his destiny might be. And presently peace descended; this keen scientific air seemed alone fit to breathe, and only this high tragedy worthy of a heroic and manly breast. Indeed the truth is a great cathartic and wonderfully relieves the vital distress of existence. We stand as on a mountain-top, and the spectacle, so out of scale with all our petty troubles, silences and overpowers the heart, expanding it for a moment into boundless sympathy with the universe.

Nevertheless, the moral problem is not solved. It is not solved for mankind at large, which remains no less distracted than it was before. Nor is it solved even for the single spirit. There is a radical and necessary recalcitrancy in the finite soul in the face of all this cosmic pomp and all this cosmic pressure: a recalcitrancy to which Spinoza was less sensitive than some other masters of the spiritual life, perhaps because he was more positivistic by temperament and less specifically religious. At any rate many a holy man has known more suffering than Spinoza found in the long work of salvation, more uncertainty, and also, in the end, a more lyrical and warmer happiness. For in the first place, as I said in the beginning, a really naked spirit cannot assume that the world is thoroughly intelligible. There may be surds, there may be hard facts, there may be dark abysses before which intelligence must be silent, for fear of going mad. And in the second place, even if to the intellect all things should prove perspicuous, the intellect is not the whole of human nature, nor even the whole of pure spirit in man. Reason may be the *differentia* of man; it is surely not his essence. His essence, at best, is animality qualified by reason. And from this animality the highest flights of reason are by no means separable. The very life of spirit springs from animal predicaments: it moves by imposing on events a perspective and a moral urgency proper to some particular creature or some particular interest.

Good, as Spinoza would tell us, is an epithet which we assign to whatsoever increases our perfection. Such a doctrine might seem egotistical, but is simply biological; and on its moral side, the maxim is a greater charter of liberty and justice than ever politician framed. For it follows that every good pursued is genuinely good, and the perfection of every creature equally perfection. Every good therefore is a good forever to a really clarified, just, and disinterested spirit; such a spirit cannot rest in the satisfaction of any special faculty, such as intelligence, nor of any special art, such as philosophy. That the intellect might be perfectly happy in contemplating the truth of the universe, does not render the universe good to every other faculty; good to the heart, good to the flesh, good to the eye, good to the conscience or the sense of justice. Of all systems an optimistic system is the most oppressive. Would it not be a bitter mockery if, in the words of Bradley, this were the best of possible worlds, and everything in it a necessary evil? The universal good by which the spirit, in its rapt moments, feels overwhelmed, if it is not to be a mystical illusion, cannot fall short of being the sum of all those perfections, infinitely various, to which all living things severally aspire. A glint or symbol of this universal good may be found in any moment of perfect happiness visiting any breast: but it is impossible unreservedly to love or worship anything, be it the universe or any part of it, unless we find in the end that this thing is completely good: I mean, unless it is perfect after its kind and a friend to itself, and unless at the same time it is beneficent universally, and a friend to everything else. Pure spirit would be lame, and evidently biassed by some biological accident, if it did not love every good loved anywhere by anybody. These varied perfections are rivals and enemies in the press of the world, where there seems not to be matter or time enough for everything: but to impartial spirit no good can render another good odious. Physically, one good may exclude another: nature and natural morality must choose between them, or be dissolved into chaos: but in eternity the most opposite goods are not enemies; rather little brothers and sisters, as all odd creatures were to St. Francis. And that all these various perfections are not actually attainable is a material accident, painful but not confusing to a free spirit. Their contrariety increases sorrow, but does not diminish love; the very pain is a fresh homage to the beauty missed, and a proof of loyalty; so that the more the spirit suffers the more clearly, when it unravels its suffering, it understands what it loves. Every perfection then shines, washed and clear, separate and uncontaminated: yet all compatible, each in its place, and harmonious. To love things spiritually, that is to say, intelligently and disinterestedly, means to love the love in them, to worship the good which they pursue, and to see them all prophetically in their possible beauty. To love things as they are would be a mockery of things: a true lover must love them as they would wish to be. For nothing is quite happy as it is, and the first act of true sympathy must be to move with the object of love towards its happiness.

Universal good, then, the whole of that to which all things aspire, is something merely potential; and if we wish to make a religion of love, after the manner of Socrates, we must take universal good, not universal power, for the object of our religion. This religion would need to be more imaginative, more poetical, than that of Spinoza, and the word God, if we still used it, would have to mean for us not the universe, but the good of the universe. There would not be a universe worshipped, but a universe praying; and the flame of the whole fire, the whole seminal and generative movement of nature, would be the love of God. This love would be erotic; it would be really love and not something wingless called by that name. It would bring celestial glimpses not to be retained, but culminating in moments of unspeakable rapture, in a union with all good, in which the soul would vanish as an object because, as an organ, it had found its perfect employment.

For there is a mystery here, the mystery of seeming to attain emotionally the logically unattainable. Universal good is something dispersed, various, contrary to itself in its opposite embodiments; nevertheless, to the mystic, it seems a single living object, the One Beloved, a good to be embraced all at once, finally and forever, leaving not the least shred of anything good outside. Yet I think this mystery may be easily solved. Spirit is essentially synthetic; and just as all the known and unknown forces of nature make, in relation to experience and destiny, one single omnificent power; and just as all facts and all the relations between facts compose for the historical and prophetic mind one unalterable realm of truth; so exactly, for the lover, all objects of love form a single ineffable good. He may say that he sees all beauties in a single face, that all beauties else are nothing to him; yet perhaps in this hyperbole he may be doing his secret heart an injustice. Beauty here may be silently teaching him to discern beauty everywhere, because in all instances of love only the sheer love counts in his eyes: and in the very absoluteness of his love he may feel an infinite promise. His ecstasy, which passes for a fulfilment, remains a sort of agony: and though itself visionary, it may, by its influence, free his heart from trivial or accidental attachments and lead it instead to a universal charity. Beggars in Catholic and Moslem countries used to beg an alms, sometimes, for the love of God. It was a potent appeal; because God, according to the Socratic tradition, was the good to which all creation moved; so that any one who loved deeply, and loved God, could not fail, by a necessary inclusion, to love the good which all creatures lived by pursuing, no matter how repulsive these creatures might be to natural human feeling.

Thus the absolute love of anything involves the love of universal good; and the love of universal good involves the love of every creature.

Such, in brief, seems to me the prospect open to a mind that examines its moral condition without any preconceptions. Perhaps an empirical critic, strictly reducing all objects to the functions which they have in experience, might see in my meagre inventory all the elements of religion. Mankind, he might say, in thinking of God or the gods have always meant the power in events: as when people say: *God willing.* Sometimes they have also meant the truth, as when people say: *God knows.* And perhaps a few mystics may have meant the good, or the supreme object of love, union with whom they felt would be perfect happiness. I should then have merely changed the language of traditional religion a little, translated its myths into their pragmatic equivalents, and reduced religion to its true essence. But no: I make no such professions: they would be plainly sophistical. The functions which objects have in experience no doubt open to us different avenues to those objects: but the objects themselves, if they exist, are not mere names for those functions. They are objects of faith: and the religion of mankind, like their science, has always been founded on faith. Now there is no faith invoked in the examination of conscience which I have made before you this evening: and therefore, properly speaking, what I come to is not religion. Nor is it exactly philosophy, since I offer no hypotheses about the nature of the universe or about the nature of knowledge. Yet to be quite sincere, I think that in this examination of conscience there is a sort of secret or private philosophy perhaps more philosophical than the other: and while I set up no gods, not even Spinoza's infinite *Deus sive Natura,* I do consider on what subjects and to what end we might consult those gods, if we found that they existed: and surely the aspiration that would prompt us, in that case, to worship the gods, would be our truest heart-bond and our ultimate religion.

If then any of us who are so minded should ever hear the summons of a liturgical religion calling to us: *Sursum corda, Lift up your hearts,* we might sincerely answer, *Habemus ad Dominum, Our hearts by nature are addressed to the Lord.* For we recognize universal power, and respect it, since on it we depend for our existence and fortunes. We look also with unfeigned and watchful allegiance towards universal truth, in which all the works of power are eternally defined and recorded; since in so far as we are able to discover it, the truth raises all things for us into the light, into the language of spirit. And finally, when power takes on the form of life, and begins to circle about and pursue some type of perfection, spirit in us necessarily loves these perfections, since spirit is aspiration become conscious, and they are the goals of life: and in so far as any of these goals of life can be defined or attained anywhere, even if only in prophetic fancy, they become glory, or become beauty, and spirit in us necessarily worships them: not the troubled glories and brief perfections of this world only, but rather that desired perfection, that eternal beauty, which lies sealed in the heart of each living thing.

JOHN DEWEY

ﭏ

Introduction

JOHN DEWEY conceives of philosophy as the intellectual expression of a conflict in culture. Its function is to locate the sources of these conflicts, and to offer a broad and general solution for them. Every philosophy, no matter how abstract or technical in its mode of statement, or how detached it may appear to be, is, in reality, an argument and a plea for certain social ideals. The philosopher is a prophet, but a prophet who attempts to give his particular view of the ideal an articulate and objective form.

Thus the philosophies of Plato and Aristotle are in essence a reasoned defense of the values of Greek civilization against the sceptical opinions and subversive forces that were soon to overthrow it, while the great *Summae* of Aquinas were an attempt to weld together in one comprehensive synthesis the wisdom of the ancients and the living faith of the Church. These particular philosophies were conservative, they sought to define and perpetuate an existing ideal. Other philosophies, such as those of Descartes or of Marx, are progressive; their primary interest is to outline a new set of values; they are the heralds of a change in the climate of opinion and the pattern of culture. In every case, when we try to plant ourselves at the center of a philosophy to see what, really, it is all about, we shall find that it is concerned with the attempt to "resolve" in some way or other "live issues" created by conflicts within the society of which the philosopher is a part.

Dewey himself belongs obviously in the camp of the progressive philosophers. Throughout all of his writing there runs one pervasive thread, the mediation of social change. If we can define the ends he envisages and the means by which they might be produced, we shall understand his philosophy. Then we can see how his contributions to a great variety of fields fit together as parts of his whole view of what constitutes progress in our society.

The first thing to say, therefore, about Dewey's philosophy is that it is concerned with the pressing and insistent problems of American democracy. In this respect Dewey invites comparison with another American philosopher of an earlier age, Thomas Jefferson. What Jefferson was interested in is what interests Dewey. Jefferson regarded democracy as the greatest social experiment ever undertaken. Dewey sees that the experiment is now in a new and critical phase. Jefferson, like Dewey, realized that the primary conflict in our society is that between traditional institutions, religious and political, and the new science which made democracy possible. Jefferson and Dewey share the faith in the common man, a belief in the unique worth of each person. Each of them knows that the primary means to the realization of a democratic society is to be found in education. It is through education and only through the processes of education that improvement from one generation to the next is possible. And both hope for a future in which through the "use of socially organized intelligence in the conduct of public affairs" the democratic way of life will become "a commonplace of living" for everybody.

But beyond this basis of fundamental agreement there is a great point of difference. During the generations that intervened between these two men the fringe of small rural communities on the Atlantic seaboard which was the America that Jefferson knew developed into a great urban and industrial country, a world power. Jefferson foresaw the difficulties that would confront the infant democracy with such a future, and his opposition to Hamilton's policy of furthering manufactures was founded upon them. In a letter to James Madison he said, "I think our governments will remain virtuous for many centuries; as long as they are chiefly agricultural; and this will be as long as there shall be vacant lands in any part of America. When they get piled upon one another in large cities, as in Europe, they will become corrupt as in Europe. Above all things I hope that the education of the common man will be attended to; convinced that on their good sense we may rely with the most security for the preservation of a due degree of liberty." [1] What Jefferson would have prevented inexorably occurred. And its occurrence generated the fundamental concern of Dewey's philosophy, to discover the means of realizing the ideals of Jefferson in an urban and industrial civilization.

The span of Dewey's own life coincides with the later and more dramatic part of this transformation of our culture. He was born on the eve of the great war that was to ensure the triumph in America of industrialism and economic enterprise, in the year that Darwin published his *Origin of Species,* the book which marked the coming of age of modern science. He grew up in the environment of the older America, in the Vermont town of Burlington. Here life was still largely unaffected by the newer science and by modern industrialism. From this small community with its simple and intimate round of handicraft and agricultural occupations, the form of society that Jefferson knew,

[1] Here quoted from James Truslow Adams's *Jeffersonian Principles and Hamiltonian Principles* (Boston, 1932), p. 18.

he was to go out into the complex world created by modern science and mass-production industries, to the first American university, the newly founded Johns Hopkins, to the fermenting democracy of the Middle West, in his years of teaching at the Universities of Michigan and Minnesota, then to the great industrial and commercial cities of Chicago and New York. Dewey has said in an autobiographical essay that the forces which influenced him came "from persons and from situations" rather than from books. It was the transition from the America of his boyhood to the new America of his maturity that created the basic problems and formed the central theme of his philosophy.

The thesis of this philosophy can be expressed in one sentence: *A general application of the methods of science, to every possible field of inquiry, is the only adequate means of solving the problems of an industrial democracy.* This was Dewey's eventual conclusion, but the road to it was a long and a hard one, and to work it out is not merely the labor of one man's prolific career, it is the task of generations. For Dewey's philosophy is not another "system"; it is the development and application of a *method*. Whoever understands and accepts Dewey's philosophy does not take over a body of doctrine. In fact, he is not *given* anything except *examples* of a patient and thorough effort to apply the method of intelligence to those problems which are of basic human concern. This is a continuing task that invites coöperation. Like science itself, it admits of indefinite extension. At seventy, after nearly half a century of reflection and writing, Dewey could say that his philosophy "was still too much in process of change to lend itself to [definitive] record." [2]

One cannot then give a summary description of Dewey's "thought" in the usual style of the histories of philosophy. [3] What one can do (inadequately of course in these few pages) is to sketch the development of his thinking, to indicate how he arrived at his conception of philosophic method and what are some of the ways in which he has proceeded to apply it.

When Dewey was an undergraduate, during the late seventies, at the University of Vermont, philosophy in America was still in what Professor Morris Cohen has called its "glacial age." The Scottish "common-sense realism" introduced into this country before the Revolution by President Witherspoon of Princeton was designed primarily as a

---

[2] Sidney Hook, *John Dewey—An Intellectual Portrait* (New York, 1939), p. 20.

[3] At the risk of contradicting myself, I must admit that more than one commentator *has* defined it—for example the German critic, cited by Dewey in the preface to *The Influence of Darwin on Philosophy and Other Essays*, who described "pragmatism" as "Epistemologically, nominalism; psychologically, voluntarism; cosmologically, energism; metaphysically, agnosticism; ethically, meliorism on the basis of the Bentham-Mill utilitarianism."

defense of Christian faith against the deism, materialism, and scepticism of the eighteenth century. Favored by the peculiar American combination of church and college, it became here the orthodox academic philosophy grafted on to protestantism. For a hundred years it was taught in virtually all the New England colleges as an arid and abstract rationalization of theological doctrines.

Such a philosophy could only ignore or evade all the new and vital developments of science.

"The storm which broke the stagnant air and aroused many American minds from this dogmatic torpor," says Professor Cohen, "came with the controversy over evolution which followed the publication of Lyell's *Geology,* Darwin's *Origin of Species,* and Spencer's *First Principles.* The evolutionary philosophy was flanked on the left by the empirical or positivistic philosophy of Comte, Mill, Lewes, Buckle, and Bain and on the right by the dialectic evolutionism of Hegel. The work of John Fiske, the leader of the evolutionary host, of Chauncey Wright, who nobly represented scientific empiricism and of William T. Harris, the saintly and practical minded Hegelian, united to give American philosophy a wider basis. With these the history of the modern period of American philosophy begins." [4]

It was to these new currents of opinion that Dewey responded.

After graduation Dewey taught high school for three years and for a part of this time also engaged in private study with his old professor, H. A. P. Torrey. During this period he wrote several articles which he sent to Harris who had established the first philosophical periodical in the country, the *Journal of Speculative Philosophy.* With the sympathetic encouragement of these two men he decided to undertake that new thing in America, graduate work, at the recently founded Johns Hopkins University.

There the contending winds of doctrine were blowing hard. The professor of philosophy, George Sylvester Morris, was enthusiastically promulgating his own version of Hegelianism in an environment dominated by the ideals of scientific research and generally hostile to "metaphysics." In England and in America Hegel's work had belatedly produced a revival of philosophic thought. As Dewey himself says, "This movement was at the time the vital and constructive one in philosophy." Charles Peirce and G. Stanley Hall were also teaching at Johns Hopkins. But Dewey seems at that time to have regarded Peirce as entirely devoted to formal logic, a subject in which he had no interest. From Hall, a hard-headed adherent of positive science who had nothing but contempt for Hegelian speculation, he did acquire an abiding interest in psychology. It was in this atmosphere that Dewey became committed to Hegelianism. If one may venture to reconstruct

[4] *The Cambridge History of American Literature* (New York, 1933), Vol. III, pp. 229-30.

the situation, it must have appeared to him then that his only choice was between Hegelian "idealism" and no philosophy at all. The alternative that offered itself was a "scientific empiricism" which postponed all attempts at the solution of ultimate problems in favor of an immediate program of piecemeal experiments.

It was as a better means of defending religious traditions and of putting science in its proper subordinate place that German idealism came so rapidly to supplant the moribund Scotch realism within academic halls. Here was a way, it seemed, by which one could keep the faith and believe in "evolution" too. But it was not in the main a desire to compromise the conflict then raging between "science" and "religion" (although this interest does seem to be dominant in some of his early writings) that led Dewey to accept Hegelian idealism. He had already come to feel "that any genuinely sound religious experience could and should adapt itself to whatever beliefs one found oneself intellectually entitled to hold." [5] What interested him was Hegel's treatment of human culture, of institutions and the arts. In Hegelian idealism, and particularly in Thomas Hill Green's version of it, Dewey found, he thought, a basis for his social idealism. Years later, speaking of the unification of knowledge, Dewey said, "The need . . . is practical and human rather than intrinsic to science itself; the latter is content as long as it can move to new problems and discoveries. The need for direction of action in large social fields is the source of a genuine demand for unification of scientific conclusions." [6] Dewey, then, at this stage was, like Marx, a "left-wing Hegelian" (though they developed very differently). Each of them thought he had found in Hegel the clue to the means of utilizing the results of science in the interests of social progress.

Professor Morris left the uncongenial environment of Johns Hopkins in 1884 to return to the University of Michigan. Shortly afterwards he invited Dewey to join him as his younger colleague. There in his formative years Dewey continued to develop under Morris's influence. [7]

Throughout this period Dewey was attempting what he later realized to be impossible, a consistent synthesis of his Hegelian idealism with the results of science. He was trying to bring the experimentalism of Hall within the framework of his own metaphysics. His way of

[5] "From Absolutism to Experimentalism." In *Contemporary American Philosophy*, edited by George P. Adams and Wm. Pepperell Montague (New York, 1930), Vol. II, p. 19.

[6] *The Quest for Certainty* (New York, 1929), p. 312.

[7] President Gilman of Johns Hopkins was overtly hostile to Morris, who was equally opposed to Gilman's positivism. Gilman, who took a friendly personal interest in the graduate students, once tried to dissuade Dewey, for his own good, from continuing the study of philosophy.

doing this was to develop what he called "the objective method in psychology." What he meant by that was:

Mind has not remained a passive spectator of the universe, but has produced and is producing certain results. These results are objective, can be studied as all objective historical facts may be, and are permanent. They are the most fixed, certain, and universal signs to us of the way in which mind works. Such objective manifestations of mind are, in the realm of intelligence, phenomena like language and science; in that of will, social and political institutions; in that of feeling, art; in that of the whole self, religion.[8]

A 'psychology' of this broad sort would be, Dewey thought, the "central science" from which one could derive, in contrast to the formalism of ordinary logic and ethics, a "real" science of man's actual processes of thinking and conduct.

In working this out over a period of about fifteen years Dewey gradually worked himself out of it. In applying this "objective method in psychology" to the problems of ethics, he finally realized that a philosophy which presumes that "the ideal is already and eternally a property of the real" can never be made consistent with the belief that men can act here and now to make their world a better place to live in.

While he was engaged in revising his views on ethics, an adventitious influence came to his rescue.[9] William James's brilliant and original *Principles of Psychology* (1890) gave an entirely new orientation to Dewey's thought. What Dewey discovered in James was the naturalistic basis for the practical idealism that was coming increasingly to dominate his thinking.

Dewey perceived that there were two distinct trends of thought in this profound work. On the surface it was an ingenious development of the traditional psychology of 'ideas,' a graphic and picturesque description of the life of the mind. But below this descriptive level there ran a deeper current: James, a trained physiologist who had come to intellectual maturity in the generation when the writings of Spencer and Darwin were exerting their greatest influence, could not help regarding this life of the mind not as something self-subsistent but as the effect of prior causes. And what could these "causes" be but the obscure and ill-known strains and tensions within the body? This in itself was nothing new. 'Behaviorism,' a biological conception of the psyche, was as old, at least, as Aristotle. What James did was to restate this ancient view with new force and conviction by deriving it from the doctrine of evolution. If mind does gradually emerge as the slow cumulative effect of certain kinds of interaction between organisms

[8] *Psychology* (New York, 1887), pp. 11-12.
[9] This transition is exhibited in the two works: *The Outlines of a Critical Theory of Ethics* (1891); *The Study of Ethics: A Syllabus* (1894).

and their environments, then the key to an understanding of all mental activity is to be found in the fact that organisms behave, as we say, "intelligently" in certain situations. Intelligence becomes a "fact" open to observation like any other natural fact. It is a distinctive kind of behavior, a certain mode of interaction between the live creature and its environment. That mode is one in which the organism in its present actions takes account of future consequences. As James puts it: *"The pursuance of future ends and the choice of means for their attainment are thus the mark and criterion of the presence of mentality* in a phenomenon." [10]

The full implications of this definition of intelligence are enormous. By accepting them Dewey abandoned completely the 'absolute idealism' which had governed his earlier thinking. Values and purposes are either inherent in the structure of reality itself, are *there* to be gradually apprehended and realized by our finite minds, or these values and purposes are created by man in his efforts to "adapt" himself to the world of nature and of society within which he lives and moves and has his being. What these values shall be is not predetermined by the appeal to some antecedent reality or cosmic purpose. They *occur* as effects or products of the conflicts that arise and the choices which are made in the particular situations of daily life. Because these choices are real, "evolution" becomes, wherever intelligence emerges, purposive. With man intelligence has reached a level where he may, within the limits of the forces at his disposal, control the future. But this is always a piecemeal control and the ends-in-view of limited human beings must always vary with the changing situation. Values are altered as knowledge develops.

A philosophy which accepts this evolutionary definition of intelligence thus "forswears enquiry after absolute origins and absolute finalities in order to explore specific values and the specific conditions that generate them." [11] If this is the rôle of philosophy, then method, the method of intelligence, is supreme. Philosophy must "become a method of locating and interpreting the more serious of the conflicts that occur in life and a method of projecting ways for dealing with them: a method of moral and political diagnosis and prognosis." [12]

On the technical side, this evolutionary definition of intelligence provides the major premise from which Dewey's reconstructions of the various fields of philosophy are derived. His many articles and books on logic and the philosophy of science, on ethics and social philosophy, on education, art and religion all represent a systematic and detailed working out of this principle.

[10] *Principles of Psychology*, Vol. I, p. 2. (Italics in original.)
[11] *The Influence of Darwin on Philosophy*, p. 13. Below, p. 341.
[12] *Ibid.*, p. 17. Below, p. 343.

There is one basic thesis, however, that underlies all of these detailed analyses. It is to exhibit Dewey's treatment of this problem that the bulk of these selections have been chosen. This is the problem, implicit in James's definition of intelligence, of the relation between knowledge and values. The emergence in modern times of experimental science resulted in a new kind of knowledge that seemed utterly at variance with our traditional beliefs. The results of the new science were too upsetting; segregation seemed on the whole easier than assimilation; the consequence was what one might fairly call (for it is a tragic malady of thought) a schizophrenic strain that runs through all our culture. This pathological dualism is exemplified by the fact that the remark, "Science has nothing to say about 'values'; it merely tells us how things occur" is generally accepted as a commonplace. Yet if this innocent-appearing commonplace is true, then any effort to control natural and social events in the interests of human ideals becomes impossible and James's definition of intelligence is absurd. On that definition, all "knowing" is motivated by the intention to alter certain factors in a present situation in such a way that the future will be different than it otherwise would have been; that is, all knowing is an attempt to discover and utilize the means of achieving certain purposes, of realizing a set of values. So far as the dissociation of knowledge and values does in fact exist knowledge is impotent and the "values" are compensatory.

For Dewey then, the "problem of restoring integration and coöperation between man's beliefs about the world in which he lives and his beliefs about the values and purposes that should direct his conduct is the deepest problem of modern life." [13] The basic theme of Dewey's thought is: the transformation of the function and objectives of knowing through the development of experimental methods in the sciences and the problem of applying these methods to the reconstruction of our traditional values. All of his writings are devoted to this purpose, to show how we may apply our intelligence to every primary concern of life.

The method of intelligence is the pragmatic or instrumentalist method. This method of persistently testing the meaning and worth of ideas, customs, institutions, in the light of their consequences, not just the immediate personal consequences, but their broad social consequences, leads us to the conception of a new society, one in which appeal to the supernatural is unnecessary, because ignorance, insecurity, oppression and disorder have disappeared, a society in which the individual is not divided within himself by trying to think in terms of two contradictory universes of discourse at the same time, a society

---

[13] *The Quest for Certainty,* p. 255. Below, p. 361.

no longer split into a set of warring classes dissipating their energies in fratricidal strife, but one where, as Francis Bacon said over three centuries ago, "we have established forever a true and lawful marriage between the empirical and rational faculties, the unkind and illstarred divorce of which has thrown into confusion all the affairs of the human family."

Here, Dewey would submit, is the basis for a genuinely adult human faith; that by the complete and thoroughgoing application of the method of intelligence we may destroy superstition, purge tradition, abandon compensatory rationalizations and illusions, and discover the means by which a genuinely coöperative society, one in which every individual shall have ample opportunity for the realization of his potentialities, may be achieved.

GAIL KENNEDY

AMHERST COLLEGE

Supplementary Note

With regard to the paragraphs on James on pages 332 f.: In writing the *Psychology* James adopted as his official position common-sense dualism,—that mind is distinct from the body and that each is capable of influencing the other. However, there were many places, as in his treatment of the emotions, where, out of respect for the facts, he was forced to be inconsistent. James never abandoned the conviction that the primary function of mind is to guide our actions, but he did eventually become convinced that the terms "consciousness" and "state of mind" must denote a function, not an entity. On this point, see his essay, "Does 'Consciousness' Exist?" (pp. 148-160 above), and Dewey's paper, "The Vanishing Subject in the Psychology of James," reprinted in *Problems of Men.*

1. The Influence of Darwinism on Philosophy [1]

THAT THE PUBLICATION of the "Origin of Species" marked an epoch in the development of the natural sciences is well known to the layman. That the combination of the very words origin and species embodied an intellectual revolt and introduced a new intellectual temper is easily overlooked by the expert. The conceptions that had reigned in the philosophy of nature and knowledge for two thousand years, the conceptions that had become the familiar furniture of the mind, rested on the assumption of the superiority of the fixed and final; they rested upon treating change and origin as signs of defect and unreality. In laying hands upon the sacred ark of absolute permanency, in treating the forms that had been regarded as types of fixity and perfection as originating and passing away, the "Origin of Species" introduced a mode of thinking that in the end was bound to transform the logic of knowledge, and hence the treatment of morals, politics, and religion.

No wonder, then, that the publication of Darwin's book, a half century ago, precipitated a crisis. The true nature of the controversy is easily concealed from us, however, by the theological clamor that attended it. The vivid and popular features of the anti-Darwinian row tended to leave the impression that the issue was between science on one side and theology on the other. Such was not the case—the issue lay primarily within science itself, as Darwin himself early recognized. The theological outcry he discounted from the start, hardly noticing it save as it bore upon the "feelings of his female relatives." But for two decades before final publication he contemplated the possibility of being put down by his scientific peers as a fool or as crazy; and he set, as the measure of his success, the degree in which he should affect three men of science: Lyell in geology, Hooker in botany, and Huxley in zoölogy.

Religious considerations lent fervor to the controversy, but they did not provoke it. Intellectually, religious emotions are not creative but conservative. They attach themselves readily to the current view of the world and consecrate it. They steep and dye intellectual fabrics in the seething vat of emotions; they do not form their warp and woof. There is not, I think, an instance of any large idea about the world being independently generated by religion. Although the ideas that rose up like armed men against Darwinism owed their intensity to religious

[1] One of a course of public lectures on "Charles Darwin and His Influence on Science" given at Columbia University in the winter and spring of 1909. Reprinted from *The Influence of Darwin on Philosophy and Other Essays in Contemporary Thought* (New York, 1910), by permission of the publishers, Henry Holt and Company, Inc. Copyright, John Dewey, 1937. Max Fisch notes that Dewey had been present twenty-five years earlier for Charles Peirce's JHU Metaphysical Club lecture, "Design and Chance," delivered on the 25th anniversary of the publication of "Origin of Species" (*The Dewey Newsletter*, April 1976, pp. 3–4).

associations, their origin and meaning are to be sought in science and philosophy, not in religion.

II

Few words in our language foreshorten intellectual history as much as does the word species. The Greeks, in initiating the intellectual life of Europe, were impressed by characteristic traits of the life of plants and animals; so impressed indeed that they made these traits the key to defining nature and to explaining mind and society. And truly, life is so wonderful that a seemingly successful reading of its mystery might well lead men to believe that the key to the secrets of heaven and earth was in their hands. The Greek rendering of this mystery, the Greek formulation of the aim and standard of knowledge, was in the course of time embodied in the word species, and it controlled philosophy for two thousand years. To understand the intellectual face-about expressed in the phrase "Origin of Species," we must, then, understand the long dominant idea against which it is a protest.

Consider how men were impressed by the facts of life. Their eyes fell upon certain things slight in bulk, and frail in structure. To every appearance, these perceived things were inert and passive. Suddenly, under certain circumstances, these things—henceforth known as seeds or eggs or germs—begin to change, to change rapidly in size, form, and qualities. Rapid and extensive changes occur, however, in many things—as when wood is touched by fire. But the changes in the living thing are orderly; they are cumulative; they tend constantly in one direction; they do not, like other changes, destroy or consume, or pass fruitless into wandering flux; they realize and fulfil. Each successive stage, no matter how unlike its predecessor, preserves its net effect and also prepares the way for a fuller activity on the part of its successor. In living beings, changes do not happen as they seem to happen elsewhere, any which way; the earlier changes are regulated in view of later results. This progressive organization does not cease till there is achieved a true final term, a *telos*, a completed, perfected end. This final form exercises in turn a plenitude of functions, not the least noteworthy of which is production of germs like those from which it took its own origin, germs capable of the same cycle of self-fulfilling activity.

But the whole miraculous tale is not yet told. The same drama is enacted to the same destiny in countless myriads of individuals so sundered in time, so severed in space, that they have no opportunity for mutual consultation and no means of interaction. As an old writer quaintly said, "things of the same kind go through the same formalities" —celebrate, as it were, the same ceremonial rites.

This formal activity which operates throughout a series of changes and holds them to a single course; which subordinates their aimless flux to its own perfect manifestation; which, leaping the boundaries of space and time, keeps individuals distant in space and remote in time to a uniform type of structure and function: this principle seemed to give insight into the very nature of reality itself. To it Aristotle gave the name, *eidos*. This term the scholastics translated as *species*.

The force of this term was deepened by its application to everything in the universe that observes order in flux and manifests constancy through change. From the casual drift of daily weather, through the uneven recurrence of seasons and unequal return of seed time and harvest, up to the majestic sweep of the heavens—the image of eternity in time—and from this to the unchanging pure and contemplative intelligence beyond nature lies one unbroken fulfilment of ends. Nature as a whole is a progressive realization of purpose strictly comparable to the realization of purpose in any single plant or animal.

The conception of *eidos*, species, a fixed form and final cause, was the central principle of knowledge as well as of nature. Upon it rested the logic of science. Change as change is mere flux and lapse; it insults intelligence. Genuinely to know is to grasp a permanent end that realizes itself through changes, holding them thereby within the metes and bounds of fixed truth. Completely to know is to relate all special forms to their one single end and good: pure contemplative intelligence. Since, however, the scene of nature which directly confronts us is in change, nature as directly and practically experienced does not satisfy the conditions of knowledge. Human experience is in flux, and hence the instrumentalities of sense-perception and of inference based upon observation are condemned in advance. Science is compelled to aim at realities lying behind and beyond the processes of nature, and to carry on its search for these realities by means of rational forms transcending ordinary modes of perception and inference.

There are, indeed, but two alternative courses. We must either find the appropriate objects and organs of knowledge in the mutual interactions of changing things; or else, to escape the infection of change, we *must* seek them in some transcendent and supernal region. The human mind, deliberately as it were, exhausted the logic of the changeless, the final, and the transcendent, before it essayed adventure on the pathless wastes of generation and transformation. We dispose all too easily of the efforts of the schoolmen to interpret nature and mind in terms of real essences, hidden forms, and occult faculties, forgetful of the seriousness and dignity of the ideas that lay behind. We dispose of them by laughing at the famous gentleman who accounted for the fact that opium put people to sleep on the ground it had a dormitive faculty. But the doctrine, held in our own day, that knowledge of the plant that yields the poppy consists in referring the peculiarities of an individual to a type, to a universal form, a doctrine so firmly established that any other method of knowing was conceived to be unphilosophical and unscientific, is a survival of precisely the same logic. This identity of conception in the scholastic and anti-Darwinian theory may well suggest greater sympathy for what has become unfamiliar as well as greater humility regarding the further unfamiliarities that history has in store.

Darwin was not, of course, the first to question the classic philosophy of nature and of knowledge. The beginnings of the revolution are in the physical science of the sixteenth and seventeenth centuries. When Galileo said: "It is my opinion that the earth is very noble and admirable by reason of so many and so different alterations and generations which are incessantly made therein," he expressed the changed temper that was coming over the world; the transfer of interest from the permanent to the changing. When Descartes said: "The nature of physical things is much more easily conceived when they are beheld coming gradually into existence, than when they are only considered as produced at once in a finished and perfect state," the modern world became self-conscious of the logic that was henceforth to control it, the logic of which Darwin's "Origin of Species" is the latest scientific achievement. Without the methods of Copernicus, Kepler, Galileo, and their successors in astronomy, physics, and chemistry, Darwin would have been helpless in the organic sciences. But prior to Darwin the impact of the new scientific method upon life, mind, and politics, had been arrested, because between these ideal or moral interests and the inorganic world intervened the kingdom of plants and animals. The gates of the garden of life were barred to the new ideas; and only through this garden was there access to mind and politics. The influence of Darwin upon philosophy resides in his having conquered the phenomena of life for the principle of transition, and thereby freed the new logic for application to mind and morals and life. When he said of species what Galileo had said of the earth, *e pur se muove,* he emancipated, once for all, genetic and experimental ideas as an organon of asking questions and looking for explanations.

III

The exact bearings upon philosophy of the new logical outlook are, of course, as yet, uncertain and inchoate. We live in the twilight of intellectual transition. One must add the rashness of the prophet to the stubbornness of the partizan to venture a systematic exposition of the influence upon philosophy of the Darwinian method. At best, we can but inquire as to its general bearing—the effect upon mental temper and complexion, upon that body of half-conscious, half-instinctive intellectual aversions and preferences which determine, after all, our more deliberate intellectual enterprises. In this vague inquiry there happens to exist as a kind of touchstone a problem of long historic currency that has also been much discussed in Darwinian literature. I refer to the old problem of design *versus* chance, mind *versus* matter, as the causal explanation, first or final, of things.

As we have already seen, the classic notion of species carried with it the idea of purpose. In all living forms, a specific type is present directing the earlier stages of growth to the realization of its own perfection. Since this purposive regulative principle is not visible to the senses, it follows that it must be an ideal or rational force. Since, however, the perfect form is gradually approximated through the sensible changes, it also follows that in and through a sensible realm a rational ideal force is working out its own ultimate manifestation. These inferences were extended to nature: (a) She does nothing in vain; but all for an ulterior purpose. (b) Within natural sensible events there is therefore contained a spiritual causal force, which as spiritual escapes perception, but is apprehended by an enlightened reason. (c) The manifestation of this principle brings about a subordination of matter and sense to its own realization, and this ultimate fulfilment is the goal of nature and man. The design argument thus operated in two directions. Purposefulness accounted for the intelligibility of nature and the possibility of science, while the absolute or cosmic character of this purposefulness gave sanction and worth to the moral and religious endeavors of man. Science was underpinned and morals authorized by one and the same principle, and their mutual agreement was eternally guaranteed.

This philosophy remained, in spite of sceptical and polemic outbursts, the official and the regnant philosophy of Europe for over two thousand years. The expulsion of fixed first and final causes from astronomy, physics, and chemistry had indeed given the doctrine something of a shock. But, on the other hand, increased acquaintance with the details of plant and animal life operated as a counterbalance and perhaps even strengthened the argument from design. The marvelous adaptations of organisms to their environment, of organs to the organism, of unlike parts of a complex organ—like the eye—to the organ itself; the foreshadowing by lower forms of the higher; the preparation in earlier stages of growth for organs that only later had their functioning—these things were increasingly recognized with the progress of botany, zoölogy, paleontology, and embryology. Together, they added such prestige to the design argument that by the late eighteenth century it was, as approved by the sciences of organic life, the central point of theistic and idealistic philosophy.

The Darwinian principle of natural selection cut straight under this philosophy. If all organic adaptations are due simply to constant variation and the elimination of those variations which are harmful in the struggle for existence that is brought about by excessive reproduction, there is no call for a prior intelligent causal force to plan and preordain them. Hostile critics charged Darwin with materialism and with making chance the cause of the universe.

Some naturalists, like Asa Gray, favored the Darwinian principle and attempted to reconcile it with design. Gray held to what may be called design on the installment plan. If we conceive the "stream of variations" to be itself intended, we may suppose that each successive variation was designed from the first to be selected. In that case, variation, struggle and selection simply define the mechanism of "secondary causes" through which the "first cause" acts; and the doctrine of design is none the worse off because we know more of its *modus operandi*.

Darwin could not accept this mediating proposal. He admits or rather he asserts that it is "impossible to conceive this immense and wonderful universe including man with his capacity of looking far backwards and far into futurity as the result of blind chance or necessity." * But nevertheless he holds that since variations are in useless as well as useful directions, and since the latter are sifted out simply by the stress of the conditions of struggle for existence, the design argument as applied to living beings is unjustifiable; and its lack of support there deprives it of scientific value as applied to nature in general. If the variations of the pigeon, which under artificial selection give the pouter pigeon, are not preordained for the sake of the breeder, by what logic do we argue that variations resulting in natural species are pre-designed? †

IV

So much for some of the more obvious facts of the discussion of design *versus* chance, as causal principles of nature and of life as a whole. We brought up this discussion, you recall, as a crucial instance. What does our touchstone indicate as to the bearing of Darwinian ideas upon philosophy? In the first place, the new logic outlaws, flanks, dismisses—what you will—one type of problems and substitutes for it another type. Philosophy forswears inquiry after absolute origins and absolute finalities in order to explore specific values and the specific conditions that generate them.

Darwin concluded that the impossibility of assigning the world to chance as a whole and to design in its parts indicated the insolubility of the question. Two radically different reasons, however, may be given as to why a problem is insoluble. One reason is that the problem is too high for intelligence; the other is that the question in its very

* "Life and Letters," Vol. I, p. 282; *cf.* 285.
† "Life and Letters," Vol. II, pp. 146, 170, 245; Vol. I, pp. 283-84. See also the closing portion of his "Variations of Animals and Plants under Domestication."

asking makes assumptions that render the question meaningless. The latter alternative is unerringly pointed to in the celebrated case of design *versus* chance. Once admit that the sole verifiable or fruitful object of knowledge is the particular set of changes that generate the object of study together with the consequences that then flow from it, and no intelligible question can be asked about what, by assumption, lies outside. To assert—as is often asserted—that specific values of particular truth, social bonds and forms of beauty, if they can be shown to be generated by concretely knowable conditions, are meaningless and in vain; to assert that they are justified only when they and their particular causes and effects have all at once been gathered up into some inclusive first cause and some exhaustive final goal, is intellectual atavism. Such argumentation is reversion to the logic that explained the extinction of fire by water through the formal essence of aqueousness and the quenching of thirst by water through the final cause of aqueousness. Whether used in the case of the special event or that of life as a whole, such logic only abstracts some aspect of the existing course of events in order to reduplicate it as a petrified eternal principle by which to explain the very changes of which it is the formalization.

When Henry Sidgwick casually remarked in a letter that as he grew older his interest in what or who made the world was altering into interest in what kind of a world it is anyway, his voicing of a common experience of our own day illustrates also the nature of that intellectual transformation effected by the Darwinian logic. Interest shifts from the wholesale essence back of special changes to the question of how special changes serve and defeat concrete purposes; shifts from an intelligence that shaped things once for all to the particular intelligences which things are even now shaping; shifts from an ultimate goal of good to the direct increments of justice and happiness that intelligent administration of existent conditions may beget and that present carelessness or stupidity will destroy or forego.

In the second place, the classic type of logic inevitably set philosophy upon proving that life *must* have certain qualities and values—no matter how experience presents the matter—because of some remote cause and eventual goal. The duty of wholesale justification inevitably accompanies all thinking that makes the meaning of special occurrences depend upon something that once and for all lies behind them. The habit of derogating from present meanings and uses prevents our looking the facts of experience in the face; it prevents serious acknowledgment of the evils they present and serious concern with the goods they promise but do not as yet fulfil. It turns thought to the business of finding a wholesale transcendent remedy for the one and guarantee for the other. One is reminded of the way many moralists and theologians greeted Herbert Spencer's recognition of an unknowable energy from which welled up the phenomenal physical processes without and the conscious operations within. Merely because Spencer labeled his unknowable energy "God," this faded piece of metaphysical goods was greeted as an important and grateful concession to the reality of the spiritual realm. Were it not for the deep hold of the habit of seeking justification for ideal values in the remote and transcendent, surely this reference of them to an unknowable absolute would be despised in comparison with the demonstrations of experience that knowable energies are daily generating about us precious values.

The displacing of this wholesale type of philosophy will doubtless not arrive by sheer logical disproof, but rather by growing recognition of its futility. Were it a thousand times true that opium produces sleep because of its dormitive energy, yet the inducing of sleep in the tired, and the recovery to waking life of the poisoned, would not be thereby one least step forwarded. And were it a thousand times dialectically demonstrated that life as a whole is regulated by a transcendent principle to a final inclusive goal, none the less truth and error, health and disease, good and evil, hope and fear in the concrete, would remain just what and where they now are. To improve our education, to ameliorate our manners, to advance our politics, we must have recourse to specific conditions of generation.

Finally, the new logic introduces responsibility into the intellectual life. To idealize and rationalize the universe at large is after all a confession of inability to master the courses of things that specifically concern us. As long as mankind suffered from this impotency, it naturally shifted a burden of responsibility that it could not carry over to the more competent shoulders of the transcendent cause. But if insight into specific conditions of value and into specific consequences of ideas is possible, philosophy must in time become a method of locating and interpreting the more serious of the conflicts that occur in life, and a method of projecting ways for dealing with them: a method of moral and political diagnosis and prognosis.

The claim to formulate *a priori* the legislative constitution of the universe is by its nature a claim that may lead to elaborate dialectic developments. But it is also one that removes these very conclusions from subjection to experimental test, for, by definition, these results make no differences in the detailed course of events. But a philosophy that humbles its pretensions to the work of projecting hypotheses for the education and conduct of mind, individual and social, is thereby subjected to test by the way in which the ideas it propounds work out in practice. In having modesty forced upon it, philosophy also acquires responsibility.

Doubtless I seem to have violated the implied promise of my earlier remarks and to have turned both prophet and partizan. But in anticipating the direction of the transformations in philosophy to be wrought by the Darwinian genetic and experimental logic, I do not profess to speak for any save those who yield themselves consciously or unconsciously to this logic. No one can fairly deny that at present there are two effects of the Darwinian mode of thinking. On the one hand there are making many sincere and vital efforts to revise our traditional philosophic conceptions in accordance with its demands. On the other hand, there is as definitely a recrudescence of absolutistic philosophies; an assertion of a type of philosophic knowing distinct from that of the sciences, one which opens to us another kind of reality from that to which the sciences give access; an appeal through experience to something that essentially goes beyond experience. This reaction affects popular creeds and religious movements as well as technical philosophies. The very conquest of the biological sciences by the new ideas has led many to proclaim an explicit and rigid separation of philosophy from science.

Old ideas give way slowly; for they are more than abstract logical forms and categories. They are habits, predispositions, deeply engrained attitudes of aversion and preference. Moreover, the conviction persists—though history shows it to be a hallucination—that all the questions that the human mind has asked are questions that can be answered in terms of the alternatives that the questions themselves present. But in fact intellectual progress usually occurs through sheer abandonment of questions together with both of the alternatives they assume—an abandonment that results from their decreasing vitality and a change of urgent interest. We do not solve them: we get over them. Old questions are solved by disappearing, evaporating, while new questions corresponding to the changed attitude of endeavor and preference take their place. Doubtless the greatest dissolvent in contemporary thought of old questions, the greatest precipitant of new methods, new intentions, new problems, is the one effected by the scientific revolution that found its climax in the "Origin of Species."

2. The Supremacy of Method [2]

UNCERTAINTY IS PRIMARILY a practical matter. It signifies uncertainty of the *issue* of present experiences; these are fraught with future peril as well as inherently objectionable. Action to get rid of the objectionable has no warrant of success and is itself perilous. The intrinsic troublesome and uncertain quality of situations lies in the fact that

[2] From *The Quest for Certainty* (New York, Minton, Balch & Co., 1929), ch. IX, "The Supremacy of Method," and ch. IV, "The Art of Acceptance and the Art of Control." By permission of the publishers, G. P. Putnam's Sons.

they hold outcomes in suspense; they move to evil or to good fortune. The natural tendency of man is to do something at once; there is impatience with suspense, and lust for immediate action. When action lacks means for control of external conditions, it takes the form of acts which are the prototypes of rite and cult. Intelligence signifies that direct action has become indirect. It continues to be overt, but it is directed into channels of examination of conditions, and doings that are tentative and preparatory. Instead of rushing to "do something about it," action centers upon finding out something about obstacles and resources and upon projecting inchoate later modes of definite response. Thinking has been well called deferred action. But not all action is deferred; only that which is final and in so far productive of irretrievable consequences. Deferred action is present exploratory action.

The first and most obvious effect of this change in the quality of action is that the dubious or problematic situation becomes *a* problem. The risky character that pervades a situation as a whole is translated into an object of inquiry that locates what the trouble is, and hence facilitates projection of methods and means of dealing with it. Only after expertness has been gained in special fields of inquiry does the mind set out at once from problems: even then in novel cases, there is a preliminary period of groping through a situation which is characterized throughout by confusion, instead of presenting a clear-cut problem for investigation.

Many definitions of mind and thinking have been given. I know of but one that goes to the heart of the matter:—response to the doubtful as such. No inanimate thing reacts to things *as* problematic. Its behavior to other things is capable of description in terms of what is determinately there. Under given conditions, it just reacts or does not react. Its reactions merely enstate a new set of conditions, in which reactions continue without regard to the nature of their outcome. It makes no difference, so to say, to a stone what are the results of its interactions with other things. It enjoys the advantage that it makes no difference how it reacts, even if the effect is its own pulverization. It requires no argument to show that the case is different with a living organism. To live signifies that a connected continuity of acts is effected in which preceding ones prepare the conditions under which later ones occur. There is a chain of cause and effects, of course, in what happens with inanimate things. But for living creatures, the chain has a particular cumulative continuity, or else death ensues.

As organisms become more complex in structure and thus related to a more complex environment, the importance of a particular act in establishing conditions favorable to subsequent acts that sustain the continuity of the life process, becomes at once more difficult and more imperative. A juncture may be so critical that the right or wrong present move signifies life or death. Conditions of the environment become more ambivalent: it is more uncertain what sort of action they call for in the interests of living. Behavior is thus compelled to become more hesitant and wary, more expectant and preparatory. In the degree that responses take place to the doubtful *as* the doubtful, they acquire *mental* quality. If they are such as to have a directed tendency to change the precarious and problematic into the secure and resolved, they are *intellectual* as well as mental. Acts are then relatively more instrumental and less consummatory or final; even the latter are haunted by a sense of what may issue from them.

This conception of the mental brings to unity various modes of response; emotional, volitional and intellectual. It is usual to say that there is no fundamental difference among these activities—that they are all different phases or aspects of a common action of mind. But I know of but one way of making this assertion good: that in which they are seen to be distinctive modes of response to the uncertain. The emotional aspect of responsive behavior is its *immediate* quality. When we are confronted with the precarious, an ebb and flow of emotion marks a disturbance of the even tenor of existence. Emotions are conditioned by the indeterminateness of present situations with respect to their issue. Fear and hope, joy and sorrow, aversion and desire, as perturbations, are qualities of a divided response. They involve concern, solicitude, for what the present situation may *become.* "Care" signifies two quite different things: fret, worry and anxiety, and cherishing attention to that in whose potentialities we are interested. These two meanings represent different poles of reactive behavior to a present having a future which is ambiguous. Elation and depression, moreover, manifest themselves only under conditions wherein not everything from start to finish is completely determined and certain. They may occur at a final moment of triumph or defeat, but this moment is one of victory or frustration in connection with a previous course of affairs whose issue was in suspense. Love for a Being so perfect and complete that our regard for it can make no difference to it is not so much affection as (a fact which the scholastics saw) it is concern for the destiny of our own souls. Hate that is sheer antagonism without any element of uncertainty is not an emotion, but is an energy devoted to ruthless destruction. Aversion is a state of affectivity only in connection with an obstruction offered by the disliked object or person to an end made uncertain by it.

The volitional phase of mental life is notoriously connected with the emotional. The only difference is that the latter is the immediate, the cross-sectional, aspect of response to the uncertain and precarious, while the volitional phase is the tendency of the reaction to modify indeterminate, ambiguous conditions in the direction of a preferred and favored outcome; to actualize one of its possibilities rather than another. Emotion is a hindrance or an aid to resolute will according as it is overwhelming in its immediacy or as it marks a gathering together of energy to deal with the situation whose issue is in doubt. Desire, purpose, planning, choice, have no meaning save in conditions where something is at stake, and where action in one direction rather than another may eventuate in bringing into existence a new situation which fulfills a need.

The intellectual phase of mental action is identical with an *indirect* mode of response, one whose purpose is to locate the nature of the trouble and form an idea of how it may be dealt with—so that operations may be directed in view of an intended solution. Take any incident of experience you choose, seeing a color, reading a book, listening to conversation, manipulating apparatus, studying a lesson, and it has or has not intellectual, cognitive, quality according as there is deliberative endeavor to deal with the indeterminate so as to dispose of it, to settle it. Anything that may be called knowledge, or a known object, marks a question answered, a difficulty disposed of, a confusion cleared up, an inconsistency reduced to coherence, a perplexity mastered. Without reference to this mediating element, what is called knowledge is but direct and unswerving action or else a possessive enjoyment. Similarly, thinking is the actual transition from the problematic to the secure, as far as that is intentionally guided. There is no separate "mind" gifted in and of itself with a faculty of thought; such a conception of thought ends in postulating the mystery of a power outside of nature and yet able to intervene within it. Thinking is objectively discoverable as that mode of serial responsive behavior to a problematic situation in which transition to the relatively settled and clear is effected.

The concrete pathologies of belief, its failures and perversions, whether of defect or excess, spring from failure to observe and adhere to the principle that knowledge is the completed resolution of the inherently indeterminate or doubtful. The commonest fallacy is to suppose that since the state of doubt is accompanied by a feeling of uncertainty, knowledge arises when this feeling gives way to one of assurance. Thinking then ceases to be an effort to effect change in the objective situation and is replaced by various devices which generate a change in feeling or "consciousness." Tendency to premature judgment, jumping at conclusions, excessive love of simplicity, making over of evidence to suit desire, taking the familiar for the clear, etc., all spring from confusing the feeling of certitude with a certified situation. Thought hastens toward the settled and is only too likely to force the pace. The natural man dislikes the dis-ease which accompanies the doubtful and is ready to take almost any means to end it. Uncertainty is got rid of by fair means or foul. Long exposure to danger breeds an overpowering love of security. Love for security, translated into a desire not to be disturbed and unsettled, leads to dogmatism, to acceptance of beliefs upon authority, to intolerance and fanaticism on one side and to irresponsible dependence and sloth on the other.

Here is where ordinary thinking and thinking that is scrupulous diverge from each other. The natural man is impatient with doubt and suspense: he impatiently hurries to be shut of it. A disciplined mind takes delight in the problematic, and cherishes it until a way out is found that approves itself upon examination. The questionable becomes an active questioning, a search; desire for the emotion of certitude gives place to quest for the objects by which the obscure and unsettled may be developed into the stable and clear. The scientific attitude may almost be defined as that which is capable of enjoying the doubtful; scientific method is, in one aspect, a technique for making a productive use of doubt by converting it into operations of definite inquiry....

... Just what did the new experimental method do to the qualitative objects of ordinary experience? Forget the conclusions of Greek philosophy, put out of the mind all theories about knowledge and about reality. Take the simple direct facts: Here are the colored, resounding, fragrant, lovable, attractive, beautiful things of nature which we enjoy, and which we suffer when they are hateful, ugly, disgusting. Just what is the effect upon them wrought by physical science?

If we consent for the time being to denude the mind of philosophical and metaphysical presuppositions, and take the matter in the most simple and naïve way possible, I think our answer, stated in technical terms, will be that it *substitutes data for objects*. (It is not meant that this outcome is the whole effect of the experimental method; that as we saw at the outset is complex; but that the first effect as far as stripping away qualities is concerned is of this nature.) That Greek science operated with *objects* in the sense of the stars, rocks, trees, rain, warm and cold days of ordinary experience is evident enough. What is signified by saying that the first effect of experimentation was to reduce these things from the status of objects to that of data may not be so clear.* By data is signified subject-matter for *further* interpretation; something to be thought about. *Objects* are finalities; they are complete, finished; they call for thought only in the way of definition, classification, logical arrangement, subsumption in syllogisms, etc. But data signify "material to serve"; they are indications, evidence, signs, clues to and of something still to be reached; they are intermediate, not ultimate; means, not finalities.

* For this shift from objects to data see G. H. Mead's essay in the volume entitled *Creative Intelligence* (New York, 1917).

In a less technical way the matter may be stated as follows: The subject-matter which had been taken as satisfying the demands of knowledge, as the material with which to frame solutions, became something which set *problems*. Hot and cold, wet and dry, light and heavy, instead of being self-evident matters with which to explain phenomena, were things to be investigated; they were "effects," not causal principles; they set question marks instead of supplying answers. The differences between the earth, the region of the planets, and the heavenly ether, instead of supplying ultimate principles which could be used to mark off and classify things, were something to be explained and to bring under identical principles. Greek and medieval science formed an art of accepting things as they are enjoyed and suffered. Modern experimental science is an art of control.

The remarkable difference between the attitude which accepts the objects of ordinary perception, use and enjoyment as final, as culminations of natural processes and that which takes them as starting points for reflection and investigation, is one which reaches far beyond the technicalities of science. It marks a revolution in the whole spirit of life, in the entire attitude taken toward whatever is found in existence. When the things which exist around us, which we touch, see, hear and taste are regarded as interrogations for which an answer must be sought (and must be sought by means of deliberate introduction of changes till they are reshaped into something different), nature as it already exists ceases to be something which must be accepted and submitted to, endured or enjoyed, just as it is. It is now something to be modified, to be intentionally controlled. It is material to act upon so as to transform it into new objects which better answer our needs. Nature as it exists at any particular time is a challenge, rather than a completion; it provides possible starting points and opportunities rather than final ends.

In short, there is a change from knowing as an esthetic enjoyment of the properties of nature regarded as a work of divine art, to knowing as a means of secular control—that is, a method of purposefully introducing changes which will alter the direction of the course of events. Nature as it exists at a given time is material for arts to be brought to bear upon it to reshape it, rather than already a finished work of art. Thus the changed attitude toward change to which reference was made has a much wider meaning than that which the new science offered as a technical pursuit. When correlations of changes are made the goal of knowledge, the fulfillment of its aim in discovery of these correlations, is equivalent to placing in our hands an instrument of control. When one change is given, and we know with measured accuracy its connection with another change, we have the potential means of producing or averting that other event. The esthetic attitude is of necessity directed to what is already there; to what is finished, complete. The attitude of control looks to the future, to production.

The same point is stated in another way in saying that the reduction of given objects to data for a knowing or an investigation still to be undertaken liberates man from subjection to the past. The scientific attitude, as an attitude of interest in change instead of interest in isolated and complete fixities, is necessarily alert for problems; every new question is an opportunity for further experimental inquiries—for effecting more directed change. There is nothing which a scientific mind would more regret than reaching a condition in which there were no more problems. That state would be the death of science, not its perfected life. We have only to contrast this disposition with that which prevails in morals and politics to realize the difference which has already been made, as well as to appreciate how limited its development still is. For in higher practical matters we still live in dread of change and of problems. Like men of olden time—with respect to natural phenomena—we prefer to accept and endure or to enjoy—as the case may happen to be—what is, what we find in possession of the field, and at most, to arrange it under concepts, and thus give it the form of rationality.

Before the rise of experimental method, change was simply an inevitable evil; the world of phenomenal existence, that is of change, while an inferior realm compared with the changeless, was nevertheless there and had to be accepted practically as it happened to occur. The wise man if he were sufficiently endowed by fortune would have as little to do with such things as possible, turning away from them to the rational realm. Qualitative forms and complete ends determined by nature are not amenable to human control. They are grateful when they happen to be enjoyed, but for human purposes nature means fortune, and fortune is the contrary of art. A good that happens is welcome. Goods, however, can be made secure in existence only through regulation of processes of change, a regulation dependent upon knowledge of their relations. While the abolition of fixed tendencies toward definite ends has been mourned by many as if it involved a despiritualization of nature, it is in fact a precondition of the projection of new ends and of the possibility of realizing them through intentional activity. Objects which are not fixed goals of nature and which have no inherent defining forms become candidates for receiving new qualities; means for serving new purposes. Until natural objects were denuded of determinate ends which were regarded as the proper outcome of the intrinsic tendency of nature's own operations, nature could not become a plastic material of human desires and purposes.

Such considerations as these are implicit in that changed attitude which by experimental analysis reduces objects to data: the aim of science becomes discovery of constant relations among changes in place of definition of objects immutable beyond the possibility of alteration. It is interested in the mechanism of occurrences instead of in final causes. In dealing with the proximate instead of with the ultimate, knowledge deals with the world in which we live, the world which is experienced, instead of attempting through the intellect to escape to a higher realm. Experimental knowledge is a mode of doing, and like all doing takes place at a time, in a place, and under specifiable conditions in connection with a definite problem.

The notion that the findings of science are a disclosure of the inherent properties of the ultimate real, of existence at large, is a survival of the older metaphysics. It is because of injection of an irrelevant philosophy into interpretation of the conclusions of science that the latter are thought to eliminate qualities and values from nature. Thus is created the standing problem of modern philosophy:—the relation of science to the things we prize and love and which have authority in the direction of conduct. The same injection, in treating the results of mathematical-mechanistic science as a definition of natural reality in its own intrinsic nature, accounts for the antagonism shown to naturalism, and for the feeling that it is the business of philosophy to demonstrate the being of a realm beyond nature, one not subject to the conditions which mark all natural objects. Drop the conception that knowledge is knowledge only when it is a disclosure and definition of the properties of fixed and antecedent reality; interpret the aim and test of knowing by what happens in the actual procedures of scientific inquiry, and the supposed need and problem vanish.

For scientific inquiry always starts from things of the environment experienced in our everyday life, with things we see, handle, use, enjoy and suffer from. This is the ordinary qualitative world. But instead of accepting the qualities and values—the ends and forms—of this world as providing the objects of knowledge, subject to their being given a certain logical arrangement, experimental inquiry treats them as offering a challenge to thought. They are the materials of problems not of solutions. They are *to be* known, rather than objects of knowledge. The first step in knowing is to locate the problems which need solution. This step is performed by altering obvious and given qualities. These are effects; they are things *to be* understood, and they are understood in terms of their generation. The search for "efficient causes" instead of for final causes, for extrinsic relations instead of intrinsic forms, constitutes the aim of science. But the search does not signify a quest for reality in contrast with experience of the unreal and phenomenal. It signifies a search for those relations upon which the *occurrence* of real qualities and values depends, by means of which we can regulate their occurrence. To call existences as they are directly and qualitatively experienced "phenomena" is not to assign to them a metaphysical status. It is to indicate that they set the problem of ascertaining the relations of interaction upon which their occurrence depends. . . .

We have seen that situations are precarious and perilous because the persistence of life-activity depends upon the influence which present acts have upon future acts. The continuity of a life-process is secured only as acts performed render the environment favorable to subsequent organic acts. The formal generalized statement of this fact is as follows: The occurrence of problematic and unsettled situations is due to the *characteristic union of the discrete or individual and the continuous or relational.* All perceived objects are individualized. They are, as such, wholes complete in themselves. Everything directly experienced is qualitatively unique; it has its own focus about which subject-matter is arranged, and this focus never exactly recurs. While every such situation shades off indefinitely, or is not sharply marked off from others, yet the pattern of arrangement of content is never exactly twice alike.

If the interactions involved in having such an individualized situation in experience were wholly final or consummatory, there would be no such thing as a situation which is problematic. In being individual and complete in itself, just what it is and nothing else, it would be discrete in the sense in which discreteness signifies complete isolation. Obscurity, for example, would be a final quality, like any other quality and as good as any other—just as the dusk of twilight is enjoyed instead of being troublesome until we need to see something the dusk interferes with seeing. Every situation has vagueness attending it, as it shades off from a sharper focus into what is indefinite; for vagueness is added quality and not something objectionable except as it obstructs gaining an eventual object.

There are situations in which self-enclosed, discrete, individualized characters dominate. They constitute the subject-matter of esthetic experience; and every experience is esthetic in as far as it is final or arouses no search for some other experience. When this complete quality is conspicuous the experience is denominated esthetic. The fine arts have as their purpose the construction of objects of just such experiences; and under some conditions the completeness of the object enjoyed gives the experience a quality so intense that it is justly termed religious. Peace and harmony suffuse the entire universe gathered up into the situation having a particular focus and pattern. These qualities mark any experience in as far as its final character dominates; in so far a mystic experience is simply an accentuated intensification of a quality of experience repeatedly had in the rhythm of experiences.

Interactions, however, are not isolated. No experienced situation can retain indefinitely its character of finality, for the interrelations that constitute it are, because they are interactions, themselves changing. They produce a change in what is experienced. The effort to maintain directly a consummatory experience or to repeat it exactly is the source of unreal sentimentality and of insincerity. In the continuous ongoing of life, objects part with something of their final character and become conditions of subsequent experiences. There is regulation of the change in the degree in which a causal character is rendered preparatory and instrumental.

In other words, all experienced objects have a double status. They are individualized, consummatory, whether in the way of enjoyment or of suffering. They are also involved in a continuity of interactions and changes, and hence are causes and potential means of later experiences. Because of this dual capacity, they become problematic. Immediately and directly they are just what they are; but as transitions to and possibilities of later experiences they are uncertain. There is a divided response; part of the organic activity is directed to them for what they immediately are, and part to them as transitive means of other experienced objects. We react to them both as finalities and in preparatory ways, and the two reactions do not harmonize.

This two-fold character of experienced objects is the source of their problematic character. Each of us can recall many occasions when he has been perplexed by disagreement between things directly present and their potential value as signs and means; when he has been torn between absorption in what is now enjoyed and the need of altering it so as to prepare for something likely to come. If we state the point in a formal way, it is signified that there is an incompatibility between the traits of an object in its direct individual and unique nature and those traits that belong to it in its relations or continuities. This incompatibility can be removed only by actions which temporarily reconstruct what is given and constitute a new object having both individuality and the internal coherence of continuity in a series.

Previous discussion has been a statement of the chief factors that operate in bringing about this reconstruction—of resolving a problematic situation: Acts of analytic reduction of the gross total situation to determine data—qualities that locate the nature of the problem; formation of ideas or hypotheses to direct further operations that reveal new material; deductions and calculations that organize the new and old subject-matter together; operations that finally determine the existence of a new integrated situation with added meaning, and in so doing test or prove the ideas that have been employed.

Without retraversing that discussion, I wish to add a few words on one point involved in it. Nothing is more familiar than the standardized objects of reference designated by common nouns. Their distinction from proper names shows that they are not singular or individual, not existing things. Yet "*the* table" is both more familiar and seemingly more substantial than *this* table, the individual. "This" undergoes change all the time. It is interacting with other things and with me, who am not exactly the same person as when I last wrote upon it. "This" is an indefinitely multiple and varied series of "thises."

But save in extreme cases, these changes are indifferent, negligible, from the standpoint of means for consequences. *The* table is precisely the constancy among the serial "thises" of whatever serves as an instrument for a single end. *Knowledge* is concerned wholly with this constant, this standardized and averaged set of properties and relations:— just as esthetic perception is occupied with "this" in its individuality, irrespective of value in use. In the degree in which reactions are inchoate and unformed, "this" tends to be the buzzing, blooming confusion of which James wrote. As habits form, action is stereotyped into a fairly constant series of acts having a common end in view; *the* table serves a single use, in spite of individual variations. A group of properties is set aside, corresponding to the abiding end and single mode of use which form *the* object, in distinction from "this" of unique experiences. *The* object is an abstraction, but unless it is hypostatized it is not a vicious abstraction. It designates selected relations of things which, with respect to their mode of operation, are constant within the limits practically important. Moreover, the abstracted object has a consequence *in* the individualized experiences, one that is immediate and not merely instrumental to them. It marks an ordering and organizing of responses in a single focused way in virtue of which the original blur is definitized and rendered significant. Without habits dealing with recurrent and constant uses of things for abiding purposes, immediate esthetic perception would have neither rich nor clear meanings immanent within it.

The scientific or physical object marks an extension of the same sort of operation. *The* table, as *not* a table but as a swarm of molecules in motions of specified velocities and accelerations, corresponds to a liberated generalization of the purposes which *the* object may serve. "Table" signifies a definite but restricted set of uses; stated in the physical terms of science it is thought of in a wider environment and free from any specified set of uses; out of relation to any particular individualized experience. The abstraction is as legitimate as is that which gives rise to the idea of *the* table, for it consists of standardized relations or interactions. It is even more useful or more widely instrumental. For it has connection with an indefinite variety of unspecified but possible consummatory individual observations and enjoyments. It waits like a servant, idle for a time, but ready to be called upon as special occasion arises. When this standardized constant, the result of series of operations and expressing an indefinite multitude of possible relations among concrete things, is treated as the reality of nature, an instrument made for a purpose is hypostatized into a substance complete and self-sufficient in isolation. Then the fullness of qualities present in individual situations have to be treated as subjective impressions mysteriously produced in mind by the real object or else as products of a mysterious creative faculty of consciousness.

The bearing of the conclusion upon the qualitative values of experienced objects is evident. Interactions of things with the organism eventuate in objects perceived to be colored and sonorous. They also result in qualities that make the object hateful or delightful. All these qualities, taken as directly perceived or enjoyed, are terminal effects of natural interactions. They are individualized culminations that give static quality to a network of changes. Thus "tertiary" qualities (as they have been happily termed by Mr. Santayana), those which, in psychological analysis, we call affectional and emotional, are as much products of the doings of nature as are color, sound, pressure, perceived size and distance. But their very consummatory quality stands in the way of using the things they qualify as signs of other things. Intellectually they are even more in the way than are "secondary" qualities. With respect to preparatory acts they are useless; when they are treated as signs and means they work injury to thought and discovery. When not experienced, they are projected in thought as ends to be reached and in that dependence upon thought they are felt to be peculiarly mental. But only if *the* object, the physical object, instrumental in character, is supposed to define "the real" in an exhaustive way, do they cease to be for the philosopher what they are for the common man:—real qualities of natural objects. This view forms the only complete and unadulterated realism.

The problem which is supposed to exist between two tables, one that of direct perception and use and the other that of physics (to take the favorite illustration of recent discussion) is thus illusory. The perceived and used table is the only table, for it alone has both individuality of form—without which nothing can exist or be perceived, and also includes within itself a continuum of relations or interactions brought to a focus. We may perhaps employ more instructively an illustration derived from the supposed contrast between an object experienced in perception as it is rendered by a poet and the same object described by a physicist. There is the instance of a body of water where the movement of the wind over its surface is reflected in sunlight. As an object of science, it is reported as follows: "Etherial vibrations of various wave lengths, reflected at different angles from the disturbed interface between air and water, reached our eyes and by photo-electric action caused appropriate stimuli to travel along optic nerves to a brain center." Such a statement, however, includes ordinary objects of individual perceptions; water, air, brain and nerves. Consequently, it must be reduced still further; when so reduced it consists of mathematical functions between certain physical constants having no counterpart in ordinary perception.*

It is worth while at this point to recur to the metric character of the physical object. Defining metric traits are reached by a series of operations of which they express the statistically constant outcome; they are not the result of a single act. Hence the physical object cannot be taken to be a single or individual thing in existence. Metric definitions are also, in large measure, reached by indirect measurements, by calculation. In other words, the conception of the physical object is, in considerable degree, the outcome of complex operations of comparison and translation. In consequence, while the physical object is *not* any one of the things compared, it enables things qualitatively unlike and individual to be treated as if they were members of a comprehensive, homogeneous, or non-qualitative system. The possibility of control of the *occurrence* of individualized objects is thereby increased. At the same time, the latter gain added meaning, for the import of the scheme of continuity of relationships with other things is incorporated within them. The procedure of physics itself, not any metaphysical or epistemological theory, discloses that physical objects cannot be individual existential objects. In consequence, it is absurd to put them in opposition to the qualitatively individual objects of concrete experience.

The vogue of the philosophy that identifies the object of knowledge as such with the reality of the subject-matter of experience makes it advisable to carry the discussion further. Physical science submits the things of ordinary experience to specifiable operations. The result are objects of thought stated in numbers, where the numbers in question permit inclusion within complex systems of equations and other mathematical functions. In the physical object everything is ignored but the relations expressed by these numbers. It is safe to assert that no physicist *while at work* ever thought of denying the full reality of the things of ordinary, coarse experience. He pays no attention to their qualities except as they are signs of operations to be performed and of inference to relations to be drawn. But in these capacities he has to admit their full reality on pain of having, logically, to deny reality to the conclusions of his operative inferences. He takes the instruments he employs, including his own sensory-motor organs and measuring instruments,

---

* The illustration is borrowed from Eddington, *The Nature of the Physical World;* see pp. 316-319. It is indicative of the hold which the older tradition of knowledge as the exclusive revelation of reality has obtained, that Eddington finds no way to combine this account with the poetic account, save to suppose that while the scientific statement describes reality as it is "in itself," the creative activity of mind adds to this skeleton the qualities characterizing an object in direct experience.

to be real in the ordinary sense of the word. If he denied the reality of these things as they are had in ordinary non-cognitive perceptual experience, the conclusions reached by them would be equally discredited. Moreover, the numbers which define his metric object are themselves results of noting interactions or connections among perceived things. It would be the height of absurdity to assert the reality of these relations while denying the reality of the things between which they hold. If the latter are "subjective" what becomes of the former? Finally, observation is resorted to for verification. It is a strange world in which the conception of the real has to be corroborated by reference to that the reality of which is made dubious by the conception. To common sense these comments may seem wholly superfluous. But since common sense may also hold the doctrine from which flow the conclusions to which the critical comments are apposite, common sense should first ask whether it holds that knowledge is a disclosure of the antecedently real? If it entertains this belief, then the dismissal by science of the experienced object to a limbo of unreality, or subjectivity or the phenomenal—whatever terms be used—results logically from his own position.

Our discussion involves a summary as well as some repetition of points previously made. Its significance lies in the liberation which comes when knowing, in all its phases, conditions and organs, is understood after the pattern provided by experimental inquiry, instead of upon the groundwork of ideas framed before such knowing had a systematic career opened to it. For according to the pattern set by the practice of knowing, knowledge is the fruit of the undertakings that transform a problematic situation into a resolved one. Its procedure is public, a part and partner of the Nature in which all interactions exist. But experienced situations come about in two ways and are of two distinct types. Some take place with only a minimum of regulation, with little foresight, preparation and intent. Others occur because, in part, of the prior occurrence of intelligent action. Both kinds are *had;* they are undergone, enjoyed or suffered. The first are not known; they are not understood; they are dispensations of fortune or providence. The second have, as they are experienced, meanings that present the funded outcome of operations that substitute definite continuity for experienced discontinuity and for the fragmentary quality due to isolation. Dream, insanity and fantasy are natural products, as "real" as anything else in the world. The acts of intentional regulation which constitute thinking are also natural developments, and so are the experienced things in which they eventuate. But the latter are resolutions of the problems set by objects experienced without intent and purpose; hence they have a security and fullness of meaning the first lack. Nothing happens, as Aristotle and the scholastics said, without an end—

without a terminal effectuation. *Every* experienced object is, in some sense, such a closing and consummatory closing episode: alike the doubtful and secure, the trivial and significant, the true and mistaken, the confused and ordered. Only when the ends are closing termini of *intelligent operations* of thinking are they ends in the honorific sense. We always experience individual objects, but only the individual things which are fruits of intelligent action have in them intrinsic order and fullness of qualities.

The conditions and processes of nature generate uncertainty and its risks as truly as nature affords security and means of insurance against perils. Nature is characterized by a constant mixture of the precarious and the stable. This mixture gives poignancy to existence. If existence were either completely necessary or completely contingent, there would be neither comedy nor tragedy in life, nor need of the will to live. The significance of morals and politics, of the arts both technical and fine, of religion and of science itself as inquiry and discovery, all have their source and meaning in the union in Nature of the settled and the unsettled, the stable and the hazardous. Apart from this union, there are no such things as "ends," either as consummations or as those ends-in-view we call purposes. There is only a block universe, either something ended and admitting of no change, or else a predestined march of events. There is no such thing as fulfillment where there is no risk of failure, and no defeat where there is no promise of possible achievement. . . .

Physical inquiry has been taken as typical of the nature of knowing. The selection is justified because the operations of physical knowledge are so perfected and its scheme of symbols so well devised. But it would be misinterpreted if it were taken to mean that science is the only valid kind of knowledge; it is just an intensified form of knowing in which are written large the essential characters of any knowing. It is in addition the most powerful tool we possess for developing other modes of knowledge. But we know with respect to any subject-matter whatsoever in the degree in which we are able deliberately to transform doubtful situations into resolved ones. Physical knowledge has the advantage of its specialized character, its whole-hearted devotion to a single purpose. The attitude involved in it, its method, has not as yet gone far beyond its own precincts. Beliefs current in morals, politics and religion, are marked by dread of change and by the feeling that order and regulative authority can be had only through reference to fixed standards accepted as finalities, because referring to fixed antecedent realities. Outside of physical inquiry, we shy from problems; we dislike uncovering serious difficulties in their full depth and reach; we prefer to accept what is and muddle along. Hence our social and moral "sciences" consist largely in putting facts as they are into conceptual systems framed at large. Our logic in social and humane subjects is still largely that of definition and classification as until the seventeenth century it was in natural science. For the most part the lesson of experimental inquiry has still to be learned in the things of chief concern.

We are, socially, in a condition of division and confusion because our best authenticated knowledge is obtained by directed practice, while this method is still limited to things aloof from man or concerning him only in the technologies of industries. The rest of our practice in matters that come home to us most closely and deeply is regulated not by intelligent operations, but by tradition, self-interest and accidental circumstance. The most significant phase of physical science, that which concerns its method, is unapplied in social practice, while its technical results are utilized by those in positions of privileged advantage to serve their own private or class ends. Of the many consequences that result, the state of education is perhaps the most significant. As the means of the general institution of intelligent action, it holds the key to orderly social reconstruction. But inculcation of fixed conclusions rather than development of intelligence as a method of action still dominates its processes. Devotion to training in technical and mechanical skills on one hand and to laying in a store of abstract information on the other is to one who has the power to read the scene an almost perfect illustration of the significance of the historic separation of knowledge and action, theory and practice. As long as the isolation of knowledge and practice holds sway, this division of aims and dissipation of energy, of which the state of education is typical, will persist. The effective condition of the integration of all divided purposes and conflicts of belief is the realization that intelligent action is the sole ultimate resource of mankind in every field whatsoever.

It is not claimed, therefore, that there is *no* philosophical problem of the relation of physical science to the things of ordinary experience. It is asserted that the problem *in the form* in which it has chiefly occupied modern philosophy is an artificial one, due to the continued assumption of premises formed in an earlier period of history and now having no relevancy to the state of physical inquiry. Clearing the ground of this unreal problem, however, only imposes upon philosophy the consideration of a problem which is urgently practical, growing out of the conditions of contemporary life. What revisions and surrenders of current beliefs about authoritative ends and values are demanded by the method and conclusions of natural science? What possibilities of controlled transformation of the content of present belief and practice in human institutions and associations are indicated by the control of natural energies which natural science has effected? These questions are as genuine and imperative as the traditional problem is artificial and futile.

3. The Construction of Good [3]

WE SAW AT the outset of our discussion that insecurity generates the quest for certainty. Consequences issue from every experience, and they are the source of our interest in what is present. Absence of arts of regulation diverted the search for security into irrelevant modes of practice, into rite and cult; thought was devoted to discovery of omens rather than of signs of what is to occur. Gradually there was differentiation of two realms, one higher, consisting of the powers which determine human destiny in all important affairs. With this religion was concerned. The other consisted of the prosaic matters in which man relied upon his own skill and his matter-of-fact insight. Philosophy inherited the idea of this division. Meanwhile in Greece many of the arts had attained a state of development which raised them above a merely routine state; there were intimations of measure, order and regularity in materials dealt with which give intimations of underlying rationality. Because of the growth of mathematics, there arose also the ideal of a purely rational knowledge, intrinsically solid and worthy and the means by which the intimations of rationality within changing phenomena could be comprehended within science. For the intellectual class the stay and consolation, the warrant of certainty, provided by religion was henceforth found in intellectual demonstration of the reality of the objects of an ideal realm.

With the expansion of Christianity, ethico-religious traits came to dominate the purely rational ones. The ultimate authoritative standards for regulation of the dispositions and purposes of the human will were fused with those which satisfied the demands for necessary and universal truth. The authority of ultimate Being was, moreover, represented on earth by the Church; that which in its nature transcended intellect was made known by a revelation of which the Church was the interpreter and guardian. The system endured for centuries. While it endured, it provided an integration of belief and conduct for the western world. Unity of thought and practice extended down to every detail of the management of life; efficacy of its operation did not depend upon thought. It was guaranteed by the most powerful and authoritative of all social institutions.

Its seemingly solid foundation was, however, undermined by the conclusions of modern science. They effected, both in themselves and

[3] *The Quest for Certainty* (New York, Minton, Balch & Co., 1929), ch. X. By permission of the publishers, G. P. Putnam's Sons.

even more in the new interests and activities they generated, a breach between what man is concerned with here and now and the faith concerning ultimate reality which, in determining his ultimate and eternal destiny, had previously given regulation to his present life. The problem of restoring integration and coöperation between man's beliefs about the world in which he lives and his beliefs about the values and purposes that should direct his conduct is the deepest problem of modern life. It is the problem of any philosophy that is not isolated from that life.

The attention which has been given to the fact that in its experimental procedure science has surrendered the separation between knowing and doing has its source in the fact that there is now provided within a limited, specialized and technical field the possibility and earnest, as far as theory is concerned, of effecting the needed integration in the wider field of collective human experience. Philosophy is called upon to be the theory of the practice, through ideas sufficiently definite to be operative in experimental endeavor, by which the integration may be made secure in actual experience. Its central problem is the relation that exists between the beliefs about the nature of things due to natural science and beliefs about values—using that word to designate whatever is taken to have rightful authority in the direction of conduct. A philosophy which should take up this problem is struck first of all by the fact that beliefs about values are pretty much in the position in which beliefs about nature were before the scientific revolution. There is either a basic distrust of the capacity of experience to develop its own regulative standards, and an appeal to what philosophers call eternal values, in order to ensure regulation of belief and action; or there is acceptance of enjoyments actually experienced irrespective of the method or operation by which they are brought into existence. Complete bifurcation between rationalistic method and an empirical method has its final and most deeply human significance in the ways in which good and bad are thought of and acted for and upon.

As far as technical philosophy reflects this situation, there is division of theories of values into two kinds. On the one hand, goods and evils, in every region of life, as they are concretely experienced, are regarded as characteristic of an inferior order of Being—intrinsically inferior. Just because they are things of human experience, their worth must be estimated by reference to standards and ideals derived from ultimate reality. Their defects and perversion are attributed to the same fact; they are to be corrected and controlled through adoption of methods of conduct derived from loyalty to the requirements of Supreme Being. This philosophic formulation gets actuality and force from the fact that it is a rendering of the beliefs of men in general as far as they have come under the influence of institutional religion. Just as rational conceptions were once superimposed upon observed and temporal phenomena, so eternal values are superimposed upon experienced goods. In one case as in the other, the alternative is supposed to be confusion and lawlessness. Philosophers suppose these eternal values are known by reason; the mass of persons that they are divinely revealed.

Nevertheless, with the expansion of secular interests, temporal values have enormously multiplied; they absorb more and more attention and energy. The sense of transcendent values has become enfeebled; instead of permeating all things in life, it is more and more restricted to special times and acts. The authority of the church to declare and impose divine will and purpose has narrowed. Whatever men say and profess, their tendency in the presence of actual evils is to resort to natural and empirical means to remedy them. But in formal belief, the old doctrine of the inherently disturbed and unworthy character of the goods and standards of ordinary experience persists. This divergence between what men do and what they nominally profess is closely connected with the confusions and conflicts of modern thought.

It is not meant to assert that no attempts have been made to replace the older theory regarding the authority of immutable and transcendent values by conceptions more congruous with the practices of daily life. The contrary is the case. The utilitarian theory, to take one instance, has had great power. The idealistic school is the only one in contemporary philosophies, with the exception of one form of neo-realism, that makes much of the notion of a reality which is all one with ultimate moral and religious values. But this school is also the one most concerned with the conservation of "spiritual" life. Equally significant is the fact that empirical theories retain the notion that thought and judgment are concerned with values that are experienced independently of them. For these theories, emotional satisfactions occupy the same place that sensations hold in traditional empiricism. Values are constituted by liking and enjoyment; to be enjoyed and to be a value are two names for one and the same fact. Since science has extruded values from its objects, these empirical theories do everything possible to emphasize their purely subjective character of value. A psychological theory of desire and liking is supposed to cover the whole ground of the theory of values; in it, immediate feeling is the counterpart of immediate sensation.

I shall not object to this empirical theory as far as it connects the theory of values with concrete experiences of desire and satisfaction. The idea that there is such a connection is the only way known to me by which the pallid remoteness of the rationalistic theory, and the only too glaring presence of the institutional theory of transcendental values can be escaped. The objection is that the theory in question holds down value to objects *antecedently* enjoyed, apart from reference to the method by which they come into existence; it takes enjoyments which are casual because unregulated by intelligent operations to be values in and of themselves. Operational thinking needs to be applied to the judgment of values just as it has now finally been applied in conceptions of physical objects. Experimental empiricism in the field of ideas of good and bad is demanded to meet the conditions of the present situation.

The scientific revolution came about when material of direct and uncontrolled experience was taken as problematic; as supplying material to be transformed by reflective operations into known objects. The contrast between experienced and known objects was found to be a temporal one; namely, one between empirical subject-matters which were had or "given" prior to the acts of experimental variation and redisposition and those which succeeded these acts and issued from them. The notion of an act whether of sense or thought which supplied a valid measure of thought in immediate knowledge was discredited. Consequences of operations became the important thing. The suggestion almost imperatively follows that escape from the defects of transcendental absolutism is not to be had by setting up as values enjoyments that happen anyhow, but in defining value by enjoyments which are the consequences of intelligent action. Without the intervention of thought, enjoyments are not values but problematic goods, becoming values when they re-issue in a changed form from intelligent behavior. The fundamental trouble with the current empirical theory of values is that it merely formulates and justifies the socially prevailing habit of regarding enjoyments as they are actually experienced as values in and of themselves. It completely side-steps the question of regulation of these enjoyments. This issue involves nothing less than the problem of the directed reconstruction of economic, political and religious institutions.

There was seemingly a paradox involved in the notion that if we turned our backs upon the immediately perceived qualities of things, we should be enabled to form valid conceptions of objects, and that these conceptions could be used to bring about a more secure and more significant experience of them. But the method terminated in disclosing the connections or interactions upon which perceived objects, viewed as events, depend. Formal analogy suggests that we regard our direct and original experience of things liked and enjoyed as only *possibilities* of values to be achieved; that enjoyment becomes a value when we discover the relations upon which its presence depends. Such a causal and operational definition gives only a conception of a value, not a value itself. But the utilization of the conception in action results in an object having secure and significant value.

The formal statement may be given concrete content by pointing to

the difference between the enjoyed and the enjoyable, the desired and
the desirable, the satis*fying* and the satis*factory*. To say that something
is enjoyed is to make a statement about a fact, something already in
existence; it is not to judge the value of that fact. There is no difference between such a proposition and one which says that something
is sweet or sour, red or black. It is just correct or incorrect and that is
the end of the matter. But to call an object a value is to assert that it
satisfies or fulfills certain conditions. Function and status in meeting
conditions is a different matter from bare existence. The fact that something is desired only raises the *question* of its desirability; it does not
settle it. Only a child in the degree of his immaturity thinks to settle
the question of desirability by reiterated proclamation: "I want it, I
want it, I want it." What is objected to in the current empirical theory
of values is not connection of them with desire and enjoyment but
failure to distinguish between enjoyments of radically different sorts.
There are many common expressions in which the difference of the two
kinds is clearly recognized. Take for example the difference between
the ideas of "satisfying" and "satisfactory." To say that something satisfies is to report something as an isolated finality. To assert that it is
satis*factory* is to define it in its connections and interactions. The fact
that it pleases or is immediately congenial poses a problem to judgment. How shall the satisfaction be rated? Is it a value or is it not?
Is it something to be prized and cherished, *to be* enjoyed? Not stern
moralists alone but everyday experience informs us that finding satisfaction in a thing may be a warning, a summons to be on the lookout
for consequences. To declare something satis*factory* is to assert that
it meets specifiable conditions. It is, in effect, a judgment that the
thing "will do." It involves a prediction; it contemplates a future in
which the thing will continue to serve; it *will* do. It asserts a consequence the thing will actively institute; it will *do*. That it is satisfying
is the content of a proposition of fact; that it is satisfactory is a judgment, an estimate, an appraisal. It denotes an attitude *to be* taken,
that of striving to perpetuate and to make secure.

It is worth notice that besides the instances given, there are many
other recognitions in ordinary speech of the distinction. The endings
"able," "worthy" and "ful" are cases in point. Noted and notable, noteworthy; remarked and remarkable; advised and advisable; wondered
at and wonderful; pleasing and beautiful; loved and lovable; blamed
and blameable, blameworthy; objected to and objectionable; esteemed
and estimable; admired and admirable; shamed and shameful; honored
and honorable; approved and approvable, worthy of approbation, etc.
The multiplication of words adds nothing to the force of the distinction. But it aids in conveying a sense of the fundamental character
of the distinction; of the difference between mere report of an already

existent fact and judgment as to the importance and need of bringing a fact into existence; or, if it is already there, of sustaining it in existence. The latter is a genuine practical judgment, and marks the only type of judgment that has to do with the direction of action. Whether or no we reserve the term "value" for the latter (as seems to me proper) is a minor matter; that the distinction be acknowledged as the key to understanding the relation of values to the direction of conduct is the important thing.

This element of direction by an idea of value applies to science as well as anywhere else. For in every scientific undertaking, there is passed a constant succession of estimates; such as "it is worth treating these facts as data or evidence; it is advisable to try this experiment; to make that observation; to entertain such and such a hypothesis; to perform this calculation," etc.

The word "taste" has perhaps got too completely associated with arbitrary liking to express the nature of judgments of value. But if the word be used in the sense of an appreciation at once cultivated and active, one may say that the formation of taste is the chief matter wherever values enter in, whether intellectual, esthetic or moral. Relatively immediate judgments, which we call tact or to which we give the name of intuition, do not precede reflective inquiry, but are the funded products of much thoughtful experience. Expertness of taste is at once the result and the reward of constant exercise of thinking. Instead of there being no disputing about tastes, they are the one thing worth disputing about, if by "dispute" is signified discussion involving reflective inquiry. Taste, if we use the word in its best sense, is the outcome of experience brought cumulatively to bear on the intelligent appreciation of the real worth of likings and enjoyments. There is nothing in which a person so completely reveals himself as in the things which he judges enjoyable and desirable. Such judgments are the sole alternative to the domination of belief by impulse, chance, blind habit and self-interest. The formation of a cultivated and effectively operative good judgment or taste with respect to what is esthetically admirable, intellectually acceptable and morally approvable is the supreme task set to human beings by the incidents of experience.

Propositions about what is or has been liked are of instrumental value in reaching judgments of value, in as far as the conditions and consequences of the thing liked are thought about. In themselves they make no claims; they put forth no demand upon subsequent attitudes and acts; they profess no authority to direct. If one likes a thing he likes it; that *is* a point about which there can be no dispute:—although it is not so easy to state just *what* is liked as is frequently assumed. A judgment about what is *to be* desired and enjoyed is, on the other hand, a claim on future action; it possesses *de jure* and not merely *de facto* quality. It is a matter of frequent experience that likings and enjoyments are of all kinds, and that many are such as reflective judgments condemn. By way of self-justification and "rationalization," an enjoyment creates a tendency to assert that the thing enjoyed is a value. This assertion of validity adds authority to the fact. It is a decision that the object has a right to exist and hence a claim upon action to further its existence.

The analogy between the status of the theory of values and the theory of ideas about natural objects before the rise of experimental inquiry may be carried further. The sensationalistic theory of the origin and test of thought evoked, by way of reaction, the transcendental theory of *a priori* ideas. For it failed utterly to account for objective connection, order and regularity in objects observed. Similarly, any doctrine that identifies the mere fact of being liked with the value of the object liked so fails to give direction to conduct when direction is needed that it automatically calls forth the assertion that there are values eternally in Being that are the standards of all judgments and the obligatory ends of all action. Without the introduction of operational thinking, we oscillate between a theory that, in order to save the objectivity of judgments of values, isolates them from experience and nature, and a theory that, in order to save their concrete and human significance, reduces them to mere statements about our own feelings.

Not even the most devoted adherents of the notion that enjoyment and value are equivalent facts would venture to assert that because we have once liked a thing we should go on liking it; they are compelled to introduce the idea that *some* tastes are to be cultivated. Logically, there is no ground for introducing the idea of cultivation; liking is liking, and one is as good as another. If enjoyments *are* values, the judgment of value cannot regulate the form which liking takes; it cannot regulate its own conditions. Desire and purpose, and hence action, are left without guidance, although the question of regulation of their formation is the supreme problem of practical life. Values (to sum up) may be connected inherently with liking, and yet not with *every* liking but only with those that judgment has approved, after examination of the relation upon which the object liked depends. A casual liking is one that happens without knowledge of how it occurs nor to what effect. The difference between it and one which is sought because of a judgment that it is worth having and is to be striven for, makes just the difference between enjoyments which are accidental and enjoyments that have value and hence a claim upon our attitude and conduct.

In any case, the alternative rationalistic theory does not afford the guidance for the sake of which eternal and immutable norms are appealed to. The scientist finds no help in determining the probable truth of some proposed theory by comparing it with a standard of absolute truth and immutable being. He has to rely upon definite operations undertaken under definite conditions—upon method. We can hardly imagine an architect getting aid in the construction of a building from an ideal at large, though we can understand his framing an ideal on the basis of knowledge of actual conditions and needs. Nor does the ideal of perfect beauty in antecedent Being give direction to a painter in producing a particular work of art. In morals, absolute perfection does not seem to be more than a generalized hypostatization of the recognition that there is a good to be sought, an obligation to be met— both being concrete matters. Nor is the defect in this respect merely negative. An examination of history would reveal, I am confident, that these general and remote schemes of value actually obtain a content definite enough and near enough to concrete situations as to afford guidance in action only by consecrating some institution or dogma already having social currency. Concreteness is gained, but it is by protecting from inquiry some accepted standard which perhaps is outworn and in need of criticism.

When theories of values do not afford intellectual assistance in framing ideas and beliefs about values that are adequate to direct action, the gap must be filled by other means. If intelligent method is lacking, prejudice, the pressure of immediate circumstance, self-interest and class-interest, traditional customs, institutions of accidental historic origin, are *not* lacking, and they tend to take the place of intelligence. Thus we are led to our main proposition: *Judgments about values are judgments about the conditions and the results of experienced objects; judgments about that which should regulate the formation of our desires, affections and enjoyments.* For whatever decides their formation will determine the main course of our conduct, personal and social.

If it sounds strange to hear that we should frame our judgments as to what has value by considering the connections in existence of what we like and enjoy, the reply is not far to seek. As long as we do not engage in this inquiry enjoyments (values if we choose to apply that term) are casual; they are given by "nature," not constructed by art. Like natural objects in their qualitative existence, they at most only supply material for elaboration in rational discourse. A *feeling* of good or excellence is as far removed from goodness in fact as a feeling that objects are intellectually thus and so is removed from their being actually so. To recognize that the truth of natural objects can be reached only by the greatest care in selecting and arranging directed operations, and then to suppose that values can be truly determined by the mere fact of liking seems to leave us in an incredible position. All the serious perplexities of life come back to the genuine difficulty of forming a judgment as to the values of the situation; they come back to a conflict of goods. Only dogmatism can suppose that serious moral conflict is between something clearly bad and something known to be good, and that uncertainty lies wholly in the will of the one choosing. Most conflicts of importance are conflicts between things which are or have been satisfying, not between good and evil. And to suppose that we can make a hierarchical table of values at large once for all, a kind of catalogue in which they are arranged in an order of ascending or descending worth, is to indulge in a gloss on our inability to frame intelligent judgments in the concrete. Or else it is to dignify customary choice and prejudice by a title of honor.

The alternative to definition, classification and systematization of satisfactions just as they happen to occur is judgment of them by means of the relations under which they occur. If we know the conditions under which the act of liking, of desire and enjoyment, takes place, we are in a position to know what are the consequences of that act. The difference between the desired and the desirable, the admired and the admirable, becomes effective at just this point. Consider the difference between the proposition "That thing has been eaten," and the judgment "That thing is edible." The former statement involves no knowledge of any relation except the one stated; while we are able to judge of the edibility of anything only when we have a knowledge of its interactions with other things sufficient to enable us to foresee its probable effects when it is taken into the organism and produces effects there.

To assume that anything can be known in isolation from its connections with other things is to identify knowing with merely having some object before perception or in feeling, and is thus to lose the key to the traits that distinguish an object as known. It is futile, even silly, to suppose that some quality that is directly present constitutes the whole of the thing presenting the quality. It does not do so when the quality is that of being hot or fluid or heavy, and it does not when the quality is that of giving pleasure, or being enjoyed. Such qualities are, once more, effects, ends in the sense of closing termini of processes involving causal connections. They are something to be investigated, challenges to inquiry and judgment. The more connections and interactions we ascertain, the more we *know* the object in question. Thinking is search for these connections. Heat experienced as a consequence of directed operations has a meaning quite different from the heat that is casually experienced without knowledge of how it came about. The same is true of enjoyments. Enjoyments that issue from conduct directed by insight into relations have a meaning and a validity due to the way in which they are experienced. Such enjoyments are not repented of; they generate no after-taste of bitterness. Even in the midst of direct enjoyment, there is a sense of validity, of authorization, which intensifies the enjoyment. There is solicitude for perpetuation of the *object* having value which is radically different from mere anxiety to perpetuate the *feeling* of enjoyment.

Such statements as we have been making are, therefore, far from implying that there are values apart from things actually enjoyed as good. To find a thing enjoy*able* is, so to say, a *plus* enjoyment. We saw that it was foolish to treat the scientific object as a rival to or substitute for the perceived object, since the former is intermediate between uncertain and settled situations and those experienced under conditions of greater control. In the same way, judgment of the value of an object to be experienced is instrumental to appreciation of it when it is realized. But the notion that every object that happens to satisfy has an equal claim with every other to be a value is like supposing that every object of perception has the same cognitive force as every other. There is no knowledge without perception; but objects perceived are *known* only when they are determined as consequences of connective operations. There is no value except where there is satisfaction, but there have to be certain conditions fulfilled to transform a satisfaction into a value.

The time will come when it will be found passing strange that we of this age should take such pains to control by every means at command the formation of ideas of physical things, even those most remote from human concern, and yet are content with haphazard beliefs about the qualities of objects that regulate our deepest interests; that we are scrupulous as to methods of forming ideas of natural objects, and either dogmatic or else driven by immediate conditions in framing those about values. There is, by implication, if not explicitly, a prevalent notion that values are already well known and that all which is lacking is the will to cultivate them in the order of their worth. In fact the most profound lack is not the will to act upon goods already known but the will to know what they are.

It is not a dream that it is possible to exercise some degree of regulation of the occurrence of enjoyments which are of value. Realization of the possibility is exemplified, for example, in the technologies and arts of industrial life—that is, up to a definite limit. Men desired heat, light, and speed of transit and of communication beyond what nature provides of itself. These things have been attained not by lauding the enjoyment of these things and preaching their desirability, but by study of the conditions of their manifestation. Knowledge of relations having been obtained, ability to produce followed, and enjoyment ensued as a matter of course. It is, however, an old story that enjoyment of these things as goods is no warrant of their bringing only good in their train. As Plato was given to pointing out, the physician may know how to heal and the orator to persuade, but the ulterior knowledge of whether it is better for a man to be healed or to be persuaded to the orator's opinion remains unsettled. Here there appears the split between what are traditionally and conventionally called the values of the baser arts and the higher values of the truly personal and humane arts.

With respect to the former, there is no assumption that they can be had and enjoyed without definite operative knowledge. With respect to them it is also clear that the degree in which we value them is measurable by the pains taken to control the conditions of their occurrence. With respect to the latter, it is assumed that no one who is honest can be in doubt what they are; that by revelation, or conscience, or the instruction of others, or immediate feeling, they are clear beyond question. And instead of action in their behalf being taken to be a measure of the extent in which things *are* values to us, it is assumed that the difficulty is to persuade men to act upon what they already know to be good. Knowledge of conditions and consequences is regarded as wholly indifferent to judging what is of serious value, though it is useful in a prudential way in trying to actualize it. In consequence, the existence of values that are by common consent of a secondary and technical sort are under a fair degree of control, while those denominated supreme and imperative are subject to all the winds of impulse, custom and arbitrary authority.

This distinction between higher and lower types of value is itself something to be looked into. Why should there be a sharp division made between some goods as physical and material and others as ideal and "spiritual"? The question touches the whole dualism of the material and the ideal at its root. To denominate anything "matter" or "material" is not in truth to disparage it. It is, if the designation is correctly applied, a way of indicating that the thing in question is a condition or means of the existence of something else. And disparagement of effective means is practically synonymous with disregard of the things that are termed, in eulogistic fashion, ideal and spiritual. For the latter terms if they have any concrete application at all signify something which is a desirable consummation of conditions, a cherished fulfillment of means. The sharp separation between material and ideal good thus deprives the latter of the underpinning of effective support while it opens the way for treating things which should be employed as means as ends in themselves. For since men cannot after all live without some measure of possession of such matters as health and wealth, the latter things will be viewed as values and ends in isolation unless they are treated as integral constituents of the goods that are deemed supreme and final.

The relations that determine the occurrence of what human beings experience, especially when social connections are taken into account, are indefinitely wider and more complex than those that determine the events termed physical; the latter are the outcome of definite selective operations. This is the reason why we know something about remote objects like the stars better than we know significantly characteristic things about our own bodies and minds. We forget the infinite number of things we do not know about the stars, or rather that what we call a star is itself the product of the elimination, enforced and deliberate, of most of the traits that belong to an actual existence. The amount of knowledge we possess about stars would not seem very great or very important if it were carried over to human beings and exhausted our knowledge of them. It is inevitable that genuine knowledge of man and society should lag far behind physical knowledge.

But this difference is not a ground for making a sharp division between the two, nor does it account for the fact that we make so little use of the experimental method of forming our ideas and beliefs about the concerns of man in his characteristic social relations. For this separation religions and philosophies must admit some responsibility. They have erected a distinction between a narrower scope of relations and a wider and fuller one into a difference of kind, naming one kind material, and the other mental and moral. They have charged themselves gratuitously with the office of diffusing belief in the necessity of the division, and with instilling contempt for the material as something inferior in kind in its intrinsic nature and worth. Formal philosophies undergo evaporation of their technical solid contents; in a thinner and more viable form they find their way into the minds of those who know nothing of their original forms. When these diffuse and, so to say, airy emanations re-crystallize in the popular mind they form a hard deposit of opinion that alters slowly and with great difficulty.

What difference would it actually make in the arts of conduct, personal and social, if the experimental theory were adopted not as a mere theory, but as a part of the working equipment of habitual attitudes on the part of everyone? It would be impossible, even were time given, to answer the question in adequate detail, just as men could not foretell in advance the consequences for knowledge of adopting the experimental method. It is the nature of the method that it has to be tried. But there are generic lines of difference which, within the limits of time at disposal, may be sketched.

Change from forming ideas and judgments of value on the basis of conformity to antecedent objects, to constructing enjoyable objects directed by knowledge of consequences, is a change from looking to the past to looking to the future. I do not for a moment suppose that the experiences of the past, personal and social, are of no importance. For without them we should not be able to frame any ideas whatever of the conditions under which objects are enjoyed nor any estimate of the consequences of esteeming and liking them. But past experiences are significant in giving us intellectual instrumentalities of judging just these points. They are tools, not finalities. Reflection upon what we have liked and have enjoyed is a necessity. But it tells us nothing about the *value* of these things until enjoyments are themselves reflectively controlled, or, until, as they are now recalled, we form the best judgment possible about what led us to like this sort of thing and what has issued from the fact that we liked it.

We are not, then, to get away from enjoyments experienced in the past and from recall of them, but from the notion that they are the arbiters of things to be further enjoyed. At present, the arbiter is found in the past, although there are many ways of interpreting what in the past is authoritative. Nominally, the most influential conception doubtless is that of a revelation once had or a perfect life once lived. Reliance upon precedent, upon institutions created in the past, especially in law, upon rules of morals that have come to us through unexamined customs, upon uncriticized tradition, are other forms of dependence. It is not for a moment suggested that we can get away from customs and established institutions. A mere break would doubtless result simply in chaos. But there is no danger of such a break. Mankind is too inertly conservative both by constitution and by education to give the idea of this danger actuality. What there is genuine danger of is that the force of new conditions will produce disruption externally and mechanically: this is an ever present danger. The prospect is increased, not mitigated, by that conservatism which insists upon the adequacy of old standards to meet new conditions. What is needed is intelligent examination of the consequences that are actually effected by inherited institutions and customs, in order that there may be intelligent consideration of the ways in which they are to be intentionally modified in behalf of generation of different consequences.

This is the significant meaning of transfer of experimental method from the technical field of physical experience to the wider field of human life. We trust the method in forming our beliefs about things not directly connected with human life. In effect, we distrust it in moral, political and economic affairs. In the fine arts, there are many signs of a change. In the past, such a change has often been an omen and precursor of changes in other human attitudes. But, generally speaking, the idea of actively adopting experimental method in social affairs, in the matters deemed of most enduring and ultimate worth, strikes most persons as a surrender of all standards and regulative authority. But in principle, experimental method does not signify random and aimless action; it implies direction by ideas and knowledge. The question at issue is a practical one. Are there in existence the ideas and the knowledge that permit experimental method to be effectively used in social interests and affairs?

Where will regulation come from if we surrender familiar and traditionally prized values as our directive standards? Very largely from the findings of the natural sciences. For one of the effects of the separation drawn between knowledge and action is to deprive scientific knowledge of its proper service as a guide of conduct—except once more in those technological fields which have been degraded to an inferior rank. Of course, the complexity of the conditions upon which objects of human and liberal value depend is a great obstacle, and it would be too optimistic to say that we have as yet enough knowledge of the scientific type to enable us to regulate our judgments of value very extensively. But we have more knowledge than we try to put to use, and until we try more systematically we shall not know what are the important gaps in our sciences judged from the point of view of their moral and humane use.

For moralists usually draw a sharp line between the field of the natural sciences and the conduct that is regarded as moral. But a moral that frames its judgments of value on the basis of consequences must depend in a most intimate manner upon the conclusions of science. For the knowledge of the relations between changes which enable us to connect things as antecedents and consequences *is* science. The narrow scope which moralists often give to morals, their isolation of some conduct as virtuous and vicious from other large ranges of conduct, those having to do with health and vigor, business, education, with all the affairs in which desires and affection are implicated, is perpetuated by this habit of exclusion of the subject-matter of natural science from a rôle in formation of moral standards and ideals. The same attitude operates in the other direction to keep natural science a technical specialty, and it works unconsciously to encourage its use exclusively in regions where it can be turned to personal and class advantage, as in war and trade.

Another great difference to be made by carrying the experimental habit into all matter of practice is that it cuts the roots of what is often called subjectivism, but which is better termed egoism. The subjective attitude is much more widespread than would be inferred from the philosophies which have that label attached. It is as rampant in realistic philosophies as in any others, sometimes even more so, although disguised from those who hold these philosophies under the cover of reverence of and enjoyment of ultimate values. For the implication of placing the standard of thought and knowledge in antecedent existence is that our thought makes no difference in what is significantly real. It then affects only our own attitude toward it.

This constant throwing of emphasis back upon a change made in ourselves instead of one made in the world in which we live seems to me the essence of what is objectionable in "subjectivism." Its taint hangs about even Platonic realism with its insistent evangelical dwelling upon the change made within the mind by contemplation of the realm of essence, and its depreciation of action as transient and all but sordid—a concession to the necessities of organic existence. All the theories which put conversion "of the eye of the soul" in the place of a conversion of natural and social objects that modifies goods actually experienced, [are] a retreat and escape from existence—and this retraction into self is, once more, the heart of subjective egoisms. The typical example is perhaps the other-worldliness found in religions whose chief concern is with the salvation of the personal soul. But other-worldliness is found as well in estheticism and in all seclusion within ivory towers.

It is not in the least implied that change in personal attitudes, in the disposition of the "subject," is not of great importance. Such change, on the contrary, is involved in any attempt to modify the conditions of the environment. But there is a radical difference between a change in the self that is cultivated and valued as an end, and one that is a means to alteration, through action, of objective conditions. The Aristotelian-medieval conviction that highest bliss is found in contemplative possession of ultimate Being presents an ideal attractive to some types of mind; it sets forth a refined sort of enjoyment. It is a doctrine congenial to minds that despair of the effort involved in creation of a better world of daily experience. It is, apart from theological attachments, a doctrine sure to recur when social conditions are so troubled as to make actual endeavor seem hopeless. But the subjectivism so externally marked in modern thought as compared with ancient is either a development of the old doctrine under new conditions or is of merely technical import. The medieval version of the doctrine at least had the active support of a great social institution by means of which man could be brought into the state of mind that prepared him for ultimate enjoyment of eternal Being. It had a certain solidity and depth which is lacking in modern theories that would attain the result by merely emotional or speculative procedures, or by any means not demanding a change in objective existence so as to render objects of value more empirically secure.

The nature in detail of the revolution that would be wrought by carrying into the region of values the principle now embodied in scientific practice cannot be told; to attempt it would violate the fundamental idea that we know only after we have acted and in consequence of the outcome of action. But it would surely effect a transfer of attention and energy from the subjective to the objective. Men would think of themselves as agents not as ends; ends would be found in experienced enjoyment of the fruits of a transforming activity. In as far as the subjectivity of modern thought represents a discovery of the part played by personal responses, organic and acquired, in the causal production of the qualities and values of objects, it marks the possibility of a decisive gain. It puts us in possession of some of the conditions that control the occurrence of experienced objects, and thereby it supplies us with an instrument of regulation. There is something querulous in the sweeping denial that things as experienced, as perceived and enjoyed, in any way depend upon interaction with human selves. The error of doctrines that have exploited the part played by personal and subjective reactions in determining what is perceived and enjoyed lies either in exaggerating this factor of constitution into the sole condition —as happens in subjective idealism—or else in treating it as a finality instead of, as with all knowledge, an instrument in direction of further action.

A third significant change that would issue from carrying over experimental method from physics to man concerns the import of standards, principles, rules. With the transfer, these, and all tenets and creeds about good and goods, would be recognized to be hypotheses. Instead of being rigidly fixed, they would be treated as intellectual instruments to be tested and confirmed—and altered—through consequences effected by acting upon them. They would lose all pretence of finality—the ulterior source of dogmatism. It is both astonishing and depressing that so much of the energy of mankind has gone into fighting for (with weapons of the flesh as well as of the spirit) the truth of creeds, religions, moral and political, as distinct from what has gone into effort to try creeds by putting them to the test of acting upon them. The change would do away with the intolerance and fanaticism that attend the notion that beliefs and judgments are capable of inherent truth and authority; inherent in the sense of being independent of what they lead to when used as directive principles. The transformation does not imply merely that men are responsible for acting upon what they profess to believe; that is an old doctrine. It goes much further. Any belief as such is tentative, hypothetical; it is not just to be acted upon, but is to be *framed* with reference to its office as a guide to action. Consequently, it should be the last thing in the world to be picked up casually and then clung to rigidly. When it is apprehended as a tool and only a tool, an instrumentality of direction, the same scrupulous attention will go to its formation as now goes into the making of instruments of precision in technical fields. Men, instead of being proud of accepting and asserting beliefs and "principles" on the ground of loyalty, will be as ashamed of that procedure as they would now be to confess their assent to a scientific theory out of reverence for Newton or Helmholz or whomever, without regard to evidence.

If one stops to consider the matter, is there not something strange in the fact that men should consider loyalty to "laws," principles, standards, ideals to be an inherent virtue, accounted unto them for righteousness? It is as if they were making up for some secret sense of weakness by rigidity and intensity of insistent attachment. A moral law, like a law in physics, is not something to swear by and stick to at all hazards; it is a formula of the way to respond when specified conditions present themselves. Its soundness and pertinence are tested by what happens when it is acted upon. Its claim or authority rests finally upon the imperativeness of the situation that has to be dealt with, not upon its own intrinsic nature—as any tool achieves dignity in the measure of needs served by it. The idea that adherence to standards external to experienced objects is the only alternative to confusion and lawlessness was once held in science. But knowledge became steadily progressive when it was abandoned, and clews and tests found within concrete acts and objects were employed. The test of consequences is more exacting than that afforded by fixed general rules. In addition, it secures constant development, for when new acts are tried new results are experienced, while the lauded immutability of eternal ideals and norms is in itself a denial of the possibility of development and improvement.

The various modifications that would result from adoption in social and humane subjects of the experimental way of thinking are perhaps summed up in saying that it would place *method and means* upon the level of importance that has, in the past, been imputed exclusively to ends. Means have been regarded as menial, and the useful as the servile. Means have been treated as poor relations to be endured, but not inherently welcome. The very meaning of the word "ideals" is significant of the divorce which has obtained between means and ends. "Ideals" are thought to be remote and inaccessible of attainment; they are too high and fine to be sullied by realization. They serve vaguely to arouse "aspiration," but they do not evoke and direct strivings for embodiment in actual existence. They hover in an indefinite way over the actual scene; they are expiring ghosts of a once significant kingdom of divine reality whose rule penetrated to every detail of life.

It is impossible to form a just estimate of the paralysis of effort that has been produced by indifference to means. Logically, it is truistic that lack of consideration for means signifies that so-called ends are not taken seriously. It is as if one professed devotion to painting pictures conjoined with contempt for canvas, brush and paints; or love of music on condition that no instruments, whether the voice or something external, be used to make sounds. The good workman in the arts is known by his respect for his tools and by his interest in perfecting his technique. The glorification in the arts of ends at the expense of means would be taken to be a sign of complete insincerity or even insanity. Ends separated from means are either sentimental indulgences or if they happen to exist are merely accidental. The ineffectiveness in action of "ideals" is due precisely to the supposition that means and ends are not on exactly the same level with respect to the attention and care they demand.

It is, however, much easier to point out the formal contradiction implied in ideals that are professed without equal regard for the instruments and techniques of their realization, than it is to appreciate the concrete ways in which belief in their separation has found its way into life and borne corrupt and poisonous fruits. The separation marks the form in which the traditional divorce of theory and practice has expressed itself in actual life. It accounts for the relative impotency of arts concerned with enduring human welfare. Sentimental attachment and subjective eulogy take the place of action. For there is no art without tools and instrumental agencies. But it also explains the fact that in actual behavior, energies devoted to matters nominally thought to be inferior, material and sordid, engross attention and interest. After a polite and pious deference has been paid to "ideals," men feel free to devote themselves to matters which are more immediate and pressing.

It is usual to condemn the amount of attention paid by people in general to material ease, comfort, wealth, and success gained by competition, on the ground that they give to mere means the attention that ought to be given to ends, or that they have taken for ends things which in reality are only means. Criticisms of the place which economic interest and action occupy in present life are full of complaints that men allow lower aims to usurp the place that belongs to higher and ideal values. The final source of the trouble is, however, that moral and spiritual "leaders" have propagated the notion that ideal ends may be cultivated in isolation from "material" means, as if means and material were not synonymous. While they condemn men for giving to means the thought and energy that ought to go to ends, the condemnation should go to them. For they have not taught their followers to think of material and economic activities as *really* means. They have been unwilling to frame their conception of the values that should be regulative of human conduct on the basis of the actual conditions and operations by which alone values can be actualized.

Practical needs are imminent; with the mass of mankind they are imperative. Moreover, speaking generally, men are formed to act rather than to theorize. Since the ideal ends are so remotely and accidentally connected with immediate and urgent conditions that need attention, after lip service is given to them, men naturally devote themselves to the latter. If a bird in the hand is worth two in a neighboring bush, an actuality in hand is worth, for the direction of conduct, many ideals that are so remote as to be invisible and inaccessible. Men hoist the banner of the ideal, and then march in the direction that concrete conditions suggest and reward.

Deliberate insincerity and hypocrisy are rare. But the notion that action and sentiment are inherently unified in the constitution of human nature has nothing to justify it. Integration is something to be achieved. Division of attitudes and responses, compartmentalizing of interests, is easily acquired. It goes deep just because the acquisition is unconscious, a matter of habitual adaptation to conditions. Theory separated from concrete doing and making is empty and futile; practice then becomes an immediate seizure of opportunities and enjoyments which conditions afford without the direction which theory—knowledge and ideas—has power to supply. The problem of the relation of theory and practice is not a problem of theory alone; it is that, but it is also the most practical problem of life. For it is the question of how intelligence may inform action, and how action may bear the fruit of increased insight into meaning: a clear view of the values that are worth while and of the means by which they are to be made secure in experienced objects. Construction of ideals in general and their sentimental glorification are easy; the responsibilities both of studious thought and of action are shirked. Persons having the advantage of positions of leisure and who find pleasure in abstract theorizing—a most delightful indulgence to those to whom it appeals—have a large measure of liability for a cultivated diffusion of ideals and aims that are separated from the conditions which are the means of actualization. Then other persons who find themselves in positions of social power and authority readily claim to be the bearers and defenders of ideal ends in church and state. They then use the prestige and authority their representative capacity as guardians of the highest ends confers on them to cover actions taken in behalf of the harshest and narrowest of material ends.

The present state of industrial life seems to give a fair index of the existing separation of means and ends. Isolation of economics from ideal ends, whether of morals or of organized social life, was proclaimed by Aristotle. Certain things, he said, are conditions of a worthy life, personal and social, but are not constituents of it. The economic life of man, concerned with satisfaction of wants, is of this nature. Men have wants and they must be satisfied. But they are only prerequisites of a good life, not intrinsic elements in it. Most philosophers have not been so frank nor perhaps so logical. But upon the whole, economics has been treated as on a lower level than either morals or politics. Yet the life which men, women and children actually lead, the opportunities open to them, the values they are capable of enjoying, their education, their share in all the things of art and science, are mainly determined by economic conditions. Hence we can hardly expect a moral system which ignores economic conditions to be other than remote and empty.

Industrial life is correspondingly brutalized by failure to equate it as the means by which social and cultural values are realized. That the economic life, thus exiled from the pale of higher values, takes revenge by declaring that it is the only social reality, and by means of the doctrine of materialistic determination of institutions and conduct in all fields, denies to deliberate morals and politics any share of causal regulation, is not surprising.

When economists were told that their subject-matter was merely material, they naturally thought they could be "scientific" only by excluding all reference to distinctively human values. Material wants, efforts to satisfy them, even the scientifically regulated technologies highly developed in industrial activity, are then taken to form a complete and closed field. If any reference to social ends and values is introduced it is by way of an external addition, mainly hortatory. That economic life largely determines the conditions under which mankind has access to concrete values may be recognized or it may not be. In either case, the notion that it is the means to be utilized in order to secure significant values as the common and shared possession of mankind is alien and inoperative. To many persons, the idea that the ends professed by morals are impotent save as they are connected with the working machinery of economic life seems like deflowering the purity of moral values and obligations.

The social and moral effects of the separation of theory and practice have been merely hinted at. They are so manifold and so pervasive that an adequate consideration of them would involve nothing less than a survey of the whole field of morals, economics and politics. It cannot be justly stated that these effects are in fact direct consequences of the quest for certainty by thought and knowledge isolated from action. For, as we have seen, this quest was itself a reflex product of actual conditions. But it may be truly asserted that this quest, undertaken in religion and philosophy, has had results which have reinforced the conditions which originally brought it about. Moreover, search for safety and consolation amid the perils of life by means other than intelligent action, by feeling and thought alone, began when actual means of control were lacking, when arts were undeveloped. It had then a relative historic justification that is now lacking. The primary problem for thinking which lays claim to be philosophic in its breadth and depth is to assist in bringing about a reconstruction of all beliefs rooted in a basic separation of knowledge and action; to develop a system of operative ideas congruous with present knowledge and with present facilities of control over natural events and energies.

We have noted more than once how modern philosophy has been absorbed in the problem of effecting an adjustment between the conclusions of natural science and the beliefs and values that have authority in the direction of life. The genuine and poignant issue does not reside where philosophers for the most part have placed it. It does not consist in accommodation to each other of two realms, one physical and the other ideal and spiritual, nor in the reconciliation of the "categories" of theoretical and practical reason. It is found in that isolation of executive means and ideal interests which has grown up under the influence of the separation of theory and practice. For this, by nature, involves the separation of the material and the spiritual. Its solution, therefore, can be found only in action wherein the phenomena of material and economic life are equated with the purposes that command the loyalties of affection and purpose, and in which ends and ideals are framed in terms of the possibilities of actually experienced situations. But while the solution cannot be found in "thought" alone, it can be furthered by thinking which is operative—which frames and defines ideas in terms of what may be done, and which uses the conclusions of science as instrumentalities. William James was well within the bounds of moderation when he said that looking forward instead of backward, looking to what the world and life might become instead of to what they have been, is an alteration in the "seat of authority."

It was incidentally remarked earlier in our discussion that the serious defect in the current empirical philosophy of values, the one which identifies them with things actually enjoyed irrespective of the conditions upon which they depend, is that it formulates and in so far consecrates the conditions of our present social experience. Throughout these chapters, primary attention has perforce been given to the methods and statements of philosophic theories. But these statements are technical and specialized in formulation only. In origin, content and import they are reflections of some condition or some phase of concrete human experience. Just as the theory of the separation of theory and practice has a practical origin and a momentous practical consequence, so the empirical theory that values are identical with whatever men actually enjoy, no matter how or what, formulates an aspect, and an undesirable one, of the present social situation.

For while our discussion has given more attention to the other type of philosophical doctrine, that which holds that regulative and authoritative standards are found in transcendent eternal values, it has not passed in silence over the fact that actually the greater part of the activities of the greater number of human beings is spent in effort to seize upon and hold onto such enjoyments as the actual scene permits. Their energies and their enjoyments are controlled in fact, but they are controlled by external conditions rather than by intelligent judgment and endeavor. If philosophies have any influence over the thoughts and acts of men, it is a serious matter that the most widely held empirical theory should in effect justify this state of things by identifying values with the objects of any interest as such. As long as the only theories of value placed before us for intellectual assent alternate between sending us to a realm of eternal and fixed values and sending us to enjoyments such as actually obtain, the formulation, even as only a theory, of an experimental empiricism which finds values to be identical with goods that are the fruit of intelligently directed activity has its measure of practical significance.

4. Science and Society [4]

THE SIGNIFICANT outward forms of the civilization of the western world are the product of the machine and its technology. Indirectly, they are the product of the scientific revolution which took place in the seventeenth century. In its effect upon men's external habits, dominant interests, the conditions under which they work and associate, whether in the family, the factory, the state, or internationally, science is by far the most potent social factor in the modern world. It operates, however, through its undesigned effects rather than as a transforming influence of men's thoughts and purposes. This contrast between outer and inner operation is the great contradiction in our lives. Habits of thought and desire remain in substance what they were before the rise of science, while the conditions under which they take effect have been radically altered by science.

When we look at the external social consequences of science, we find it impossible to apprehend the extent or gauge the rapidity of their occurrence. Alfred North Whitehead has recently called attention to the progressive shortening of the time-span of social change. That due to basic conditions seems to be of the order of half a million years; that due to lesser physical conditions, like alterations in climate, to be of the order of five thousand years. Until almost our own day the time-span of sporadic technological changes was of the order of five hundred years; according to him, no great technological changes took place between, say, 100 A.D. and 1400 A.D. With the introduction of steam-power, the fifty years from 1780 to 1830 were marked by more changes than are found in any previous thousand years. The advance of chemical techniques and in use of electricity and radio-energy in the last forty years makes even this last change seem slow and awkward.

Domestic life, political institutions, international relations and personal contacts are shifting with kaleidoscopic rapidity before our eyes. We cannot appreciate and weigh the changes; they occur too swiftly. We do not have time to take them in. No sooner do we begin to understand the meaning of one such change than another comes and displaces the former. Our minds are dulled by the sudden and repeated

[4] An essay from the volume *Philosophy and Civilization* (New York, 1931). By permission of the publishers, G. P. Putnam's Sons.

impacts. Externally, science through its applications is manufacturing the conditions of our institutions at such a speed that we are too bewildered to know what sort of civilization is in process of making.

Because of this confusion, we cannot even draw up a ledger account of social gains and losses due to the operation of science. But at least we know that the earlier optimism which thought that the advance of natural science was to dispel superstition, ignorance, and oppression, by placing reason on the throne, was unjustified. Some superstitions have given way, but the mechanical devices due to science have made it possible to spread new kinds of error and delusion among a larger multitude. The fact is that it is foolish to try to draw up a debit and credit account for science. To do so is to mythologize; it is to personify science and impute to it a will and an energy on its own account. In truth science is strictly impersonal; a method and a body of knowledge. It owes its operation and its consequences to the human beings who use it. It adapts itself passively to the purposes and desires which animate these human beings. It lends itself with equal impartiality to the kindly offices of medicine and hygiene and the destructive deeds of war. It elevates some through opening new horizons; it depresses others by making them slaves of machines operated for the pecuniary gain of owners.

The neutrality of science to the uses made of it renders it silly to talk about its bankruptcy, or to worship it as the usherer in of a new age. In the degree in which we realize this fact, we shall devote our attention to the human purposes and motives which control its application. Science is an instrument, a method, a body of technique. While it is an end for those inquirers who are engaged in its pursuit, in the large human sense it is a means, a tool. For what ends shall it be used? Shall it be used deliberately, systematically, for the promotion of social well-being, or shall it be employed primarily for private aggrandizement, leaving its larger social results to chance? Shall the scientific attitude be used to create new mental and moral attitudes, or shall it continue to be subordinated to service of desires, purposes and institutions which were formed before science came into existence? Can the attitudes which control the use of science be themselves so influenced by scientific technique that they will harmonize with its spirit?

The beginning of wisdom is, I repeat, the realization that science itself is an instrument which is indifferent to the external uses to which it is put. Steam and electricity remain natural forces when they operate through mechanisms; the only problem is the purposes for which men set the mechanisms to work. The essential technique of gunpowder is the same whether it be used to blast rocks from the quarry to build better human habitations, or to hurl death upon men at war with one another. The airplane binds men at a distance in closer bonds of intercourse and understanding, or it rains missiles of death upon hapless populations. We are forced to consider the relation of human ideas and ideals to the social consequences which are produced by science as an instrument.

The problem involved is the greatest which civilization has ever had to face. It is, without exaggeration, the most serious issue of contemporary life. Here is the instrumentality, the most powerful, for good and evil, the world has ever known. What are we going to do with it? Shall we leave our underlying aims unaffected by it, treating it merely as a means by which uncoöperative individuals may advance their own fortunes? Shall we try to improve the hearts of men without regard to the new methods which science puts at our disposal? There are those, men in high position in church and state, who urge this course. They trust to a transforming influence of a morals and religion which have not been affected by science to change human desire and purpose, so that they will employ science and machine technology for beneficent social ends. The recent Encyclical of the Pope is a classic document in expression of a point of view which would rely wholly upon inner regeneration to protect society from the injurious uses to which science may be put. Quite apart from any ecclesiastical connection, there are many "intellectuals" who appeal to inner "spiritual" concepts, totally divorced from scientific intelligence, to effect the needed work. But there is another alternative: to take the method of science home into our own controlling attitudes and dispositions, to employ the new techniques as means of directing our thoughts and efforts to a planned control of social forces.

Science and machine technology are young from the standpoint of human history. Though vast in stature, they are infants in age. Three hundred years are but a moment in comparison with thousands of centuries man has lived on the earth. In view of the inertia of institutions and of the mental habits they breed, it is not surprising that the new technique of apparatus and calculation, which is the essence of science, has made so little impression on underlying human attitudes. The momentum of traditions and purposes that preceded its rise took possession of the new instrument and turned it to their ends. Moreover, science had to struggle for existence. It had powerful enemies in church and state. It needed friends and it welcomed alliance with the rising capitalism which it so effectively promoted. If it tended to foster secularism and to create predominantly material interests, it could still be argued that it was in essential harmony with traditional morals and religion. But there were lacking the conditions which are indispensable to the serious application of scientific method in reconstruction of fundamental beliefs and attitudes. In addition, the development of the new science was attended with so many internal difficulties that energy had to go to perfecting the instrument just as an instrument. Because of all these circumstances the fact that science was used in behalf of old interests is nothing to be wondered at.

The conditions have now changed, radically so. The claims of natural science in the physical field are undisputed. Indeed, its prestige is so great that an almost superstitious aura gathers about its name and work. Its progress is no longer dependent upon the adventurous inquiry of a few untrammeled souls. Not only are universities organized to promote scientific research and learning, but one may almost imagine the university laboratories abolished and still feel confident of the continued advance of science. The development of industry has compelled the inclusion of scientific inquiry within the processes of production and distribution. We find in the public prints as many demonstrations of the benefits of science from a business point of view as there are proofs of its harmony with religion.

It is not possible that, under such conditions, the subordination of scientific techniques to purposes and institutions that flourished before its rise can indefinitely continue. In all affairs there comes a time when a cycle of growth reaches maturity. When this stage is reached, the period of protective nursing comes to an end. The problem of securing proper use succeeds to that of securing conditions of growth. Now that science has established itself and has created a new social environment, it has (if I may for the moment personify it) to face the issue of its social responsibilities. Speaking without personification, we who have a powerful and perfected instrument in our hands, one which is determining the quality of social changes, must ask what changes we want to see achieved and what we want to see averted. We must, in short, plan its social effects with the same care with which in the past we have planned its physical operation and consequences. Till now we have employed science absent-mindedly as far as its effects upon human beings are concerned. The present situation with its extraordinary control of natural energies and its totally unplanned and haphazard social economy is a dire demonstration of the folly of continuing this course.

The social effects of the application of science have been accidental, even though they are intrinsic to the private and unorganized motives which we have permitted to control that application. It would be hard to find a better proof that such is the fact than the vogue of the theory that such unregulated use of science is in accord with "natural law," and that all effort at planned control of its social effects is an interference with nature. The use which has been made of a peculiar idea of personal liberty to justify the dominion of accident in social affairs is another convincing proof. The doctrine that the most potent instrument of widespread, enduring, and objective social changes must be left at the mercy of purely private desires for purely personal gain is a doctrine of anarchy. Our present insecurity of life is the fruit of the adoption in practice of this anarchic doctrine.

The technologies of industry have flowed from the intrinsic nature of science. For that is itself essentially a technology of apparatus, materials and numbers. But the pecuniary aims which have decided the social results of the use of these technologies have not flowed from the inherent nature of science. They have been derived from institutions and attendant mental and moral habits which were entrenched before there was any such thing as science and the machine. In consequence, science has operated as a means for extending the influence of the institution of private property and connected legal relations far beyond their former limits. It has operated as a device to carry an enormous load of stocks and bonds and to make the reward of investment in the way of profit and power one out of all proportion to that accruing from actual work and service.

Here lies the heart of our present social problem. Science has hardly been used to modify men's fundamental acts and attitudes in social matters. It has been used to extend enormously the scope and power of interests and values which anteceded its rise. Here is the contradiction in our civilization. The potentiality of science as the most powerful instrument of control which has ever existed puts to mankind its one outstanding present challenge.

There is one field in which science has been somewhat systematically employed as an agent of social control. Condorcet, writing during the French Revolution in the prison from which he went to the guillotine, hailed the invention of the calculus of probabilities as the opening of a new era. He saw in this new mathematical technique the promise of methods of insurance which should distribute evenly and widely the impact of the disasters to which humanity is subject. Insurance against death, fire, hurricanes and so on have in a measure confirmed his prediction. Nevertheless, in large and important social areas, we have only made the merest beginning of the method of insurance against the hazards of life and death. Insurance against the risks of maternity, of sickness, old age, unemployment, is still rudimentary; its idea is fought by all reactionary forces. Witness the obstacles against which social insurance with respect to accidents incurred in industrial employment had to contend. The anarchy called natural law and personal liberty still operates with success against a planned social use of the resources of scientific knowledge.

Yet insurance against perils and hazards is the place where the application of science has gone the furthest, not the least, distance in present society. The fact that motor cars kill and maim more persons yearly than all factories, shops, and farms is a fair symbol of how backward we are in that province where we have done most. Here, however, is one field in which at least the idea of planned use of scientific knowledge for social welfare has received recognition. We no longer regard plagues, famine and disease as visitations of necessary "natural law" or of a power beyond nature. By preventive means of medicine and public hygiene as well as by various remedial measures we have in idea, if not in fact, placed technique in the stead of magic and chance and uncontrollable necessity in this one area of life. And yet, as I have said, here is where the socially planned use of science has made the most, not least, progress. Were it not for the youth of science and the historically demonstrated slowness of all basic mental and moral change, we could hardly find language to express astonishment at the situation in which we have an extensive and precise control of physical energies and conditions, and in which we leave the social consequences of their operation to chance, laissez-faire, privileged pecuniary status, and the inertia of tradition and old institutions.

Condorcet thought and worked in the Baconian strain. But the Baconian ideal of the systematic organization of all knowledge, the planned control of discovery and invention, for the relief and advancement of the human estate, remains almost as purely an ideal as when Francis Bacon put it forward centuries ago. And this is true in spite of the fact that the physical and mathematical technique upon which a planned control of social results depends has made in the meantime incalculable progress. The conclusion is inevitable. The outer arena of life has been transformed by science. The effectively working mind and character of man have hardly been touched.

Consider that phase of social action where science might theoretically be supposed to have taken effect most rapidly, namely, education. In dealing with the young, it would seem as if scientific methods might at once take effect in transformation of mental attitudes, without meeting the obstacles which have to be overcome in dealing with adults. In higher education, in universities and technical schools, a great amount of research is done and much scientific knowledge is imparted. But it is a principle of modern psychology that the basic attitudes of mind are formed in the earlier years. And I venture the assertion that for the most part the formation of intellectual habits in elementary education, in the home and school, is hardly affected by scientific method. Even in our so-called progressive schools, science is usually treated as a side line, an ornamental extra, not as the chief means of developing the right mental attitudes. It is treated generally as one more body of ready-made information to be acquired by traditional methods, or else as an occasional diversion. That it is the method of all effective mental approach and attack in all subjects has not gained even a foothold. Yet if scientific method is not something esoteric but is a realization of the most effective operation of intelligence, it should be axiomatic that the development of scientific attitudes of thought, observation, and inquiry is the chief business of study and learning.

Two phases of the contradiction inhering in our civilization may be especially mentioned. We have long been committed in theory and words to the principle of democracy. But criticism of democracy, assertions that it is failing to work and even to exist are everywhere rife. In the last few months we have become accustomed to similar assertions regarding our economic and industrial system. Mr. Ivy Lee for example, in a recent commencement address, entitled *This Hour of Bewilderment*, quoted from a representative clergyman, a railway president, and a publicist, to the effect that our capitalistic system is on trial. And yet the statements had to do with only one feature of that system: the prevalence of unemployment and attendant insecurity. It is not necessary for me to invade the territory of economics and politics. The essential fact is that if both democracy and capitalism are on trial, it is in reality our collective intelligence which is on trial. We have displayed enough intelligence in the physical field to create the new and powerful instrument of science and technology. We have not as yet had enough intelligence to use this instrument deliberately and systematically to control its social operations and consequences.

The first lesson which the use of scientific method teaches is that control is coördinate with knowledge and understanding. Where there is technique there is the possibility of administering forces and conditions in the region where the technique applies. Our lack of control in the sphere of human relations, national, domestic, international, requires no emphasis of notice. It is proof that we have not begun to operate scientifically in such matters. The public press is full of discussion of the five-year plan and the ten-year plan in Russia. But the fact that the plan is being tried by a country which has a dictatorship foreign to all our beliefs tends to divert attention from the fundamental consideration. The point for us is not this political setting nor its communistic context. It is that by the use of all available resources of knowledge and experts an attempt is being made at organized social planning and control. Were we to forget for the moment the special Russian political setting, we should see here an effort to use coördinated knowledge and technical skill to direct economic resources toward social order and stability.

To hold that such organized planning is possible only in a communistic society is to surrender the case to communism. Upon any other basis, the effort of Russia is a challenge and a warning to those who live under another political and economic regime. It is a call to use our more advanced knowledge and technology in scientific thinking about our own needs, problems, evils, and possibilities so as to achieve some degree of control of the social consequences which the application of science is, willy-nilly, bringing about. What stands in the way is a lot of outworn traditions, moth-eaten slogans and catchwords, that do substitute duty for thought, as well as our entrenched predatory self-interest. We shall only make a real beginning in intelligent thought when we cease mouthing platitudes; stop confining our ideas to antitheses of individualism and socialism, capitalism and communism, and realize that the issue is between chaos and order, chance and control: the haphazard use and the planned use of scientific techniques.

Thus the statement with which we began, namely, that we are living in a world of change extraordinary in range and speed, is only half true. It holds of the outward applications of science. It does not hold of our intellectual and moral attitudes. About physical conditions and energies we think scientifically; at least, some men do, and the results of their thinking enter into the experiences of all of us. But the entrenched and stubborn institutions of the past stand in the way of our thinking scientifically about human relations and social issues. Our mental habits in these respects are dominated by institutions of family, state, church, and business that were formed long before men had an effective technique of inquiry and validation. It is this contradiction from which we suffer today.

Disaster follows in its wake. It is impossible to overstate the mental confusion and the practical disorder which are bound to result when external and physical effects are planned and regulated, while the attitudes of mind upon which the direction of external results depends are left to the medley of chance, tradition, and dogma. It is a common saying that our physical science has far outrun our social knowledge; that our physical skill has become exact and comprehensive while our humane arts are vague, opinionated, and narrow. The fundamental trouble, however, is not lack of sufficient information about social facts, but unwillingness to adopt the scientific attitude in what we do know. Men floundered in a morass of opinion about physical matters for thousands of years. It was when they began to use their ideas experimentally and to create a technique or direction of experimentation that physical science advanced with system and surety. No amount of mere fact-finding develops science nor the scientific attitude in either physics or social affairs. Facts merely amassed and piled up are dead; a burden which only adds to confusion. When ideas, hypotheses, begin to play upon facts, when they are methods for experimental use in action, then light dawns; then it becomes possible to discriminate significant from trivial facts, and relations take the place of isolated scraps. Just as soon as we begin to use the knowledge and skills we have to control social consequences in the interest of shared abundant and secured life, we shall cease to complain of the backwardness of social knowledge. We shall take the road which leads to the assured building up of social science just as men built up physical science when they actively used the techniques of tools and numbers in physical experimentation.

In spite, then, of all the record of the past, the great scientific revolution is still to come. It will ensue when men collectively and coöperatively organize their knowledge for application to achieve and make secure social values; when they systematically use scientific procedures for the control of human relationships and the direction of the social effects of our vast technological machinery. Great as have been the social changes of the last century, they are not to be compared with those which will emerge when our faith in scientific method is made manifest in social works. We are living in a period of depression. The intellectual function of trouble is to lead men to think. The depression is a small price to pay if it induces us to think about the cause of the disorder, confusion, and insecurity which are the outstanding traits of our social life. If we do not go back to their cause, namely our half-way and accidental use of science, mankind will pass through depressions, for they are the graphic record of our unplanned social life. The story of the achievement of science in physical control is evidence of the possibility of control in social affairs. It is our human intelligence and human courage which are on trial; it is incredible that men who have brought the technique of physical discovery, invention, and use to such a pitch of perfection will abdicate in the face of the infinitely more important human problem.

5. Creative Democracy—The Task Before Us [5]

UNDER PRESENT circumstances I cannot hope to conceal the fact that I have managed to exist eighty years. Mention of the fact may suggest to you a more important fact—namely, that events of the utmost significance for the destiny of this country have taken place during the past four-fifths of a century, a period that covers more than half of its national life in its present form. For obvious reasons I shall not attempt a summary of even the more important of these events. I refer here to them because of their bearing upon the issue to which this country committed itself when the nation took shape—the creation of democracy, an issue which is now as urgent as it was a hundred and fifty years ago when the most experienced and wisest men of the country

[5] A paper read at a meeting in honor of his eightieth birthday in 1939 and published in the volume, The Philosopher of the Common Man: Essays in Honor of John Dewey to celebrate his Eightieth Birthday (New York, 1940). Reprinted by permission of the publishers, G. P. Putnam's Sons.

gathered to take stock of conditions and to create the political structure of a self-governing society.

For the net import of the changes that have taken place in these later years is that ways of life and institutions which were once the natural, almost the inevitable, products of fortunate conditions have now to be won by conscious and resolute effort. Not all the country was in a pioneer state eighty years ago. But it was still, save perhaps in a few large cities, so close to the pioneer stage of American life that the traditions of the pioneer, indeed of the frontier, were active agencies in forming the thoughts and shaping the beliefs of those who were born into its life. In imagination at least the country was still having an open frontier, one of unused and unappropriated resources. It was a country of physical opportunity and invitation. Even so, there was more than a marvelous conjunction of physical circumstances involved in bringing to birth this new nation. There was in existence a group of men who were capable of readapting older institutions and ideas to meet the situations provided by new physical conditions—a group of men extraordinarily gifted in political inventiveness.

At the present time, the frontier is moral, not physical. The period of free lands that seemed boundless in extent has vanished. Unused resources are now human rather than material. They are found in the waste of grown men and women who are without the chance to work, and in the young men and young women who find doors closed where there was once opportunity. The crisis that one hundred and fifty years ago called out social and political inventiveness is with us in a form which puts a heavier demand on human creativeness.

At all events this is what I mean when I say that we now have to re-create by deliberate and determined endeavor the kind of democracy which in its origin one hundred and fifty years ago was largely the product of a fortunate combination of men and circumstances. We have lived for a long time upon the heritage that came to us from the happy conjunction of men and events in an earlier day. The present state of the world is more than a reminder that we have now to put forth every energy of our own to prove worthy of our heritage. It is a challenge to do for the critical and complex conditions of today what the men of an earlier day did for simpler conditions.

If I emphasize that the task can be accomplished only by inventive effort and creative activity, it is in part because the depth of the present crisis is due in considerable part to the fact that for a long period we acted as if our democracy were something that perpetuated itself automatically; as if our ancestors had succeeded in setting up a machine that solved the problem of perpetual motion in politics. We acted as if democracy were something that took place mainly at Washington and Albany—or some other state capital—under the impetus of what happened when men and women went to the polls once a year or so—which is a somewhat extreme way of saying that we have had the habit of thinking of democracy as a kind of political mechanism that will work as long as citizens are reasonably faithful in performing political duties.

Of late years we have heard more and more frequently that this is not enough; that democracy is a way of life. This saying gets down to hard pan. But I am not sure that something of the externality of the old idea does not cling to the new and better statement. In any case we can escape from this external way of thinking only as we realize in thought and act that democracy is a *personal* way of individual life; that it signifies the possession and continual use of certain attitudes, forming personal character and determining desire and purpose in all the relations of life. Instead of thinking of our own dispositions and habits as accommodated to certain institutions we have to learn to think of the latter as expressions, projections, and extensions of habitually dominant personal attitudes.

Democracy as a personal, an individual, way of life involves nothing fundamentally new. But when applied it puts a new practical meaning in old ideas. Put into effect it signifies that powerful present enemies of democracy can be successfully met only by the creation of personal attitudes in individual human beings; that we must get over our tendency to think that its defense can be found in any external means whatever, whether military or civil, if they are separated from individual attitudes so deep-seated as to constitute personal character.

Democracy is a way of life controlled by a working faith in the possibilities of human nature. Belief in the Common Man is a familiar article in the democratic creed. That belief is without basis and significance save as it means faith in the potentialities of human nature as that nature is exhibited in every human being irrespective of race, color, sex, birth, and family, of material or cultural wealth. This faith may be enacted in statutes, but it is only on paper unless it is put in force in the attitudes which human beings display to one another in all the incidents and relations of daily life. To denounce Naziism for intolerance, cruelty and stimulation of hatred amounts to fostering insincerity if, in our personal relations to other persons, if, in our daily walk and conversation, we are moved by racial, color, or other class prejudice; indeed, by anything save a generous belief in their possibilities as human beings, a belief which brings with it the need for providing conditions which will enable these capacities to reach fulfilment. The democratic faith in human equality is belief that every human being, independent of the quantity or range of his personal endowment, has the right to equal opportunity with every other person for development of whatever gifts he has. The democratic belief in the principle of leadership is a generous one. It is universal. It is belief in the capacity of every person to lead his own life free from coercion and imposition by others provided right conditions are supplied.

Democracy is a way of personal life controlled not merely by faith in human nature in general but by faith in the capacity of human beings for intelligent judgment and action if proper conditions are furnished. I have been accused more than once and from opposed quarters of an undue, a utopian, faith in the possibilities of intelligence and in education as a correlate of intelligence. At all events, I did not invent this faith. I acquired it from my surroundings as far as those surroundings were animated by the democratic spirit. For what is the faith of democracy in the rôle of consultation, of conference, of persuasion, of discussion, in formation of public opinion, which in the long run is self-corrective, except faith in the capacity of the intelligence of the common man to respond with common sense to the free play of facts and ideas which are secured by effective guarantees of free inquiry, free assembly, and free communication? I am willing to leave to upholders of totalitarian states of the right and the left the view that faith in the capacities of intelligence is utopian. For the faith is so deeply embedded in the methods which are intrinsic to democracy that when a professed democrat denies the faith he convicts himself of treachery to his profession.

When I think of the conditions under which men and women are living in many foreign countries today, fear of espionage, with danger hanging over the meeting of friends for friendly conversation in private gatherings, I am inclined to believe that the heart and final guarantee of democracy is in free gatherings of neighbors on the street corner to discuss back and forth what is read in uncensored news of the day, and in gatherings of friends in the living rooms of houses and apartments to converse freely with one another. Intolerance, abuse, calling of names because of differences of opinion about religion or politics or business, as well as because of differences of race, color, wealth, or degree of culture, are treason to the democratic way of life. For everything which bars freedom and fullness of communication sets up barriers that divide human beings into sets and cliques, into antagonistic sects and factions, and thereby undermines the democratic way of life. Merely legal guarantees of the civil liberties of free belief, free expression, free assembly are of little avail if in daily life freedom of communication, the give and take of ideas, facts, experiences, is choked by mutual suspicion, by abuse, by fear and hatred. These things destroy the essential condition of the democratic way of living even more effectually than open coercion, which—as the example of totalitarian state proves—is effective only when it succeeds in breeding hate, suspicion, intolerance in the minds of individual human beings.

Finally, given the two conditions just mentioned, democracy as a way of life is controlled by personal faith in personal day-by-day working together with others. Democracy is the belief that even when needs and ends or consequences are different for each individual, the habit of amicable coöperation—which may include, as in sport, rivalry and competition—is itself a priceless addition to life. To take as far as possible every conflict which arises—and they are bound to arise—out of the atmosphere and medium of force, of violence as a means of settlement, into that of discussion and of intelligence, is to treat those who disagree—even profoundly—with us as those from whom we may learn, and in so far, as friends. A genuinely democratic faith in peace is faith in the possibility of conducting disputes, controversies, and conflicts as coöperative undertakings in which both parties learn by giving the other a chance to express itself, instead of having one party conquer by forceful suppression of the other—a suppression which is none the less one of violence when it takes place by psychological means of ridicule, abuse, intimidation, instead of by overt imprisonment or in concentration camps. To coöperate by giving differences a chance to show themselves because of the belief that the expression of difference is not only a right of the other persons but is a means of enriching one's own life-experience, is inherent in the democratic personal way of life.

If what has been said is charged with being a set of moral commonplaces, my only reply is that that is just the point in saying them. For to get rid of the habit of thinking of democracy as something institutional and external and to acquire the habit of treating it as a way of personal life is to realize that democracy is a moral ideal and so far as it becomes a fact is a moral fact. It is to realize that democracy is a reality only as it is indeed a commonplace of living.

Since my adult years have been given to the pursuit of philosophy, I shall ask your indulgence if in concluding I state briefly the democratic faith in the formal terms of a philosophic position. So stated, democracy is belief in the ability of human experience to generate the aims and methods by which further experience will grow in ordered richness. Every other form of moral and social faith rests upon the idea that experience must be subjected at some point or other to some form of external control; to some "authority" alleged to exist outside the processes of experience. Democracy is the faith that the process of experience is more important than any special result attained, so that special results achieved are of ultimate value only as they are used to enrich and order the ongoing process. Since the process of experience is capable of being educative, faith in democracy is all one with faith in experience and education. All ends and values that are cut off from the ongoing process become arrests, fixations. They strive to fixate what has been gained instead of using it to open the road and point the way to new and better experiences.

If one asks what is meant by experience in this connection, my reply is that it is that free interaction of individual human beings with surrounding conditions, especially the human surroundings, which develops and satisfies need and desire by increasing knowledge of things as they are. Knowledge of conditions as they are is the only solid ground for communication and sharing; all other communication means the subjection of some persons to the personal opinion of other persons. Need and desire—out of which grow purpose and direction of energy—go beyond what exists, and hence beyond knowledge, beyond science. They continually open the way into the unexplored and unattained future.

Democracy as compared with other ways of life is the sole way of living which believes wholeheartedly in the process of experience as end and as means; as that which is capable of generating the science which is the sole dependable authority for the direction of further experience and which releases emotions, needs, and desires so as to call into being the things that have not existed in the past. For every way of life that fails in its democracy limits the contacts, the exchanges, the communications, the interactions by which experience is steadied while it is also enlarged and enriched. The task of this release and enrichment is one that has to be carried on day by day. Since it is one that can have no end till experience itself comes to an end, the task of democracy is forever that of creation of a freer and more humane experience in which all share and to which all contribute.

VI

ALFRED NORTH WHITEHEAD

⅍

Introduction

THE LAST THINKER represented in this book is an Englishman. His life in America did not begin until 1924, when he was sixty-three years old; and he always remained a British subject. Thus the editorial correctness of including him is open to doubt. But he did compose most of his philosophy here, and in the opinion of competent judges his is the only philosophical synthesis ever produced in this country that compares with Europe's greatest. Its affinity with the other achievements of our classic period is strong; and its influence, though worldwide, has certainly been greatest here (perhaps least in England). Hence it is best to acquaint the reader with his work.

I

The life of Alfred North Whitehead demonstrates that academic walls do not a prison make. He was born into a family of schoolmasters and clergymen at Ramsgate, a village on the east coast of Kent, in 1861. Before he left home for Sherborne (one of England's oldest schools), he often accompanied his father on visits to the local schools which the father headed. After Sherborne came Trinity College, Cambridge—Isaac Newton's college. Whitehead taught mathematics there for a quarter of a century, then for thirteen years at the University of London. Finally came thirteen more years of teaching, this time as professor of philosophy at Harvard. After his retirement in 1937 he continued to serve his adopted university as a Senior Fellow, and to live in a small apartment near the Harvard Yard. There he died in his eighty-seventh year. It sounds a most unexciting life, so unexciting as to rouse a suspicion that the emphasis on *adventure* in his philosophy must have been a professor's compensatory gesture.

The adventure was real. In 1910 Whitehead, author of A *Treatise on Universal Algebra* (1898) and Fellow of the Royal Society, had finished his statutory term as Lecturer at Trinity. The first two volumes of *Principia Mathematica* by Whitehead and Russell were in the press; the great intellectual adventure of deducing the fundamental concepts and principles of mathematics from a new statement of the basis of formal logic was drawing to a close. Whitehead now abandoned Cambridge for London—without first securing a position there. London was a different world, where he was in the thick of "the problem of higher education in a modern industrial civilization." [1] His interest in this problem drew him into administrative connections with several technical schools as well as into the Faculty of Science (of which he became Dean) at the University of London. When the time for his retirement approached, he moved across the Atlantic to enter a third world. This opportunity was probably the best thing that could have happened to him. A whole generation of his English pupils had been nearly wiped out by the First World War, which also took his own youngest son. At any rate this Victorian Englishman,[2] with an extreme modesty that was ingrained, attributed his philosophic achievements to the new stimulus which America provided.

Of course a philosopher's important adventures are to be found in his works rather than in his biography. As a mathematician, Whitehead had been more interested in making new syntheses than in spinning out additional truths with the intellectual apparatus that he found at hand. He suspected that mathematics was narrowly defined as "the science of number and quantity," and his is one of the great names in the enlargement of the very meaning of mathematics that has occurred in the last hundred years. This was his main concern during two decades beginning in 1891. He next was to write the fourth volume of *Principia Mathematica,* which was to be devoted to geometry. He never completed it. A more interesting and challenging question was, What are the foundations of geometry, considered not as a purely mathematical, but as a physical science? Back in 1905 Whitehead had used the symbolism of *Principia* to restate the Newtonian theory of the relations between space, time and matter, and to propose alternative theories; [3] but his point of view then was purely mathematical or logical; and his work had little effect. A dozen years later the whole Newtonian scheme had broken down, and the big question was what the new philosophy of physics would be. Whitehead thought Einstein's contribution was a brilliant mathematical theory erected upon basic empirical meanings that were narrowly restricted to laboratory operations plus conventions. His own adventure, in the latter half of his stay in London, was the ambitious philosophical one of replacing the

---

[1] *Cf.* his "Autobiographical Notes" (*The Philosophy of Alfred North Whitehead,* ed. P. A. Schilpp, p. 12; or Whitehead, *Essays in Science and Philosophy,* p. 12). A biographical study, recently begun by the present writer, will probably give Mrs. Whitehead a large role in the move to London.

[2] So he sometimes referred to himself: *Essays in Science and Philosophy,* p. 115.

[3] "On Mathematical Concepts of the Material World," *Philos. Transactions, Royal Soc. of London,* series A, CCV, 1906 (reprinted in the Northrop and Gross Whitehead anthology). For an account of this magnificent memoir, see W. Mays, in Ivor Leclerc, ed., *The Relevance of Whitehead* (1961), pp. 235-260; or V. Lowe, *Understanding Whitehead* (1962), Ch. 7, Sect. i-iv.

Newtonian concept of nature with another erected upon the broadest possible empirical foundation.[4]

This was still, from a philosophical point of view, a limited enterprise. As Whitehead said, it was not metaphysics but "pan-physics." [5] But his mind would not stop there for long. Since youth he had been familiar with broad philosophical issues, and throughout his years as a mathematician his conversation, reading and reflection had recognized no professional limits. In the first book that he wrote in America, *Science and the Modern World,* Whitehead showed the theoretical reason for carrying the criticism and replacement of the Newtonian concepts farther. Newton's success had established the reign of what Whitehead called "scientific materialism"—the mechanical philosophy of nature resulting from the work of the great seventeenth-century scientists. (One of Whitehead's expositions of it is given in our Selection, "Nature Lifeless.") Dualism was its immediate result: the material world fitted this scheme of ideas, values were outside it. But as the applications of the scheme increased, scientific materialism became a

---

[4] The work appeared in three books published between 1919 and 1922: *An Enquiry Concerning the Principles of Natural Knowledge, The Concept of Nature,* and *The Principle of Relativity.* The second is the best known and the easiest to read, though the first is the most important. The exact statement of Whitehead's empirical premises is a complex matter. They center round certain universal relations between passing events, which are what we directly perceive: for example, one event is observed to extend over another. (Whitehead adopted the position— later modified in his metaphysics—that the Nature which science studies is just "the terminus of sense-perception," rather than something behind that.) He defined the scientific concepts of space, time and motion by ingenious applications of mathematical logic to such perceived relations, in accordance with the "method of extensive abstraction" which he invented. Also involved is the general relation between percipient events and perceived events. Whitehead ran afoul of philosophical idealists by insisting on tackling this without appealing to the *mental* character of the percipient event. Naturally he was welcomed by the anti-idealist camp of new realists, to whom he was sympathetic; and commentators on twentieth century philosophy began to misrepresent Whitehead as merely one of this group. Others turned him into a philosopher of the flux whom Bergson had inspired to reform physics.

Whitehead's elaboration of new foundations for physics was not an affair of philosophy and mathematical logic only. On his non-Einsteinian basis, he worked out a special and (in *The Principle of Relativity*) a general theory of relativity. His formulae generally agreed with Einstein's except for minute quantities not then, and probably not now, observable. Whitehead's theory had certain advantages and certain disadvantages. One main reason why physicists preferred Einstein's is that Whitehead's procedure contradicted the rising doctrine of operationism by defining spatio-temporal relations and entities without referring to measurement. See Ch. IV of Whitehead's *Enquiry* or Part IV, Ch. V, §IV of his *Process and Reality.*

[5] *The Principle of Relativity,* 3-6; *cf. The Concept of Nature,* 4 f., 28 f., 32, 48. It is a mistake to think that this pan-physics contains "Whitehead's philosophy of science," or of space, time, or causality; his later books must be taken into account. Unfortunately specialists lost much of their interest in Whitehead when his later books appeared, because of their metaphysical nature and concern with religion.

dominant force affecting morals, politics, poetry, the entire civilization of the occident. Whitehead sketched its career as the exciting story of an idea that mankind had got hold of and "could neither live with nor live without." [6] Idealistic philosophers did not dethrone it; like the orthodox theologians, they assumed that this was the final scientific truth about nature, and then strove to mitigate it by arguing that nature presupposed something beyond nature. That did not hinder materialism, backed by the power and prestige of science, from controlling human affairs; while philosophy, like religion, became merely consoling. In the twentieth century, however, scientific materialism broke up from the inside:—"What is the use of talking about a mechanical explanation when you do not know what you mean by mechanics?" wrote Whitehead. "The only way of mitigating mechanism is by the discovery that it is not mechanism." The discovery appeared imminent. Could not the dualism be overcome at last by some new conception of "the nature of things," which would express the aesthetic and purposive character of immediate experience at the same time that it provided a more adequate frame of reference, basically neither mechanistic nor materialistic, for natural science?

In the mid-twenties there was a fair expectation among educated, thoughtful Americans that this could be accomplished by a philosophical scientist of sufficient genius. So when Whitehead in *Science and the Modern World* combined his historical criticism of the Newtonian world-view with a sketch of such a new conception, the book was immediately hailed. But the full statement which appeared four years later in *Process and Reality: An Essay in Cosmology*, was too intricate and many-faceted for popularity. Furthermore, the doctrine became increasingly prevalent that the gap between matter and value can be bridged without cosmology by fearlessly applying the scientist's experimental *method* of thinking to questions of value. Compared with John Dewey's influence, Whitehead's has been small.

In the preface to *Process and Reality* there is a passage which shows the method and temper of Whitehead's great enterprise.

In putting out these results, four strong impressions dominate my mind: First, that the movement of historical, and philosophical, criticism of detached questions, which on the whole has dominated the last two centuries, has done its work, and requires to be supplemented by a more sustained effort of constructive thought. Secondly, that the true method of philosophical construction is to frame a scheme of ideas, the best that one can, and unflinchingly to explore the interpretation of experience in terms of that scheme. Thirdly, that all constructive thought, on the various special topics

[6] Read, in *Science and the Modern World*, especially the third and the famous fifth and thirteenth chapters. The quotations in this paragraph are from pages 72, 23, and 107 of the first edition (The Macmillan Company).

of scientific interest, is dominated by some such scheme, unacknowledged, but no less influential in guiding the imagination. The importance of philosophy lies in its sustained effort to make such schemes explicit, and thereby capable of criticism and improvement.

There remains the final reflection, how shallow, puny, and imperfect are efforts to sound the depths in the nature of things. In philosophical discussion, the merest hint of dogmatic certainty as to finality of statement is an exhibition of folly.

Whitehead called this method that of "speculative philosophy." For reasons which will appear, he named his scheme of ideas "the philosophy of organism."

In 1933 Whitehead published *Adventures of Ideas*—the third and last of his major philosophical works, and for the average reader the most rewarding one. There the new metaphysics was used, and illustrated, in understanding civilization and the history of civilization. The book might be called Whitehead's testament of wisdom.

The philosophy of organism is not only complex and elaborate, but also—for the sake of system, greater precision, and freedom from bondage to orthodox meanings—highly technical. Its presentation by an adequate series of passages from *Process and Reality* is out of the question. We shall therefore supplement the Selections by attempting here an account of the structure of Whitehead's metaphysical system.[7] All but the main concepts will be omitted; these will be presented sympathetically, with some fullness and a little comment, as a bald statement of them would be unintelligible. Whitehead thought of his work as *indicating*, rather than precisely defining, a new conception of reality;[8] we shall make no attempt to reduce such ambiguity. The justification for asking the student to put up with these difficulties, and with being at first quite baffled, is that Whitehead's philosophy

. . . is exciting because of the way he depicts reality; and because he depicts reality, not man alone. In this philosophy, the basic fact is everywhere some process of self-realization, which grows out of previous processes and itself adds a new pulse of individuality and a new value to the world. . . .

But can you construct a system of the world on this basis? The amazing thing is that Whitehead did just that.[9]

II

Though Whitehead's metaphysics—as this quotation implies—is pluralistic, no monist ever insisted more strongly than he that nothing in

---

[7] This account will be easier to follow if the Selection, "Nature Alive," is read first.

[8] See pp. 445–447 of the Selections for his argument that this must be the case, to some extent, in every metaphysical endeavor, and most of all in a new system.

[9] V. Lowe, "The Philosophy of Whitehead," *Antioch Rev.* VIII, 1948, p. 226 (p. 16 in Lowe, *Understanding Whitehead*, Baltimore, 1962).

the world exists in independence of other things. In fact, he repeatedly criticizes traditional monisms for not carrying this principle far enough; they exempted eternal being from dependence on temporal beings. Independent existence is a myth, whether you ascribe it to God or to a particle of matter in Newtonian physics, to persons, to nations, to things, or to meanings. To understand is to see things together, and to see them as, in Whitehead's favorite phrase, "requiring each other." [10]

Each pulse of existence—Whitehead calls them "actual entities"— requires the antecedent others as its constituents, yet achieves individuality as a unique, finite synthesis; and when its growth is completed, stays in the universe as one of the infinite number of settled facts from which the individuals of the future will arise. "The many become one, and are increased by one." The ultimate character pervading the universe is a drive towards the endless production of new syntheses. Whitehead calls this drive "creativity." It is "the underlying energy of process." Nothing escapes it; the universe consists entirely of its creatures, its individualized embodiments.

But creativity is not a thing or an agency external to these actual embodiments. Rather it is "that ultimate notion of the highest generality" which actuality exhibits. Apart from that exhibition it does not exist. Like Aristotle's "matter," creativity has no character of its own, but is perfectly protean:—"It cannot be characterized, because all characters are more special than itself." Nor can its universal presence be explained in terms of anything else; it must be seen by direct, intuitive experience.

The doctrine that all actualities alike are in the grip of creativity suggests a general principle which Whitehead thinks every metaphysical scheme, so far as it is coherent, must follow. The principle is that there is but one kind of actuality.

'Actual entities'—also termed 'actual occasions'—are the final real things of which the world is made up. There is no going behind actual entities to find anything more real. They differ among themselves: God is an actual entity, and so is the most trivial puff of existence in far-off empty space. But, though there are gradations of importance, and diversities of function, yet in the principles which actuality exemplifies all are on the same level.[11]

This statement represents an ideal which Whitehead, so far as the concept of God is concerned, does not entirely achieve. But he is distinguished by his conscious adoption and pursuit of it, in place of the more traditional, dualistic doctrine of inferior and superior realities.

---

[10] See his discussion of the "coherence" of philosophical systems, in §§ I, II of the Selection on "Speculative Philosophy," below.

[11] *Process and Reality*, ₐ27 f. (ₑ24 f.). (The subscripts, here and in future references to this book, refer to the American edition [Macmillan Co., 1929] and the English edition [Cambridge University Press, 1929] respectively.)

Our experience of the universe does not, at first glance, present any obvious prototype of actual entities. Selves, monads, material atoms, and Aristotelian substances have been tried out in the history of philosophy. Whitehead develops a theory of a different entity—an *experience*. The doctrine that experience comes in drops or pulses, each of which has a unique character and an indivisible unity, is to be found in the writings of William James; but James never outlined a metaphysics on this basis. In any case, Whitehead had motives of his own for adopting the working hypothesis that "all final individual actualities have the metaphysical character of occasions of experience."

There was the anti-dualistic motive: belief that some such actualities are without any experience of their own, when joined to the fact that the human existence with which philosophic thought must begin is just a series of experiences, makes it impossible to think of these extremes as contrasting but connected instances of one basic kind of actuality. But on Whitehead's hypothesis, "the direct evidence as to the connectedness of one's immediate present occasion of experience with one's immediately past occasions, can be validly used to suggest categories applying to the connectedness of all occasions in nature." [12]

Secondly, we instinctively feel that we live in a world of "throbbing actualities"; and such "direct persuasions" are the ultimate touchstones of philosophic theory.

Thirdly, Whitehead does not wish to think that intrinsic value is an exclusive property of superior beings; rather it belongs to even "the most trivial puff of existence." In human life, he finds value not far off, but at hand as the living essence of present experience. If every puff of existence is a pulse of some kind of immediate experience, there can be no final dualism of value and fact in the universe.

A fourth reason why Whitehead chose occasions of experience for his "actual entities" emerges as a reader becomes familiar with his thought. It is his love of concrete immediacy. An immediate experience, in its living occurrence at this moment—that, to this rationalist's way of thinking, is a full fact, in comparison with which all other things are pale abstractions. It is a mistake for philosophers to begin with substances which appear solid and obvious to them, like the material body or the soul, and then, almost as if it were an afterthought, bring in transient experiences to provide these with an adventitious historical filling. The transient experiences *are* the ultimate realities.

But experience is not restricted to consciousness. "We experience the universe, and we analyze in our consciousness a minute selection of its details." Like most psychologists today, Whitehead thinks of consciousness as a variable factor which heightens an organism's discrimination

[12] *Adventures of Ideas* (New York, The Macmillan Co., 1933, and Cambridge, Cambridge Univ. Press, 1933), p. 284.

of some part of its world. Consciousness is no basic category for him, because it is so far from being essential to every drop of experience in the cosmos, that it is not even found in every human experience. The same remark applies—the tradition of modern philosophy to the contrary notwithstanding—to thought and sense-perception.

The chief meaning intended by calling every actual entity a pulse of *experience* is that the entity has an immediate existence in and for itself. "Experience" is "the self-enjoyment of being one among many, and of being one arising out of the composition of many." Each appropriation of an item of the many into the arising unity of enjoyment is a "feeling" or "prehension" (literally, a grasping) of that item, and the process of composition is a "concrescence" (growing together) of prehensions. Pages 427-428 and 431-435 of the Selections give the general idea intended by these concepts. We turn to the theory of them.

The appropriated "many" are "objects," existing before the process begins; the "one" is the privately experiencing "subject." Thus "the subject-object relation is the fundamental structural pattern of experience." This does not mean that Whitehead defends what William James, in his essay, "Does Consciousness Exist?", led so many twentieth century philosophers to reject. Whitehead indeed thinks it obvious that experience is a relation between private centers of experience and public objects experienced. But there are three big differences between his theory of this relation and the views which James attacked.

(1) In the earlier views this was a cognitive relation of a conscious mind to objects known. Whitehead's fundamental relation of prehension is something broader and more elemental, the generally unconscious emotional feeling by which one bit of life responds to other realities. An essential factor in every prehension is its "subjective form" —the affective tone with which that subject now experiences that object. An example is the unconscious annoyance with which you experienced this page when you turned to it and saw another solid mass of print. Everything in your environment contributes something both to the tone of your experience and to its content.

(2) A prehension is not so much a relation as a relating, or transition, which carries the object into the make-up of the subject.[13] Whitehead's "feelings" are not states, but " 'vectors'; for they feel what is *there* and transform it into what is *here*." [14] He was writing a theoretical transcript of the fact that you feel this moment of experience to be your very own, yet derived from a world without. By taking that elemental assurance at its face value, he was able to accept a primary

[13] Thus there is some analogy between "prehension" and the "felt transition" of which James wrote. See pp. 160 f. above.

[14] *Process and Reality*, ₂133 (₀121). Vectors, in physical theory, are quantities which have direction as well as magnitude: *e.g.*, forces or velocities.

rule of modern philosophy—that the evidence for an external world can be found only within occasions of experience—without being drawn into solipsism.

Prehensions, like vectors, should be symbolized by arrows. The arrows run from the past [15] to the present—for the "there" is antecedent, however slightly, in time as well as external in space to the "here"— and *from* objects *to* a subject. The method is realistic, not idealistic: Whitehead remarks that instead of describing, in Kantian fashion, how subjective data pass into the appearance of an objective world, he describes how subjective experience emerges from an objective world.

(3) For Whitehead the subject which enjoys an experience does not exist beforehand, neither is it created from the outside; it creates itself in that very process of experiencing. The process starts with the multitude of environmental objects awaiting unification in a fresh perspective, moves through stages of partial integration, and concludes as a fully determinate synthesis, effected by a concrescence of feelings. "The point to be noticed is that the actual entity, in a state of process during which it is not fully definite, determines its own ultimate definiteness. This is the whole point of moral responsibility."[16] It is also the point of the descriptive term, "organism," which Whitehead applies to actual entities, and which supplies the very name of his philosophy. He means that an organism determines the eventual character and integration of its own parts. Its growth is motivated by a living—if generally unconscious—aim at that outcome. So the brief course of each pulse of experience is guided by an internal teleology.

Many philosophers consider Whitehead's doctrine of a self-creating experiencer unintelligible. It certainly contradicts the mode of thought to which we are accustomed—*first* a permanent subject, *then* an experience for it. But how did the subject originally come into being? Whitehead looks upon process as not only the appearance of new patterns among things, but the becoming of new subjects, which are completely individual, self-contained units of feeling. "The ancient doctrine that 'no one crosses the same river twice' is extended. No thinker thinks twice; and, to put the matter more generally, no subject experiences twice." "The universe is thus a creative advance into novelty. The alternative to this doctrine is a static morphological universe." [17]

---

[15] Except—see p. 405 below—in the case of "conceptual prehension."

[16] *Process and Reality*, ₄390 (₆361). The following partial analogy may be of help:—"A pulse of existence does, in miniature, what a human being normally accomplishes in the course of his life: the world gives him his material, his many alternative potentialities, and of these he fashions *his* personality, which embodies the perspective and the feeling with which he now takes in the world. So does each pulse of experience unwittingly create its own final unity, complete its own perspective of the world."—V. Lowe, *Understanding Whitehead* (1962), p. 20.

[17] *Process and Reality*, ₄43 (₆40); ₄340 (₆314).

Whitehead pictures reality as cumulative. When, upon the completion of an actual occasion, the creativity of the universe moves on to the next birth, it carries that occasion with it as an "object" which all future occasions are obliged to prehend. They will feel it as an efficient cause—as the immanence of the past in their immediacies of becoming. The end of an occasion's private life—its "perishing"—is the beginning of its public career.

If you get a general notion of what is meant by perishing, you will have accomplished an apprehension of what you mean by memory and causality, what you mean when you feel that what we are is of infinite importance, because as we perish we are immortal.[18]

Part of the appeal of Whitehead's metaphysics lies in this, that through his conception of pulses of experience as the ultimate facts, he invests the passage of time with life and motion, with pathos, and with a majesty rivalled in no other philosophy of change, and in few eternalistic ones.

Our experience does not usually discriminate a single actual entity as its object, but rather a whole nexus of them united by their prehensions. That is how you experience your body or your past personal history. "The ultimate facts of immediate actual experience," then, "are actual entities, prehensions, and nexūs.[19] All else is, for our experience, derivative abstraction." In Whitehead's cosmology, however, some types of derivative abstractions are constituents in every actual entity. Propositions are such; in every experience, conscious or unconscious, they function as "lures proposed for feeling." (Whitehead cites "There is beef for dinner today" as an example of a "quite ordinary proposition.") Because human beings think it important to consciously judge some propositions true or false, all propositions have traditionally been treated as units of thought or discourse, and supposed to be the concern of logicians alone. But we have no space for Whitehead's highly original theory of propositions as factors in natural processes, or for the theory of the meaning of truth which issues from it.

We shall confine attention to a simpler and more important type of abstract entity. The entertainment of propositions is but one of the ways in which "eternal objects" are ingredients in experience. A Platonic strain, of which Whitehead was thoroughly aware, is native to his thought; these eternal objects, uncreated and undated, are his version of Plato's timeless ideal "forms." They are patterns and qualities like roundness or squareness, greenness or redness, courage or cowardice. The fact that every actual occasion in its process of becoming acquires a definite character to the exclusion of other possible charac-

---

[18] *Essays in Science and Philosophy,* p. 117.
[19] Plural of "nexus." The quotation is from *Process and Reality,* ₐ30 (ₐ26).

ters is explained as its selection of *these* eternal objects for feeling and its rejection ("negative prehension") of *those*.[20]

For Whitehead as for Aristotle, process is the realizing of selected antecedent potentialities, or it is unexplainable. "Pure potentials for the specific determination of fact"—that is what eternal objects are. And that is all they are. The ideal is nothing more than a *possibility* (good *or* bad) *for* the actual. Whitehead so emphatically repudiates the Platonic tendency to think of the realm of forms as constituting a superior, self-sufficient type of existence, that he interprets even the propositions of mathematics as statements about certain possible forms *of process*.

As an anti-dualist, Whitehead rejects the doctrine that mind and body are distinct, disparate entities. He generalizes the mind-body problem, and suggests that a certain contrast between two modes of activity exists within every actual occasion. An occasion is a pulse of experience, so of course its "physical pole" cannot consist of matter, in the sense of a permanent unfeeling substance; and consciousness is too slight and occasional to define the "mental pole." [21] The physical activity of each occasion is rather its absorption of the actual occasions of the past, its direct *rapport* with the environment from which it sprang; and its mental side is its own creativeness, its desire for and realization of ideal forms (including its own terminal pattern) by means of which it makes a novel, unified reaction to its inheritance. (So there are two species of prehensions in Whitehead's system: "physical prehensions" of actual occasions and "conceptual prehensions" of eternal objects.) Each occasion is a fusion of the already actual and the ideal.

The subjective forms of conceptual prehensions are "valuations," up or down; this or that possibility is felt to be important or trivial or irrelevant, or not wanted. We see again how, in trying to make theory correspond to the character of immediate experience, Whitehead insists that emotional feeling, not pure cognition of a neutral datum, is basic. Except for mathematical patterns, the data are not neutral either: red is a possibility of warmth, blue of coolness.

An eternal object, as a form of definiteness, may be realized in one actual occasion after another, through each prehending that form in its predecessor. A nexus composed of one, or simultaneously of many, such strands, Whitehead aptly calls a "society of occasions," which has that eternal object for its "defining characteristic." Such a process of inheri-

---

[20] This is not as fantastic as it sounds; actualities inherit habits of selection, and these habits are so strong that scientists call them laws of nature.

[21] These terms are prominent in *Process and Reality*. Whitehead privately regretted that he had used them; too many readers thought they referred to substantially separate parts of each actual occasion.

tance seems to be the essence of every human "society," in the usual meaning of the word. But the general principle has a much wider application; through it, a metaphysics of drops of experience can define personal identity, and a philosophy of process can account for *things* —for frogs and mountains, electrons and planets—which are certainly neither becomings nor forms. They are societies of becomings. Thus personal minds and material bodies finally appear in the philosophy of organism, but as variable complexes rather than metaphysical absolutes.

Though Whitehead's philosophy is very much a philosophy of change, we must notice that according to it the ultimate members of the universe do not, strictly speaking, change—i.e., alter some of their properties while retaining their identities. Because it is a process of self-realization, an actual occasion can only become itself, and then "perish." Whatever changes is a serial "society" of such occasions, and its persistence during the change is not due to any underlying *substance*—Whitehead eliminates that notion—but to retention of one *form* (the defining characteristic) while others vary.

The differences between the kinds of things in nature then go back to the different contrasts, repetitions, divisions, or modes of integration involved in the chains of prehensions by which actual occasions make up societies with different defining characteristics. Whitehead sketched the main principles involved.[22] His universe exhibits societies arising and decaying, societies within other societies which sustain them (consider the animal body), societies on all scales of magnitude. The *structure* of Nature comes out well—in fact beautifully—in this philosophy of the flux.

The bare statement of Whitehead's theory of actual entities, apart from its elaboration, takes the form in *Process and Reality* of thirty-six principles—twenty-seven "Categories of Explanation" and nine "Categoreal Obligations." Many of his Categories of Explanation have appeared, unnamed, in our exposition. Before we go farther, we must draw attention to three others. The nature of the Categoreal Obligations will be explained later.

The principle that "no two actual entities originate from an identical universe" is one that we should expect in a philosophy of process. An actual occasion's "universe"—also called its "actual world"—is the nexus of all those occasions which have already become and are available for feeling.[23] This nexus is *its* past, and is not quite the same as the past of any other occasion. The part that is the same for both, each

---

[22] It is not only readers interested in natural science who should find the chapter in *Process and Reality* on "The Order of Nature" fascinating.

[23] Contemporary occasions are precisely those, neither of which can feel the other as a cause.

will absorb into its unique perspective from its unique standpoint in the cosmos.

The "principle of relativity" applies the doctrine of the relativity of all things to the very definition of "being." The being of any kind of entity is its potentiality for being an element in a becoming. That means: for being felt in an occasion of experience. So, according to Whitehead's cosmology, "There is nothing in the real world which is merely an inert fact. Every reality is there for feeling: it promotes feeling; and it is felt." [24]

It should now be evident that Whitehead's metaphysical concepts are intended to show the interpenetration of "being," "becoming," and "perishing." Becoming draws on being (or "process" on "reality"); and what becomes, perishes. Becoming is the central notion; for the universe, at every moment, consists solely of becomings. Only actual entities *act*. Hence the "ontological principle":

Every condition to which the process of becoming conforms in any particular instance, has its reason *either* in the character of some actual entity in the actual world of that concrescence, *or* in the character of the subject which is in process of concrescence. . . . This ontological principle means that actual entities are the only *reasons;* so that to search for a *reason* is to search for one or more actual entities. [25]

The effect of this fundamental doctrine is to put all thought into an ontological context. In the last analysis, there is no such thing as a disembodied reason; no principles of order—in logic, science, epistemology, even in ethics or aesthetics—have any reality except what they derive from one or more actualities whose active characters they express.

Then what of the realm of eternal objects in Whitehead's system? By the ontological principle, there must be an eternal actual entity whose active character that realm expresses. Whitehead naturally calls this entity "God"; more exactly, this consideration defines the "primordial" side of God's nature, which is "the unconditioned actuality of conceptual feeling at the base of things." Thus "the universe has a side which is mental and permanent." Whitehead's God is not a creator God, and is "not *before* all creation, but *with* all creation"—i.e., immanent in every concrescence at its very beginning. His ordering of the eternal objects—he does not create them either—bestows a certain character to all eternity on the creativity of the universe. Here is how Whitehead asks us to conceive this character:

[24] *Process and Reality*, ₐ472 (ₑ439). In this consists the reality even of spatio-temporal relations: see p. 413, below. But there is danger of reading too much into the term, "feeling." Its technical definition is "positive prehension"; thus to be "felt" means to be included in an integrative, partly self-creative atom of process, as part of the internal essence of that process.

[25] *Process and Reality*, ₐ36 f. (ₑ33).

Enlarge your view of the final fact which is permanent amid change. . . . This ultimate fact includes in its appetitive vision all possibilities of order, possibilities at once incompatible and unlimited with a fecundity beyond imagination. Finite transience stages this welter of incompatibles in their ordered relevance to the flux of epochs . . . The notion of the one perfection of order, which is (I believe) Plato's doctrine, must go the way of the one possible geometry. The universe is more various, more Hegelian.[26]

Whitehead seems never to have considered atheism as a serious alternative in metaphysics. An atheist would naturally suggest that all the potentialities for any occasion are derived from its historic environment. A "society," in Whitehead's cosmology, is built on this sort of derivation. Why then need the occasion also draw upon a God? The answer is that if the past provided everything for the present, nothing new could appear. Novelty and adventure were too real to Whitehead to permit him to say, like the materialists, that the apparently new is a reconfiguration of the old. Yet his thoroughgoing rationalism did not permit him to say that novelty just happens. His religious humility told him whence it came.

Throughout his philosophy, Whitehead contrasts the compulsion of what is with the persuasive lure of what might be. God's action on the world is primarily persuasive: he offers to each occasion its possibilities of value. The theory that each occasion creates itself by realizing an aim internal to it, however, requires that the germ of this aim be initially established at that spot in the temporal world by God; otherwise the occasion's self-creation could never commence, since nothing can come from nowhere. Whitehead's position is that the initial aim partially defines the goal which is best in the given situation, and that the temporal occasion itself does the rest. God thus functions as the "Principle of Concretion," in that he initiates the move toward a definite outcome from an indeterminate situation.

Whitehead calls actual occasions the "cells" of the universe. As in biology, the "cells" are organic wholes which can be analyzed both genetically and morphologically. These two analyses make up the detailed theory of actual occasions in *Process and Reality.*

The genetic analysis is the analysis of the self-creation of an experiencing "subject." In the first phase of its self-genesis an actual occasion merely receives the antecedent universe of occasions as data for integration. None of these can be absorbed in its entirety, but only so far as is consistent with present prehension of the others. In a continuing chain of occasions the past progressively fades, but, like energy radi-

[26] *Essays in Science and Philosophy,* p. 118. On the meaning of "flux of epochs," see Selections, p. 429.

ated from afar, never disappears. Thus the datum for physical feeling by a new occasion consists of some of the constituent feelings of every occasion in its "actual world." The first phase of the new occasion's life is an unconscious "sympathy" [27] with its ancestors. The occasion then begins to put the stamp of its developing individuality on this material: the intermediate phase is "a ferment of qualitative valuation" effected by conceptual feelings, some of them automatically derived from the physical feelings of the first phase, others introduced because of their contribution toward a novel unification. All these are integrated and reintegrated with each other until at the end of the concrescence we have but one complex, integral feeling—"the 'satisfaction' of the creative urge." This final phase includes the occasion's anticipatory feeling of the future as necessarily embodying this present existence.

The difference between the universe as felt in the first phase and as felt in the last is the difference, for that occasion, between the plural public "reality" which it found and the integral, privately experienced "appearance" into which it transformed that reality. Since the difference is the work of the "mental pole," we may say that Whitehead has generalized the modern doctrine that mentality is a unifying, transforming agency. He also makes it a simplifying agency. By an actual entity with a strong intensity of conceptual feeling, the qualities common to many individual occasions in its immediate environment can be "fused into one dominating impression" which masks the differences between those occasions. That is why a world which is really a multitude of atoms of process appears to us as composed of grosser qualitative objects.

In the language of physics, the simplest "physical feelings" are units of energy transference; or, rather, the physicist's idea that energy is transmitted according to quantum conditions is an abstraction from the concrete facts of the universe, which are individual occasions of experience connected by their "physical feelings." Whitehead's principles governing the integration of physical and conceptual feelings, and the way in which an actual occasion's conceptual feelings are physically felt by that occasion's successors in a "society" (so that appearance merges into reality), constitute an original treatment of the interaction of the physical and the mental, which has been such a problem for modern philosophy. We must leave it to the interested student to look up Whitehead's elucidation of "the higher phases of experience," and, in particular, of consciousness.

[27] As we would say "in the language appropriate to the higher stages of experience" (*Process and Reality*, ₂246, ₂227). But the word fits Whitehead's technical meaning, namely, feeling another's feeling with a similar "subjective form." This is prominently illustrated in the relation between your present drop of experience and that which you enjoyed a second earlier.

Taken as a whole, this theory of the internal course of process is remarkable in three respects. Efficient causation and teleology are nicely linked in Whitehead's cosmology: the former expresses the transition from completed to nascent becomings, while the latter is the urge toward self-completion, and toward a future career, within each becoming. Nevertheless the system is first and foremost a new teleology, for it makes every activity, in its immediate occurrence, purposive. The main postulates of the genetic theory—the "Categoreal Obligations"—are the conditions to which every concrescence must conform if it is to achieve a fully determinate end as a unity of feeling. These conditions are very general and do not specify the content of this unity. Each occasion has its own aim, and that is what renders it an individual in a pluralistic universe.

In this concept of existences as teleological processes, Whitehead thought, we find the proper way for the philosopher to perform his task, now that the basic idea of physics has become the flux of energy rather than the particle of Newtonian matter. It is obvious that "physical science is an abstraction"; but to say this and nothing more would be "a confession of philosophic failure." Whitehead conceives physical energy as "an abstraction from the complex energy, emotional and purposeful, inherent in the subjective form of the final synthesis in which each occasion completes itself." [28]

Second, this teleology is evidently a universal quantum-theory of *growth*. Whitehead, though sympathetic with Bergson's reaction against materialism, was teaching by example that it *is* possible for theoretical concepts to express the inner growth of things. His conception of growth has points of similarity with Hegel's, but differs in having no use for "contradiction," and in presenting a hierarchy of categories of feeling rather than a hierarchy of categories of thought.

Third, the principles of this teleology are, broadly speaking, aesthetic principles. The culmination of each concrescence, being an integrated pattern of feeling, is an aesthetic achievement. "The ultimate creative purpose" is "that each unification shall achieve some maximum depth of intensity of feeling, subject to the conditions of its concrescence." God's immanence in the world provides novel possibilities of contrast to this end. The conditions of synthesis are not the dialectical antagonism of opposites, but aesthetic contrast among ideal forms, and between these forms and the occasion's inheritance. The latter contrast is exhibited at its simplest in the wave-vibration which is so prominent in nature. The superiority of a living over an inanimate nexus of occasions is that it does not refuse so much of the novelty in its environment, but adapts it to itself by a massive imposition of new conceptual

[28] *Adventures of Ideas,* p. 239.

feeling, thus transforming threatened incompatibilities into contrasts. The very notion of "order" in an occasion's environment is relative to the syntheses which that environment permits; adaptability to an end is what makes the difference between order and disorder. (*Regularity* is a secondary meaning of order, definable by reference to "societies.")

The distinctive character of occasions of *human* experience, to which we now turn, is the great difference between "appearance" and "reality." The genetic process is based on feelings of the causal efficacy of the antecedent environment, and more especially of the body; it generates the appearance called "sense-perception." Of sense-data Whitehead says:

Unfortunately the learned tradition of philosophy has missed their main characteristic, which is their enormous emotional significance. The vicious notion has been introduced of mere receptive entertainment, which for no obvious reason by reflection acquires an affective tone. The very opposite is the true explanation. The true doctrine of sense-perception is that the qualitative characters of affective tones inherent in the bodily functionings are transmuted into the characters of [external] regions.

Our developed consciousness fastens on the sensum as datum: our basic animal experience entertains it as a type of subjective feeling. The experience starts as that smelly feeling, and is developed by mentality into the feeling of that smell.[20]

Sense-data, according to this account, are indeed received from the external world, but only in the form of innumerable faint pulses of emotion. The actual occasions in the various organs of the animal body, acting as selective amplifiers, gather these pulses together and get from them sizeable feelings; and these—e.g., the eye's enjoyment of a reddish feeling—are intensified and transmuted by the complex occasions of the brain into definite colors, smells, and other instances of qualitative eternal objects, definitely arranged in a space defined by prolongation of the spatial relations experienced inside the brain. In this process the original physical feelings of causal efficacy are submerged (not eliminated) by an inrush of conceptual feelings, so that the throbbing causal world of the immediate past now appears as a passive display of qualities "presented" to our senses. Whitehead calls this new kind of experience "perception in the mode of presentational immediacy."

The higher animals have learned to interpret these sense-qualities, thus perceived, as symbols of the actualities in the external world— actualities which are themselves perceived only by vague feelings of their causal agency. The epistemology of sense-perception is the theory of this "symbolic reference." The recognition of these two levels of

[29] *Adventures of Ideas,* pp. 276, 315.

perception distinguishes Whitehead's epistemology from other realistic ones.

The practical advantage of sense-perception over causal feeling lies in its superior clarity and definiteness. And of course natural science would be impossible without it. For Whitehead scientific theory refers to causal processes, not, as the positivists think, to correlations of sense-data; but science is accurate for the same reason that it is no substitute for metaphysics—its observations are limited to experience in the mode of presentational immediacy; and science is important because it systematically interprets sense-data as indicators of causal processes.

Presentational immediacy, in addition to its practical value, has the aesthetic value of a vivid qualitative display. Although unconscious feeling is the stuff of nature for Whitehead, his theory of "appearance" is what especially brings home the gloriousness of his philosophy—and that even as this theory emphasizes the fusion of conceptual feeling with physical nature. We cannot go into his discussion of the aesthetics of appearance. This passage will suggest what is meant:

> The lesson of the transmutation of causal efficacy into presentational immediacy is that great ends are reached by life in the present; life novel and immediate, but deriving its richness by its full inheritance from the rightly organized animal body. It is by reason of the body, with its miracle of order, that the treasures of the past environment are poured into the living occasion. The final percipient route of occasions is perhaps some thread of happenings wandering in "empty" space amid the interstices of the brain. It toils not, neither does it spin. It receives from the past; it lives in the present. It is shaken by its intensities of private feeling, adversion or aversion. In its turn, this culmination of bodily life transmits itself as an element of novelty throughout the avenues of the body. Its sole use to the body is its vivid originality: it is the organ of novelty.[30]

The morphological analysis of an actual occasion is the analysis of the occasion as completed, no longer having any process of its own; it is only an "object"—a complex, permanent potentiality for being an ingredient in future becomings. Each concrescence is an indivisible creative act; and so the temporal advance of the universe is not continuous, but discrete. But in retrospect and as a potentiality for the future, the physical side (though not the mental) of each atom of process is infinitely divisible. The theory of this divisibility is the theory of space-time—a subject on which Whitehead was expert, original, and involved.

Space-time, he holds, is not a fact prior to process, but a feature of process, an abstract system of perspectives (feeling is always perspectival). It is no actuality, but a continuum of potentialities—of potential routes for the transmission of physical feeling. (The transmission of

[30] Process and Reality, .515 f. (.480 f.).

purely mental feeling is not bound by it.) "Actuality is incurably atomic"; but potentialities can form a continuum.

Each actual occasion prehends the space-time continuum in its infinite entirety; that, says Whitehead, is nothing but an example of the general principle (also illustrated by prehension of qualitative eternal objects) that "actual fact includes in its own constitution real potentiality which is referent beyond itself." There is a similarity to and a difference from Kant's doctrine of space and time as forms of intuition; each occasion inherits this network of potential relatedness from its past, actualizes a portion of it, and (if it has any substantial experience in the mode of presentational immediacy) redefines the network and projects it upon the contemporary world.

There is one "extensive continuum," and space and time are its two aspects.[31] When we consider the infinity of the universe, it would be rash to ascribe to this continuum more than very general properties of extensiveness and divisibility. The dimensional and metric relationships to which we are accustomed (you and Einstein alike) are only local; they define various finite "societies." [32]

Whitehead does not say what the time-span of an actual occasion is, even in the "cosmic epoch" in which we live. The theory of actual occasions is a *general way* of thinking about the pluralistic process of the universe; it suggests basic concepts, but does not automatically apply them. The "specious present" of human experience and the quantum events of physics are perhaps the best samples of actual occasions now discernible.

The philosophy of organism culminates in a new metaphysical theology.[33]

The most general formulation of the religious problem is the question whether the process of the temporal world passes into the formation of other actualities, bound together in an order in which novelty does not mean loss

—as it does in the temporal world. Whitehead thought anything like proof was impossible here; [34] with great diffidence he sketched the sort of other "order" which his metaphysics suggests, and in which he deeply believed.

[31] We ordinarily think of space and time in terms of points and instants; but these surely are abstractions; actual occasions occupy regions. So Whitehead in *Process and Reality* (Part IV, Chaps. II and III) defined these ideal elements in terms derived from a general relation of "extensive connection" among regions.

[32] Further on this point, see Selections, p. 429.

[33] *Process and Reality*, Part V. This short Part, though often technical, is a fine expression of wisdom and of religious feeling. The quotation which follows is from ₐ517 (₀481 f.).

[34] *Cf.* Selections, p. 469.

Evidently the question is one of permanence; but it is not merely that, for permanence without freshness is deadening. And to oppose a permanent Reality to transient realities is to brand the latter as inexplicable illusions. The problem is the double one of conceiving "actuality with permanence, requiring fluency as its completion; and actuality with fluency, requiring permanence as its completion." Whitehead's solution is his doctrine of "the consequent nature of God." God's primordial nature is but one half of his being—the permanent side, which embraces the infinity of eternal forms and seeks fluency. The temporal world is a pluralistic world of activities, creatively arising, then fading away. But "by reason of the relativity of all things," every new actual occasion in that world reacts on God—is felt by him. The content of a temporal occasion is its antecedent world synthesized and somewhat transformed by a new mode of feeling; the consequent nature of God consists of the temporal occasions transformed by an inclusive mode of feeling derived from his all-embracing primordial nature, so as to be united in a conscious, infinitely wide harmony of feeling which grows without any fading of its members. It is a creative advance devoid of "perishing."

The theme of Cosmology, which is the basis of all religions, is the story of the dynamic effort of the World passing into everlasting unity, and of the static majesty of God's vision, accomplishing its purpose of completion by absorption of the World's multiplicity of effort.[35]

It is important to note the interdependence of God and the world, and the final emphasis on creativity:

Neither God, nor the World, reaches static completion. Both are in the grip of the ultimate metaphysical ground, the creative advance into novelty. Either of them, God and the World, is the instrument of novelty for the other.

The story requires a final chapter:

... the principle of universal relativity [or interdependence] is not to be stopped at the consequent nature of God. ... For the perfected actuality passes back into the temporal world ["according to its gradation of relevance

[35] *Process and Reality*, .529 f. (.494). The next quotation is from the same page. Whitehead thought his conception of the consequent nature of God was close to F. H. Bradley's conception of Reality. Referring to God's primordial nature as "the lure for feeling, the eternal urge of desire" (*Process and Reality*, .522 f. [.487]), Whitehead noticed a similarity there to Aristotle's conception of the "prime mover."

The "Eros" spoken of in the close of the selection on "Peace" (p. 470, below) is the primordial nature of God, the "Unity of Appearance" is his consequent nature, and the "Supreme Adventure" is the union of the two. The interaction of God and the World was also the subject of the last philosophical paper Whitehead wrote, "Immortality." The student will find it in *Essays in Science and Philosophy* or in Schilpp, *The Philosophy of Alfred North Whitehead*.

to the various concrescent occasions"], and qualifies this world so that each temporal actuality includes it as an immediate fact of relevant experience.[36]

Whitehead has evidently been concerned to embody the finer intuitions of religion in his cosmology. From these he emphatically excludes the notion of omnipotence. God in his primordial nature is rather "the divine persuasion, by reason of which ideals are effective and forms of order evolve." [37] His consequent nature perfects and saves the world. And its passing into the world is God's love, whereby "the kingdom of heaven is with us today."

Any doctrine of an omnipotent God would also undermine the assertion of freedom and novelty in the temporal world. And it would be contrary to Whitehead's basic metaphysical orientation, which is directed toward showing how God and the World, and the poles of every other perennial antithesis, can be reconceived so as to require each other. With regard to modern philosophy, Whitehead intended his fundamental concepts to be so inclusive in scope, and so interlocked, as to overcome all its traditional dualisms. Subject and object, unity and plurality, teleology and causality, the mental and the physical, immanence and transcendence, value and matter-of-fact—these are united in every "actual entity." And the separation of man from nature is replaced by a magnificent theory of that immediate union with nature to which, Whitehead was convinced, man's experience directly testifies.

III

Whitehead's metaphysics was probably molded quite as much by his convictions about social life and the history of civilization as by his interpretation of the contrast between Newtonian and recent physics. Thus his doctrine that every actual entity incorporates its past but makes a spontaneous, novel reaction to it, reflects his perception of two ubiquitous factors in social life—the trend toward a continuation of the past, and the impulse to deviate therefrom. Whitehead's feeling for history is illustrated in his tacit assumption that perennial ideas of high generality always embody important truths. When he asserts that, though process is universal, yet "The essence of the universe is more than process," he explains that "The alternative metaphysical doctrine, of reality devoid of process, would never have held the belief of great men, unless it expressed some fundamental aspect of our experience." [38] Whitehead's philosophy, for all the novelty of its outcome, is not the radical departure of an iconoclast, but a broad, and perhaps culminat-

[36] *Process and Reality*, ₂532 (₂496 f.).
[37] *Adventures of Ideas*, 214 (below, p. 453).
[38] *Modes of Thought*, p. 137. See *Process and Reality*, Preface and Part II, Ch. I, §I.

ing, unification of the European tradition. It is not merely eclectic, for every traditional idea is redesigned. The whole is sustained by the strongest rationalistic faith [39] that we are likely to see in an original thinker for some time, and enlivened by an intense feeling for the freshness and creativity of existence.

The result has been rather too big for absorption. There is no Whiteheadian school except in theology, and there only in a very general sense. The philosophy of organism can neither be incorporated in any contemporary movement, nor accurately represented as the joint influence of recent thinkers on its author. There is in Whitehead a touch of Bergson, a touch of James, a touch of Samuel Alexander; more of Wordsworth, and above all of Plato. His sympathies were wide; his work was his own.

Whitehead's doctrines of the universality of value and of experience in the cosmos are closer to idealism than to any other type of philosophy. And, referring to his metaphysical theology, he wrote in the Preface to *Process and Reality* that "it becomes natural at this point to ask whether the type of thought involved be not a transformation of some main doctrines of Absolute Idealism onto a realistic basis." Yet, since his working position is not only realistic, but pluralistic and temporalistic, his is emphatically an idealism without a "block universe." There is also a naturalistic strain in Whitehead: he views man and his higher faculties as quite unessential to the process of the universe.

The full reach of Whitehead's metaphysics has by no means been indicated in this Introduction. For example, the "problem of induction" has not been mentioned. One of Whitehead's intentions in elaborating his theory of the "perishing" of actual occasions and their prehensive unification in "societies" was to provide a basis for solving that notorious problem. Students specializing in the philosophy of science must look into this topic for themselves.[40]

Neither have we mentioned the views on education which go with Whitehead's philosophy. Just as he teaches that the universe is alive and that there are no inert facts, so he insists that the pupils in the schools are alive and that there must be no attempt to stock their minds with "inert ideas." The student of education will find rewarding ideas in the essays on that subject—brilliant and untechnical—which Whitehead wrote between 1912 and 1936.[41]

A philosophy of life founded on Whitehead's metaphysics would

---

[39] See Selections, p. 443, below.

[40] They might begin with Whitehead's paper on "Uniformity and Contingency" (in *Essays in Science and Philosophy* or *Proc. of the Aristotelian Soc.*, n.s. XXIII, 1922-23), and Ch. III of *Science and the Modern World*.

[41] Almost all of them are reprinted either in *The Aims of Education and Other Essays* (New York, The Macmillan Co., 1929) or in Part III of *Essays in Science and Philosophy* (New York, Philosophical Library, 1947).

enjoin respect not only for all men, but for all beings. But Whitehead, unlike most systematic philosophers, never wrote an essay or a chapter on ethical theory; in fact he disliked the subject. His cosmology implicitly contains a theory of value, but the emphasis is on beauty more than goodness. Sheer existence is a value, and beauty of some sort is the unconscious aim of each pulse of existence. The reaction of moralists to Whitehead's statement that beauty is "the one aim which by its very nature is self-justifying" can easily be imagined. One implication of his work, however, is that instead of separating ethics and aesthetics we should bring them together in such notions as "harmony," "feeling," and "adventure."

VICTOR LOWE

JOHNS HOPKINS UNIVERSITY

1. Nature and Life [1]

I. *Nature Lifeless*

PHILOSOPHY IS THE product of wonder. The effort after the general characterization of the world around us is the romance of human thought. The correct statement seems so easy, so obvious, and yet it is always eluding us. We inherit the traditional doctrine; we can detect the oversights, the superstitions, the rash generalizations of the past ages. We know so well what we mean and yet we remain so curiously uncertain about the formulation of any detail of our knowledge. This word "detail" lies at the heart of the whole difficulty. You cannot talk vaguely about Nature in general. We must fix upon details within Nature and discuss their essences and their types of interconnection. The world around is complex, composed of details. We have to settle upon the primary types of detail in terms of which we endeavor to express our understanding of Nature. We have to analyze and to abstract, and to understand the natural status of our abstractions. At first sight there are sharp-cut classes within which we can sort the various types of things and characters of things which we find in Nature. Every age manages to find modes of classification which seem fundamental starting points for the researches of the special sciences. Each succeeding age discovers that the primary classifications of its predecessors will not work. In this way a doubt is thrown upon all formulations of laws of Nature which assume these classifications as firm starting points. A problem arises. Philosophy is the search for its solution. . . . [2]

For example, we can conceive Nature as composed of permanent things—namely, bits of matter, moving about in space which otherwise is empty. This way of thinking about Nature has an obvious consonance with common-sense observation. There are chairs, tables, bits of rock,

---

[1] The greater part (pp. 1-5, 6-11, 12-14, 15, 19-20, 22-28, 30-32, 34-46) of *Nature and Life* (Univ. of Chicago Press, 1934). The headings, "Nature Lifeless" and "Nature Alive," are taken from the reprint in *Modes of Thought* (New York, The Macmillan Co., 1938), where they first appeared.

Unless otherwise noted, the headings and sub-heads throughout these selections are the editor's. Obvious typographical errors have been corrected, and on page 432 a very long paragraph has been broken in two. The editor's footnotes are indicated by numbers, Whitehead's by asterisks. A few of Whitehead's notes have been omitted, as unnecessary for the purpose of this volume.

[2] "You cannot think without abstractions; accordingly, it is of the utmost importance to be vigilant in critically revising your *modes* of abstraction. It is here that philosophy finds its niche as essential to the healthy progress of society. It is the critic of abstractions. A civilisation which cannot burst through its current abstractions is doomed to sterility after a very limited period of progress." (Whitehead, *Science and the Modern World,* New York, The Macmillan Company, 1925, pp. 85–86).

oceans, animal bodies, vegetable bodies, planets, and suns. The enduring self-identity of a house, of a farm, of an animal body, is a presupposition of social intercourse. It is assumed in legal theory. It lies at the base of all literature. A bit of matter is thus conceived as a passive fact, an individual reality which is the same at an instant, or throughout a second, an hour, or a year. Such a material, individual reality supports its various qualifications such as shape, locomotion, color, or smell, etc. The occurrences of Nature consist in the changes in these qualifications, and more particularly in the changes of motion. The connection between such bits of matter consists purely of spatial relations. Thus, the importance of motion arises from its change of the sole mode of interconnection of material things. Mankind then proceeds to discuss these spatial relations and discovers geometry. The geometrical character of space is conceived as the one way in which Nature imposes determinate relations upon all bits of matter which are the sole occupants of space. In itself, space is conceived as unchanging from eternity to eternity, and as homogeneous from infinity to infinity. Thus, we compose a straightforward characterization of Nature, which is consonant to common sense, and can be verified at each moment of our existence. We sit for hours in the same chair, in the same house, with the same animal body. The dimensions of the room are defined by its spatial relations. There are colors, sounds, scents, partly abiding and partly changing. Also, the major facts of change are defined by locomotion of the animal bodies and of the inorganic furniture. Within this general concept of Nature, there have somehow to be interwoven the further concepts of life and mind.

I have been endeavoring to sketch the general common-sense notion of the universe, which about the beginning of the sixteenth century, say in the year 1500 A.D., was in process of formation among the more progressive thinkers of the European population. It was partly an inheritance from Greek thought and from medieval thought. Partly it was based on the deliverance of direct observation, at any moment verified in the world around us. It was the presupposed support supplying the terms in which the answers to all further questions were found. Among these further questions, the most fundamental and the most obvious are those concerning the laws of locomotion, the meaning of life, the meaning of mentality, and the interrelations of matter, life, and mentality. When we examine the procedures of the great men in the sixteenth and seventeenth centuries, we find them presupposing this general common-sense notion of the universe, and endeavoring to answer all questions in the terms it supplies.

I suggest that there can be no doubt but that this general notion expresses large, all-pervading truths about the world around us. The only question is as to how fundamental these truths may be. In other words, we have to ask what large features of the universe cannot be expressed in these terms. We have also to ask whether we cannot find some other set of notions which will explain the importance of this common-sense notion, and will also explain its relations to those other features ignored by the common-sense notion.

When we survey the subsequent course of scientific thought through-out the seventeenth century up to the present day, two curious facts emerge. In the first place, the development of natural science has gradually discarded every single feature of the original common-sense notion. Nothing whatever remains of it, considered as expressing the primary features in terms of which the universe is to be interpreted. The obvious common-sense notion has been entirely destroyed, so far as concerns its function as the basis for all interpretation. One by one, every item has been dethroned.

There is a second characteristic of subsequent thought which is equally prominent. This common-sense notion still reigns supreme in the work-a-day life of mankind. It dominates the market place, the playgrounds, the law courts, and in fact the whole sociological inter-course of mankind. It is supreme in literature and is assumed in all the humanistic sciences. Thus, the science of Nature stands opposed to the presuppositions of humanism. Where some conciliation is attempted, it often assumes some sort of mysticism. But in general there is no conciliation.

Indeed, even when we confine attention to natural science, no special science ever is grounded upon the conciliation of presuppositions belonging to all the various sciences of Nature. Each science confines itself to a fragment of the evidence and weaves its theories in terms of notions suggested by that fragment. Such a procedure is necessary by reason of the limitations of human ability. But its dangers should always be kept in mind. For example, the increasing departmentaliza-tion of universities during the last hundred years, however necessary for administrative purposes, tends to trivialize the mentality of the teaching profession. The result of this effective survival of two ways of thought is a patch-work procedure.

Presuppositions from the two points of view are interwoven sporadi-cally. Every special science has to assume results from other sciences. For example, biology presupposes physics. It will usually be the case that these loans really belong to the state of science thirty or forty years earlier. The presuppositions of the physics of my boyhood are today powerful influences in the mentality of physiologists. Indeed, we do not need even to bring in the physiologists. The presuppositions of yesterday's physics remain in the minds of physicists, although their explicit doctrines taken in detail deny them. . . .

The first item to be abandoned was the set of qualifications which we distinguish in sense-perception—namely, color, sound, scent, and analogous qualifications. The transmission theories for light and sound introduced the doctrine of secondary qualities. The color and the sound were no longer in nature. They are the mental reactions of the percipient to internal bodily locomotions. Thus, nature is left with bits of matter, qualified by mass, spatial relations, and the change of such relations.

This loss of the secondary qualities was a severe restriction to Nature, for its value to the percipient was reduced to its function as a mere agent of excitement. Also, the derived mental excitement was not primarily concerned with factors in Nature. The colors and the sounds were secondary factors supplied by the mental reaction. But the curious fact remained that these secondary factors are perceived as related by the spatiality which is the grand substratum of Nature. Hume was, I think, the first philosopher who explicitly pointed out this curious hybrid character of our perceptions, according to the current doctrine of the perception of secondary qualities. Though, of course, this hybrid characteristic was tacitly presupposed by Locke when he conceived color as a secondary quality of the things in Nature. I believe that any cosmological doctrine which is faithful to the facts has to admit this artificial character of sense-perception. Namely, when we perceive the red rose we are associating our enjoyment of red derived from one source with our enjoyment of a spatial region derived from another source. The conclusion that I draw is that sense-perception, for all its practical importance, is very superficial in its disclosure of the nature of things. This conclusion is supported by the character of delusiveness —that is, of illusion—which persistently clings to sense-perception. For example, our perception of stars which years ago may have vanished, our perceptions of images in mirrors or by refraction, our double vision, our visions under the influence of drugs. My quarrel with modern epistemology concerns its exclusive stress upon sense-perception for the provision of data respecting Nature. Sense-perception does not provide the data in terms of which we interpret it.

This conclusion that pure sense-perception does not provide the data for its own interpretation was the great discovery embodied in Hume's philosophy. This discovery is the reason why Hume's Treatise will remain as the irrefutable basis for all subsequent philosophic thought.

Another item in the common-sense doctrine concerns empty space and locomotion. In the first place, the transmission of light and sound shows that space apparently empty is the theater of activities which we do not directly perceive. This conclusion was explained by the supposition of types of subtle matter, namely, the ether, which we cannot directly perceive. In the second place, this conclusion, and the obvious behavior of gross ordinary matter, show us that the motions of matter are in some way conditioned by the spatial relations of material bodies to each other. It was here that Newton supplied the great synthesis upon which science was based for more than two centuries. Newton's laws of motion provided a skeleton framework within which more particular laws for the interconnection of bodily motions could be inserted. He also supplied one example of such a particular law in his great law of gravitation, which depended upon mutual distances.

Newton's methodology for physics was an overwhelming success. But the forces which he introduced left Nature still without meaning or value. In the essence of a material body—in its mass, motion, and shape—there was no reason for the law of gravitation. Even if the particular forces could be conceived as the accidents of a cosmic epoch, there was no reason in the Newtonian concepts of mass and motion why material bodies should be connected by any stress between them. Yet the notion of stresses, as essential connections between bodies, was a fundamental factor in the Newtonian concept of Nature. What Newton left for empirical investigation was the determination of the particular stresses now existing. In this determination he made a magnificent beginning by isolating the stresses indicated by his law of gravitation. But he left no hint why, in the nature of things, there should be any stresses at all. The arbitrary motions of the bodies were thus explained by the arbitrary stress between material bodies, conjoined with their spatiality, their mass, and their initial states of motion. By introducing stresses—in particular the law of gravitation—instead of the welter of detailed transformations of motion, he greatly increased the systematic aspect of Nature. But he left all the factors of the system—more particularly, mass and stress—in the position of detached facts devoid of any reason for their compresence. He thus illustrated a great philosophic truth, that a dead Nature can give no reasons. All ultimate reasons are in terms of aim at value. A dead Nature aims at nothing. It is the essence of life that it exists for its own sake, as the intrinsic reaping of value.

Thus for Newtonians, Nature yielded no reasons: it could yield no reasons. Combining Newton and Hume we obtain a barren concept, namely, a field of perception devoid of any data for its own interpretation, and a system of interpretation devoid of any reason for the concurrence of its factors. It is this situation that modern philosophy from Kant onward has in its various ways sought to render intelligible. My own belief is that this situation is a *reductio ad absurdum,* and should not be accepted as the basis for philosophic speculation. Kant was the first philosopher who in this way combined Newton and Hume. He accepted them both, and his three Critiques were his endeavor to render intelligible this Hume-Newton situation. But the Hume-Newton situation is the primary presupposition for all modern philosophic thought. Any endeavor to go behind it is, in philosophic discussion, almost angrily rejected as unintelligible.

My aim in these lectures is briefly to point out how both Newton's contribution and Hume's contribution are, each in their way, gravely defective. They are right as far as they go. But they omit those aspects of the universe as experienced, and of our modes of experiencing, which jointly lead to the more penetrating ways of understanding. In the recent situations at Washington, D.C.,[3] the Hume-Newton modes of thought can only discern a complex transition of sensa, and an entangled locomotion of molecules, while the deepest intuition of the whole world discerns the President of the United States inaugurating a new chapter in the history of mankind. In such ways the Hume-Newton interpretation omits our intuitive modes of understanding.

I now pass on to the influence of modern science in discrediting the remaining items of the primary common-sense notion with which science in the sixteenth century started its career. But in the present-day reconstruction of physics fragments of the Newtonian concepts are stubbornly retained. The result is to reduce modern physics to a sort of mystic chant over an unintelligible universe. This chant has the exact merits of the old magic ceremonies which flourished in ancient Mesopotamia and later in Europe. One of the earliest fragments of writing which has survived is a report from a Babylonian astrologer to the king, stating the favorable days to turn cattle into the fields, as deduced by his observations of the stars. This mystic relation of observation, theory, and practice is exactly the present position of science in modern life, according to the prevalent scientific philosophy.

The notion of empty space, the mere vehicle of spatial interconnections, has been eliminated from recent science. The whole spatial universe is a field of force—or, in other words, a field of incessant activity. The mathematical formulae of physics express the mathematical relations realized in this activity. . . . The modern point of view is expressed in terms of energy, activity, and the vibratory differentiations of space-time. Any local agitation shakes the whole universe. The distant effects are minute, but they are there. The concept of matter presupposed simple location. Each bit of matter was self-contained, localized in a region with a passive, static network of spatial relations, entwined in a uniform relational system from infinity to infinity and from eternity to eternity. But in the modern concept the group of agitations which we term matter is fused into its environment. There is no possibility of a detached, self-contained local existence. The environment enters into the nature of each thing. Some elements in the nature of a complete

[3] This lecture was written in 1933.

set of agitations may remain stable as those agitations are propelled through a changing environment. But such stability is only the case in a general, average way. This average fact is the reason why we find the same chair, the same rock, and the same planet, enduring for days, or for centuries, or for millions of years. In this average fact, the time-factor takes the aspect of endurance, and change is a detail. The fundamental fact, according to the physics of the present day, is that the environment with its peculiarities seeps into the group-agitation which we term matter, and the group-agitations extend their character to the environment. In truth, the notion of the self-contained particle of matter, self-sufficient within its local habitation, is an abstraction. Now an abstraction is nothing else than the omission of part of the truth. The abstraction is well founded when the conclusions drawn from it are not vitiated by the omitted truth.

This general deduction from the modern doctrine of physics vitiates many conclusions drawn from the applications of physics to other sciences, such as physiology, or even such as physics itself. For example, when geneticists conceive genes as the determinants of heredity. The analogy of the old concept of matter sometimes leads them to ignore the influence of the particular animal body in which they are functioning. They presuppose that a pellet of matter remains in all respects self-identical whatever be its changes of environment. So far as modern physics is concerned, such characteristics may, or may not, effect changes in the genes, changes which are important in certain respects, though not in others. Thus, no *a priori* argument as to the inheritance of characters can be drawn from the mere doctrine of genes. In fact, recently, physiologists have found that genes are modified in some respects by their environment. The presuppositions of the old common-sense view survive, even when the view itself has been abandoned as a fundamental description.

This survival of fragments of older doctrines is also exemplified in the modern use of the term space-time. . . . The fashionable notion that the new physics has reduced all physical laws to the statement of geometrical relations is quite ridiculous. It has done the opposite. In the place of the Aristotelian notion of the procession of forms, it has substituted the notion of the forms of process. . . .

*   *   *

Finally, we are left with a fundamental question as yet undiscussed. What are those primary types of things in terms of which the process of the universe is to be understood? Suppose we agree that Nature discloses to the scientific scrutiny merely activities and process. What does this mean? These activities fade into each other. They arise and then pass away. What is being enacted? What is effected? It cannot be that these are merely the formulae of the multiplication table—in the words of a great philosopher,[4] merely a bloodless dance of categories. Nature is full-blooded. Real facts are happening. Physical Nature, as studied in science, is to be looked upon as a complex of the more stable interrelations between the real facts of the real universe.

This lecture has been confined to Nature under an abstraction in which all reference to life was suppressed. The effect of this abstraction has been that dynamics, physics, and chemistry were the sciences which guided our gradual transition from the full common-sense notions of the sixteenth century to the concept of Nature suggested by the speculative physics of the present day. This change of view, occupying four centuries, may be characterized as the transition from space and matter as the fundamental notions to process conceived as a complex of activity with internal relations between its various factors. The older point of view enables us to abstract from change and to conceive of the full reality of Nature *at an instant,* in abstraction from any temporal duration and characterized as to its interrelations solely by the instantaneous distribution of matter in space. . . .

For the modern view process, activity, and change are the matter of fact. At an instant there is nothing. Each instant is only a way of grouping matters of fact. Thus, since there are no instants, conceived as simple primary entities, there is no Nature at an instant. Thus, all the interrelations of matters of fact must involve transition in their essence. All realization involves implication in the creative advance.

The discussion in this lecture is only the prolegomenon for the attempt to answer the fundamental question—How do we add content to the notion of bare activity? Activity for what, producing what, activity involving what?

The next lecture will introduce the concept of life, and will thus enable us to conceive of Nature more concretely, without abstraction.

II. Nature Alive

The status of life in Nature is the standing problem of philosophy and of science. Indeed, it is the central meeting point of all the strains of systematic thought, humanistic, naturalistic, philosophic. The very meaning of life is in doubt. When we understand it, we shall also understand its status in the world. But its essence and its status are alike baffling.

After all, this conclusion is not very different from our conclusion respecting Nature, considered in abstraction from the notion of life. We were left with the notion of an activity in which nothing is effected. Also this activity, thus considered, discloses no ground for its own

[4] F. H. Bradley.

coherence. There is merely a formula for succession. But there is an absence of understandable causation to give a reason for that formula for that succession. Of course, it is always possible to work one's self into a state of complete contentment with an ultimate irrationality. The popular positivistic philosophy adopts this attitude.

The weakness of this positivism is the way in which we all welcome the detached fragments of explanation attained in our present stage of civilization. Suppose that a hundred thousand years ago our ancestors had been wise positivists. They sought for no reasons. What they had observed was sheer matter of fact. It was the development of no necessity. They would have searched for no reasons underlying facts immediately observed. Civilization would never have developed. Our varied powers of detailed observation of the world would have remained dormant. For the peculiarity of a reason is that the intellectual development of its consequences suggests consequences beyond the topics already observed. The extension of observation waits upon some dim apprehension of reasonable connection. For example, the observation of insects on flowers dimly suggests some congruity between the natures of insects and of flowers, and thus leads to a wealth of observation from which whole branches of science have developed. But a consistent positivist should be content with the observed facts—namely, insects visiting flowers. It is a fact of charming simplicity. There is nothing further to be said upon the matter, according to the doctrine of a positivist. At present the scientific world is suffering from a bad attack of muddle-headed positivism, which arbitrarily applies its doctrine and arbitrarily escapes from it. The whole doctrine of life in Nature has suffered from this positivist taint. We are told that there is the routine described in physical and chemical formulae, and that in the process of Nature there is nothing else.

The origin of this persuasion is the dualism which gradually developed in European thought in respect to mind and Nature. At the beginning of the modern period Descartes expresses this dualism with the utmost distinctness. For him, there are material substances with spatial relations, and mental substances. The mental substances are external to the material substances. Neither type requires the other type for the completion of its essence. Their unexplained interrelations are unnecessary for their respective existences. In truth, this formulation of the problem in terms of minds and matter is unfortunate. It omits the lower forms of life, such as vegetation and the lower animal types. These forms touch upon human mentality at their highest, and upon inorganic Nature at their lowest.

The effect of this sharp division between Nature and life has poisoned all subsequent philosophy. Even when the coördinate existence of the two types of actualities is abandoned, there is no proper fusion of the two in most modern schools of thought. For some, Nature is mere appearance and mind is the sole reality. For others, physical Nature is the sole reality and mind is an epiphenomenon. Here the phrases "mere appearance" and "epiphenomenon" obviously carry the implication of slight importance for the understanding of the final nature of things.

The doctrine that I am maintaining is that neither physical Nature nor life can be understood unless we fuse them together as essential factors in the composition of "really real" things whose interconnections and individual characters constitute the universe.

The first step in the argument must be to form some concept of what life can mean. Also, we require that the deficiencies in our concept of physical Nature should be supplied by its fusion with life. And we require that, on the other hand, the notion of life should involve the notion of physical Nature.

Now as a first approximation the notion of life implies a certain absoluteness of self-enjoyment. This must mean a certain immediate individuality, which is a complex process of appropriating into a unity of existence the many data presented as relevant by the physical processes of nature. Life implies the absolute, individual self-enjoyment arising out of this process of appropriation. I have, in my recent writings, used the word "prehension" to express this process of appropriation. Also, I have termed each individual act of immediate self-enjoyment an "occasion of experience." I hold that these unities of existence, these occasions of experience, are the really real things which in their collective unity compose the evolving universe, ever plunging into the creative advance.

But these are forward references to the issue of the argument. As a first approximation we have conceived life as implying absolute, individual self-enjoyment of a process of appropriation. The data appropriated are provided by the antecedent functioning of the universe. Thus, the occasion of experience is absolute in respect to its immediate self-enjoyment. How it deals with its data is to be understood without reference to any other concurrent occasions. Thus, the occasion, in reference to its internal process, requires no contemporary process in order to exist. In fact this mutual independence in the internal process of self-adjustment is the definition of contemporaneousness.

This concept of self-enjoyment does not exhaust that aspect of process here termed "life." Process for its intelligibility involves the notion of a creative activity belonging to the very essence of each occasion. It is the process of eliciting into actual being factors in the universe which antecedently to that process exist only in the mode of unrealized potentialities. The process of self-creation is the transformation of the potential into the actual, and the fact of such transformation includes the immediacy of self-enjoyment.

Thus, in conceiving the function of life in an occasion of experience, we must discriminate the actualized data presented by the antecedent world, the non-actualized potentialities which lie ready to promote their fusion into a new unity of experience, and the immediacy of self-enjoyment which belongs to the creative fusion of those data with those potentialities. This is the doctrine of the creative advance whereby it belongs to the essence of the universe, that it passes into a future. It is nonsense to conceive of Nature as a static fact, even for an instant devoid of duration. There is no Nature apart from transition, and there is no transition apart from temporal duration. This is the reason why the notion of an instant of time, conceived as a primary simple fact, is nonsense.

But even yet we have not exhausted the notion of creation which is essential to the understanding of Nature. We must add yet another character to our description of life. This missing characteristic is "aim." By this term "aim" is meant the exclusion of the boundless wealth of alternative potentiality, and the inclusion of that definite factor of novelty which constitutes the selected way of entertaining those data in that process of unification. The aim is at that complex of feeling which is the enjoyment of those data in that way. "That way of enjoyment" is selected from the boundless wealth of alternatives. It has been aimed at for actualization in that process.

Thus, the characteristics of life are absolute self-enjoyment, creative activity, aim. Here "aim" evidently involves the entertainment of the purely ideal so as to be directive of the creative process. Also, the enjoyment belongs to the process and is not a characteristic of any static result. The aim is at the enjoyment belonging to the process.

The question at once arises as to whether this factor of life in Nature, as thus interpreted, corresponds to anything that we observe in Nature. . . .

Science can find no individual enjoyment in Nature; science can find no aim in Nature; science can find no creativity in Nature; it finds mere rules of succession. These negations are true of natural science. They are inherent in its methodology. The reason for this blindness of physical science lies in the fact that such science only deals with half the evidence provided by human experience. It divides the seamless coat —or, to change the metaphor into a happier form, it examines the coat, which is superficial, and neglects the body which is fundamental.

The disastrous separation of body and mind which has been fixed on European thought by Descartes is responsible for this blindness of science. In one sense the abstraction has been a happy one, in that it has allowed the simplest things to be considered first, for about ten generations. Now these simplest things are those widespread habits of Nature that dominate the whole stretch of the universe within our remotest, vaguest observation. None of these laws of Nature gives the slightest evidence of necessity. They are the modes of procedure which within the scale of our observations do in fact prevail. I mean the fact that the extensiveness of the universe is dimensional, the fact that the number of spatial dimensions is three, the spatial laws of geometry, the ultimate formulae for physical occurrences. There is no necessity in any of these ways of behaviour. They exist as average, regulative conditions because the majority of actualities are swaying each other to modes of interconnection exemplifying those laws. New modes of self-expression may be gaining ground. We cannot tell. But, to judge by all analogy, after a sufficient span of existence our present laws will fade into unimportance. New interests will dominate. In our present sense of the term, our spatio-physical epoch will pass into that background of the past, which conditions all things dimly and without evident effect on the decision of prominent relations.

These massive laws, at present prevailing, are the general physical laws of inorganic nature. At a certain scale of observation they are prevalent without hint of interference. The formation of suns, the motions of planets, the geologic changes on the earth, seem to proceed with a massive impetus which excludes any hint of modification by other agencies. To this extent sense-perception on which science relies discloses no aim in Nature.

Yet it is untrue to state that the general observation of mankind, in which sense-perception is only one factor, discloses no aim. The exact contrary is the case. All explanations of the sociological functionings of mankind include "aim" as an essential factor in explanation. For example, in a criminal trial where the evidence is circumstantial the demonstration of motive is one chief reliance of the prosecution. In such a trial would the defense plead the doctrine that purpose could not direct the motions of the body, and that to indict the thief for stealing was analogous to indicting the sun for rising? Again no statesman can conduct international relations without some estimate—implicit or explicit in his consciousness—of the types of patriotism respectively prevalent in various nations and in the statesmen of these nations. A lost dog can be seen trying to find his master or trying to find his way home. In fact we are *directly* conscious of our purposes as *directive* of our actions. Apart from such direction no doctrine could in any sense be acted upon. The notions entertained mentally would have no effect upon bodily actions. Thus, what happens would happen in complete indifference to the entertainment of such notions.

Scientific reasoning is completely dominated by the presupposition that mental functionings are not properly part of Nature. Accordingly it disregards all those mental antecedents which mankind habitually presuppose as effective in guiding cosmological functionings. As a method this procedure is entirely justifiable, provided that we recognize the limitations involved. These limitations are both obvious and undefined. The gradual eliciting of their definition is the hope of philosophy. . . .

Again, another consideration arises. How do we observe Nature? Also, what is the proper analysis of an observation? The conventional answer to this question is that we perceive Nature through our senses. Also, in the analysis of sense-perception we are apt to concentrate upon its most clear-cut instance, namely, sight. Now visual perception is the final product of evolution. It belongs to high-grade animals—to vertebrates and to the more advanced type of insects. There are numberless living things which afford no evidence of possessing sight. Yet they show every sign of taking account of their environment in the way proper to living things. Also, human beings shut off sight with peculiar ease, by closing their eyes or by the calamity of blindness. The information provided by mere sight is peculiarly barren—namely, external regions disclosed as colored. There is no necessary transition of colors, and no necessary selection of regions, and no necessary mutual adaptation of the display of colors. Sight at any instant merely provides the passive fact of regions variously colored. If we have memories, we observe the transition of colors. But there is nothing intrinsic to the mere colored regions which provides any hint of internal activity whereby change can be understood. It is from this experience that our conception of a spatial distribution of passive material substances arises. Nature is thus described as made up of vacuous bits of matter with no internal values, and merely hurrying through space.

But there are two accompaniments of this experience which should make us suspicious of accepting it at its face value as any direct disclosure of the metaphysical nature of things. In the first place, even in visual experience we are also aware of the intervention of the body. We know directly that we see *with our eyes*. That is a vague feeling, but extremely important. Second, every type of crucial experiment proves that what we see, and where we see it, depend entirely upon the physiological functioning of our body. Any method of making our body function internally in a given way will provide us with an assigned visual sensation. The body is supremely indifferent to the happenings of Nature a short way off, where it places its visual sensa.

Now, the same is true of all other modes of sensation, only to a greater extent. All sense-perception is merely one outcome of the dependence of our experience upon bodily functionings. Thus, if we wish to understand the relation of our personal experience to the activities of Nature, the proper procedure is to examine the dependence of our personal experiences upon our personal bodies.

Let us ask about our overwhelming persuasions as to our own personal body-mind relation. In the first place, there is the claim to unity. The human individual is one fact, body and mind. This claim to unity is the fundamental fact, always presupposed, rarely explicitly formulated. I am experiencing and my body is mine. In the second place, the functioning of our body has a much wider influence than the mere production of sense-experience. We find ourselves in a healthy enjoyment of life by reason of the healthy functionings of our internal organs —heart, lungs, bowels, kidneys, etc. The emotional state arises just because they are not providing any sensa directly associated with themselves. Even in sight, we enjoy our vision because there is no eyestrain. Also, we enjoy our general state of life because we have no stomach ache. I am insisting that the enjoyment of health, good or bad, is a positive feeling only casually associated with particular sensa. For example, you can enjoy the ease with which your eyes are functioning even when you are looking at a bad picture or a vulgar building. This direct feeling of the derivation of emotion from the body is among our fundamental experiences. There are emotions of various types—but every type of emotion is at least modified by derivation from the body. It is for physiologists to analyze in detail the modes of bodily functioning. For philosophy, the one fundamental fact is that the whole complexity of mental experience is either derived or modified by such functioning. Also, our basic feeling is this sense of derivation, which leads to our claim for unity, body and mind.

But our immediate experience also claims derivation from another source, and equally claims a unity founded upon this alternative source of derivation. This second source is our own state of mind directly preceding the immediate present of our conscious experience. A quarter of a second ago we were entertaining such and such ideas, we were enjoying such and such emotions, and we were making such and such observations of external fact. In our present state of mind we are continuing that previous state. The word "continuing" states only half the truth. In one sense it is too weak, and in another sense it overstates. It is too weak because we not only continue, but we claim absolute identity with our previous state. It was our very identical self in that state of mind, which is, of course, the basis of our present experience a quarter of a second later. In another sense the word "continuing" overstates. For we do not quite continue in our preceding state of experience. New elements have intervened. All of these new elements are provided by our bodily functionings. We fuse these new elements with the basic stuff of experience provided by our state of mind a quarter of a second ago. Also, as we have already agreed, we claim an identification with our body. Thus, our experience in the present discloses its own nature as with two sources of derivation, namely, the body and the antecedent experiential functionings. Also, there is a claim for identification with each of these sources. The body is mine, and the antecedent experience is mine. Still more, there is only one ego, to claim the body and to claim the stream of experience. I submit that we have here the fundamental basic persuasion on which we found the whole practice of our existence. While we exist, body and soul are inescapable elements in our being, each with the full reality of our own immediate self.

But neither body nor soul possess the sharp observational definition which at first sight we attribute to them. Our knowledge of the body places it as a complex unity of happenings within the larger field of Nature. But its demarcation from the rest of Nature is vague in the extreme. The body consists of the coördinated functionings of billions of molecules. It belongs to the structural essence of the body that, in an indefinite number of ways, it is always losing molecules and gaining molecules. When we consider the question with microscopic accuracy, there is no definite boundary to determine where the body begins and external Nature ends. Again, the body can lose whole limbs, and yet we claim identity with the same body. Also, the vital functions of the cells in the amputated limb ebb slowly. Indeed, the limb survives in separation from the body for an immense time compared to the internal vibratory periods of its molecules. Also, apart from such catastrophes, the body requires the environment in order to exist. Thus, there is a unity of the body with the environment, as well as a unity of body and soul into one person.

But in conceiving our personal identity we are apt to emphasize rather the soul than the body. The one individual is that coördinated stream of personal experiences which is my thread of life or your thread of life. It is that succession of self-realization, each occasion with its direct memory of its past and with its anticipation of the future. That claim to enduring self-identity is our self-assertion of personal identity.

Yet, when we examine this notion of the soul, it discloses itself as even vaguer than our definition of the body. First, the continuity of the soul—so far as concerns consciousness—has to leap gaps in time. We sleep or we are stunned. And yet it is the same person who recovers consciousness. We trust to memory, and we ground our trust on the continuity of the functionings of Nature, more especially on the continuity of our body. Thus, Nature in general and the body in particular provide the stuff for the personal endurance of the soul. Again, there is a curious variation in the vividness of the successive occasions of the soul's existence. We are living at full stretch with a keen observation of external occurrence; then external attention dies away and we are lost in meditation; the meditation gradually weakens in vivid presentation —we doze; we dream; we sleep with a total lapse of the stream of consciousness. These functionings of the soul are diverse, variable, and discontinuous. The claim to the unity of the soul is analogous to the claim to the unity of the body, and is analogous to the claim to the unity of body and soul, and is analogous to the claim to the community of the body with an external Nature. It is the task of philosophic speculation to conceive the happenings of the universe so as to render understandable the outlook of physical science and to combine this outlook with these direct persuasions representing the basic facts upon which epistemology must build. The weakness of the epistemology of the eighteenth and nineteenth centuries was that it based itself purely upon a narrow formulation of sense-perception. Also, among the various modes of sensation, visual experience was picked out as the typical example. The result was to exclude all the really fundamental factors constituting our experience.

In such an epistemology we are far from the complex data which philosophic speculation has to account for in a system rendering the whole understandable. Consider the types of community of body and soul, of body and Nature, of soul and Nature, or successive occasions of bodily existence, or the soul's existence. These fundamental interconnections have one very remarkable characteristic. Let us ask what is the function of the external world for the stream of experience which constitutes the soul. This world, thus experienced, is the basic fact within those experiences. All the emotions, and purposes, and enjoyments, proper to the individual existence of the soul are nothing other than the soul's reactions to this experienced world which lies at the base of the soul's existence. Thus, in a sense, the experienced world is one complex factor in the composition of many factors constituting the essence of the soul. We can phrase this shortly by saying that in one sense the world is in the soul.

But there is an antithetical doctrine balancing this primary truth. Namely, our experience of the world involves the exhibition of the soul itself as one of the components within the world. Thus, there is a dual aspect to the relationship of an occasion of experience as one relatum and the experienced world as another relatum. The world is included within the occasion in one sense, and the occasion is included in the world in another sense. For example, I am in the room, and the room is an item in my present experience. But my present experience is what I now am.

But this baffling antithetical relation extends to all the connections which we have been discussing. For example, consider the enduring self-identity of the soul. The soul is nothing else than the succession of my occasions of experience, extending from birth to the present moment. Now, at this instant, I am the complete person embodying all these occasions. They are mine. On the other hand, it is equally true that my immediate occasion of experience, at the present moment, is only one among the stream of occasions which constitutes my soul. Again, the world for me is nothing else than how the functionings of my body present it for my experience. The world is thus wholly to be discerned within those functionings. Knowledge of the world is nothing else than an analysis of the functionings. And yet, on the other hand, the body is merely one society of functionings within the universal society of the world. We have to construe the world in terms of the bodily society, and the bodily society in terms of the general functionings of the world.

Thus, as disclosed in the fundamental essence of our experience, the togetherness of things involves some doctrine of mutual immanence. In some sense or other, this community of the actualities of the world means that each happening is a factor in the nature of every other happening. After all, this is the only way in which we can understand notions habitually employed in daily life. Consider our notion of "causation." How can one event be the cause of another? In the first place, no event can be wholly and solely the cause of another event. The whole antecedent world conspires to produce a new occasion. But some one occasion in an important way conditions the formation of a successor. How can we understand this process of conditioning?

The mere notion of transferring a quality is entirely unintelligible. Suppose that two occurrences may be in fact detached so that one of them is comprehensible without reference to the other. Then all notion of causation between them, or of conditioning, becomes unintelligible. There is—with this supposition—no reason why the possession of any quality by one of them should in any way influence the possession of that quality, or of any other quality, by the other. With such a doctrine the play and interplay of qualitative succession in the world becomes a blank fact from which no conclusions can be drawn as to past, present, or future, beyond the range of direct observation. Such a positivistic belief is quite self-consistent, provided that we do not include in it any hopes for the future or regrets for the past. Science is then without any importance. Also effort is foolish, because it determines nothing. The only intelligible doctrine of causation is founded on the doctrine of immanence. Each occasion presupposes the antecedent world as active in its own nature. This is the reason why events have a determinate status relatively to each other. Also, it is the reason why the qualitative energies of the past are combined into a pattern of qualitative energies in each present occasion. This is the doctrine of causation. It is the reason why it belongs to the essence of each occasion that it is *where* it is. It is the reason for the transference of character from occasion to occasion. It is the reason for the relative stability of laws of Nature, some laws for a wider environment, some laws for a narrower environment. It is the reason why—as we have already noted—in our direct apprehension of the world around us we find that curious habit of claiming a twofold unity with the observed data. We are in the world and the world is in us. Our immediate occasion is in the society of occasions forming the soul, and our soul is in our present occasion. The body is ours, and we are an activity within our body. This fact of observation, vague but imperative, is the foundation of the connexity of the world, and of the transmission of its types of order.

In this survey of the observational data in terms of which our philosophic cosmology must be founded we have brought together the conclusions of physical science, and those habitual persuasions dominating the sociological functionings of mankind. These persuasions also guide the humanism of literature, of art, and of religion. Mere existence has never entered into the consciousness of man, except as the remote terminus of an abstraction in thought. Descartes' "Cogito, ergo sum" is wrongly translated, "I *think* therefore I am." It is never bare thought or bare existence that we are aware of. I find myself as essentially a unity of emotions, enjoyments, hopes, fears, regrets, valuations of alternatives, decisions—all of them subjective reactions to the environment as active in my nature. My unity—which is Descartes' "I am"—is my process of shaping this welter of material into a consistent pattern of feelings. The individual enjoyment is what I am in my rôle of a natural activity, as I shape the activities of the environment into a new creation, which is myself at this moment; and yet, as being myself, it is a continuation of the antecedent world. If we stress the rôle of the environment, this process is causation. If we stress the rôle of my immediate pattern of active enjoyment, this process is self-creation. If we stress the rôle of the conceptual anticipation of a future whose existence is a necessity in the Nature of the present, this process is the teleological aim at some ideal in the future. This aim, however, is not really beyond the present process. For the aim at the future is an enjoyment in the present. It thus effectively conditions the immediate self-creation of the new creature.

We can now again ask the final question as put forward at the close of the former lecture. Physical science has reduced Nature to activity, and has discovered abstract mathematical formulae which are illustrated in these activities of Nature. But the fundamental question remains: How do we add content to the notion of bare activity? This question can only be answered by fusing life with Nature.

In the first place, we must distinguish life from mentality. Mentality involves conceptual experience, and is only one variable ingredient in life.[5] The sort of functioning here termed "conceptual experience" is the entertainment of possibilities for ideal realization in abstraction from any sheer physical realization. The most obvious example of conceptual experience is the entertainment of alternatives. Life lies below this grade of mentality. Life is the enjoyment of emotion, derived from the past and aimed at the future. It is the enjoyment of emotion which was then, which is now, and which will be then. This vector character is of the essence of such entertainment. The emotion transcends the present in two ways. It issues from, and it issues toward. It is received, it is enjoyed, and it is passed along, from moment to moment. Each occasion is an activity of concern, in the Quaker sense of that term. It is the conjunction of transcendence and immanence. The occasion is concerned, in the way of feeling and aim, with things that in their own essence lie beyond it; although these things in their present functions are factors in the concern of that occasion. Thus, each occasion, although engaged in its own immediate self-realization, is concerned with the universe.

The process is always a process of modification by reason of the numberless avenues of supply, and by reason of the numberless modes of qualitative texture. The unity of emotion, which is the unity of the present occasion, is a patterned texture of qualities, always shifting as it is passed into the future. The creative activity aims at preservation of the components and at preservation of intensity. The modifications of pattern, the dismissal into elimination, are in obedience to this aim.

In so far as conceptual mentality does not intervene, the grand patterns pervading the environment are passed on with the inherited modes of adjustment. Here we find the patterns of activity studied by the physicists and chemists. Mentality is merely latent in all these occasions as thus studied. In the case of inorganic Nature any sporadic flashes are inoperative so far as our powers of discernment are concerned. The lowest stages of effective mentality, controlled by the inheritance of physical pattern, involve the faint direction of emphasis by unconscious ideal aim. The various examples of the higher forms of life exhibit the variety of grades of effectiveness of mentality. In the social habits of animals there is evidence of flashes of mentality in the past which have degenerated into physical habits. Finally, in the higher mammals and more particularly in mankind, we have clear evidence of mentality habitually effective. In our own experience, our knowledge consciously entertained and systematized can only mean such mentality, directly observed.

The qualities entertained as objects in conceptual activity are of the

---

[5] In Whitehead's metaphysical system, as expounded in *Process and Reality*, the terms *mental* and *conceptual* appear to be used in a broader sense, which is explained in our Introduction, pp. 405, 409.

nature of catalytic agents, in the sense in which that phrase is used in chemistry. They modify the aesthetic process by which the occasion constitutes itself out of the many streams of feeling received from the past. It is not necessary to assume that conceptions introduce additional sources of measurable energy. They may do so; for the doctrine of the conservation of energy is not based upon exhaustive measurements. But the operation of mentality is primarily to be conceived as a diversion of the flow of energy.

In these lectures I have not entered upon systematic metaphysical cosmology. The object of the lectures is to indicate those elements in our experience in terms of which such a cosmology should be constructed. The key notion, from which such construction should start, is that the energetic activity considered in physics is the emotional intensity entertained in life. . . .

2. Speculative Philosophy [6]

I

. . . SPECULATIVE PHILOSOPHY is the endeavour to frame a coherent, logical, necessary system of general ideas in terms of which every element of our experience can be interpreted. By this notion of 'interpretation' I mean that everything of which we are conscious, as enjoyed, perceived, willed, or thought, shall have the character of a particular instance of the general scheme. Thus the philosophical scheme should be coherent, logical, and, in respect to its interpretation, applicable and adequate. Here 'applicable' means that some items of experience are thus interpretable, and 'adequate' means that there are no items incapable of such interpretation.

'Coherence,' as here employed, means that the fundamental ideas, in terms of which the scheme is developed, presuppose each other so that in isolation they are meaningless. This requirement does not mean that they are definable in terms of each other; it means that what is indefinable in one such notion cannot be abstracted from its relevance to the other notions. It is the ideal of speculative philosophy that its fundamental notions shall not seem capable of abstraction from each other. In other words, it is presupposed that no entity can be conceived in complete abstraction from the system of the universe, and that it is the business of speculative philosophy to exhibit this truth. This character is its coherence.

---

[6] The first chapter, "Speculative Philosophy," of *Process and Reality* (copyright 1929 by The Macmillan Company and used with their permission). A few short passages (some of them references to later parts of the book) have been omitted. They may be found on pp. 4, 10, 11, 13, 14, 17, 18, and 19 of the original.

The term 'logical' has its ordinary meaning, including 'logical' consistency, or lack of contradiction, the definition of constructs in logical terms, the exemplification of general logical notions in specific instances, and the principles of inference. It will be observed that logical notions must themselves find their places in the scheme of philosophic notions.

It will also be noticed that this ideal of speculative philosophy has its rational side and its empirical side. The rational side is expressed by the terms 'coherent' and 'logical.' The empirical side is expressed by the terms 'applicable' and 'adequate.' But the two sides are bound together by clearing away an ambiguity which remains in the previous explanation of the term 'adequate.' The adequacy of the scheme over every item does not mean adequacy over such items as happen to have been considered. It means that the texture of observed experience, as illustrating the philosophic scheme, is such that all related experience must exhibit the same texture. Thus the philosophic scheme should be 'necessary,' in the sense of bearing in itself its own warrant of universality throughout all experience, provided that we confine ourselves to that which communicates with immediate matter of fact. But what does not so communicate is unknowable, and the unknowable is unknown; and so this universality defined by 'communication' can suffice.

This doctrine of necessity in universality means that there is an essence to the universe which forbids relationships beyond itself, as a violation of its rationality. Speculative philosophy seeks that essence.

II

Philosophers can never hope finally to formulate these metaphysical first principles. Weakness of insight and deficiencies of language stand in the way inexorably. Words and phrases must be stretched towards a generality foreign to their ordinary usage; and however such elements of language be stabilized as technicalities, they remain metaphors mutely appealing for an imaginative leap.

There is no first principle which is in itself unknowable, not to be captured by a flash of insight. But, putting aside the difficulties of language, deficiency in imaginative penetration forbids progress in any form other than that of an asymptotic approach to a scheme of principles, only definable in terms of the ideal which they should satisfy.

The difficulty has its seat in the empirical side of philosophy. Our datum is the actual world, including ourselves; and this actual world spreads itself for observation in the guise of the topic of our immediate experience. The elucidation of immediate experience is the sole justification for any thought; and the starting point for thought is the analytic observation of components of this experience. But we are not conscious of any clear-cut complete analysis of immediate experience, in terms of the various details which comprise its definiteness. We habitually observe by the method of difference. Sometimes we see an elephant, and sometimes we do not. The result is that an elephant, when present, is noticed. Facility of observation depends on the fact that the object observed is important when present, and sometimes is absent.

The metaphysical first principles can never fail of exemplification. We can never catch the actual world taking a holiday from their sway. Thus, for the discovery of metaphysics, the method of pinning down thought to the strict systematization of detailed discrimination, already effected by antecedent observation, breaks down. This collapse of the method of rigid empiricism is not confined to metaphysics. It occurs whenever we seek the larger generalities. In natural science this rigid method is the Baconian method of induction, a method which, if consistently pursued, would have left science where it found it. What Bacon omitted was the play of a free imagination, controlled by the requirements of coherence and logic. The true method of discovery is like the flight of an aeroplane. It starts from the ground of particular observation; it makes a flight in the thin air of imaginative generalization; and it again lands for renewed observation rendered acute by rational interpretation. The reason for the success of this method of imaginative rationalization is that, when the method of difference fails, factors which are constantly present may yet be observed under the influence of imaginative thought. Such thought supplies the differences which the direct observation lacks. It can even play with inconsistency; and can thus throw light on the consistent, and persistent, elements in experience by comparison with what in imagination is inconsistent with them. The negative judgment is the peak of mentality. But the conditions for the success of imaginative construction must be rigidly adhered to. In the first place, this construction must have its origin in the generalization of particular factors discerned in particular topics of human interest; for example, in physics, or in physiology, or in psychology, or in aesthetics, or in ethical beliefs, or in sociology, or in languages conceived as storehouses of human experience. In this way the prime requisite, that anyhow there shall be some important application, is secured. The success of the imaginative experiment is always to be tested by the applicability of its results beyond the restricted locus from which it originated. In default of such extended application, a generalization started from physics, for example, remains merely an alternative expression of notions applicable to physics. The partially successful philosophic generalization will, if derived from physics, find applications in fields of experience beyond physics. It will enlighten observation in those remote fields, so that general principles can be discerned as in process of illustration, which in the absence of the imaginative generalization are obscured by their persistent exemplification.

Thus the first requisite is to proceed by the method of generalization so that certainly there is some application; and the test of some success is application beyond the immediate origin. In other words, some synoptic vision has been gained.

In this description of philosophic method, the term 'philosophic generalization' has meant 'the utilization of specific notions, applying to a restricted group of facts, for the divination of the generic notions which apply to all facts.'

In its use of this method natural science has shown a curious mixture of rationalism and irrationalism. Its prevalent tone of thought has been ardently rationalistic within its own borders, and dogmatically irrational beyond those borders. In practice such an attitude tends to become a dogmatic denial that there are any factors in the world not fully expressible in terms of its own primary notions devoid of further generalization. Such a denial is the self-denial of thought.[7]

The second condition for the success of imaginative construction is unflinching pursuit of the two rationalistic ideals, coherence and logical perfection.

[7] "... we have to discriminate between the weight to be given to scientific opinion in the selection of its methods, and its trustworthiness in formulating judgments of the understanding [philosophic judgments]. The slightest scrutiny of the history of natural science shows that current scientific opinion is nearly infallible in the former case, and is invariably wrong in the latter case. The man with a method good for purposes of his dominant interests, is a pathological case in respect to his wider judgment on the coördination of this method with a more complete experience. Priests and scientists, statesmen and men of business, philosophers and mathematicians, are all alike in this respect. We all start by being empiricists. But our empiricism is confined within our immediate interests. The more clearly we grasp the intellectual analysis of a way regulating procedure for the sake of those interests, the more decidedly we reject the inclusion of evidence which refuses to be immediately harmonized with the method before us. Some of the major disasters of mankind have been produced by the narrowness of men with a good methodology. Ulysses has no use for Plato, and the bones of his companions are strewn on many a reef and many an isle." "Obscurantism is the refusal to speculate freely on the limitations of traditional methods. It is more than that: it is the negation of the importance of such speculation, the insistence on incidental dangers. A few generations ago the clergy, or to speak more accurately, large sections of the clergy were the standing examples of obscurantism. Today their place has been taken by scientists—

By merit raised to that bad eminence.

The obscurantists of any generation are in the main constituted by the greater part of the practitioners of the dominant methodology. Today scientific methods are dominant, and scientists are the obscurantists." (From *The Function of Reason* [copyright 1929 by Princeton University Press and used with their permission], pp. 8, 34-35, where the immediate topic of discussion is the practically unanimous opinion of physiologists that the concept of purpose must be kept out of attempts to understand living organisms. Whitehead's criticism is expressed in general terms, and the reader will easily think of other cases of methodolatry, in and outside of science, to which it applies.)

Logical perfection does not here require any detailed explanation. An example of its importance is afforded by the rôle of mathematics in the restricted field of natural science. The history of mathematics exhibits the generalization of special notions observed in particular instances. In any branches of mathematics, the notions presuppose each other. It is a remarkable characteristic of the history of thought that branches of mathematics developed under the pure imaginative impulse, thus controlled, finally receive their important application. Time may be wanted. Conic sections had to wait for eighteen hundred years. In more recent years, the theory of probability, the theory of tensors, the theory of matrices are cases in point.

The requirement of coherence is the great preservative of rationalistic sanity. But the validity of its criticism is not always admitted. If we consider philosophical controversies, we shall find that disputants tend to require coherence from their adversaries, and to grant dispensations to themselves. It has been remarked that a system of philosophy is never refuted; it is only abandoned. The reason is that logical contradictions, except as temporary slips of the mind—plentiful, though temporary—are the most gratuitous of errors; and usually they are trivial. Thus, after criticism, systems do not exhibit mere illogicalities. They suffer from inadequacy and incoherence. Failure to include some obvious elements of experience in the scope of the system is met by boldly denying the facts. Also while a philosophical system retains any charm of novelty, it enjoys a plenary indulgence for its failures in coherence. But after a system has acquired orthodoxy, and is taught with authority, it receives a sharper criticism. Its denials and its incoherences are found intolerable, and a reaction sets in.

Incoherence is the arbitrary disconnection of first principles. In modern philosophy Descartes' two kinds of substance, corporeal and mental, illustrate incoherence. There is, in Descartes' philosophy, no reason why there should not be a one-substance world, only corporeal, or a one-substance world, only mental. According to Descartes, a substantial individual 'requires nothing but itself in order to exist.' Thus this system makes a virtue of its incoherence. But on the other hand, the facts seem connected, while Descartes' system does not; for example, in the treatment of the body-mind problem. The Cartesian system obviously says something that is true. But its notions are too abstract to penetrate into the nature of things. . . .

III

In its turn every philosophy will suffer a deposition. But the bundle of philosophic systems expresses a variety of general truths about the universe, awaiting coördination and assignment of their various spheres of validity. Such progress in coördination is provided by the advance of philosophy; and in this sense philosophy has advanced from Plato onwards. According to this account of the achievement of rationalism, the chief error in philosophy is overstatement. The aim at generalization is sound, but the estimate of success is exaggerated. There are two main forms of such overstatement. One form is what I have termed elsewhere, the 'fallacy of misplaced concreteness.' * This fallacy consists in neglecting the degree of abstraction involved when an actual entity is considered merely so far as it exemplifies certain categories of thought. There are aspects of actualities which are simply ignored so long as we restrict thought to these categories. Thus the success of a philosophy is to be measured by its comparative avoidance of this fallacy, when thought is restricted within its categories.

The other form of overstatement consists in a false estimate of logical procedure in respect to certainty, and in respect to premises. Philosophy has been haunted by the unfortunate notion that its method is dogmatically to indicate premises which are severally clear, distinct, and certain; and to erect upon those premises a deductive system of thought.

But the accurate expression of the final generalities is the goal of discussion and not its origin. Philosophy has been misled by the example of mathematics; and even in mathematics the statement of the ultimate logical principles is beset with difficulties, as yet insuperable. The verification of a rationalistic scheme is to be sought in its general success, and not in the peculiar certainty, or initial clarity, of its first principles. In this connection the misuse of the *ex absurdo* argument has to be noted; much philosophical reasoning is vitiated by it. The only logical conclusion to be drawn, when a contradiction issues from a train of reasoning, is that at least one of the premises involved in the inference is false. It is rashly assumed without further question that the peccant premise can at once be located. In mathematics this assumption is often justified, and philosophers have been thereby misled. But in the absence of a well-defined categoreal scheme of entities, issuing in a satisfactory metaphysical system, every premise in a philosophical argument is under suspicion.

Philosophy will not regain its proper status until the gradual elaboration of categoreal schemes, definitely stated at each stage of progress, is recognized as its proper objective. There may be rival schemes, inconsistent among themselves; each with its own merits and its own failures. It will then be the purpose of research to conciliate the differences. Metaphysical categories are not dogmatic statements of the obvious; they are tentative formulations of the ultimate generalities.

If we consider any scheme of philosophic categories as one complex

---

* Cf. *Science and the Modern World,* Ch. III.

assertion, and apply to it the logician's alternative, true or false, the answer must be that the scheme is false. The same answer must be given to a like question respecting the existing formulated principles of any science.

The scheme is true with unformulated qualifications, exceptions, limitations, and new interpretations in terms of more general notions. We do not yet know how to recast the scheme into a logical truth. But the scheme is a matrix from which true propositions applicable to particular circumstances can be derived. We can at present only trust our trained instincts as to the discrimination of the circumstances in respect to which the scheme is valid.

The use of such a matrix is to argue from it boldly and with rigid logic. The scheme should therefore be stated with the utmost precision and definiteness, to allow of such argumentation. The conclusion of the argument should then be confronted with circumstances to which it should apply.

The primary advantage thus gained is that experience is not interrogated with the benumbing repression of common sense. The observation acquires an enhanced penetration by reason of the expectation evoked by the conclusion of the argument. . . .

After the initial basis of a rational life, with a civilized language, has been laid, all productive thought has proceeded either by the poetic insight of artists, or by the imaginative elaboration of schemes of thought capable of utilization as logical premises. In some measure or other, progress is always a transcendence of what is obvious.

Rationalism never shakes off its status of an experimental adventure. The combined influences of mathematics and religion, which have so greatly contributed to the rise of philosophy, have also had the unfortunate effect of yoking it with static dogmatism. Rationalism is an adventure in the clarification of thought, progressive and never final. But it is an adventure in which even partial success has importance.

[8] [That we fail to find in experience any elements intrinsically incapable of exhibition as examples of general theory, is the hope of rationalism. This hope is not a metaphysical premise. It is the faith which forms the motive for the pursuit of all sciences alike, including metaphysics.

In so far as metaphysics enables us to apprehend the rationality of things, the claim is justified. It is always open to us, having regard to the imperfections of all metaphysical systems, to lose hope at the exact point where we find ourselves. The preservation of such faith must depend on an ultimate moral intuition into the nature of intellectual

[8] Brackets mark the insertion here of two relevant paragraphs—much too important to be given in a footnote—from another part of *Process and Reality* (The Macmillan Co., 1929), p. 67.

action—that it should embody the adventure of hope. Such an intuition marks the point where metaphysics—and indeed every science—gains assurance from religion and passes over into religion. But in itself the faith does not embody a premise from which the theory starts; it is an ideal which is seeking satisfaction. In so far as we believe that doctrine, we are rationalists.]

IV

... The study of philosophy is a voyage towards the larger generalities. For this reason in the infancy of science, when the main stress lay in the discovery of the most general ideas usefully applicable to the subject-matter in question, philosophy was not sharply distinguished from science. To this day, a new science with any substantial novelty in its notions is considered to be in some way peculiarly philosophical. In their later stages, apart from occasional disturbances, most sciences accept without question the general notions in terms of which they develop. The main stress is laid on the adjustment and the direct verification of more special statements. In such periods scientists repudiate philosophy; Newton, justly satisfied with his physical principles, disclaimed metaphysics.

The fate of Newtonian physics warns us that there is a development in scientific first principles, and that their original forms can only be saved by interpretations of meaning and limitations of their field of application—interpretations and limitations unsuspected during the first period of successful employment. One chapter in the history of culture is concerned with the growth of generalities. In such a chapter it is seen that the older generalities, like the older hills, are worn down and diminished in height, surpassed by younger rivals.

Thus one aim of philosophy is to challenge the half-truths constituting the scientific first principles. The systematization of knowledge cannot be conducted in watertight compartments. All general truths condition each other; and the limits of their application cannot be adequately defined apart from their correlation by yet wider generalities. The criticism of principles must chiefly take the form of determining the proper meanings to be assigned to the fundamental notions of the various sciences, when these notions are considered in respect to their status relatively to each other. The determination of this status requires a generality transcending any special subject-matter.

If we may trust the Pythagorean tradition, the rise of European philosophy was largely promoted by the development of mathematics into a science of abstract generality. But in its subsequent development the method of philosophy has also been vitiated by the example of mathematics. The primary method of mathematics is deduction; the primary method of philosophy is descriptive generalization. Under the influence of mathematics, deduction has been foisted onto philosophy as its standard method, instead of taking its true place as an essential auxiliary mode of verification whereby to test the scope of generalities. This misapprehension of philosophic method has veiled the very considerable success of philosophy in providing generic notions which add lucidity to our apprehension of the facts of experience. The depositions of Plato, Aristotle, Thomas Aquinas, Descartes, Spinoza, Leibnitz, Locke, Berkeley, Hume, Kant, Hegel, merely mean that ideas which these men introduced into the philosophic tradition must be construed with limitations, adaptations, and inversions, either unknown to them, or even explicitly repudiated by them. A new idea introduces a new alternative; and we are not less indebted to a thinker when we adopt the alternative which he discarded. Philosophy never reverts to its old position after the shock of a great philosopher.

V

Every science must devise its own instruments. The tool required for philosophy is language. Thus philosophy redesigns language in the same way that, in a physical science, pre-existing appliances are redesigned. It is exactly at this point that the appeal to facts is a difficult operation. This appeal is not solely to the expression of the facts in current verbal statements. The adequacy of such sentences is the main question at issue. It is true that the general agreement of mankind as to experienced facts is best expressed in language. But the language of literature breaks down precisely at the task of expressing in explicit form the larger generalities—the very generalities which metaphysics seeks to express.

The point is that every proposition refers to a universe exhibiting some general systematic metaphysical character. Apart from this background, the separate entities which go to form the proposition, and the proposition as a whole, are without determinate character. Nothing has been defined, because every definite entity requires a systematic universe to supply its requisite status. Thus every proposition proposing a fact must, in its complete analysis, propose the general character of the universe required for that fact. There are no self-sustained facts, floating in nonentity. . . . A proposition can embody partial truth because it only demands a certain type of systematic environment, which is presupposed in its meaning. It does not refer to the universe in all its detail. . . .

The technical language of philosophy represents attempts of various schools of thought to obtain explicit expression of general ideas presupposed by the facts of experience. It follows that any novelty in metaphysical doctrines exhibits some measure of disagreement with statements of the facts to be found in current philosophical literature.

The extent of disagreement measures the extent of metaphysical divergence. It is, therefore, no valid criticism on one metaphysical school to point out that its doctrines do not follow from the verbal expression of the facts accepted by another school. The whole contention is that the doctrines in question supply a closer approach to fully expressed propositions. . . .

[9] [Philosophy has been afflicted by the dogmatic fallacy, which is the belief that the principles of its working hypotheses are clear, obvious, and irreformable. Then, as a reaction from this fallacy, it has swayed to the other extreme which is the fallacy of discarding method. Philosophers boast that they uphold no system. They are then a prey to the delusive clarities of detached expressions which it is the very purpose of their science to surmount. Another type of reaction is to assume, often tacitly, that if there can be any intellectual analysis it must proceed according to some one discarded dogmatic method, and thence to deduce that intellect is intrinsically tied to erroneous fictions. This type is illustrated by the anti-intellectualism of Nietzsche and Bergson, and tinges American Pragmatism.]

Whatever is found in 'practice' must lie within the scope of the metaphysical description. When the description fails to include the 'practice,' the metaphysics is inadequate and requires revision. There can be no appeal to practice to supplement metaphysics, so long as we remain contented with our metaphysical doctrines. Metaphysics is nothing but the description of the generalities which apply to all the details of practice.

No metaphysical system can hope entirely to satisfy these pragmatic tests. At the best such a system will remain only an approximation to the general truths which are sought. In particular, there are no precisely stated axiomatic certainties from which to start. There is not even the language in which to frame them. The only possible procedure is to start from verbal expressions which, when taken by themselves with the current meaning of their words, are ill-defined and ambiguous. These are not premises to be immediately reasoned from apart from elucidation by further discussion; they are endeavours to state general principles which will be exemplified in the subsequent description of the facts of experience. This subsequent elaboration should elucidate the meanings to be assigned to the words and phrases employed. Such meanings are incapable of accurate apprehension apart from a correspondingly accurate apprehension of the metaphysical background which the universe provides for them. But no language can be anything but elliptical, requiring a leap of the imagination to understand its meaning in its relevance to immediate experience. The position of

[9] This inserted paragraph is from *Adventures of Ideas* (New York, The Macmillan Co., 1933), p. 287.

metaphysics in the development of culture cannot be understood without remembering that no verbal statement is the adequate expression of a proposition.

An old established metaphysical system gains a false air of adequate precision from the fact that its words and phrases have passed into current literature. Thus propositions expressed in its language are more easily correlated to our flitting intuitions into metaphysical truth. When we trust these verbal statements and argue as though they adequately analysed meaning, we are led into difficulties which take the shape of negations of what in practice is presupposed. But when they are proposed as first principles they assume an unmerited air of sober obviousness. . . .

VI

It has been an objection to speculative philosophy that it is over-ambitious. Rationalism, it is admitted, is the method by which advance is made within the limits of particular sciences. It is, however, held that this limited success must not encourage attempts to frame ambitious schemes expressive of the general nature of things.

One alleged justification of this criticism is ill-success: European thought is represented as littered with metaphysical systems, abandoned and unreconciled.

Such an assertion tacitly fastens upon philosophy the old dogmatic test. The same criterion would fasten ill-success upon science. We no more retain the physics of the seventeenth century than we do the Cartesian philosophy of that century. Yet within limits, both systems express important truths. Also we are beginning to understand the wider categories which define their limits of correct application. Of course, in that century, dogmatic views held sway; so that the validity both of the physical notions, and of the Cartesian notions, was misconceived. Mankind never quite knows what it is after. When we survey the history of thought, and likewise the history of practice, we find that one idea after another is tried out, its limitations defined, and its core of truth elicited. . . . The proper test is not that of finality, but of progress.

But the main objection, dating from the sixteenth century and receiving final expression from Francis Bacon, is the uselessness of philosophic speculation. The position taken by this objection is that we ought to describe detailed matter of fact, and elicit the laws with a generality strictly limited to the systematization of these described details. General interpretation, it is held, has no bearing upon this procedure; and thus any system of general interpretation, be it true or false, remains intrinsically barren. Unfortunately for this objection, there are no brute, self-contained matters of fact, capable of being understood apart from interpretation as an element in a system. Whenever we attempt to express the matter of immediate experience, we find that its understanding leads us beyond itself, to its contemporaries, to its past, to its future, and to the universals in terms of which its definiteness is exhibited. But such universals, by their very character of universality, embody the potentiality of other facts with variant types of definiteness. Thus the understanding of the immediate brute fact requires its metaphysical interpretation as an item in a world with some systematic relation to it. When thought comes upon the scene, it finds the interpretations as matters of practice. Philosophy does not initiate interpretations. Its search for a rationalistic scheme is the search for more adequate criticism, and for more adequate justification, of the interpretations which we perforce employ. Our habitual experience is a complex of failure and success in the enterprise of interpretation. If we desire a record of uninterpreted experience, we must ask a stone to record its autobiography. Every scientific memoir in its record of the 'facts' is shot through and through with interpretation. The methodology of rational interpretation is the product of the fitful vagueness of consciousness. Elements which shine with immediate distinctness, in some circumstances, retire into penumbral shadow in other circumstances, and into black darkness on other occasions. And yet all occasions proclaim themselves as actualities within the flux of a solid world, demanding a unity of interpretation.

Philosophy is the self-correction by consciousness of its own initial excess of subjectivity. Each actual occasion contributes to the circumstances of its origin additional formative elements deepening its own peculiar individuality. Consciousness is only the last and greatest of such elements by which the selective character of the individual obscures the external totality from which it originates and which it embodies. An actual individual, of such higher grade, has truck with the totality of things by reason of its sheer actuality; but it has attained its individual depth of being by a selective emphasis limited to its own purposes. The task of philosophy is to recover the totality obscured by the selection. It replaces in rational experience what has been submerged in the higher sensitive experience and has been sunk yet deeper by the initial operations of consciousness itself. The selectiveness of individual experience is moral so far as it conforms to the balance of importance disclosed in the rational vision; and conversely the conversion of the intellectual insight into an emotional force corrects the sensitive experience in the direction of morality. The correction is in proportion to the rationality of the insight.

Morality of outlook is inseparably conjoined with generality of outlook. The antithesis between the general good and the individual interest can be abolished only when the individual is such that its interest is the general good, thus exemplifying the loss of the minor intensities in order to find them again with finer composition in a wider sweep of interest.

Philosophy frees itself from the taint of ineffectiveness by its close relations with religion and with science, natural and sociological. It attains its chief importance by fusing the two, namely, religion and science, into one rational scheme of thought. Religion should connect the rational generality of philosophy with the emotions and purposes springing out of existence in a particular society, in a particular epoch, and conditioned by particular antecedents. Religion is the translation of general ideas into particular thoughts, particular emotions, and particular purposes; it is directed to the end of stretching individual interest beyond its self-defeating particularity. Philosophy finds religion, and modifies it; and conversely religion is among the data of experience which philosophy must weave into its own scheme. Religion is an ultimate craving to infuse into the insistent particularity of emotion that non-temporal generality which primarily belongs to conceptual thought alone. In the higher organisms the differences of tempo between the mere emotions and the conceptual experiences produce a life-tedium, unless this supreme fusion has been effected. The two sides of the organism require a reconciliation in which emotional experiences illustrate a conceptual justification, and conceptual experiences find an emotional illustration.

This demand for an intellectual justification of brute experience has also been the motive power in the advance of European science. In this sense scientific interest is only a variant form of religious interest. Any survey of the scientific devotion to 'truth,' as an ideal, will confirm this statement. There is, however, a grave divergence between science and religion in respect to the phases of individual experience with which they are concerned. Religion is centered upon the harmony of rational thought with the sensitive reaction to the percepta from which experience originates. Science is concerned with the harmony of rational thought with the percepta themselves. When science deals with emotions, the emotions in question are percepta and not immediate passions—other people's emotion and not our own; at least our own in recollection, and not in immediacy. Religion deals with the formation of the experiencing subject; whereas science deals with the objects, which are the data forming the primary phase in this experience. The subject originates from, and amid, given conditions; science conciliates thought with this primary matter of fact; and religion conciliates the thought involved in the process with the sensitive reaction involved in that same process. The process is nothing else than the experiencing subject itself. In this explanation it is presumed that an experiencing subject is one occasion of sensitive reaction to an actual world. Science finds religious experiences among its percepta; and religion finds scientific concepts among the conceptual experiences to be fused with particular sensitive reactions.

The conclusion of this discussion is, first, the assertion of the old doctrine that breadth of thought reacting with intensity of sensitive experience stands out as an ultimate claim of existence; secondly, the assertion that empirically the development of self-justifying thoughts has been achieved by the complex process of generalizing from particular topics, of imaginatively schematizing the generalizations, and finally by renewed comparison of the imagined scheme with the direct experience to which it should apply.

There is no justification for checking generalization at any particular stage. Each phase of generalization exhibits its own peculiar simplicities which stand out just at that stage, and at no other stage. There are simplicities connected with the motion of a bar of steel which are obscured if we refuse to abstract from the individual molecules; and there are certain simplicities concerning the behaviour of men which are obscured if we refuse to abstract from the individual peculiarities of particular specimens. In the same way, there are certain general truths, about the actual things in the common world of activity, which will be obscured when attention is confined to some particular detailed mode of considering them. These general truths, involved in the meaning of every particular notion respecting the actions of things, are the subject matter for speculative philosophy.

Philosophy destroys its usefulness when it indulges in brilliant feats of explaining away. It is then trespassing with the wrong equipment upon the field of particular sciences. Its ultimate appeal is to the general consciousness of what in practice we experience. Whatever thread of presupposition characterizes social expression throughout the various epochs of rational society, must find its place in philosophic theory. Speculative boldness must be balanced by complete humility before logic, and before fact. It is a disease of philosophy when it is neither bold nor humble, but merely a reflection of the temperamental presuppositions of exceptional personalities.

Analogously, we do not trust any recasting of scientific theory depending upon a single performance of an aberrant experiment, unrepeated. The ultimate test is always widespread, recurrent experience; and the more general the rationalistic scheme, the more important is this final appeal.

The useful function of philosophy is to promote the most general systematization of civilized thought. There is a constant reaction between specialism and common sense. It is the part of the special sciences to modify common sense. Philosophy is the welding of imagination and common sense into a restraint upon specialists, and also into an enlargement of their imaginations. By providing the generic notions philosophy should make it easier to conceive the infinite variety of specific instances which rest unrealized in the womb of nature.

3. Religion

Religion and Science [10]

[WITH REGARD TO] the questions in which there is a variance between science and religion ... if we have any sense of perspective and of the history of thought, we shall wait and refrain from mutual anathemas.

We should wait: but we should not wait passively, or in despair. The clash is a sign that there are wider truths and finer perspectives within which a reconciliation of a deeper religion and a more subtle science will be found.

... Remember the widely different aspects of events which are dealt with in science and in religion respectively. Science is concerned with the general conditions which are observed to regulate physical phenomena; whereas religion is wholly wrapped up in the contemplation of moral and aesthetic values. On the one side there is the law of gravitation, and on the other the contemplation of the beauty of holiness. What one side sees, the other misses; and vice versa.

Consider, for example, the lives of John Wesley and of Saint Francis of Assisi. For physical science you have in these lives merely ordinary examples of the operation of the principles of physiological chemistry, and of the dynamics of nervous reactions: for religion you have lives of the most profound significance in the history of the world. Can you be surprised that, in the absence of a perfect and complete phrasing of the principles of science and of the principles of religion which apply to these specific cases, the accounts of these lives from these divergent standpoints should involve discrepancies? It would be a miracle if it were not so.

It would, however, be missing the point to think that we need not trouble ourselves about the conflict between science and religion. In an intellectual age there can be no active interest which puts aside all hope of a vision of the harmony of truth. To acquiesce in discrepancy is destructive of candour, and of moral cleanliness. It belongs to the self-respect of intellect to pursue every tangle of thought to its final unravelment. If you check that impulse, you will get no religion and no science from an awakened thoughtfulness. The important question is, In what spirit are we going to face the issue? ...

[10] From the chapter bearing this title in *Science and the Modern World* (Copyright, 1925 by the Macmillan Co. and used with their permission.) pp. 264–266, 270–271.

... When Darwin or Einstein proclaim theories which modify our ideas, it is a triumph for science. We do not go about saying that there is another defeat for science, because its old ideas have been abandoned. We know that another step of scientific insight has been gained.

Religion will not regain its old power until it can face change in the same spirit as does science. Its principles may be eternal, but the expression of those principles requires continual development. This evolution of religion is in the main a disengagement of its own proper ideas from the adventitious notions which have crept into it by reason of the expression of its own ideas in terms of the imaginative picture of the world entertained in previous ages. Such a release of religion from the bonds of imperfect science is all to the good. It stresses its own genuine message. . . .

Religion Defined [11]

... Your character is developed according to your faith. This is the primary religious truth from which no one can escape. Religion is force of belief cleansing the inward parts. For this reason the primary religious virtue is sincerity, a penetrating sincerity.

A religion, on its doctrinal side, can thus be defined as a system of general truths which have the effect of transforming character when they are sincerely held and vividly apprehended.

In the long run your character and your conduct of life depend upon your intimate convictions. Life is an internal fact for its own sake, before it is an external fact relating itself to others. The conduct of external life is conditioned by environment, but it receives its final quality, on which its worth depends, from the internal life which is the self-realization of existence. Religion is the art and the theory of the internal life of man, so far as it depends on the man himself and on what is permanent in the nature of things.

This doctrine is the direct negation of the theory that religion is primarily a social fact. Social facts are of great importance to religion, because there is no such thing as absolutely independent existence. You cannot abstract society from man; most psychology is herd-psychology. But all collective emotions leave untouched the awful ultimate fact, which is the human being, consciously alone with itself, for its own sake.

Religion is what the individual does with his own solitariness. It runs through three stages, if it evolves to its final satisfaction. It is the transition from God the void to God the enemy, and from God the enemy to God the companion.

[11] The greater part (pp. 15-18) of the section which bears this title in *Religion in the Making* (Copyright, 1926 by the Macmillan Company and used with their permission.)

Thus religion is solitariness; and if you are never solitary, you are never religious. Collective enthusiasms, revivals, institutions, churches, rituals, bibles, codes of behaviour, are the trappings of religion, its passing forms. They may be useful, or harmful; they may be authoritatively ordained, or merely temporary expedients. But the end of religion is beyond all this.

Accordingly, what should emerge from religion is individual worth of character. But worth is positive or negative, good or bad. Religion is by no means necessarily good. It may be very evil. The fact of evil, interwoven with the texture of the world, shows that in the nature of things there remains effectiveness for degradation. In your religious experience the God with whom you have made terms may be the God of destruction, the God who leaves in his wake the loss of the greater reality.

In considering religion, we should not be obsessed by the idea of its necessary goodness. This is a dangerous delusion. The point to notice is its transcendent importance; and the fact of this importance is abundantly made evident by the appeal to history.

Plato and Jesus [12]

[Plato published his conviction,] towards the end of his life,* that the divine element in the world is to be conceived as a persuasive agency and not as a coercive agency. This doctrine should be looked upon as one of the greatest intellectual discoveries in the history of religion. . . . The alternative doctrine, prevalent then and now, sees either in the many gods or in the one God, the final coercive forces wielding the thunder. By a metaphysical sublimation of this doctrine of God as the supreme agency of compulsion, he is transformed into the one supreme reality, omnipotently disposing a wholly derivative world. Plato wavered inconsistently between these diverse conceptions. But he does finally enunciate without qualification the doctrine of the divine persuasion, by reason of which ideals are effective in the world and forms of order evolve.

. . . The essence of Christianity is the appeal to the life of Christ as a revelation of the nature of God and of his agency in the world. The record is fragmentary, inconsistent, and uncertain. . . . But there can be no doubt as to what elements in the record have evoked a response from all that is best in human nature. The Mother, the Child, and the bare manger: the lowly man, homeless and self-forgetful, with his message of peace, love, and sympathy: the suffering, the agony, the tender

[12] *Adventures of Ideas*, pp. 213-214. (Copyright, 1933 by the Macmillan Company and used with their permission.)
* *Cf.* the *Sophist* and the *Timaeus*.

words as life ebbed, the final despair: and the whole with the authority of supreme victory.

I need not elaborate. Can there be any doubt that the power of Christianity lies in its revelation in act, of that which Plato divined in theory?

4. Civilization

The Rôle of General Ideas [13]

THE GREAT classical civilization is remarkable for two facts. First, it constituted a culmination of slavery, especially at the height of the Roman Empire. . . . [Secondly,] it was the first period which introduced moral principles forming an effective criticism of the whole system. . . .

We see here the first stage of the introduction of great ideas. They start as speculative suggestions in the minds of a small, gifted group. [E.g., the group of Greek thinkers gathered around Plato, who in his concept of the soul introduced "notions from which all claims for freedom must spring. His general concept of the psychic factors in the Universe stressed them as the source of all spontaneity, and ultimately as the ground of all life and motion." [14]] They acquire a limited application to human life at the hands of various sets of leaders with special functions in the social structure. ["The Stoic lawyers of the Roman Empire introduced a legal reformation largely motived by the principle that human nature has essential rights." [15]] A whole literature arises which explains how inspiring is the general idea, and how slight need be its effect in disturbing a comfortable society. Some transition has been produced by the agency of the new idea. But on the whole the social system has been inoculated against the full infection of the new principle. It takes its place among the interesting notions which have a restricted application.

But a general idea is always a danger to the existing order. The whole bundle of its conceivable special embodiments in various usages of society constitutes a program of reform. At any moment the smouldering unhappiness of mankind may seize on some such program and initiate a period of rapid change guided by the light of its doctrines.

[13] From Ch. II, "The Human Soul," of Adventures of Ideas, pp. 16-19, 21, 24, 26, 29-31—except for the last paragraph of this section of selections, which is from p. 105. (Copyright, 1933 by the Macmillan Company and used with their permission.) The chapter presents Whitehead's favorite illustration of the social rôle of a general idea—the part played by the idea of the essential worth of each human soul, in gradually eliminating the slavery on which ancient civilization was founded. We have had to omit his discussion of the religious and secular forms which this idea took in the eighteenth and nineteenth centuries.

[14] Whitehead, Adventures of Ideas, p. 64. By permission of The Macmillan Company.

[15] Adventures of Ideas, pp. 16-17. By permission of The Macmillan Company.

In this way, the conception of the dignity of human nature was quietly energizing in the minds of Roman officials, producing somewhat better government and nerving men like Marcus Aurelius to rise to the height of their appointed task. It was a worthy moral force, but society had been inoculated against its revolutionary application. For six hundred years, the ideal of the intellectual and moral grandeur of the human soul had haunted the ancient Mediterranean world. It had in a way transformed the moral ideas of mankind: it had readjusted religions: and yet it had failed to close with the basic weakness of the civilization in which it flourished. It was the faint light of the dawn of a new order of life.

In the midst of this period of progress and decadence, Christianity arose.... [It] rapidly assimilated the Platonic doctrine of the human soul. The philosophy and the religion were very congenial to each other in their respective teachings; although, as was natural, the religious version was much more specialized than the philosophic version. We have here an example of the principle that dominates the history of ideas. There will be a general idea in the background flittingly, waveringly, realized by the few in its full generality—or perhaps never expressed in any adequate universal form with persuasive force. Such persuasive expression depends on the accidents of genius; for example, it depends on the chance that a man like Plato appears. But this general idea, whether expressed or implicitly just below the surface of consciousness, embodies itself in special expression after special expression. It condescends so as to lose the magnificence of its generality, but it gains in the force of its peculiar adaptation to the concrete circumstances of a particular age. It is a hidden driving force, haunting humanity, and ever appearing in specialized guise as compulsory on action by reason of its appeal to the uneasy conscience of the age. The force of the appeal lies in the fact that the specialized principle of immediate conduct exemplifies the grandeur of the wider truth arising from the very nature of the order of things, a truth which mankind has grown to the stature of being able to feel though perhaps as yet unable to frame in fortunate expression....

In ethical ideals we find the supreme example of consciously formulated ideas acting as a driving force effecting transitions from social state to social state. Such ideas are at once gadflies irritating, and beacons luring, the victims among whom they dwell. The conscious agency of such ideas should be contrasted with senseless forces, floods, barbarians, and mechanical devices. The great transitions are due to a coincidence of forces derived from both sides of the world, its physical and its spiritual natures. Mere physical nature lets loose a flood, but it requires intelligence to provide a system of irrigation....

The slow issue of general ideas into practical consequences is not wholly due to inefficiency of human character. There is a problem to be solved, and its complexity is habitually ignored by impetuous seekers. The difficulty is just this:—It may be impossible to conceive a reorganization of society adequate for the removal of some admitted evil without destroying the social organization and the civilization which depends on it. . . .

. . . A great idea is not to be conceived as merely waiting for enough good men to carry it into practical effect. That is a childish view of the history of ideas. The ideal in the background is promoting the gradual growth of the requisite communal customs, adequate to sustain the load of its exemplification. . . .

Human life is driven forward by its dim apprehension of notions too general for its existing language. Such ideas cannot be grasped singly, one by one in isolation. They require that mankind advances in its apprehension of the general nature of things, so as to conceive systems of ideas elucidating each other. But the growth of generality of apprehension is the slowest of all evolutionary changes. It is the task of philosophy to promote this growth in mentality. In so far as there is success, the specialized applications of great ideas are purified from their gross associations with savage fancies. The Carthaginians were a great civilized trading nation. . . . Yet, when Plato was speculating, this great people could so conceive the supreme powers of the Universe that they sacrificed their children to Moloch as an act of religious propitiation. The growth in generality of understanding makes such savagery impossible in corresponding civilizations today. . . .

The history of ideas is a history of mistakes. But through all mistakes it is also the history of the gradual purification of conduct. When there is progress in the development of favourable order, we find conduct protected from relapse into brutalization by the increasing agency of ideas consciously entertained. In this way Plato is justified in his saying, The creation of the world—that is to say, the world of civilized order— is the victory of persuasion over force.

. . . The worth of men consists in their liability to persuasion. They can persuade and can be persuaded by the disclosure of alternatives, the better and the worse. Civilization is the maintenance of social order, by its own inherent persuasiveness as embodying the nobler alternative. The recourse to force, however unavoidable, is a disclosure of the failure of civilization, either in the general society or in a remnant of individuals. Thus in a live civilization there is always an element of unrest. For sensitiveness to ideas means curiosity, adventure, change. Civilized order survives on its merits, and is transformed by its power of recognizing its imperfections.

Adventure [16]

The foundation of all understanding of sociological theory—that is to say, of all understanding of human life—is that no static maintenance of perfection is possible. This axiom is rooted in the nature of things. Advance or Decadence are the only choices offered to mankind. The pure conservative is fighting against the essence of the universe. This doctrine requires justification. It is implicitly denied in the learned tradition derived from ancient thought.

The doctrine is founded upon three metaphysical principles. One principle is that the very essence of real actuality—that is, of the completely real—is *process*. Thus each actual thing is only to be understood in terms of its becoming and perishing. There is no halt in which the actuality is just its static self, accidentally played upon by qualifications derived from the shift of circumstances. The converse is the truth.

The static notion, here rejected, is derived by two different paths from ancient thought. Plato in the earlier period of his thought, deceived by the beauty of mathematics intelligible in unchanging perfection, conceived of a super-world of ideas, forever perfect and forever interwoven. In his latest phase he sometimes repudiates the notion, though he never consistently banishes it from his thought. His later Dialogues circle round seven notions, namely—The Ideas, The Physical Elements, The Psyche, The Eros, The Harmony, The Mathematical Relations, The Receptacle. I mention them because I hold that all philosophy is in fact an endeavour to obtain a coherent system out of some modification of these notions. . . .

. . . In the modern development of these seven metaphysical notions, we should start from the notion of actuality as in its essence a process. This process involves a physical side which is the perishing of the past as it transforms itself into a new creation. It also involves a mental side which is the Soul entertaining ideas.

The Soul thereby by synthesis creates a new fact which is the Appearance [17] woven out of the old and the new—a compound of reception and anticipation, which in its turn passes into the future. The final synthesis of these three complexes is the end to which its indwelling Eros [18] urges the soul. Its good resides in the realization of a strength of many feelings fortifying each other as they meet in the novel unity. Its evil lies in the clash of vivid feelings, denying to each other their proper expansion. Its triviality lies in the anaesthesia by

[16] Approximately half (pp. 353-360) of the chapter which bears this title in *Adventures of Ideas*. By permission of The Macmillan Company.

[17] On the meaning of this term, see p. 468 below, and pp. 405, 409, 411 f. of the Introduction to these Selections.

[18] I.e., "the urge towards the realization of ideal perfection" (*Adventures of Ideas*, p. 354).

which evil is avoided. In this way through sheer omission, fewer, fainter feelings constitute the final Appearance. Evil is the half-way house between perfection and triviality. It is the violence of strength against strength.

Aristotle introduced the static fallacy by another concept which has infected all subsequent philosophy. He conceived of primary substances as the static foundations which received the impress of qualification. In the case of human experience, a modern version of the same notion is Locke's metaphor of the mind as an 'empty cabinet' receiving the impress of ideas. Thus for Locke the reality does not reside in the process but in the static recipient of process. According to the versions of Aristotle and Locke, one primary substance cannot be a component in the nature of another primary substance. Thus the interconnections of primary substances must be devoid of the substantial reality of the primary substances themselves. With this doctrine, the conjunction of actualities has, in various shapes, been a problem throughout modern philosophy—both for metaphysics and for epistemology. The taint of Aristotelian Logic has thrown the whole emphasis of metaphysical thought upon substantives and adjectives, to the neglect of prepositions and conjunctions. This Aristotelian doctrine is in this book summarily denied. The process is itself the actuality, and requires no antecedent static cabinet. Also the processes of the past, in their perishing, are themselves energizing as the complex origin of each novel occasion. The past is the reality at the base of each new actuality. The process is its absorption into a new unity with ideals and with anticipation, by the operation of the creative Eros.

I now pass to the second metaphysical principle. It is the doctrine that every occasion of actuality is in its own nature finite. There is no totality which is the harmony of all perfections. Whatever is realized in any one occasion of experience necessarily excludes the unbounded welter of contrary possibilities. There are always 'others,' which might have been and are not. This finiteness is not the result of evil, or of imperfection. It results from the fact that there are possibilities of harmony which either produce evil in joint realization, or are incapable of such conjunction. This doctrine is a commonplace in the fine arts. It also is—or should be—a commonplace of political philosophy. History can only be understood by seeing it as the theatre of diverse groups of idealists respectively urging ideals incompatible for conjoint realization. You cannot form any historical judgment of right or wrong by considering each group separately. The evil lies in the attempted conjunction.

This principle of intrinsic incompatibility has an important bearing upon our conception of the nature of God. The concept of impossibility such that God himself cannot surmount it, has been for centuries quite familiar to theologians. Indeed, apart from it there would be difficulty in conceiving any determinate divine nature. But curiously enough, so far as I know, this notion of incompatibility has never been applied to ideals in the Divine realization. We must conceive the Divine Eros as the active entertainment of all ideals, with the urge to their finite realization, each in its due season. Thus a process must be inherent in God's nature, whereby his infinity is acquiring realization.

It is unnecessary to pursue theology further. But the point stands out that the conceptual entertainment of incompatibilities is possible, and so is their conceptual comparison. Also there is the synthesis of conceptual entertainment with physical realization. The idea conceptually entertained may be identical with the idea exemplified in the physical fact; or it may be different, compatible or incompatible. This synthesis of the ideal with the real is just what happens in each finite occasion.

Thus in every civilization at its culmination we should find a large measure of realization of a certain type of perfection. This type will be complex and will admit of variation of detail, this way or that. The culmination can maintain itself at its height so long as fresh experimentation within the type is possible. But when these minor variations are exhausted, one of two things must happen. Perhaps the society in question lacks imaginative force. Staleness then sets in. Repetition produces a gradual lowering of vivid appreciation. Convention dominates. A learned orthodoxy suppresses adventure.... There may be high survival power. For decadence, undisturbed by originality or by external forces, is a slow process. But the values of life are slowly ebbing. There remains the show of civilization, without any of its realities.

There is an alternative to this slow decline. A race may exhaust a form of civilization without having exhausted its own creative springs of originality. In that case, a quick period of transition may set in, which may or may not be accompanied by dislocations involving widespread unhappiness. Such periods are Europe at the close of the Middle Ages, Europe during the comparatively long Reformation Period, Europe at the end of the eighteenth century. Also let us hope that our present epoch is to be viewed as a period of change to a new direction of civilization, involving in its dislocations a minimum of human misery. And yet surely the misery of the Great War [19] was sufficient for any change of epoch.

These quick transitions to new types of civilization are only possible when thought has run ahead of realization. The vigour of the race has then pushed forward into the adventure of imagination, so as to anticipate the physical adventures of exploration. The world dreams of

[19] Of 1914-18.

things to come, and then in due season arouses itself to their realization. Indeed all physical adventure which is entered upon of set purpose involves an adventure of thought regarding things as yet unrealized. Before Columbus set sail for America, he had dreamt of the far East, and of the round world, and of the trackless ocean. Adventure rarely reaches its predetermined end. Columbus never reached China. But he discovered America.

Sometimes adventure is acting within limits. It can then calculate its end, and reach it. Such adventures are the ripples of change within one type of civilization, by which an epoch of given type preserves its freshness. But, given the vigour of adventure, sooner or later the leap of imagination reaches beyond the safe limits of the epoch, and beyond the safe limits of learned rules of taste. It then produces the dislocations and confusions marking the advent of new ideals for civilized effort.

A race preserves its vigour so long as it harbours a real contrast between what has been and what may be; and so long as it is nerved by the vigour to adventure beyond the safeties of the past. Without adventure civilization is in full decay.

It is for this reason that the definition of culture as the knowledge of the best that has been said and done, is so dangerous by reason of its omission. It omits the great fact that in their day the great achievements of the past were the adventures of the past. Only the adventurous can understand the greatness of the past. In its day, the literature of the past was an adventure. Aeschylus, Sophocles, Euripides were adventurers in the world of thought. To read their plays without any sense of new ways of understanding the world and of savouring its emotions is to miss the vividness which constitutes their whole value. But adventures are to the adventurous. Thus a passive knowledge of the past loses the whole value of its message. A living civilization requires learning; but it lies beyond it. . . .[20]

Peace [21]

SECTION I. . . . Finally, in this . . . last Part of the book, those essential qualities, whose joint realization in social life constitutes civilization, are being considered. Four such qualities have, so far, been examined: —Truth, Beauty, Adventure, Art.

[20] Whitehead's exposition of the third of the "three metaphysical principles" on which he said (p. 475, above) that his doctrine of Adventure is founded, is here omitted, because its connection with that doctrine appears to be indirect. The omitted principle, which he calls "the principle of Individuality," may be roughly summarized as asserting that the idea of harmony, in its fullest meaning, stands for a harmony not merely of patterned qualities, but of individual actualities; so Art which presents such harmonies is essential to Civilization.

[21] The last chapter of *Adventures of Ideas* (New York, 1933). The title is Whitehead's. By permission of The Macmillan Company.

SECTION II. Something is still lacking. It is difficult to state it in terms that are wide enough. Also, where clearly distinguished and exposed in all its bearings, it assumes an air of exaggeration. Habitually it is lurking on the edge of consciousness, a modifying agency. . . . Apart from it, the pursuit of 'Truth, Beauty, Adventure, Art,' can be ruthless, hard, cruel; and thus, as the history of the Italian Renaissance illustrates, lacking in some essential quality of civilization. The notions of 'tenderness' and of 'love' are too narrow, important though they be. We require the concept of some more general quality, from which 'tenderness' emerges as a specialization. We are in a way seeking for the notion of a Harmony of Harmonies, which shall bind together the other four qualities, so as to exclude from our notion of civilization the restless egotism with which they have often in fact been pursued. 'Impersonality' is too dead a notion, and 'Tenderness' too narrow. I choose the term 'Peace' for that Harmony of Harmonies which calms destructive turbulence and completes civilization. Thus a society is to be termed civilized whose members participate in the five qualities— Truth, Beauty, Adventure, Art, Peace.

SECTION III. The Peace that is here meant is not the negative conception of anaesthesia. It is a positive feeling which crowns the 'life and motion' of the soul. It is hard to define and difficult to speak of. It is not a hope for the future, nor is it an interest in present details. It is a broadening of feeling due to the emergence of some deep metaphysical insight, unverbalized and yet momentous in its coördination of values. Its first effect is the removal of the stress of acquisitive feeling arising from the soul's preoccupation with itself. Thus Peace carries with it a surpassing of personality. There is an inversion of relative values. It is primarily a trust in the efficacy of Beauty. It is a sense that fineness of achievement is as it were a key unlocking treasures that the narrow nature of things would keep remote. There is thus involved a grasp of infinitude, an appeal beyond boundaries. Its emotional effect is the subsidence of turbulence which inhibits. More accurately, it preserves the springs of energy, and at the same time masters them for the avoidance of paralyzing distractions. The trust in the self-justification of Beauty introduces faith, where reason fails to reveal the details.

The experience of Peace is largely beyond the control of purpose. It comes as a gift. The deliberate aim at Peace very easily passes into its bastard substitute, Anaesthesia. In other words, in the place of a quality of 'life and motion,' there is substituted their destruction. Thus Peace is the removal of inhibition and not its introduction. It results in a wider sweep of conscious interest. It enlarges the field of attention. Thus Peace is self-control at its widest—at the width where the 'self' has been lost, and interest has been transferred to coördinations wider than personality. Here the real motive interests of the spirit are meant, and not the superficial play of discursive ideas. Peace is helped by such superficial width, and also promotes it. In fact it is largely for this reason that Peace is so essential for civilization. It is the barrier against narrowness. One of its fruits is that passion whose existence Hume denied, the love of mankind as such.

SECTION IV. The meaning of Peace is most clearly understood by considering it in its relation to the tragic issues which are essential in the nature of things. Peace is the understanding of tragedy, and at the same time its preservation.

We have seen that there can be no real halt of civilization in the indefinite repetition of a perfected ideal. Staleness sets in. And this fatigue is nothing other than the creeping growth of anaesthesia, whereby that social group is gradually sinking towards nothingness. The defining characteristics are losing their importance. There may be no pain or conscious loss. There is merely a slow paralysis of surprise. And apart from surprise, intensity of feeling collapses.

Decay, Transition, Loss, Displacement belong to the essence of the Creative Advance. The new direction of aim is initiated by Spontaneity, an element of confusion. The enduring Societies [22] with their rise, culmination, and decay, are devices to combine the necessities of Harmony and Freshness. There is the deep underlying Harmony of Nature, as it were a fluid, flexible support; and on its surface the ripples of social efforts, harmonizing and clashing in their aims at ways of satisfaction. The lower types of physical objects can have a vast endurance of inorganic life. The higher types, involving animal life and the dominance of a personality primarily mental, preserve their zest by the quick succession of stages from birth, culmination, to death. As soon as high consciousness is reached, the enjoyment of existence is entwined with pain, frustration, loss, tragedy. Amid the passing of so much beauty, so much heroism, so much daring, Peace is then the intuition of permanence. It keeps vivid the sensitiveness to the tragedy; and it sees the tragedy as a living agent persuading the world to aim at fineness beyond the faded level of surrounding fact. Each tragedy is the disclosure of an ideal—What might have been, and was not: What can be. The tragedy was not in vain. This survival power in motive force, by reason of appeal to reserves of Beauty, marks the difference between the tragic evil and the gross evil. The inner feeling belonging to this grasp of the service of tragedy is Peace—the purification of the emotions.

SECTION V. The deepest definition of Youth is, Life as yet untouched by tragedy. And the finest flower of youth is to know the lesson in

---

[22] I.e., things of nature, each a group of processes. See pp. 466 f., below; also p. 405 of our Introduction for the definition of the term, and p. 410 for the relevance of "Harmony and Freshness" to Societies.

advance of the experience, undimmed. The question here for discussion is how the intuition of Peace asserts itself apart from its disclosure in tragedy. Evidently observation of the earlier stages of personal life will afford the clearest evidence.

Youth is distinguished for its whole-hearted absorption in personal enjoyments and personal discomforts. Quick pleasure and quick pain, quick laughter and quick tears, quick absence of care, and quick diffidence, quick courage and quick fear, are conjointly characters of youth. In other words, immediate absorption in its own occupations. On this side, Youth is too chequered to be termed a happy period. It is vivid rather than happy. The memories of youth are better to live through, than is youth itself. For except in extreme cases, memory is apt to count the sunny hours. Youth is not peaceful in any ordinary sense of that term. In youth despair is overwhelming. There is then no tomorrow, no memory of disasters survived.

The short-sightedness of youth matches the scantiness of its experience. The issues of its action are beyond its ken, perhaps with literature supplying a delusory sense of knowledge. Thus generosity and cruelty are equally natural, by reason of the fact that their full effects lie beyond conscious anticipation.

All this is the veriest commonplace in the characterization of youth. Nor does the modern wealth of social literature in any fundamental way alter the case. The reason for its statement here is to note that these features of character belong to all animals at all ages, including human beings at every stage of their lives. The differences only lie in relative proportions. Also the success of language in conveying information is vastly over-rated, especially in learned circles. Not only is language highly elliptical, but also nothing can supply the defect of first-hand experience of types cognate to the things explicitly mentioned. The general truth of Hume's doctrine as to the necessity of first-hand impressions is inexorable.

There is another side. Youth is peculiarly susceptible to appeals for beauty of conduct. It understands motives which presuppose the irrelevance of its own person. Such motives are understood as contributing to the magnification of its own interests. Its very search for personal experience thus elicits impersonality, self-forgetfulness. Youth forgets itself in its own ardour. Of course, not always. For it can fall in love. But the test of the better nature, so happily plentiful, is that love passes from selfishness to devotion. The higher forms of love break down the narrow self-regarding motives.

When youth has once grasped where Beauty dwells—with a real knowledge and not as a mere matter of literary phraseology in some poetic, scriptural, or psychological version—when youth has once grasped, its self-surrender is absolute. The vision may pass. It may traverse consciousness in a flash. Some natures may never permit it to emerge into attention. But youth is peculiarly liable to the vision of that Peace, which is the harmony of the soul's activities with ideal aims that lie beyond any personal satisfaction.

SECTION VI. The vigour of civilized societies is preserved by the widespread sense that high aims are worth while. Vigorous societies harbour a certain extravagance of objectives, so that men wander beyond the safe provision of personal gratifications. All strong interests easily become impersonal, the love of a good job well done. There is a sense of harmony about such an accomplishment, the Peace brought by something worth while. Such personal gratification arises from aim beyond personality.

The converse tendency is at least equally noticeable; the egotistic desire for fame—'that last infirmity'—is an inversion of the social impulse, and yet presupposes it. The tendency shows itself in the trivialities of child-life, as well as in the career of some conqueror before whom mankind trembled. In the widest sense, it is the craving for sympathy. It involves the feeling that each act of experience is a central reality, claiming all things as its own. The world has then no justification except as a satisfaction of such claims. But the point is that the desire for admiring attention becomes futile except in the presence of an audience fit to render it. The pathology of feeling, so often exemplified, consists in the destruction of the audience for the sake of the fame. There is also, of course, the sheer love of command, finally devoid of high purpose. The complexity of human motive, the entwinement of its threads, is infinite. The point, which is here relevant, is that the zest of human adventure presupposes for its material a scheme of things with a worth beyond any single occasion. However perverted, there is required for zest that craving to stand conspicuous in this scheme of things as well as the purely personal pleasure in the exercise of faculties. It is the final contentment aimed at by the soul in its retreat to egoism, as distinct from anaesthesia. In this, it is beyond human analysis to detect exactly where the perversion begins to taint the intuition of Peace. Milton's phrase states the whole conclusion— 'That last infirmity of noble mind.'

Fame is a cold, hard notion. Another half-way house between the extreme ecstasy of Peace and the extreme of selfish desire, is the love of particular individual things. Such love is the completion almost necessary for finite reality, and all reality is in some way finite. In the extreme of love, such as mother's love, all personal desire is transferred to the thing loved, as a desire for its perfection. Personal life has here evidently passed beyond itself, but with explicit, definite limitation to particular realities. . . . This aspect of personal love is simply a clinging to a condition for selfish happiness. There is no transcendence of personality.

But some closeness of status, such as the relation of parent to child or the relation of marriage, can produce the love of self-devotion where the potentialities of the loved object are felt passionately as a claim that it find itself in a friendly Universe. Such love is really an intense feeling as to how the harmony of the world should be realized in particular objects. It is the feeling as to what would happen if right could triumph in a beautiful world, with discord routed. It is the passionate desire for the beautiful result, in this instance. Such love is distracting, nerve-racking. But, unless darkened by utter despair, it involves deep feeling of an aim in the Universe, winning such triumph as is possible to it. It is the sense of Eros, hovering between Peace as the crown of Youth and Peace as the issue of Tragedy.

SECTION VII. The general health of social life is taken care of by formularized moral precepts, and formularized religious beliefs and religious institutions. All of these explicitly express the doctrine that the perfection of life resides in aims beyond the individual person in question.

It is a doctrine of great generality, capable of a large variety of specializations, not all of them mutually consistent. For example, consider the patriotism of the Roman farmers, in the full vigour of the Republic. Certainly Regulus did not return to Carthage, with the certainty of torture and death, cherishing any mystic notions of another life—either a Christian Heaven or a Buddhist Nirvana. He was a practical man, and his ideal aim was the Roman Republic flourishing in this world. But this aim transcended his individual personality; for this aim he entirely sacrificed every gratification bounded by such limits. For him there was something in the world which could not be expressed as sheer personal gratification—and yet in thus sacrificing himself, his personal existence rose to its full height. He may have been mistaken in his estimate of the worth of the Roman Republic. The point is that with that belief, he achieved magnificence by the sacrifice of himself.

In this estimate, Regulus has not in any way proved himself to be exceptional. His conduct showed heroism that is unusual. But his estimate of the worth of such conduct has evoked widest assent. The Roman farmers agreed; and generation after generation, amid all the changes of history, have agreed by the instinctive pulse of emotion as the tale is handed down.

Moral codes have suffered from the exaggerated claims made for them. The dogmatic fallacy has here done its worst. Each such code has been put out by a God on a mountain top, or by a Saint in a cave, or by a divine Despot on a throne, or, at the lowest, by ancestors with a wisdom beyond later question. In any case, each code is incapable of improvement; and unfortunately in details they fail to agree either with each other or with our existing moral intuitions. The result is that the world is shocked, or amused, by the sight of saintly old people hindering in the name of morality the removal of obvious brutalities from a legal system. Some *Acta Sanctorum* go ill with civilization.

The details of these codes are relative to the social circumstances of the immediate environment—life at a certain date on 'the fertile fringe' of the Arabian desert, life on the lower slopes of the Himalayan Mountains, life on the plains of China, or on the plains of India, life on the delta of some great river. Again the meaning of the critical terms is shifting and ambiguous, for example, the notions of ownership, family, marriage, murder, God. Conduct which in one environment and at one stage produces its measure of harmonious satisfaction, in other surroundings at another stage is destructively degrading. Each society has its own type of perfection, and puts up with certain blots, at that stage inevitable. Thus the notion that there are certain regulative notions, sufficiently precise to prescribe details of conduct, for all reasonable beings on Earth, in every planet, and in every star-system, is at once to be put aside. That is the notion of the one type of perfection at which the Universe aims. All realization of the Good is finite, and necessarily excludes certain other types.

But what these codes do witness to, and what their interpretation by seers of various races throughout history does witness to, is the aim at a social perfection. Such a realized fact is conceived as an abiding perfection in the nature of things, a treasure for all ages. It is not a romance of thought, it is a fact of Nature. For example, in one sense the Roman Republic declined and fell; in another sense, it stands a stubborn fact in the Universe. To perish is to assume a new function in the process of generation. Devotion to the Republic magnified the type of personal satisfactions for those who conformed their purposes to its maintenance. Such conformation of purpose to ideal[s] beyond personal limitations is the conception of that Peace with which the wise man can face his fate, master of his soul.

SECTION VIII. The wide scope of the notion of 'society' requires attention. Transcendence begins with the leap from the actuality of the immediate occasion to the notion of personal existence, which is a society of occasions. In terms of human life, the soul is a society. Care for the future of personal existence, regret or pride in its past, are alike feelings which leap beyond the bounds of the sheer actuality of the present. It is in the nature of the present that it should thus transcend itself by reason of the immanence in it of the 'other.' But there is no necessity as to the scale of emphasis that this fact of nature should receive. It belongs to the civilization of consciousness to magnify the large sweep of harmony.

Beyond the soul there are other societies, and societies of societies. There is the animal body ministering to the soul: there are families, groups of families, nations, species, groups involving different species associated in the joint enterprise of keeping alive. These various societies, each in its measure, claim loyalties and loves. In human history the various responses to these claims disclose the essential transcendence of each individual actuality beyond itself. The stubborn reality of the absolute self-attainment of each individual is bound up with a relativity which it issues from and issues into. The analysis of the various strands of relativity is the analysis of the social structure of the Universe, as in this epoch.

Although particular codes of morality reflect, more or less imperfectly, the special circumstances of social structure concerned, it is natural to seek for some highly general principles underlying all such codes. Such generalities should reflect the very notions of the harmonizing of harmonies, and of particular individual actualities as the sole authentic reality. These are the principles of the generality of harmony, and of the importance of the individual. The first means 'order,' and the second means 'love.' Between the two there is a suggestion of opposition. For 'order' is impersonal; and love, above all things, is personal. The antithesis is solved by rating types of order in relative importance according to their success in magnifying the individual actualities, that is to say, in promoting strength of experience. Also in rating the individual on the double basis, partly on the intrinsic strength of its own experience, and partly on its influence in the promotion of a high-grade type of order. These two grounds in part coalesce. For a weak individual exerts a weak influence. The essence of Peace is that the individual whose strength of experience is founded upon this ultimate intuition, thereby is extending the influence of the source of all order.

The moral code is the behaviour-patterns which in the environment for which it is designed will promote the evolution of that environment towards its proper perfection.

SECTION IX. The attainment of Truth belongs to the essence of Peace. By this it is meant, that the intuition constituting the realization of Peace has as its objective that Harmony whose inter-connections involve Truth. A defect in Truth is a limitation to Harmony. There can be no secure efficacy in the Beauty which hides within itself the dislocations of falsehood.

The truth or falsehood of propositions is not directly to the point in this demand for Truth. Since each proposition is yoked to a contradictory proposition, and since of these one must be true and the other false, there are necessarily as many false as there are true propositions.

This bare 'truth or falsehood' of propositions is a comparatively superficial factor affecting the discursive interests of the intellect. The essential truth that Peace demands is the conformation of Appearance to Reality. There is the Reality from which the occasion of experience springs—a Reality of inescapable, stubborn fact; and there is the Appearance with which the occasion attains its final individuality—an Appearance including its adjustment of the Universe by simplification, valuation, transmutation, anticipation. A feeling of dislocation of Appearance from Reality is the final destructive force, robbing life of its zest for adventure. It spells the decadence of civilization, by stripping from it the very reason for its existence.

There can be no necessity governing this conformation. Sense-perception, which dominates the appearance of things, in its own nature re-arranges, and thus in a way distorts. Also there can be no mere blunt truth about the Appearance which it provides. In its own nature Sense-perception is an interpretation, and this interpretation may be completely misleading. If there were a necessary conformation of Appearance to Reality, then Morality would vanish. There is no morality about the multiplication table, whose items are necessarily linked. Art would also be a meaningless term. For it presupposes the efficacy of purpose. Art is an issue of Adventure.

The question for discussion is whether there exists any factor in the Universe constituting a general drive towards the conformation of Appearance to Reality. This drive would then constitute a factor in each occasion persuading an aim at such truth as is proper to the special appearance in question. This concept of truth, proper to each special appearance, would mean that the appearance has not built itself up by the inclusion of elements that are foreign to the reality from which it springs. The appearance will then be a generalization and an adaptation of emphasis; but not an importation of qualities and relations without any corresponding exemplification in the reality. This concept of truth is in fact the denial of the doctrine of Appearance which lies on the surface of Kant's *Critique of Pure Reason*. . . .

SECTION X. The answer to this question must issue from a survey of the factors in terms of which individual experience has been interpreted:—The antecedent World from which each occasion springs, a World of many occasions presenting for the new creature harmonies and discords: the easy road of Anaesthesia by which discordant factors are dismissed into irrelevance: the activity of the mental poles [23] in building conceptual experience into patterns of feeling which rescue discords from loss: the spontaneity of the mental action and its persuasion by a sense of relevance: the selective nature of consciousness and

[23] See Introduction, p. 405.

its initial failure to discriminate the deeper sources of feeling: that there is no agency in abstraction from actual occasions, and that existence involves implication in agency: the sense of a unity of many occasions with a value beyond that of any individual occasion; for example, the soul, the complete animal, the social group of animals, the material body, the physical epoch: the aim at immediate individual contentment.

The justification for the suggestion derived from this group of factors must mainly rest upon their direct elucidation of first-hand experience. They are not, and should not be, the result of an argument. For all argument must rest upon premises more fundamental than the conclusions. Discussion of fundamental notions is merely for the purpose of disclosing their coherence, their compatibility, and the specializations which can be derived from their conjunction.

The above set of metaphysical notions rests itself upon the ordinary, average experience of mankind, properly interpreted. But there is a further set for which the appeal lies to occasions and modes of experience which in some degree are exceptional. It must be remembered that the present level of average waking human experience was at one time exceptional among the ancestors of mankind. We are justified therefore in appealing to those modes of experience which in our direct judgment stand above the average level. The gradual emergence of such modes, and their effect on human history, have been among the themes of this book in its appeal to history. We have found the growth of Art: its gradual sublimation into the pursuit of Truth and Beauty: the sublimation of the egoistic aim by its inclusion of the transcendent whole: the youthful zest in the transcendent aim: the sense of tragedy: the sense of evil: the persuasion towards Adventure beyond achieved perfection: the sense of Peace.

SECTION XI. The concept of Civilization, as developed up to this stage, remains inherently incomplete. No logical argument can demonstrate this gap. Such arguments are merely subsidiary helps for the conscious realization of metaphysical intuitions.—*Non in dialectica complacuit Deo salvum facere populum suum.*[24] This saying, quoted by Cardinal Newman,[25] should be the motto of every metaphysician. He is seeking, amid the dim recesses of his ape-like consciousness and beyond the reach of dictionary language, for the premises implicit in all reasoning. The speculative methods of metaphysics are dangerous, easily perverted. So is all Adventure; but Adventure belongs to the essence of civilization.

The incompleteness of the concept relates to the notion of Transcendence, the feeling essential for Adventure, Zest, and Peace. This

[24] It is not by dialectic that God has been pleased to save His people.
[25] From St. Ambrose, on the title-page of Newman's *Grammar of Assent.*

feeling requires for its understanding that we supplement the notion of the Eros by including it in the concept of an Adventure in the Universe as One. This Adventure embraces all particular occasions but as an actual fact stands beyond any one of them. It is, as it were, the complement to Plato's Receptacle, its exact opposite, yet equally required for the unity of all things. In every way, it is contrary to the Receptacle. The Receptacle is bare of all forms: the Unity of Adventure includes the Eros which is the living urge towards all possibilities, claiming the goodness of their realization. The Platonic Receptacle is void, abstract from all individual occasions: The Unity of Adventure includes among its components all individual realities, each with the importance of the personal or social fact to which it belongs. Such individual importance in the components belongs to the essence of Beauty. In this Supreme Adventure, the Reality which the Adventure transmutes into its Unity of Appearance requires the real occasions of the advancing world each claiming its due share of attention. This Appearance, thus enjoyed, is the final Beauty with which the Universe achieves its justification. This Beauty has always within it the renewal derived from the Advance of the Temporal World. It is the immanence of the Great Fact including this initial Eros and this final Beauty which constitutes the zest of self-forgetful transcendence belonging to Civilization at its height.

At the heart of the nature of things, there are always the dream of youth and the harvest of tragedy. The Adventure of the Universe starts with the dream and reaps tragic Beauty. This is the secret of the union of Zest with Peace:—That the suffering attains its end in a Harmony of Harmonies. The immediate experience of this Final Fact, with its union of Youth and Tragedy, is the sense of Peace. In this way the World receives its persuasion towards such perfections as are possible for its diverse individual occasions.

Appendix

Suggestions for Further Reading

General

Histories

Blau, Joseph L., *Men and Movements in American Philosophy*. New York: Prentice-Hall, 1952.

Cohen, Morris R., *American Thought: A Critical Sketch*. Glencoe, Illinois: The Free Press, 1954.

Commager, Henry Steele, *The American Mind: An Interpretation of American Thought and Character since the 1880's*. New Haven: Yale University Press, 1950. (Bibliographies.)

Curti, Merle, *The Growth of American Thought*. New York: Harper & Brothers, 1943; 2d ed., 1951. (Bibliographies.)

Gabriel, Ralph Henry, *The Course of American Democratic Thought*. New York: Ronald Press, 1940; 2d ed., 1956.

Hofstadter, Richard, *Social Darwinism in American Thought*. Philadelphia: University of Pennsylvania Press, 1944. Revised paperback edition, Boston: Beacon Press, 1955.

Moore, Edward C., *American Pragmatism: Peirce, James, and Dewey*. New York: Colombia University Press, 1961.

Passmore, John, *A Hundred Years of Philosophy*. London: Gerald Duckworth & Co., 1957. (Primarily of English philosophy; secondarily of American and continental European philosophy in relation to English philosophy.)

Reck, Andrew J., *Recent American Philosophy: Studies of Ten Representative Thinkers*. New York: Pantheon Books, 1964. (Perry, Hocking, Mead, Boodin, Urban, Parker, Sellars, Lovejoy, Jordan, Brightman.)

Schneider, Herbert W., *A History of American Philosophy*. New York: Columbia University Press, 1946; 2d. ed., with added chapters, 1963. (1st ed. still valuable for bibliographies and index.)

Smith, John E., *The Spirit of American Philosophy*. New York: Oxford University Press, 1963. (Peirce, James, Royce, Dewey, Whitehead.)

Struik, Dirk J., *Yankee Science in the Making*. New, revised edition. New York: Collier Books, 1962.

Townsend, Harvey G., *Philosophical Ideas in the United States*. Cincinnati: American Book Co., 1934.

Werkmeister, W. H., *A History of Philosophical Ideas in America*. New York: Ronald Press, 1949. (Analytic summaries of major texts of classic period.)

White, Morton G., *Social Thought in America*. New York: Viking Press, 1949. (Dewey, Veblen, Holmes, Beard, Robinson.)

Wiener, Philip P., *Evolution and the Founders of Pragmatism*. Cambridge, Mass.: Harvard University Press, 1949.

Anthologies

Anderson, Paul R., and Fisch, Max H., *Philosophy in America from the Puritans to James, with representative selections.* New York: D. Appleton-Century Co., 1939.

Barrett, William, and Aiken, Henry D. (eds.), *Philosophy in the Twentieth Century.* 2 vols. New York: Random House, 1962.

Blau, Joseph L. (ed.), *American Philosophic Addresses 1700-1900.* New York: Columbia University Press, 1946.

Frankel, Charles (ed.), *The Golden Age of American Philosophy.* New York: George Braziller, 1960.

Konvitz, Milton R., and Kennedy, Gail eds.), *The American Pragmatists.* New York: Meridian Books, 1960. (Emerson, James, Peirce, Holmes, Dewey, Mead, Bridgman, Lewis, Kallen, Hook.

Miller, Perry (ed.), *American Thought, Civil War to World War I.* New York: Rinehart & Co., 1954.

Muelder, Walter G.; Sears, Laurence; and Schlabach, Anne V., *The Development of American Philosophy.* 2d ed. Boston: Houghton Mifflin Co., 1960.

Peterfreund, Sheldon P., *An Introduction to American Philosophy.* New York: Odyssey Press, 1959. (For beginners in philosophy.)

Collections of a General Character

Adams, G. P., and Montague, W. P. (eds.), *Contemporary American Philosophy: Personal Statements.* 2 vols. New York: The Macmillan Co., 1930.

Black, Max (ed.), *Philosophy in America.* Ithaca, New York: Cornell University Press, 1965.

Hook, Sidney (ed.), *American Philosophers at Work: The Philosophic Scene in the United States.* New York: Criterion Books, 1956.

Kallen, H. M., and Hook, Sidney (eds.), *American Philosophy Today and Tomorrow.* New York: Lee Furman, 1935.

Schlesinger, Arthur M., Jr., and White, Morton (eds.), *Paths of American Thought.* Boston: Houghton Mifflin Co., 1963.

Collections Representing Particular Movements

Barrett, Clifford (ed.), *Contemporary Idealism in America.* New York: The Macmillan Co., 1932.

Drake, Durant, and others, *Essays in Critical Realism: A Co-operative Study of the Problem of Knowledge.* New York: The Macmillan Co., 1920.

Holt, Edwin B., and others, *The New Realism: Coöperative Studies in Philosophy.* New York: The Macmillan Co., 1912.

Krikorian, Yervant H. (ed.), *Naturalism and the Human Spirit.* New York: Columbia University Press, 1944.

Sellars, R. W., and others, *Philosophy for the Future: The Quest of Modern Materialism.* New York: The Macmillan Co., 1949.

Representative Journals

Journal of Speculative Philosophy (22 vols., 1867-93, edited by W. T. Harris; index to vols. 1-15 in vol. 15, 1881).

Ethics (1890–; formerly *International Journal of Ethics*)

The Monist (1890-1936; 1962–; index to vols. 1-30, 1921)

The Philosophical Review (1892–; index to vols. 1-35, 1927)
The Journal of Philosophy (1904–; index to vols. 1-50, 1962; to vols. 51-60, 1964)

1. Chauncey Wright

Madden, Edward H. (ed.), *The Philosophical Writings of Chauncey Wright: Representative Selections*. New York: The Liberal Arts Press, 1958.

Madden, Edward H., *Chauncey Wright and the Foundations of Pragmatism*. Seattle: University of Washington Press, 1963.

Madden, Edward H., *Chauncey Wright*. New York: Washington Square Press, 1964.

(See also Wiener under Histories above.)

2. Peirce

Peirce's most important papers have been published in the *Collected Papers of Charles Sanders Peirce*, eight volumes. Volumes I-VI were edited by Charles Hartshorne and Paul Weiss, Harvard University Press, 1931-1935; Volumes VII and VIII were edited by Arthur W. Burks, Harvard University Press, 1958. The volumes are: (I) *Principles of Philosophy*, (II) *Elements of Logic*, (III) *Exact Logic*, (IV) *The Simplest Mathematics*, (V) *Pragmatism and Pragmaticism*, (VI) *Scientific Metaphysics*, (VII) *Science and Philosophy*, and (VIII) *Reviews, Correspondence, and Bibliography*.

Volume VIII contains a long bibliography of Peirce's writings. This is supplemented by additions and a bibliography of writings about Peirce, prepared by Max Fisch and published in *Studies in the Philosophy of Charles Sanders Peirce*, Second Series, edited by Edward Moore and Richard Robin; University of Massachusetts Press, 1964. This volume contains a number of interesting essays on Peirce, as does the earlier *Studies in the Philosophy of Charles Sanders Peirce*, edited by Philip Wiener and Frederic Young, Harvard University Press, 1952.

There are many books devoted entirely to Peirce. Among the best are W. B. Gallie, *Peirce and Pragmatism* (Penguin, 1952), Thomas A. Goudge, *The Thought of C. S. Peirce* (University of Toronto Press, 1950), Manley Thompson, *The Pragmatic Philosophy of C. S. Peirce* (University of Chicago Press, 1953), and Murray G. Murphey, *The Development of Peirce's Philosophy* (Harvard University Press, 1961). Max Fisch is preparing a biography.

There are several one-volume editions of Peirce's writings: Justus Buchler, *The Philosophy of Peirce, Selected Writings* (Kegan Paul, etc., 1940); Morris R. Cohen, *Chance, Love, and Logic* (George Braziller, 1956); Vincent Tomas, *Charles S. Peirce, Essays in the Philosophy of Science* (Liberal Arts, 1957), and Philip P. Wiener, *Values in a Universe of Chance: Selected Writings of C. S. Peirce* (Doubleday Anchor, 1958).

3. James

For a nearly complete list of James's writings see R. B. Perry, *Annotated Bibliography of the Writings of William James* (1920). The following list makes no pretense of completeness, but merely indicates works most likely to be of interest to readers of this volume.

a) James's works

The best over-all account of James's general position is contained in *Pragmatism* (1907). The theory of truth set forth there engendered opposition to which James replied in *The Meaning of Truth* (1909). *The Will to Believe* (1897) besides containing the essay of that title and "The Moral Philosopher and the Moral Life" includes a variety of interesting non-technical essays. *Essays in Radical Empiricism* (1912) develops the point of view set forth in "Does 'Consciousness' Exist?" James's philosophy and psychology of religion are presented in *The Varieties of Religious Experience* (1902). James's monumental *Principles of Psychology* (1890) anticipates later expressions of many of James's opinions and has philosophical as well as psychological importance; see ch. 28 especially. James's interest and skill in practical psychology is manifest in *Essays on Faith and Morals* (1943), selected by R. B. Perry from various lectures and books by James.

b) James in relation to other philosophers

The fullest and most interesting account of James's development is R. B. Perry's *Thought and Character of William James* (1935). Perry gives much of James's correspondence and a running account of his life and opinions. It is not necessary to read this book as a whole; one may gain enjoyment as well as insight into James's character and views from a reading of any part of it. The chapters dealing with James's relations with Royce, Dewey, Santayana, and Peirce should be of particular interest to readers of this book. For a comparison of James's views with those of Whitehead, see Victor Lowe, "William James and Whitehead's Doctrine of Prehensions," *Journal of Philosophy*, vol. 38 (1941), pp. 113-126. *The Letters of William James*, ed. by his son Henry James (1920), affords many interesting glimpses of James's relationship to his contemporaries in philosophy and psychology. The affiliations and affinities of phenomenology and existentialism with the philosophy of James are explored by Herbert Spiegelberg, *The Phenomenological Movement* (1960), I, 66-69, 111-117, and by James M. Edie, "Notes on the Philosophical Anthropology of William James," in the volume edited by Edie, *Invitation to Phenomenolgy: Studies in the Philosophy of Experience* (1965).

c) Discussions of James's works

A vast literature, much of it polemical, has accumulated about the idea of pragmatism. The lead essay of Arthur O. Lovejoy's *The Thirteen Pragmatisms and other Essays* (1963) answers the demand for clarification of the term "pragmatism." Other essays in this volume bear directly on the interpretation of James's philosophy. George Santayana's *Character and Opinion in the United States*, ch. III, contains an estimate of James which is on the whole unsympathetic. (In this connection, see John J. Fisher, "Santayana on James: A Conflict of Views on Philosophy," *American Philosophical Quarterly* 2: 1-7, 1965.) Bertrand Russell's *Philosophical Essays*, chs. IV and V, attack "The Will to Believe" and James's theory of truth. John Dewey, who made a somewhat different interpretation of pragmatism, sets forth his meaning in an essay "What Pragmatism Means by Practical," in his *Essays in Experimental Logic*. John A. Passmore's *A Hundred Years of Philosophy* (1957) contains a good digest and estimate of James's thought in relation to contemporaries such as Henri Bergson, Renouvier and some of his followers such as F. C. S. Schiller. The centenary of James's birth was the occasion for two collections of essays, the first of which is particularly valuable: *In Commemoration of William James, 1842-1942* (Columbia University Press, 1942); *William James, The Man and the Thinker* (University of Wisconsin Press, 1942). Edward C. Moore's *William James* in the Great American Thinkers series (1965) is a fresh interpretation and criticism of his major works.

4. Royce

A bibliography of Royce's published writings up to his death, compiled by Benjamin Rand, is included in *Papers in Honor of Josiah Royce* (1916), ed. J. E. Creighton, pp. 287-293. The same may also be found in *Philos. Rev.* 25(1916), pp. 515-521. J. Loewenberg compiled a list of Royce's numerous unpublished writings in *Philos. Rev.* 26 (1917), pp. 578–582. The most complete and recent bibliography of Royce's writings is to be found in "A Critical Annotated Bibliography of the Published works of Josiah Royce," by Frank M. Oppenheim, S. J., in *The Modern Schoolman* 41: 339-365, 1964.

Most of Royce's major philosophical works are mentioned in the text and notes of the Royce Introduction above. Attention is called here only to some of his less well known books: *California from the Conquest in 1846 to the Second Vigilance Committee in San Francisco: A Study of American Character* (1886); *The Feud of Oakfield Creek: A Novel of California Life* (1887); *The Spirit of Modern Philosophy* (1892); *Studies of Good and Evil: A Series of Essays upon Problems of Life and Philosophy* (1898); *The Conception of Immortality* (1900); *Outlines of Psychology* (1903); *Herbert Spencer, on Estimate and Review* (1904); *Race Questions, Provincialism, and Other American Problems* (1908); *William James and Other Essays on the Philosophy of Life* (1911); *The Sources of Religious Insight* (1912); *Lectures on Modern Idealism*, ed. by J. Loewenberg (1919); *Fugitive Essays*, ed. by J. Loewenberg (1925). The major writings on logic are collected in *Royce's Logical Essays* ed. by Daniel S. Robinson (1951).

The volume of *Papers in Honor of Josiah Royce* (also in *Philos. Rev.* 25(1916), pp. 229-522) contains essays on many aspects of his thought. Those by G. H. Howison, John Dewey, Mary Whiton Calkins, E. G. Spaulding, Morris R. Cohen, C. I. Lewis, J. Loewenberg, Richard C. Cabot, E. A. Singer, and W. E. Hocking are especially recommended.

Suberb sketches of the Royce-James relationship are to be found in R. B. Perry, *In the Spirit of William James* (1938), ch. 1, and in the same author's *The Thought and Character of William James* (1935), I, chs. 49-51. Vol. II of this work includes, in Appendices V and VI, documents on "Discussion of the Absolute, James and Royce, 1899," and "Royce's Criticisms of 'The Meaning of the Word Truth,' 1908." Much of the Royce-James correspondence is published in *The Letters of William James,* ed. by Henry James (1920).

Selected bibliographies listing articles and books by and about Royce are to be found in Vincent Buranelli's *Josiah Royce* (1964), pp. 160-166; and in *Royce on the Human Self*, by James Harry Cotton (1954), pp. 305-311. Buranelli's book is a very readable "intellectual sketch" of Royce with emphasis on his career as a writer. Cotton's book serves as a general introduction to Royce's philosophy.

Royce's Metaphysics by Gabriel Marcel (tr. by Virginia and Gordon Ringer, 1956) is a prescient interpretation and keen analysis—the best commentary on Royce to date. John E. Smith's *Royce's Social Infinite* (1950) is an informed account of the last phase of Royce's thought. Peter Fuss in *The Moral Philosophy of Josiah Royce* (1965) shows that he had a well developed ethics and argues that it is independent of his metaphysics and probably incompatible with the earlier form of it, though compatible with the later.

Sympathetic expositions of Royce's philosophy are to be found in J. H. Muirhead's *The Platonic Tradition in Anglo-Saxon Philosophy* (1931), Part III, chs. 4-8, and in ch. 10 of G. W. Cunningham, *The Idealistic Argument in Recent British and American Philosophy* (1938). The books of Mary Whiton Calkins and W. E. Hocking bespeak the influence of Royce on several generations of his students. *Contemporary Idealism in America*, ed. by Clifford Barrett (1932), contains Hocking's essay on "The ontological argument in Royce and others." A critique of Royce's epistemology is to be found in A. C. Ewing's: *Idealism: A Critical Survey* (1934) pp. 49-59.

Between 1890 and 1920 Royce's system as a whole or in part was a constant target of criticism by pragmatists, realists and naturalists. William James, neighbor and foeman, concentrated much of his fire in *Pragmatism* (1907) and *A Pluralistic Universe* (1909). R. B. Perry countered for realism in "Professor Royce's Refutation of Realism and Pluralism," *the Monist*, 12(1902), pp. 446-458. George S. Fullerton carried the attack for naturalism in his *System of Metaphysics* (1940), pp. 585-597, and in *The World We Live In* (1912) chs. 14 and 15. An article by George H. Mead, "The Philosophies of Royce, James and Dewey in Their American Setting," (Internat. J. of Ethics 40, 1929-30, pp. 211-231), presents an instructive comparison. Chapter four of George Santayana's *Character and Opinion in the United States* (1920) is an appraisal by one who was out of sympathy with both the person and the philosophy of Josiah Royce.

Josiah Royce's Seminar, 1913-1914, as Recorded in the Notebooks of Harry T. Costello, edited by Grover Smith (1963), is a vivid record of his teaching.

5. SANTAYANA

Readers with little formal training in philosophy may wish to begin with some of Santayana's more literary and less systematic writings, such as his poems, his novel *The Last Puritan, Three Philosophical Poets, Dialogues in Limbo, Soliloquies in England, Character and Opinion in the United States*, or *The Idea of Christ in the Gospels*. Three anthologies of his work are also available: *Little Essays Drawn from the Writings of George Santayana*, by Logan Pearsall Smith with the collaboration of the author (1920); *The Philosophy of Santayana*, edited by Irwin Edman, new and greatly enlarged edition (1953); and *The Wisdom of George Santayana*, edited by Ira D.

Cardiff with a preface by the author (1964; first edition, *Atoms of Thought*, 1950). There is also a collection of *Essays in Literary Criticism of George Santayana*, edited by Irving Singer (1956), with an introductory essay on Santayana as a literary critic.

The most complete bibliography of Santayana's writings is in *The Philosophy of George Santayana*, in the Library of Living Philosophers, edited by Paul A. Schilpp, 1940; 2d ed., 1951. This volume contains an autobiographical sketch by Santayana, eighteen essays by interpreters and critics of his work, and a reply of more than a hundred pages by him. It is the most useful single volume for the serious student.

Santayana's chief work after *The Life of Reason, Scepticism and Animal Faith*, and *Realms of Being*, was *Dominations and Powers: Reflections on Liberty, Society and Government* (1951). An issue of *The Journal of Philosophy* (49: 201-239, 1952) was given over to reflections on it by six reviewers. See also R. Boynton, "Poetic Approach to Politics: A Study in the Political Theory of George Santayana." *Journal of Politics* 20: 676-694, 1958; and Jean H. Faurot, "The Political Thought of George Santayana," *The Western Political Quarterly* 14: 663-675, 1961.

Santayana's last major effort was a one-volume abridgment of *The Life of Reason* (1954). (The preface to the 2d ed., 1922, was not retained but is still of great interest.) A one-volume edition of *Realms of Being* had appeared in 1942, with a new introduction. There is now a one-volume edition also of *Persons and Places* (1963), Santayana's autobiography, which had originally appeared in three volumes (1944, 1945, 1953).

Santayana several times sketched his system in brief. See, for examples, "Preface to Realms of Being" in *The Realm of Essence* (1927) and in the one-volume edition; "Some Meanings of the Word 'Is'" and "Literal and Symbolic Knowledge" in *Obiter Scripta* (1936); "On Metaphysical Projection" and "Human Symbols for Matter" in *The Idler and His Works* (1957); and, earliest of all. "System in Lectures 1909-1910," *Review of Metaphysics* 10: 626-659, 1956-57.

No thorough expository and critical treatment of Santayana's general philosophical position by a single author has yet been published. Special aspects are treated in G. W. Howgate's *George Santayana* (1938), whose emphasis is literary; *The Moral Philosophy of George Santayana*, by M. K. Munitz (1939); *Santayana and the Sense of Beauty*, by W. E. Arnett (1955); and *Santayana's Aesthetics: A Critical Introduction*, by Irving Singer (1957). There are two more general accounts by Roman Catholic scholars: *The Mind of Santayana*, by Richard Butler, O. P. (1955), and *The Essential Wisdom of Santayana*, by Thomas N. Munson, S. J. (1962); the latter has a useful list of writings about Santayana. There are approaches to biography in Howgate's book; in Mossie May Kirkwood's *Santayana: Saint of the Imagination* (1961); and in Daniel Cory's *Santayana: The Later Years, A Portrait with Letters* (1963). Cory had previously edited *The Letters of George Santayana* (1955). He was Santayana's secretary, literary executor, and heir, and had helped him assemble *Dominations and Powers* and abridge *The Life of Reason*.

The centenary of Santayana's birth was honored by a double number of *The Journal of Philosophy* (61: 5-69, 1964). See also the memorial addresses in an earlier number (51: 29-64, 1954). *Dialogue on George Santayana*, edited by Corliss Lamont (1959), records an amusing conversation of seven American philosophers who had known him.

An edition of Santayana's Ph.D. thesis, *Lotze's System of Philosophy* (1889), is being prepared by Paul G. Kuntz.

6. DEWEY

Dewey's writings over a period of more than sixty-five years are so voluminous that only the most important of them can be mentioned here. A comprehensive bibliography of writings by and about him has been compiled by Milton Halsey Thomas, *John Dewey: A Centennial Bibliography* (Chicago, 1962). A less complete bibliography covering Dewey's own writings to its date of publication, is in *The Philosophy of John Dewey*, edited by Paul Arthur Schilpp (Evanston and Chicago, 1939).

There are three excellent brief accounts of Dewey's philosophy as a whole: one by Dewey himself, *Reconstruction in Philosophy* (New York, 1920), and two more recent books which take his important later work into account, Sidney Hook's *John Dewey: An Intellectual Portrait* (New York, 1939), and George R. Geiger's *John Dewey in Perspective* (New York, 1958). A volume of selections from Dewey's writings has been published in the Modern Library by Joseph Ratner under the title, *Intelligence in the Modern World: John Dewey's Philosophy* (New York, 1939). Other anthologies are: Irwin Edman, *John Dewey: His Contribution to the American Tradition* (Indianapolis, 1955) and Richard J. Bernstein, *John Dewey on Experience, Nature and Freedom* (New York, 1960). The cooperative volume, *Creative Intelligence: Essays in the Pragmatic Attitude* (New York, 1917), is an early presentation of "instrumentalism" by Dewey and seven of his associates in developing this new point of view.

Dewey's own account of his intellectual development, "From Absolutism to Experimentalism," is in volume two of *Contemporary American Philosopy: Personal Statements* (New York, 1930), edited by George P. Adams and W. P. Montague. The best detailed study of this transition is Morton G. White's *The Origin of Dewey's Instrumentalism* (New York, 1943). A biographical sketch, edited by Jane M. Dewey, which gives additional details of value, is in *The Philosophy of John Dewey*.

There have been many critical essays written about various aspects of Dewey's thought. A representative collection of these will be found in Paul Arthur Schilpp (editor), *The Philosophy of John Dewey*, together with a long reply by Dewey to his critics entitled "Experience, Knowledge and Value: A Rejoinder." Other volumes devoted to Dewey's thought are: *John Dewey, the Man and His Philosophy* (Cambridge, Mass., 1930); *Essays in Honor of John Dewey, On the Occasion of His Seventieth Birthday* (New York, 1929); *The Philosopher of the Common Man: Essays in Honor of John Dewey to celebrate His Eightieth Birthday* (New York, 1940); *Essays for John Dewey's Ninetieth Birthday* (Urbana, 1950); *John Dewey: Philosopher of Science and Freedom* (New York, 1950); *John Dewey and the Experimental Spirit in Philosophy* (New York, 1959).

The writings of Dewey may be roughly divided in accordance with the topics of which they treat. Usually, Dewey has written many articles on each of these subjects as well as the books here mentioned.

The most general and the most profound statement of Dewey's philosophy is in his *Experience and Nature* (Chicago, 1925; 2d ed., New York, 1929); in the second edition Chapter One is completely rewritten.

In the field of logic, his most important books are the *Essays in Experimental Logic* (Chicago, 1916)—a collection of articles written over the period 1900-1916—and his monumental *Logic: The Theory of Inquiry* (New York, 1938). A brief popular statement of Dewey's theory of inquiry is *How We Think* (Boston, 1910); a second edition, thoroughly revised and rewritten, was published in 1933. Dewey, who did not regard anything he wrote as "definitive," continued to study problems of logic and theory of knowledge, at this period in active collaboration with Arthur F. Bentley. Parts of these results were published under the title, *Knowing and the Known* (Boston, 1949). Sidney Ratner and Jules Altman have published a comprehensive selection from their letters, *John Dewey and Arthur F. Bentley: A Philosophical Correspondence* (Rutgers, 1964).

Dewey's definitive exposition of his philosophy of science is *The Quest for Certainty* (New York, 1929), from which excerpts are printed in this volume.

In ethics and value theory, his principal writings are: *Ethics* (New York, 1908), written in collaboration with James H. Tufts (the second edition of this book in 1932 was entirely rewritten); *Human Nature and Conduct: An Introduction to Social Psychology* (New York, 1922); and a monograph entitled "Theory of Valuation" in the *International Encyclopedia of Unified Science*, Vol. II No. 4 (Chicago, 1939). This last work should be read in conjunction with the *Logic*.

One of Dewey's greatest books, and perhaps the best introduction to his philosophy, is *Art as Experience* (New York, 1934).

Human Nature and Conduct may be considered the preface to Dewey's social and political thought. His most important books on this subject are: *German Philosophy and Politics* (New York, 1915), *The Public and Its Problems* (New York, 1927), *Characters and Events: Popular Essays in Social and Political Philosophy*, edited by Joseph Ratner (2 vols., New York, 1929); *Individualism Old and New* (New York, 1930); *Liberalism and Social Action* (New York, 1935); *Freedom and Culture* (New York, 1939).

In the closely allied field of education Dewey's classic work is *Democracy and Education* (New York, 1916). Other important writings are: *The School and Society* (Chicago, 1899, revised edition, 1915); *Schools of Tomorrow* (New York, 1915), written in collaboration with Evelyn Dewey; *The Sources of a Science of Education* (New York, 1929); *The Way Out of Educational Confusion* (Cambridge, Mass., 1931); *Experience and Education* (New York, 1938); and *Education Today* (New York, 1940), a collection of essays edited by Joseph Ratner, Katherine Camp Mayhew and Anna Camp Edwards have given a detailed account of the laboratory school at the University of Chicago in *The Dewey School* (New York, 1936). Volumes of selections from his writings on education have been edited by Martin S. Dworkin, *Dewey on Education* (New York, 1959) and Reginald D. Archambault, *John Dewey on Education* (New York, 1964). Melvin C. Baker's *Foundations of John Dewey's Educational Theory* (New York, 1955) is a good systematic study. Lawrence A. Cremin's *The Transformation of the School* (New York, 1961) is a brilliant historical interpretation of progressive education.

Dewey made a clear and simple statement of his philosophy of religion in *A Common Faith* (New Haven, 1934).

Many of Dewey's most important essays have been collected in the following volumes: *The Influence of Darwin on Philosophy and Other Essays*

(New York, 1910); *Philosophy and Civilization* (New York, 1931); *Problems of Men* (New York, 1946).

7. WHITEHEAD

By Whitehead.—A nearly complete bibliography of Whitehead's writings, with a list of the most significant reviews of his books, may be found in *The Philosophy of Alfred North Whitehead*, edited by P. A. Schilpp, 2nd ed., 1951. A critical edition of his philosophical works has been undertaken by Ivor Leclerc. Leclerc has completed the first task, a critical edition of *Process and Reality*, but it is unpublished at the time of this writing.

Alfred North Whitehead: An Anthology, ed. F. S. C. Northrop and Mason W. Cross (1953), is a superb large collection of chapters from all periods of his work. Like almost all of Whitehead's books and many of the books about his philosophy, it is available in paperback as well as hard cover. The student whose time for further reading is quite limited may pick from Northrup and Gross a series of chapters which especially interests him, or follow the suggestions made in various footnotes to our Introduction to the Whitehead selections, above, or go through one of Whitehead's four short philosophical books. These are: *Religion in the Making* (1926); *Symbolism, Its Meaning and Effect* (1927), which sketches Whitehead's doctrine of two levels of perception and his general conception of symbolism; *The Function of Reason* (1929), an untechnical discussion of the relation between the physical and mental aspects of life, and between the latter's practical and speculative functions; *Modes of Thought* (1938), a free presentation of Whitehead's philosophic attitude, in which his system is left aside. Whitehead's chief works are described on pp. 395-399, above.

In *Process and Reality* Whitehead's procedure is one that is usual among mathematicians: he presents all his axioms and fundamental terms before applying any part of the apparatus to any topic. In this case it makes heavy reading. Donald W. Sherburne, in *A Key to Whitehead's Process and Reality* (1966), has arranged passages from various parts of the book so as to provide substantial understanding of a basic idea before its companions are introduced. The resulting "linear" exposition, accompanied by an extensive Glossary and Index, is a great help to students. It uses slightly more than one third of Whitehead's text.

The Interpretation of Science: Selected Essays, ed. A. H. Johnson (1961) is a handy collection of Whitehead's shorter writings on this subject.

Biographical.—Whitehead wrote a few pages of autobiographical notes and some vivid descriptions of his English environment and education; these are most readily found as the first four pieces in his *Essays in Science and Philosophy* (1947—the paperback reprint is named *Science and Philosophy*). The finest sketch of the philosopher is by his Harvard colleague W. E. Hocking: "Whitehead as I Knew Him," in George L. Kline, ed., *Alfred North Whitehead: Essays on His Philosophy* (1963). Bertrand Russell, who was Whitehead's pupil in mathematics, later his collaborator, has a fine chapter on him in *Portraits from Memory* (1956). The longer memorial essays by C. D. Broad and Dorothy Emmet in *Mind* (LVII, 1948), and by E. T. Whittaker in *Obituary Notices of Fellows of the Royal Society* (VI, 1948), are excellent. On Whitehead in his last years, see

Lucien Price's *Dialogues of Alfred North Whitehead* (1954). Victor Lowe has begun work toward a biographical study.

On Whitehead's Philosophy and its Uses.—There is no book-length commentary on *Process and Reality*. The earliest books about Whitehead's metaphysics are still useful: Dorothy Emmet, *Whitehead's Philosophy of Organism* (1932) and R. Das, *The Philosophy of Whitehead* (1938) reprinted 1964). Another accurate exposition is by A. H. Johnson: *Whitehead's Theory of Reality* (1952). The most valuable book for a student who comes to Whitehead from Aristotle and the history of metaphysics is *Whitehead's Metaphysics: An Introductory Exposition*, by Ivor Leclerc (1958). The most detailed analysis is offered by William A. Christian, in *An Interpretation of Whitehead's Metaphysics* (1959); the last third of this book is devoted to Whitehead's philosophical theology, and takes issue with Hartshorne's view of it. Wolfe Mays, in *The Philosophy of Whitehead* (1959), takes the memoir of 1905 (see p. 396, above) as the key to *Process and Reality,* and so construes Whitehead's system to be neither "as outrageous nor as metaphysical as some philosophers have made it out to be"; this forced view exemplified the prevailing English disapproval of what Whitehead appeared to be writing in America. The only extended review of his work as a whole is Part II of Victor Lowe's *Understanding Whitehead* (1962). Bertrand Russell has set down his recollection of his ten-year collaboration with Whitehead in "Whitehead and *Principia Mathematica*" (*Mind,* LVII, 1948, p. 137f.); see also his two chapters on that work in *My Philosophical Development* (1959).

Articles on various aspects of Whitehead's philosophy are so numerous that we must be content to list four collections of them, each of which contains ten or more studies for the advanced student: *The Philosophy of Alfred North Whitehead* (Vol. III of *The Library of Living Philosophers*), ed. P. A. Schilpp (1941; 2nd ed., with an essay by C. I. Lewis, 1951); *The Relevance of Whitehead,* ed. Leclerc (1961); *Alfred North Whitehead: Essays on His Philosophy,* ed. George L. Kline (1963—includes Corrigenda for *Process and Reality* and a letter in which Whitehead explained his doctrine of "eternal objects"); *Process and Divinity: The Hartshorne Festschrift,* ed. William L. Reese and Eugene Freeman (1964). In the development of his own metaphysics and theology Charles Hartshorne has acclaimed Whitehead's (and Peirce's); see, for example, *Reality as Social Process* (1953).

Whitehead's Philosophy of Science, by Robert M. Palter (1960), is the authoritative book on Whitehead's philosophy of physics. Biologists will be interested in the use made of Whitehead's principles in *A Contribution to the Theory of the Living Organism,* by W. E. Agar (1943, 2nd ed. 1951). A striking application of Whitehead's concepts is William Morgan's, in "The Organization of a Story and a Tale" (*Jour. of Amer. Folklore,* 58, 1945, pp. 169-194—with a Preface by Whitehead). In the philosophical disciplines, *A Whiteheadian Aesthetic* by Donald W. Sherburne (1961) is outstanding.

Catalogues of books published in the United States in 1965 show three under the subject-heading, "Whitehead." One was written by a theologian, one by an educator, and one by a physicist. It would be a great mistake for the serious student to ignore such works; Whitehead held that the value of abstract thought lies in its wide applicability. The books in question are: *A Christian Natural Theology, Based on the Thought of Alfred North Whitehead,* by John B. Cobb, Jr.; *Whitehead on Education,* by Harold B.

Dunkel; *Experience and Conceptual Activity: A Philosophical Essay Based Upon the Writings of Alfred North Whitehead,* by J. M. Burgers. All three begin with sound expositions of the philosophy of organism, then apply it well for their own purposes. Only Cobb is explicitly much concerned to amend and extend Whitehead. Burgers refrains from theology; a physicist of distinction who is especially interested in the status of life and value in nature, he keeps Whitehead's vocabulary to a minimum, and by using the languages of everyday life and current physical science presents the argument for a Whiteheadian rather than a physicalistic world-view in terms most perspicuous for our generation.

For students familiar with quantum theory, there is a comparative study by A. Shimony, "Quantum Physics (in its present form) and the Philosophy of Whitehead," in Max Black, ed., *Philosophy in America,* pp. 240-261 (1965); as first published in R. S. Cohen, ed., *Boston Studies in the Philosophy of Science,* Vol. 2 (1965), it is followed by Burgers's comments. Students who know Freudian theory should read pp. 166-175, by William C. Lewis, in Greenfield and Lewis, eds., *Psychoanalysis and Current Biological Thought* (1965); Dr. Lewis finds Whitehead on the causal and symbolic modes of experience indispensable for psychoanalytic theory.

Whitehead's Relation to Other American Philosophers.—See Victor Lowe, "Peirce and Whitehead as Metaphysicians," *Studies in the Philosophy of Charles Sanders Peirce, Second Series,* ed. Edward C. Moore and Richard S. Robin (1964); also "William James and Whitehead's Doctrine of Prehensions," in Lowe, *Understanding Whitehead,* Ch. 13. Hocking's "Whitehead as I Knew Him" (George L. Kline, ed., *Alfred North Whitehead: Essays on His Philosophy,* 1963) sheds light on Whitehead and Royce (pp. 9-14). In *Process and Reality* Whitehead made some use of *Scepticism and Animal Faith* as a foil; see index entries under "Santayana." John Dewey's paper, "Whitehead's Philosophy," *Philos. Rev.,* XLVI (1937), is probably the best published expression of Dewey's reaction to Whitehead; it is followed by Whitehead's reply, under the heading, "Remarks."

Index

This index approaches completeness in respect of personal names but falls far short of it in respect of subject headings and even in respect of page references under the headings which are included. The serious student will extend it as his purposes may require. (The Preface and Appendix are not indexed.)

Harvard University, 1, 2, 3, 16, 41, 42, 183, 258
Health, 320ff.
Heat, 90
Hedonism, 310f.
Hegel, G. W. F., 1, 17, 18, 19, 21, 23, 34, 68, 98, 112, 183, 194, 330, 331, 408, 410, 445
Hegesias, 310
Heine, Heinrich, 176
Helium, 135
Helmholtz, H. L. F., 375
Heraclitus, 270
Heredity, 91, 99, 424
Heresy-hunting, 32, 68f.
Heterogeneity, 91
Heuretic science, 32
Hierarchy of good, 300
Historical criticism, 101
Historical economics, 11
Historic route, 22
History, 11, 24, 93, 202f., 219, 282, 233; of ideas, 456
Hobbes, Thomas, 88
Hodgson, Shadworth, 130
Holmes, Oliver Wendell, 9
Holmes, Oliver Wendell, Jr., 2, 6, 7, 8, 9, 10, 12, 14, 15, 41
Homogeneity, 91
Hooker, J. D., 336
Hope, 37; community of, 205; adventure of, 444
Howgate, G. W., 258
Howison, G. H., 129, 187, 188, 196
"How to Make Our Ideas Clear," 42, 44, 52, 70–87, 129
Humanism, 420, 435
Humanities, 212, 225, 227, 241
Humanity, religion of, 173, 241
Hume, David, 1, 8, 48, 121, 130, 138, 260, 298, 421, 422f., 445, 462, 463
Huxley, T. H., 139, 141, 336
Huygens, Christian, 90
Hylopathy, 94
Hypostatization, 354f.
Hypothesis, 15, 16, 90, 102, 108, 117, 165, 236ff., 353, 375, 446; live or dead, 136f., 140; moral, 143f.; religious, 145ff.

"I," 260. See also Personal identity, Self
Idealism, 5, 17, 18, 21, 22, 27f., 38, 95, 121, 164, 181–256, 257, 269, 331, 362, 397, 403, 416; absolute, 5, 181, 333, 416; objective, 21, 22, 95, 181; subjective, 46, 375
Ideal society, 264
Ideals, 168, 170, 173–180, 202, 206, 376f.
Ideas, 15f., 23, 25, 28, 78, 82, 93, 133, 151, 188, 189ff., 201, 214, 260, 261, 263, 280, 332, 457; weapons, 26, 28; not mirrors, 28; amphibious, 263; general, rôle of, 454–456; "adventures" of, 454–470. See also Consequences, Difference-making, Plans of Action, "Working"
Ideation, impulse and, 264
Identity, personal, 22f., 260, 406, 431f.
Ideomotor action, 10, 189
Image, 283, 320
Imagination, 439, 450, 459f.
Immanence, 434, 436
Immediacy, 277, 346, 401; of self-enjoyment, 428
Immediate consciousness, 75
Immediate experience, 155f., 164, 398, 401, 405, 431, 438, 448
Immediate individuality, 427
Immediate knowledge, 19f., 28, 363
Immediate perception, 160
Immortality, 44, 404, 414
Imperative, 171
Impersonality, 463ff.
Impressions, 316f., 320
Impulse, 263, 297f., 306, 314; and ideation, 264
Incarnation, 296
Incoherence, 441
Indefinite community, 37
Indian philosophy, 270
Individual, 22, 448; world and, 189ff.
Individualism, 36, 44f.
Individuality, principle of, 460
Individuation, principle of, 188, 190, 200ff., 294
Induction, 49, 101, 102, 103, 104, 105, 235ff., 416
Inductive logic, 132